The New Certificate Geography Series

ADVANCED LEVEL

THE MEDITERRANEAN LANDS

The New Certificate Geography Series

ADVANCED LEVEL

THE
MEDITERRANEAN LANDS

J. J. BRANIGAN, M.A., F.R.G.S.

*Formerly Deputy Headmaster and Head of Geography
and Geology Departments, St Bede's Grammar School,
Bradford*

and

H. R. JARRETT, B.A., M.Sc. (Econ.), Ph.D., F.R.G.S.

*Formerly Senior Lecturer in Geography, University
of Newcastle, N.S.W.*

MACDONALD & EVANS LTD
8 John Street, London WC1

1969

First published May 1969

©

MACDONALD & EVANS LTD
1969

S.B.N. 7121 1339 8

The New Certificate Geography Series

ADVANCED LEVEL

Australasia
Africa
Europe
Latin America
North America
The United States
of America
Monsoon Asia
The Soviet Union

Another volume in the series
is in the course of preparation

The British Isles

Printed in Great Britain by Fletcher & Son Ltd, Norwich

AUTHORS' PREFACE

THIS survey of the geography of the Mediterranean lands includes the whole of all the countries (except France) which abut on or are islands in the Mediterranean Sea, even where considerable areas of some of them such as Yugoslavia or Algeria are definitely "extra-Mediterranean." France is a special case; it is usually treated as a Western European country with a small "Mediterranean" component. In this book only Mediterranean France is considered. Portugal, outside the Mediterranean basin but forming part of the Iberian peninsula, and Jordan, landlocked but westward-looking and an essential piece of the Levant lands, are included within the scope of our survey. The book has been compiled specially by the authors of the two volumes *Europe* and *Africa*, in this series, in an attempt to show the Mediterranean lands as a geographical unity, and not merely as separate and unrelated marginal portions of Europe, Africa and Asia.

The work is planned primarily for the Sixth Form students of geography who are presenting the region or part of it at the Advanced Level of the G.C.E., and their interests are always in the forefront. At the same time, it is hoped that the book in its treatment of the political, social, and economic problems of the emergent countries around the Mediterranean will be of some value to the general reader. Widespread changes are taking place everywhere in the region, and some of the developments such as the closure of the Suez Canal, the Arab–Israeli conflict, the political problems of Greece and Cyprus, and the economic resurgence of North Africa, to mention only a few, are having impacts which are felt far beyond the Mediterranean shores.

The book is in two parts. Part One consists of eight chapters of general geography and is the result of close collaboration between the two authors. It deals first with the structure, relief, climate, soil and natural vegetation of the Mediterranean region as a whole, and then considers in some detail the human response to these physical factors. Wherever they are relevant, short introductions are given to related topics such as air mass climatology, soil formation and characteristics, plant adaptations, cultural patterns of human settlement, or population problems, which may be included in other branches of geography studied in the Sixth Form, but which are introduced here in definite relation to the Mediterranean lands.

Part Two of the book deals with regional geography. The countries lying to the north of the Mediterranean are examined first, followed by those of North Africa, and then by the lands situated at the eastern end of the sea. Much of the detail of the European and African countries has already appeared in *Europe* and *Africa*, but the authors have revised, enlarged and in many cases completely rewritten their chapters so as to bring them in line with the general aim of the book. The chapters on the Levant lands, by the author of *Europe*, are entirely new. In the Maghrib and the Levant, the countries are first grouped on a major regional basis and then examined individually; and all the Mediterranean countries are subdivided and surveyed along traditional lines of physical, human and regional geography. Inevitably, there is some repetition of material given in Part One of the book; sometimes this is done deliberately, but in any case it may be of advantage to view various aspects of our survey from different angles.

The relationship between history and geography is of very great importance in a study of the Mediterranean lands, the more so since from the region we draw our heritage of Western civilisation. Consequently, due prominence is given throughout to the historical factors which have helped to bring each of the Mediterranean lands into existence and to the political and economic factors which sustain them. Every effort has been made to give as up-to-date information as possible, but in both political and economic fields there are such rapid changes around the Mediterranean that it is difficult to keep abreast all the time. Constant reappraisal is imperative, for example, of the economies of North Africa and the Levant lands.

The latest available statistics of physical, economic and social geography have been used, but statistical tables have purposely been reduced to a minimum and relevant figures included in the text, where they are of more value. Maps and diagrams have been specially drawn to illustrate the text, and with very few exceptions every place-name mentioned in the text is shown on them. Where there are alternative names or where names have been changed both forms are given at least once in the book; and where temperature figures are mentioned both Centigrade and Fahrenheit readings are shown. Sample study questions, many of them set by Examination Boards, are added at the end of most chapters, and a "Short Guide to Further Reading and Study" is placed at the end of the book.

In view of the prospective adoption of the metric system in the U.K., metric equivalents of heights and distances are given, and a brief conversion table of Imperial and metric units is included as an appendix.

The authors wish to express once more their thanks for the help given by so many people in the compilation of their books on *Europe* and *Africa*, on which much of the present work is based. We are indebted especially to the authors of the works included in the bibliography who have beaten out paths for us and made our task easier. We are grateful to the Government departments of many countries which have provided information and photographs, and to the Examining Boards which have allowed questions set by them to be reproduced.

J.J.B.
H.R.J.

March, 1969

CONTENTS

PART ONE

THE GEOGRAPHICAL FRAMEWORK

LIST OF ILLUSTRATIONS

LIST OF TABLES

PART ONE

THE GEOGRAPHICAL FRAMEWORK

Chapter I

THE MEDITERRANEAN BASIN

INTRODUCTORY

FROM the dawn of history the Mediterranean Sea and the lands which surround it have played a most significant part in the evolution of a succession of civilisations, the latest of which (and the most highly developed) being the one we live in today. To the ancient peoples of Mesopotamia, Babylonia, Syria, Palestine and Egypt, the Mediterranean was "The Great Sea," yet they knew very little about it; their knowledge was confined to its eastern waters, the area which we call the Levant. To the ancient Greeks and more especially to the Romans, for whom it was at the heart of their empire, it became *Mare Internum*, the "interior sea," and later the Italians named it *Mare Nostrum*, "our sea." The name "Mediterranean," which means "in the middle of the land," does not appear to have come into general use until about the beginning of the Christian era. It describes admirably this almost landlocked sea, while it also gives some prominence to the *terra*, the land which surrounds it. All this seems to suggest that the Mediterranean Sea may have some kind of unifying influence on the countries which border it or come closely within its scope.

The following chapters will attempt to show that this is undoubtedly the case. Over most of the Mediterranean borderlands there is a large degree of physical, climatic, historical, and economic unity. But first it is necessary to define the area covered in this book. The terms "Mediterranean region" and "area of Mediterranean climate," so familiar to most students and often used almost as synonymous in meaning, can be very misleading and even completely erroneous if applied indiscriminately to the Mediterranean lands as a whole. All geographers recognise that there is a "Mediterranean region," but they limit this term in the strict sense to those areas which experience the true "Mediterranean climate." We shall discuss later the limits which should be set to these areas; meanwhile we may note that they are sometimes said to embrace the extensive region in which the olive grows. More loosely, the term "Mediterranean region" is occasionally applied to all the region enclosed by the Alpine fold mountains which encircle much of the sea; but since this excludes parts of the Iberian peninsula and of Yugoslavia, the whole of the African "shield" countries of Libya and Egypt, and the Asiatic plateaus of Turkey, Syria, Lebanon, Israel and Jordan, it can hardly be regarded as a satisfactory definition.

The title of the present book is *The Mediterranean Lands*, and the scope of the work includes all countries which open to the Mediterranean Sea

3

or are associated with it, with the exception of France. Mediterranean France forms so distinctive a unit that it is given completely independent consideration. Portugal, on the other hand, although it lies outside the Mediterranean basin, is viewed as part of our study, since structurally it is part of the Iberian peninsula, and its climate is "Mediterranean." Jordan is included as one of the Levant lands in spite of having no Mediterranean seaboard, partly because of its orientation towards the Mediterranean, partly because of its historical, social, and economic impact on Israel. Yugoslavia lies for the most part shut off from Mediterranean influences, and eastern Turkey is on the fringe of "continental" Asia, but both countries are here considered as within the scope of this book since they have long Mediterranean seaboards. Similarly, the Saharan desert portions of Morocco, Algeria and Tunisia, although far from the Mediterranean Sea, are included in relation to these countries, while Libya and Egypt can hardly be excluded from our study, since each has a Mediterranean coastline, albeit of desert character. Moreover, in the case of Egypt, its strategic importance as the guardian of the Suez Canal and its large population together invest the country with more than ordinary significance in the Mediterranean basin.

PHYSICAL CHARACTERISTICS OF THE SEA BASIN

The Mediterranean Sea (*see* Fig. 1) occupies a basin between southern Europe and northern Africa, and bounded in the east by part of Southwest Asia. More than 2250 miles (3600 m) from end to end and with an area of 1,146,000 square miles (2,979,600 sq. km), it is all that remains of a great ocean known as the Tethys, which in early geological times stretched halfway round the globe south of Eurasia. The present sea took roughly the form we know today in late Cretaceous and early Tertiary times, as a result, apparently, of a movement northwards of the African shield towards Eurasia. This northward migration compressed the layers of sedimentary rocks on the floor of the Tethys geosyncline and folded, faulted and uplifted them to form the mountain ranges of the Alpine system which today encloses much of the Mediterranean basin, especially in the west. At the same time, some parts of the folded sedimentaries, together with broken-off portions of the proto-continents, were forced downwards to form deep hollows in the floor of the basin; others, such as Corsica and Sardinia, fragmental pieces of the ancient mainland, were left upstanding above sea-level.

Mountain folds are found throughout the length of the Mediterranean along its European borders, and on the African side from the Atlantic to the Gulf of Gabès, but east of this there are no encircling ranges in Libya and Egypt. Here the African shield as far as the Sinai peninsula drops from a tableland by a series of faulted terraces to the coast, and this step-like formation is continued northwards in the floor of the sea. The eastern margins of the Mediterranean are also lacking in mountain folds of any

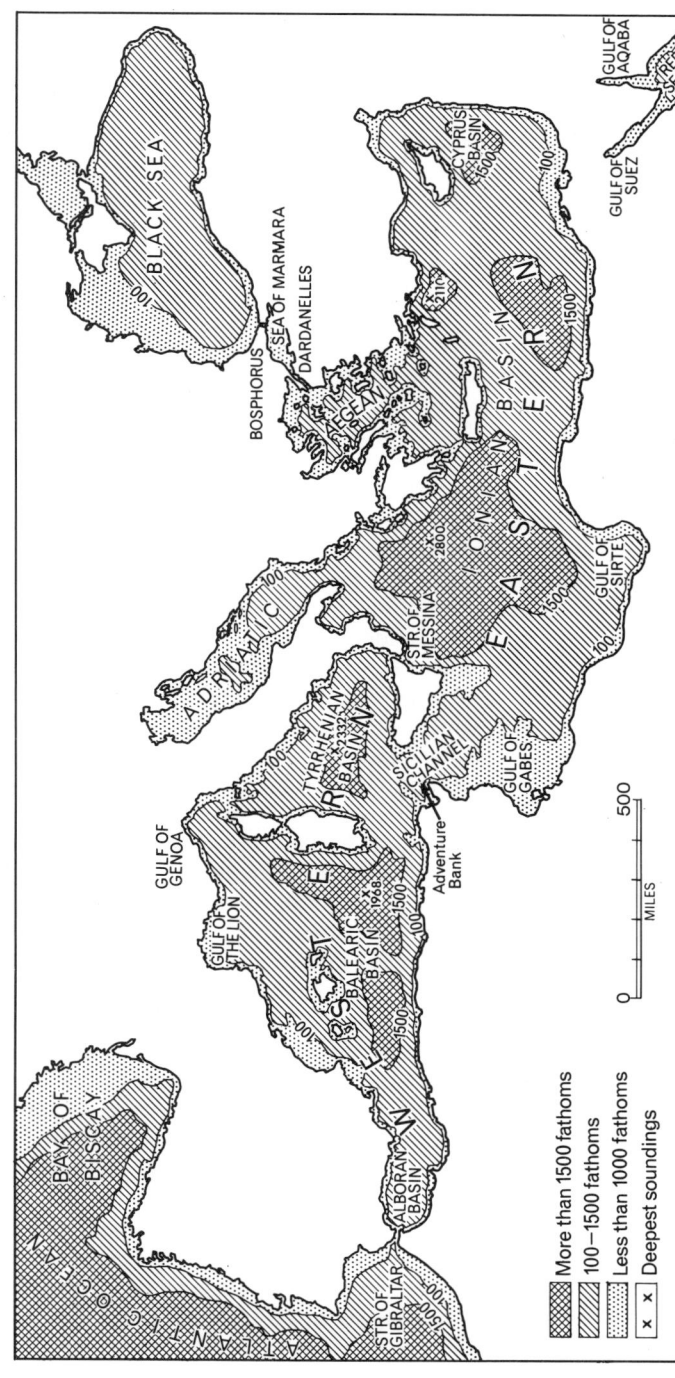

FIG. I.—The Mediterranean Sea: the chief basins and their subdivisions; the 100-fathom and 1500-fathom bathymetric contours.

size. The Arabian shield, which in the Levant lands underlies sedimentaries of considerable thickness in some places, lay outside the region most
affected by the Alpine mountain-building "storm," and although there
was some folding of the sedimentaries, only in Lebanon was it sufficiently
intense to produce high mountains; even there only one peak rises to
more than 10,000 ft (Qernus es Sauda, 10,030 ft, 3057 m). Along the
south of Turkey, however, fully developed Alpine folds are encountered
again, and they continue eastwards beyond the Turkish boundary; they
can be regarded as extensions of the Alpine folds of southern Europe.

SUBSIDIARY BASINS

Within the Mediterranean basin as a whole several subsidiary basins may
be distinguished. The main basin is first of all divided in two, the Western
and Eastern Mediterranean basins, by Italy, Sicily, and a submarine ridge
known as the Adventure Bank which runs from Sicily to Cape Bon at a
depth of not more than 200 fathoms (366 m).

The Western basin stretches from the Strait of Gibraltar to the Sicilian
Channel. At its western end the Strait of Gibraltar, which is only 9·22 miles
(14·83 km) across at its narrowest point, is floored by a sill which rises to
within 200 fathoms (366 m) of the sea surface and prevents the deepest
waters of the Mediterranean flowing outwards to the Atlantic. The
Western basin may be further divided into three smaller basins. Between
Gibraltar and the barren, volcanic island of Alboran which lies north of
Melilla is a small basin, sometimes called the Alboran basin, with a depth
of 790 fathoms (1445 m), while to the east of the island the Balearic basin
extends to Corsica and Sardinia and reaches a maximum depth of 1968
fathoms (3598 m). The floor of this basin is broken by a ridge from which
rise the Balearic Islands. These islands belong to the Alpine fold system
and are continuations of the Betic Cordillera of southern Spain. Corsica
and Sardinia, however, together with the Estérel and Maures massifs of
south-east France, are fractured pieces of an old continental mass, probably of Hercynian age, with characteristic pre-Cambrian gneisses, schists
and granites. Parts of the African coast in Morocco and Algeria appear to
be of a similar age and origin. The remainder of the Western Mediterranean basin is known as the Tyrrhenian basin. It is not as large in area as
the Balearic basin and its floor slopes more gradually downwards from its
surrounding coasts, but it has a much larger proportion of deep water,
much of the basin being at a greater depth than 1850 fathoms (3383 m).
Its deepest point is 2332 fathoms (4265 m), about 50 miles (80 Km) south-
west of the island of Ponziane and roughly midway between the islands
of Capri and Sardinia.

Most of the Eastern Mediterranean basin is occupied by the Ionian basin
which stretches from the Sicilian Channel almost to the Levantine coast;
a slight submarine ridge which extends southwards from Cyprus, however, here shuts off a small basin 1250 fathoms (2286 m) deep. The Ionian
basin is comparatively shallow on its southern side where the faulted

terraces of the African shield extend seawards, and especially where the submarine portion of the Nile delta reaches to the north; but the northern half of the basin has the greatest depths in the whole of the Mediterranean, reaching 2110 fathoms (3859 m) near the island of Rhodes, and 2800 fathoms (5121 m), the deepest part of the sea floor so far discovered, 65 miles (104 km) west of Cape Matapan (Tainaron) in Greece. It will be noted that these deeps lie on the outer side of a great arc of folded mountains which may be traced from the Pindus in Greece, through Crete and Rhodes to the Taurus in Turkey; the juxtaposition of fold mountains and submarine trenches and a liability to earthquake action (*see* below) together present a pattern reminiscent, though on a much smaller scale, of similar physical phenomena which occur along the east coasts of Japan and the Philippines, and also in the West Indies.

In the north of the eastern Mediterranean there are two extensions to the Ionian basin, the Adriatic and Aegean seas. Neither of these constitutes a separate basin, and each offers many interesting contrasts to the other. The Adriatic seems to have been formed as a lowland between the mountain folds of the Apennines and the Italian and Dinaric Alps, and flooded by the waters of the Mediterranean. At one time the sea extended into the area now occupied by the eastern half of the north Italian plain, but the abundant silts deposited by the Po and its tributaries and by other Alpine rivers filled the northern portion of the sea to produce the plain of Lombardy and to build the extensive Po delta. The filling-in process continues; the delta is increasing in size and the silts carried further out to sea have constructed a kind of submarine shelf which now extends in shallow waters as far as the "heel" of Italy. This shelf, however, for some reason not yet fully explained, is interrupted by a deep trench which cuts across the floor of the sea between Pescara in Italy and Sibenik in Yugoslavia. An axis of tectonic movement runs the whole length of the Adriatic; whereas the Italian side of the narrow sea is rising and giving all the signs of an emergent coast, *i.e.*, a piedmont plain and few or no coastal openings, the Dalmatian seaboard on the eastern side of the Adriatic, with its festoons of islands, truncated mountain ranges and extensive inlets, is obviously developing as a result of submergence.

The island-studded Aegean Sea, the second of the northward extensions of the Ionian basin, was formed probably by the faulting and sinking of two ancient massifs during the late Tertiary period. The Cyclades are fragments of the more southern of these fractured crustal blocks; a northern block is represented by the island of Thásos and by scattered fragments of ancient rock along the Macedonian and Thracian coastlands. Possibly the Rhodope massif in southern Bulgaria belonged to the same block. The break-up of the southern block was accompanied by volcanic activity; the harbour of Mílos is an extinct crater, and Thíra has soils developed from lava. With the foundering of the ancient blocks, a transgression of the Mediterranean waters reached far to the north, penetrating along the valleys of the rivers Vardar, Morava and Struma to the foot of the Balkan mountains. A further epeirogenic (vertical) movement towards the end of the Tertiary uplifted the northern portion of the region causing the waters to retreat and forming the present coastline of the Aegean, while the great amount of silt brought down by rivers during the Quaternary Ice Age and deposited on the sea floor has made the northern portion of the Aegean very shallow.

The Sea of Marmara, although strictly not a part of the Mediterranean Sea, is included here because it lies within the confines of Turkey, a Mediterranean land, and it was formed by the same earth movements which gave birth to the Aegean. It lies in an area of 4500 square miles (11,700 sq. km) of subsidence permanently flooded by the waters of the Black Sea, to which it is connected by the Bosphorus, a passage 20 miles long (32 km) and from 800 yards to $2\frac{3}{4}$ miles wide (4·4 km). The Sea of Marmara flows to the Aegean via the Dardanelles (Hellespont), a drowned river valley 40 miles long (64 km) and up to 4 miles wide (6·4 km), carved in soft Cretaceous and Tertiary rocks.

The Eastern and Western basins of the Mediterranean are connected by two deep channels north and south of Sicily. To the north is the Strait of Messina which at its northern end is little more than 2 miles wide (3·2 km). In summer there is little difficulty in navigating this passage, but in winter, partly because of treacherous winds and partly because of dangerous cross-currents formed over a submarine ridge, small boats risk a hazardous journey. The southern passage from west to east is the Sicilian Channel, about 100 miles wide (160 km). It lies over a submarine ridge which connects Sicily with the Maouin peninsula of Tunisia. The small islands of Pantelleria, Linosa, and Lampedusa are upstanding portions of the ridge; and near the eastern end of the channel, and until recent years considered to be in a commanding strategic position, are the Maltese Islands.

The Western Mediterranean basin is much smaller than the Eastern, and on the whole it lies about 5 degrees of latitude further north, a factor which has considerable influence on climate and development, as will be considered later in more detail. The Western basin, too, is more regular in shape and structure than the Eastern; it has few islands and these are generally larger than those in the east, where the numerous archipelagoes and long openings such as the Aegean and Adriatic seas find no counterpart in the west.

PHYSICAL GEOLOGY OF THE REGION—AN OUTLINE

It has already been noted that the Mediterranean Sea is all that is left of a great ocean which in Mesozoic times stretched along the south of a land mass which may be thought of as Eurasia, although in that era it bore little resemblance in outline to its present shape. Far to the south the Tethys, as the ocean is called, was bounded by a vast continental block known to geologists as Gondwanaland, which included the extensive shield which later broke up and formed most of Africa, large portions of Arabia, the

Deccan of India, the South American plateaus of Brazil and Guiana, and most of Australia. All these areas are composed of Archaean rocks which resisted folding in any of the major tectonic movements which have affected the earth's surface, and so today there are few fold mountains in any of them.

To the north of the Tethys stretched Laurasia, the name given to a land mass which may be considered to comprise the origins of Europe, Asia and much of North America. The proto-European section of this land mass had in the course of its existence prior to the formation of the Mediterranean basin undergone at least three mountain-building revolutions, the Charnian in pre-Cambrian times, the Caledonian in the late Silurian and early Devonian, and the Hercynian in the late Carboniferous and early Permian. From the completion of the Hercynian orogenesis there were well over 100 million years of quiescence, during which there were no major earth movements; and in this time sediments eroded from the giant Hercynian ranges and other bordering lands were swept into the Tethys to form sandstones, clays, and shales; and these, together with the limestones and chalks developed from a rich marine life, became deep layers of sedimentary rocks on the floor of the ocean, which was now in fact a gigantic geosyncline.

At some time, estimated variously by geologists from the late Jurassic to the middle Cretaceous, the continental land mass of Gondwanaland began to move north and break up. The reasons for this "continental drift" are still unknown, but the result as far as we are concerned was that one portion of the land mass, the African and Arabian shields, gradually drew near to the "European" part of Laurasia. The sedimentaries on the floor of Tethys were buckled into folds, some simple, some complex, and on the north of the ocean the folds were forced out of the water and pressed against the worn-down and very rigid stumps of the Hercynian ranges in the south of the northern land mass, to form high mountain chains. On the southern edge of the Tethys, folds were crumpled along the front of the advancing Gondwanaland, but these resulted in mountain ranges of less height. Another result of the meeting of the two land masses, in addition to the building of mountains, was to trap a vast lake of sea water and give birth to the Mediterranean Sea.

Around the Mediterranean, then, we can trace two series of fold mountains, one to the north and one to the south. The northern series is known as the Alpides, the southern one the Dinarides, while the whole mountain-building movement is normally called the Alpine or Tertiary orogenesis (see Fig. 2). In some places between the Alpides and Dinarides were enclosed Hercynian blocks fractured and separated by the Alpine thrust. Some of the blocks were forced up, some down, the German names horst being given to those uplifted, and graben to the areas of subsidence. In the Mediterranean region the "mesetas" of Spain and Morocco, the Rhodope and Char massifs in the Balkan peninsula, and the Anatolian Plateau in Turkey are horsts of Hercynian origin, while the islands of

Corsica and Sardinia and the French massifs of Estérel and Maures are apparently of the same age. Notable graben include the Balearic basin of the western Mediterranean and the Black Sea basin. The final result of all the movements given above was the obliteration of the Tethys and its transformation into the Mediterranean Sea.

The Alpides consist of the Betic Cordillera, the Cantabrians and Pyrenees in Spain, the main ranges of the Alps in south-east France, Switzerland and Austria, the great curve of the Carpathians, Transylvanian Alps, and Balkan mountains (Stara Planina), the Yaila mountains in the Crimea, and the Caucasus (*see* Fig. 3). Beyond the Caucasus the Alpides continue eastwards far into Asia—to the northern Pamirs and ranges such as the Tian Shan.

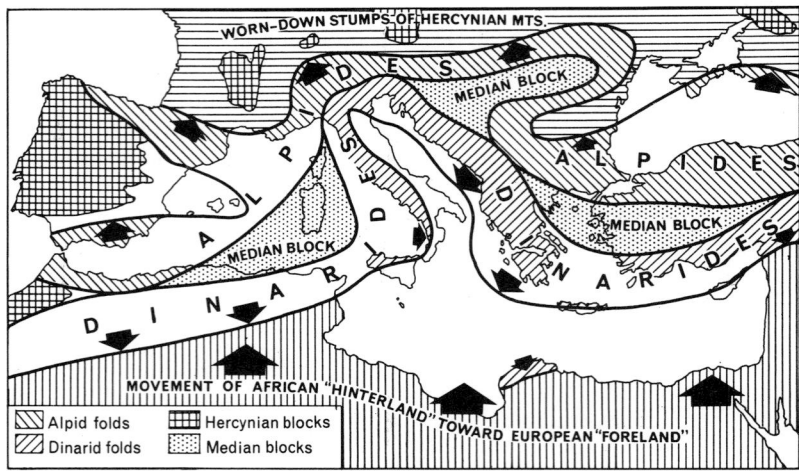

FIG. 2.—The Alpides and Dinarides: together they make up the Alpine mountain system. The median blocks, also known as median masses and Zwischengebirge, are intermontane areas of simple structure, uplifted or down-thrust between the two series of folds. Small arrows show direction of folding.

The Dinarides include the Atlas ranges in north-west Africa, much of Sicily, the Apennines and the southern ranges of the Alps in Italy, the Dinaric Alps and Pindus mountains in the Balkan peninsula, the island of Crete, and the Taurus mountains in Asia Minor. Asiatic continuations of the Dinarides appear to include the Zagros and the lofty Himalayas, but as yet the exact relationship of the Tertiary ranges of Asia to those of Europe has not been fully established.

The formation of the complete Alpine system took millions of years, and ranges were uplifted at long intervals. The Atlas and Caucasus are the oldest folds, dating as far back as the late Jurassic. The Pyrenees, Dinaric Alps and Taurus belong to the late Cretaceous; and the early and middle Tertiary saw the main uplift of the Alps, Carpathians and their

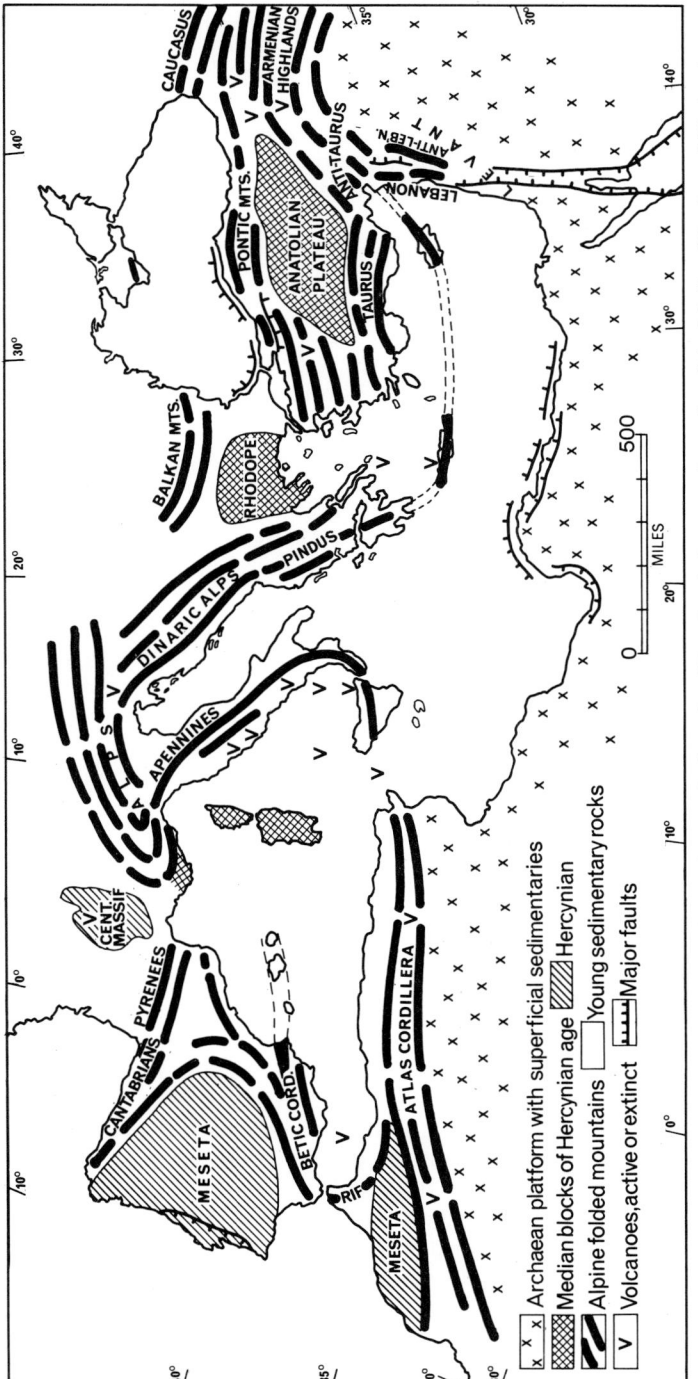

Fig. 3.—The Mediterranean lands: structure. The Archaean Platform is of Pre-Cambrian age; the rocks of the Median Blocks and Hercynian are Carbo–Permian; rocks of Triassic, Rhaetic, Jurassic, Cretaceous and Tertiary age make up the Alps and most of the lowlands; superficial deposits of Quaternary along coasts and river valleys; Quaternary volcanics in Italy and Armenia; fragmental Cambrian in N.W. Iberia.

continuations eastwards, and a second movement of the Pyrenees. Some parts of the orogenic belts show two phases of uplift. The Rif mountains of north Morocco, for instance, appear to join across the Strait of Gibraltar with the southern ranges of the Betic Cordillera. The Rif folding, however, was later than and subsidiary to the main uplift of the Alpides and Dinarides, whose principal ranges continue independently to the west and are terminated abruptly at the Atlantic Ocean.

The folds of the Alpides and Dinarides lie in a series of great arcs, such as are seen very well in the Carpathian-Balkans and the Apennines-Atlas. Where the northern and southern series approach each other closely, as they do in northern Italy, the tremendous pressures produced a complicated system of folds which were broken and forced northwards on top of each other in vast overthrusts and nappes, best exemplified in Switzerland. These have so dislocated the original folds as to make it extremely difficult to reconstruct the mountain-building process in this area. Nappes are found also in the Rif Atlas, the Betic Cordillera, the Apennines, the Carpathians and the Dinaric Alps.

The folding of the Alpides was complicated by the resistance of the worn-down Hercynian system to the north; consequently the geology of the Alpides is very much more complex than that of the Dinarides. There seems little doubt that the relatively rigid structure of the Hercynians was a major factor in determining the shape of the whole of the Alpine system. The difficulty of reconstruction is increased also by the presence in most of the folds of crystalline rocks far older than the predominant limestones, and disclosed by a very long period of erosion. Such crystalline rocks, invariably of Hercynian age, occur in the highest peaks in Morocco, Spain, Switzerland, France (Mont Blanc, 15,681 ft, 4780 m), and the Caucasus. These last are the highest mountains in Europe, and have Hercynian fragments in the loftiest peak, Mt Elbruz (18,467 ft, 5629 m). It has been suggested that in Mesozoic times considerable tracts of the southern Hercynians were submerged beneath the waters of the Tethys and covered with sedimentaries, but that some areas remained uncovered, as islands. When the major mountain uplift occurred, these were caught up in the folds, and appear today as inliers high in the Alpine ranges.

At the time when the folds of the Alpine system were rising, the forces of denudation were very active and sediments were being deposited in shallow seas on the flanks of the emergent mountains. These deposits, mostly clays and sandstones, are today known as *flysch*. Flysch is found in largest amounts north of the Alps; in the Mediterranean region it occurs chiefly in the Apennines. Erosion has continued to be rapid, especially during the Ice Age, and more in the Alpides than in the Dinarides. This being the case, and since the northern series of ranges are in general higher than the southern, one must conclude that for the Alpides to have attained their present altitude, there must have been a slow, continuous elevation of their folds subsequent to the original orogenesis or uplift. Stability seems now to have been reached in the Alpides, if we consider the absence of earth movements in recent geological times; the Dinarides, however, are still very unstable, as is shown by the frequency of earth tremors and major earthquakes and the number of active volcanoes in or near their folds (*see* below).

During the Ice Age, most of the Alpides were glaciated, but the Dinarides suffered to a much less extent. The mountains of the northern series show all the characteristics associated with valley glaciers; there are even today many peaks in the Pyrenees, Italian Alps and eastern Turkey perpetually covered by snow, and in the high valleys of the French and Swiss Alps there are some quite extensive glaciers. In the Dinarides, however, signs of glaciation are much less marked; and although snow may rest for many months on the higher peaks, only rarely does it persist throughout the summer, and there are consequently no glaciers.

One result of glaciation was to make the Alpides more open to human penetration and settlement than the Dinarides, by reason of the deep valleys carved by the ice. Although the actual peaks are very high, numerous passes make the ranges easy to cross, and from early times the Alps, Pyrenees, Carpathians and Stara Planina have supported large numbers of people. The Dinarides, on the other hand, have been less eroded than the Alpides; they are not so faulted and broken by dislocation; they were less affected by the Ice Age; and they are located in a drier climate, with less powerful erosive agents. The limestones of the Dinarides have weathered into rugged and often almost impenetrable masses with precipitous slopes, as in the central Apennines and the ranges to the east of the Adriatic Sea. Such areas have only a scanty population.

The lands bordering the southern side of the Eastern Mediterranean basin, that is, from the Gulf of Gabès eastwards, and the countries which lie along its eastern margin are situated away from the region affected by Alpine folding and present a striking contrast in structure and relief to that already described. They form part of the ancient, stable platform of Gondwanaland, which had a large share in the Alpine folding. The Archaean rocks which comprise the basement of most of Africa and Arabia were resistant to folding, and so it may be said that in general these land masses have flattish surfaces, and a monotony of relief not found elsewhere around the Mediterranean. Although it resisted folding, however, the ancient platform underwent several periods of subsidence and uplift, during which marine transgressions by the Tethys resulted in the deposition of sedimentaries on the Archaean floor, especially in the north. The principal mountain ranges are shown in Fig. 4.

During early Tertiary times, and in a way comparable to that which produced the fractures and dislocations in the Hercynian system in Eurasia, the stresses set up by the Alpine "storm" caused extensive faulting and fissuring in northern Gondwanaland. Arabia broke away from the main body of the ancient continent, and the trough of subsidence between the two land masses was drowned, so producing the Red Sea, the Gulf of Aden, and the rift valley which contains the Dead Sea and the river Jordan.

The Great Rift Valley in Africa, which extends southwards to Lake Malawi (Nyasa), is part of the same trough. Faulting led to the formation of horsts, graben and downthrow basins; and sub-aerial erosion of the sedimentary rocks which rested on the horsts has resulted in low hill ranges such as are found in Cyrenaica and north-west Egypt. In Israel, Lebanon and Syria the surface sedimentaries were thrown into slight anticlinals, as in the hills of Judaea or the more lofty Lebanon and Anti-Lebanon mountains. In the south of Israel and Jordan, the younger sedimentaries form a very thin

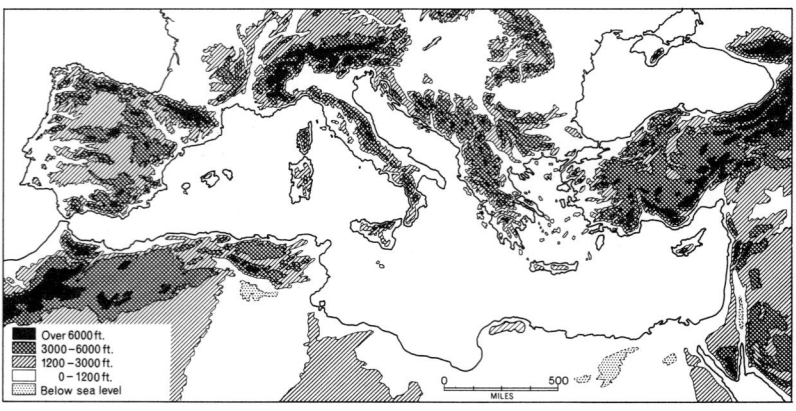

FIG. 4.—The Mediterranean lands: relief.

layer and in some places have been eroded completely, exposing the Archaean basement. Northwards in the Levant lands there was fracturing in both north–south and east–west directions, so that there is a series of detached upland masses separated by lowlands such as the Plain of Esdraelon in Israel, the Bekaa in Lebanon and the plains of Akkar and Bukeia in Syria.

EARTHQUAKES AND VULCANICITY

As we have seen, the whole area covered by the Mediterranean Sea and its neighbouring lands is geologically very young. The first movements of the Alpine orogenesis were in late Jurassic and early Cretaceous times, but the fold mountains so characteristic of the region date in the main from the beginning of the Tertiary period, roughly 50 million years ago. The consequence is that seismically the region remains unstable in many parts and is still in a process of settling down. This is shown by the large number of earthquakes, many of disastrous proportions, experienced in quite recent times, and by numerous volcanoes, some still active.

Earth movements within the folded ranges themselves are rare, but the presence of volcanic rocks in the eastern Alps and the Atlas mountains, and the numerous displacements along the faults, show that this was not always so. Most tectonic movements associated with the Alpine system occur, however, in districts adjacent to the folds, that is, along faults in the Hercynian blocks in Eurasia and in the Afro-Arabian shields, the two land masses which cracked and foundered in giving birth to the mountain system. A great fault in Portugal, for instance, stretches north–south from the mouth of the river Douro to Cape St Vincent, and a downthrow on the seaward side gave rise to the lowlands of that country. Slight earth tremors are still frequent along the line of the fault, and in 1755 a violent earthquake destroyed the city of Lisbon. A fault in Thessaly, south of the Rhodope massif, led to major earth tremors in 1954; and movement along the faults of fractured and dislocated fragments of the same ancient block resulted in 1962 in the destruction of Skopje in Yugoslavia, with the loss of over 1000 lives. The eastern end of the Anatolian plateau in Asia Minor is extremely unstable, with major earthquakes registered at Erzincan in 1939 and around the small town of Varto in 1966. The last-named movement had its epicentre south of Erzerum and west of Lake Van, and was the most disastrous shock experienced in the Mediterreanean region in modern times, killing 2394 people, injuring many more, and rendering about 100,000 homeless. Along the African coast, earthquake disturbances occur along faults in Algeria and Libya, the most serious in recent years being at Orleansville (now El Asnam) in 1954 and at Barce, where in 1963 300 people were killed and 15,000 made homeless. In Sicily, the city of Messina was almost destroyed by earthquake in 1908, and in January, 1968, Montevago, in the west of the island, was the centre of shocks which resulted in great destruction and the loss of more than 400 lives.

The original subsidence or uplift of fractured blocks of the ancient land masses was often accompanied by the extrusion of lava and the building of volcanic cones. Much of western Sardinia has a cover of tuffs and lava, with Mt Ferru, an extinct volcano, rising to over 3000 feet (900 m). The lava complex at the western end of the Great Atlas and the extinct volcano on the barren island of Alboran, isolated midway between Spain and Morocco, originated at roughly the same period. The break-up and dislocation of the Hercynian block of which the Rhodope forms a major portion was accompanied by an outpouring of lava, and its final collapse was marked in the southern Aegean Sea by the growth of volcanic cones such as occur in the islands of Aegina and Santorin in the Cyclades. The highlands of western Arabia are due largely to the lava outflow and cone formation which accompanied the subsidence of the Red Sea rift valley, and smaller rifts in Lebanon and western Syria led to the widespread lava sheets, mainly of basalt, in northern Jordan and the Hauran plateau in south Syria.

The vulcanicity mentioned so far dates chiefly from Tertiary times, but in Asia Minor the results of both Tertiary and the more recent Quaternary earth movements can be seen. The foundering of the Black Sea basin in the Pliocene led to extensive faulting along the southern coastline and to the extrusion of the lava sheets which cover much of the region between Samsun and Trabzon (Trebizond), an area which is still liable to disastrous earthquakes. In the south of Turkey, the closely packed folds of the Taurus mountains, which rise like a wall behind the Mediterranean coast, show few signs of igneous activity, but the eastern ranges, east of Cape Anamur, include huge sheets of lava, culminating in the Quaternary volcanic area of Erciyas Daglari (Ercies mountains) where there are peaks of over 11,000 feet (3350 m). Lava sheets form a complete cover for the northern portion of the Anti-Taurus, the parallel fold ranges which strike towards the north-east corner of the Mediterranean.

North of the Taurus the plateau of Anatolia has an altitude generally between 3000 and 5000 ft (900–1500 m). Above this undulating surface rise scattered highlands to a further 5000 ft (1500 m); these are usually small horsts with extinct Tertiary volcanic cones flanking them. To the north of Ankara sheets of basalt are further indications of igneous activity, and throughout the plateau there are valuable igneous intrusions of gold, chromium and manganese. An eastward continuation of the Anatolian plateau, known as the plateau of Armenia, has a fairly level and generally inhospitable character which it owes to Quaternary outpourings of lava so vast as to fill entire valleys. In one part volcanic cones were built, the largest being the extinct Mt Ararat (16,916 ft, 5156 m), and the dormant Mt Nimrut (Nimrud). One eruption of Nimrut resulted in the blocking of a river valley and the formation of the aretic (inland drainage) basin of Lake Van.

Present-day volcanic activity in the Mediterranean region is usually associated with the active volcanoes in peninsular and insular Italy, where there are also remains of Tertiary eruptions. In south Tuscany and Umbria, for instance, there are extinct Tertiary cones and calderas, some of the latter being occupied by lakes such as Bolzano, while further south the Agro Romano in the lower Tiber basin is dotted with many low hills of volcanic origin. Further south again, the plain of Naples is a basin of subsidence filled in by Quaternary activity which still continues. North-west of the city of Naples is the wreck of an immense volcanic crater, the Phlegraean Fields, where there are hot, sulphurous springs (*solfatare*) and occasional spurts of liquid lava. In the south of the plain the active volcano of Vesuvius (3891 ft, 1186 m) has erupted frequently in modern times; its most violent outburst was in A.D. 79, when an explosion blew off a large section of the crater. The town of Herculaneum was buried in hot ash and another town, Pompeii, was completely covered by mud washed down the mountain slopes by torrential rains which often accompany volcanic eruptions.

In the Lipari Islands there are several active volcanoes, notably Stromboli, "the lighthouse of the Mediterranean," and Vulcano, which has given its name to all volcanoes. The Strait of Messina, between Sicily and the mainland, is notorious for earthquakes; the towns of Reggio and Messina, on opposite sides of the strait, have suffered severely on many occasions, the latest in 1908. South-west of Messina the massive volcano of Etna (10,739 ft, 3356 m) is almost continuously active; and in south-east Sicily a cover of basic lavas and tuffs on the low plateau of Monti Iblei is an indication of former activity. About 30 miles (48 km) roughly north of Palermo in western Sicily is the lonely, extinct volcanic island of Ustica; and on the south side of the submarine ridge which connects Sicily to north Africa the volcanic peak of Pantelleria rises above the waters.

STUDY QUESTIONS

1. Write a short account of the geological movements which led to the formation of the basin of the Mediterranean Sea.

2. What do you understand by (a) Alpides, (b) Dinarides, (c) Gondwanaland? To what degree have all three been factors in determining the present shape of the Mediterranean Sea basin?

3. Compare and contrast the physical features of the marginal lands of the Eastern and Western basins of the Mediterranean Sea.

4. "From a seismic point of view, some parts of the Mediterranean lands are among the most unstable in the world." Write a short essay to show the truth of this statement.

5. Give an account of volcanic and earthquake action in the region of the Mediterranean Sea.

Chapter II

THE MEDITERRANEAN SEA

WE have already noted that the waters of the Mediterranean Sea cover an area of 1,146,000 square miles (2,979,600 sq. km) in two great, inter-connected, tectonic basins which stretch roughly east–west for 2250 miles (3600 km) and which separate Europe from Africa; and because the exit through the Strait of Gibraltar to the Atlantic is so narrow, the Mediterranean is usually regarded as an inland sea—the largest in the world. The smaller western portion of the sea, with a maximum width of 470 miles (752 km), is bounded on the east by peninsular Italy and the fractured land bridge of which Sicily is the main upstanding part. The Eastern basin of the Mediterranean, 420 miles (672 km) at its widest, is much less regular in shape than the Western, especially in the north where the Adriatic and Aegean seas project into the Euro-Asiatic land mass. As a whole, the Mediterranean lies between latitudes 30 and 45 degrees N., but it is impor-tant to note that whereas the line of 40 degrees N. runs through the middle of the Western basin, the eastern Mediterranean lies astride 35 degrees N., and that this more southerly position has led to marked climatic and hydro-graphic differences between east and west.

The most notable hydrographic features of the Mediterranean to be con-sidered here are those relating to temperature, salinity, tidal ranges and currents, in all of which the sea has peculiarities which stand in sharp con-trast to corresponding phenomena observed in the neighbouring Atlantic Ocean.

TEMPERATURE

Temperatures of surface waters in the Mediterranean to a depth of about 50 fathoms (91 m) are remarkably high and uniform throughout. The mean annual isotherm of 65° F (18·3° C) runs from Gibraltar to the north of Sardinia and then through the Strait of Messina to the Gulf of Corinth; that of 70° F (21·1° C) cuts across the south-east of the sea from Cyrenaica to Israel. Although mean annual temperatures are often very misleading when applied to land surfaces, for they may disguise big differences between winter and summer heat, on the sea the far slower changes and the much smaller range of temperature experienced between winter and summer make the figures more meaningful. This is especially the case in the Mediterranean, where seasonal and local variations are never large.

In general, surface temperatures are highest at all times in the Eastern Mediterranean basin. Midsummer readings of over 80° F (26·7° C) are common in the surface waters off the southern Levant lands and in the rest of the basin they rarely fall as low even as 60° F (15·6° C). In winter temperatures fall from 58° F (14·4° C) near the coast of Egypt to 54° F (12·2° C) in the southern approaches to the Aegean and Adriatic seas. In the northern Aegean, where there is an inflow of colder water from the Black Sea, and also in the very shallow waters of the northern Adriatic which are cooled by the *bora* (*see* p. 38), winter temperatures may be much lower, sometimes less than 40° F (4·4° C). Temperatures in the Western Mediterranean basin range from 68° F (20° C) in summer along the African coast to 53° F (11·7° C) in winter off north-east Spain, with somewhat cooler waters in both seasons inside the Strait of Gibraltar through which there is a surface inflow from the Atlantic. All these temperatures, especially those of summer, are higher than might be expected in surface waters of comparable latitudes in other parts of the world.

Just as remarkable are the high temperatures which prevail with little seasonal variation at lower levels in the sea. At a depth of 100 fathoms (183 m) temperatures fall gradually from 60° F (15·6° C) off the Levant lands to 55° F (12·8° C) east of Gibraltar, and at 200 fathoms (366 m) there is a fall between the same places from 58° F (14·4° C) to 55° F (12·8° C). The temperatures at all depths near Gibraltar are very uniform and are lower than those found in the rest of the Western Mediterranean basin, as a result of the Atlantic inflow already mentioned. Elsewhere in the Western basin the average at 200 fathoms (366 m) is 56° F (13·3° C). At depths greater than 250 fathoms (457 km) temperatures are practically uniform to the sea floor, 55·5° F (13·1° C) in the Western basin, 56·5° F (13·6° C) in the Eastern. The temperature observed at the bottom of the "Pola Deep" (2046 fathoms—3742 m) south-west of Cape Matapan was 56·3° F (13·5° C).

The high temperatures in the depths of the Mediterranean are attributable (i) to the sills at the straits of Gibraltar and the Bosphorus/Dardanelles which allow cooler waters to enter only in the surface layers, and (ii) to the cumulative effects of summer insolation. Because of the sills the deep basins probably contain much of the same water which was trapped at the period of the Alpine "storm"; and the lower levels of the Mediterranean have become in effect a vast reservoir of heat and an important climatic control, especially in winter (*see* Chapter III).

SALINITY

The inflows of water into the Mediterranean from the Atlantic Ocean and Black Sea already mentioned are necessitated by very rapid evaporation from the surface of the almost enclosed sea. In the case of the Black Sea constantly augmented by accretions from rivers, the normal discharge of its waters into the Mediterranean is made greater by virtue of the high rate of evaporation in the Eastern basin, but from the Western basin there is no outward flow of surface waters at all to the Atlantic, largely because the contribution from rivers is insufficient to compensate for the loss by evaporation. At both ends of the Mediterranean, however, there is an outflow of deep, very saline water over the enclosing sills, greater in the Strait of Gibraltar than through the Dardanelles, but insignificant in either case as compared with the surface inflows. The outflow of deep waters is caused by differences in salinity at great depths. High insolation in summer leads to increased salinity in the surface waters; these sink to augment the very salty waters in the depths and there is a corresponding upwelling of slightly less saline layers and an escape over the sills. The water which flows outwards over the Gibraltar sill is much more saline and heavier

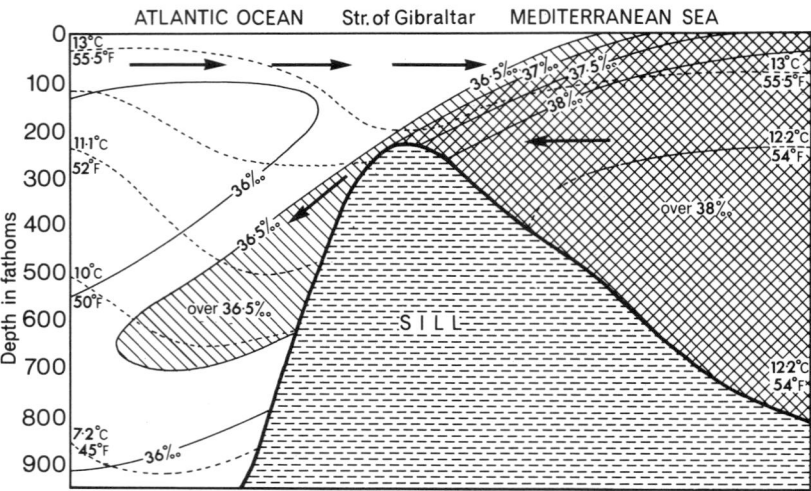

FIG. 5.—Strait of Gibraltar: currents, salinity and water temperatures. There is a contrast at lower levels on opposite sides of the sill in (i) salinity (in parts per thousand), (ii) in temperature (given in degrees Fahrenheit and Centigrade). (*Based on Schott.*)

than the corresponding layer in the Atlantic and it enters the ocean as a kind of submarine waterfall (*see* Fig. 5).

The total volume of fresh water added annually by rainfall and rivers (of which only the Rhône, Po and Nile contribute substantial amounts), is only about one-quarter of what is required to maintain the present level of the Mediterranean. The remainder is provided by the Atlantic and the Black Sea. The Atlantic contributes the major part, probably 71% of the total evaporation loss, and a further 4% comes from the Black Sea. Three-quarters of the water which feeds the Mediterranean, therefore, is already saline when it enters the sea, coming as it does either from the Atlantic, which has an average salinity near the Strait of Gibraltar of 36 *pro mille* (36 parts of salt to 1000 parts of water), or from the Black Sea, whose average salinity near its exit is 20 *pro mille*. Invasions of saline water on this scale, allied with a high rate of evaporation, produce an average salinity in the

Mediterranean far greater than that normal in comparable latitudes in the open ocean.

In the extreme west of the Mediterranean the salinity of the surface water is 36·3 *pro mille* and there is an increase eastwards to 37·6 *pro mille* east of Sardinia and to 39·0 *pro mille* or more off the coast of the Levant lands; the distribution of lower or higher salinity coincides more or less with that of temperature. At lower levels of the sea records of salinity are rather scanty, but observations made by various expeditions seem to show an average of 38·2 *pro mille* for the whole of the Mediterranean deeper than 200 fathoms (366 m), with the highest salinity, 39·0 *pro mille*, in the deeps south of Crete. It has been further observed that the more saline waters of the Eastern basin sink slowly and appear to creep westwards along the sea floor near the African coast as a kind of counter-current to the eastward movement of the surface waters in the same region (*see* below). It is part of this deep-sea movement which upwells and flows to the Atlantic across the Gibraltar sill.

TIDES AND CURRENTS

There is little to be said about tides in the Mediterranean. Greek and Roman classical literature contains no reference to them at all, for the Mediterreanean is almost tideless. Nowhere is the tidal range more than 5 ft and usually it is less than 3 ft (1·5–0·9 m). The greatest ranges are at the heads of narrow openings, especially where there are shallows, such as in the Adriatic and the narrow gulfs in the north and east of the Aegean. The wider gulfs of Gabès, Sidra and Adalia have ranges of about 4 ft (1·2 m). These figures may be compared with spring tide ranges of 14 ft (4·3 m) on the Tyne, 20 ft (6·1 m) at London, 27 ft (8·2 m) at Liverpool, and 45 ft (13·7 m) at the head of the Bristol Channel.

There is also an absence of distinct marine currents in the main body of the Mediterranean. We have noted, however, the two inflows of water through the straits at each end of the sea. The large volume of water required from the Atlantic enters as a current flowing at about 4 miles (6·4 km) per hour, but the amount which comes from the Black Sea is small and should be considered to form a weak drift rather than a definite current. In general, what circulation of water can be distinguished in the Mediterranean has an anti-clockwise direction (*see* Fig. 6). The "Atlantic" current may be traced along the north African coast, while the "Black Sea" drift moves to the west along the coast of Europe. This direction of flow, together with a negligible amount of tidal scour, is responsible for the formation of sand-spits which project eastwards along the African coast and westwards in Europe.

Although the drift along the European coast is hardly noticeable elsewhere, the restriction of waters caused by the narrow Strait of Messina leads to a tidal race of about 6 miles (9·6 km) per hour in the channel. This, together with the whirlpools set up by the peculiar configuration of the coast, especially on the Sicilian side, was greatly feared by the ancients, and in the *Odyssey* gave rise to the idea of two dangerous monsters, Scylla and Charybdis, who lived under rocks and three times a day swallowed and threw up the waters of the sea, engulfing ships and mariners.

In addition to the general coastwise circulation in the Mediterranean, local surface currents may be developed, either in the open sea by the direct action of wind or near the coast as the result of wind heaping

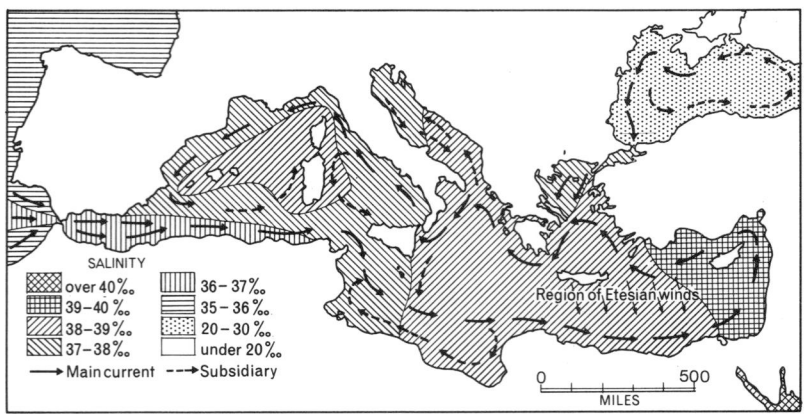

Fig. 6.—The Mediterranean Sea: salinity and surface currents; showing (i) increase of salinity eastwards, (ii) low salinity of Black Sea, (iii) general anti-clockwise circulation of surface currents, (iv) development of inner circulatory current system. (*Based on Schott.*)

water against the land. Nowhere do they reach the dignity of a distinct current system, but they are usually sufficient to obliterate the feeble tides characteristic of the Mediterranean.

COASTLINES

The youthful character of the Mediterranean, the origin, structure and variety of the lands which form its boundaries, the peculiar climatic factors which obtain over most of its area, the Ice Age and its aftermath, and the almost complete absence of tides and currents in its waters, together have produced a wide variety of coastal types, and this makes it very difficult to attempt to formulate any simple, systematised description of its coastlines. Even so, it is possible to discover coastlines of emergence and submergence, of concordance and discordance, of erosion and deposition and to relate them to the factors causing them. This is attempted in a general way in this section; details of coastlines of individual countries are given in later chapters.

Coasts developed as a result of the fracture of ancient massifs are usually cliff-lined and unbroken, except where indentations occur as a result of erosion along the faults. The hard rocks of which such massifs are composed yield little rock-waste, and except at the heads of narrow gulfs the cliffs descend directly into the sea with no intervening beach. Coasts like this occur in Corsica and Sardinia, along the Maures massif in south-east France, and in Asia Minor east of the Aegean Sea. A succession of parallel faults in the last has resulted in a greatly indented coastline, the openings in which have the appearance of rias (see below). Cross faults and subsidences in this area have given rise to cliff-grit, offshore islands, of which Samos, Khios and Lesvos are good examples.

Most of the coastlines of the Western Mediterranean basin and those of the northern side of the Eastern basin have been developed in association with the uplift of Alpine folded mountains. Where the trend of the folds is roughly parallel to the coast, that is, longitudinal or concordant, there is generally an absence of coastal openings, and if the mountains are near enough to the sea, there may be cliffs. Concordant coasts are found along the southern coast of Spain (see Fig. 7), in parts of the French and Italian rivieras, in south Turkey, and in Algeria and Morocco. The coast of Dalmatia is concordant, but with departures from the normal type. After the concordant coast is developed, submergence by the sea may result in the drowning of coastal ranges and the penetration of its waters into the inner valleys may give rise to a coast with long, winding, narrow indentations, bordered by festoons of elongated islands. This happened along the coast of Dalmatia in Yugoslavia, but in addition the drowning was accompanied by the solution of the component limestones, thus accentuating the broken character of the coast.

Where the trend of folding of mountain ranges is truncated at the junction of land and sea, the result is designated as transverse or discordant, and is marked by an alternation of headlands and narrow openings, the latter in most cases being known as rias. The best examples of this type of coastline in the Mediterranean are in the south of Greece and north-east Tunisia.

Coastlines which cannot be classified as either concordant or discordant, that is, low-lying coasts with no neighbouring mountains or those formed by the fracture and dislocation of ancient blocks, are known as neutral. The coastline of Africa east of the Gulf of Gabès is a good example of a neutral coast. Inland, the ancient African block, a plateau which in places is over 1650 feet (500 m) above sea-level, descends by a series of faulted terraces to a narrow coastal plain, and similar terraces continue northwards to form the sea floor. The coastline is extremely regular, but although it is cliff-girt in some parts, it is not as precipitous as in most of the massifs mentioned previously.

Similar in structure to the African seaboard but with a thicker cover of Tertiary limestones, the coastline of the Levant is also very regular, except where mountain spurs reach the sea, as in the case of Mount Carmel. In the north oscillation of sea level has resulted in wave-cut platforms which may be distinguished on the western slopes of the Jebel Ansariya (Ansariyeh) in Syria, and in the shallow waters near the coast this process of

FIG. 7.—Spain: Tossa de Mar, a small fishing village and holiday resort in north-east Spain. The rugged coast, the cliffs of massive limestone and the small sheltered beach are typical of most of the littoral of the western Mediterranean.

marine erosion is continuing. Parts of the coast of Lebanon are cliff-lined, but southwards from Mount Carmel a low-lying coastal plain, which widens in southern Israel to about 50 miles (80 km), sinks gradually under the sea. The plain is the result of north–south faulting which produced a series of downthrow basins and terraces towards the Mediterranean. The seaward margin of the terraces has been levelled and smoothed by a cover of loess and fine sand blown from North Africa. All three types of coast, concordant, discordant and neutral, may be distinguished in the Levant.

A further way of classifying coastlines is to distinguish *submergent coasts* and *emergent coasts*. A rise of sea level or a depression of the land leads to the submergence of a landscape which had already been shaped by erosion. The drowning of a region of hills and valleys gives an indented coastline with headlands and offshore islands, such as that of Dalmatia; or if the original landscape had a chain of high mountains very near the coast, submergence would lead to a rocky, cliff-bound coastline, similar to those of concordance mentioned above. Submergence of plains, on the other hand, results in very broad bays. The gulfs of Gabès and Sidra were possibly formed in this way, but bays of this type are rare in the Mediterranean. A fall of sea level or an elevation of the land leads to a retreat of the sea and the emergence of part of the sea floor; since the latter is essentially covered with sediments it usually has a smooth surface, and when uplifted it becomes a broad, featureless plain. The most notable example of an emergent coast in the Mediterranean region is that on the east of peninsular Italy, where a slow uplift still continues. As already noted (*see* page 7), there seems to be an axis of earth movement along the line of the Adriatic, on the west of which there is uplift and on the east depression. The western coasts of Dalmatia and Greece are slowly subsiding.

The shape of the Mediterranean was determined in the first place by the earth movements which culminated in the Alpine mountain-building revolution, but the present configuration of most of its coastlines is due mainly to the results of the Quaternary Ice Age. During the Pleistocene an area of nearly 8 million square miles in the north of North America and Eurasia was covered by a thick ice sheet, and there was also a subsidiary ice cap which radiated from the Alps. Smaller ice fields developed in the Pyrenees, Atlas, central Apennines and Pindus mountains. So much water was locked up in the various ice caps that the surface level of all oceans and seas including the Mediterranean was lowered by an estimated 300 feet (90 m). Elba, Sicily and most of the coastal islands in the Aegean became once more parts of the adjacent mainlands and some extinct volcanic cones and calderas on the sea floor west of peninsular Italy were made visible. The rise in sea level which followed the melting of the Ice Age glaciers was accompanied by the deposition of silt in gigantic proportions along the coasts, but except in sheltered positions such as at the head of the Adriatic, which was at that time greatly enlarged, it was carried away from the land and spread over the sea floor. There seems little doubt that much of the Plain of Lombardy and some of the lowlands along the northern Aegean owe their existence mainly to this post-glacial period, and that the numerous islands and coastal inlets, especially in the Eastern Mediterranean basin, are the results of marine transgressions in post-Pleistocene times.

The coastline of the Mediterranean continues to be modified, not so much by earth movements, although in some parts there are frequent earthquakes, as by the deposition of silt. The vast majority of rivers entering the Mediterranean have little water during the summer, but in winter they may become raging torrents. Only those like the Rhône and Po, whose sources lie far back in the Alps, and which in consequence are fed by summer rains and snow-melt, and the Nile, which has its maximum flow during the summer monsoon, pour any substantial amount of water into the Mediterranean in the hot season. All of them, however, large and small, bring down enormous amounts of silt and, in the tideless sea, tend to build deltas. In the case of the Nile it should be noted that the greatly increased use of its waters for irrigation in recent years and the construction of dams and barrages has reduced the volume of flow in its lower course to a mere trickle compared with that of former times.

The constructive action of rivers has had a material effect on all the coasts of "Alpine" character, notably when it occurs in conjunction with feeble sea currents and lack of tides. Deltas have been extended seawards and today help to form coastal plains which may range in size from a few square miles to the large area of the Plain of Lombardy. Currents and wave action are responsible for the formation of spits and offshore bars which on the European side trend from east to west and on the African side from west to east. In the course of time spits and bars may coalesce to form lagoons, as has happened along the French coast west of the Rhône delta; or they may impede the easy passage of smaller streams and cause the development of swamps such as the Pontine and Maremma marshes in Italy, and many in Albania and Greece.

The Mediterranean coastlands on the European side and to a less degree in the Maghrib (Morocco, Algeria, Tunisia) present a kaleidoscope of mountains, hills, tiny plains and sea; scenes of classic beauty under a clear, blue sky. A voyage along the European shores reveals a succession of villages and farms clinging precariously to steep slopes, where agriculture is possible only with the aid of terracing and where tree crops are more common than cereals or vegetables. The plains of deposition are dwarfed by the ring of mountains behind them and vary greatly in development. Some, such as those in peninsular Italy, the Cheliff of Algeria, and along the lower course of the river Medjerda in Tunisia, were originally malarial swamps and are only now being recovered; others show the rectilinear outlines of land reclaimed in the past, small-holdings each with its isolated homestead. Still others have a look of permanence, with irrigation systems and a rich cover of orchard and field crops.

On the south side of the Mediterranean the African coast east of the Gulf of Gabès shows few signs of deposition until the Nile delta. Here the vast amounts of silt brought down by the river have built up a delta extending 150 miles (240 km) along its seaward base and 100 miles (160 km) inland to its apex; it is the largest delta in the Mediterranean. Most of its surface has been reclaimed, but there are still extensive marshes and saline flats behind spits and lagoons which fringe the coast, especially in the area bordering Lake Manzala. Wind, waves and current have also caused long spits and offshore bars east of Port Said, enclosing the brackish lagoon, Sabkhet el Bardawil. North and east of the Nile delta thick deposits of sediments cover the sea floor, so that for 50 miles (80 km) from the coast the south-east Mediterranean is shallow; depths greater than 25 fathoms

(46 m) are rare in these coastal waters. In this south-eastern region, too, large quantities of blown sand have built dunes along the coasts of the Gaza strip of Egypt and southern Israel.

LAND AND SEA GATEWAYS

The great east–west extent of the Mediterranean made it an important highway far earlier than the land routes which lead from the sea. Traffic within the boundaries of the Mediterranean itself and by its eastern gateway through the Straits to the Black Sea preceded by centuries any common use of the Strait of Gibraltar which led to the stormy Atlantic Ocean. The western gateway was not very attractive to early mariners, partly because the inflowing Gibraltar current and adverse winds hindered navigation, and partly because the sailors of those times feared the unknown which lay beyond the Pillars of Hercules, as the headlands on both sides of the Strait of Gibraltar were called; not until the fifteenth and sixteenth centuries was there any regular use made by shipping of this passage to the Atlantic. The opening of an artificial gateway, the Suez Canal, in 1869, provided a third passage by water from the Mediterranean, this time via the Red Sea to the Indian Ocean. The new gateway in conjunction with the Strait of Gibraltar opened up a continuous sea route from the Atlantic to the Far East. The Mediterranean Sea became part of a commercial highway of first-class international importance. With the completion of the canal, too, land routes leading from the sea through the Alpine ranges to Central and Western Europe, up to then of more historical and political import than of economic value, began to be developed as major pathways of commerce.

Unfortunately, there are not many easy passages through the mountains which encompass so much of the Mediterranean. In the Western basin the Rhône valley giving access to North-west Europe is the most important. The Bochetta Pass behind Genoa leads to the north Italian plain and thence, by several Alpine passes traversed by roads and railways, to Switzerland, France and West Germany. A third route leads through the Gate of Carcassonne towards the Bay of Biscay, but although it gives connection with Bordeaux it has little more than local importance. In the Eastern basin there are passes of increasing value near the head of the Adriatic, opening a way to the Danubian lands, and in the north of the Aegean the Morava–Vardar "corridor" serves a similar purpose.

In the Levant, part of the "Fertile Crescent" forms a broad route from the coast of Syria via the Euphrates valley to the Persian Gulf. In ancient times this route had great historical significance and through the centuries it has been a highway for camel caravans. Today its chief value is as an outlet to the Mediterranean for the Persian Gulf oil-fields; it has become a route of very great economic importance. The exploitation of oilfields brought sudden wealth to a backward region, but at the same time caused it to have serious political problems. More will be said later about the historical, political and economic aspects of all the land routes opening from the Mediterranean.

On the African side of the sea the Nile valley offers the only easy passage to the interior, but it has never been a commercial route of any importance except to Egypt. Elsewhere the coast is backed either by the Sahara Desert or, in the west, by the difficult Atlas ranges. Settlement has been confined mainly to a narrow coastal strip, and only in recent years has there been any organised penetration inland, and then mainly to exploit the mineral resources of the desert.

STUDY QUESTIONS

1. From the point of view of (a) salinity, (b) tides and currents, (c) climatic influence, contrast the Mediterranean Sea with any other European sea.

2. Write a short account of (a) temperature distribution and (b) variations in salinity in the waters of the Mediterranean Sea.

3. Under the headings (a) concordant, (b) discordant, (c) neutral, attempt a classification of the coastlines surrounding the Mediterranean Sea. Illustrate your answer by means of a sketch map and diagrams.

4. With special reference to the Mediterranean marginal lands, give examples of emergent and submergent coastlines, deltaic swamps and plains of deposition, and explain their formation.

5. Write a short essay on "Tides and Currents in the Mediterranean Sea."

Chapter III

CLIMATE

MAINLY because of the position and form of the Mediterranean Sea, the lands around this body of water are one of the most clearly defined climatic units in the world. In summer, following the northward march of the sun, the Mediterranean region, situated between latitudes 30 and 45 degrees N., lies in the belt of north-east trade winds and of high pressure, and it is therefore dry. In winter, with the retreat of the sun south of the equator, the region falls under the general influence of the westerlies and the depressions associated with them, and is wet. Many of the depressions travel the whole length of the Mediterranean from west to east, and most of the winter rain typical of the region owes its origin to them. It may be said in general that the Mediterranean region has a temperate and changeable climate for the winter half of the year and a more uniform climate of the "hot desert" type during the summer. The main characteristics of the Mediterranean climate may be summarised under four headings: *winter rain, summer drought, mild winters* (over 43° F (6·1° C)) and *hot summers* (over 70° F (21·1° C)). It is also noteworthy that long periods of sunshine and cloudless skies are experienced at all seasons. Within the lands described in this book, however, there are many departures from this norm, some caused by distance from the main body of the Mediterranean Sea and some by relief.

The Mediterranean extends over 2250 miles (3600 km) from west to east and in that distance the total annual rainfall near sea-level decreases from 35·1 in. at Gibraltar to 15·3 in. at Athens and to a mere 3·3 in. at Port Said; the decrease in annual rainfall eastwards is due mainly, but not entirely, to increasing distance from the Atlantic. Patterns of rainfall distribution (like those of temperature variation) are affected also by relief. Where mountain ranges lie athwart moisture-bearing winds, such as in the Italian and Balkan peninsulas, along the Black Sea coast of Turkey and in Morocco, their windward slopes may have rainfall totals greater than many "wet" areas of north-west Europe. On the other hand, mountain ranges often act as rainfall barriers, and cast extensive rain shadows. Corfu for instance, on the west side of Greece, has an annual rainfall of 50·3 in., whereas Athens, on the east, has 15·3 in.

Sometimes mountains shut off areas so completely from Mediterranean influences as to result in a climate far removed from what is considered the norm for the whole region; such areas include the plain of northern Italy and the northern interior of Yugoslavia. Frequently, too, extensive plateaus such as the Meseta of Spain and the plateaus of Anatolia and Algeria develop "continental" climates in miniature. It is in the seasonal incidence of rainfall that most differences from the normal Mediterranean climate are found. Some areas such as the Lombardy Plain and the Spanish Meseta receive more rain in the summer than in the winter half of the year. The Biscayan portion of the Iberian peninsula has a "Cool Temperate Western Marginal" climate with rain at all seasons; and wide expanses of Syria, Jordan, Egypt, Libya and Algeria are hot deserts, although here it must be said that most of their scanty rains come in winter.

In all the enclosed and elevated regions winter temperatures are lower than the Mediterranean averages given above for that season. Burgos (Spain), for instance, has a January mean of 36° F (2·2° C), Ankara (Turkey) 28° F (−2·2° C), Alessandria (north Italy) 31° F (−0·6° C) and Géryville (Algeria) 39° F (3·9° C). Summers are also apt to be very hot indeed away from the moderating influence of the sea; this is illustrated by the September mean of 85° F (29·4° C) for Marrakesh and the July mean of 92° F (33·3° C) for Biskra. When the sirocco (see below, page 38) blows in Algeria temperatures of over 100° F (37·8° C) are usual.

It is these frequent variations in the Mediterranean lands from the generally accepted idea of the "Mediterranean type" of climate that have led most geographers to avoid that title and substitute "Warm Temperate Western Marginal" type, which can be applied more accurately to comparable climates in other parts of the world, for example, in central California and central Chile. In this book, the term "Mediterranean climate" will continue to be used, but with certain restrictions; it will be limited so as to apply only to those areas in which the olive flourishes and will usually be designated as "true" or "typical" (see Fig. 10). Regions such as the Spanish Meseta, the continental portion of Italy and the Plateau of the Shotts in Algeria will be regarded as sub-Mediterranean; and those in which the climate varies substantially from the typical, as in the Biscayan coastlands, the eastern portion of Asia Minor, and the hot deserts, will be called extra-Mediterranean.

AIR MASSES

Any examination of the climate of the Mediterranean lands must first of all have regard to the juxtaposition of the various air masses which overlie the region. A consideration of air masses is of fundamental importance in any study of climate, and in a transitional region like the Mediterranean, this is especially the case. Taken in conjunction with the size and position of the Alpine mountain system, air masses are the dominant factors in determining the general characteristics of the climate of the Mediterranean lands, as well as bringing about many of the peculiarities in temperature and rainfall régimes to be found in them. This being so, it will be useful at this point to introduce a short summary of the general principles of air mass climatology and frontal development. For further information on details any advanced book on climatology or meteorology should be consulted.

If the air which rests on large areas of land or water remains relatively undisturbed for any length of time it takes on some of the qualities of temperature and humidity of the surface on which it lies. Temperature will depend largely upon distance from the equator and humidity on whether or not the air mass concerned rests upon the ocean. From the point of view of temperature air masses are classified as "tropical" or "polar," and of humidity as "maritime" or "continental," and so it becomes possible to treat any given air mass under one of four headings:

1. *Polar maritime* (abbreviated to P.m.). This air mass develops over cold seas far from the equator. It is cool and moist, and as it moves into lower latitudes it becomes increasingly unstable.

2. *Polar continental* (P.c.). This originates in polar regions or, in winter, over the interior of continents such as Eurasia and North America, and is cold, dry and very stable.

3. *Tropical maritime* (T.m.), which moves outwards above oceans in sub-tropical or "Horse" latitudes. It has the form of a great mass of warm, moist and stable air; it may, however, become unstable if it drifts over land which is warmer than the air mass.

4. *Tropical continental* (T.c.) air occurs over low latitude deserts and is hot and dry—markedly so in summer when the high temperatures of the lower layers may, however, set up convection currents and cause instability.

All air masses develop in *source regions* of high pressure and from these source regions *air streams* spread outwards to areas of lower pressure until ultimately they come into conflict with others. If the converging air streams are of similar character, such as in the equatorial regions where the tropical maritime air masses of the northern hemisphere approach those of the southern hemisphere, the *zone of convergence* is one of calm and very moist air; a well-known example of this is the belt of equatorial calms and rainfall we call the doldrums. If on the other hand the two air streams which arrive in juxtaposition are of contrasting character and if they are strongly developed (for example, if a tropical maritime converges on a polar maritime) a sharp boundary known as a *front* develops between them, and transfer of heat and moisture takes place from one air stream to the other along the line of the front. The main bodies of the air masses retain their original characteristics of temperature and humidity to a great degree, but at the front between the two contrasting air streams, because of the difference in temperature on its opposite sides, there may be quick variations in pressure and moisture content, which not infrequently bring about rapid and sometimes striking changes in weather. It is convergences and fronts such as these which are largely responsible for the variable weather of Western Europe, and in winter for that of the Mediterranean lands.

If air streams of contrasting character such as polar and maritime meet, the warm air slides over the colder, to form what is called a *warm front*, a line of discontinuity which is marked by extensive cloudiness and a probability of rain. Behind the warm front in a depression there is usually a *warm sector* of tropical air, in the rear of which is the *cold front*. Here the polar air stream forces itself under the warmer tropical air, so lifting it, reducing its temperature, and causing condensation and rain, but to a less extent than at the warm front. As a result of this lifting process, warm and cold fronts may coalesce, so that a mass of cold air lies under the whole of the warm sector. The front so formed combines the characteristics of the original warm and cold fronts and is called an *occluded front*.

Frontal development is very pronounced in the depressions which are born in the broad zone of convergence of T.m. and P.m. air streams in the north Atlantic along what is known as the Polar Front. Here originates the succession of depressions which, as noted, dominates the climate of Western Europe at all seasons and which, in winter, influences the Mediterranean region, especially in the west.

Further east in the Mediterranean there is a winter convergence of tropical maritime and polar continental air. The belt of discontinuity between polar and tropical air streams which in winter extends along the whole length of the northern half of the Mediterranean region is usually known as the Mediterranean Front, but strictly this name should be reserved to the western end of the zone, which is an extension of the Polar Front. One reason for the reservation is that the winter convergence zone in the Eastern Mediterranean basin is between two relatively dry air streams and frontal development is not so pronounced.

In summer, much of the Mediterranean region comes under the influence of the rather inactive zone of convergence between tropical maritime and tropical continental air masses, inactive because the zone is situated along the southern limits of the Mediterranean lands and the air in it is relatively dry. All four types of air mass have a share in the climate of the Mediterranean lands. Because of the seasonal contrasts which result from their interaction, they will now be examined in more detail with regard to (i) summer and (ii) winter conditions in the region (*see* Fig. 8).

SUMMER

In summer the tropical maritime air mass which is usually associated with the Azores high pressure system moves north with the sun, and at the same time spreads eastwards over the Western basin of the Mediterranean. The tropical continental dry air which is normally over the Sahara is pushed southwards from its winter location, so that the zone of convergence between the two air streams becomes centred near the Tropic of Cancer. Over the Sahara the line of discontinuity may be marked by instability and a high degree of convection, and this may give rise to the sudden summer rainstorms experienced in the desert. The moist air of the tropical maritime may also affect all the coastlands of the African side of the Mediterranean as far as Libya, but in general the air over the Mediterranean lands in summer is remarkably stable. Although moist, its passage across the hot north of Africa precludes condensation except in the form

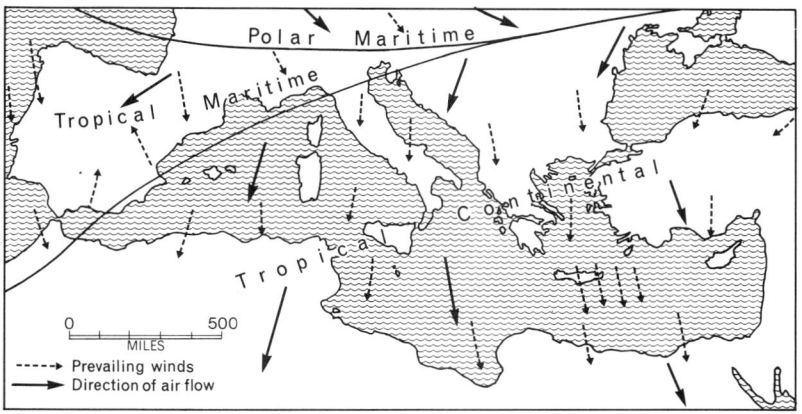

FIG. 8 (a).—The Mediterranean lands: air masses, summer; prevailing winds, July.

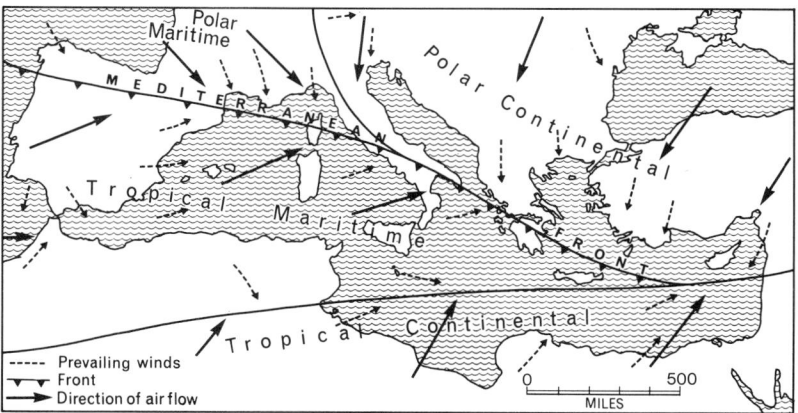

FIG. 8 (b).—The Mediterranean lands: air masses, winter; prevailing winds, January.
See also Fig. 9 showing local winds.

of heavy dews, and so there is an absence of rain in summer. Moreover, because the Azores *centre* of high pressure has moved north of the Mediterranean basin, the western sea has prevailing north or north-east winds, offshore and therefore dry on the European side. Before these winds reach the African coast they have crossed the Mediterranean and have greatly increased their moisture content under the hot sun, but the still higher temperatures they encounter over the land to the south enable them rather to pick up moisture than to deposit rain. There are exceptions to this in mountainous districts and in areas near the Atlantic, which may have slight summer rain. Elsewhere along the African coastlands precipitation is mainly in the form of dew, the result of large diurnal ranges of temperature.

The Eastern basin of the Mediterranean is affected in summer by the monsoonal wind system of South-west Asia. In Asia Minor the winds belong to the northern drier sector of the immense monsoonal depression, and arrive at the Mediterranean as north or north-west winds which are almost completely dry and very stable. There is some adiabatic warming caused by the increase of pressure as the winds descend from the coastal highlands to traverse the eastern Mediterranean, but evaporation during the short passage over the sea is insufficient to increase humidity to the point of giving rain to the coastlands of the Levant. It is enough, however, to form clouds during the daytime, a phenomenon rarely seen in summer in the western Mediterranean, and to give heavy deposits of dew.

The north-westerlies which blow in summer over the Aegean were known to the ancient Greeks as "Etesian" winds (Gr. *etesios*, annual). In Egypt the prevailing winds are from the north throughout the year. It is interesting to note that because of this it is possible at almost any time to sail *up* the river and to drift *downstream* with the current; this feature undoubtedly had much to do with the early emergence of Egypt as a unified state. In the Levant lands the winds are from the north-west, and their humidity is high enough to give a noteworthy precipitation of dew at night, especially near the coast, where in the morning the roofs of buildings are apt to be streaming with moisture. All the eastern and south-eastern coastal regions are marked in summer by an unpleasant combination of high temperatures and excessive humidity; inland, with a further increase in temperature, the relative humidity of the air is lowered and the wind becomes dry and scorching.

In summer, then, both Western and Eastern basins of the Mediterranean lie in the track of northerly winds. The Western basin, within the orbit of the Azores high pressure system, has north-easterly trade winds; the Eastern basin, influenced by the Asiatic low pressure monsoonal circulation, has north or north-westerly winds. In both basins the result is the same—conditions which may approach complete drought. There are exceptions to this general rule wherever there are local variations from the normal distribution of pressure. These occur mainly on the European side in the sub-Mediterranean and extra-Mediterranean parts of Iberia, Italy, the Balkan peninsula and Asia Minor; here there may be a greater incidence of summer rain than elsewhere around the Mediterranean.

WINTER

In winter the positions and effects of air masses are altogether different from those of summer. Topography, too, especially the disposition of mountain ranges in relation to rain-bearing winds, has a greater influence on the climate of Mediterranean lands than in the warmer season.

The southward migration of the sun with the onset of winter in the northern hemisphere is accompanied by a corresponding movement of the polar maritime air mass, and by the development of the polar continental air mass over Central Asia and Eastern Europe. The air over the Western Mediterranean basin is warmer than the average for its latitude because of the vast reservoir of heat contained in its waters and it becomes a more or less stagnant pool of low pressure. To it flow the tropical maritime and the cooler but still moist polar maritime air streams from the Atlantic, and in their zone of convergence, that is, along the Polar Front and its extension, the Mediterranean Front, cyclonic depressions are formed. The fronts developed in these account for most of the rains of the Mediterranean winter.

The Eastern Mediterranean basin, several degrees of latitude further south, experiences in winter consistently higher pressure than the Western basin, and its air is not as humid. At this end of the sea there is a zone of convergence between the southern edges of the polar continental air stream, which has spread from the cold heart of Asia, and the northern boundary of the tropical continental air stream from Africa, but lack of humidity in the convergence zone here is not favourable to the production of rain-giving depressions and of frontal development. The Eastern basin depends for its rain either on depressions which force their way from the Atlantic into the rather inactive convergence zone between the two continental air streams, or on those depressions which have their origin within the Mediterranean basin itself; for minor centres of low pressure sometimes develop locally in the Gulf of the Lion, the Gulf of Genoa, the southern Adriatic, the southern Aegean, and near Crete, and their depressions may carry "cold front" rain eastwards.

Occasionally a Polar Front depression moves south-eastwards across western Europe towards the Mediterranean. Some of them pass through the Gate of Carcassonne, others are checked by the Alps. Where the mountains deny an easy passage of the depressions to the Mediterranean, the air in their north-western quadrants may cross over and reach the sea as north winds. Wherever the north winds are channelled along passages through the mountains they are cold and violent, for example, the *mistral* which blows down the Rhône corridor, the *bora* at the head of the Adriatic, and the *vardarac* down the Vardar valley (*see also* the section on "Local Winds," page 37). The thermal contrast between the cold air of these winds and the warmer air of the Mediterranean results in minor centres of instability with secondary depressions and local rain-bearing winds such as are experienced on the west of the Italian and Balkan peninsulas. In areas, too, where mountains are flanked by lowlands, as in the north Italian plain, or by the sea, as in the northern Aegean or in south Turkey, steep temperature gradients may cause small but important cyclonic disturbances.

All depressions in the Mediterranean move from west to east, although some of those developed locally as in the Gulf of Genoa and west of Cyprus may remain stationary for some time before moving eastwards and filling up. The main paths of depressions, "storm tracks," are along the European side, nearer to the Mediterranean Front, which is estimated to be responsible for 60% of all Mediterranean cyclonic disturbances. The southern half of the sea is affected more by Polar Front depressions which enter from the Atlantic via the Gibraltar gateway. These are relatively few in number, and in consequence the African side of the Mediterranean has less rain than the European coastlands. Moreover, by the time those which are able to penetrate to the Eastern basin arrive there, they are weak and almost ineffective as sources of rain. In the Levant lands, most of the precipitation in winter is brought by depressions formed locally in the southern Aegean or near Cyprus. Their cyclonic rains are augmented by relief rain wherever coastal regions are backed by mountains or plateaus, notably in Syria and Lebanon.

WINDS

GENERAL

Throughout the summer, as we have seen, the prevailing winds in all Mediterranean lands are from the north. In the Western basin they are largely north-easterlies; hence the oft-repeated statement that the Mediterranean lands lie in the "trade wind belt" in summer. This is true for the Western basin, but the Etesian winds, the steady stream of northerly air in the eastern Mediterranean, blowing with the greatest regularity in June, July and August, are not trade winds; they form part of the summer monsoonal system of South-west Asia. The Etesian winds were used by mariners and traders of classical times to carry their ships southwards from Crete and the city states of Greece to the Barka peninsula in Cyrenaica. The return journey utilised the coastal current past the Nile delta, then north and west back to the Aegean, one of the earliest trade circuits to come into existence. We have noted, too (page 34), the use made of the northerly wind by sailors on the river Nile. In the Levant lands the prevailing winds come more from the north-west in summer. Their direction is affected by the low pressure centred over South-west Asia.

During the day the Etesian winds are much stronger than at night, for the intense insolation in north Africa and the interior of the Levant lands adds the effects of sea breezes to the normal air flow. When they reach the coast the winds are unpleasantly damp; clouds may form during the day, but no rain falls; the cooler nights may cause mists and heavy dew. Throughout the Mediterranean, the prevailing north-easterlies or northerlies are affected in summer by land and sea breezes. Along the European coasts the prevailing winds are diminished in strength and sometimes completely masked by sea breezes during the day, and along the African coasts they are reinforced. At night, land breezes have the reverse effect.

During the winter, atmospheric pressure over the Mediterranean tends to be low compared with that in Western and Central Europe to the north and Africa to the south. In consequence, most of the winds on the European side have a northerly component, whereas in the south of the region they come more from the south. In addition, there are winds from other directions associated with the depressions which traverse the Mediterranean in winter; and local pockets of high pressure, that is, of divergence, which build up in the Iberian peninsula, the interior of the Balkan peninsula, and the plateaus of Anatolia and Armenia, may give rise to winds from any quarter. In general, the northerly winds on the European margin are cold and boisterous, for they come mainly from the north-west quadrants of depressions and are associated with cold fronts. The southerlies from Africa are warm, desiccating and dusty, for usually they belong to the south-east quadrants and warm sectors of depressions.

LOCAL WINDS

Where winter winds follow the general principles of circulation but have been accentuated by local variations of temperature, pressure and humidity, they have been given specific names (*see* Fig. 9). The mistral, bora and vardarac have already been mentioned as cold, violent winds which visit respectively the lower Rhône valley, the northern Adriatic

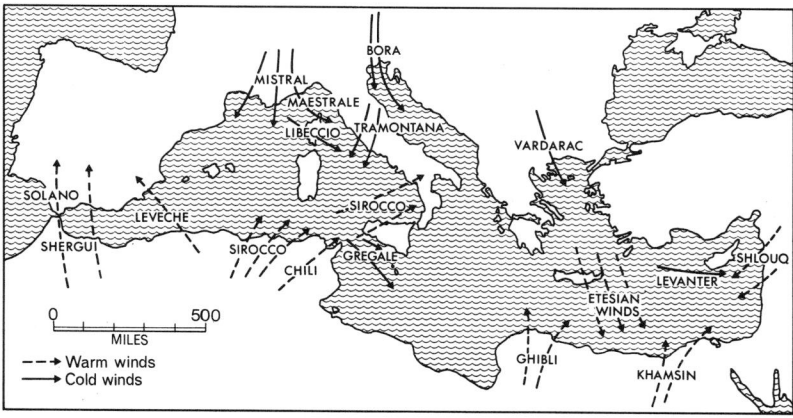

FIG. 9.—The Mediterranean lands: local winds. With the exception of the Etesian winds, which blow in June, July and August, the local winds blow mostly in winter and spring.

and the northern Aegean. The *mistral* is most prominent in Mediterranean France, but its effects may be felt as far west as the Ebro delta and eastwards to Liguria and Sardinia, where it is called the *maestrale*. It attains its greatest strength and frequency in Provence and Languedoc, that is, in the neighbourhood of the Rhône delta, where in winter it blows on an average one day in two; the record at Marseille is 175 days in the year. Over the land, the mistral is usually associated with cloudless skies, brilliant sunshine, intense dryness and piercing cold. With the passage of a depression over the Gulf of Lions or a rapid rise of pressure following a snowfall on the central massif of France, it becomes violently stormy. It has been known to blow trains off viaducts. Houses are orientated so that doors and windows face away from the mistral. At sea, where the mistral may become part of the cold front of a passing depression, it may lead to torrential rain and hail.

Similar in character is the *bora*, which is felt to the full in Istria and the north Dalmatian coastland. Cold air on the Carso plateau slides down to the Adriatic where the pressure is much less. In its descent it is warmed and dried, much as in the case of the föhn of Switzerland; but unlike the föhn, the bora is so cold in its inception that the rise in temperature still leaves it below 40° F (4·4° C) at sea-level. During a bora, temperature on the Carso may be well below freezing point and at Trieste 35° F (1·7° C) or less, with the wind at gale force. The January mean temperature for Trieste is 39° F (3·9° C), which makes it sub-Mediterranean; and from it we may infer that winter temperatures in the whole of the northern Adriatic are dominated by the bora. In contrast, Dubrovnik, at the southern end of the Dalmatian coast, has a January average of 48° F (8·9° C), which is much higher for that month than most European stations in the Eastern Mediterranean basin. The *vardarac*, which affects the plain of the lower Vardar but not as seriously, reduces the January mean for Salonica (Thessaloníki) to 41° F (4·5° C).

The *tramontana* (It. "through the mountains") is a cold north wind which blows from the northern Apennines to the coastal regions of Tuscany, bringing raw, blustery weather. The same districts may experience the *libeccio*, a west or south-west wind which is born in the Gulf of Lions and traverses Corsica. It is cool and wet, but less unpleasant than the mistral or the tramontana. In the central Mediterranean Sea, caused possibly by the increased instability in depressions passing over the narrow Sicilian Channel, the *gregale* is a boisterous north-west wind, usually accompanied by rain. In the east of the eastern Mediterranean, drawn to the low pressure centre which occasionally develops south of Cyprus, blows the *levanter*, a cool, blustery wind from the east.

The winds which blow in winter on the south side of the Mediterranean are associated, we have seen, with the front quadrants of eastward-moving depressions, and hence are arriving from the African mainland. The generic name for all such dry, hot, dusty, gusty south or south-east winds from the desert is *sirocco (scirocco)*, but this name is usually reserved for the wind which descends to the eastern Algerian Tell and then blows across Sicily and southern Italy. In Algeria the sirocco may be scorchingly hot, drying up vegetation and presenting problems to farmers, but in Sicily and Italy, after picking up moisture from the sea, it is oppressively humid and enervating. It is dust-laden, and the addition of water vapour may cause dusty mists or showers of muddy rain. The "blood-rains" experienced in southern Italy are coloured by their content of red, desert dust swept northwards by the sirocco.

Other names for the sirocco are the *chili* in Tunisia, the *ghibli* in western Libya, the *khamsin* in Egypt, the *shlouq* in Syria and Lebanon, the *leveche* in western Algeria, and the *solano* or *shergui* in Morocco. The khamsin (Ar. "fifty") originates in the Sahara and blows in Egypt intermittently for about fifty days during March, April and May, filling the air with dusty sand. The leveche, blowing mainly to Murcia and Alicante in Spain, and the solano, to southern Spain and Gibraltar, have too short sea passages to affect materially their original characteristics, and arrive in the Iberian peninsula hot, dry and dust-laden; rarely, however, do they penetrate beyond the southern mountain rim.

TEMPERATURE

A preliminary word of warning is necessary in connection with the reading and comparison of all temperature figures. Mean annual temperatures, which along the Mediterranean coasts may vary from 56° F (13·3° C) to 77° F (25·0° C), give no indication of the monthly or seasonal distribution of heat and may be very misleading unless taken in conjunction with other readings. London, for instance, has a mean annual temperature of 49·7° F (9·7° C), which is the same as that of Budapest in central Europe and higher than the annual mean of Burgos (48·9° F; 9·4° C) in Spain. The annual figures disguise the fact that winters are cooler and summers warmer in Budapest and Burgos than in London.

Annual *ranges* of temperature are more useful, for they are of assistance in deciding whether or not a climate is equable or extreme; but again, unless the mean temperatures of the warmest and coldest months are known, they are of little further value. The annual range in London is 24° F (13·3° C), as compared with 23° F (12·8° C) in Alexandria. which is nearly 20° F (11·1° C) warmer in every month in the year. It is always better, therefore, to consult tables of monthly or seasonal average temperatures before drawing any conclusions (*see* Fig. 10). In the following paragraphs constant reference should be made to the table on pages 42–43.

The proximity of the Atlantic Ocean limits the annual range of temperature in the western Mediterranean lands. Essaouria (Mogador), which is additionally affected by the cool Canaries Current, has a range of only 11° F (6·1° C); Gibraltar and Lisbon each has a range of 20° F (11·1° C) and Algiers 24° F (13·3° C). Along the greater part of the African coastlands warm winters result in small ranges; Tobruk has 13° F (7·0° C), Alexandria 23° F (12·8° C), Cairo 27° F (15·0° C) and Tunis 30° F (16·6° C). European stations along the coasts of the Western Mediterranean basin usually have ranges of less than 30° F (16·6° C); Barcelona, Marseille and Nice each has 28° F (15·5° C); Palermo has 26° F (14·4° C). In the eastern Mediterranean, with greater distance from Atlantic influences, ranges along the European coast are greater, Salonica with 38° F (21·1° C) and Izmir with 35° F (19·4° C) being representative.

Sub-Mediterranean regions, partially shut off from Mediterranean influences, have ranges considerably above the average for coastal stations. Milan has a range of 43° F (23·8° C) and Alessandria 44° F (24·4° C); Madrid's range of 36° F (20·0° C) is much greater than that of any Iberian coastal station. The interior and elevated positions of Ankara and Aleppo

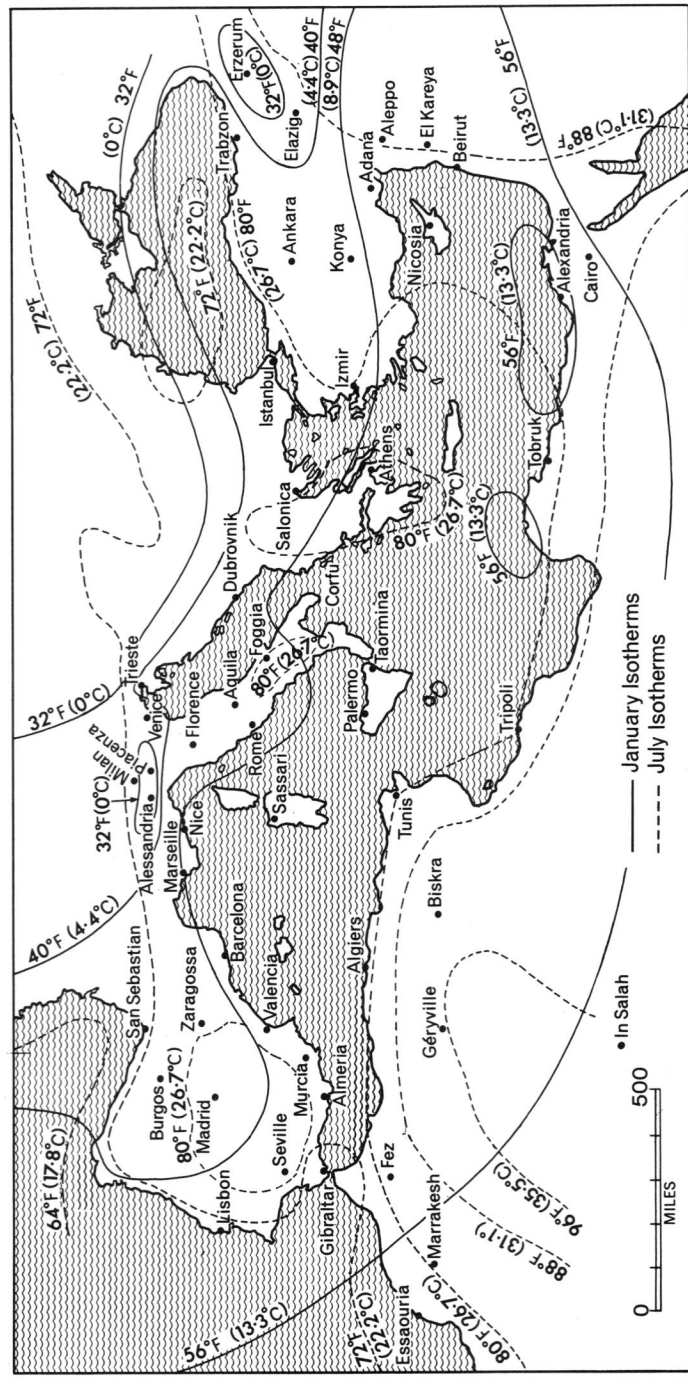

FIG. 10.—The Mediterranean lands: January and July isotherms. The stations shown are mentioned in the text or in Table I.

have led to ranges of 45° F (25·0° C) and 47° F (26·1° C) respectively, while in Africa comparable situations give ranges of 36° F (20·0° C) in Constantine and 40° F (22·2° C) in Géryville. Eastern Turkey is almost continental in its ranges; Elâzig (El Aziz) has a range of 58° F (32·2° C), and some parts of Turkish Armenia have still wider differences between summer and winter mean temperatures. These stations should be considered as extra-Mediterranean. Extra-Mediterranean places on the Biscayan coast, however, have very small ranges. San Sebastian's range of 22° F (12·2° C) is characteristic and is comparable with the low ranges found all along the coasts of Western Europe.

SUMMER TEMPERATURES

In general, the mean temperature for the months of May, June, July and August in the Western Mediterranean basin is rarely below 60° F (15·6° C), and in most places this average is maintained until October (*see* Table I). The hottest month in Mediterranean France, Italy, most of Iberia, and the parts of North Africa removed from maritime influence is usually July; elsewhere it is August. In Essaouria the mean temperature for September, the warmest month, is 68° F (20·0° C), which is very low for a station so far south. The Biscayan region, too, has summer temperatures well below the Mediterranean average and approximating more to those found further north in Western Europe. The highest temperatures are registered in Africa, as might be expected, and the summer heat is experienced well into the autumn. Algiers, for instance, has average temperatures over 60° F (15·6° C) from April to November inclusive.

Summer temperatures in the Eastern Mediterranean basin are higher on the whole than in the Western basin, partly because of the greater store of heat in the waters of the sea, and partly because of lower latitudes, greater continentality and more limited Atlantic influences. There is a greater tendency, too, for the summer to be prolonged even to November, especially in Africa and the southern Levant. The hottest month in these two regions is August; elsewhere it is July. Temperatures in these two months rarely fall below an average of 75° F (23·9° C), and in the interior of Libya and Egypt there are July means of 90° F (32·2° C) or more. Outstanding among stations with a true Mediterranean climate is Nicosia with an average in July of 90° F (32·2° C).

In the Mediterranean region perhaps more than in most parts of the world, monthly averages of temperature such as are given above may be deceptive unless due regard is given also to diurnal ranges. The same warning applies to the winter averages given later, but not to the same degree. In the Western Mediterranean basin temperature maxima in July and August often rise during the day as high as 95° F (35·0° C) and in the cloudless nights are correspondingly low. Still higher midday temperatures are registered in the Eastern basin, where the thermometer frequently rises above 100° F (37·8° C) near the coasts of Africa and the southern Levant and may reach 110° F (43·3° C) or 120° F (48·9° C) in interior

TABLE I

Mean Monthly Temperatures

	Altitude (feet)	Jan °F	Jan °C	Apr °F	Apr °C	July °F	July °C	Oct °F	Oct °C
Western (north)									
Lisbon . . .	66	51	10·6	58	14·4	70	21·1	62	16·7
Seville . . .	74	50	10·0	63	17·2	84*	28·9*	67	19·4
Gibraltar. . .	49	54	12·2	61	16·1	74*	23·3*	65	18·3
Almeria . . .		53	11·7	60	15·6	78*	25·6*	67	19·4
Murcia . . .	197	50	10·0	61	16·1	79	26·1	66	18·9
Barcelona . .	135	47	8·3	56	13·3	75*	23·9*	62	16·7
Valencia . . .	75	51	10·6	59	15·0	76	24·4	65	18·3
Marseille. . .	246	44	6·7	55	12·8	72	22·2	58	14·4
Nice . . .	66	46	7·8	57	13·9	74	23·3	61	16·1
Florence . . .	240	41	5·0	56	13·3	76	24·4	59	15·0
Aquila . . .	735	36	2·2	52	11·1	72*	22·2*	56	13·3
Rome . . .	164	45	7·2	57	13·9	77	25·0	62	16·7
Palermo . . .	230	51	10·6	58	14·4	77*	25·0*	67	19·4
Sassari . . .	224	47	8·3	57	13·9	77*	25·0*	64	17·8
Western (south)									
Essaouria. . .	33	57	13·9	63	17·2	68†	20·0†	67	19·4
Fez . . .	1542	52	11·1	67	19·4	85*	29·4*	70	21·1
Algiers . . .	72	53	11·7	61	16·1	78*	25·6*	69	20·6
Tunis . . .	141	50	10·0	59	15·0	80*	26·7*	68	20·0
Eastern (north)									
Taormina . .	260	52	11·1	61	16·1	81	27·2	68	20·0
Foggia . . .	74	43	6·1	58	14·4	80	26·7	64	17·8
Dubrovnik . .	49	48	8·9	57	13·9	77	25·0	65	18·3
Corfu . . .	98	51	10·6	60	15·6	79*	26·1*	68	20·0
Athens . . .	351	48	8·9	59	15·0	81	27·2	66	18·9
Salonica . . .	128	41	5·0	58	14·4	79	26·1	63	17·2
Istanbul . . .	246	41	5·0	52	11·1	73	22·8	61	16·1
Izmir . . .	65	46	7·8	59	15·0	81	27·2	66	18·9
Eastern (east)									
Nicosia . . .		50	10·0	66	18·9	90	32·2	74	23·3
Adana . . .		48	8·9	63	17·2	83*	28·3*	71	21·7
Beirut . . .		56	13·3	66	18·9	84*	28·9*	76	24·4
Aleppo . . .	1000	42	5·6	61	16·1	89*	31·7*	67	19·4
El Kareya . .		41	5·0	56	13·3	72*	22·2*	63	17·2
Eastern (south)									
Tripoli . . .	56	53	11·7	65	18·3	80*	26·7*	74	23·3
Alexandria . .	105	58	14·4	66	18·9	81*	27·2*	75	23·9
Sub-Mediterranean									
Burgos . . .	2882	36	2·2	48	8·9	66*	18·9*	51	10·6
Madrid . . .	2149	40	4·4	52	11·1	76	24·4	55	12·8
Zaragoza . .	772	42	5·6	56	13·3	76	24·4	58	14·4

	Altitude (feet)	Jan F°	Jan C°	Apr F°	Apr C°	July F°	July C°	Oct F°	Oct C°
Sub-Mediterranean									
Milan . . .	482	32	0·0	55	12·8	75	23·9	56	13·3
Alessandria . .	322	31	−0·6	55	12·8	75	23·9	55	12·8
Piacenza . . .	163	32	0·0	53	11·7	73	22·8	55	12·8
Venice . . .	10	39	3·9	55	12·8	74	23·3	59	15·0
Trieste . . .	220	39	3·9	54	12·2	73	22·8	58	14·4
Trabzon . . .		45	7·2	51	10·6	73	22·8	64	17·8
Extra-Mediterranean									
San Sebastian . .		45	7·2	54	12·2	67	19·4	60	15·6
Konya . . .		30	−1·1	52	11·1	74	23·3	56	13·3
Elâzig . . .		19	−7·2	52	11·1	77	25·0	59	15·0
In Salah . . .	1080	54	12·2	70	21·1	98	36·6	80	26·7
Biskra . . .	410	51	10·6	70	21·1	89	31·7	70	21·1
Cairo . . .	380	55	12·8	70	21·1	82	27·7	74	23·3
For Comparison									
London . . .	18	39	3·9	47	8·3	63	17·2	50	10·0
Valentia . . .	30	44	6·7	48	8·9	59	15·0	52	11·1
Bergen . . .	66	34	1·1	42	5·6	58	14·4	45	7·2
Vienna . . .	656	29	−1·7	49	9·4	67	19·4	50	10·0
Moscow . . .	480	12	−11·1	38	3·3	66	18·9	40	4·4

★ Temperature for August (hottest month)
† Temperature for September (hottest month)

steppe and desert, and also in deep, sheltered valleys. During the night the temperature in these areas may fall to the comparatively low reading of 60° F (15·6° C) or less. The burnous, a long, loose cloak of woollen stuff with a hood, is worn by the Arabs in North Africa and the Middle East to protect the wearers against these wide differences between day and night temperatures.

WINTER TEMPERATURES

Everywhere at low altitudes the mildness of the Mediterranean winter is well marked. Most coastal stations have a mean temperature for the coldest month of about 50° F (10·0° C) and some have 55° (12·8° C) or more (*see* Table I). For the whole of the Mediterranean lands the winter average is 43° F (6·1° C). The comparatively high temperatures for the latitudes are due primarily to the vast amount of heat stored in the waters of the sea and to the slow cooling of the surface layers. On the whole, coastal lowlands and islands south of latitude 40 degrees N. rarely suffer frost, and "cold waves" or "Northers" such as are experienced in California, which is another "Mediterranean" land, and in Florida and the Gulf of Mexico,

[*Courtesy of the Spanish Ministry of Information.*

FIG. 11.—Spain: the valley of Baro, Santander. A view of the region with an extra-Mediterranean climate, taken in the spring. The fruit trees are in blossom and are reminiscent of southern England; the Cantabrian mountains, still snow-capped, are in the background.

are unknown in the Western Mediterranean basin. They may blow occasionally in the Eastern basin in Asia Minor, the Levant and Egypt, where they are associated with cold fronts in the rear of depressions.

A good index to the non-occurrence of killing frosts is the presence of the olive, and the limits of distribution of this tree are in consequence often taken as the boundaries of the true Mediterranean climate. The olive can withstand slight frost or light snowfall but will not tolerate long-continued periods below freezing point; neither will it survive prolonged rains in summer. The lemon is another frost indicator, but because it is wholly intolerant of frost its distribution is more limited, and is not used as a criterion of climate except in a restricted sense. The fact that the lemon is produced in commercial quantities in Murcia, the huertas of southern Spain, Sicily, the "toe" of Italy, the coastal plains of Lebanon and parts of the Maghrib, shows that all these are virtually frost-free.

The coldest month everywhere is January; and because of the slow loss of heat from the waters of the Mediterranean during the winter months, with a consequent reduction in their warmth-giving capacity, the return in spring to higher temperatures on adjacent lands is delayed. Average temperatures for April are lower than for October, but there is a rapid increase in May, when means generally range from 60° F (15·6° C) to over 70° F (21·1° C). The relatively mild winter and the delayed approach in spring to scorchingly high temperatures, taken in conjunction with the high proportion of annual rainfall in these two seasons, are of great significance in Mediterranean agriculture. Together, they ensure excellent conditions for good crops of wheat and other temperate cereals and most vegetables, which are grown as cool season crops. The slow onset of winter, too, with a gradual loss of heat and a minimum of rain in autumn, is of value in the cultivation of fruits such as citrus fruits which require a long ripening time. The temperatures and rainfall of late winter and spring also favour the growth of vines, plums and tobacco, some of which may be dried in the open air in the ensuing hot, dry summer to produce currants, raisins and prunes.

Away from the coasts, for example, in the Spanish Meseta, the north Italian plain, the Alps, the Dinarides, Macedonia, Thessaly, Turkey and on the Plateau of the Shotts, the characteristic winter mildness disappears, and temperatures may fall below freezing point for long periods (*see* Fig. 11). In Milan the January mean is 32° F (0·0° C), in Géryville 39° F (3·9° C), in Madrid 40° F (4·4° C), in Salonica 41° F (5·0° C), and in Erzerum the very low average of 12° F (−11·1° C). Moreover, although the winter diurnal range in most parts of the Mediterranean lands is less than it is in the summer months, in the sub-Mediterranean and extra-Mediterranean regions it is much greater. For instance, while the average daily maximum in Erzerum in January is 34° F (1·1° C), the average minimum is −10° F (−23·3° C), a mean diurnal range of 44° F (24·4° C). Low winter readings along the European coast are the result mainly of cold winds such as the mistral and bora, which are drawn from the north by Mediterranean low pressure, or of temperature inversions in places where coastal plains are backed by mountains. A notable case of the latter is Florence, where the cold air of the tramontana slides down the western side of the Apennines to reduce the January mean of the city to 41° F (5·0° C) and to give it more than 30 frosty days per annum. Rome suffers from the tramontana in the same way but to a less degree.

The sub-Mediterranean plain of north Italy, shut off from maritime influences by the northern Apennines, has widespread frost in January, Milan and Piacenza with averages of 32° F (0·0° C) and Alessandria with 31° F (−0·6° C) being typical. The extra-Mediterranean region of eastern Turkey, so far removed from the sea that it may be looked on as continental, has winter temperatures reminiscent of central Siberia. Kars, for instance, near the eastern border of Turkish Armenia, has a January mean of 9° F (−12·8° C) and an average night minimum of −5° F (−20·6° C). In eastern Anatolia and Armenia the temperature may remain below freezing point throughout December, January and February. Snow falls frequently in winter in all these areas and on all high mountains throughout the Mediterranean lands. The Italian and Dinaric Alps and most of the Apennines are snowclad for ten weeks or more, and the Sierra Nevada (Sp. "snowy range") and Atlas for about two months. The Plateau of the Shotts in Algeria is often swept by northerly winds in winter, and these winds send temperatures down well below freezing point; severe snow-storms are not uncommon at this season.

On the other hand, the coastal margins of Africa and the Levant, affected in winter mainly by southerly winds, may have January means of more than 10° F (5·5° C) above the general average of 43° F (6·1° C) for the whole of the Mediterranean lands. For instance, Beirut has a January mean of 56° F (13·3° C), Alexandria 58° F (14·4° C), Cairo 55° F (12·8° C), and Tripoli 53° F (11·7° C).

SUNSHINE AND HUMIDITY

One of the striking climatic features of the Mediterranean region is the large percentage of sunshine received at all seasons. In the dry summer the sun beats down from a sky unobscured by cloud, and in winter the rain-bearing depressions are relatively small in area and are interspersed with long periods of sunshine and blue skies. Over the region south of latitude 40 degrees N. the annual total of sunshine is more than 2500 hours. North of this, the sub-Mediterranean areas included, the annual total rarely falls below 2250 hours, and even in extra-Mediterranean "pluviose" Iberia it tops 2000 hours. These figures should be compared with the annual total of 1500 hours in the sunniest part of southern England.

The high incidence of sunshine and the warm winters have always attracted holiday-making tourists from the colder, cloudier, bleaker Western Europe, especially to those parts of the Mediterranean coast which are sheltered from northerly winds by neighbouring mountain ranges. The most famous of these sheltered stretches, known as *rivieras*, is the Côte d'Azur in France. With the development of rapid air transport the tourist industry has also grown enormously in the Costa Brava and Costa del Sol in Spain, the Riviera di Ponente and Riviera di Levante in north-west Italy, and the Adriatic rivieras of Rimini–Pesaro in Italy and Sibenik–Split in Yugoslavia. The archaeological treasures of an ancient civilisation have long drawn tourists and specialists to Egypt; today the tourist invasion is extending over much of the remainder of North Africa, especially in Morocco and Tunisia; even the Isle of Djerba (the island of Tennyson's Lotos Eaters) is now within the tourist orbit.

The dry, clear atmosphere with abundant sunshine in summer may be an attraction to holiday-makers, but to the native worker it presents a problem. The intense direct insolation causes a cessation of human activity for several hours in the middle of the scorching summer days; farm workers are forced to take shelter and rest, and in the towns offices and shops are closed, streets are deserted, and factories, except where they are air-conditioned, are at a standstill. Arduous labour, both indoors and out, is confined to the early morning and the cool of the evening; the middle of the day is given over to the *siesta* (Sp. "afternoon sleep") or the *dolce far niente* (It. "sweet idleness").

One advantage of the prolonged sunshine and drying winds is the quick oxidation and blowing away of ordure and offensive refuse. In areas where sanitation is primitive or defective—and in the Mediterranean region these are widespread—germ-infested dirt is literally burnt and blown away by the hot wind, so that the dangers of diphtheria, cholera and other intestinal epidemic diseases are much reduced. On the other hand, many of the coastal plains, turned into swamps and marshes by heavy winter rains and imperfect drainage, are liable to become breeding places of the *Anopheles* mosquito which carries the virus of malaria. This disease was a scourge in the Mediterranean coastlands until modern methods of drainage almost eliminated the pest.

In winter, when the sun is shining for long periods between showers, cool breezes in the northern coastlands of the Mediterranean give weather eminently suitable for both plant and animal life and with an invigorating effect on man. It has been described as "a cool climate where the sun is hot." With this in mind rather than the scorching and often enervating summers, many writers have described the Mediterranean climate as the ideal for human activity and have pointed to the many civilisations born in the region and the glories of art, literature and science we have inherited from its early inhabitants. In terms of human geography, the Mediterranean is a "region of increment," where man can produce his requirements for life with less continuous labour than elsewhere, and where he has sufficient leisure to occupy himself with such liberal pursuits as sculpture, painting, literature and natural philosophy, for which some Mediterranean countries were famous in classical times.

High temperatures and persistent winds over the large area of the Mediterranean Sea lead to rapid evaporation and a high degree of humidity, especially in summer. This is not so noticeable on the European side, for there the prevailing winds are offshore; but along the eastern and southern coastlands, where onshore winds have crossed the sea, there is a most oppressive combination of heat and exceptionally high humidity from June to September. During these months the damp heat of daytime makes life in the Egyptian and Levantine coastal regions almost unbearable. At night, with a rapid fall in temperature, there are heavy deposits of dew which in places may amount in total to an appreciable percentage of the annual precipitation. This is notably the case in Syria and Lebanon, and to a less degree in southern Israel and the Sinai peninsula. Houses are equipped with cisterns to collect the heavy dews, and in the fields the farmer in some places can use the deposits to grow crops without the aid of irrigation.

In European Mediterranean lands the humidity is not as high and the summers not as oppressive, except in Sicily and southern Italy during the sirocco (*see* page 38). The Spanish Meseta and the plateaus of Turkey and Algeria have the lowest humidity in summer; the dry heat and parching winds result in arid stretches of steppe and semi-desert.

RAINFALL

Regions lying between latitudes 30 and 45 degrees on the western side of continental land masses are exceptional in that their hot season coincides with drought; elsewhere in the world maximum heat is accompanied by greatest precipitation. The regions which have their rainfall almost exclusively in winter are central California, central Chile, south-west Cape of Good Hope, south-west West Australia, southern South Australia and the Mediterranean lands. Of these, only the last is of large area, and this fact is due to the deep penetration of the land by the sea (*see* Fig. 12).

The reasons for the seasonal distribution of precipitation in the Mediterranean lands have been discussed under "Air Masses" (*see* page 30), and note has been made of those areas which are truly "Mediterranean" (*i.e.*, with an almost complete summer drought) and those which are marginal (sub-Mediterranean and extra-Mediterranean, which may have summer rains). Cyclonic and relief rains are the types of precipitation usually experienced in the Mediterranean, though convectional rains are common in the marginal regions. In the latter, thunderstorms with heavy downpours of rain and hail are frequent and account for much of the summer rainfall of the north Italian plain and the scanty winter rain of the African deserts.

The incidence and unreliability of Mediterranean rainfall are noteworthy. Annual or seasonal totals (*see* Table II) disguise the fact that a great deal of rain may fall in a short period of time, often during the course of a single storm. The average monthly rainfall shown in a table of totals may represent only three or four short torrential downpours. Cloudbursts, with as much as 4 in. of rain in as many hours, are regular features of the Eastern Mediterranean basin; in marginal lands persistent heavy rain for several days in succession may have disastrous results. In the autumn of 1966, for example, continuous rain in the Dolomites caused landslides and streams of mud which created havoc in road communications and threatened to engulf mountain villages; the river Po burst its banks and flooded its delta; and the river Arno overflowed and inundated Florence to a depth of many feet, with incalculable resultant damage to the treasures of museums and art galleries and to the homes and workshops of craftsmen. In the case of the Po delta the flooding was accentuated by Adriatic storms which broke the dykes protecting reclaimed land; thousands of acres of good farmland were invaded by sea and river water, and many villages had to be abandoned.

Not only may the winter rains come in a few short bursts, but the annual totals may vary considerably. This is more the case in the southern and eastern coastlands of the Mediterranean, where an average figure, say of 15 in. as given in a table, may include actual annual totals of as high as 30 in. or as low as 5 in. Along the northern coastlands the variation in annual totals is not as great, but rainfall is still so unreliable in amount as to necessitate the use of irrigation in most lowlands. Moreover, since the

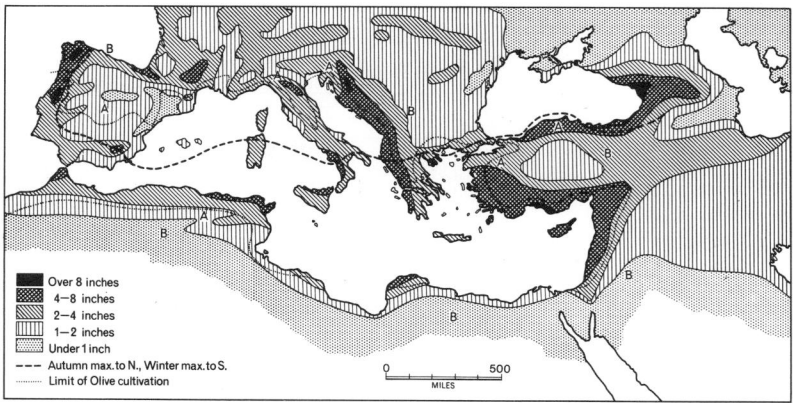

Fig. 12 (a).—Mediterranean lands: rainfall in January. North of the broken line maximum rainfall occurs in September, October, November; south of it in December, January, February. Areas marked A are "sub-Mediterranean"; B are "extra-Mediterranean."

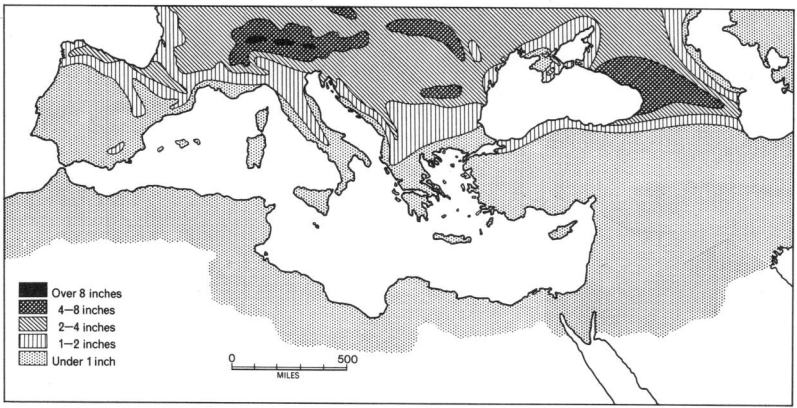

Fig. 12 (b).—The Mediterranean lands: rainfall in July, which shows an almost universal drought.

rain may come in sharp, heavy bursts, the amount lost by rapid surface run-off and evaporation reduces its *effective* value, that is, what is retained by the soil, sometimes by as much as 50%.

Partly because of its unreliability, it is not easy to formulate any genera-lised account of the total annual rainfall and its distribution in Mediter-ranean lands. On the whole, the rainfall decreases from west to east and from north to south, but there are many notable exceptions where moun-tain ranges or plateau slopes lie across the path of rain-bearing winds. In the west, Gibraltar has an annual total of 35·1 in. of rain and Algiers 30·0 in. Eastwards, this is reduced to 21·5 in. at Salonica and 20·0 in. at Nicosia, and along the Libyan and Egyptian coasts to less than 10 in., Alexandria

TABLE II

Mean Annual Rainfall and Seasonal Percentages

	Annual total (inches)	Seasonal percentages			
		Spring	Summer	Autumn	Winter
Western (north)					
Lisbon . . .	27·1	26	4	32	38
Seville . . .	19·5	31	3	30	36
Gibraltar . .	35·1	26	2	31	41
Almeria . .	9·7	28	6	29	37
Barcelona . .	21·4	25	18	37	20
Valencia . .	16·1	23	14	40	23
Marseille . .	22·6	26	11	40	23
Genoa . . .	44·1	22	13	37	28
Sassari . . .	23·2	26	4	34	36
Florence . .	30·6	26	15	33	26
Aquila . . .	29·4	27	15	32	26
Naples . . .	32·6	23	8	36	33
Western (south)					
Essaouria . .	13·2	25	1	31	43
Fez . . .	9·4	34	5	25	36
Algiers . . .	30·0	24	3	29	44
Tunis . . .	18·0	29	7	27	37
Eastern (north)					
Taormina . .	29·2	22	3	31	44
Foggia . . .	19·0	24	17	33	26
Dubrovnik . .	59·2	24	11	33	32
Corfu . .	50·3	18	4	35	43
Athens . . .	15·3	18	8	35	39
Salonica . .	21·5	27	18	30	25
Istanbul . . .	28·8	18	14	30	38
Izmir . . .	26·0	23	2	22	53
Eastern (east)					
Nicosia . .	20·0	18	0	21	61
Adana . . .	23·8	27	6	21	46
Beirut . . .	37·7	17	1	20	62
Aleppo . . .	14·5	21	0	17	62
Jerusalem . .	24·8	21	0	11	68
El Kareya . .	56·7	23	1	15	61
Eastern (south)					
Tripoli . . .	16·3	10	1	29	60
Benghazi . .	10·1	10	0	26	64
Alexandria . .	8·1	9	0	21	70
Port Said . .	3·3	18	0	18	64
Sub-Mediterranean					
Burgos . .	21·7	32	17	27	24
Madrid . .	16·5	30	14	32	24
Zaragoza . .	11·5	30	20	30	20

	Annual total (inches)	Seasonal percentages			
		Spring	Summer	Autumn	Winter
Sub-Mediterranean					
Milan . . .	39·7	26	24	31	19
Padua . . .	33·9	26	25	29	20
Venice . . .	29·8	30	21	29	20
Trieste . . .	43·0	22	25	35	18
Belgrade . .	24·4	17	28	32	23
Skopje . . .	19·6	22	25	26	27
Trabzon . .	33·4	19	18	35	28
Extra-Mediterranean					
San Sebastian . .	57·8	19	21	31	29
Konya . . .	11·3	34	13	19	34
Elâzig . . .	17·4	41	6	22	31
Biskra . . .	6·9	38	10	26	26
Cairo . . .	1·3	31	0	15	54
For Comparison					
London . .	24·5	20	27	28	25
Bergen . . .	81·0	18	21	32	29
Vienna . . .	24·5	26	34	21	19
Moscow . .	21·0	22	37	24	17

having 8·1 in. and Port Said 3·3 in. In contrast, the mountains of Dalmatia commonly receive more than 100 in. of rainfall annually; the yearly total of 183 in. near Kotor (Cattaro) in Yugoslavia makes this district the wettest in the Mediterranean lands and possibly in the whole of Europe.

Rain shadow effects are prominent in most Mediterranean lands. Stations on the eastern sides of peninsulas have invariably less precipitation than those on the west. Lisbon, for example, has 27·1 in. as compared with 9·7 in. in Almeria on the other side of the Iberian peninsula; in Italy, Naples has 32·6 in. in contrast to Foggia's 19·0 in. and in Greece Corfu has 50·3 in. to 15.3 in. at Athens. The totals for Naples and Corfu are relatively high for their positions in the Mediterranean and are due to the mountains which rise behind the towns. Sharp rain shadows are produced also by the Atlas ranges. The Plateau of the Shotts, in the rain shadow of the Moroccan Atlas and the Tell Atlas, has an annual rainfall which rarely exceeds 20 in. and may be as low as 10 in., as compared with 30·0 in. at Algiers. The north-facing slopes of the Saharan Atlas have 20 in., whereas Biskra to the south has only 6·9 in. It should be noted, too, that rain shadow effects are not limited to mountainous districts. Essaouria, for instance, on the Atlantic coast of Morocco, has an annual total of 13·2 in., but Marrakesh, about 100 miles (160 km) inland and situated in the down-faulted Haouz (*see* page 359), has 9·3 in. The great depth of the Jordan rift valley gives rise to a much diminished rainfall, Jericho, for example, having an annual total of no more than 5 in.

The winter rainfall régime varies from west to east. In the eastern half of Spain, the whole of Mediterranean France, and most of peninsular Italy north of Naples, the greater percentage of precipitation is in autumn and early winter, and the same applies to much of the coastal districts on both sides of the Adriatic. A simple winter (December to February) maximum occurs in the west and south of the Iberian peninsula, Sardinia, southern Italy, Sicily, most of Greece, the western and southern coastlands of Turkey, and all the Levantine and North African lands. In the Levant the rainy season is considered to begin in October or November, but the coming of the first showers of "early rain," as it is called in the Old Testament, is by no means certain; in Palestine it may be delayed until early December. The early rain is followed by a comparatively dry period until late December or early January when the main fall commences and lasts to March or April. The wettest month near the coast of the Levant is January, but near the eastern borders of Jordan there is often a March maximum. In Israel the "latter rain," though not a maximum, normally occurs in April; in Scriptural days its failure heralded disaster, for the last showers of the rainy season assured "the fulness of the yearly harvest" (Jer. v. 24).

Sub-Mediterranean regions such as the Spanish Meseta, the north Italian plain, the Alps and the northern Adriatic coasts, have generally more rain in the summer half of the year than in the winter half, and in most there are two peaks of maximum fall. The Meseta has maxima in spring and autumn, that of spring being the greater and associated with thunderstorms. Madrid has 30% of its total fall of 16·5 in. in spring and 32% in autumn; 54% falls in the winter half of the year. Zaragoza (11·5 in.), in a rain shadow in the Ebro valley, receives 50% of its total in each half of the year. In the north Italian plain the rainfall peaks are unevenly distributed; Milan has its maxima in May and October, Venice in April and November, and Trieste and Padua in June and October. Annual totals here are much greater than the Mediterranean average, Milan having 39·7 in. and Trieste 43·0 in. Most of the summer rains of the sub-Mediterranean regions are convectional; the winter precipitation coincides with the passage of the more active depressions along the Mediterranean basin.

Stations in the northern Aegean have also a substantial percentage of their annual rainfall in summer, Salonika with 18% of its 21·5 in. during June, July and August, and Istanbul, with 14% of its 28·8 in. in the same months, being typical. Skopje (19·6 in.) and Belgrade (24·4 in.), away from the coast, lie transitionally between Mediterranean and Central European régimes; in Skopje almost as much rain falls in the winter half of the year (49%) as in the summer six months; Belgrade, further from the coast, receives 60% of its total from June to November inclusive. The

Black Sea coast of Turkey has rain at all seasons and totals may be high. Rize has an annual fall of 105·3 in., of which 65·8 in. comes in the months from September to February inclusive; only April and May have less than 6 in.

The extra-Mediterranean Biscayan coast of Iberia has a rainfall régime like that of Western Europe. Precipitations shows no marked periodicity, occurring at all seasons but usually with a minimum in spring. Annual totals are high, especially on the seaward side of the Cantabrians, Santiago in the west having 62·0 in. and San Sebastian in the east 57·8 in. The central and eastern plateaus of Turkey, also extra-Mediterranean, are in the rain shadow of bordering mountains and have low rainfalls; Elâzig with 17·4 in. annually and Konya with 11·3 in. are typical. Further east, however, in spite of its greater continentality, the mountain knot near the borders of Armenia is somewhat wetter. The driest months on these plateaus are July, August and September; the wettest period is in spring and early summer, similar to the incidence in the steppe further east in Asia. The Saharan regions of North Africa and the dry interior of Levantine lands are also extra-Mediterranean, but they have most of their rain in winter. The totals, however, are small, so small that their climate is classed as hot desert.

On the mountains and high plateaus which comprise much of the surface of the Mediterranean lands, winter precipitation may take the form of snow. Altitude, aspect and distance from the warm waters of the Mediterranean Sea are the governing factors in the amount and duration of the fall. In the Cantabrians, far away from Mediterranean influences, and in the Pyrenees and Italian Alps which are sub-Mediterranean, snowfall is heavy and continues throughout the winter half of the year. The heaviest falls are in the eastern Alps, where depths of 15 ft (4·5 m) may be found at altitudes of over 6000 ft (1800 m); many peaks in these ranges are permanently snowcapped. The mountains of Yugoslavia, Greek Macedonia, Thrace and Lebanon, and most of the encircling ranges and plateaus of Turkey are snowclad for periods which vary from three to six months, but the falls are lighter and there is no permanent capping.

Further south in the Mediterranean region the Apennines and Sierra Nevada have heavy falls. The central Apennines may be closed to road traffic for weeks on end and winter sports are a feature in Abruzzi and Molise; in the Sierra Nevada a few patches of snow may remain throughout the summer. The Plateau of the Shotts (3000–4000 ft, 900–1200 m) experiences severe snowstorms, and on the windward side of the High Atlas in Morocco slopes above 10,000 ft (3000 m) are covered with snow for most of the year. Snow showers are common in winter on the Spanish Meseta and the north Italian plain, but at low altitudes elsewhere in the Mediterranean lands this form of precipitation is rare. A few showers may occur along the northern coastlands, and southern Italy and Greece may see snow once or twice a year, but in some districts in the southern and eastern Mediterranean lands snowfall is unknown.

RIVER RÉGIMES

The value of rivers must be measured substantially in terms of their *régime*, a comprehensive term which has reference to the pattern of water discharge through the year over the whole of the basins of the rivers concerned and of the behaviour of the water. Such matters as times of high discharge, low discharge and the carrying of silt are all included within the compass of river régime; and since these aspects are closely related to climate, it is appropriate to include in this chapter a short account of the régimes of Mediterranean rivers.

The contrast between summer drought and winter rains in the Mediterranean region is reflected in the river régimes. During the dry summers there is little or no water in many of the rivers; some become mere trickles flowing through wide, pebble-strewn beds. In winter the intensity of the rain, coming in short, sharp bursts, produces swollen and raging torrents with two periods of high water, one at the beginning, the other at the end, of the season. Over most of the Mediterranean the winter rains are heavier near the beginning of the season, but the run-off is reduced because the dry, porous surface soils, parched by the scorching summer sun, soak up large quantities of water, and so the rise in the level of the rivers, although substantial, is not as great as might be expected. The end of the winter is marked in many places by the "latter rain," which causes the water level to rise again in the rivers. In the mountains, where the rains are most intensive, the slopes, usually without a protective cover of vegetation, are stripped of much of their soil, and the rivers enter the lowlands turbid and silt-laden.

This is the typical régime of such rivers as the Douro, Tagus and Guadiana in Spain, the short rivers of southern Italy, Sicily, Greece, the Levant and the African coast. But many rivers receive additional water from snow melting on the mountains bordering the Mediterranean, so that their régime is modified. Their flow of high water is continued into the early summer and their period of low water is correspondingly shortened. Outstanding in this category are the Rhône and Po, which receive so much melt-water from the Alps that their even flow continues throughout the summer; consequently their régimes are more like those of British rivers. Among other rivers whose régimes are modified by snow-melt are the Ebro (from the Cantabrians and Pyrenees), Guadalquivir (Sierra Nevada), Tiber and Arno (Apennines), Vardar (Macedonian highlands), Struma (Rhodope), Menderes (Taurus), and Oum er Rbia (High Atlas) (*see* Fig. 13).

The régimes of the wadis in the desert areas of Mediterranean lands are relatively simple. The Arabic word *wadi* means the dried-up bed of a torrent. Its use as an element in the Spanish river names *Guada*lquivir and *Guadi*ana is suggestive of their low water in summer; in Morocco the term *oued* has the same meaning. For most of the time these water-courses in Africa are empty. Sudden cooling of the atmosphere by cyclonic or

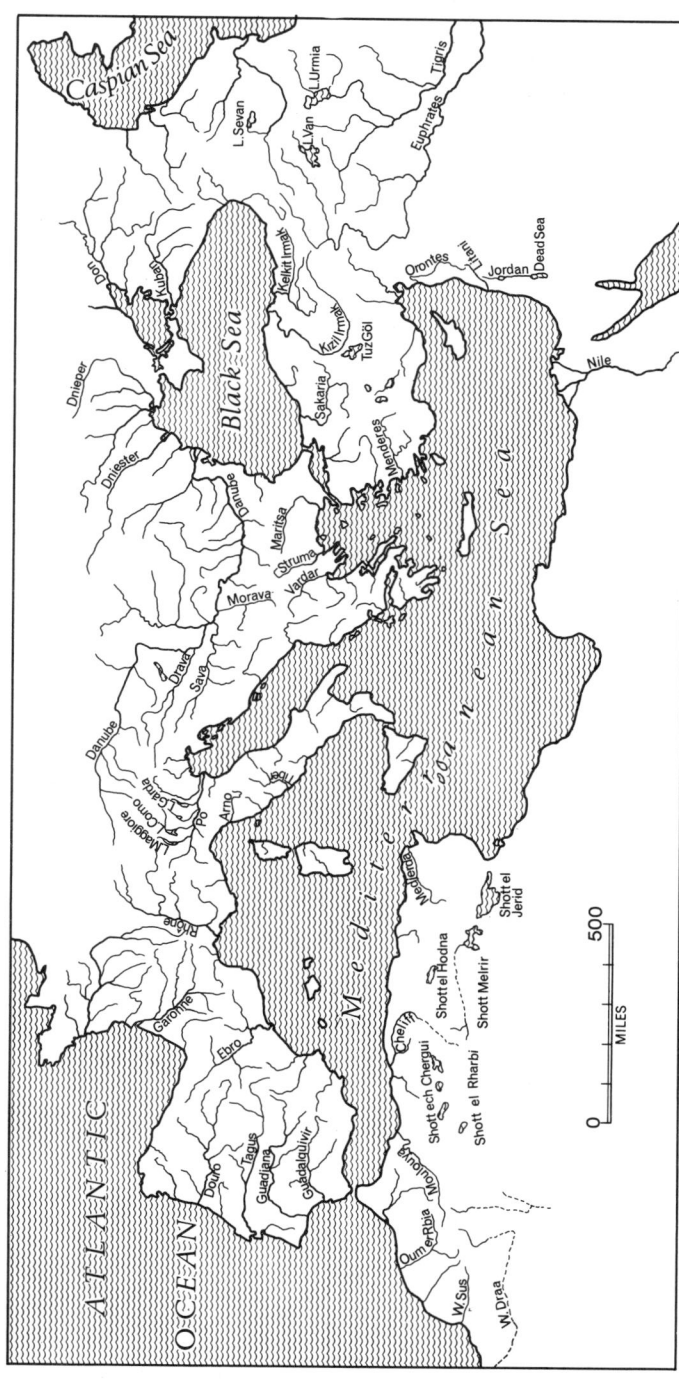

Fig. 13.—The Mediterranean rivers.

convectional air movements may result in violent downpours of rain which fill the wadis to the brim in the region of the storms, and produce raging torrents which may overflow their banks. Very soon, however, the waters of the wadi decrease in volume and within a distance of a few miles may have dried up by evaporation or been swallowed by the thirsty sands. Occasionally the flood waters move for many miles along a wadi. The Wadi Saoura, for example, which leads southwards from the Atlas, has sometimes flowed for as much as 500 miles (800 km) from the mountains. It supports an almost continuous line of date palms pointing towards the heart of the Sahara, and where 'water is more abundant than usual, as at Beni Abbès, notable oases have developed along its course.

Besides being agents of soil erosion in their upper courses and having silt-choked lower courses which often terminate in coastal swamps and deltas, the steep gradients and wide variations in volume have caused most Mediterranean rivers to incise their beds deeply in their middle courses, thus reducing their value for navigation and irrigation and necessitating much bridge-building. A further disability arises from the fact that they are at their lowest level in the hot, dry summer, for this means that their usefulness for irrigation, where it is possible, is at a minimum at the time when water is most urgently needed.

A consideration of the régime of the river Nile has been purposely omitted here. The Nile, which in contrast to the rivers given above has its maximum flow in summer, can be included as a Mediterranean river only because its waters enter the Mediterranean Sea. It receives no tributary waters when flowing through Egypt, and its régime is governed mainly by climatic factors which obtain in regions far from the Mediterranean. Nevertheless, the river is of such vital importance in the economy of Egypt that an account of its régime cannot be neglected; it is treated at length in the chapter on Egypt (pages 454 f.).

STUDY QUESTIONS

1. Describe the rainfall régime of the Mediterranean region. Give reasons for the seasonal variations you mention, and discuss the differences in total annual rainfall that are found in stations around the Mediterranean Sea. (O. & C.)

2. Give a reasoned account of the main climatic contrasts which may occur between the European, Asiatic and North African marginal lands of the Mediterranean.

3. What do you understand by "air masses" as the term is used in climatology? Give an account of the distribution of air masses over the Mediterranean lands in (a) summer, (b) winter.

4. Select *three* of the following and explain the reasons for their location and occurrence: Etesian winds, mistral, sirocco, bora.

5. The following climatic statistics are those of three stations (A, B, C) in the Mediterranean lands:

		J	F	M	A	M	J	Jy	A	S	O	N	D

Station A

| Temp. | °F. | 53 | 55 | 58 | 61 | 66 | 71 | 77 | 78 | 75 | 69 | 62 | 56 |
| Rain | in. | 4·2 | 3·5 | 3·5 | 2·3 | 1·3 | 0·6 | 0·1 | 0·3 | 1·1 | 3·1 | 4·6 | 5·4 |

Station B

| Temp. | °F. | 39 | 39 | 47 | 55 | 63 | 70 | 74 | 74 | 69 | 59 | 51 | 41 |
| Rain | in. | 2·3 | 1·6 | 3·0 | 3·1 | 2·8 | 2·9 | 1·5 | 2·0 | 2·8 | 2·6 | 3·0 | 2·2 |

Station C

| Temp. | °F. | 55 | 57 | 63 | 70 | 76 | 80 | 82 | 82 | 78 | 74 | 65 | 58 |
| Rain | in. | 0·3 | 0·2 | 0·2 | 0·2 | 0 | 0 | 0 | 0 | 0 | 0·1 | 0·1 | 0·2 |

(*a*) Point out the similarities and differences in temperature and rainfall conditions at the three stations and try to locate the stations.

(*b*) How far do they suggest that the title "Mediterranean climate" as applied to the Mediterranean marginal lands is misleading?

6. "Hot, dry summers and mild, wet winters are characteristic of the Mediterranean climate." In a short and reasoned answer show the limitations of this statement.

7. Select *two* rivers flowing into the Mediterranean Sea, one with a simple régime and the other with a complex régime, and in each case give a reasoned account of its régime.

Chapter IV

SOILS

FORMATION

SOIL may be defined as that part of the earth's mantle which can support plant life and therefore, indirectly, animal life; some forms of life actually exist within the soil itself and are essential to its formation. Soil is merely a thin veneer rarely more than a few feet thick, yet it is so vital to our very existence that we must know as much as we can about its character and adopt all the means possible to maintain its usefulness.

Soil is a complex mixture of mineral and organic products. Its development begins with the physical breakdown of surface rocks into small particles which are then colonised by bacteria and mosses. At a later stage, mould begins to accumulate; other plant life takes root, grows, dies and decomposes to form *humus*; air and water enter and are retained, if only for a short time; and burrowing animals stir up the surface layers. With the decay of dead plant and animal life, organic acids are formed, and these react with the mineral contents of the rocks and with themselves to form soils. Bacteria enter into the process by assisting in the decomposition of organic life. Soil formation, then, involves a series of chemical reactions, some very complex; and since all chemical changes depend on varying amounts of heat and moisture, it is immediately clear that the development of soil rests to a large degree on temperature and rainfall, that is, on climate. In fact, it is now recognised that although the parent rock, the natural vegetation and the presence of bacteria are important, the dominant factor in soil formation is climate. For instance, soils evolved in tropical climates, with faster chemical reactions, are quite different from those in temperate or cold regions, although the parent rock in each case may be the same. Soils which are closely related in type to their parent rocks are known as *immature* or *azonal*, while those which have evolved over a lengthy period in response to climatic factors are known as *mature* or *zonal* (*see* below, p. 65).

The most important requisites for the development of a useful soil are as follows:

1. *Mineral particles*

These are derived from the underlying parent rock or are transported from elsewhere. They form the framework of the soil and at the same time give it body, and in certain cases act as necessary plant foods. Potash, nitrates and phosphates, for example, in their soluble form are taken in by plant roots to make growth possible (*see* Fig. 14, showing a chemical fertiliser factory).

2. Air

In a useful soil air is present between the mineral particles. Without it, as may be the case in some water-logged soils, the bacteria essential to the development of good soils cannot live. Instead, anaerobic bacteria take over and help to produce "sour" soils which are useless for agriculture.

3. Water

Water must be present in a useful soil, but it is important that it should be correct in amount. As we have just seen, if too much water is present the soil becomes water-logged and useless, while if the soil is completely

[*Courtesy of Montecatini Edison S.p.A.*

FIG. 14.—Italy: chemical fertiliser plant at Campofranco, near Caltanissetta in Sicily. Potassic minerals which are brought from San Cataldo are processed to produce potassium sulphate, a valuable fertiliser which has brought marked benefits to Italian agriculture. Note the type of vegetation in the foreground.

dry the bacteria will die, humus dry out and be lost, and true soil characteristics disappear. A good soil has films of water attached to the various mineral particles so that air is still free to circulate through the interstices which remain.

4. Humus

This is derived from organic matter which decomposes in a soil. One might reasonably expect that it would *form* most prolifically under dense vegetation such as equatorial rain forest (selva), but it *accumulates* most in "temperate" climatic conditions, for instance, under grasslands of the steppe or prairie type. The reason for this distinction is that humus is destroyed by great heat. In equatorial regions the amount of humus is by no means commensurate with the luxuriance of the selva because the hot, wet conditions cause a too rapid decay. In the temperate grasslands, with a small summer rainfall, the decaying process is slow and continuous, leaching is not excessive, and the annual grasses provide a constant supply of new humus. Some of the best soils under temperate grasslands have a humus content of 10% whereas under tropical forest there is usually less than 2% . Dry conditions are not favourable to the formation of humus, for in such circumstances the natural vegetation is sparse. In Mediterranean regions, for instance, soils have only a small percentage of humus, for here the natural vegetation consists mainly of low-growing shrubs and trees, with little grass. Moreover, under the strong sunshine of summer the soil in many areas becomes baked and the humus is literally burnt away. In cold climatic conditions, which in the Mediterranean lands are found at high altitudes, there is insufficient vegetation to provide the raw material for the formation of humus.

5. *Micro-fauna*
The chief organisms under this heading are bacteria, which are largely responsible for the decomposition of organic matter and the formation of humus. Other bacteria produce nitrites by combining atmospheric nitrogen with other substances, and the nitrites in turn are changed by other bacteria into nitrates—a valuable fertiliser. In some cases bacteria directly help plant growth; this is particularly the case with legumes (peas, beans), for bacteria live on the roots of these plants, extract nitrogen from the air in the soil, and make it available for plant growth.

6. *Macro-fauna*
Included under this heading are earthworms and ants which move enormous amounts of earth each year. We are all familiar with the worm-casts seen on English lawns. These are small compared with some found in other parts of the world; they may reach several inches in height in some tropical countries, *e.g.*, Natal and Ceylon, where there are species of worm up to 6 ft long. Some kinds of ants make underground nests; galleries and chambers are hollowed out in the soil and connected to the surface by tiny openings. Other ants construct their nests in the form of ant-hills sometimes many feet high. All these activities, as well as the earth movements caused by burrowing animals such as rabbits, moles and foxes, help to aerate soils and improve them by mixing. It appears likely, too, that worms and ants actually add substances to soils and thereby increase their usefulness.

SOIL CHARACTERISTICS

Soils have many characteristics which make them vary from one another. These include texture, structure, thickness, colour and the percentage of lime found in them.

TEXTURE

This is concerned with the sorts of mineral or other particles found in a soil. Some soils consist of coarse particles such as sand; others, such as clays, consist of very fine particles; and some are a mixture of coarse and fine particles as, for example, in silts or alluvium. In some soils there are still finer particles of inorganic colloids or colloidal clays, but usually colloids, which are mainly of organic origin, are found as a gelatinous coating on the surface of mineral particles.

STRUCTURE

This is concerned with the way the particles are arranged in a soil. Usually they cohere into granules or groups in what is known as flocculation, and on this depends to a great extent whether the soil is permeable or impermeable. In sandy soils the spaces (pores) between the particles are greater than those in clayey soils and will allow water to penetrate and percolate more freely; and when the particles are grouped into floccules the degree of permeability or impermeability is increased. Fine clays soon become waterlogged, whereas very sandy soils may allow water to drain away so quickly that they are of little practical value. The best soils for arable farming are those in which the particles are irregular both in shape and arrangement, that is, where there is a mixture of sand and clay, and where they are present in roughly equal proportions. Such a soil is called a *loam* or, if there is a significant amount of lime in the mixture, a *marl*. Mixed soils with a large proportion of sands are known as *light soils*, and those with a disproportion of clays as *heavy soils*.

THICKNESS

The amount of soil overlying the parent rock may vary in depth from a few inches to several feet, dependent on the nature of the bedrock, the length of time the soil has been developing, the speed of mechanical and chemical breakdown, the climate and the overlying vegetation. The thickest soil layers are found in cool temperate grassland regions, where there are frequent summer rains and a temperature sufficiently moderate to prevent rapid evaporation. In the Ukraine, for instance, the famous "black earth" (*chernozem*) may reach a thickness of 40 in. (102 cm). In regions of more pronounced aridity, however, and especially where temperatures are high, the solid cover may be only a few inches thick, as on the edges of hot deserts. Soils are relatively thin also under a vegetative cover of forest, in warmer regions because of rapid evaporation from the surface soils, in cooler regions because low temperatures slow down the rate of chemical action. Under coniferous forests, for example, the soil (*podsol*) is often waterlogged and rarely more than 10 inches (25 cm) thick.

Most of the soils of the Mediterranean lands are thin, since climatic conditions, which may be said to range from sub-humid to semi-arid, are adverse to good soil development. Moreover, the accidented relief of so much of the area prevents the accumulation of soil. Soils developed on mountain slopes are eroded and washed down by winter storms to the lowlands and valleys. Consequently, there is a poor, thin cover of soil on the slopes, but in favoured areas at lower levels there may be a thick accumulation of potentially fertile soils. Such areas include the north Italian plain, the many small coastal plains of Iberia, the Maghrib, Italy, Greece, Turkey and the Levant, and the deltas of the Rhône and Nile. In the case of the last-named, however, it must be remembered that its soils are not "Mediterranean" in origin.

COLOUR

The colour of soils is so useful a characteristic that it is often used to designate soil types (see below). It depends on the mineral and organic content of the soil, and varies almost entirely with the relative abundance or paucity of different iron and aluminium compounds and humus. With a high percentage of iron hydroxide soil has a red colour, and with decreasing amounts of iron the colour ranges through various shades of brown to yellow. Humus or decayed vegetable matter has the effect of producing darker shades of all these; it is to the high humus content (10 to 15%) that chernozem owes its black colour. Mediterranean soils are sparsely supplied with humus, and so their colour is lighter—grey-brown, brown or red. As aridity increases there is less vegetative cover, less humus, and therefore a lighter soil colour.

LIME

The amount of lime found in a soil is very important, for it encourages the process of flocculation. But lime is very soluble, and so in rainy regions it may be leached from the surface layers of the soil. Soils deficient in lime but having a high percentage of iron and aluminium hydroxides are called *pedalfers* (*Al*, aluminium, *Fe*, iron); they are known also as non-lime-accumulating or acidic soils and are low in fertility. In practice, they may be improved by the addition of lime. Soils rich in lime in their upper layers are *pedocals* (*Ca*, calcium), and are lime-accumulating or alkaline. Pronounced pedocalic soils are found in regions deficient in rainfall, and if water can be supplied may be very productive even if the humus content is low; for it may be supposed that if the lime has not been dissolved and leached other useful minerals such as phosphates and potash may be present. In most cases the soils of the Mediterranean lands are pedocalic. In northern Iberia, however, that is, in an extra-Mediterranean region, the higher incidence of rainfall has leached much of the soluble salts, including those of iron, from the upper layers of the soil and has carried them downwards. Such impoverished soils are said to be *podsolised*, and tend to be brown or browny-grey in colour. They are of medium fertility; nevertheless, if they are limed they are agriculturally of great value.

SOIL PROFILE

In the majority of regions where cultivation has been carried on for thousands of years, as in most of the Mediterranean lands, the soil may seem to be uniform throughout its depth, yet this is not the case. In all soils, and best to be seen in virgin zonal soils, a vertical cutting reveals a characteristic layering which is known as the *soil profile* (*see* Fig. 15). This is divided downwards from the surface into three zones of varying thickness, known respectively as the A, B and C horizons. The *A horizon*,

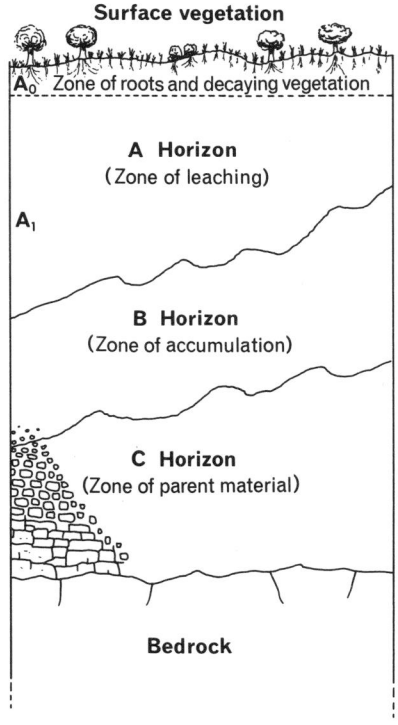

Surface vegetation

A_0 Zone of roots and decaying vegetation

A Horizon
(Zone of leaching)

A_1

B Horizon
(Zone of accumulation)

C Horizon
(Zone of parent material)

Bedrock

Fig. 15.—Soil profile.

called also the zone of leaching, is the layer in which rainwater and snow-melt have the greatest effect, where chemical and bacterial action is most active, and where rotting vegetation is transformed into humus; and it is the zone which is of paramount importance to man. It is subdivided into the A_0 horizon, which is really the zone of roots and decaying vegetation, and the A_1 horizon, where the soil is more fully developed.

The moisture which penetrates the surface of the soil carries down soluble minerals and humus in a colloidal solution to the lower levels of the A horizon, and where rainfall is persistent and evaporation low there may be excessive leaching of the zone and an accumulation and possible precipitation of the mineral salts lower down, in what is the B *horizon* or zone of accumulation. This is what takes place in podsols, and accounts for the bleached or ashy-grey appearance of the surface soils. Where rainfall is seasonal, as in the greater part of the Mediterranean lands, the leaching is not so pronounced, and the mineral salts which were carried down by the winter rains may rise again towards the surface by capillary movement during the dry summer; so that soils formed under these conditions are potentially productive. The salts precipitated in the upper part of the B horizon of podsols may form a concretionary layer òr *hard pan* which leads to water-logging and the formation of peaty swamps; in the podsolised soils of the Mediterranean, however, hard pan is rarely evident and in any case is thin enough to be broken by ploughing.

In the soils of drier regions there may also be a precipitation of salts and a formation of hard pan, but in these cases the concretion forms in the A horizon from salts moving upwards by capillary action. The conditions most favourable to its formation are a winter rainfall of about 25–30 in. followed by a complete drought in summer, and where intense insolation in the dry season may result in surface temperatures of well over 150° F (65·5° C). Such conditions may be found in parts of eastern Turkey, around Saida in Lebanon, and along the flanks of the mountains of Syria, Israel and Jordan. Here during the wet season colloidal compounds are washed down to lower levels in the horizon, and in the complete dryness and high temperatures of the following summer are brought back to the topsoil by capillary movement; and by a peculiar chemical action the colloids are precipitated so as to envelop the soil floccules near the surface and cement them together. The resultant hard pan may be thick and near enough to the surface to cause winter swamps; at the least, it limits cultivation to shallow-rooted plants such as cereals. In some areas farmers have overcome the handicap of hard pan by boring holes in it and planting olive and other deep-rooting fruit trees in the openings thus formed.

Here and there in North Africa and the Middle East there are layers of hard pan of such thickness or of such a nature that it is considered unlikely that they could have been formed under present climatic conditions. Near Saida, for instance, there is a depth of hard pan over 13 ft (4 m) thick, and in the hinterland of Tobruk in Libya there is a cemented layer actually on the surface. These are now usually regarded as relict laterite, the tropical equivalent of podsol, from which the A horizon has been completely eroded during some earlier and moister climatic period.

The B horizon of the soil profile is succeeded by the *C horizon*, the zone of parent material which rests on the bedrock. It may be looked upon as a zone of rotting rock in which mechanical processes of decay are of far greater importance than chemical action. In this horizon the development of soil is just beginning and the pieces of broken rock bear as yet little resemblance to the soil of the B horizon and still less to that of the topsoil. As was noted earlier, bedrock and to a slight degree the components of the C horizon of widely different rocks may finish up in the A horizon as soils of the same type. For instance, terra rossa may be found in some parts of the Mediterranean developed from bedrock as different as limestone and basalt.

SOIL TYPES

We have seen how soils are developed from parent rocks under the influence of climate, humus and bacteria, and since all these factors and their combinations vary considerably from one part of the world to another, the number of different soils which can be distinguished is very great. At the same time, using as a basis the discoveries of Russian soil scientists (pedologists), it has been found possible to classify zonal soils under a relatively few headings, e.g., tundra soils, podsols, chernozems, brown soils, chestnut soils, yellow soils, red soils, laterites and desert soils. Such groupings are known as *zonal*, as they occur in zones or belts which may be extensive in both length and breadth (*see* Fig. 16). Some soils, such as those formed by the deposition of alluvium, the breakdown of recent volcanic extrusions, or in isolated hollows in deserts, do not follow the normal process of soil evolution and cannot be included in a zonal classification; in consequence, they are known as *azonal*.

ZONAL SOILS

The chief zonal types or major groupings of soil found in the Mediterranean lands are (1) grey-brown podsolic soils, (2) brown forest soils, (3) red soils, (4) chestnut soils, and (5) desert soils.

1. Grey-brown podsolic soils

Some account has been given of this soil, which belongs more to regions outside the limits of true Mediterranean climate. Podsolic soils occur in northern Portugal and on both sides of the Cantabrian–Pyrenean mountains in Spain and Mediterranean France, and to a less degree in parts of Yugoslavia, where rain occurs at all seasons and summer temperatures are not as high as in regions further south. The soils have a slightly bleached character with a low humus content, and are of medium fertility; but by careful cultivation they have been made very productive.

2. Brown forest soils

Essentially a product of cool, temperate, humid climates, these are ideally developed under deciduous forests such as used to cover large areas of Western Europe. In the Mediterranean lands this type is limited to cooler and damper areas, where deciduous forests are the natural cover; they occur at their best in the north Italian plain, the Algerian Tell, north-west Morocco, southern Portugal and much of the Spanish Meseta, and a broad belt along the Aegean and Black Sea coasts of Turkey. The soils are various shades of brown in colour, dependent on the amount of humus and

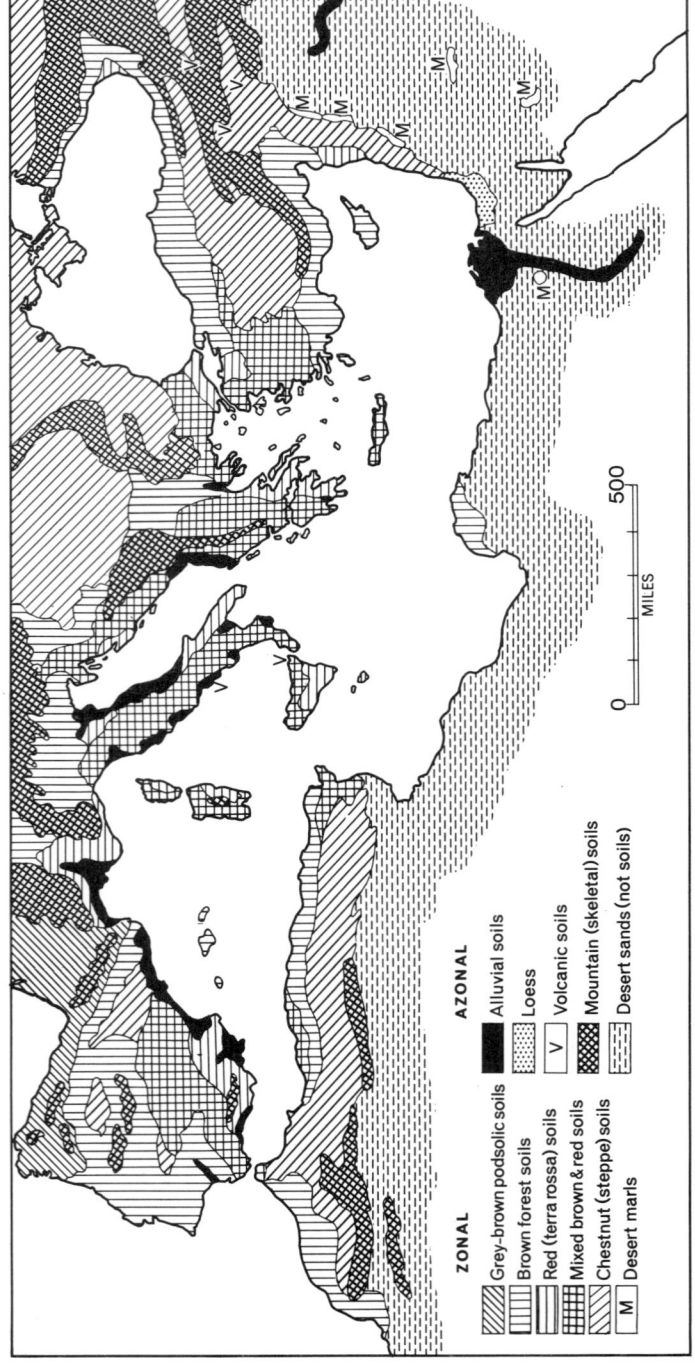

ZONAL

Grey-brown podsolic soils
Brown forest soils
Red (terra rossa) soils
Mixed brown & red soils
Chestnut (steppe) soils
Desert marls

AZONAL

Alluvial soils
Loess
Volcanic soils
Mountain (skeletal) soils
Desert sands (not soils)

0   500
MILES

FIG. 16.—The Mediterranean lands: soils. A generalised distribution of the main types.

decomposition in the A horizon, and this in turn is affected by slight differences in climatic conditions. They are more fertile than podsolic soils.

3. Red soils or terra rossa

Where the climatic régime is typically Mediterranean, and especially but not exclusively where the parent rock is limestone, the brown forest soils tend to be mixed with soil of a reddish colour, known as terra rossa. This mixture, or terra rossa alone, is the most characteristic soil of the Mediterranean lands, especially on the European side. Patches of pure terra rossa occur in south-east Spain, the lower Rhône valley, the eastern flanks of the Apennines, Sicily, Corsica, Sardinia, eastern Greece, Syria and eastern Turkey. The mixed reddish-brown soils lie in close proximity to the terra rossa, covering large areas of the eastern Spanish Meseta, most of Corsica, Sardinia and Greece, the Apennine ranges and northern Sicily. They are found extensively inside the belt of brown soils in Turkey, and have developed also in the valleys of Dalmatia, the northern Levant lands and the western Tell. Terra rossa is a rather heavy, clayey soil, rich in lime and sesquioxides of iron, aluminium and silicon, but poor in humus. Where it is evolved on underlying limestones, the high iron content gives it a bright red colour, but where the parent rock is basalt or serpentine it has a darker red tint. In the more mountainous parts of Asia Minor, where there is a greater rainfall, the iron hydroxides are leached from the topsoil, and the reddish colour is replaced by yellow. Terra rossa and the mixed red and brown soils are deficient in humus, and are of low fertility. Nevertheless, they are of great value to the Mediterranean farmers, for cereals grow well in them and they can support olives, vines and other fruit trees.

4. Chestnut soils

Under the steppe vegetation of the Danubian plains of Yugoslavia and the eastern Anatolian plateau are soils of a dark chestnut colour, formed in regions of light summer rainfall and heat. In some ways they are reminiscent of chernozem, but their humus content is rarely more than 5% and they are far inferior in fertility to black earth. They are better, however, than most Mediterranean soils and yield excellent crops of cereals. In the drier and hotter steppe lands of Syria, Lebanon and Israel, the soils are light chestnut in colour and have a much shallower profile; and since the plant cover is less dense they have sometimes no more than 1% humus. Moreover, as conditions become drier towards the neighbouring deserts, the light-chestnut soils tend to become more and more saline.

5. Desert soils

These are better described as marls or limy clays. They were developed originally under moister climatic conditions, probably in river valleys and lake basins. Desert marls, which are not to be confused with desert sands, occur in scattered patches in the Syrian, Arabian and Saharan deserts. They are pale brown, grey and even white in colour, extremely saline and almost entirely lacking in humus. They can support a scanty salt-resistant vegetation and, where the saline content is lower, may be made fit for cultivation. This is made possible by a plentiful supply of irrigation water, sometimes carried long distances, which is used first to wash away the surplus alkali salts and later, after cultivation has commenced, to keep the soil clear of further accumulations. Reclamation of desert marls has taken place in some localities in Egypt and Libya, especially in the vicinity of the larger oases, and ambitious projects are in course of fulfilment or are planned in Syria, Israel and Jordan.

AZONAL SOILS

Most of the coastal plains skirting the Mediterranean, some inland troughs and the floors of river valleys are composed of alluvium deposited by rivers in flood or discharging into a tideless sea to form deltas. The *alluvial soils* which are evolved are usually heavy clays, rich in humus, and very fertile. This is notably the case in reclaimed coastal swamps such as the Pontine and Maremma in western peninsular Italy, where dense marsh vegetation has supplied large quantities of humus. In Tuscany, the Plain of Naples and other areas in which volcanic activity, past or present, has occurred, there are soils which have developed from the decomposition of lavas and tuffs. For want of a better title, they are here designated as *volcanic soils*. Their fertility depends on their age. In Tuscany and the eastern Plain of Naples, for instance, the soils are mature and among the most fertile in the Mediterranean, and there are similar but less productive soils in south-east Sicily. Near Mounts Vesuvius and Etna, however, the soils are too young to have more than a minimum value, and in the immediate vicinity of the volcanoes the breakdown of lavas and ash has hardly commenced. How long it takes a soil to develop is not known, but it is certain that the soil formed on volcanic rocks takes far longer to mature than that on alluvium, given the same climatic conditions.

Another type of azonal soil is that which is developed on *loess*. In or near deserts where wind erosion is more active than that occasioned by water, particles of desert marls and dust from desert sands may be whirled high in the air and carried considerable distances by dust storms. When they are deposited they may form accumulations of loess, such as are found as dunes in the north of the Sinai peninsula and the Negev (Negeb); or the particles may be forced down by a more humid atmosphere to mix with the native soils of the European peninsulas and the Levant lands. Loess is a mixture of sand, silt and clay, and where moisture is available it develops into a very fertile soil. In the form of dunes it has limited potentiality, especially in regions of low rainfall such as those mentioned above, but in Israel irrigation has made it possible for some of the dunes to support orchards of citrus fruits and vines. Where loess forms a cover over or is mixed with other soils, the resulting loam is rich and, where irrigation water is available, yields good crops.

An interesting fact which has relation to all types of soil has recently come to light. It has been found that plants normally take only about 5% of their constituent materials directly from the soil; the other 95% is produced by the process of photosynthesis of sunlight, air and water, operating through their leaves. This fact, unsuspected until a short time ago, might seem to suggest that soil fertility has less importance than is usually credited to it. This is not so. If soils are poor in quality, the whole growth of the plant suffers, sometimes seriously; photosynthesis cannot make good any deficiencies in the soil.

SOILS AND MEDITERRANEAN AGRICULTURE

Three features should be noted in connection with the soils and agriculture of Mediterranean lands: (1) a widespread shortage of humus, (2) the danger of soil erosion, and (3) the necessity for irrigation.

1. *Shortage of humus*

The high temperatures of summer literally burn away most of the organic matter in the A horizon of soils, and so the chances of accumulation of decaying natural or cultivated vegetation are minimised. Animal manures, which also form an important source of humus, are not plentiful, for in general the Mediterranean has poor pastures. In any case, manure suffers the same rapid oxidation as dead vegetation, so much so that dried dung is used as household fuel in many places and the ashes then strewn on the fields. This practice is said to be only little less effective than to allow the dried-up manure to decompose naturally. Artificial fertilisers are not a complete answer to a shortage of humus; indeed, they may lead to new problems if used injudiciously. Capillary action in the dry summers may cause a precipitation of their soluble salts as a temporary hard pan in the topsoil, and in the rains of winter they may be leached excessively. Most Mediterranean soils are deficient in humus and are not naturally very fertile. Their relative productivity, however, and the importance in world markets of the crops produced on them are indications of the care with which they are cultivated, rather than of any great inherent fertility.

2. *The danger of soil erosion*

This means the risk of the removal of surface soil by wind or water, the normal weathering agents. It generally takes place after the ground has been broken up by ploughing and made easier to carry away. In humid regions, *i.e.*, where rain falls at all seasons, the soil particles are more coherent, and the loss by erosion is slow; in carefully cultivated soils there may even be no loss at all. Humid regions, too, may have a more complete cover of vegetation, which helps to inhibit erosion. Where there is seasonal drought, however, or where the total annual rainfall is small, soil erosion either by wind or water presents a major problem to the cultivator. It is especially intense if the rainfall comes in torrential showers. It has been computed, for example, that Algeria loses the equivalent of 250 acres of arable land *per day* because of soil erosion (*see also* page 384).

Over most of the Mediterranean soil erosion is a legacy of the torrential rains of winter. Much of the land is mountainous and steeply sloping, so that the thin layer of incipient soil on the slopes is washed to the lowlands whence it is carried away by rivers in flood to build up river flats, coastal swamps and deltas, or to be lost in the sea. Consequently, the soils on slopes are poor and thin, except where they are kept in place artificially by the building of retaining walls (terracing) as shown in Fig. 17. Lowland soils, too, parched and powdery during the dry summer, may be blown away by wind, and in winter they are gullied by rains and rivers sometimes to such an extent as to produce "badlands." The total amount of soil lost in this way is incalculable. Governments everywhere are alive to the problem, and active measures, such as contour ploughing, crop alternation and the fixation of gully soils by fast-growing plants, are being encouraged in all countries which suffer from this type of soil erosion.

The loss of soil in the Mediterranean lands has been accentuated by the cutting down of forests or the ploughing of grasslands, so destroying the binding power of their roots and exposing the loosened soil to the devastation of swiftly flowing water. Similar results follow over-grazing on grasslands and the rearing of goats on mountain slopes. Goats are the great enemies of Mediterranean forests, nibbling bushes, tree seedlings and the lower branches of trees, even in the most inaccessible places, and leaving still greater areas of soil open to easy erosion.

The regions most subject to soil erosion by water are the Meseta of Spain, the whole of peninsular Italy, Sicily, peninsular Greece, Cyprus, much of the coastal areas of Asia Minor and the northern Levant lands, and the Maghrib, but few Mediterranean countries are completely free from this type of denudation.

Soil erosion by wind occurs chiefly along the drier southern and eastern margins of the Mediterranean, where dust-laden winds and the formation of dunes and loess have already been noted. Deflation by wind is common also in all Mediterranean lands which have wide stretches of relatively flat land and only a thin vegetative cover, such as the south and east of the Spanish Meseta, the Plateau of the Shotts, the plains of Sicily and Cyprus, the plateaus of Asia Minor and of the Levant interior. The wind can remove only dry, incoherent particles, and so, along the European margins where summer rains are sufficient to bind the soil together in the period of greatest insolation and maximum desiccation, wind erosion has far less effect than in those parts of the Mediterranean lands which have rain mainly in winter.

Because fine particles of soil are washed or blown away, many Mediterranean soils are pronouncedly stony in character, sometimes to such a degree that to English eyes they look almost useless. Mediterranean farmers have discovered, however, that a loose covering of stones can act as a mulch, keeping the underneath soil moist, and encouraging a type of

[*Courtesy of the French Embassy.*

FIG. 17.—Mediterranean France: this view is typical of terracing in most countries around the Mediterranean coastlands of Europe.

dry farming. It is often good farming, therefore, to cultivate stony soils, especially for tree crops; olives and vines, for instance, often seem to be growing from a bed of dry stones.

3. *The necessity for irrigation*

With the exception of a belt along the Biscayan and Atlantic coasts, the Mediterranean lands generally have seasonal distribution of rainfall or a total annual precipitation which is unsatisfactory for cultivation all the year, even where temperatures are suitable. In some areas of deficient rainfall "dry farming" is practised, that is, using the rainfall of two years for one crop; the two-year rotation of crop followed by fallow is a type of dry farming. In most parts, however, a shortage of water is made good by irrigation. Even in some of the valleys of the Italian and Yugoslavian Alps and in the eastern Plain of Lombardy, where annual rainfall totals are relatively high and summers comparatively wet, farmers must resort to irrigation. It is essential as a general rule that all Mediterranean lands should store some of the rains of winter for use in summer. More will be said later about irrigation systems and methods in individual countries; in particular, irrigation in Egypt, since it is not "Mediterranean" in type, deserves special treatment. Careful attention is paid to it in Chapter XXII. Here we shall discuss Mediterranean irrigation in general.

Irrigation has been practised for thousands of years in the Nile valley and the Middle East, and it was gradually introduced to all the countries of North Africa. In its older, more primitive forms it depended simply on the annual inundation of land by the flooding of rivers. To prevent the flood waters flowing away too quickly, earthen walls were constructed so as to make vast, shallow basins adjoining the rivers. In course of time these were inter-connected by systems of canals, and in this way water was taken to basins further from the rivers, so extending the scope of the flood waters (*see also* page 462). This "basin" irrigation, as it is called, although it permitted the spread of river silts and the consequent enrichment of the soils, was limited in duration to the drying-up period following floods. At other times, artificial watering depended on various water-lifting devices such as shadufs, sakias (water-wheels), and Archimedean screws, powered by human labour or by mules or camels.

Today, basin irrigation has been replaced almost everywhere by the conservation of flood waters in huge reservoirs blocked by barrages or giant dams. These make water available throughout the year in the system known as "perennial" irrigation. Cultivation is no longer confined to a few crops immediately following the flood season but is possible all the year, so that two, three, or even four crops may be grown in succession. Water-lifting is still practised, but most of the old, primitive devices have been replaced by modern pumps, the latest being driven by diesel engines. Pumps are especially valuable where the water supply is from wells, which in due course have been driven deeper and deeper. Modern dams have been constructed and more are under construction in Egypt, Israel,

Jordan, Syria, Lebanon and Turkey, and in all cases the impounded waters are used also for the generation of hydro-electric power. Water-pumps are found mainly in the Levant lands, Libya and Algeria.

Along the European marginal lands irrigation was developed later than in those mentioned above, but even before the Christian era there were already primitive canal systems using river water in Spain, southern France, Italy and Greece. Most were the work of individual landowners and were limited to a few hundred square yards; none offered any comparison with the large areas covered by irrigation systems in the Arab lands. New knowledge and impetus came with the Arab invasions of Sicily, southern Italy and the Iberian peninsula, particularly in the last, where the invaders remained for 400 years and introduced irrigation systems similar to those in North Africa. In addition, they imported plants such as citrus fruits, cotton and sugar cane, and imposed laws of water usage, some of which are still in force.

Modern dam construction has greatly increased the areas under irrigation in southern Europe, especially in Spain, central and southern Italy, and Yugoslavia; in every country more and more land is coming under the plough. Rivers are being diverted, deep wells bored, and new sources are being tapped and the waters conserved. In connection with this last, it should be remembered that in the limestone mountain ranges which are so numerous around the Mediterranean, rains and surface water may disappear through "joints" to flow underground and possibly collect in huge, natural subterranean reservoirs. Most of this water in the past has fed rivers flowing in deeply etched valleys where irrigation is difficult. Today, by carefully constructed channels and controls, the water may be carried long distances to more suitable surface areas, and hitherto unproductive land has been transformed into fruitful farms. Examples of this type of water supply occur in Algeria, the Sierra Nevada and the central sierras of the Meseta in Spain, the Apennines in Italy, the Karst in Yugoslavia, the Pindus in Greece, and the islands of Crete and Cyprus. It is a most expensive method of water conservation and use; schemes of this type are not numerous, and most have a very limited extent.

Irrigation in lands around the Mediterranean is not an unmixed blessing. It is true that it enables land to be used for crops where none would grow before, and in poor land it will raise both quantity and quality, but it is also a fact that some potentially useful soils may be rendered sterile by injudicious addition of irrigation water, and also that carelessly constructed canals may have deleterious results. In chestnut soils, for instance, especially where there is an admixture of loess, irrigation has immediate beneficial results, but unless there is careful control of the amount of water added, there may be a slow accumulation of mineral salts in the upper soil and in time this may be inimical to plant life. Too much irrigation water in any type of soil may leach the useful mineral salts and make the ground sour and infertile. Imperfectly made or badly sited canals may allow the entry of saline waters which taint and render harmful the normal supply.

Water from wells, especially deep ones, is often brackish and unfit for use in irrigation.

Besides these, a new danger has emerged, mainly in the drier parts of Egypt and the Middle East. The vast surface of permanent water in reservoirs and perennial canals has become a fresh breeding place for mosquitoes and parasitic worms, so that, according to some authorities, there is serious increase in their vicinity of malaria and bilharziasis. The worst aspects of these drawbacks to irrigation are encountered in lands with desert or semi-desert climatic conditions and where educational standards are low, but some of them may be met in more progressive regions with a true Mediterranean climate.

A further problem in some areas is of quite a different nature. Where the traditional way of life is semi-nomadic or transhumant it is not uncommon for herdsmen to pasture their stock on the lowlands during the winter months and move to higher levels at other times of the year. Difficulties arise when substantial areas of lowland pastures are ploughed, irrigated and used for crop growing and other agricultural purposes, for these lands are then no longer available to the transhumant for winter feed. The way of life of the stock rearer can be totally upset in these circumstances, and great hardship caused. This is especially so in parts of Morocco, where it has become a pressing problem (*see* page 371).

The difficulties and problems which have followed in the train of irrigation in the lands around the Mediterranean are, however, vastly outweighed by its advantages. The use of irrigation has become a serious scientific study, since it is now increasingly recognised that it involves far more than merely to conserve water and convey it to areas deficient in rainfall. Due regard must also be given to the type and mineral content of the water used, to the kind of soil for which it is intended, to any local climatic variations or anomalies, to the varieties of plants which are to be grown, and to existing patterns of social life and land use. Irrigation has become the field, not only of civil engineers, economists and financiers, but of soil chemists and ecologists. Wherever it is practised extensively, it is now under strict governmental supervision. Water supply, storage and distribution are carefully controlled and watched over by specially trained officials; and everywhere attempts are being made with the help of increased education and legislation to correct many of the mistakes made in the past.

STUDY QUESTIONS

1. Write a short essay on "Soil types in the Mediterranean region."

2. What is meant by soil erosion? Illustrating your answer by reference to the Mediterranean lands, explain concisely (a) the ways in which soil erosion may be caused, and (b) how it is being combated.

3. Write short notes on *four* of the following: pedocals, terra rossa, loess, humus, flocculation, azonal soils.

4. Discuss the part played by irrigation in the rural economy of the Mediterranean lands. (London.)

Chapter V

NATURAL VEGETATION

THE different climates found within the limits of the Mediterranean lands (Mediterranean, sub-Mediterranean and extra-Mediterranean), the variety of soils and the accidented relief are the main factors affecting the distribution of natural vegetation. There is ample evidence, however, that climatic changes during and after the Quaternary Ice Age were responsible for a plant revolution in the lands around the Mediterranean Sea, and some consideration should therefore be given to the effects of these changes on the present natural vegetation. Moreover, within the past 5000 years man has been responsible for such profound changes in the areas in which he has settled as to make it appropriate to include him also as an important factor in the distribution and diversity of natural vegetation.

It is generally accepted that in the middle Tertiary the whole of Western and Central Europe and most of the Mediterranean lands were covered by luxuriant tropical or sub-tropical forest, similar to the forests found nowadays in Florida and South-east Asia. With the onset of cooler conditions in the Pliocene, culminating with the vast ice sheets of the Pleistocene, this forest was gradually exterminated in Europe as far south as the Pyrenean–Alpine mountain barrier, and in the areas not covered by ice it was replaced by tundra. First in the process of extermination was the more delicate plant life near the Scandinavian centres of glaciation, and as temperatures continued to fall and the ice sheets advanced southwards only the tougher types of tree were able to survive. These tended to assume a zoned character very much like that of today, with the more resistant conifers nearer the ice and deciduous trees and broad-leaved evergreens further away. The retreat of the forests southwards was checked by the twofold barrier of mountain ranges and the broad Mediterranean Sea, except from the Balkan region eastwards, where the ranges are lower and less continuous and allowed some of the northern species to penetrate and flourish. At the period of maximum glaciation all the less hardy species, even of the conifers, were unable to survive in the harsh conditions of the mountains, and tundra fringed the southern edges of the Pyrenees and Alps. South of the tundra the hardiest conifers covered the northern Meseta of Spain and much of the northern half of the Italian peninsula, and coniferous forest stretched also across the continental part of the Balkan lands.

During the Glacial Epoch temperatures fell everywhere around the Mediterranean. In the early Quaternary the region away from the northern mountain rim had a cool to cold temperate climate, with more oceanic influence and rainfall than today, especially in the Western basin. In these circumstances, most sub-tropical plants which had flourished before the Ice Age disappeared, together with many species of deciduous and ever-green trees. Some sub-tropical varieties managed to survive in sheltered pockets on the southward-facing tips of peninsulas, on the south coasts of islands, and along the Tell of north-west Africa, and there were further survivals on the Atlantic coasts north and south of the Strait of Gibraltar. On the whole, however, most of the Mediterranean lands in the climatic conditions then obtaining were well forested, in the north and at high altitudes by conifers, followed further south and on lower slopes first by deciduous and then by broad-leaved evergreen trees. The variety of species, however, was far more restricted than before the Ice Age.

Since the last phase of the Quaternary Ice Age the climate of the Medi-terranean lands has gradually evolved to the predominant winter-rain/ summer-drought type and this has brought in its train many changes in natural vegetation. In the first place, the melting of the ice in the moun-tains allowed a return of plant life along the northern rim of the basin, a recolonisation which was encouraged by a spread of genera from the the south and also from outside the basin in the north-east. In the latter the incomplete mountain barrier in the Balkan lands and Asia Minor had al-ready played a part, for some pre-glacial species which had penetrated there had managed to survive; these now began to drift towards and colo-nise more western regions, and seeds of steppe grasses and bulbous plants, of new deciduous and coniferous trees and of shrubs were blown from Eastern Europe and Western Asia into the Mediterranean lands. It is sug-gested, for instance, that the Judas tree, which is a type of rock rose, was exterminated in Europe during the Ice Age, except in the Balkan penin-sula; today it may be found as far west as Mediterranean France. Cedars and cypress also survived in the north-east and began to move westwards, but the typical Mediterranean climate is not really favourable to their growth; both may occur in the western Mediterranean lands as far as the Strait of Gibraltar, but their distribution is patchy and sporadic and confined to slopes which have more than the average rainfall. At the western end of the Mediterranean the climate of south Portugal remained sufficiently genial during the Ice Age for the cork-oak to survive there, and thence it spread to the north coast of Africa, eastern Spain and western Italy.

PLANT ADAPTATIONS

Perhaps the most important result of the evolution in climate to that which is typical of the Mediterranean today was the necessity of plant life to adapt itself to the new conditions and also to the new types of soil which developed. The normal optimum climatic conditions for plant growth include the coincidence of heat and moisture, but in the Mediterranean climate high temperatures and rainfall are rarely concomitant. The great-est heat is accompanied by drought, and rain comes mainly in the cool season, when normally in temperate climates plant life is dormant and resting. Plants in the Mediterranean had to change their rhythm of growth in such a way as to allow greatest activity and development when temperatures were at their lowest, and they must needs adapt themselves to combat the desiccating effects of the long, hot summers. Fortunately, winter temperatures in the Mediterranean region average more than 43° F (6·1° C), and this is warm enough to permit plant growth, but only very slowly. Mediterranean trees take longer to mature than those in regions where heat and moisture coincide, and many of them have a gnarled and stunted appearance.

Plants can withstand long periods of heat and drought (a) by completing their cycle of growth wholly within the mild, wet winters and the warm and still moist springs, or (b) by modifications in their structure. Natural grasses, for example, germinate in late autumn, grow to fruition and shed their seeds during the winter and spring, and are shrivelled by the hot sun of summer. Cultivated grasses may have a similar cycle; wheat and barley were developed from wild grasses in Mesopotamia, and both appeared in very early times in the Mediterranean in the Levant and North Africa and spread quickly to all parts of the basin as winter crops. Other plants which have a short cycle of activity in the cool season are those which store food and moisture for the summer drought in bulbs, tubers and rhizomes (swollen roots); such include tulips, lilies, narcissi and irises, which may be found growing wild in most Mediterranean countries.

Structural modifications in Mediterranean plant life have the purpose of searching for moisture in the summer or of preventing a too rapid transpiration at all times. In the former the adaptation is the development of long roots which can reach the water preserved in lower soil horizons or which spread sideways for long distances near the surface of the soil. Among the better-known examples of plants which have roots penetrating deeply are the vine, olive, Aleppo pine, walnut and kermes oak. In places in the Levant, penetration is helped artificially by breaking holes through hard pan which may occur a short distance below the soil surface and planting olives in the gaps thus made. In the Levant, too, are found plants with wide-spreading roots within a few inches of the surface so that the very heavy dews deposited during the summer nights may be utilised.

Plants which have adapted themselves not so much to obtain moisture as to minimise transpiration are common. The cork oak, for example, effects the conservation of moisture by developing a thick bark; the thick, leathery leaves of the laurel and evergreen oak serve the same purpose. In some plants, such as the olive, the leaves are reduced in size; in others, like many genera of thorn bushes, the leaves are mere spikes. Many plants have leaves covered with hairs or with a resinous exudation, adaptations which provide an insulating layer against the scorching sun. A large number of shrubs are aromatic or fragrant, and are deciduous. The hyssop, lavender, sage and thyme, for example, shed their leaves in summer, and in that season appear to be dead. The same applies to many plants of the desert edges, which in the dry summer look like dried sticks.

The tamarisk is a semi-desert bush with a normal withered and dead appearance; after a brief shower, however, its spiny leaves begin to exude a sticky sap.

TYPES AND DISTRIBUTION OF VEGETATION

Whereas a description of the *types* of natural vegetation found in the Mediterranean lands presents little difficulty, a satisfactory account of their *distribution* is not so easy. Not only are we concerned with different climatic types (Mediterranean, sub-Mediterranean and extra-Mediterranean) which have their own characteristic vegetational types, but in each climatic region there are also local variations from the normal factors of temperature and rainfall and consequently in the plant life found there. This is especially noticeable in the region of true Mediterranean climate, for here the distribution of vegetational types is complicated by the relief. In peninsular Italy, for example, the central Apennines rise to over 9000 feet (2700 m) above sea-level, and the resultant low temperatures and high rainfall have given a succession upwards of deciduous, coniferous and Alpine vegetation not usually associated with a "Mediterranean" region; and the same sequence is to be found on the windward slopes of the Atlas in north-west Africa. In the typical Mediterranean region, too, man in the past 5000 years has so interfered with the vegetation pattern as to make it very difficult to describe its *natural* distribution.

The types of natural vegetation found in the Mediterranean lands may be classified as follows (*see* Fig. 18): (1) broad-leaved evergreen forest, (2) stunted and degenerate woodland, (3) deciduous forest, (4) aquatic grasses and reeds, (5) coniferous forest, (6) grassland, including steppe, (7) dry steppe and semi-desert, (8) desert, and (9) Alpine vegetation. Of these, (1), (2) and (4) fall within the limits of the true winter-rain/summer-drought climate, and so does a subdivision of (3); (7) for the most part lies outside true Mediterranean climatic conditions, and (8) almost entirely so. The remainder, although they belong mainly to sub-Mediterranean and extra-Mediterranean regions, may occur fragmentally in true Mediterranean areas.

TRUE MEDITERRANEAN TYPES

1. *Broad-leaved evergreen forest*

This lies entirely within the limits of cultivation of the olive and may be regarded as the type most characteristic of Mediterranean vegetation. The chief trees are evergreen oaks of various kinds, the most numerous being the holm oak (*Quercus ilex*), the cork oak (*Q. suber*) and the kermes oak (*Q. coccifera*). The holm oak, whose leaves resemble those of holly (*Ilex Aquifolium*) and which for that reason is sometimes called the holly-oak, has a distribution around the Mediterranean somewhat wider than that of the olive, except that it is not found in the Levant and that it has extended its range to the sub-Mediterranean Biscayan and Atlantic coastlands. The

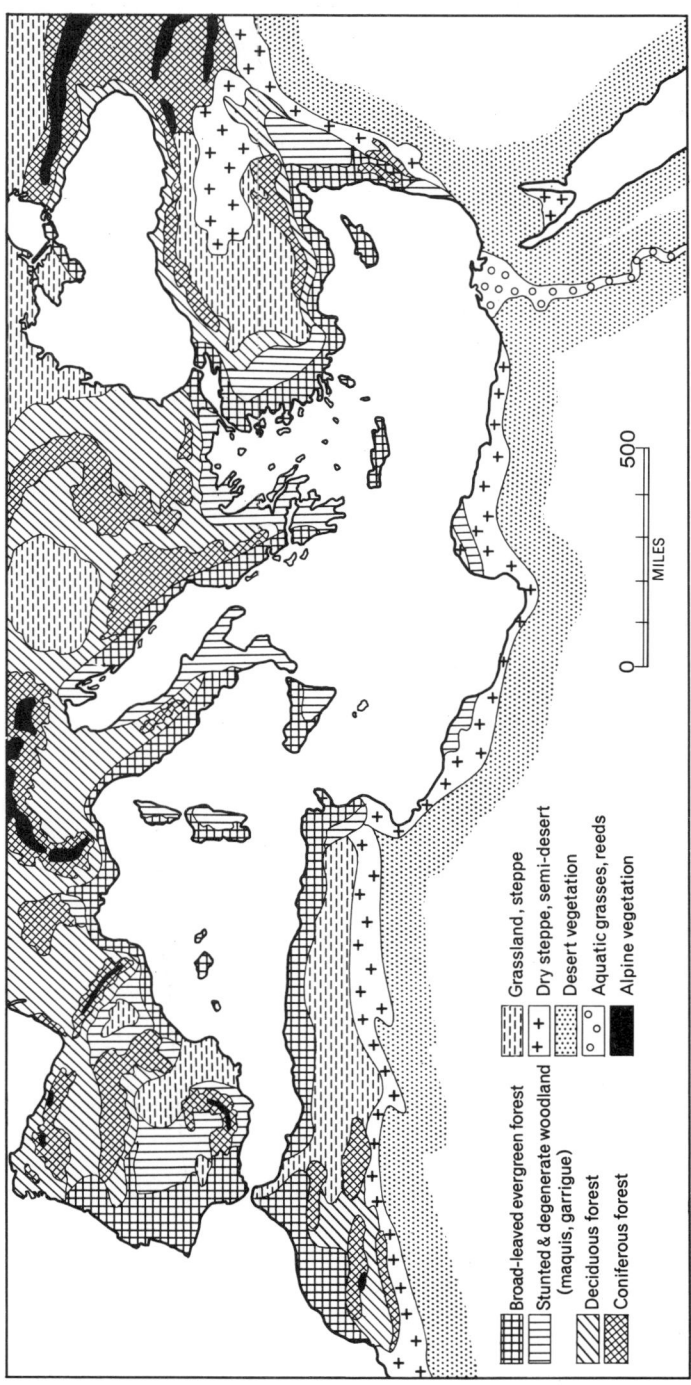

Grassland, steppe

Dry steppe, semi-desert

Desert vegetation

Aquatic grasses, reeds

Alpine vegetation

Broad-leaved evergreen forest

Stunted & degenerate woodland
(maquis, garrigue)

Deciduous forest

Coniferous forest

500

MILES

0

FIG. 18.—The Mediterranean lands: natural vegetation.

cork-oak, although it is xerophilous, that is, tolerant of a droughty habitat, seems to prefer the moister atmosphere found in the Western Mediterranean basin; it occurs extensively in the western half of the Iberian peninsula and along the coastlands of the Maghrib, and there are small concentrations in north-east Spain, Sardinia, Tuscany and north-east Sicily. In the Eastern basin its distribution is limited to the Dalmatian littoral. The kermes oak is found mainly in North Africa and the Levant, but its distribution extends also to most countries along the north of the Mediterranean, a notable exception being Italy, where it rarely occurs. The kermes has a more stunted appearance than most other evergreen oaks and its timber is of little economic value. On its leaves, however, breed coccus insects, known to the Persians and Arabs as *kermes* (*qirmiz*), the female bodies of which are used as a red dye-stuff similar to cochineal.

Most of the original broad-leaved evergreen forest has been cut down and replaced by cultivated trees or the land left derelict, so that today there are only a few representative stands. The main distribution of evergreen oaks nowadays is in areas with too little rain for agriculture; exceptions may occur where the oaks are of economic value, as in the case of the cork-oak in Portugal and North Africa, or where the land under the oak forests, although unsuitable for general cultivation, could support more valuable fruit trees. In the Eastern Mediterranean basin, the oaks over wide stretches have been replaced by olive groves.

The trees in the evergreen forests are widely spaced, as if to avoid competition in the search for water, and between the trees is a dense mat of xerophilous shrubs and small trees. Shrubs such as broom, rosemary, myrtle, gorse, privet, rock-rose (*cistus*) and laurel form a ground vegetation, and above them rise the taller fig, wild olive, terebinth and arbutus. Scattered throughout the forest are such bulbous plants as narcissi, tulips and lilies. In places where the summer drought is too intense or the soils too thin for major tree growth, evergreen oaks are extremely stunted or disappear completely, and their place may be taken by the wild olive (olivaster), the carob or locust-tree (*Ceratonia Siliqua*), known also as the algarroba (Ar. *al kharrūbah*, hence "carob"), and the lentisk or mastic tree (L. *lentiscus*). Most of these occur in the Eastern basin, but may be found also in small numbers in Sicily, the "toe" and "heel" of Italy, and the Maghrib. The wild olive has a distribution similar to the cultivated variety; the greatest numbers today are in the south of Italy and the Peloponnesus. The beans of the wild carob provide useful fodder for cattle, and from the lentisk is obtained a pale yellow gum used in the manufacture of varnish.

2. *Stunted and degenerate woodland*

Although we have stated that the most characteristic type of vegetation around the Mediterranean is broad-leaved evergreens, the tangle of undergrowth which lies beneath the taller trees must be regarded as equally typical. In fact, because so much of the evergreen forest has been cleared, or the trees destroyed by the depredations of goats, the largest areas of natural vegetation in lands with a Mediterranean climate are varieties of this "undergrowth," but without tall trees. It may be said to represent a degeneration of the evergreen forest described above, and is usually an extensive and virtually impenetrable tangle of woody, thorny shrubs and dwarfed and twisted trees rising to a height of not more than 10 ft (3 m). It is best developed in Calabria and Corsica in the western Mediterranean; it occurs also in western Spain, parts of the Algerian Tell, Istria and the Aegean coastlands of Turkey; and still more degenerate forms cover large areas of southern Italy, Spain and Greece. Various names are given to this type of vegetation. To the French it is known as *maquis*, and this is the term normally used in textbooks; the Italians call it *macchia* and the Spaniards *mattoral*. Maquis is usually associated with siliceous soils; where the soils are derived from limestones, there is a further degeneration into *garrigue* (*garigue*). Garrigue occurs extensively in Mediterranean France, Algeria and Tunisia in the Western basin, and in all the lands to the north and east of the Eastern basin. The thickets in garrigue are more low-growing and discontinuous than in maquis; bulbous plants are more common; and desert plants such as cactus and aloe (agave), brought from America by the Spaniards, add to the prickly confusion. In some of the deeper, more enclosed valleys in the west of Asia Minor, garrigue still further degenerates to a low-growing, spiny thorn scrub known as *phrygana*.

3. Deciduous forest

Here we must distinguish two groups: (a) deciduous trees which occur in the region with a Mediterranean climate, and (b) those found in sub- and extra-Mediterranean areas.

(a) Generally speaking, deciduous trees are not suited to a true Mediterranean climate, and within the area of summer drought they are normally found above the limit of olive cultivation, that is, where it is cooler and more likely to have precipitation caused by higher altitudes. This varies from 1000 feet to 2000 feet (300–600 m), depending on position in the Mediterranean, and on aspect. In peninsular Italy, for example, deciduous oaks mixed with alders and ash occur at about 1000 feet (300 m) on the Apennines, and these are succeeded to more than 3000 feet (900 m) by the edible chestnut, and from thence upwards by the beech. Deciduous forests are found at similar altitudes in Greece, Dalmatia and the south coasts of Turkey, and at somewhat greater heights in the Betic Cordillera and the Atlas. In the Eastern basin around the Aegean and in the Levant, oaks are the main species, and are mixed with elm, wild plum, wild cherry and chestnut. The acorns of the valonia oak (*Quercus Aegilops*), which is indigenous to Greece and the coasts of the Levant, provide one of the richest of tanning materials. In this region, incidentally, the oak forests may degenerate into a kind of *deciduous* maquis, as for example in Macedonia.

(b) Along the northern limit of olive cultivation there is a transition from evergreen to deciduous trees following the change from Mediterranean to sub-Mediterranean climatic conditions. A belt of deciduous forest stretched originally from north-west Spain south of the Cantabrians, through the north Italian plain to Dalmatia and Albania. The belt today is widest in "pluviose" Spain and north-west Portugal where it extends to the extra-Mediterranean coastal areas of northern Spain. It narrows south of the Pyrenees and the Maritime Alps, widens again in the north Italian plain, and spreads over the mountainous border of Yugoslavia to the extra-Mediterranean part of that country. It appears again in the mountains of Thrace and widens in the sub-Mediterranean Taurus and plateau districts of Turkey. In the west the chief varieties are similar to those in Britain— oak, ash, elm, beech, chestnut—with occasional migrants such as hazel, wild cherry, laburnum and edible chestnut. In the northern Italian plain there was a predominance of oaks, but most of these have been cleared for agriculture and for such tree crops as grapes, almonds, walnuts, peaches, cherries and mulberries, the last for sericulture.

In the Eastern basin the Turkey oak (Q. Cerris) is an important deciduous tree. It abounds all over the Turkish peninsula and forms a large portion of the vast forests that clothe the slopes of the Taurus ranges and the south shores of the Black Sea. It is common in Italy and Sardinia, and occurs also in Mediterranean France. Its wood is hard, heavy and of fine grain, excellent for indoor work, and it is also employed in the building of ships in Greece and Turkey.

Deciduous trees yield comparatively large amounts of humus, and fertile soils may develop under them. In the course of time they have been cleared for cultivation over most of the belt outlined above, especially in the plain of north Italy. In the Italian Alps the natural cover up to about 2000 ft (600 m) is also deciduous forest, but here too there has been much clearance on the sunnier slopes for tree crops. The cleared areas in the Biscayan lands have a greater annual rainfall than the Mediterranean and it comes at all seasons. The soils suffer more leaching and are somewhat posolised; fortunately, however, they can be enriched by plentiful supplies of animal manure from the dairying districts, and in Galicia by seaweed gathered along the coast. Where deciduous forests have been cleared in the mountains and valleys east of the Karst in Yugoslavia there are now vineyards and fields of wheat, potatoes and sugar beet.

4. *Aquatic grasses and reeds*

Aquatic grasses, mainly of the reed type, grow extensively on the deltas of the Rhône, Po and Nile, sometimes so closely together as to impede the passage of silt and so help the deltas to extend. In parts of the Nile delta, the banks of distributaries are lined with a dense cover of giant reeds and lotus lilies. The lower course of the Nile was at one time the source of papyrus, the "reed of Egypt," which provided writing material for the ancient Egyptians. Today, the plant is extinct in Lower Egypt, but is found in the Upper Nile regions and in Ethiopia. Marram grass (*Psamma arenaria*) is well known as a useful sand-binder on the shores of the British

Isles; it grows naturally along the coasts of Mediterranean Europe and North Africa. *Lygeum Spartum*, a tough grass which grows in rocky soils in the Western basin, has adapted itself anomalously to the sands of the sea shore almost everywhere in the Eastern basin of the Mediterranean.

SUB- AND EXTRA-MEDITERRANEAN TYPES

5. *Coniferous forest*

Above the deciduous forests in the northern Mediterranean and in the north-facing Atlas ranges, conifers make their appearance; and they may be found too elsewhere in the region of true Mediterranean climate where mountains are high enough, as in the Sierra Nevada and Apennines and in parts of the Levant (*see* Fig. 19). The lower limit of conifers varies in altitude with climatic conditions; in the west of the Mediterranean there is usually a zone of mixed deciduous and coniferous trees from about 1500 ft (460 m) upwards, but in the interior of the Balkan peninsula, where winters are colder, conifers may be found lower down the mountain slopes. One variety of pine, the cluster pine or pinaster, frequently occurs near sea-level. All the conifers have been exploited through the centuries for building construction, shipbuilding and furniture, and more recently for railway sleepers, harbour works, and pulp and paper mills, so that many areas have been deforested, with subsequent soil erosion. As a result many mountain slopes in the Dolomites, Calabria, Sardinia, Greece and Lebanon consist simply of bare rock. The danger of soil erosion is being met today by planned cutting, conservation and reafforestation.

The white or silver fir (*Abies pectinata*) is one of the commonest conifers in the mountains of southern Europe. There are extensive stands in the Italian Alps up to an altitude of 4000 ft (1200 m) and it is plentiful in the Pyrenees and Apennines. It is a lofty tree, growing to over 100 ft (30 m) in height, and was much prized by the Romans for masts or wherever long stretches of timber were required. It appears to be the true "Abies" of the Latin writers—the "pulcherrima abies" (most beautiful tree) of Virgil. Other kinds of fir are found in the Atlas, Sierra Nevada, Pindus and Taurus mountains.

There are many varieties of pine around the Mediterranean. In the west the silver fir is mixed above 1500 ft (460 m) with the maritime or cluster pine (*Pinus Pinaster*), sometimes called the pinaster. This conifer also thrives near sea-level; it grows vigorously, withstands the force of gales, and is at home in sandy soils, and as a result is often planted to bind drift-sands and dunes. It was employed to afforest the drift-sands of the Landes in France, and was introduced into England, where it has become naturalised in the Isle of Purbeck and other parts of the south. In our latitudes, incidentally, summer temperatures are not high enough to allow the formation in the cluster pine of any useful resinous products. In the Mediterranean, however, where the pinaster grows naturally on sandy soils from Spain to the Levant, it has been used widely for afforestation; the trees reach a height of 40–80 ft (12–24 m), and besides providing timber in once treeless districts are a source of turpentine.

The northern pine (*P. Sylvestris*), known in North-west Europe as the Scotch fir, grows at the highest altitudes in the Mediterranean Lands. In the Pyrenees it occurs above 5600 ft (1600 m), and on the forest-slopes of Etna it is said to be present above 7000 ft (2130 m). One of the noblest of the group is the Corsican pine (*P. Laricio*), which attains a height of 100–150 ft (30–45 m). It abounds in Corsica and is more or less abundant in the Cantabrians and Pyrenees, in the Maritime Alps in France, and the Italian Alps. It grows also in the higher parts of the mountains of Cyprus. It has been used with some success to bind the drift-sands of the Bay of Biscay, but is not as good for the purpose as the cluster pine. At high altitudes in the central Apennines and the mountains of Yugoslavia the commonest conifers are the Austrian pine (*P. austriaca*) and its near relative the black pine (*P. nigra*), which have penetrated from southern Austria, and there are cognate species in the Pindus, Crete and Turkey.

The Pyrenean pine (*P. pyrenaica*) attains a large size on the mountains of northern Spain, whence its distribution extends along the Mediterranean to Asia Minor; the Calabrian pine (*P. Brutia*) may be regarded as being the same species, but as its name suggests, is found in more southern districts, such as south Italy and south Spain. The Aleppo pine (*P. halepensis*) occurs mainly in the Eastern basin. It can withstand high temperatures and desiccating winds, and is useful for afforestation in the drought-stricken lands of the east. It frequently is found in association with garrigue, but in a stunted form. The stone pine or umbrella pine (*P. Pinea*) grows everywhere in the north of the Mediterranean between 2000 and 3000 ft (600–900 m) and extends its distribution in Italy to the western slopes of the Apennines and in Spain to the central Sierras. Like the Aleppo pine, it can endure long periods of drought, and occurs often in maquis. The presence of pines in maquis or garrigue suggests that these degenerate woodlands need not be associated always with broad-leaved evergreen forests, but may have developed from the undergrowth of pine forests which have long since disappeared. The umbrella pine receives its name from its shape. It has a spreading, rounded canopy of light green foliage supported on a long and often branchless trunk, and forms a striking feature in many Mediterranean landscapes.

Other coniferous trees and shrubs include cypresses, cedars and junipers. These are more typical of the high coniferous forests of north-west Africa and the Levant than are firs and pines, but the latter are not entirely missing. The Aleppo pine, as its name suggests, is a native of the northern Levant, and the Morocco fir (*Abies marocana*) is abundant in the Atlas mountains. The common cypress (*Cupressus sempervirens*) has been known throughout the Mediterranean since classical times. The largest stands are in the Tuscan Apennines and on the drier slopes of the mountains which encircle the plateau of Anatolia; the species occurs abundantly in the dry hollows and high eastern slopes of Corfu. The cedar of Lebanon (*Cedrus*

Libani) is perhaps the best known of that genus. It is a tall tree from 50 to 80 ft (15–24 m) high, and in Lebanon it is found in stately groves rather than in continuous forests at an altitude of about 6000 ft (1800 m). It grows in great abundance on the higher slopes of the Taurus and Anti-Taurus ranges, and is common in Crete and Syria. In the Atlas mountains the Atlantic cedar (*C. Atlantica*) occurs everywhere between 4000 and 6000 ft (1200–1800 m). The cedar of Lebanon was used by Solomon in the construction of his Temple in Jerusalem; it is less well known that he imported cypress and pine from the same country.

There are many species of juniper around the Mediterranean. They are evergreen bushy shrubs with a more or less aromatic odour and bear cones (usually called berries) from which oil may be pressed. The common juniper (*Juniperus communis*) grows at considerable elevations in southern Europe—from 4000 to 8000 ft (1200–2400 m) in the Alps, Apennines, Pyrenees and Sierra Nevada—and it occurs abundantly in the Taurus and Anti-Taurus. Its berries yield oil of juniper, which is akin to turpentine, and its very aromatic wood is used for ornamental work. Juniper berries are used also to flavour gin, a name derived from *juniper* through the Fr. *genièvre*. *J. thurifera* is the incense juniper of Spain and Portugal, and *J. phoenicia* and *J. lycia* from the Levant and Asia Minor may also be burnt as incense. One species of juniper (*J. drupacea*) which grows in Asia Minor has large, edible fruits, known in the East as *habhel*.

6. Grassland and steppe

Within the limits of true Mediterranean climate there is a paucity of natural grassland; indeed throughout the Mediterranean lands, including the areas of sub- and extra-Mediterranean climate, extensive stretches of grassland are unusual. There are good grasslands along the Biscayan coast of Spain where rain falls at all seasons; in the valleys of Galicia and on the Asturian plain dairying is a major occupation. Similarly, in the foothills of the Piedmont in north-west Italy, with a summer maximum of rainfall, cattle-rearing for dairy produce is important. In the plain of northern Italy there are meadows in the flood-plain of the river Po, but in many places they are being ploughed for the cultivation of rice; further north, in the sub-Alpine zone, the original cover of oak forest was cut down, and in its place there are now poor grasses and heath on which sheep are reared.

The plains of the Sava, Danube and Tisza in Yugoslavia, with a more continental climate than most other Mediterranean lands, had a natural vegetation of steppe, but with the exception of a few remnants in the Bačka and the Banat, these have largely been ploughed for agriculture. True steppe is found on the plateau of Anatolia in Turkey, and this gradually changes eastwards into arid steppe in parts of Armenia; arid steppe occurs also in Syria and Jordan (*see* below). Steppe vegetation evolves in climatic conditions characterised by wide seasonal variations in temperature and low rainfall. Trees are absent, and the landscape is one of various species of grasses and bulbous plants. Following the rains of winter, the steppe is a scene of luxuriant growth; but this lasts only for a couple of months and begins to wither with the approach of the hot, rainless summer. In autumn only hardy bushes and thorny plants show signs of life, and in general the steppe looks barren and scorched. The annual growth and decay of grasses leads to an accumulation of humus in the top layer of the soil, but because of insufficient rainfall, and also because much of the dead organic matter is destroyed by the heat of the sun, the soils do not develop into true black chernozem, such as is found on the northern side of the Black Sea, but have a chestnut brown colour. They are not as fertile as chernozem; nevertheless, if water is available, they can be made most productive, and considerable areas of the Turkish steppe are now under cultivation.

Above the tree-line and in clearings at high altitudes in most Mediterranean mountain ranges there are pastures used for summer grazing of cattle, sheep and goats. The best "high pastures" are on sub- or extra-Mediterranean mountains, such as the Cantabrians, Maritime and Italian Alps, the highlands of Yugoslavia, and the Taurus and eastern ranges of Turkey, and in all of these seasonal migrations of men and animals (transhumance) is common. Within the region of true Mediterranean climate, the chief high pastures are in the central Apennines, especially in Abruzzi and Molise, in the Iberian mountains of the north-east Meseta, and on the windward slopes of the Atlas ranges in Morocco and Algeria. The grass of the high pastures which have summer rain may grow long enough to produce hay, but this is rarely the case in the areas of summer drought.

7. Dry steppe and semi-desert

The most extensive regions of purely Mediterranean grasses are in the south and east of the Spanish Meseta and on the Plateau of the Shotts in Algeria, where climatic conditions are semi-arid and trees will not grow, and where even the xerophilous shrubs of maquis are widely spaced in discontinuous patches. The main vegetative cover in these regions is a tough, tussocky grass (*Stipa tenacissima*), called *esparto* by the Spaniards and *alfa* by the Arabs. It is indigenous to the south of Spain and the north of Africa, and is especially abundant in the rugged and sterile parts of Murcia and Valencia, flourishing best in sandy, ferruginous soils. It grows also in dry, sunny situations along the Algerian and Tunisian coasts. In its scattered, grey-green clumps, esparto bears no resemblance to the grasses we know in the fields of North-west Europe; the nearest approach is the ornamental feather-grass of gardens. The main stems grow to a height of 3 or 4 ft (1 m), and leaves from 6 in. to 3 ft (15–90 cm) in length branch from the stem. When young, the plant serves as food for cattle or sheep, but after a few years' growth it acquires great toughness of texture. On account of their tenacity of fibre and flexibility the leaves for centuries have been employed in the making of such useful articles as baskets, sandals, ropes and mats, and today they are an important raw material for paper-making

They are generally obtained during the dry summer months, as at other times their adherence to the stems is so firm as often to cause the uprooting of the plants in the attempt to remove them. Another grass (*Lygeum Spartum*), with stiff rush-like leaves, which grows in rocky soils of plateaus and high plains in Andalusia, southern Portugal, Morocco, Algeria and Tunisia, is also a source of esparto.

South of the esparto region of the Plateau of the Shotts, there is a transition zone of similar vegetation, but much more xerophilous and patchy as rainfall decreases, and with more artemisia such as sagebrush and wormwood. This is semi-desert, on which nomadic Bedouin herdsmen eke out a precarious existence. Here and there, in the damper valleys or wadis, an occasional oasis with date-palms and a few cultivated fields break the barren monotony. A narrow belt of semi-desert borders the African coast east of the Gulf of Gabès as far as the Nile delta; and although living conditions are difficult, it is sufficiently habitable to support most of the population of Libya. In Turkey, the steppe described above merges eastwards into dry steppe, in which bulbous plants are not as common, grasses are poorer, and artemisia more frequent. By the middle of summer, the vegetation begins to dry up and fade, so that by the end of August the region looks scorched, and the stems of the dried grass stick up like the bristles of a brush. In the Levant, a narrow zone of dry steppe and semi-desert lies along the western edge of the Syrian desert in Syria and Jordan; and parts of the Sinai Peninsula in Egypt are similar but drier.

8. *Desert vegetation*

The most arid areas of the Mediterranean lands are the Saharan regions of Morocco, Algeria, Tunisia, Libya and Egypt, the Syrian desert in eastern Syria and Jordan, and the Negev of Israel. In these desert conditions plants show the furthest degree of adaptation to heat and drought. Few parts of the desert are entirely devoid of vegetative life, and there are more varieties of plants than one might expect; but all of them have their leaves reduced to spines, none grows to more than a few feet in height, and the majority look like dried sticks after a short period of drought. The most important growths are many varieties of tamarisk, some sickly-looking acacias, and the ubiquitous camel-thorn (*Alhagi maurorum*), a manna-yielding plant which camels eat greedily. Manna (Hebr. *mān hū*, what is it? or *man*, a gift) is a sweet sap which exudes from several types of plant and hardens to sugary globules which are edible. In the Old Testament it was the food of the Israelites in the wilderness and was probably collected from a variety of tamarisk. On both banks of the Nile and in desert oases the date-palm (*Phoenix dactylifera*) is characteristic; it should be regarded more as a cultivated tree than as a natural growth, since from the remotest antiquity it has been cared for and prized as a source of food. In the oases of Syria and Jordan the date-palm is non-fruiting, and is gradually being replaced by vines and olives. It has been introduced to the northern shores of the Mediterranean, but as the fruit does not ripen so far north, the trees there are used only to supply leaves for the Christian Palm Sunday and the Jewish Passover.

9. *Alpine flora*

Above the tree-limit and the mountain pastures of the Alps and other high ranges, there is an extensive Alpine flora which has adapted itself to the extreme cold and may be found even on islands of rock above the snow-line. Earlier in the chapter it was mentioned that the Alps during the Quaternary Ice Age formed a natural boundary between the flora of northern Europe and of the Mediterranean region; and the presence at high altitudes of northern species as well as endemic varieties emphasises this feature. The northern element contains many saxifrages, "cushion-plants" of compact, moss-like growth, and dwarfed groundsel (*Erigeron alpinus*), azalea (*Azalea procumbens*), willow (*Salix retusa*), and juniper (*Juniperus nana*), such as may be found in sub-arctic regions. The more truly "Mediterranean" Alpine flora, such as occurs in the Pyrenees, Atlas, and other ranges in the eastern Mediterranean, is represented in the Alps and elsewhere by a multitude of tiny flowering plants, which are akin to some growing much lower down their slopes or have affinities to many bulbous plants found in the steppe. Tiny crocuses (*Crocus vernus*), colchicums (*Colchicum alpinum*), heathers (*Erica carnea*), and edelweiss (*Leontopodium alpinum*) are representative. It is worth noting that edelweiss is also found plentifully in the Siberian steppe, but that there it is a much bigger plant. Most of the Alpine flora flower freely, and in the summer the high plateaus and peaks of most of the Mediterranean present a very beautiful picture. There are about 700 species of Alpine flora, and of these roughly one-third belong to the northern element.

SUMMARY

There are several points of interest which should be remembered about the distribution of natural vegetation in the Mediterranean lands:

1. Man and his animals have so destroyed the natural vegetative cover of the region with a true Mediterranean climate that it is hard to realise that many of the areas of maquis and garrigue were originally forests of evergreen or deciduous oaks, and that the time since their clearance has been too short for tall trees to re-establish themselves even if they were allowed to do so by the goats.

2. The landscape as we see it today has little or no resemblance to the natural aspect. A typical landscape along most coasts of the Mediterranean would certainly show some relics of past vegetation, such as patches of maquis or trees such as the umbrella pine, holm oak and Lombardy poplar, but most of the area in its terraced fields and orchards would demonstrate the overwhelming influence of man. Only on the higher slopes of mountains is there any extensive cover of natural vegetation, and even there man has made changes by lumbering and by enlarging the high pastures.

3. Man is still making alterations to the natural landscape. He is replacing forests where his ancestors cut them down; he is reclaiming maquis by burning and subsequent modern irrigation schemes; he is controlling rivers and draining swamps; and he is introducing new and useful varieties of plant life.

4. With regard to this last, it is well to remember that many products of Mediterranean agriculture are not "Mediterranean" at all. Wheat, wine, olive oil and citrus fruits are regarded as characteristic of Mediterranean regions, yet of these only the olive is positively indigenous. The vine probably was introduced in early times from Persia; wheat came originally from Mesopotamia; and the orange was brought either by the Arabs from India or by the Portuguese from China. The Arabs were also responsible for the coming of cotton, sugar cane, lemons and rice into the Mediterranean, and the Spaniards brought maize, tobacco, and such maquis shrubs as aloe and cactus from the Americas. In recent times, various forms of eucalyptus, an Australian genus of the myrtle family, have been introduced into the Mediterranean coastlands, especially in the Levant. The eucalyptus, a very tall relation of the common myrtle (*Myrtus communis*) which is a low-growing evergreen shrub found wild in many Mediterranean countries, is eminently suited to heat and drought, and is used for afforestation and to form wind-breaks. Eucalypts also take up from the soil very large amounts of moisture (more so than the majority of other types of tree) and pass it to the atmosphere by transpiration. For this reason they are valuable in assisting to drain swamps, and have been used for this purpose, for example, in the Cheliff valley in Algeria.

STUDY QUESTIONS

1. Discuss briefly how plant life in the Mediterranean lands has adapted itself to its climatic environment.

2. Attempt a classification and description of natural forests in the Mediterranean lands.

3. Explain why large areas of the Mediterranean lands have a surface cover of maquis or garrigue. Give an account of their distribution *or* draw an illustrative sketch map.

4. Show how the natural vegetation of the Mediterranean lands has been affected (*a*) by the Quaternary Ice Age, (*b*) by man.

Chapter VI

HUMAN RESPONSE: HISTORICAL AND SOCIAL

THE next three chapters are concerned with the advent of man into the Mediterranean lands and his response to his physical environment, that is, the ways in which he adapted himself to the surroundings in which he settled. In this chapter his response will be examined briefly from the *historical* and *social* points of view, and in the following two chapters there is a more extensive consideration of his *economic* response.

HISTORICAL GEOGRAPHY

PREHISTORIC SETTLEMENT

The skeletal remains of palaeolithic (Old Stone Age) man have been found extensively in south-west France, the interior of the Iberian peninsula, and Italy south of Tuscany, and probably are representative of the earliest inhabitants of the Mediterranean lands. Among them would doubtlessly be many migrants from more northern areas of Europe, driven southwards by the advancing ice sheets of the last phase of the Glacial Epoch. These people were rather short in stature, but were all dolichocephalic or long-headed. There is no direct evidence of their colouring, but it is thought they had dark skins and black hair.

After the Ice Age, climatic conditions improved in the lands around the Mediterranean, but deteriorated in the interior of North Africa and South-west Asia, which became drier, more desert-like and less hospitable to man. Movements of people began from these areas to the shores of the Mediterranean, especially to the northern side, which they reached by land bridges which were still in existence at the Gibraltar and Black Sea straits. The majority of these neolithic (New Stone Age) immigrants were distinctly dolichocephalic, with dark skins, dark, wavy hair, and varied stature, but mostly on the short side; they are known collectively to ethnologists as the Mediterranean race. They mixed peacefully with such of the palaeolithic inhabitants as still remained, and interbreeding seems to have resulted in some modifications in physical characteristics, *e.g.*, in the shape of the head, which became mesocephalic (intermediate, less long-headed).

A second wave of neolithic migration brought large numbers of people from further afield in South-west Asia and possibly from Central Asia. These were markedly brachycephalic (broad-headed) and are known as the Alpine race, for they penetrated and settled in all parts of the European

Alps. In the course of time, some of these Alpine people moved into the Mediterranean area, and these incursions may account for the medium heads and brown eyes of many in southern France and northern Italy, and for the tall, dark, brachycephalic people, sometimes called the Dinaric sub-race, found in the western Balkan peninsula, the eastern plain of Lombardy and the eastern Alps. In the eastern Mediterranean lands, later arrivals of various Alpine sub-races from the central Asiatic highlands either displaced the original Mediterranean race or so mingled with it as to destroy its distinctive character. The chief of these migrants were the Armenoid sub-race, best typified by the present-day inhabitants of Armenia, but found also throughout Asia Minor, the Levant coastlands and the lower Nile valley. They are extremely brachycephalic and have dark, frizzy hair, dark brown eyes, thick lips and a long, hooked nose.

THE BIRTH OF CIVILISATION

Archaeological discoveries show that the most ancient civilisations known to us developed almost contemporaneously in Egypt and Babylonia, which lie at opposite ends of a long, narrow, curving strip of comparatively fertile land which we call the "Fertile Crescent" (*see* Fig. 132). Egypt became a united country about 3300 B.C., with its capital at Memphis, and by 2300 B.C. had developed a unique civilisation, with its emphasis on religion, art and civil organisation. The Egyptians invented hieroglyphics or picture-writing, and recorded events on papyrus made from reeds. They made use of stone as a building material, constructed the pyramids at Giza, and carved and erected the giant statuary for which the country is renowned; and in the centuries following the Pyramid Age, the Faiyum was reclaimed, Lake Moeris was regulated for irrigation, and the copper mines in the south of Sinai were exploited. The ancient Egyptians, it is thought, were of Hamitic stock which migrated originally from the Caucasus, whereas the Egyptians of today are mainly descended from Semites who moved in from Arabia.

The Babylonians, who lived in lower Mesopotamia, were originally two peoples, in the north the warlike Akkadians whose forebears were Arabian Semites, and in the south the more cultured Sumerians who came originally from the Iranian plateau as part of the Armenoid migration. Excavations seem to show there were civilised city states along the lower Euphrates before 3000 B.C.; and by about 2637 B.C., when both peoples were united by Akkadian conquest into one nation, with its capital at Babylon, the Sumerians had already a wonderfully advanced civilisation. They were the creators of a well-organised system of canal irrigation; they were sculptors, architects and workers in metals; and they invented cuneiform writing by which they kept records of their laws, history and trading accounts. The Babylonian civilisation had a profound influence on all the countries of the Middle East, even when their empire had crumbled and been replaced, firstly by the Assyrians after 729 B.C., and later when a

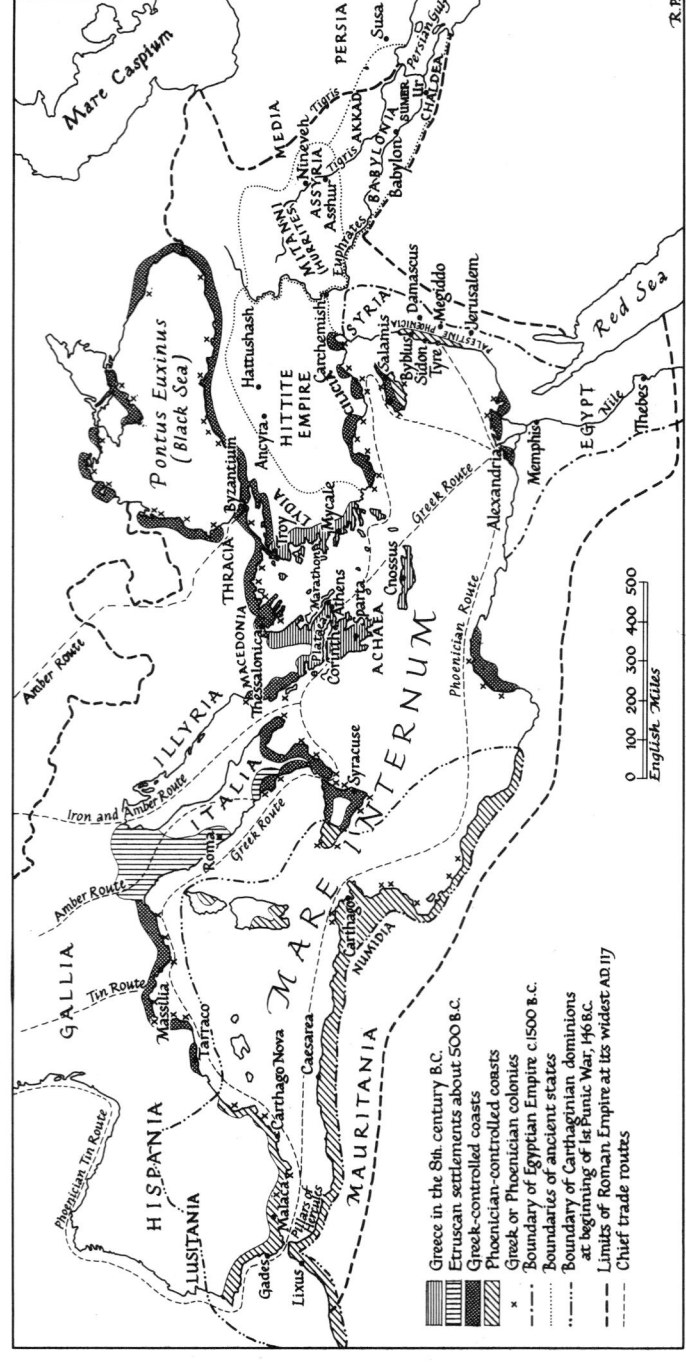

FIG. 19.—The Mediterranean lands: ancient history.

short-lived Babylonian (Neo-Babylonian, Chaldean) revival was destroyed by the Persians in 538 B.C.

The Persians were already masters of part of Asia Minor, and eastwards their empire stretched to the banks of the Indus; now, by the defeat of the Neo-Babylonians, their dominions reached from the Aegean to India. By 525 B.C., Egypt was added to the Persian Empire, and in 481 B.C. Persian armies passed through Thrace and Macedonia, entered Greece and occupied Athens. At this time the Persians had the largest empire the world had known and the best administrative organisation. Further advance into Europe was stopped, however, by an alliance in Greece of Athenians and Spartans. In 480 B.C. the Athenian fleet inflicted a crushing defeat on the Persian navy at Salamis in one of the most decisive battles in history, and on land the combined Greek forces were victorious in the following year at Plataea and Mycale. The Persians withdrew from Europe, and from that time their empire began to shrink. Their contributions to civilisation included the "law of the Medes and Persians which altereth not," that is, an order once given by the emperor could not be revoked. Every part of the empire enjoyed equal rights and paid the same taxes, the revenue from which was used for the public good; and local forms of religion and government were respected. A first-class system of roads was constructed to facilitate communication between Susa, the capital, and distant parts of the empire; and while the Persians occupied Egypt, they dug a canal from the river Nile to the Red Sea.

In 338 B.C., however, a new people entered the scene. Philip of Macedonia marched south with his army to unite all Greece (known as Hellas) under his leadership, and four years later his son, Alexander (the Great), embarked on his career of conquest. He advanced via Thrace into Asia Minor, conquered the Levant, and marched into Egypt where he crushed the Persians. The Egyptians accepted Alexander as a great deliverer, and named the city of Alexandria after him. He now turned towards Persia itself. In a series of quick campaigns culminating in a decisive victory at Gaugamela, 331 B.C., he broke the Persian power for ever. When Alexander died at Babylon, 323 B.C., his empire extended from Hellas and Egypt to the banks of the river Indus. After his death his dominions were split among his generals, and Hellas suffered decline. Egypt, however, prospered under the Macedonian Ptolemy and his successors (332–30 B.C.), and Alexandria became a centre of commerce and culture.

An immediate result of the spread of Alexander's empire was the Hellenisation of Egypt and the Middle East. To understand the meaning of this term it is necessary to go back a little in history. By 1300 B.C. Greece was in the hands of the Achaeans, a people who came from the north. In the next 200 years the Achaeans became sea-traders competing with rivals from the coast of Asia Minor and Phoenicia. The struggle for trade led to war with Troy (Ilium) in which the Achaeans were successful, but their casualties were so great that they were not able to withstand an invasion by the Dorians, another northern tribe who had learnt the use of iron. Their advance, from 1100 B.C. onwards, was accompanied by the erection of city states, the most important of which were Sparta, Argos, Corinth and Thebes, and by the enslavement of the Achaeans in the occupied territory. Outside the line of invasion was the Ionian city state of Athens, "Ionian" being the name given to Achaeans who had not been enslaved. Later the term was applied also to trading colonies such as Ephesus and Miletus in Asia Minor. Dorians and Ionians adopted a common speech and culture and became known as Hellenes and their country as Hellas, but although on occasions they combined to face a common enemy, they never really amalgamated into one nation.

This is seen very well in the struggle for supremacy in trade and prestige between Athens and Sparta, which became respectively the dominant Ionian and Dorian city states. Athens was a democracy, that is, it was governed according to the wishes of its citizens. It was a peace-loving city in which philosophers, poets, sculptors and architects encouraged a culture based on the best from the civilisations of Egypt, Crete and Babylonia. Sparta, on the other hand, was an oligarchy, that is, ruled by a small, exclusive class, whose claims to be part of the government were based on military prowess and skill. Later, Roman ideas of military discipline and tactics were developed from those of Sparta; and the hardy, rigorous and frugal way of life which its citizens were forced to follow is known today as "spartan."

After the decisive victory of the Athenian fleet at Salamis (see above), Athens became the acknowledged leader of most of Hellas, with a powerful navy and mercantile marine fleet, but Sparta, which had strong land forces, organised the Peloponnesian League in the south of Hellas, and as a result of two wars (431–405 B.C.) dominated the Athenians for 30 years. During this period of subjection, however, the Athenians continued as traders and explorers throughout the Mediterranean, and at home their culture was advanced by such great scholars as Socrates, Plato, Aristotle, Sophocles, Demosthenes and Xenophon. This was the culture found and accepted by Alexander the Great and carried by his forces throughout the Middle East. His empire soon broke up into several portions, but Greek kings maintained themselves in Egypt, Syria and Asia Minor, and proceeded to plant their Hellenistic culture among the ancient peoples of these lands. Greek manners and ideas and the use of the Greek language went on spreading for centuries throughout the Middle East; this is what is meant by "Hellenisation."

The last of the ancient civilisations to develop around the Mediterranean was that of the Romans. In the centuries following their successful rebellion against the Etruscans (509 B.C.), the Romans subdued the whole of the Italian peninsula and took possession of the Greek trading colonies which had been planted in the "toe" and "heel" of Italy. In the meantime, the Carthaginians had become a great naval power, controlling all maritime trade in the western Mediterranean. Carthage was a Phoenician colony established in Tunisia about 822 B.C. It became independent of the mother country about the same time as Rome began to emerge as a power, and inevitably its merchant fleet came into conflict with the ships of Rome, which had begun to sail from the newly-acquired Greek trading stations. Commercial rivalry led finally in 268 B.C. to the Punic Wars (L. *Poenus* or *Punicus*, a Phoenician, and hence a Carthaginian) which dragged on until the final victory of the Romans and the complete destruction of Carthage in 146 B.C.

As a result of their victory the Romans were now in almost uncontested control of Mediterranean trade and commerce. The luxurious woven cloths of Carthage became a Roman commodity; the sale of black slaves, ivory, metals, precious stones and other products of central Africa, brought to the Mediterranean shores by camel caravan, passed into Roman hands, and so did the copper and silver found in Spain at Huelva and Cartagena (New Carthage); and the fertile land around the ruins of Carthage was developed as a vast granary for Rome. Within 20 years of the fall of Carthage, Rome was master also of Spain, Greece, Macedonia, and much of Asia Minor and North Africa. This movement of Roman troops eastwards brought them within the sphere of Hellenic culture and changed completely the Roman way of life. Greek concepts of democracy, science and the arts were superimposed on the Roman militaristic culture; and the enormous wealth brought back from vanquished countries enabled the Romans to embark on a wide programme of emulation of the Greeks, especially in civic reform and architecture (*see* Fig. 20). In the first century of the Christian era, the Roman Empire reached its maximum size, extending from the Persian Gulf to the borders of Scotland, and from the Strait of Gibraltar to the Caucasus mountains. For the only time in history the Mediterranean lands were united at that period as a single political entity, with the sea and magnificent trunk roads as dominant unifying factors.

The next few centuries saw the decline and breaking up of the Roman Empire, and the beginning of a period of political, social and economic backwardness in all the Mediterranean lands which was to last until the early years of the nineteenth century. From the beginning of the fourth century there were continuous incursions into the western Mediterranean lands of such barbarian tribes from the north as the Visigoths, Ostrogoths, Vandals and Franks (*see* Fig. 21). In the seventh and eight centuries the armies of Islam conquered most of the Levant and the countries of North Africa and occupied all but a small portion of the Iberian peninsula; and the fourteenth century witnessed the foundation of the Ottoman Empire and the commencement of Turkish domination of the eastern Mediterranean which was to continue until the early years of the present century. More is said later in the book of the impact of all these peoples on the history of individual countries. Here it is necessary to note only that their entry into the Mediterranean lands had a profoundly deleterious effect on the cultures already in existence; the name of the Vandals, for instance, has been perpetuated because of their ruthless and wilful destruction of life and property; and the Ottoman Turks, at times almost equally savage, were cruelly oppressive and entirely indifferent to the welfare of their subject peoples, burning their cities and crops, cutting down their forests, and by mass executions sometimes leaving large areas completely depopulated and derelict. Of great significance in the history of the Mediterranean lands is the fact that none of these invading peoples, with the possible exception of the Moorish Arabs whose contributions to architecture, water

[*Courtesy of the Turkish Embassy.*

FIG. 20.—Turkey: Pergamum, the Grand Theatre on the Acropolis. Pergamum (modern Bergama, 55 miles north of Izmír) was founded by Greek colonists on a lofty, isolated hill in a broad, fertile valley, and by the third century B.C. was the capital of the region. It was renowned for its school of sculpture. The remains shown are of a Roman theatre, an amphitheatre and a circus.

supply and agricultural products such as citrus fruits, sugar cane and cotton were of benefit to Spain, had a well-developed culture of its own to replace that which was destroyed. The cultures of Greece and Rome were almost obliterated in the eastern Mediterranean lands; and in the western Mediterranean the conflict between Islamic Moors and Christian Spain, the warlike ambitions of France, Austria and Spain to control Italy, and the discovery of America and of new routes to the Far East, halted the course of civilisation and turned the region into an economic and social backwater. Only within the past two centuries have the Mediterranean lands begun to climb again towards the position of dignity they held in ancient times.

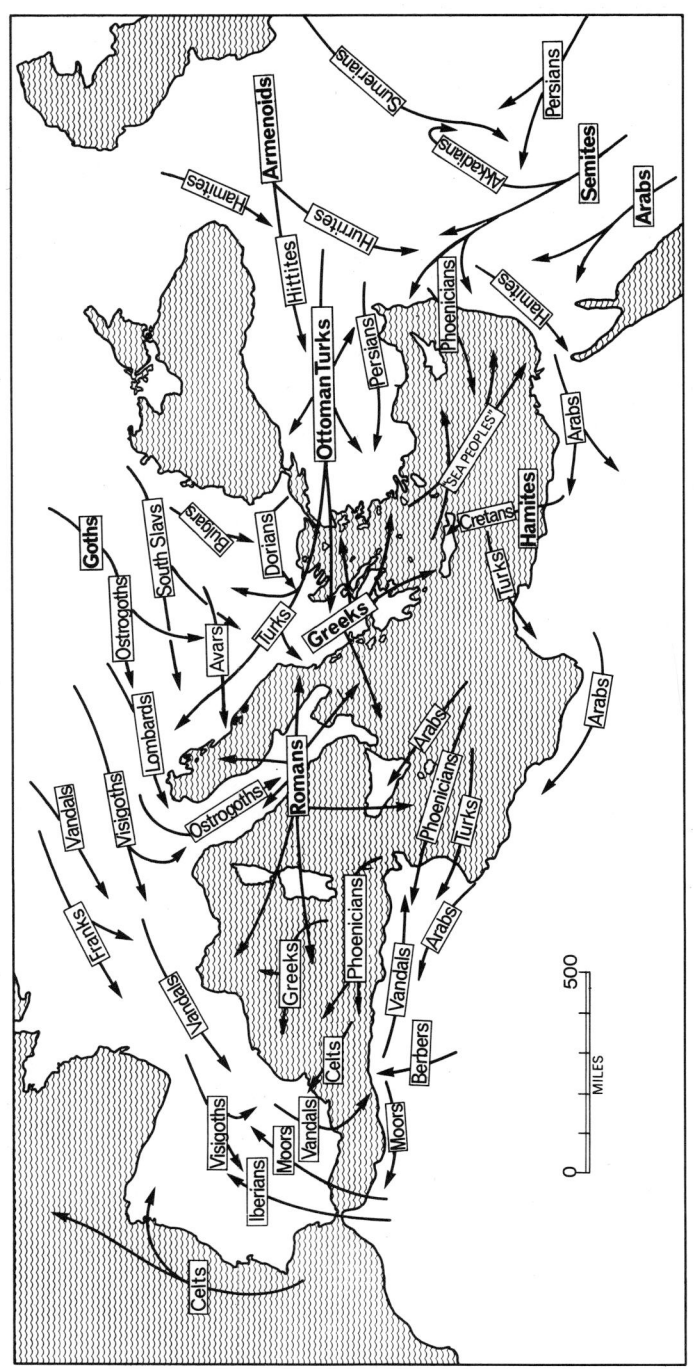

FIG. 21.—The Mediterranean lands: movements of peoples.

MEDITERRANEAN CIVILISATIONS—A CRITICAL SURVEY

The Mediterranean basin is the cradle of Western civilisation, but exactly why this should be so has not yet been completely demonstrated. We may, however, discern two common factors in the development of most of the earliest civilised cultures: the presence of very fertile, well-watered river lowlands surrounded by less inviting steppe, semi-desert and desert, and the mass movement of peoples into them. The Babylonian and Egyptian civilisations grew in river valleys which were subject to flooding and had great fertility, and in environments which gave opportunity for sedentary occupations such as the selection and growth of food crops and the building of permanent dwellings, in contrast with the pastoral nomadism of surrounding regions. But why the two civilisations developed almost contemporaneously in regions hundreds of miles apart and why they showed roughly comparable advances in religious thought and practice, massive architecture, art (including writing) and social organisation, are questions which cannot be answered convincingly. We note that in the case of Babylonia, where the plains of Mesopotamia are more open to invasion, the inhabitants had perforce to develop an efficient system of military strength to safeguard themselves from attacks which could come from any direction; whereas in Egypt, where the river valley was protected east and west by desert, attacks were likely only along narrow fronts from the north and south, and in point of fact were invariably from the north. So it was that in spite of their relatively superior military organisations the civilisations based on the Tigris and Euphrates valleys were shorter-lived than that of Egypt, the Babylonian culture being supplanted by those of Assyria and Persia, and all three being outlived by that of the Nile. It is suggested that the evolution of the Egyptian civilisation was largely the result of the isolation of Egypt (*see* Chapter XXI).

On the other hand, it is confidently suggested that civilisation develops best where there is contact and exchange of ideas with other peoples, and possibly with interbreeding. The rise of the Babylonian, Assyrian and Persian empires has been attributed in part to the fusion of the various races which entered the region. Mass movements of peoples invariably preceded and accompanied the earliest civilisations. These were caused primarily by pressure of population on the lands in which they lived, or by long-continued drought which forced a search for a new and more favoured home. For instance, we read in the Scriptures (Gen. xi, xii) how shortly after 2000 B.C. a branch of Aramaean nomads made the long journey from Ur on the lower Euphrates to settle at Haran in northern Mesopotamia, and how from there a small tribe led by Abraham moved southwards through the Levant to make a home in the hills of Judaea. Later (Gen. xlii) we learn they were driven into Egypt by a drought which lasted for seven years; and after a settlement of 400 years in Goshen, near the Nile delta, how about 1200 B.C. they returned to invade and occupy Canaan (Exodus; Joshua).

One obvious result of successive migrations of people was the inter-mingling of diverse racial strains along the main routes of movement, so that in time the physical characteristics of the population ceased to give any clue to its ethnic origin. Today, for example, in all the countries bordering the eastern Mediterranean, one may observe marked differences in stature, colouring and facial characteristics; their peoples may be differentiated as Arab or Turk or Hebrew, but these are now only linguistic or cultural terms, and have little relation to racial origins. The process of admixture and of submergence of ethnic distinguishing features was accentuated in western Asia Minor and the Levant by the general tendency for early migrations to continue towards the west via the Fertile Crescent and to be halted, at least temporarily, on the Mediterranean margins.

It is suggested that this fusion of races led to an increase of mental activity, natural curiosity and inventive genius, and to consequent cultural development; and point is given to this by the fact that the advent of mixed peoples to the shores of the Mediterranean was the prelude to further civilisations. As the older cultures of the Middle East began to decline, new ones began to emerge in Phoenicia, Asia Minor, Cyprus, Crete and Greece. This westward march of civilisation was later continued to Rome, to Gothic and Moorish Spain, and ultimately to what we know as Western civilisation; and everywhere, it should be noted, its development was accompanied by fusions of different peoples.

There is little doubt, too, that the mental stimulus so necessary for the evolution of civilisation was encouraged in the eastern Mediterranean lands by the climatic rhythm and the annual renewal of fertile silts by flooding rivers. The Mediterranean lands are "regions of increment," where man's labours on flooded fields or during winter rains should ensure sufficient food supplies to last during periods of summer drought, and therefore, it is argued, enough leisure to develop a knowledge of science, philosophy, literature and the arts. It is further suggested that the increase in agricultural output, occasioned by the invention of irrigation, bridges and paved roads, was a factor in the growth of town life, for these advances meant that a scattered rural population could produce enough surplus foodstuffs to support urban communities, in exchange for services such as military protection. In other words, the growth of cities is a natural accompaniment to the evolution of a civilisation. The Babylonian civilisation grew up around the city states of Babel (Babylon) and Ur, and that of Egypt around Memphis and Thebes.

The conquest of the Mediterranean Sea must also be included as a civilising factor. The Phoenician, Greek, Minoan (Cretan) and Roman fleets carried between them knowledge of their cultures to all parts of the Mediterranean and beyond. Their mariners and merchants brought back new ideas, new products, and new information about foreign customs and ways of life which could possibly be assimilated into and improve their own cultures; for, as we have already noted, civilisation thrives on contacts with other peoples. The Phoenician and Greek cultures were spread by trading colonies in well-chosen positions, but neither Greeks nor Phoenicians were colonists in the modern sense; their overseas activities were confined mainly to coastal settlements which were occupied primarily for commercial purposes. Greek colonies were erected in Sicily, southern Italy, Mediterranean France and eastern Spain, and eastwards along the coasts of the Straits and the Black Sea; the Phoenicians (afterwards the Carthaginians) traded chiefly along the coasts of North Africa, western Sicily, Sardinia, and southern Spain. Many modern ports were born at this time; among those founded by the Greeks are Byzantium (Istanbul), Tarentum (Taranto), Neapolis (Naples), Massilia (Marseille), Tarraco (Tarragona) and Saguntum (Valencia), and by the Phoenicians are Malaca (Málaga), Gades (Cádiz) and Carthage (Tunis, near its ruins). All these colonies were taken over later by the Romans.

An outstanding feature in the evolution of Mediterranean civilisation was the number and importance of Greek city states. In the very early cultures city states were not numerous; those that prospered were large and at some distance from each other. This was possibly because the areas in which they developed were wide lowlands with few physical obstacles to prevent the expansion of a city's sphere of influence. In Greece, however, a large number of small, fertile plains segregated from each other by the accidented relief of the country encouraged the establishment of an equally large number of self-contained settlements, each with its own defensive and administrative centre, and often with its own idea of political government, as we have already seen in the cases of Athens and Sparta (see page 94). The plains in which the cities formed nuclei were, however, too small to provide a surplus of staple foods sufficient to explain the eminence in early Mediterranean commerce of such urban concentrations as Athens and Corinth, and indeed of some of the smaller city states; none of the city states was in the long run able to support itself, and food had to be imported. Shortage of foodstuffs in Greece was, therefore, one of the factors in the development of Greek colonies and overseas trading interests. Athens, for example, with Piraeus as its port, became an international market for wheat, barley, woollen textiles, pottery and silver ware; and there seems little doubt, too, that it became rich and powerful, in common with other city states, because of systematic, piratical plundering of rival colonies and of isolated merchant ships of other countries or city states.

Finally, a word must be said about the emergence of slavery as a universal and inevitable accompaniment to the movement of peoples and the rise of sedentary civilisations. In the earliest times the population of a region was sometimes completely wiped out and displaced by the advancing hordes; but as sedentary life became more commonplace and a large increase in labour was needed for agriculture and primitive industry, the work of slaves was introduced to provide food and services for the masters or freemen. In all the early Mediterranean cultures, the subjugated peoples of territories occupied by invading armies were enslaved to provide food for the victors or were led away as slaves to the invaders' homelands to work in the fields and cities. A position developed in which the freeman, who was essentially a warrior, and the slave became mutual auxiliaries, exercising different and complementary functions, each necessary to the community.

This was well demonstrated in the rise of Babylonia, Assyria and Greece, and the story of the Israelites enslaved in Egypt is familiar to all (Book of Exodus); but the role of peasant slavery in the economy of the early Mediterranean is probably seen best in the case of Rome. So long as Rome was engaged in military advance, slavery properly found its place; but as soon as the march of conquest had reached its natural limit, that is, when no more territories were being added to the empire, peasant slavery began to be modified. It had served its purpose; and when the empire started to split up and the system of warfare and defence characteristic of the Middle Ages was substituted for the movement of peoples and the aggression of antiquity, slavery gradually disappeared and was replaced by serfdom.

SOCIAL GEOGRAPHY

The aim of social geography is to examine and explain the distribution and density of population in a region—in the present case, of the Mediterranean lands. This involves a short preliminary inquiry into *modes of life* or *cultural patterns* and some aspects of *social organisation*. *Economic patterns* also enter into the picture, but as these are dealt with more fully in the next two chapters, they are introduced here only in so far as they are relevant to cultural patterns.

CULTURAL PATTERNS

In a study of cultural patterns we try to see why some areas of the earth's surface are completely uninhabited, some have a widely dispersed and possibly scanty population, some have aggregations of people into villages and small towns, and some are covered by large concentrations in cities and conurbations. In other words, we observe and try to find explanations for the distribution and density of population in an area. We look at man's habitations, whether they be caves, tents or permanent dwellings, and we observe his ways of life as a nomad, semi-nomad or sedentary dweller. We view the changes he has made in the physical landscape: the cultivated fields and orchards, the pastures with their domesticated herds and flocks, the surface workings of mines and quarries, the scars of deforestation and soil erosion, and the transformation caused by such projects as irrigation systems, hydro-electricity works, and vast networks of roads, railways and canals. We note the size, shape and number of dispersed and isolated homesteads, and of urban settlements, large and small, and we attempt some classification of them as to position, function or grouping. Much of this work is inevitably in the economic field, but it must be included if we are to form a true conspectus of the *cultural landscape*, that is, the physical or natural landscape as it has been affected by man.

In our study we observe also the speed or momentum of the changes effected by man. It may be slow in nomadic and peasant communities, or rapid where a region is becoming industrialised; or it may result in a mixture of cultures in a relatively small area. For example, in the Middle East and Algeria, one may find nomadic tribes, transhumant shepherds and peasant villages, where the way of life has changed very little since the earliest times; whereas in the cities of these regions the cultural pattern is being modified very rapidly, largely because of the impact of mineral oil and natural gas on their economies. Side by side with mosques, bazaars and native strongholds are modern factories, airports, oil and gas refineries and distillation plants, up-to-date harbour and port installations, and new systems of motor roads, railways and air lines. In such cases the cultural changes are dramatic, and modifications in the landscape are continuous; but everywhere in the Mediterranean lands there are transformations, even if they are not so momentous.

Cultural patterns are examined as they are related to *rural* and *urban landscapes*. It is not always easy, however, to decide on a dividing line between the two, especially where a small urban community is centred in a predominantly rural environment. A rural landscape may hold a large number of hamlets and villages, just as an urban landscape may have some rural components. One must note, too, that the distinction between rural and urban landscapes may vary between one country and another, and depends on the degree of cultural advance. What we in England regard as rural landscapes, say in parts of Essex, Norfolk or Somerset, would, by reason of their many small towns, situated in close proximity to each other and with numerous industrial establishments, be categorised in some under-developed Mediterranean countries as urban landscapes.

RURAL CULTURES

The most primitive way of life in the Mediterranean lands is *nomadism* based on the herding of animals. With the beginnings of sedentary life based on cultivating the land there evolved a way of life known as *semi-nomadism*. The *advent of agriculture* led gradually to the development of civilisation, to the succession of cultures outlined earlier in the chapter. Here we examine the social implications, the merits and demerits of nomadism and semi-nomadism; and with regard to agricultural communities we consider the development of *field patterns and systems, rural settlements* and *house types* in the Mediterranean lands.

Nomadism

This is the wandering of a pastoralist community in search of food for its herds and flocks. It is an adaptation of man to an environment which has been classified by H. J. Fleure as a "region of privation." In the Mediterranean lands pastoral nomads live on the desert edges of North Africa and the Levant, and are known collectively as Bedouin (Ar. *badāwin*). Nomads are organised into groups or tribes which are limited in size by the food and water resources of the district through which they wander, but which are usually large enough to protect their grazing grounds against attempted inroads by neighbouring nomad bands. Each tribe has a recognised and jealously guarded pastoral area, carefully defined by wells and wadis, and related in extent to the strength of the group and the power and prestige of its leader or *sheikh*. In North Africa, the life of the nomad is based chiefly on the rearing and use of camels, while in the Levant the nomads are typically goatherds or shepherds (Ar. *chouayia*, sheep breeders), and occasionally herders of cattle (Ar. *beggara*). Camels can move faster and travel further than sheep and cattle and can exist longer without water, and so wanderings in North Africa are more extensive and grazing grounds larger than in the Levant.

Social organisation is patriarchal, that is, dependent on decisions made by the older members of the group and announced by the sheikh, who in times of crisis may take complete control. By virtue of its patriarchal character, life among the nomads is extremely conservative, little change having taken place over thousands of years. In its insistence on marriage within the tribe, on the importance of the family or tribe rather than of individuals, and on subservience to the will of the elders, the way of life is reminiscent of Biblical times. The discipline of patriarchal rule and the experience of countless centuries have perpetuated and been the strength of this type of culture, which at its best is a struggle for survival in a harsh and inhospitable environment.

There are signs, however, that nomadism as a way of life is on the decline. It still remains the only effective culture for the majority of the inhabitants of the deserts and semi-deserts of Algeria, Libya, Egypt, Jordan and Syria, but in all these countries the political, social and economic changes of the present century have reduced the numbers of nomads very considerably and weakened their position in the economy. For a full account of their present status see P. Birot and J. Dresch: *La Méditerranée et le Moyen Orient*, on which much of the following is based.

In the first place, pastoral nomads are considered by governments to contribute in a major way to political instability in the country in which they wander. Their segregation into closely-knit groups or tribes jealously guarding their own pastoral areas has proved a weakness in modern times, for it has made difficult any form of permanent political union between tribes; rather it has led to warfare where one tribe has tried to encroach on another's territory. Moreover, tribal segregation seems to have engendered a mentality which makes it difficult for nomads to co-operate on a national level and still less internationally. Nomadism is a selfish and self-centred way of life, as the events of recent years have shown. Great efforts have been made to incorporate the tribes of the desert edges into a much-heralded Pan-Arab world, but with very little success. The nomad is more concerned with his own day-to-day struggle

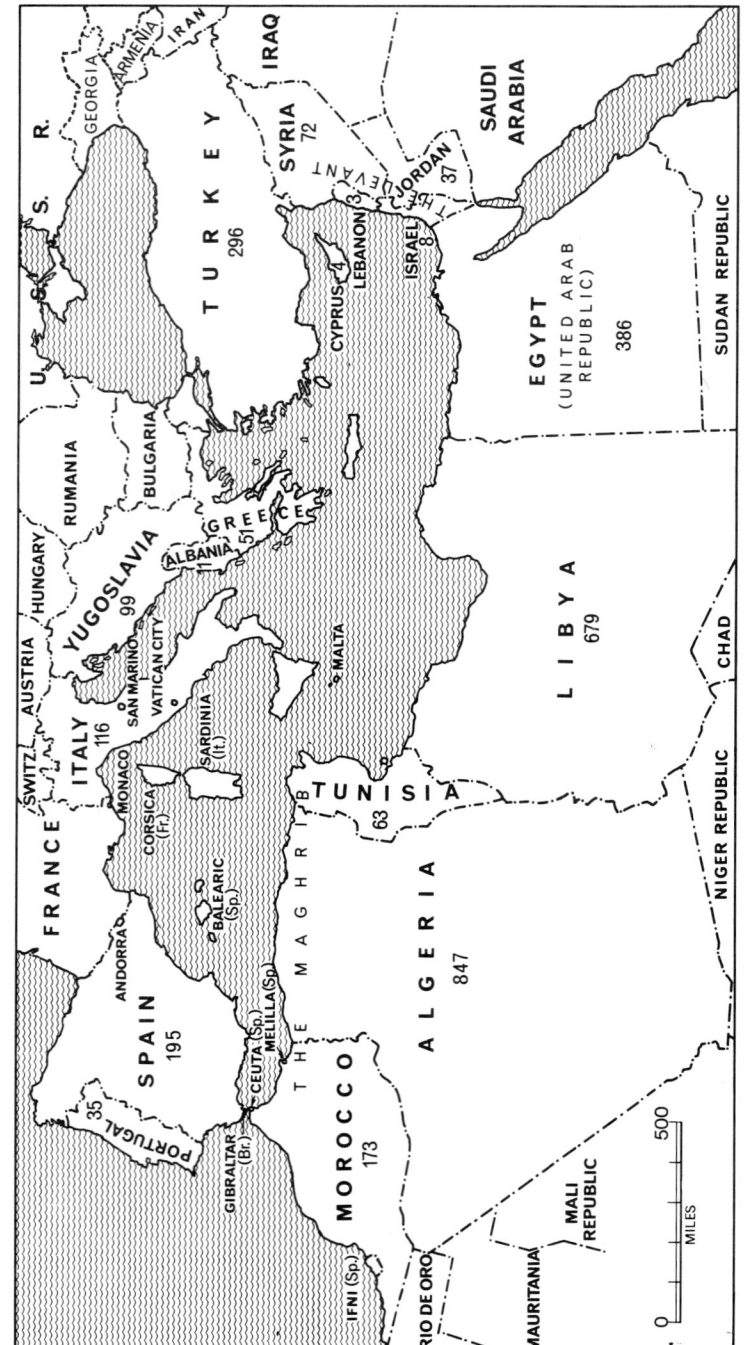

FIG. 22.—The Mediterranean lands: political divisions.   The figures show each country's area in thousands of sq. miles.

for existence than with political ambitions. In consequence, the governments of newly-emergent Arab countries are generally hostile to nomadic groups. The boundaries of these countries are shown in Fig. 22.

Governments have prescribed definite limits to each tribe's pasturage, and desert and semi-desert areas have been "pacified" and placed under the rule of law, but not without great opposition. Instability and friction were caused where international boundaries were drawn across traditional nomadic routes. Tribes tended to ignore such boundaries, and this often led to international clashes. Political systems, too, are no longer favourable to the nomad's age-old custom of taking without payment any goods he could plunder from oases or "foreign" caravans, and have taken strong measures to suppress it. Governments have tried also to convert nomads to a life of agriculture wherever this is possible; results, however, are not too encouraging, for it has been found that even if environmental difficulties are overcome, nomads who adopt a sedentary life suffer a gradual mental and physical debility which leads to an undesirable decrease in their numbers.

Economically, the position of pastoral nomads is far weaker than it used to be. New dry farming methods have led to an increase in cultivation along desert borders, so that many of their better grazing grounds are no longer available. This has reduced the quantity and quality of the products of their herds and flocks—live animals, milk (fermented into yoghourt), wool, hair, leather—so that they no longer command the same value in exchange for other foodstuffs and manufactured goods which they formerly did. A further example is to be seen in the case of salt, a traditional product of desert nomads, for there has been a great decline in its value as barter. Whereas in 1945 a single camel-load of salt could be exchanged along the southern margins of the Sahara for about six loads of sorghums or millets, ten years later it commanded only two such loads. Nomads have also lost the key position they formerly held as desert carriers. Except for local trade, the place of the camel caravan has been taken by the automobile and the railway. A modern lorry in a single journey can transport a load equal to that of 400 camels, and much more speedily and efficiently. The adverse effects of modern means of transport are felt by all nomadic groups; they are especially noticeable on the diminishing size and number of trans-desert caravans travelling between Damascus and Baghdad and across the western Sahara, where for centuries the transfer of merchandise has been organised and guarded by nomads employed for the purpose.

In a more localised way the development of new industries, particularly those connected with the exploitation of mineral oil and natural gas, is helping in the disintegration of nomadic life. The numbers so affected in individual localities may not be large, amounting for example to about 25,000 Bedouin in Algeria and Libya and 15,000 in Saudi Arabia, but in total they are by no means negligible. We must realise that the wages paid by the oil and gas companies and the conditions of life in their camps seem extraordinarily attractive to the nomad. In the Algerian Sahara, for instance, a labourer at an oil installation needs to work only 40 days in a year to earn the equivalent of his income as a nomad or even as an itinerant oasis worker in a full year. Caught up in a way of life far different from that of his ancestors, the converted nomad becomes more sophisticated in his needs and abandons his primitive culture. He may even be attracted later into the towns and cities, to work in new industrial establishments. In Algeria and Turkey, in spite of the deleterious mental and physical results on the converted nomad, already noted, it is part of the declared economic policy to encourage immigration into new towns and to guarantee work in newly-built factories.

One consequence of all these political and economic developments is that the rigidity of the ancient patriarchal system is relaxing. The younger members of a tribe, brought into contact with social and economic conditions far superior to those of their own culture, are increasingly critical of the rule of their elders and chiefs, who no longer command the respect and power of former days. They still bow to the authority of the sheikh, but they insist on changes in those aspects of his government which are feudal in character. This bid for more individual freedom and responsibility has, for the time being at least, further emphasised the lack of unity among the nomad tribes, for sometimes it has caused splits in some of the larger groups into small and mutually hostile clans. In any case, it is a further factor in the decline of nomadism, in the decay of a culture which the modern world regards as archaic and outmoded.

Semi-nomadism

As a way of life semi-nomadism lies intermediately between that of the purely pastoral nomad and that of the permanently settled agriculturist. The nomad wanders, often without apparent pattern, within the limits of his grazing grounds, his route determined by the amount of water and food available at any time and place. The semi-nomad, however, follows a distinct *seasonal* pattern of wandering and always returns to a fixed settlement or encampment. He is primarily a herdsman—and in this capacity he resembles a nomad—but he is also an agriculturist. During the winter, when vegetation is more prolific, he takes his animals in search of pasture, but always along a set route. At the end of the wet season he returns to his home, which is situated where water supplies are adequate during the dry summer; here he may cultivate crops such as olives, vines and a few vegetables. The olives and vines are harvested before the semi-nomad leaves again at the beginning of winter, but if the harvest is not completed, he may leave his flocks and return for a few days to assist. Semi-nomadism occurs in all the countries of the Maghrib and the Levant, and in Libya, Egypt and Turkey.

Transhumance

Sometimes the term *transhumance* is applied to semi-nomadism, but more properly it refers to a different way of life. In a transhumant society only the herdsmen move seasonally, often to high ground in search of summer pasture, but the community as a whole remains at the home base. Transhumance is practised widely on the European side of the Mediterranean in Spain, Mediterranean France, Italy, Greece and Yugoslavia, where agriculture has a much more prominent part in the economy of a community and the seasonal movement of animals plays a relatively minor although important role.

The advent of agriculture

Sedentary life seems to have begun when man learned to cultivate the soil, but there is as yet insufficient evidence to say when or where this first took place. We know that settled agricultural communities existed in very early times both in the Far East and the Middle East and that they grew up under widely different climatic régimes; and we acknowledge that sedentary cultivation in parts of India and China, for example, may have developed earlier with the better opportunities offered by the monsoonal summer-rain type of climate than under the winter-rain/summer-drought régime of the Mediterranean, which even now presents a real challenge to the agriculturist. Our first knowledge of agricultural communities in the Mediterranean lands is in the valleys of the rivers Nile, Euphrates and Tigris, where annual flooding of the rivers compensates for summer drought and gives a replenishment of fertile silt, and where winter warmth encourages plant life in that season, inducing man to adopt a settled way of life completely different from that of the pastoral nomad. The happy combination of plentiful water, fertile soil, propitious climate and vigorous plant growth gave a new direction to man's activities, setting him on the way to what we know as civilised life.

The first positive steps to be taken in primitive civilisation were towards the evolution of cultivated grasses as food. Wheat and barley were the initial grains to be developed; and we know that both were grown widely along the lower Nile in Egypt, the upper Euphrates in Syria, and the middle and lower Euphrates and Tigris in Iraq, as early as 3000 B.C. Today, these two are still the most important cereals in all Mediterranean lands except Egypt, Yugoslavia, Portugal and Albania, where maize, introduced from America, now takes first place. The cultivation of cereals spread from the Middle East and Egypt to all other parts of the Mediterranean long before the Christian era, and caused striking changes in the primitive rural landscapes.

Field patterns and systems

The most significant change was the appearance of fields or enclosures of land for the purpose of tillage; and in the *field pattern*, that is, the size, shape and arrangement of fields, it is still often possible to discern the influence of the distant past. Many earlier field patterns, however, have been effaced; increased demands for food by a growing population have led to a great increase in the area of cultivated land and to changes in field pat-terns. In addition, the development of urban settlement and the spate of planned agrarian reform in recent years have further obliterated the origi-nal field patterns. Nevertheless, we are able to reconstruct many of the ancient patterns, either by reference to examples still in existence, or by consulting historical sources and old maps, or by aerial photographs which show the "shadows" of earlier field boundaries.

In the Mediterranean lands the accidented relief of the coastlands—small plains separated by mountain spurs—governs the size and shape of fields in most areas. In general, fields vary greatly in size, sometimes being less than an acre, and are irregular in shape; and often there is a further haphazard subdivision of even small fields into multiform sections, so that the landscape has a marked patchwork appearance. The cultivator needs a coincidence of relatively flat land, sufficient soil cover and satisfactory water supply, together with a suitable site for his homestead. These con-ditions are commonplace in the plains, but many Mediterranean farmers have reproduced them artificially on the lower slopes of the mountains enclosing the plains. Here the thin soils have been laboriously scratched together and retained by terraced walls and houses built precariously on rocky ledges, to give a rural landscape familiar to all who have traversed the Mediterranean, with a field pattern all its own. A field pattern of a different type has developed in modern times in flood plains and deltas along the coast, where the cultivator has to contend with problems of drainage and reclamation. Here the fields are large and rectilinear in shape, and are separated by drainage ditches; and, except where urban settlements and industrial establishments have encroached on the fields, the homesteads are dispersed at regular intervals along roads which tra-verse the reclaimed areas. In many respects the field pattern resembles that of the polders in the Netherlands, and is reminiscent also of the Roman centuriation (*see* below).

Very large fields, of 100 acres (40 ha) or more, are not common around the Mediterranean. They occur mainly in plateau areas such as the north-ern Meseta of Spain, Sicily, western Turkey and Tunisia, or on the more extensive plains of central Portugal, northern Italy and Apulia. Many of them have always been tilled as agricultural units, but in some the Romans imposed a pattern of *centuriation*, that is, a division into 100 smaller rec-tangular blocks. Centuriated patterns are still extant in Italy in the Arno basin, the plain of Apulia and around Milan, and air photographs have dis-closed similar patterns, now discarded, in North Africa, Dalmatia and Andalusia. The large-field pattern in the Mediterranean lands is gradually disappearing where big estates based on a land tenure system of latifundia (*see* later) are being broken up.

In the Mediterranean lands, except in those areas which have summer rain (the Biscayan coastlands, the plain of north Italy and interior Yugo-slavia) or perennial irrigation (Egypt, Israel), drought in the hot season has dictated the adoption of the *two-field system*, with an annual rotation of one field growing wheat or other crops and the other left fallow. During the winter the fallow fields provide herbage for sheep and goats, which enrich them by their manure. In the exceptions mentioned above, there is little fallow, and there is a rotation of crops which may spread over three or more years.

As the centuries have passed, more and more emphasis has been placed in the Mediterranean lands on the cultivation of tree crops, with a resultant great modification in the original field patterns. The change in land use came about in the first place probably because poor farming techniques destroyed good cereal-producing soils; and the place of ground crops was taken by olives and vines or was left derelict and open to a transgression of maquis and garrigue. In more recent years, the better economic returns from tree crops have persuaded the farmer to extend arboriculture to rocky hillsides and other areas of thin soils unsuitable for cereals, thus further modifying the rural landscape. Olive groves mask the hills of every country from Spain to Israel, and vines are a speciality in Languedoc, Tuscany, southern Greece, western Asia Minor, Cyprus, Lebanon and the Algerian Tell. Citrus fruits have been introduced where irrigation is possible in the lowlands, and cover large areas in Andalusia, the Spanish huertas, southern Italy, Sicily, the Faiyum in Egypt and the Levantine coastlands.

One result of the development of the Mediterranean rural landscape was the almost complete disappearance of the original evergreen forest in the lowlands. Throughout history, man has attacked the forests to make room for agriculture, but not always with desirable results; for where the cleared land proved unsuitable for cultivation and was abandoned, it developed a vegetative cover, not of new forest, but of low-growing, bushy, thorny and almost useless maquis or garrigue. Further up the hill slopes the deciduous forest suffered also, but not to the same degree; for the deforested areas there received a new and artificial cover of fruit trees such as fig, peaches, walnuts and almonds, to augment the edible chestnut which grows there naturally. Above the tree line on the higher mountains, there are natural pastures to which goats and sheep may be taken in the summer. Now, by ruthless felling of coniferous trees a new line of pastures extends around the slopes at the lower limit of the conifers. These lower meadows provide halting places for animals to and from the higher pastures and yield crops of hay for consumption in winter in the lowlands.

A notable feature in the Mediterranean landscape is the absence of grassland at lower levels and the small part played by cattle. Sheep and goats are plentiful, for during the wet winters the maquis and the fallows provide enough fodder in the lowlands, and in the dry summers they are driven to the hill and mountain pastures. Cattle for draught purposes are employed widely in the peasant farms of the lowlands, but in total their numbers are not significant. Dairy cattle are not suited to a true Mediterranean climate, and are reared mainly in the sub- and extra-Mediterranean regions of the Biscayan lands, the western part of the north Italian plain, the Piedmont, and northern Yugoslavia, where rain falls at all seasons.

Patterns of rural settlement

Broadly speaking, two very different patterns of rural settlement, the *nucleated* and the *dispersed* types, are found in the Mediterranean lands. In the nucleated type the houses are grouped into villages; in the dispersed type they are scattered among the fields or arranged in tiny groupings known as hamlets (*see* Fig. 23). It is not always easy, however, to say when a hamlet is big enough to be called a village, for numbers of inhabitants are not always a sure guide. The functions and zones of influence of small aggregations of houses in relation to neighbouring settlements may be better criteria in distinguishing between hamlets and villages.

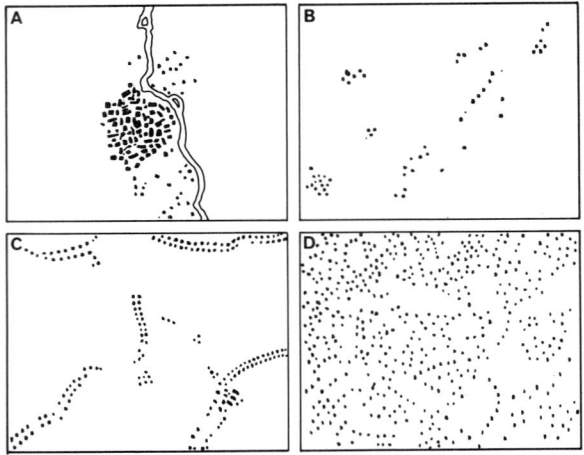

FIG. 23.—Rural settlement patterns (*after Houston*): A. Nucleated village, Andalusia, Spain; B. Small dispersed villages, Peloponnesus, Greece; C. Elongated "street" villages, Bilo Gora, Yugoslavia; D. Dispersed settlements, Galicia, Spain.

Reasons for the origin of the different patterns of rural settlement are often complex and a matter for speculation. Relief, soil and water supply are obvious physical factors, and must always be considered, but racial peculiarities and historic causes such as migrations, invasions and a need for defence may also have to be taken into account (*see* Fig. 24). Most Mediterranean villages occupy lowland sites, either in river valleys which penetrate the mountains or on coastal plains; or they are built at frequent intervals in the wide basins which occur on the surface of plateaus. In all cases the settlements have sufficient water and cultivable land to support them, and they are usually of the nucleated type. It is noticeable, however, that with good systems of irrigation, as in some parts of the richer huertas

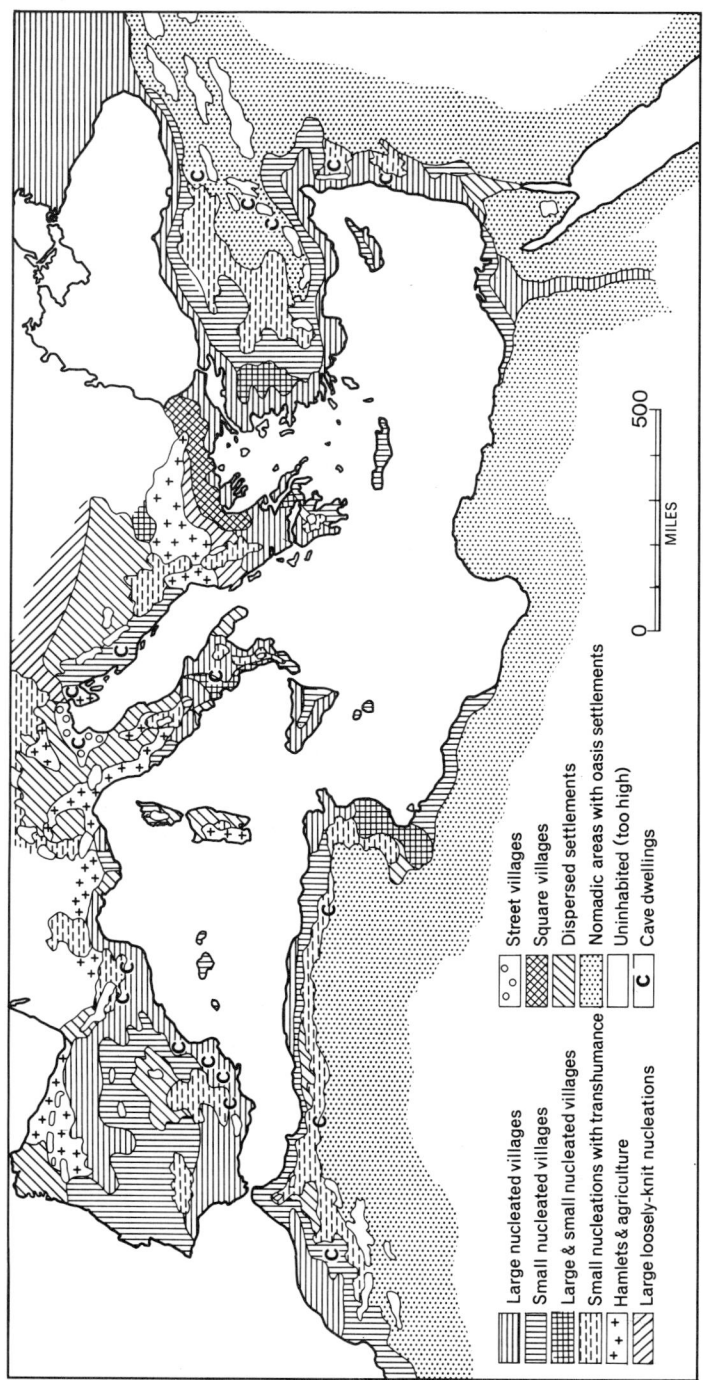

Large nucleated villages
Small nucleated villages
Large & small nucleated villages
Small nucleations with transhumance
Hamlets & agriculture
Large loosely-knit nucleations

Street villages
Square villages
Dispersed settlements
Nomadic areas with oasis settlements
Uninhabited (too high)
Cave dwellings

500

MILES

0

FIG. 24.—The Mediterranean lands: pattern of rural settlement.

of Spain and the reclaimed Pontine and Maremma marshes, nucleation gives way to dispersal; and that acute shortage of water in summer, as in the more arid regions of New Castile, the "toe" and "heel" of Italy, eastern Greece, Thrace and the rain-shadow areas of Lebanon, usually produces marked nucleation. There seems to be a distinct connection between low rainfall and the large agglomerated village. This is especially the case in the interior and west of Sicily, where availability of water supplies is of vital importance. It is suggested that the Mafia came into existence originally because they gained the control of the water which supplied the villages. Those who dared oppose the Mafia could expect no water during the summer, and this could obviously prove fatal to their material prospects and even to themselves and their families.

Although the majority of Mediterranean villages occupy comparatively level sites on the lowlands and plateaus, the mountainous character of so much of the region has led to the siting of a large number of settlements in the highlands, sometimes at considerable elevations. There is an upper limit to permanent settlement, which may range in different areas from 3000 ft to over 5000 ft (900–1500 m), and at these high altitudes the pattern tends to be one of dispersal. At lower levels, nucleated villages cling precariously to slopes or cover hill tops. There is, however, no general rule; dispersed patterns are found at both high and low altitudes throughout the northern Apennines, the Italian Alps, the mountains of Galicia and north Portugal, the ranges of Yugoslavia and the plateaus of Sardinia, whereas large nucleated villages—and even towns of considerable size such as Moreda and Lorca—occur at heights of over 3000 ft (900 m) in the Betic Cordillera; and in the central Apennines most of the people live in nucleated villages high up the slopes. Usually the sites were chosen with an eye to defence against enemies, but sometimes, as in the case of Assisi, villages were built on hill tops to avoid using cultivable lands on lower slopes and in the valleys below.

Social factors such as the terms of land tenancy sometimes determined the site of nucleated settlements. In central Portugal, southern Spain, southern Italy and Sicily, large estates were based on a feudal system of land tenure. In these *latifundia* (It. *latifondi*), some of which still exist, it was convenient for the landowner to have all his workers living near each other in a nucleated village. In contrast, share-cropping in Tuscany and tenant farming in the Middle East have led to a dispersed pattern.

Historically, the incursions of Goths, Vandals, Berbers, Arabs and Moors into the Mediterranean lands undoubtedly affected the pattern of rural settlement to a greater or less degree. The Moorish occupation of Spain, for instance, left a legacy of irregularly shaped and cluttered villages, whereas the Romans, who were neat and methodical builders, used a "gridiron" plan such as may be seen in the excavated ruins of Pompeii and in some of the present-day villages in the Po and Arno basins, the Roman Campagna and the Apulian plain. On the other hand, the incursions of the Arabs into North Africa and the Levant and of the Ottoman

Turks into the Balkan peninsula did not influence the pattern very materially, except in details of architecture and defensive works. With the advance of the Turks, some nucleated villages in the Balkans became fortresses whose thick walls were lined inside by rows of cell-like houses. Generally speaking, however, the original villages in the line of advance were abandoned, and new, large nucleations built in valleys deep in the mountains, where resistance to the enemy could more easily be maintained. The beginnings of Sarajevo, Bitola and many more villages and towns in the mountains of western Yugoslavia belong to this category. Similarly, many villages built at low levels near the coasts of Mediterranean France, Sardinia, southern Italy and Sicily were abandoned because of frequent marauding raids by Vandal pirates or Barbary corsairs, and replaced by new nucleations slightly inland on rocky and easily defended promontories.

This necessity for defence is a prominent factor in the development of settlement patterns in all the highlands around the Mediterranean. There are fortified hill-top villages in Provence, Roussillon and the Sierra Nevada; and the Maronite Christians of Lebanon owe their survival to the inaccessible, fortress-like nucleations they built high up the Lebanon mountains. In the mountainous districts of Morocco and Algeria, too, the typical village consists of flat-topped houses of mud and stone huddled closely and precariously on a steep hill slope in the shadow of the *kasbah* or fortress, so much so that it is often possible to step from the door of a house directly on to the roof of its neighbour. In the less mountainous districts of the Algerian Tell a measure of protection may be given to hamlets and villages by dense surrounding hedges of cactus and prickly pear.

In Greece and Roman Italy the first organised communities always developed in the shadow of a citadel (*acropolis*) situated on a hill. Rome was built on seven volcanic hills, one of which was topped by the citadel, and Athens lies at the foot of a high, rocky eminence crowned by the now-ruined Acropolis. We must note, however, especially in Greece, that a strong position is only one element in the subsequent development of a settlement, and that in the long run it may be outweighed by other adverse factors (*see* Fig. 25). Thebes, for example, which was founded about 1200 B.C. on a small plateau 650 ft (200 m) above the plain of Boeotia, was estimated to have had a population of 40,000 in 450 B.C., and a century later to be the most important city state. Today, Thivai, its modern equivalent, is a struggling, backward village with only 4000 inhabitants; it is a victim of remoteness, inaccessibility and neglect. Athens, on the other hand, built similarly on a hill 500 ft (150 m) high and guarded by the Acropolis, was destined to become the capital of modern Greece. In ancient times, like Thebes, it was an important commercial centre, but for several centuries prior to 1830 it was in the hands of the Turks, and during that time it was just another small provincial town set on a hill. With the advent of Greek independence and its selection as capital of the new state, it began to spread into the plains below; and today, with its port Piraeus, it is the major portion of a conurbation with a population of nearly 2 millions. The defensive factor which was prominent in the selection of its site has long since ceased to be effective, and has been replaced in modern times by the nodal position of the city and its port in relation to the trade routes of the Eastern Mediterranean. The Acropolis is no longer needed as a stronghold; its ruins are merely an attraction for tourists.

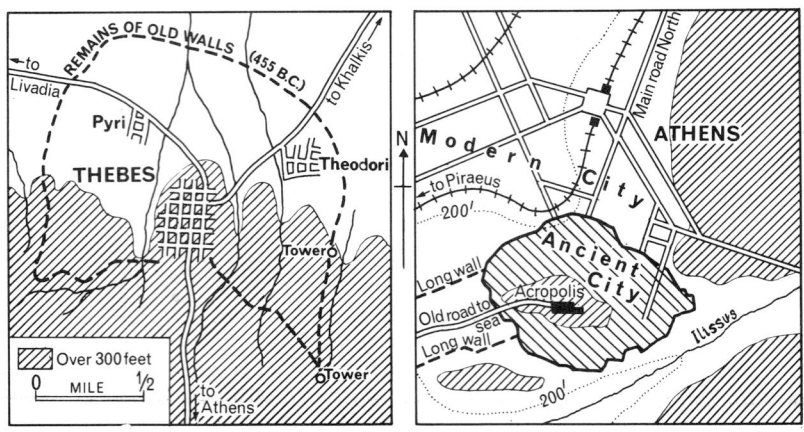

FIG. 25.—Thebes and Athens: a contrast in development. Whereas Thebes has shrunk from an estimated population of 40,000 in 455 B.C. clustered about its ancient citadel, Athens has developed into a modern city which forms a conurbation with Piraeus of nearly two million people. Theodori and Pyri are small villages inside Thebes' ancient walls.

The villages of oases in the desert regions of the Mediterranean lands, that is, in North Africa and the Levant, are usually nucleated and surrounded by thick, protective walls of sun-baked mud. Often there is a wide open space in the middle of the village, where the livestock of the community can be assembled during an attack by desert raiders; and here and sometimes outside the walls there may also be found the *caravanserai*, an extensive enclosed area where caravans are accommodated. In the Nile valley, the usual type is the nucleated village, but rarely can defence be counted as a factor in the selection of its site. Here the paramount need is to economise in the use of cultivable land, and so the houses are clustered tightly on slight rises above flood level, often on mounds composed of the remains of former villages (*see* Chapter XXI).

House types in rural settlements

(a) *Cave dwellings* are popularly associated with primitive man and not with the people of today, yet there are thousands of *troglodytes* (habitual cave-dwellers) still widely distributed in the Mediterranean lands. They may be found in natural caves which have developed in the limestones of Algeria, Morocco, Syria, Lebanon and Spain, in the last-named chiefly in the provinces of Huesca, Lerida, Granada, Almeria, Murcia and Valencia. Troglodytes live also in artificial caves cut in the travertines of Istria and Dalmatia and the volcanic tuff of Campania; and in eastern Turkey, in the Gôreme valley, not far from Nevsehir, many people live in homes carved in earth pillars. Here the early Christians made over 300 pillars into churches, cutting passages from the bases to large chapels near the summits. In some extinct volcanic districts underground caves have been cut, originally to form cemeteries. In most cases these are now used as storage cellars for wine and olive oil, but outside Rome a vast system of underground caves known as the Catacombs, which were both the home and the cemetery of Christian refugees from persecution, is preserved as a place of pilgrimage and tourist attraction.

Caves develop easily in many Mediterranean limestones, and sometimes they are roomy enough to allow subdivision into several compartments. They remain at an even temperature and because of the dry summers are rarely dank; and if the outer walls are not too thick they may be provided with such refinements as doors and glazed windows. These, however, are more common where caves have been cut artificially.

(b) *Tents* form an important element in the landscapes of all the desert margins, and they are found also in the steppe and semi-desert regions of Turkey, Syria, Lebanon and Morocco. The tents, usually black and woven from camel or goat hair, are thick enough to withstand the violent though infrequent rainstorms characteristic of the desert. Their size, indicated by the number of poles in each, depends on the wealth and social standing of the owner, and so does the quantity of carpets and cushions which, apart from cooking utensils, constitute the chief furniture. The tent, which is left open on the side away from the wind, is divided inside into two compartments, one for men, the other for women. Tents, easily erected and struck and with a minimum of impedimenta, are admirably suited to the nomadic and semi-nomadic life.

(c) *Houses* of a very primitive type, built of wattles or reeds daubed with clay or mud, are common in the delta of the Nile, and elsewhere in the Nile valley most rural houses are single-storeyed, box-like, flat-roofed structures with walls of sun-baked bricks made from a mixture of mud and chopped straw. Millet, maize or rice straw is used to thatch the roof. Wattle and daub are used also for more pretentious two- and even three-storeyed houses in eastern Greece, south-west Yugoslavia, central Italy and north-west Spain. To these simpler forms of human shelter should be added the mountain huts of transhumant pastoralists, which vary from merely four walls and a roof, all of stone, to the elaborate chalets found in some parts of the Italian and French Alps.

Over the greater part of the Mediterranean region, the rural house type must be associated with a predominantly agricultural economy, for in addition to the house being a home, it must be seen as an essential component in man's daily work. The homestead is also a storehouse and workshop, besides housing animals and equipment used in the fields; and in nucleated villages the establishments of wheelwrights, blacksmiths and other craftsmen form an intrinsic part of the household buildings.

The abundance of well-jointed limestone has led to stone-built houses almost everywhere in the countryside; in deforested regions the use of stone is universal. In all stone houses the walls are extremely thick, an insulation against summer heat, and in regions of true Mediterranean climate the flat or slightly inclined roof is usual. In the regions of heavier rainfall pitched roofs are employed, the pitch being steep in districts of heavy snow such as the Pyrenees, Alps, central Apennines and eastern Dinarics. Houses built entirely of logs are found in the forests of Bosnia and Hercegovina; and half-timbered houses are usual in parts of the Pyrenees, Apennines, Turkey, Lebanon and Algeria. Sometimes these take the form of a superstructure of timber on a stone foundation, but usually they are composed of a substantially-built wooden framework filled in with blocks of limestone.

Wherever pasture predominates in the economy the traditional house is two-storeyed. On the ground floor are the kitchen and accommodation for animals, sleeping quarters and storage rooms occupy the first floor, and hay is kept in the loft. In agricultural districts houses often have three storeys and occasionally a basement cellar where olive oil and wine are stored. The ground floor is shared by the kitchen and oil and wine presses, the living rooms and bedrooms are on the first floor, and grain and other crops are stored on the second floor. Some of the larger houses are built around a *patio* or courtyard; here the living and sleeping quarters of the family and farm labourers are on two sides of the patio, the remaining space being occupied by stores, granaries, presses, workshops, and accommodation for animals and poultry. To help air circulation, most houses have balconies and wide verandahs.

In the latifundia type of estate, the homestead sometimes approaches the status of a nucleated village. Around the owner's and steward's houses are separate store rooms, wine and oil presses, cheese dairies, barns and silos, and repair shops, together with the homes of permanent workers and a wide range of dormitories and canteens for seasonal labourers.

Near all settlements, nucleated and dispersed, space may be reserved for the open-air drying of cork, tobacco and fruits, and for the threshing and winnowing of grain; and there are sheds for the collection and temporary storage of perishable produce such as tomatoes, peaches, apricots and citrus fruits. These are then despatched to packing or processing plants in nearby towns, or to "co-operatives" which have been established in recent years in the villages themselves or in convenient positions in the open countryside.

URBAN DEVELOPMENT

The vast majority of towns and cities have passed through previous stages of growth first as hamlets and then as villages; the few exceptions are such communities as mining towns and planned "overspill" towns, "garden cities" and dormitory suburbs which have appeared in the past few decades as fully-fledged urban units. There is, however, no generally accepted distinction between a village and a town; the dictionary definition of a village as "an assemblage of houses smaller than a town" and of a town as "a populous place bigger or less rural than a village" is not very helpful. Some writers on urban geography give an arbitrary figure of 10,000 inhabitants as the dividing line between villages and towns, but whether this is accepted or not, it must be agreed that a town has physical factors such as accessibility, nodality, water supply and productive hinterland superior to those of a village. It is agreed, too, that the size, value and accessibility of a hinterland determines the development of a town into a city. Whereas a hamlet serves and is served by its immediate neighbourhood, cities like Marseille, Barcelona and Naples have hinterlands which cover large portions of their respective countries. In considering the growth of a town into a city we may also have to take into account those increasingly complex economic and sociological factors which relate to the function of the urban aggregation—its type of administration, its role in the national economy, and its cultural influence on the area it serves.

Marketing of rural produce is initially the function of the small town, which by reason of superior focal values becomes a local market linking rural and urban economies. In all agricultural areas, we find these small markets contributing to larger and still larger centres, until finally the produce reaches the city with its very much superior facilities for commerce and trade; and of course there is a return funnelling of manufactured and other goods from the city to the regional markets and ultimately to the villages and hamlets within its hinterland or zone of influence. In the Campania of Italy, for example, the regional markets of Formia, Cassino, Caserta, Benevento, Avellino and Salerno, after collecting from their tributary towns and villages, send their produce to Naples, which, by virtue of its focal situation in the Campania and its position on a excellent harbour, has become the largest city in southern Italy and a major international port. In Spain, too, the towns of Valladolid, Segovia, Salamanca, Talavera, Toledo and Tarascon are regional centres encircling and contributing to Madrid, an artificial metropolis which may not have an original site superior to many of its subsidiary markets, but which has the great advantage of centrality in the country.

Nodality, which in a geographical sense means the convergence of roads or trade routes, is an important factor in urban development. All the above-mentioned smaller markets are at minor nodal points and cities are at major positions of nodality. The most ancient cities in the Mediterranean lands were founded where routes were made to converge on permanent sources of water such as rivers and oases; in the case of rivers the largest settlements were usually where in addition the river could be crossed easily, as at Baghdad and Memphis, Hama and Homs. Aleppo, Damascus and Amman are representative of oasis nodality. All these ancient cities of the Fertile Crescent, some of them dating from before

5000 B.C., have for long been concerned with commerce along caravan routes and over the sea, as well as the trade dependent on local supplies and needs. The varied types of merchandise carried over long or short distances in this region sandwiched between the Mediterranean and the desert led to a concentration of merchants and craftsmen in these centres where water was plentiful. Gradually there developed a marked contrast between the crowded cities and the poorly-populated countryside, between urban prosperity and rural poverty, so that today there is a serious imbalance in the proportions of urban and rural populations throughout the Levant, and indeed also in the whole of North Africa. In Syria, Israel and Egypt, especially, too rapid economic expansion, foreign competition and the present political uncertainty are tending to an increase in this imbalance, with its resultant social problems of over-population and unemployment in the cities.

In Greece the earliest urban communities appeared about 2000 B.C. around easily defended strongpoints which commanded fertile plains at Athens, Thebes, Sparta and Olympia. For the most part the Greek cities were small, rarely reaching a population of 10,000, for their size was governed mainly by the ability of their agricultural hinterlands to support them, and the factor of defence was dominant. Of the original city states only Athens has developed into a major urban settlement, and this was because its nodality is not merely local, but extends to the whole of the eastern Mediterranean. With the increased use of the Mediterranean Sea as a commercial highway, many Greek and Levantine settlements on the coast grew in size and status as ports; from cities such as Athens and Corinth in Greece, and Tyre, Sidon and Byblus in Phoenicia, merchant fleets established trading posts on all sides of the Mediterranean and Black Seas. Many of the colonies had hinterlands more extensive and productive than those of the home ports, and in the course of time became independent centres of national and international trade. Outstanding modern ports of ancient Greek foundation are Alexandria, Istanbul, Naples, Marseille and Valencia; and Cádiz and Málaga were originally Phoenician colonies (*see also* page 100).

Milan is an outstanding example of urban growth at the junction of routes. Situated at the convergence of several roads and railways through the Alps and with easy access to all parts of the north Italian plain, it was already a major trading and craft centre in the Middle Ages; today it is the greatest industrial city in Italy. Madrid, as already noted, has artificial nodality; chosen as the capital of Spain because of its central position in the country, it was given a system of roads and railways radiating in all directions. A similar road network was constructed around Ankara when it became capital of Turkey.

Wide river valleys and plains are obvious places for urban growth, for they are usually fertile and give facilities for road and possibly river transport. The larger urban centres are sited at fords, bridge points and confluences, where there may be a convergence of routes, and near the river exits to the sea, where the cities act as exchange and trading points for the products of the river basins and for those brought from overseas. Seville, Valencia, Rome, Florence, Turin, Ljubljana and El Asnam are examples of bridge towns; Milan, Zaragoza, Padua, Belgrade and Niš are at river confluences; Cairo is at the head of a delta; and Lisbon, Oporto, Marseille and Alexandria are near river exits. It should be noted, however, that the larger ports of the Mediterranean basin are never exactly at the river exits, which are invariably deltas and liable to silting; Marseille, for example, is sited to the east of the Rhône delta, and Alexandria to the west of the Nile delta. The ports are where their harbours are kept clear of silt by the sea currents, feeble though these may be. Here it should be mentioned that ports may develop also at land gateways to rich agricultural or industrial hinterlands, as at Barcelona, Genoa, İzmír and Tunis; or at the convergence of maritime routes, as at Messina, Valetta, Port Said and Istanbul, at the last of which land routes give additional nodality.

Where highlands meet lowlands, especially where routes through the mountains meet others along their flanks, are places suitable for the exchange of products of widely different environments and for the growth of towns. Many of the cities of the Maghrib, such as Oran, Algiers, Constantine and Bone, are at the meeting-place of routes through the Atlas Cordillera and along the Tell; and in Italy, at intersection points along the Emilian Way, a road which traverses the length of the Po lowlands at the foot of the northern Apennines, are the regional markets of Piacenza, Parma, Reggio, Modena, Bologna, Faenza, Cesena and Rimini (see Fig. 56). At road junctions on the Flaminian Way, which makes use of the Tiber and Arno valleys to cut through the Apennines and connect Rome and Bologna, there are markets at Orvieto, Chiusi, Arezzo, Florence, Prato and Pistoia. The size of these regional markets depends partly on the extent of its own immediate hinterland and partly on the degree of its wider nodality.

Defence has already been noted as a factor in the development of the early urban growths of the Levant, Greece, Rome and their colonies, and in many of the towns and cities mentioned above there are the ruined remains of castles and fortresses. To them may be added the more recent foundation of the Moorish city of Marrakesh, situated at a strategic point and route focus near the juxtaposition of two regions of contrasting types. Here the dates, hides and skins of the drier south and south-east are still exchanged for the cereals and fruits of the moister north and north-west, but the defensive factor has disappeared in the modern development of the city. In medieval times many towns grew around fortresses and strongholds built against invasion from abroad or from neighbouring rival factions or clans. In the Iberian peninsula, towns with "Castella" (Span.) and "Castela" (Port.) as part of their names are legacies of the wars against the Moors; in Italy the powerful families of the Medicis, Gonzagas and Scaligeri were responsible for the growth and importance respectively of Florence, Mantua and Verona. In modern times, the strategic factor was uppermost in the development of Gibraltar, Ceuta and Valletta; but in these days of air and nuclear warfare the defensive factor in urban development has ceased to have any real significance.

The Mediterranean lands have very few large urban centres of recent foundations when compared with the many mushroom growths of cities in the industrial regions of Western Europe and the U.S.S.R. Where industry developed on a large scale, as in northern Italy, the Biscayan lands, and around Barcelona, it was in cities and towns already established which then increased in size and extended their functions. In North Africa, the discovery and exploitation of mineral oil and natural gas have had more permanent effects on towns and cities already in existence near the coast than in the areas of exploitation, where settlements already show signs of transience as the deposits are exhausted. Ports such as Algiers, Oran, Bougie and Arzew in Algeria, La Skhirra in Tunisia, and Sidra and Port Brega in Libya, most of which until recently had little or no economic significance, are now thriving communities with oil and gas pipeline termini, oil refineries or gas liquefaction plants, tanker connections and a host of new subsidiary and ancillary industries.

Among the cities and towns founded in the present century are those built on the reclaimed and colonised Maremma and Pontine marshes in Italy. Latina, the largest, has reached a population of over 200,000. Casablanca, in Morocco, may be regarded as of this century, for prior to its occupation by the French in 1907 it was a tiny fishing settlement. With the advent of the French, who made it their base for the conquest of Morocco, the small town entered on a phase which led to the emergence of a well-planned city in the European style, with a population today of nearly a million. Tel Aviv, too, which since 1948 has been the commercial capital of Israel, may be regarded as a new foundation rather than an expansion from its status of a small residential suburb of Jaffa. It was developed after the First World War as a better outlet than Jaffa for the fertile plain of Sharon, and gradually took over the functions of its parent, with which today it forms a conurbation of more than 400,000 people. The Red Sea ports of Eilat in Israel and Aqaba in Jordan are also modern developments of insignificant coastal settlements; and Ashdod in Israel is at present undergoing a transformation which will change it from a small regional market to the largest port in the country. In Libya a completely new foundation, Beida, planned as the federal capital of the country, is being built about 100 miles north-east of Benghazi. The new city will replace the present inconvenient alternation of the functions of federal capital between Benghazi and Tripoli, the provincial capitals respectively of Cyrenaica and Tripolitania.

DISTRIBUTION AND DENSITY OF POPULATION

The factors of relief, climate, soil, productivity, fuel and power resources, useful minerals and, very important, the degree of cultural advancement of a people, vary greatly from one Mediterranean country to another and result in big differences in the distribution and density of their populations. These are considered in dealing with individual countries later in the book; this section is concerned more with some of the characteristic features of population distribution and density in the Mediterranean lands, viewed as a whole (see Table III and Fig. 26). The features noted here are: (1) the influence of the associated factors of relief and climate, (2) the "zoning" of population in many countries, and (3) the marked contrasts in density between adjoining districts or adjacent countries.

INFLUENCE OF RELIEF AND CLIMATE

In general, as in most other parts of the world, we expect to find fewer people in the highlands of the Mediterranean lands than in the lowlands, simply because of the more difficult terrain and the harsher climate. There are many exceptions, of course, for in the highlands there may be broad shelves of productive soil capable of supporting considerable numbers of people, as in the Sierra Nevada and the Lebanon mountains; or parts of the lowlands may be desert or malarial marsh and discourage settlement. Until recent years, for instance, many of the coastal swamps of Italy, Albania and Greece were completely uninhabited. The influence of relief and climate is here considered as it applies to (1) highlands, (2) plateaus, and (3) lowlands.

1. Highlands

There is an upward limit placed by relief and climate on permanent settlement, even in isolated homesteads. In the Mediterranean lands the limit seems to be set at about 5500 ft (1700 m), and only in the Sierra Nevada and the western Atlas do any permanently occupied sites approach that height. In the Central Sierras of Spain, the Apennines, southern Greece and Lebanon the upper limit of settlement falls to 4500 ft (1370 m), and in most parts of the Pyrenees, Alps and the mountains of eastern Turkey to not much more than 3000 ft (900 m). Above these limits there are many temporary homes occupied in summer by transhumant shepherds at heights up to 10,000 ft (3000 m) in the Maghrib and 8000 ft (2400 m) in the Alps. In the highlands of the Mediterranean lands in general, it may be said there is permanent settlement everywhere up to about 3500 ft (1070 m).

Most highland peoples live on the lower slopes where agriculture is possible, but since soil development, aspect and the possibilities of terracing and irrigation vary greatly, there is an equally great variation in the distribution and density of population. The lower slopes of the central Pyrenees in Spain are developed on dry limestones in a rain shadow area, and support only a scanty population living in dispersed settlements on subsistence agriculture and transhumant sheep rearing; whereas on the Tuscan side of the central Apennines the well-watered hillsides and richer

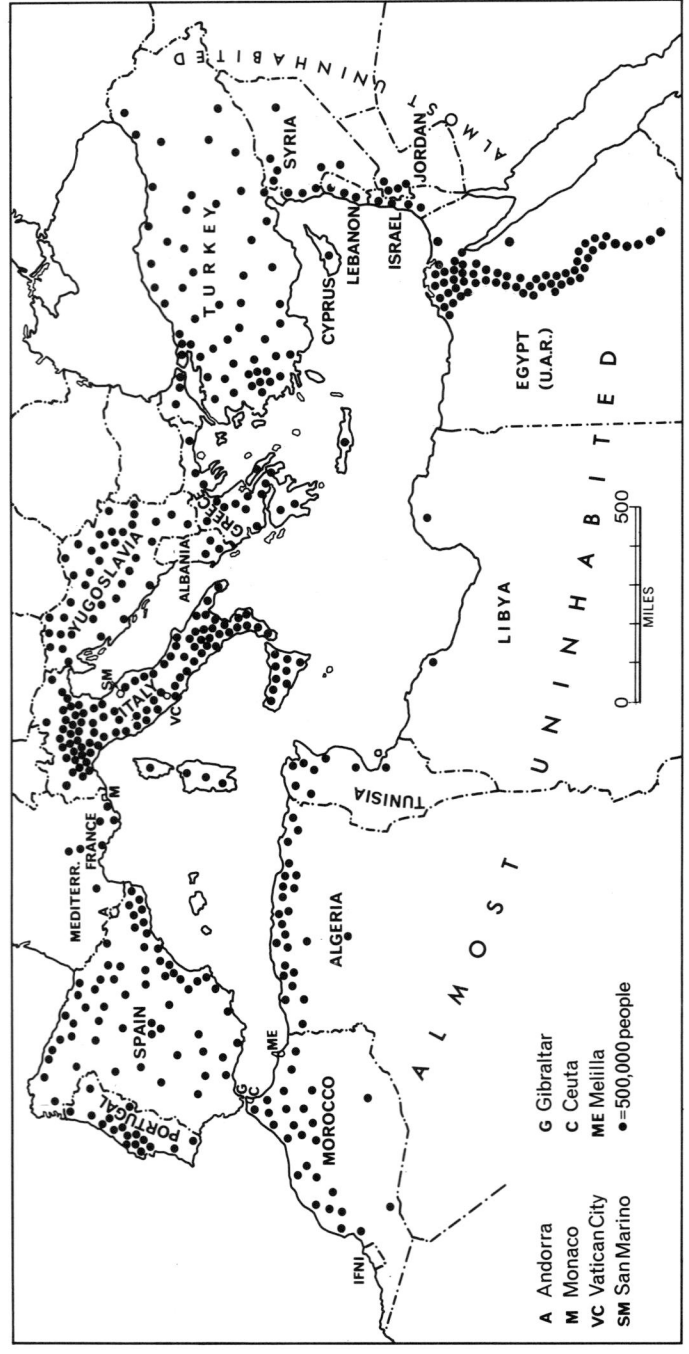

FIG. 26.—The Mediterranean lands: distribution of population.

soils have encouraged the growth of many nucleated villages and small towns at altitudes up to 3000 ft (900 m). Contrast might be made also between the scattered distribution of people on the mountain slopes of Yugoslavia, Greece and Albania, and the concentrations in the high, inter-montane basins of the Betic Cordillera, where Granada, the largest of several towns, has a population of 161,851 at an altitude of around 3000 ft (900 m).

TABLE III

Population of the Mediterranean Lands

	Area (square miles)	Population (000)	Density (persons per square mile)
Portugal . . .	34,831	8,889	255
Spain . . .	194,945	30,430	156
Gibraltar . . .	2·5	25	
Mediterranean France	24,078	4,175	173
Monaco . . .	368 acres	20	
Italy . . .	116,280	50,464	435
San Marino . .	24	18	708
Vatican City .	109 acres	1	
Yugoslavia . .	98,725	19,064	193
Albania . . .	11,101	1,814	163
Greece . . .	50,534	8,389	166
Maltese Islands . .	121	316	2,600
Morocco . .	171,300	13,323	77
Ifni . . .	750	50	67
Ceuta & Melilla	82	155	1,890
Algeria (northern) .	125,000	11,505	92
Algeria (Saharan) .	731,000	588	0·8
Tunisia . . .	63,378	4,457	70
Libya . . .	679,358	1,244	2
Egypt (U.A.R.) . (inhabited area)	386,000 (15)	30,083	80 (nearly 2000)
Turkey . . .	296,000	28,602	96
Cyprus . . .	3,572	594	164
Syria . . .	72,000	4,566	64
Lebanon . . .	3,400	1,750	548
Jordan . . .	37,730	2,017	54
Israel . . .	8,000	2,170	280

2. *Plateaus*

Largely because of their elevation, comparative isolation and climates which approach the continental, the plateaus of the Mediterranean lands are poorly peopled and have backward economies. The Meseta of Spain, a plateau which varies in height from 3200 ft (975 m) in the east to 1500 ft (450 m) in the west, has a widely distributed population based on exten-sive monoculture of cereals or on pastoralism. Settlements are usually nucleated in character, market towns and regional centres, but the overall density is low, varying between 80 and 125 persons per square mile even when the 2 million people in the Madrid area are taken into account, and comparing unfavourably with the figures of 262 in Catalonia and of 156 for the whole of Spain. This paucity of people on the plateau is mainly the result of its semi-continental climate with extremes of temperature and pronounced aridity, but it is due also to a combination of historic and social factors such as the large-estate type of land tenure. In Turkey, too, the Anatolian plateau, ranging in elevation from 2700 ft (820 m) in the west to over 5500 ft (1680 m) where it passes eastwards into Armenia, has a well-spaced distribution of population with a low density; in fact, in some parts of Armenia there are hardly any inhabitants at all. The western half of the plateau supports a large majority of the people of the plateau, partly because of its lower elevation, kindlier climate and better soils, and partly because of its past history of settlement and the present planned economic developments of the Turkish Government.

The rest of the large plateaus in the Mediterranean lands remain virtually uninhabited. Most of the plateau areas of Syria and Jordan form part of the Syrian and Arabian deserts, and have only a sprinkling of inhabitants in oases or the black tents of nomads. Similarly, in North Africa vast stretches of Algeria, Libya and Egypt lie between 1500 and 3000 ft (450–900 m) in the north of the Sahara Desert, and are peopled only by nomads, oasis dwellers and the transient workers in mineral settlements. At a higher altitude, the Plateau of the Shotts, from 3000 to 6000 ft (900–1800 m), supports only a very scanty population of semi-nomadic and nomadic pastoralists. At this point it is worth noting that because of practical difficulties in obtaining a census of wandering peoples, their numbers are often estimated by counting how many tents they possess and allowing an arbitrary figure of from four to six persons per tent. In Syria, for example, the large Sbaa tribe, which wanders between Homs and the south-eastern desert, has an estimated 3400 tents; and the Karachim, with a grazing area limited to the immediate vicinity of Homs, have only 120 tents. Within the boundaries of Syria there are 33 nomadic tribes occupying approximately 41,000 tents, which indicates a total of between 160,000 and 250,000 nomads in the country.

3. Lowlands

In examining the distribution and density of population in the plains and low-lying river valleys of the Mediterranean lands we must consider their size, their relation to neighbouring highlands, the thickness and fertility of their soils, the degree to which arboriculture is practised, the efficiency and extent of irrigation systems, the growing process of industrialisation, the proximity to the sea, and any other climatic, historical and political factors which may obtain in individual cases. All these are examined in some detail in later chapters. Here it may be sufficient to say that in general lowlands with a pronounced summer drought cannot support a dense population unless plentiful irrigation water is available, and that some riverine, deltaic and coastal areas, unreclaimed and malarial, may have too much water and few or no inhabitants.

In typical lowlands much of the surface may be covered with maquis or garrigue, and such areas are poorly peopled. In many districts, too, the emphasis placed on the production of tree crops or on single-crop agriculture as in latifundia, has resulted in a decrease in the amount of labour required and in a consequent low population density. On the other hand, where the cultivation of cereals is combined with the production of profitable commercial crops such as citrus fruits, dried fruits and fruit juices, tobacco, cotton and market produce (especially of the early or out-of-season varieties), more careful cultivation and a larger labour force are demanded, and so there are denser rural populations and a more pronounced urban development.

Finally, where the coasts of lowlands are suitable for the building of good ports and harbours, or where hydro-electric power can be provided from near-by highlands, as in the north Italian and the Barcelona districts, or where useful mineral deposits are exploited, as along the Biscayan coast, the development of commerce and industry has led to large numbers and dense concentrations of people comparable with any found elsewhere in the modern world. The process of industrialisation is visible to a greater or less extent in every Mediterranean country, and everywhere it is accompanied by a large and somewhat inexplicable upsurge in the total and density of populations, so much so, that many lowland areas are now over-populated or are in danger of that unwelcome state, as we shall see later.

ZONING OF POPULATION

In many Mediterranean countries there is a zoning of population inland and upwards from the coast to the highlands of the interior. In general, the largest numbers and densest concentrations of people are on coastal plains, or where lowlands, as in the north Italian plain, have easy access to the sea. We must remember, however, that there are long stretches of rocky coast and lagoon-dotted marshes with few inhabitants; there are areas at one time productive from which the people moved to escape the depredations of pirates and to which they are only slowly returning; and there are coastal regions in Libya and Egypt which are little removed from true desert. In wide contrast are the densely peopled huertas of Spain, the rivieras of France and Italy, the industrial and commercial foci of Barcelona, Marseille, Genoa, Naples, Algiers, Casablanca and Istanbul, and the great industrial complex in the west of the Po basin.

Zoning of population is well exemplified in Tuscany. The coastal belt, largely reclaimed marshland, has a density of less than 200 persons per square mile, which in Italy is considered low. Half the population of the province is concentrated between 100 and 1200 ft (30–365 m) above sea-level, with a density of 350–400, and another one-sixth, more concerned with tree crops, lives in a zone up to 1600 ft (490 m) and has a density of 200–350. Above that, there are still many nucleated settlements, with an overall density of about 150 per square mile. These are all big densities when compared with those of other Mediterranean countries, and are used merely to illustrate the arrangement of the population in zones. Italy, with an average density of 435 persons per square mile, is the most crowded country around the Mediterranean; the figures given for Tuscany must be related to this average.

In all lowlands the density of population varies also with the degree of agricultural productivity and takes a sharp upward trend with irrigation. In other words, zoning of population may be distinguished in many coastal plains. In the huerta of Valencia, for example, the non-irrigated districts have a density of 10 persons per square mile, which increases gradually in marginal irrigated areas, and reaches 1000 per square mile where irrigation is used to the full or industry has been developed.

REGIONAL CONTRASTS IN POPULATION DISTRIBUTION

Most striking is the contrast in Egypt between the large area of desert, virtually uninhabited, and the packed concentration of people in the Nile valley and delta, where in places there is a *rural* density of over 1000 persons per square mile and where, including towns and cities, there is an overall density of 2500 per square mile. Compare this figure with the totally misleading average of 64 persons per square mile for the whole of Egypt. Similar contrasts between a well-populated strip of country and a neighbouring desert occur in Algeria, Syria and Jordan; and in Morocco there are marked regional differences in distribution and density. Most of the people of Morocco live west and north-west of the main Atlas ranges in three groups of concentration: on the Rharb plain which is well watered by the Wadi Sebou, along the Atlantic coastal plain where the annual rainfall and the soils are better than elsewhere in the lowlands, and in a zone of foothills flanking the Atlas where mountain torrents and melting snows give a good supply of water. In these areas the density is about 100 persons per square mile, whereas south of the mountain ranges the region is sparsely peopled in oases and the damp beds of wadis, and the density averages little more than 50 per square mile. The average density for the whole country is 77 person per square mile.

The Iberian peninsula, too, provides violent regional variations in both distribution and density of populations. The greatest concentrations are in the coastal industrial regions of Catalonia, the Basque provinces, Lisbon and Oporto, the richer huertas such as Valencia and Malaga, and inland in the artificial aggregation of Madrid (*see* Fig. 40). In the immediate vicinity of all of these the population density may rise to over 350 persons per square mile, and elsewhere along the coasts of the peninsula it rarely falls below 100 per square mile. With the ascent to the plateau of the Meseta, however, there is a rapid fall both in total numbers and in density. The wheat-growing areas of Old Castile have densities decreasing from 60 to

25 per square mile, and in the arid steppe of New Castile and Extremadura the density may fall below 25 per square mile. Even the influence of Madrid does not prevent the density falling below 80 per square mile within a few miles of the city. Another noteworthy contrast is between the latifundias of Andalusia and central Portugal, which are only moderately peopled, and the densities of over 200 per square mile in parts of the mountains of Galicia and north Portugal, which are woefully overpopulated.

OVER-POPULATION

Population throughout the Mediterranean lands is increasing rapidly, the average annual rate of growth being in fact twice that of most Western European countries. This presents an ever-growing problem to most countries: how to support swelling numbers on resources which are insufficient even for present needs. The problem is urgent in Italy, the Maghrib, Egypt and all the Levant lands, and is hardly less pressing in Portugal and Greece.

Since this question of over-population occurs frequently in future chapters, perhaps its meaning should be amplified. In emergent countries —and most of the Mediterranean lands may be so called—the coming of industrial development is usually accompanied by an increase in population. If there is a corresponding increase in the production of food supplies and the utilisation of other resources, a favourable balance is preserved, but if the population grows at a faster rate than the country's resources can support, ultimately the time must arrive when either the surplus population must emigrate and thus restore the balance, or a planned economic development programme must be introduced in an effort to do so. Such plans are in existence in many Mediterranean countries, but they will take many years to complete; and since emigration is generally frowned upon by governments imbued with nationalistic ideals, the point of imbalance must surely approach. Where it has been reached and passed, the country is over-populated. Efforts may be made to reduce its impact, as in Italy, where better methods of agriculture, improved water conservation and distribution, land reclamation, development of fisheries, exploitation of power and mineral resources, and a large-scale introduction of manufacturing and processing industries have had a most beneficial effect. Once a country becomes seriously over-populated, however, all the above are merely palliatives. The evils of overcrowding—slums, disease, mass unemployment, poverty—are evident in most parts of the Mediterranean region; the problem of over-population has to be faced by all its peoples.

STUDY QUESTIONS

1. Discuss the part played by nomadism in the rural economy of some of the Mediterranean lands. Indicate the changes which are taking place in modern times in this pattern of life.

2. Write a short essay on field patterns in the Mediterranean lands.

3. Select *three* areas in the Mediterranean lands which differ widely from each other in the mode of life of their inhabitants, and show how geographical factors have exerted their influence on the people of each area you describe.

4. Explain what is meant by (*a*) nucleated, (*b*) dispersed types of rural settlement, and give some account of their distribution in the Mediterranean lands.

5. Examine the importance of site in a consideration of any *three* capital cities of the Mediterranean lands. (*Based on* O. & C.)

6. With the help of examples from the Mediterranean lands, discuss the importance of defence in the development of urban settlements.

7. Basing your answer on regions of (*a*) high, (*b*) medium and (*c*) low densities of population, write a short account of the distribution of population in the lands surrounding the Mediterranean Sea.

8. "A state has always a natural focus, but rarely a natural frontier." Illustrate this statement from the nation states around the Mediterranean. (*Based on* O. & C.)

9. What effect is industrialisation having on the distribution of population in the Mediterranean lands?

10. What is meant by over-population? Illustrate your answer by examples in the Mediterranean lands where over-population occurs for widely different reasons.

11. Discuss the geographical factors which may have contributed to the early growth of civilisation in the Eastern Mediterranean region.

Chapter VII

HUMAN RESPONSE: ECONOMIC (I)

AGRICULTURE

ECONOMIC geography deals with the production, distribution and consumption of wealth, which in this sense means not money but the things which money will buy. The study of the production of this wealth leads us to consider activities such as stock rearing, agriculture, mining and industry, while the examination of its distribution directs our attention to the special organisation of agriculture and industry, as well as trade, both national and international. This in turn involves some knowledge of types of communication and transport. Economic geography shows how man responds to the factors of his physical environment as well as to such historical and social factors as have been outlined in preceding chapters. In this chapter we shall concern ourselves with agriculture, animal husbandry and fishing in the Mediterranean lands, and in the one following with fuel and power resources, minerals, communications and the development of industries.

Before going on to a survey of the economic geography of the Mediterranean lands under these separate headings, however, it is worth while to say a few introductory words about the Mediterranean economy as a whole, to look at its development from a wide angle. Physical factors such as relief, climate and soils, dealt with in previous chapters in more detail, must be referred to again and used as a background against which we can project the historical and social patterns. Only by taking into account the interaction of all the factors can we arrive at a clear economic picture.

Traditionally, Mediterranean agriculture was based partly upon winter crops such as wheat, barley and vegetables, and partly upon summer crops from the vine and olive. Animal husbandry, too, usually of the transhumant type, has always been prominent in the agricultural landscape. Wheat and barley were favoured because other cereals require more moisture than the Mediterranean climate normally provides; and this shortage of water, together with thin soils and an accidented terrain, led to poor yields. Yields of vegetables were poor for the same reasons, while the comparatively sparse vegetation suitable for grazing and the periods of drought which occur regularly make stock rearing, even of such hardy animals as sheep and goats, somewhat precarious. Some of these difficulties of the Mediterranean peasant farmer were outlined in Chapter IV, and more will be said about them and the way they are overcome in dealing with individual countries.

Shortage of water in a district may be compensated for by irrigation, but there is an obvious limit to the supplies which can be provided artificially. Thin soils are a legacy of the climate, and little if anything can be done to increase their bulk in regions of summer drought. They can, however, be cultivated wisely, either by providing water by irrigation or by adopting the *dry farming* method (*see* Fig. 27). The practice of dry farming developed naturally from rainfall shortage and uncertainty, and

[*Courtesy of the Spanish Ministry of Information.*

Fig. 27.—Spain: the plains of Caudillo, in the province of Cuidad Real; a good example of field patterns in the *secano* (non-irrigated) region of New Castile. Note the dead-flat surface, and the absence of trees and buildings.

today it is widely in common use throughout the Mediterranean lands, even where the usable layers of the soil are comparatively thick. The most common form of dry farming demands alternate years of cropping and fallow on any piece of cultivated land, careful ploughing and harrowing being carried out in both crop and fallow years. Continued cultivation of this sort breaks up capillary action in the soil and slows down evaporation of its water content; and this means that part of the moisture received during the fallow years is retained in the soil and is available for crops in the following year. Four lots of cultivation are normal in the fallow year: the first is ploughing in autumn to open the surface to the early rains; the second is either ploughing or harrowing in midwinter to retain the moisture contributed by the heavier rains; the third is harrowing near the end of spring to catch the last showers of rainfall; and the fourth is harrowing near mid-summer to break up the surface soil, impede capillary action, and hinder the loss by evaporation during the hot summer of the moisture accumulated in the soil in the preceding months. This method of farming, known also as the two-field system (described above on page 108), despite all the care of the farmer, gives crop yields which remain generally low.

The accidented relief of the majority of the Mediterranean lands, together with the torrential showers of winter, results in disastrous soil erosion (*see* page 69), and in places where cultivation has been attempted on sloping land this has been accentuated. It is probable, for instance, that many of the extensive olive groves and vineyards now found in the region were planted on hill slopes which originally supported cereals, but had become impoverished through soil denudation. Terracing and reafforestation are employed to reduce soil losses, and in many areas very stony soils are given over to long-rooted plants such as olives and vines.

In addition to the difficulties presented by their physical environment, cultivators were often subject to raids by nomads and other marauders, while the small surpluses which were produced in some areas were commandeered in ancient times by cities such as Carthage, Athens, Rome and Alexandria. Almost constantly throughout history, as we saw in Chapter VI, peasant farmers in the Mediterranean lands have seen their fields overrun and devastated by foreign invaders, and have had to face oppression and crippling demands on the fruits of their labours by their rulers and landlords. In view of all these factors, physical and historical, it is not surprising that agriculture in the Mediterranean lands became backward and poverty-stricken.

Yet the story is not one of unbroken gloom. After the Renaissance there came not only mental and spiritual rebirth, but also a certain amount of commercial development. Agricultural surpluses began to travel further afield, especially towards north-west Europe. The main items were summer crops such as olives and olive oil, wine and fruits, chiefly figs, which could readily be preserved, winter crops of wheat, barley and some vegetables, and animal products such as wool, hides and skins. Among the vegetables were the so-called "tree onions" from Egypt and other parts of North Africa, cucumbers from Greece and Italy, and tomatoes from Spain. The tomato was first introduced into Mediterranean Europe by the Spaniards, who brought it from Peru, its native home.

With the coming of the Industrial Revolution, too, there was considerable expansion of markets. The developing industrial countries had greatly increased purchasing power. Populations were growing rapidly; in England, for instance, there was a fourfold increase in the numbers of its inhabitants during the last century, and this meant a natural market extension. Transport facilities, too, were vastly improved. As a result of these changes something approaching an economic revolution was started in the Mediterranean lands and has continued to the present day as far as agriculture is concerned.

In the first place, there was a remarkable increase in the output of such traditional summer crops as wine and dried fruits. Vegetable production also grew enormously, and there was a tremendous development in arboriculture, especially of citrus fruits, where the grape-fruit was added to the older-established orange, lemon and tangerine. The last two features were made possible because for the first time it became economic to develop new-style irrigation and provide the water that vegetables and citrus fruits require. Modern methods of irrigation are expensive, and until the market for Mediterranean agricultural products became large enough to warrant the large expenditure involved, there was little effort to make use of the surplus water from winter rains. In fact, since Roman times there had been little incentive to improve systems of irrigation. In addition to this greater control of water supply, there was a big development of dry farming techniques aimed to give increased production in areas which previously had been of minimum agricultural value. A further and by no means negligible factor in the modern growth of Mediterranean agriculture has been the increasing importance of the tourist industry, which not only brings considerable wealth to the region but also requires large quantities of foodstuffs to sustain it.

PATTERNS OF MEDITERRANEAN AGRICULTURE

Although the Mediterranean region is essentially agricultural, the areal distribution of land fit for tillage is decidedly patchy. This is especially so in Greece and peninsular Italy, where the accidented relief cuts the lowlands into small and relatively isolated parcels, but the mountainous and plateau-like character of most Mediterranean lands has a similar limiting effect, precluding the existence of many large areas of flat, or nearly flat, cultivable land. It is to be expected that high altitudes usually prevent the growing of crops, but it is also true that at lower levels the slopes are often too steep for cultivation, and frequently have a thin cover of poorly developed soils which may be subject to soil erosion. Moreover, we have already seen that in general the soils of the Mediterranean lands are not very fertile, that much of the region suffers from a distinct summer drought, and that the winter rains may be both deficient and irregular in amount. There are also extensive areas of maquis and garrigue where cultivation is impossible and where pasture, even by the omnivorous goat, is difficult.

Yet the limits imposed by relief, climate and soils have not prevented the use of every available stretch of lowland for crop production. Intermont and piedmont plains are watered by rains and by streams which feed irrigation systems; coastal plains are being increased in size by the reclamation of swamps; dry farming techniques have been introduced; and where hill or mountain slopes are not too steep and the soil cover is deep enough, the cultivable area had been extended by terracing, sometimes to altitudes of over 2000 ft (600 m).

A zoning of agricultural activities such as is shown in Fig. 28 is often noticeable. An altitude scale has been included, but since conditions vary considerably from one part of the Mediterranean to another, it must be regarded as indicating very broad limitations. Citrus fruits, for instance, are found everywhere at low altitudes, whereas the vertical distribution of the fig and olive may range from near the base of mountains in northern

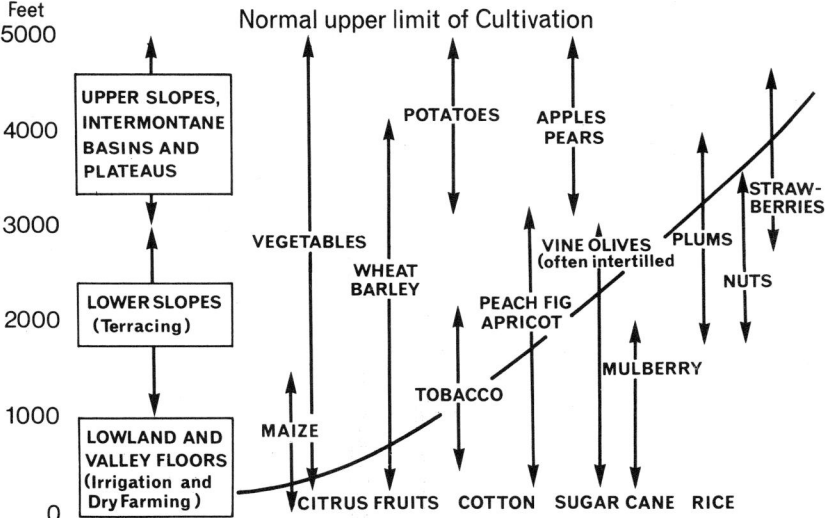

FIG. 28.—Vertical zoning of Mediterranean crops. The vertical range of some crops can be seen to vary widely, since climatic and other factors are very different from one part of the region to another.

Spain to over 5000 ft (1500 m) in southern Greece. Cereals, too, may be cultivated at levels as widely variable as the delta of the Nile and the high, intermont basins in the Betic Cordillera. The zoning shown, however, may be regarded as characteristic of those parts of the Mediterranean lands which have a true Mediterranean climate.

The largest expenses of agricultural land are in the north and west of the Spanish Meseta, the Guadalquivir and Ebro river basins, central Portugal, the lower Rhône valley, the north Italian plain, the Danubian plain in Yugoslavia, the western Anatolian plateau, the Nile valley, the Algerian Tell and the Moroccan Meseta with its adjoining lowlands. Agricultural development varies greatly in these, as it is dependent in part on differences in climate, and in part on the social and economic advancement of the inhabitants. The better seasonal distribution of rainfall in central Portugal, northern Italy and Yugoslavia, and the greater opportunities for irrigation in the Nile, Guadalquivir, Ebro and Rhône valleys have permitted a wider use of the land and a greater variety of crops than in Turkey and the Maghrib lands.

Irrigation is the key to further development, not only in the areas mentioned, but everywhere around the Mediterranean. The large areas of some of the lowlands, however, preclude any very widespread systems of artificial watering at present, either for reasons of cost and practicability or for lack of a convenient and suitable water supply. Nevertheless in the interior of Turkey, the Levant lands, Egypt, and the countries of the Maghrib, irrigation systems are in process of expansion. These are countries where drought is keenly felt and where agriculture faces great difficulties and is backward. It is in these regions, too, that tillage still competes with the pastoral nomad, and where in consequence the amount of land brought under the plough increases only slowly.

From the foregoing it is evident that agriculture around the Mediterranean is not easy. The farmer faces a constant challenge from surface, soil and climate. Over most of the region the peasant cultivator produces little more than sufficient for his own needs, and in some areas he lives at subsistence level. He grows as much as possible on a limited amount of productive land; he sticks to the crops which he knows from experience will give the biggest return in quantity and he disregards quality; he resists official efforts to change his conservatism and persists with out-of-date and backward methods of cultivation; and he exerts such pressure on his land as will inevitably result in progressive infertility. This general low standard of agriculture must be remembered in the rest of this chapter. The favoured areas of reasonably good soils and adequate water supplies, where specialised cultivation of field crops and fruit trees gives a substantial reward to the farmer, are in strong contrast to the far larger acreage where he must scratch a living.

One of the distinctive features of Mediterranean economy is the large proportion of the working population engaged in some form of agriculture. In most Mediterranean territories the proportion is rarely below 50% of the active male workers and may be as high as 80%, compared with less than 20% in the United Kingdom. Proportions vary with the degree of industrialisation and the incidence of city or urban growth, those in the more advanced countries on the European side of the Mediterranean being lower than elsewhere. The percentage of rural workers in France is 45, in Italy 48, in Greece 48, and in Cyprus 37, and it rises to 50 in Spain, 52 in Portugal and 52 in Yugoslavia. The figure given for France refers to the whole country; separate statistics are not available for Mediterranean France. The percentage given, however, which is surprisingly high for an industrialised country in Western Europe, may be regarded as representative of its Mediterranean region. The figure relating to Greece is really too low; it exaggerates the industrial advance of the country and disguises the swollen, often workless urban over-population.

In North Africa the percentage of agricultural workers is uniformly high, ranging from 65 in Egypt to 75 in Morocco. In Egypt, as in Greece,

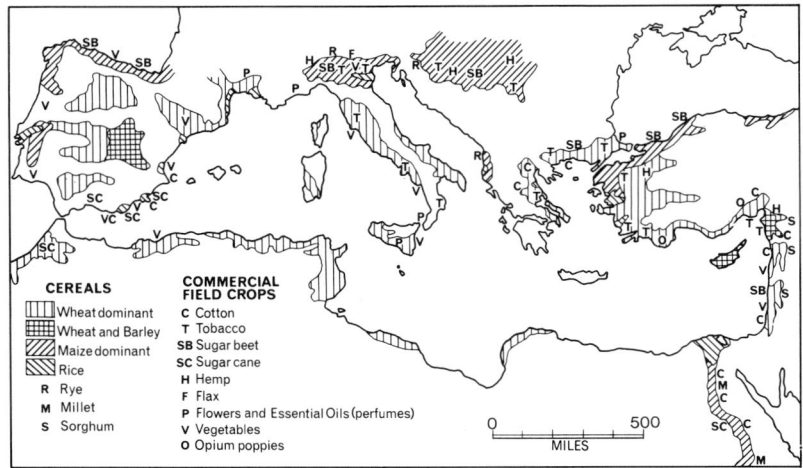

FIG. 29.—The Mediterranean lands: cereals and commercial field crops.

the figure is deceptive, cloaking as it does the tremendous overcrowding into towns and cities, especially in Cairo and Alexandria, where there are hordes of non-productive beggars and vagrants. To the east of the Mediterranean the percentages of rural workers vary from 67 in Turkey to 80 in Jordan, with a notable exception in Israel, where the latest figures show that agriculture supports only about 18% of the working population, the lowest proportion around the Mediterranean and a sign of rapid industrialisation. With regard to all these percentages, it should be noted that official statistics of labour on the land normally refer only to male workers. If we were to take account of the female and child labour which frequently is an intrinsic part of Mediterranean rural economy, many of the percentages given would have to be increased, sometimes substantially, and especially in Israel.

TYPES OF AGRICULTURE

The agricultural products of the Mediterranean lands may be divided into (1) field crops and (2) tree crops. (1) Field crops include cereals, the chief of which are wheat, barley, maize and rice, and a large variety of vegetables (*see* Fig. 29). To these foodstuffs should be added commercial crops such as cotton, tobacco, hemp and sugar. (2) Tree crops are olives, grapes, citrus fruits, peaches, apricots, figs, pomegranates and dates. Nuts and other products from stands of natural forest must also be included under this heading. Cereals are usually grown extensively and most tree crops intensively.

1. *Field crops*

Cereals. The mild, wet winters and warm springs are well suited to the cultivation of wheat and barley, which in most of the Mediterranean lands are cool season crops; and as both these cereals were first developed as food grains in the Middle East, it is not surprising that very early in history their cultivation spread westwards to all the Mediterranean coastlands.

Wheat (*see* Table IV) is the chief cereal in every Mediterranean country except Yugoslavia, Portugal, Egypt and Albania, where its production has been outstripped by that of maize. Extensive areas are under wheat in Turkey, Spain and Italy, and there are large acreages in Greece, Algeria, Morocco, Tunisia, Syria, Egypt, Portugal and Yugoslavia. In the last three, wheat follows maize in the list of cereals. In southern Italy, Sicily and parts of the Spanish Meseta, where the latifundia system of land tenure still obtains, there is almost a monoculture of wheat, but agrarian reforms are gradually inducing a more varied crop output wherever possible. The Maghrib countries, Turkey, and Syria, mainly because of more primitive techniques, have a smaller yield of wheat per acre than most other Mediterranean lands. The production of *barley*, at one time a major food crop, has declined since the beginning of the century, its place having been taken in some countries by summer crops such as maize, rice and millet. It is still important in Turkey, Spain, Morocco, Syria and Cyprus; in the last it remains the chief cereal.

Maize was introduced first to Spain after the discovery of America, of which it is a native. Thence its cultivation spread eastwards in the Mediterranean lands, for not only is it an excellent food and fodder crop, but unlike the native cereals, it can be grown in summer. It needs more water then either wheat or barley, and so its cultivation on a large scale is mainly in sub- and extra-Mediterranean areas which have summer rain, such as northern Spain, northern Italy, Yugoslavia and parts of Turkey, or where there is ample irrigation, as in Lower Egypt and central Portugal. As already noted, maize is the chief cereal grown in Yugoslavia, Egypt and Portugal; in parts of Ribatejo (Portugal) it is almost a monoculture. It is an important crop also in northern Greece, Morocco and Albania.

The increasing cultivation of *rice* round the Mediterranean is noteworthy. Lowland rice, which is the type usually grown, thrives in swampy and waterlogged soils and is tolerant of saline conditions, so it is admirably suited to deltas and salt marshes which are being reclaimed, and to coastal swamps. Rice production in the north of the Nile delta has doubled in the past ten years, and Egypt in some years has a larger tonnage of rice than of maize, which is considered its main cereal. The area under rice is mounting rapidly in the Tagus (Tejo) valley in Portugal, the Ebro delta and some of the huertas in Spain, the Rhône delta and the lagoon coastlands of Aude and Roussillon in Mediterranean France, the lower valley and delta of the Po in Italy, and the Aegean coastal plains in Turkey. Smaller amounts of rice are produced in Greece, Albania and Syria.

Not shown in Table IV are rye, millet and sorghum. *Rye*, which is one of the hardiest cereals, is not grown much around the Mediterranean. In nutritive value, as measured by the amount of gluten it contains, it stands next to wheat, a fact which may explain why it is cultivated in northern

TABLE IV

Cereals, 1964–65

	Wheat		Barley		Maize		Rice	
	Acres (000s)	Tons (metric 000s)	Acres (000s)	Tons (metric 000s)	Acres (000s)	Tons (metric 000s)	Acres (000s)	Tons (metric 000s)
Albania		60		3		192		9
Algeria (north)	5,500	1,121	1,680	359				
Cyprus		45		65				
Egypt (U.A.R.)	1,360	1,500	0·125	0·14	1,745	1,934	1,010	2,036
Greece	3,017	1,387		388	387	289		85
Israel		No	separate figures		available			
Italy	11,020	8,582		250	2,780	3,929	300	617
Jordan	742	295	229	97				
Lebanon		50						
Libya		No	separate figures		available			
Maltese Is.		No	separate figures		available			
Medit. France		No	separate figures		available			
Morocco	3,280	1,196		1,700	1,135	334		
Portugal	1,712	472	276	46	1,215	597	95	178
Spain	10,462	3,983	3,520	1,927	1,385	1,203	160	398
Syria	3,542	1,042	1,817	690				1
Tunisia	2,282	714	1,670	284		5		
Turkey	19,972	8,440	6,800	3,200	1,700	1,000	88	100
Yugoslavia	5,257	3,703	922	534	6,075	6,960		

latitudes ill-suited to the growth of wheat. It is a comparatively recent culture in Mediterranean lands. No traces of rye have been found in Egyptian monuments and there is no special name for it in the Semitic languages. Albania, with about 5000 tons annually, is the largest Mediterranean producer, with Yugoslavia (200 tons) and Italy (100 tons) a long way behind. Elsewhere, the acreage under rye is insignificant. *Millet*, which is probably a native of Egypt and Arabia, has been cultivated in these two countries and in southern Europe from prehistoric times. Its grain is small, but is produced in such profusion that a field of millet may yield five times as much in weight as a similar acreage of wheat. It is not as nutritive as wheat, however, and its cultivation in Egypt and Europe has declined. It is grown mainly in Turkey, which has an annual production of about 53,000 tons on 100,000 acres (40,400 ha). *Sorghum*, also known as great millet, Indian millet, Guinea corn, Kaffir corn and durra, is one of the most important tropical grains. Its culms (stems) and leaves afford excellent fodder for cattle, and its grain, of which the yield is very high, provides meal or flour. Sugar may also be obtained from the juice of its stems. Egypt produces annually about 750 tons of sorghum, mainly for fodder and sugar. Syria is the chief Mediterranean producer, growing annually 50,000 tons of a mixed crop of sorghum and millet on 100,000 acres (40,000 ha), again mostly for fodder.

Table IV, which shows cereal production in the Mediterranean lands in 1964–65 (the latest year for which comparable figures are available), should be read with circumspection. It is important to make comparisons between acreage and output, for this gives some idea of the yield per acre and the standard of cultivation. For instance, Italy is not only the largest producer of wheat in the Mediterranean lands, but its yield per acre (0·77 tons) is also next to the highest; this seems to imply that its farming techniques are superior to those of its neighbours. Turkey grows nearly as much wheat, but needs a far greater acreage for it. Spain has almost the same area under wheat as Italy but produces less than half its total; much of Spain's crop is *secano* wheat (*see* Fig. 27), that is, non-irrigated, and with the very low yield of less than 0·38 tons per acre. In North Africa, Egypt, with a long history of cultivation and a good irrigation supply, has a yield of 1·1 tons per acre, the highest around the Mediterranean; but backward techniques in the Maghrib lands are indicated by yields of 0·36 tons per acre in Morocco, 0·31 tons in Tunisia, and 0·20 tons in Algeria. Local variations and vagaries of climate must, of course, always be taken into consideration; in years of severe drought the yield of all cereals, except where plentiful supplies of irrigation water are available, must be very small.

Vegetables. In all areas of arable land around the Mediterranean a proportion, however small, is given over to the cultivation of vegetables, which everywhere form an essential part of the people's diet. In the majority of cases they are cool season crops. Most vegetables are consumed locally, but the fact that the mild winters enable many varieties to come to fruition early in the year, that is, when there is a shortage and consequently an increased demand in Western Europe, has led many Mediterranean districts to grow vegetables on a commercial basis and specialise in "early" or out-of-season produce. New potatoes, cauliflowers, broccoli and asparagus, which are exported from Spain, the Canary Islands, Italy, Lebanon, Israel, Algeria and parts of Portugal are among specialised products of this type. Potatoes in large quantities are grown everywhere in the cooler and wetter northern Mediterranean lands; and onions are sent out from Spain, Italy and the Canaries. Tomato cultivation is widespread and very important; the fruit enters into commerce as raw fruit, pulp and juice. Wherever plentiful water is at hand, such as between rows of citrus fruit trees, there are notable crops of melons, pumpkins, marrows and cucumbers; and around most cities there is extensive market gardening. Worthy of mention is the cultivation of garlic, a bulbous plant with a pungent taste and very strong odour, which is used for flavouring food dishes by most Mediterranean countries.

Commercial field crops. The chief crops included under this heading are cotton, tobacco, hemp and sugar. Of less importance are flax, flowers and the opium poppy. *Cotton* is easily the most valuable commercial field crop of the Mediterranean lands. It is outstanding in Egypt, where it accounts in value for nearly three-quarters of the exports; in 1965, 496,000 tons were produced, mainly in Lower Egypt. It is chiefly the renowned long-stapled variety which thrives in the long, hot summers wherever irrigation water is abundant, but in recent years other varieties, shorter stapled and with heavier yields, have been introduced with marked success (*see also* page 464). Since 1950 Turkey has become a major producer of cotton, its present annual output amounting to 320,000 tons, principally from the alluvial plains of Adana. Other important growers are Syria (95,000 tons per annum), Spain (75,000 tons), Greece (66,000 tons) and Italy (5000 tons); smaller amounts are contributed by Cyprus and Lebanon.

Tobacco grows in every Mediterranean country and is an export from nearly all of them. Most varieties of tobacco are derived from the Virginian type, seeds of which were brought from America by the Spaniards in 1558. The plant adapts itself to a great range of climatic conditions and will grow on almost all kinds of soil, but the flavour and quality of the produce are profoundly affected by very slight differences in these two factors. Sandy soils produce the bright yellow tobacco used in Virginian cigarettes, while clay soils, retentive of moisture, support heavy-cropping tobaccos which cure to a dark brown or reddish colour and are used more for cigars and pipe smoking. Generally speaking, the warm, moist springs of most parts of the Mediterranean lands give first-class conditions for tobacco cultivation, and the long drought and sunshine of the summers facilitate the open-air drying of the leaves. Racks for this purpose are a familiar sight in the Mediterranean countryside.

The chief tobacco growers, with their annual crops, are Turkey (175,000 tons), Italy (82,000 tons), Yugoslavia (66,000 tons), Greece (62,000 tons) and Algeria (15,000 tons). With smaller commercial totals are Syria (6600 tons), Lebanon (3000 tons) Israel (1500 tons) and Cyprus (800 tons). Turkey and Greece grow the special-flavoured "Turkish" tobacco, mainly in Macedonia, Thrace and the eastern Aegean coastlands, but efforts are being made in both countries to grow more of the orthodox Virginian variety which is preferred by the majority of smokers. Much of the Greek export goes to Cairo and Alexandria for the manufacture of "Egyptian" cigarettes. Italy produces two types: a dark, heavy Virginian tobacco on the heavy, clay soils of the north, and a "Turkish" type on the sandy soils of the south. The distinctive Latakia tobacco, which is usually blended with other pipe tobaccos, comes from the Saida province of northern Syria. Its black colour and peculiar flavour are the results of its being subjected during its drying to a long process of fumigation in the smoke of leafy branches of evergreen oak burnt while still green.

Both *sugar beet* and *sugar cane* are cultivated in the Mediterranean lands, the beet in the cooler, summer-rain regions in the north, the cane by means of irrigation in the hotter, drier south. The chief sugar-producing countries are Italy (1,136,000 tons per annum), Spain (524,000 tons) and Egypt (412,000 tons). Most of the sugar of Italy is from beet, grown in the northern plain. Spain has beet in the Biscayan provinces and cane in the huertas of the south. Almost all Egypt's production is from cane, grown by perennial irrigation below the Aswan Dam; a small proportion is obtained from sorghum. Sugar beet is also grown in Yugoslavia, northern Greece and Turkey, and there are small quantities of sugar cane in Lebanon and Morocco.

The satisfactory cultivation of *hemp* demands a light, rich and fertile soil (*see* Fig. 61). The plant is grown for its fibre, which is coarser and more brittle than that of flax, and is used in the manufacture of ropes, sackcloth, sailcloth and cheap carpets. The very finest hemp is produced in the Piedmont province of Italy (11,900 tons per annum); it bears a close resemblance to the more expensive flax and makes the best ropes and sailcloth. The largest grower of hemp is Yugoslavia (31,200 tons annually). It is grown also in Turkey (12,000 tons), Syria and Lebanon. Commercial hemp belongs to the species *Cannabis sativa*; in the hotter districts of Turkey and Syria some *Cannabis indica* or Indian hemp is grown, not so much for its fibre as for the resinous secretion which develops on its leaves and flowering heads. From the resin hashish is made. This is a dangerous hypnotic drug whose manufacture and sale are forbidden by the laws of most countries.

The cultivation and preparation of *flax* used to be very important in Egypt and the Levant; the manufacture of linen from its fibre is one of the most ancient textile industries. Linen was worn by all classes in ancient Egypt, and it was used as wrappings for embalmed bodies or mummies. In Genesis we read that Pharaoh clothed Joseph in "vestures of fine linen." Flax continued to be the chief fibre crop in Egypt until the end of the eighteenth century, when it was displaced by cotton. Today only a very small area in Egypt is under flax; the leading producer is now the north Italian plain. Even here its cultivation is declining yearly, and the total flax crop of all the Mediterranean lands is negligible in world commerce. Nearly everywhere it is giving way to cotton.

The other commercial field crops worthy of note are *flowers* and *opium poppies*. Both are highly specialised crops, and although they occupy only a small area, they are very profitable. Cut flowers, especially of early spring varieties such as mimosa, daffodils, narcissi and tulips, which in the Mediterranean coastlands bloom several weeks before those of Western Europe, are exported in large quantities, mainly from the "rivieras" of the Western Mediterranean basin. Of greater commercial value are flowers grown for the essential oils which may be distilled from their petals, leaves and stems, and used in the manufacture of perfumes. Mediterranean France around Grasse, Cannes and Nice is the centre of the natural perfume industry, producing rose, carnation, acacia, jasmine, orange-flower and violet oils. Nîmes in Languedoc distils oils from thyme, rosemary and lavender. Sicily produces citron and orange oils; Italy, iris and bergamot (lemon); and Turkey-in-Europe, attar of roses.

The opium poppy is cultivated in Turkey for medicinal purposes; morphine and its derivatives, one of which is heroin, are produced from the seed capsules. The acreage devoted to the poppies is small and strictly controlled by law, but the high value of the drugs often leads peasant cultivators to grow more than the legal limit and pass the surplus to traffickers in illicit drugs.

2. Tree crops

Olives. In its capacity to thrive in thin, stony soils and to withstand the heat and drought of summer, the olive is without doubt the most characteristic Mediterranean tree, so much so that the limits of its distribution are taken to coincide with those of the true Mediterranean climate (*see* page 44 and Fig. 30).

The wild olive, small in stature and with tiny, useless fruit, is found in most Mediterranean lands and eastwards as far as the Caspian Sea. It is indigenous to Syria and the seaboard of Asia Minor, and its abundance in the peninsula and islands of Greece, together with the frequent allusions to it by the earliest poets, suggests that it was native there also. It is possible, however, that in some parts of Greece, where piratical raids or foreign

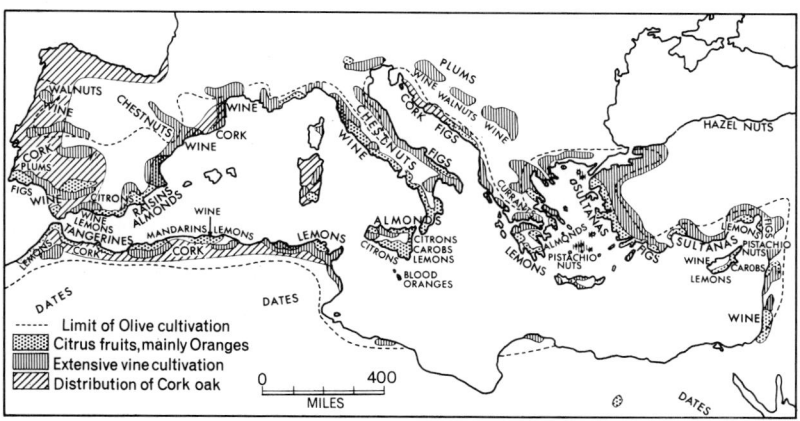

FIG. 30.—The Mediterranean lands: tree crops. Peaches, nectarines, apricots, etc., are grown widely in vine and citrus regions.

invasion led to complete depopulation of coastal settlements, the cultivated olive reverted to the wild type. The wild olive shows a marked preference for calcareous soils and a partiality for sea breezes, flourishing luxuriantly on the limestone slopes and crags which make up a large part of the Aegean coastline.

The cultivated olive is descended from the wild variety, but at what period the improvement took place it is impossible even to guess. Olive oil was already a valuable product of Syria in the days of Homer, which could be as early as the tenth century B.C., and the olive is frequently mentioned in Greek mythology as a symbol of peace and prosperity. Branches of wild olive were carried at the Panathenaea, the chief national festival of ancient Athens, and sprigs of either wild or cultivated olive were awarded to Olympic victors. Roman conquerors returning in triumph were crowned with olive sprays. In its cultivated form the olive was taken from Syria to Greece, and ultimately by Greek, Phoenician, Roman and Semitic mariners and colonists to all the coastlands of the Mediterranean.

It is more compact in shape than the wild variety and, unless confined by constant pruning, which is the usual practice, grows to a height of 30 ft (9 m); in well-tended groves it is normally not more than half this height. It differs from the wild olive, too, in that it can be grown well away from the sea coast. It is planted in rows at regular intervals, in groves which sometimes cover several square miles of the stony hillsides. Olive groves cover 4000 square miles (10,400 sq. km) of Greece, that is, nearly 8% of the total surface. The spaces between the trees are often used for annual crops, for example for wheat in Calabria, but the trees yield better if there is no intercropping. The olive fruit is eaten as a food, but its chief value is as a source of edible oil. Olive oil in most parts of the Mediterranean land forms a substitute for the butter and animal fats consumed elsewhere. Consequently a large proportion of the olives and olive oil produced around the Mediterranean does not enter into commerce, but is consumed locally. Greece, for instance, which in 1965 had an output of 47,500 tons of olives and 145,000 tons of olive oil, exported only 8500 tons of fruit and 16,500 tons of oil. Spain and Italy, which between them grow more olives than any other countries (over 4 million tons a year), actually import olive oil, and together absorb about two-thirds of the world production.

The amount of olive oil produced varies considerably from year to year. Olive trees at their best give a good crop only every other year, and where cultivation is careless they bear abundantly only at intervals of four years or more. Quality, too, depends on the care with which the olive is cultivated; the best oil is said to come from Mediterranean France, Italy and Greece. The largest producers of olives and olive oil are Spain, Italy, Greece, Portugal, Turkey and Tunisia, in that order; and they are followed by Algeria, Syria, Cyprus, Lebanon, Israel, Mediterranean France, Yugoslavia, Albania and Libya. Cultivation is increasing rapidly in North Africa, notably in Tunisia and Libya. Libya is said to have 3·4 million olive trees.

Vines. The vine is almost certainly a native of the Mediterranean lands, and its cultivation as a source of food and drink seems to be as ancient as that of the olive. In the luxurious days of the later Roman Empire it was already a well-established axiom that long and pleasant life depended on two liquids, "wine within and oil without." Grape-stones have been found among the remains of lake-dwellings in Italy and Switzerland, and dried grapes in Egyptian tombs. Today, viticulture has spread to every region of the world which has a climate similar to that around the Mediterranean Sea, and to many other countries where there is a satisfactory combination of limestone soils and hot summers, preferably with not too much rain.

The vine seems to grow best on slopes, which aid drainage. Its long roots can penetrate the drier, permeable, stony surface soils to the damper layers below the water-table. In the Mediterranean lands vineyards do not require irrigation; they cover great stretches of lower hill slopes where the thin soils are somewhat better than those needed by the olive. Most individual vineyards are small in area, only 20% of the total exceeding 5 acres, (2 ha), but they are often so clustered together as to give the appearance of one vast vineyard extending for miles. The largest vineyards are in Languedoc, where the cultivation of the vine is in places almost a monoculture. There are large vineyards also in the Algerian Tell, where until recently viticulture was increasing rapidly and rivalling that in Languedoc. With the achievement of Algerian independence, however, a mass exodus of *colons* has left many of the vineyards neglected and often abandoned.

The wide distribution of viticulture and the ease with which wine can be made from the grapes are a part explanation of the fact that wine is the ordinary drink of most Mediterranean lands. The generally poor quality of drinking water and the dangers from contamination are undoubtedly other factors which have encouraged the drinking of wine. Even where a peasant farmer does not own a vineyard in the accepted sense, he usually has a few vines growing on stretches of his land which are unsuited to arable crops, and he produces enough wine for his own use. In countries which still obey the laws of Islam or where, as in Greece, Yugoslavia and Spain, the people were for long centuries under Moslem domination, the religious interdict against alcoholic drinks led to the drying of grapes to form currants, sultanas and raisins. Today, the export of these dried products forms an important branch of viticulture. Greece has an annual output of over 70,000 tons of currants and about 40,000 tons of sultanas. Turkey produces over 70,000 tons of sultanas a year, and in Spain the influence of the Moorish occupation is seen in the drying of grapes for raisins around Murcia and Valencia.

The chief producer of grapes and wine is France, which markets annually a total of nearly 10 million tons. Of this amount Mediterranean France grows about half the crop, mainly in Languedoc, where co-operative methods are employed for making and marketing the wine. Next in order of production are Italy (8·6 million tons), Spain (3·3 million tons), Turkey (2·2 million tons), Algeria (2·0 million tons) and Portugal (1·5 million tons). Smaller totals come from Greece, Syria, Lebanon and Israel. Altogether, the countries around the Mediterranean Sea produce over 60% of the world total of grapes and wine.

Most of the wine of the Mediterranean lands corresponds to the French *vin ordinaire*, the ordinary drink of the people, and is consumed locally; but wherever the soil and climate are most favourable, vineyards produce high-class wines for the commercial market. Among the best known are sherry from the Jerez district of Spain, port wine from the Douro valley in Portugal, and table wines from the hills of Chianti, Asti, Orvieto and Frascati in Italy. The Spanish huertas of Tarragona, Murcia and Malaga also make good commercial wines, and in recent years Portugal, Cyprus and Yugoslavia have begun to export table wines. There is also a large production and export of table grapes from southern Spain, the Canaries, Algeria, southern Greece, Sicily, Turkey and Israel.

Citrus fruits. The chief citrus fruits grown in the Mediterranean lands are citrons, oranges, lemons, tangerines and grape-fruits. Mandarins, which are a small and very sweet variety of orange, are usually included in the production figures of that fruit.

All citrus fruits flourish in any moderately fertile soil if it is well drained and sufficiently moist, but they prefer stiff loams or calcareous marls. They require a mean annual temperature of 62° F (16·7° C), and so their cultivation in the Mediterranean lands, except in sheltered districts or where artificial protection is given, is mainly south of latitude 42 degrees N. Lemons, citrons and grape-fruits are more delicate and liable to frost damage than oranges and tangerines, and their distribution is limited mainly to frost-free districts. Citrus fruits depend on a plentiful water supply, and so the groves are situated for the most part in lowlands and coastal plains where irrigation is possible. The trees are well spaced in rows, and there is intercropping of melons, pumpkins and annual vegetables. If the fruit is destined for export, it is harvested before it is ripe and carefully packed in boxes; very often each fruit is wrapped separately in paper before it is packed. Much of the fruit, however, is fully ripened and either consumed in the country of origin or pulped for its juice (orange, lemon, grape-fruit) or tinned (mandarin oranges). The peel of the orange, citron and lemon is also candied, that is, encrusted with sugar, and exported for use in confectionery.

The citron is the only citrus fruit indigenous to the Mediterranean. It was known to the peoples of the Middle East in the fourth century B.C. Today it is cultivated chiefly in Sicily, in the extreme south of peninsular Italy, and around Malaga and Almeria in Spain. It is more bitter than the lemon and is rarely eaten in its raw state. Its main use is as a source of citron oil and citric acid, and for the production of candied peel.

The orange was cultivated from a remote period in northern India, but it was not grown in the Mediterranean region until the Arabs in the tenth century introduced it first to Oman, and then via Mesopotamia to Syria. From there, following the tide of Mohammedan conquest and civilisation, its cultivation spread to North Africa, Spain and Sicily. Later, oranges were brought to Italy and southern France by soldiers returning from the Crusades. These first oranges were all of the bitter variety, such as are grown today in the Guadalquivir valley for the manufacture of marmalade, and known as Seville oranges. The sweet or China orange, which had been introduced by Arab seamen to the Levant lands, was carried to Italy by the Genoese merchants of the fifteenth century, and a hundred years later it was brought directly from the Far East by Portuguese navigators, first to the Azores and then to their homeland. The numerous kinds of orange found in the world today, differing chiefly in the external shape, size and flavour of the fruit, are all probably derived from these sweet and bitter sub-species. Besides the common sweet orange, the very sweet mandarin and the Seville orange, may be mentioned the Jaffa from Israel, the blood-orange from Malta, Tunisia, Sicily and southern Italy, and the navel-orange from south-east Italy, Lebanon and Syria. More oranges are grown in the Mediterranean lands than all the other citrus fruits taken together.

The chief orange-growing countries with their annual output are Spain (1·85 million tons), Italy (1·03 million tons), Israel (460,000 tons), Egypt (350,000 tons) and Turkey (253,000 tons). With these major producers should be included Morocco and Algeria, for which separate figures for oranges are not available; they have a total output of citrus fruits respectively of 630,000 tons and 319,000 tons, of which about one-tenth is lemons, and one-quarter tangerines. A considerable proportion of the oranges of these two countries consists of mandarins. Other countries with a substantial growth of oranges are Lebanon (150,000 tons), Tunisia (60,000 tons), Cyrpus (50,000 tons) and Greece (30,000 tons). In Mediterranean France, Portugal, southern Dalmatia and Albania oranges are grown chiefly for local consumption.

The mandarin is remarkable for its very flat spheroidal fruit, the rind of which separates easily with the slightest pressure. Because of its sweetness it is much favoured for canning. *The tangerine*, whose name is derived from Tangiers, was developed in North Africa from the mandarin; it is valued for its fine fragrance.

The lemon, like the orange, is a native of northern India, and was introduced to the Mediterranean lands by the Arabs at the same time as the orange, arriving in Spain during the twelfth or thirteenth century. It is more delicate than the orange and requires frost-free conditions for its successful cultivation. Unlike the orange, too, which has a compact tree shape, the lemon is a straggly bush or small tree, 10 to 12 ft high (3 m). The lemon tree is exceedingly fruitful, a large one in Sicily or southern Spain ripening as many as 3000 fruits in favourable seasons.

The chief lemon producers are southern Italy and Sicily (562,000 tons), Lebanon (80,000 tons), Turkey (37,000 tons), Greece (28,000 tons), Tunisia (13,500 tons) and Cyprus (10,000 tons), plus Morocco and Algeria, mentioned above. The lemons of Malaga in southern Spain are highly esteemed, but they form only a small total in commerce.

The grape-fruit, whose proper name is the shaddock, is allied to the orange and the lemon, and is thought to be native to the Malay and Polynesian islands. Shaddock was the name of a sea captain who is alleged to have introduced the fruit to the West Indies. From there it was brought to the Mediterranean lands less than a century ago. The grape-fruit sometimes has a slight grape-like taste, hence its name. It is cultivated to be eaten as a breakfast fruit either raw or canned; it is also pulped for its juice. The chief Mediterranean growers are Sicily and southern Italy (61,000 tons), Cyprus (15,000 tons) and Israel.

Miscellaneous fruits. Besides citrus fruits, the Mediterranean lands export large quantities of *apricots, peaches, pomegranates and figs* (*see* Fig. 30), and from regions which are extra-Mediterranean in climate come *plums* from Yugoslavia and *dates* from North Africa. Apricots and plums are of course widely cultivated in all temperate countries; those which enter into commerce from the Mediterranean lands are often sun-dried before export, or they may be canned. Dried plums are known as *prunes*: they are prepared from a species of plum, *Prunus domestica*, which is native to the Balkan lands and Anatolia, and from which most other European kinds of plum are descended. Plums for prunes have a firm flesh, a high sugar content, low acidity, and can be dried whole, that is, with the stone, without fermentation. Yugoslavia is the main source of prunes; they are prepared also on a small scale in Portugal, Spain and Mediterranean France. Types of brandy are made from apricots and plums. Peaches require a warmer climate than apricots, and so their cultivation outside the Mediterranean lands is limited to a few favoured districts just beyond their northern boundaries. Ripe peaches are very perishable; rapid transport to foreign markets is essential. Most of the crop seen in the shops of Western Europe comes from Mediterranean France, Spain, Italy, Portugal, Algeria and Morocco. In all these countries the canning of peaches is important, and it is becoming increasingly so in Turkey, Lebanon and Israel.

The pomegranate has been grown in the Levant lands from very ancient times, and these remain the main sources of supply. The fruit, which usually attains the size of a large orange, consists of a hard, leathery rind enclosing a quantity of pulp derived from the numerous seeds. This pulp, which is filled with refreshing, acid juice, constitutes the main value of the fruit. The pomegranate has never become really popular in England. The wild fig is found in most Mediterranean lands. In its cultivated form it occurs chiefly in Italy and Turkey, and large amounts are grown also in Algeria, Syria, Jordan, Dalmatia and southern Portugal. Fresh figs form an important item of diet wherever they are grown; for export figs are usually sun-dried and then compressed into large cubical blocks.

The distribution and value of the date palm have already been noted (*see* page 87). Dates occur as a product throughout the zone of oases which stretches from Morocco through southern Algeria and Libya to Egypt. The dates of commerce come mostly from the Tozeur region of Tunisia, which has an annual output of 30,000 tons. Large quantities of dates are stoned and then compressed into cubical blocks in the same manner as figs. One variety from Tozeur, the excellent *Deglat en Nour*, "finger of light," is carefully packed in small boxes, and is prominent in Britain on the Christmas market. All parts of the date palm yield valuable economic products. The trunk furnishes timber for house-building and furniture; the leaves supply thatch; the footstalks produce a fibre from which cordage can be spun, or they may be used as fuel; and the stones from the fruit can be ground and fed to camels.

Other tree crops. In the extensive deforestation which through the centuries has occurred in the Mediterranean lands, those forest trees which yielded fruits useful as food or sources of oil were spared. In some cases their areas of growth were extended, and today they are carefully exploited. They include stands of chestnut, hazel, almond, walnut, stone pine, pistachio, carob and a type of oak producing nut galls. To them must be added the cork oak, not so much for the acorns on which large numbers of pigs are reared, as for the bark of the tree, the cork of commerce.

The Spanish or edible *chestnut* is abundant in Mediterranean Europe, chiefly in Spain and Italy. The fruit is a valuable food for the mountain dwellers of the Apennines and north-east Spain; they grind the nuts into meal for thickening vegetable soups and even for bread-making. Pigs are reared in the chestnut forests, where they feed on the fallen nuts. Some chestnuts are exported to Western Europe. In Italy, too, the nuts of the *stone pine* are used as food or pressed for oil.

Hazel nuts are common in most European countries; in the Mediterranean lands they form an important cash crop, notably along the Black Sea coasts of Turkey, which has an annual export of about 200,000 tons. *Walnuts* are exported from Yugoslavia (35,000 tons per annum), Portugal, Spain and Italy. *Almonds* are of two types, the common almond used mainly for food and the bitter almond which is a source of oil. Plantations of both kinds of almond are widely distributed in the Spanish huertas, southern Italy, Sicily, and southern Greece. *Pistachio nuts* are the fruit of trees native to Syria, whence they have spread to the other Levant lands, Turkey and Greece. They are smaller than hazel nuts and have an almond flavour. They are esteemed as a food delicacy along the eastern Mediterranean seaboard. One variety of pistachio yields small, edible *cashew nuts*; from it also, by cutting incisions in the bark, an aromatic, resinous exudation known as mastic may be obtained. This is used by the Turks as chewing gum (L. *masticare*, to chew). *Carob* or *locust beans* are a tree crop everywhere from Spain to the Levant lands, but especially in Cyprus (37,000 tons per annum). The beans or pods have a sweet taste and are a food for both men and animals. In Sicily a spirit and a syrup are made from them. *Gall nuts* are growths produced by wasps on oak trees in the northern Levant countries. They are used in the making of printer's ink.

The *cork-oak* grows in all the countries of the western Mediterranean, but its cultivation is mainly in Portugal, Spain and Algeria. The tree is evergreen and reaches a height of about 30 ft (9 m). By annual additions from within, the outer layer of bark becomes a thick, soft, homogenous mass of cork. This is stripped from the tree, the first stripping taking place 15 to 20 years after planting (*see* Fig. 31). Subsequently the bark is removed every 8 to 10 years, the quality of cork improving with each successive stripping. The trees continue to live and thrive under the operation for 150 years or more. Cork has been used since ancient times as an aid to flotation and for the soles of shoes. Surprisingly, it was not employed for stopping bottles until near the end of the seventeenth century. Ground

[*Courtesy of Portuguese State Office*

FIG. 31.—Portugal: stripping and transporting cork in the forests of Alentejo. The tractor-drawn truck is a sign of modernisation.

cork is used today for packing grapes and other soft fruits for export, as a sound insulator, and, mixed with some cementing agent, is compressed to make mats and other objects. The chief producer of commercial cork is Portugal, where one-quarter of all the forested area is covered by cork-oak.

ANIMAL HUSBANDRY

The rearing of domestic animals is subsidiary in the Mediterranean economy to the production of field and tree crops, yet it plays a prominent part everywhere. Animal husbandry may be considered from two main standpoints: (*a*) where the keeping of stock forms an intrinsic part of a complete agricultural programme, and (*b*) where it constitutes the main occupation of the rural population. The first is well exemplified in the mixed farming in most parts of Western Europe; it is far less common in the Mediterranean lands. Mixed farming as we know it occurs chiefly in Galicia, the Biscayan lands, the north Italian plain, the Piedmont foothills and the northern half of Yugoslavia, all of which are extra-Mediterranean and have a better seasonal distribution of rainfall. Turkey, Lebanon and Israel are the only other Mediterranean countries in which the rural economy approaches the mixed farming type. Normally the peasant agriculturist may keep a very few animals such as goats and mules for his own use. Under the second heading, where animal husbandry is the main occupation, flocks of sheep and goats may form part of a transhumant, semi-nomadic or true nomadic system. In the first-named, the animals are taken to mountain pastures during the dry summers and returned to the lowlands in winter. Here they feed on maquis or garrigue or, where the two-field type of cultivation is the rule, they are turned into the fallow to nibble the quick-growing weeds. Transhumance of this kind is common in Mediterranean Europe and some parts of the Maghrib, but in the Levant and elsewhere in the Maghrib it may be that although there are fixed headquarters in the lowlands, the semi-nomadic shepherds remain more or less permanently with their flocks, taking little part in community life and in tilling the land. Their seasonal migration, too, may be outwards in winter to the grazing grounds of the semi-desert. Nomadic pastoralism is confined to the semi-desert and desert regions of the Levant and North Africa (*see also* page 102).

There are few extensive areas of low-lying pasture in the Mediterranean lands. Much of the region consists of mountain ranges or high plateaus, and in any case the long, hot, dry summers are inimical to the growth of rich natural grasses. Moreover, since agriculture gives a better and quicker yield of necessary foodstuffs than pastoralism, the emphasis in all suitable areas is on tillage rather than animal husbandry. In those countries where transhumance and nomadism are dominant, it follows that a large proportion of the surface must be unfitted for cultivation. In consequence, vegetable foodstuffs are scarce, living standards are low and the economy is backward. It is significant, for instance, that organisations such as Oxfam have projects for relief and rural education in countries which are predominantly pastoral; Jordan and Libya are notable examples.

In nomadic and some transhumant regions, there is often antagonism and sometimes open strife between pastoralists and settled cultivators. This enmity is age-old, as the Old Testament story of Cain and Abel reminds us, and it results from the incessant struggle for food and life in areas of deficient and uncertain rainfall and water supply. Today, in all districts where new or improved systems of irrigation are extending the limits of cultivable land, the conflict continues, largely to the benefit of the agriculturist. Areas which until recently were regarded by the nomadic shepherd as traditionally part of his pastures are now fenced off and denied to him. The aggrieved pastoralist, in search of food, raids the fields of the settled farmer, who for the sake of peace may be driven to acknowledge the overlordship and supremacy of the more warlike nomad and pay tribute to him. In the long run, however, it is the shepherd who suffers. He has less extensive grazing grounds; his flocks decrease in numbers and quality; and he has less wool and fewer skins to sell or barter. Much of the political unrest in North Africa and the Middle East has its roots in the struggle between the pastoralist attempting to protect his traditional grazing lands and the agriculturist who is encroaching on them, backed in his efforts by the city merchants and the politicians (*see also* page 103, for the decline of nomadism).

The animals found in greatest numbers in the Mediterranean lands are sheep and goats, followed by asses and mules. The rearing of cattle and pigs is widespread but uneven in concentration (*see* Table V). With the exceptions of Turkey, Yugoslavia and Egypt, most cattle are found in the countries of the western Mediterranean; and pigs are reared least in Israel and wherever Islam is the chief religion. To Jews and Moslems the pig is "unclean," and the eating of its flesh is forbidden. The rearing of camels is confined to the arid regions of the Levant and North Africa.

SHEEP AND GOATS

Both these animals are admirably suited to Mediterranean conditions, the goat more so than the sheep. They are tolerant of the dry, hot summers, although the heat reduces the weight and quality of the sheep's fleece; they can subsist on the poorest of vegetation, where most other animals would starve; and because of their agility they can browse on steep slopes and find sustenance on what appears to be the driest of limestone crags (*see* Fig. 32(a)). The last applies especially to goats, who can maintain a foothold in the most precipitous country. In lowland areas which may be too arid and infertile for arable farming, sheep are kept on maquis or garrigue; or as already mentioned, where the two-field system of cultivation is employed they may be grazed on the fallow or in fields from which the harvest has been gathered in, and will enrich them with

TABLE V

Number of Animals, 1965

(in 000s)

	Sheep	Goats	Cattle	Pigs	Horses	Mules	Asses	Camels
Albania .	1,581	1,120	402	112	(———122———)			—
Algeria (north) .	5,360	2,020	623	62	160	188	341	103
Algeria (Sahara) .	400	350						150
Cyprus .	420	190	35	44	no figures available			—
Egypt .	1,250	723	1,390	17	45	11	950	157
France .	separate figures not available for Mediterranean France							
Greece .	9,590	5,000	1,110	621	328	224	502	—
Israel .	(———342———)		217	—	(———30———)			—
Italy .	(———8,900———)		8,900	5,000	348	289	412	—
Jordan .	no figures available							
Lebanon (1964) .	222	500	92	7	3	6	34	1
Libya .	931	1,250						94
Malta .	11	29	8	13	2	1	2	—
Morocco .	15,000	7,400	2,900	48	542	(———1,125———)		200
Portugal .	4,000	738	1,074	1,500	74	127	237	—
Spain .	17,618	2,284	3,723	5,011	345	844	538	—
Syria .	3,800	751	129	—	67	72	186	14
Tunisia .	4,000	1,001	400	10	70	50	140	100
Turkey .	32,000	21,000	13,200		1,200	216	1,900	46
Yugoslavia	9,400		5,200	7,000	1,100			

Note: San Marino is included with Italy, Gibraltar with Spain, Ifni and Spanish North Africa with Morocco.

their manure. In cultivated areas, even the poorest of peasant farmers also keeps a few goats, but does not allow them to wander uncontrolled; because of their voracious appetites they are carefully tethered away from crops and young trees. Goats in large numbers are more usually found on the garrigue of mountain slopes, or herded with sheep as on the steppe in Turkey and the semi-deserts of Syria, Libya, Algeria and Morocco. Both animals are kept for milk, meat, wool, hair and skins.

The wool of most Mediterranean flocks is of poor quality and the yield small, especially of those owned by nomads. An exception is the fleece of the merino sheep, whose wool is the finest in the world. The merino is a native of North Africa, whence it was taken to Spain by the Moors. At the end of the eighteenth century, Spain was a major exporter of wool especially to England, but after the Peninsular War (1808–14) the trade declined. Most merino wool now comes from Australia, and the export from Spain is of minor importance. Mutton and goat flesh, too, are poor in quality, since the animals are reared on inferior pastures; meat figures very low in the list of exports of all Mediterranean lands. Only the nomadic and semi-nomadic Mediterranean pastoralists, the large farmers and the more prosperous city-dwellers among the peoples may be regarded as meat eaters; for most, olive oil takes the place of animal fats and poultry that of meat.

In all Mediterranean lands where there are mountains or high plateaus, sheep-rearing is usually accompanied by transhumance. In Spain there are large seasonal movements on the Meseta, especially in Extremadura and New Castile, and notably in La Mancha in the latter. In Mediterranean France flocks are carried in summer from the scorched lowlands of the Midi to pastures on the central massif or the Pyrenees. In both France and Spain the animals travel long distances, transhumance being helped by rail and motor transport. More recently, there has been an increased use of artificial foodstuffs for summer feeding in the lowlands. These are costly, but the expense involved can be set off against the saving in transport charges and the reduced amount of labour required; as a result, the numbers of men and animals taking part in the annual migrations are declining.

Transhumance is practised also in the Apennines, the Italian and Yugoslavian Alpine ranges, central peninsular Greece and Turkey. In the Alps, the mountains of Bosnia-Hercegovina and the plateaus of eastern Turkey, away from typical Mediterranean climatic influences, the seasonal movements are up the slopes in summer, down in winter, as elsewhere, but the governing factor here is the cold of winter, not the heat of summer. In the north of peninsular Greece, the Vlach shepherds lead a way of life distinct from the rest of the country and are almost semi-nomadic. The mountains of Cyprus and the hill country of Syria, Lebanon and Israel have semi-nomadic transhumance, where the shepherds often live permanently with their flocks and eke out a precarious existence by subsistence agriculture. In Lebanon there are seasonal migrations of upwards of 20 miles.

[*Courtesy of Portuguese State Office.*

Fig. 32 (a).—Portugal: a shepherd in the Tras os Montes. All the flocks of a village are under the care of one shepherd. His over-coat is plaited from rye straw, which is also used for thatching houses. Rye is the staple cereal in this difficult mountain province.

Sheep- and goat-rearing in the more arid regions of the Levant and North Africa is predominantly nomadic in character. In these areas the numbers of animals given as official (*see* Table V) cannot be regarded as accurate, for nomads are reticent about the extent of their flocks. Indeed, the census figures for the nomads themselves are often no more than esti-mates.

The rearing of sheep and goats in Turkey deserves special mention. Both animals are reared extensively in the European part of the country, especially on the slopes of the Istranca Dağlari, and on the high plateau which occupies a large proportion of Asia Minor there are the greatest flocks of sheep and goats in the Mediterranean lands. In 1965 Turkey had 32 million sheep and 21 million goats. The coarse wools of the native sheep are not suitable for the manufacture of fine cloths. Nevertheless, their quality is being improved by the introduction of merino stock from Australia; and as a producer of wool, Turkey is second only to the United Kingdom among European countries. One quarter of the goats are of the Angora variety, whose long, fine, lustrous, silky coat is known as mohair, a valuable textile raw material which is exported in large quantities.

In the west of Turkey, that is, in western Anatolia, transhumance is common, but eastwards to the mountains of Armenia and Kurdistan there is a gradual change to nomadism. Great efforts are being made to improve agricultural techniques and extend the area under wheat and barley in the present regions of transhumance in western Anatolia, and in the east of the province it is Government policy to convert the nomads to a transhumant way of life, with a fixed headquarters or settlement where agriculture can be developed. In this, and in persuading some of the nomads to work on State farms or in industries being introduced into the towns, Turkey has been moderately successful. On the whole, however, it may be said that a large part of Anatolia and most of Armenia and Kurdistan remain the territory of the pastoralist.

The chief sheep-rearing countries after Turkey in point of numbers are Spain, Morocco, Greece, Italy and Algeria, and for goats the order is Morocco, Greece, Spain, Algeria and Italy. To obtain a truer picture of the importance of these animals in the economy of individual Mediterranean countries, however, the areas of the lands (see Table III) must also be taken into account. For instance, Albania, a small country with an area of 11,097 sq. miles (28,852 sq. km) and a total of 2,701,000 sheep and goats, has an average density of these animals of 243 per square mile; whereas Turkey, with 53 million sheep and goats, that is, more than twice as many as any other Mediterranean country, in an area of 296,000 sq. miles (769,600 sq. km), has a corresponding animal density of 179 per sq. mile. From this we conclude that Albania, over twenty times smaller than Turkey, is far more completely pastoral than the larger country.

HORSES; ASSES; MULES

The progenitors of the horse were natives of steppe or dry grassland; the mountains, forests and thickets of much of the Mediterranean lands are not as suitable for the rearing and use of horses as open stretches of grassland such as are found on the Anatolian plateau, the Danubian plains of Yugoslavia, the Mesetas of Spain and Morocco, and the plains of north Italy, Macedonia and Thrace. These are the chief rearers of horses around the Mediterranean (see Table V), but we must note also the relatively large numbers bred on the desert borders of the Levant and North Africa.

In the Mediterranean lands the horse has always been used for riding rather than for draught or as a pack animal; and although in recent years the motor car has largely displaced the horse as a means of human transport, the possession of horses is still esteemed in Arab countries as a mark of affluence and social superiority. We are familiar with the bodyguards and ceremonial troops of Arab chiefs, mounted on magnificent Arab steeds, as depicted on television and cinema screens. We are less familiar with the workaday animals which are an intrinsic part of the nomadic scene in the Levant, or with the sturdy Barb horses of Morocco and Algeria, admirably suited to their semi-desert environment.

Of far greater value than the horse, whether as draught or pack animals or for riding, are the ass, commonly called a donkey, and the mule (*see* Fig. 32 (*b*)). Biologically the ass belongs to the same family as the horse, although anatomically it differs in structure. It is descended from the wild ass of Africa. The mule is a hybrid, the offspring of an ass and a horse,

[*Courtesy of Italian State Tourist Office.*

Fig. 32 (b).—Italy: Teulada.   Grinding maize in the home by donkey-power.

usually a he-ass and a mare, and cannot reproduce itself. The offspring of a she-ass and a stallion is also a mule, but is often called a jennet, a name which strictly belongs to a small-sized horse of Spanish breeding.

Both asses and mules are hardy animals, more suited to Mediterranean conditions of relief and climate than horses. They are remarkably tolerant of heat, they can find sustenance on poor pastures, they are small in structure and can be housed in very limited space, and they are extremely sure-footed on rocky mountain paths and across broken country. This last makes them invaluable on highlands and boulder-strewn steppe. Asses are stronger than their slight physique would suggest, and can carry surprisingly heavy burdens. Mules possess the patience, endurance and sure-footedness of the ass, and the vigour and strength of the horse.

In every Mediterranean country except Spain asses are more numerous

than mules. They are the principal draught and carrying animals of peasant farmers, and may often be seen yoked with oxen to pull ploughs or
wine carts. Mules are used similarly, but they are employed especially in
difficult mountain country, where their strength and efficiency at high altitudes exceed those of asses; for this reason they are often used as military
transport where motorised vehicles would be useless. The largest numbers of asses are in Turkey, Egypt, Spain and Greece, and of mules in
Spain, Italy and Greece. Cyprus is noted for the breeding of high-class
mules. The large number of asses in some countries is explained by their
presence in the cities, where they are stabled and fed in their owners'
houses and employed for all kinds of urban transport.

CATTLE; PIGS

There are far fewer cattle in the Mediterranean lands than sheep or goats,
largely because of a paucity of rich pastures or suitable fodder. They are
found in greatest numbers in Galicia, the Biscayan lands, northern Italy,
Yugoslavia and parts of Turkey, where summer rains result in more lus-
cious grasses. Elsewhere cattle are reared in cultivated areas and fed on
vegetable refuse or, as in Egypt, herded in the reedy vegetation which
grows along rivers or on marshland. Most are dairy cattle, but dairying
as an established industry is best developed mainly in Galicia and the Piedmont province of Italy. Round most cities, however, there are usually
many dairy cattle to supply the urban population with milk and butter, so
that locally the output of dairy produce is sometimes considerable. In the
vicinity of Lisbon, Istanbul, Beirut, Tel Aviv and Cairo, this is notably the
case; even within the boundaries of the cities the cattle may be kept in
stalls and fed on waste from the markets and vegetable fields. Beef cattle
are reared chiefly in the Biscayan lands and on the steppe of Yugoslavia.
Bulls for bullfighting are bred in the Guadalquivir valley in Spain and the
Douro plains of Portugal; in the *corridas* of Portugal the bulls are not killed.
The use of cattle for draught purposes is common throughout the Mediterranean lands (*see* Figs. 58 and 64); ploughs and farm wagons drawn by
teams of oxen, sometimes yoked to asses or mules, are a familiar sight
everywhere. Turkey has the greatest number of cattle, followed by Yugoslavia, Italy, Spain, Morocco, Egypt, Greece and Portugal.

The keeping of pigs is a normal part of agricultural economy in all
temperate lands, for they can be raised in pens or sties closely adjacent to
the farmstead and fed on vegetable and animal refuse and on skimmed and
waste milk. In Mediterranean lands, however, the hot, dry summers have
kept their numbers down, and in Israel and Moslem countries a religious
ban has reduced pig-keeping to a minimum. Table V shows this very
clearly. Italy, Yugoslavia, Spain and Portugal rear most pigs. Besides those
kept in conjunction with dairy cattle, Italy has large numbers which roam
and feed on fallen chestnuts in the forests of the Apennines, and acorns
support big herds in the cork-oak forests of Portugal and Spain, and in the
common-oak forests of Serbia.

CAMELS

The camel is essentially the "ship of the desert." Camels are usually owned by nomads and employed as beasts of burden and to provide milk. They are found in greatest numbers in the countries of North Africa; in the desert regions of the Levant, however, they occur in considerable strength, even as far north as eastern Turkey. In modern times, with the advent of hard-surfaced roads and motor transport, the importance of camels as desert carriers has declined, and the large, well-guarded caravans, so familiar in the past, are seen less frequently. A camel caravan takes about three months to cross the Sahara, whereas motor vehicles accomplish the journey in a few days. Nevertheless, for the more localised traffic of desert margins, the camel remains the chief means of transport.

LAND OWNERSHIP AND TENURE

Among the factors affecting agriculture and pastoralism in the Mediterranean lands, that relating to land ownership and tenure is prominent; for centuries land ownership has been concentrated in the hands of a few. Large estates bring many evils with them, a notable one being that the owner is often an absentee, leaving the management to a steward or overseer, and showing complete indifference to the well-being of the workers, who have no possible means of improving their standard of living except by emigration.

In some countries, for example Italy, Spain, Portugal, Syria and Egypt, large estates are being broken up for the benefit of peasant farmers, but the process is slow and naturally is obstructed by the wealthy landlords. Moreover, the peasants do not always benefit by the new system. One reason for this is that the small-scale farmer is often at a disadvantage; his comparatively small purchases of seed and equipment generally have to be made at a high unit cost, for price reductions coincident with bulk buying are not available to him. Similarly, he is at a disadvantage with his selling. Usually, too, he cannot afford the large-scale mechanised equipment which is available to wealthy landlords, and this further reduces his efficiency. Indeed, if his holding is very small he is almost inevitably forced into inefficient subsistence farming and the low standard of living associated with it.

In some types of large-scale land ownership, the cultivators may be tenant farmers. Conditions for the tenants vary considerably throughout the Mediterranean. Where the State has expropriated and divided large estates and has in consequence become the landlord, the tenant in return for his rent may receive material help in the form of advice, improved seeds and the loan of machinery and equipment which he could not afford himself. In some countries, however, especially in the Levant and Egypt, he may be charged such exorbitant rents and be liable to such high taxes that the net return to himself is hardly above subsistence standard. In the better forms of tenancy the farmer is encouraged to improve his land and the variety and yield of his crops, but where the tenant is working merely to satisfy the demands of his landlord and the tax gatherer, he becomes dispirited and lacking in initiative, and very low standards of life are perpetuated.

One system of tenancy is known as share-cropping or *mètayage*. Here the landlord provides seeds and implements, and receives an agreed proportion of the crops after taxes are paid. This might appear to be a reasonably good system, for the landlord is involved in the success or failure of the crops, and the tenant is safeguarded against unreasonable demands. In practice, however, it is a very poor system, largely because the share-cropper and landlord are both concerned more with quantity of crops and a quick financial return than with quality and a judicious use of the land. The result is that a minimum of attention is paid to the soil, which becomes progressively impoverished and worn out. Returns become poorer and the onset of poverty even more vicious as the years go by.

Where the peasant farmer is also the owner of his land, the laws of inheritance in many countries have resulted in such fragmentation that many farms consist of very few acres of minute and widely separated fields, some of which may be on stony hillsides. Some countries, notably France, are attempting by legislation to effect exchanges of fields, so as to make the reorganised farms more compact, and are forbidding further fragmentation. Farms of this kind are small; peasant farmers with more than ten acres are counted as prosperous in most Mediterranean lands, and in some Arab countries holdings may be no more than a couple of hundred square yards. In all parts, except the more favoured sub-Mediterranean regions and those of specialised citriculture, the peasant farmer can grow little more than he requires for his own use, and this applies no matter what his terms of land tenancy may be. Any small surplus is swallowed up by the provision of clothing and household necessities; improved farming implements and fertilisers are beyond the peasant's means, and he has no possible chance to accumulate capital. The land is overworked; quantity becomes of more importance than quality; and with an increasingly high birthrate everywhere in the Mediterranean lands, there is severe rural overpopulation.

Poverty strides throughout the region, and is most obvious in those parts such as the southern portions of the European peninsulas and the whole of the eastern and southern coastlands of the Mediterranean, where there is the greatest dependence on agriculture. Moreover, these are the areas with the lowest standards of agricultural practice and the most serious rural overcrowding.

Sad to say, conditions in the more backward areas of the Mediterranean are such that any short-term promises of amelioration are doomed to be fruitless. Even the introduction of manufacturing or other industry seems to provide only temporary relief, as is shown in the north Italian plain and around Naples. The building of new factories creates a demand for labour which cannot be satisfied by the urban population. This is followed by a surge of immigrants into the cities from the over-peopled farmlands, all looking for social security and better standards of living. Their success brings a further influx of would-be workers, but the development of industry is too limited or too slow to absorb them, and perforce they join the ranks of unemployed in the cities. In northern Italy the index of urban unemployment has risen alarmingly in recent years, and there is now urban as well as rural over-population; in Naples there are thousands of homeless beggars who cannot find a living either in the city or in the rich countryside around; and in Cairo the swarms of mendicants present a serious problem to the city authorities.

This gloomy picture is lightened somewhat by the long-term efforts being made by all governments to effect agrarian reforms and, by encouraging the exploitation of mineral and water resources and fostering new industries, to give a better balance to the whole economy. The wisdom of planned growth is realised, and some countries are actively engaged in long-term development plans. In Italy the *Cassa per il Mezzogiorno*, the Fund for the Development of the South, was inaugurated in 1950 and still continues. Yugoslavia in 1947 adopted the first Five-year Plan of Economic Development and has just commenced its fifth in the series. A four-year economic development plan was decreed for Tunisia in 1965, and a three-year plan, started in Morocco in 1966, gives priority to agriculture, tourism and professional training. Turkey is engaged in a series of five-year plans, and in Syria, with a view to relieving rural over-population, there has been partial nationalisation and supervision of industry since 1963. Spain, Portugal and Greece are in process of introducing agrarian reforms as a preliminary to a much wider development and distribution of industry, and Jordan has an ambitious programme of terracing hillsides, planting fruit trees and providing extensive irrigation.

All these efforts must in the long run bring some economic relief and an easement of social distress, but the best results will not materialise until standards of education are lifted, especially in rural areas. In many countries, notably in the Levant and North Africa, up to 50% of the working population may be illiterate, so that Government schemes and regulations for reform have to be explained orally or demonstrated practically, often against native prejudice and tradition, and with inevitable delays and frustration. In addition all the schemes for amelioration are costly. The provision of necessary transport facilities and means of communication involves vast expenditure and investment of capital, and money is wanted for drainage projects, irrigation and hydro-electrical engineering, mineral exploration and exploitation, and for the mechanisation of agriculture where it is possible. But none of the Mediterranean lands is rich; all must depend on capital from abroad.

Fortunately, this is forthcoming in large quantities, especially from the U.S.A. and U.S.S.R.; Greece, Israel and Spain are benefiting greatly from the former, Egypt and Syria are receiving aid from the latter. Great Britain has investments in most Mediterranean countries, but notably in Malta, Israel, Greece and Libya. Albania looks for help from Communist China. The discoveries of oil and natural gas in North Africa brought a flood of investment from and development by all the major Western powers. Large sums of money have been poured into the establishment of light industries in all the Mediterranean lands and a beginning made in heavy engineering; and these, using a surplus of rural labour resultant on agrarian reforms, are helping to bring about a better balance between industry and agriculture. It is, however, a long, slow process of readjustment.

FISHING

Since every Mediterranean country except Jordan abuts on the sea, it might be presumed that fishing would be important, especially where shorelines are long, as in Italy and Greece. Yet the fishing industry within the Mediterranean basin plays only a very small part in the economy of the countries surrounding it. The more valuable fisheries lie outside the basin along the Atlantic coasts of Spain, Portugal and Morocco. This is because of the deficiency of plankton and other fish food in the almost landlocked sea, and the high degree of salinity of its waters, especially in the eastern basin. Within the Mediterranean there is very little deep-sea fishing except for tunny, which migrates from American waters in early summer and appears in the Western basin, where Algeria, Tunisia, Sicily, Sardinia, Mediterranean France and south-eastern Spain share in the catch. Sardines, sprats and anchovies are of local importance throughout the western Mediterranean and along the northern shores of the Eastern basin, and here and there varieties such as stone fish and tiny octopuses, unknown in northern waters, are caught for local consumption.

Inshore fishing for crabs, lobsters, shrimps, prawns and oysters is carried on everywhere within the Mediterranean basin and along the Atlantic shores; the rocky coasts of Galicia and north Portugal are noted for their abundance of shellfish. In Atlantic waters, Morocco, Portugal and Spain share in the most important sardine fisheries in the world; the Portuguese canneries at Setúbal and along the Algarve coast have almost a monopoly in the export of sardines to the United Kingdom. Spain and Portugal have also long-distance cod-fishing fleets which visit the Newfoundland Grand Banks.

Other marine products of the Mediterranean are sponges and red coral. Sponges are harvested in the shallow waters of the southern Adriatic and eastern Aegean seas, and along the Tunisian and Libyan coasts. The chief supply comes from the waters around the Dodecanese islands, where sponge-diving is a traditional occupation. Red coral, which is used in making brooches, necklaces and other decorative articles, is abundant in waters up to 50 ft deep off the coasts of the Maghrib, Catalonia, Corsica, Sardinia and Provence, and near Naples and Leghorn.

Inland fishing is of considerable importance, especially in the Middle

East and North Africa. All countries make use of fish in rivers and lakes, but in these two regions the tendency for the population to concentrate near rivers and freshwater lakes has sometimes made inland fishing more important than sea fishing. In Egypt, for instance, the lakes in the Nile delta and Faiyum have a yield far in excess of that of its Mediterranean waters; and in Israel, Lake Tiberias teems with fish. Some countries, too, notably Israel, have constructed artificial fishponds and stocked them with fish such as carp. More than three-fifths of Israel's total catch is from fishponds.

STUDY QUESTIONS

1. Outline the significance of irrigation in the human geography of the Mediterranean lands. (London.)

2. What are the physical and climatic problems which may face the agriculturist in the Mediterranean lands? How does he attempt to solve them?

3. Discuss the part played by transhumance in the rural economy of the Mediterranean lands. (London.)

4. Explain the significance of wheat, wine, vegetable oil and fruit in the economic geography of the Mediterranean lands.

5. Discuss the geographical factors (physical and human) which underlie the distribution of viticulture in the Mediterranean lands. (London.)

6. Describe and account for the cultivation and distribution of *three* of the following in the Mediterranean lands: cotton, wheat, maize, tobacco, lemons.

7. Write a short essay on animal husbandry in the Mediterranean lands.

8. With special reference to the Mediterranean lands, give a reasoned account of *two* of the following: (*a*) dry farming, (*b*) deforestation, (*c*) land tenure, (*d*) rice cultivation.

9. "There is a growing tendency in some of the Mediterranean lands for wheat and barley to be replaced or supplemented as food crops by maize and rice." Expand this statement, and show in which countries it is true.

10. Which are the chief commercial crops grown around the Mediterranean? Give an account of their distribution and of the physical and human conditions necessary for their successful cultivation.

11. "The large-scale cultivation of trees is a most important part of the Mediterranean rural economy." Enlarge on this statement with special reference to any *one* Mediterranean country.

12. Write an account of the distribution and cultivation of citrus fruits around the Mediterranean.

13. Make a broad survey of sheep-rearing in the Mediterranean lands, relating your answer to nomadism, semi-nomadism and transhumance.

14. Write descriptive notes on *three* of the following as they apply to the Mediterranean lands: (*a*) the use of animals in transport, (*b*) fishing as part of the economy, (*c*) the commercial collection of nuts, (*d*) cork oak, (*e*) rural poverty.

Chapter VIII

HUMAN RESPONSE: ECONOMIC (II)

INDUSTRIAL DEVELOPMENT

THE opening of the Suez Canal in 1869 was an event of major importance in the industrial history of the Mediterranean lands. Up to this date every country in the region had for centuries been socially, economically and politically in a state of decline, although early in the nineteenth century there were vague signs of a recrudescence. Great Britain and France had begun to interest themselves in Egypt, and France had taken over control first of Algeria and later of Tunisia. Their motives, however, were suspect; they certainly brought some slight benefits to the African countries, but their main purpose was to increase their own spheres of influence and trade. In the middle of the century the growth of nationalism and the striving for independence in Italy and the Balkan states was to have far-reaching results on the European side of the Mediterranean. By 1866, Italy, for long divided, had become a single independent sovereign kingdom; and with the gradual overthrow of the Ottoman Turks in south-east Europe, Greece and some of the states which now comprise Yugoslavia achieved independence. Freedom, however, did not bring prosperity. The new countries remained wretchedly poor, their economies were backward, and there seemed little immediate prospect of improvement.

A change for the better came with the impact on the Mediterranean lands of the Industrial Revolution in Western Europe and with the vastly improved rail and water transport made possible by the technological advance which formed part of it, and of which the cutting of the Suez Canal was a consequence. The Mediterranean Sea ceased to be a maritime cul-de-sac, and became the chief highway of commerce between Western Europe and the Far East. Shipping began to abandon the longer, more hazardous route around the Cape of Good Hope in favour of the shorter, safer voyage via the Mediterranean and Red Seas. With the construction of the roads and railways through gaps and tunnels in the mountain rim on the north, trade soon began to pour into the Mediterranean from the rejuvenated ports of Marseille, Genoa, Trieste, Salonika and Constantinople (Istanbul). Industries such as shipbuilding and repairing received new life; around Barcelona and in north Italy textile industries based on local supplies of wool, silk and flax were given renewed impetus; and food processing and manufactures based on agricultural produce, encouraged by demands from Western Europe, took root and flourished in all the ports.

In this present century the movement to industrialisation has continued in all the Mediterranean lands. At first, progress was slow and hesitant, mainly because power resources were lacking. Coal deposits are scanty, and for as long as coal had to be imported, industries which depended on it as a fuel remained poorly developed and restricted to a few areas near the major ports. The first moves towards industry lay in an increase of the old-established manufactures mentioned above, and in the exploitation of non-ferrous minerals such as copper, mercury, sulphur and bauxite, whose unprocessed ores were exported to Western Europe. The Mediterranean lands became primarily suppliers of raw materials rather than industrial regions in their own right.

The advent of hydro-electricity as a means of power heralded the beginning of a new era. Water-power potential is great in all the high mountains on the north of the Mediterranean and to a less degree in those of the Maghrib; and although the value of rivers with a Mediterranean régime is low, it has been found possible in many instances to store enough winter precipitation to keep most hydro-electricity stations running throughout the year. One result of the new source of power was to make the older industrial regions and districts, such as those in north Italy and north-east Spain, comparable in development with some in Western Europe. Another effect, of far greater general significance, was the birth of completely new industrial installations in areas where previously there were none at all. This was especially the case in parts of Spain, Portugal, peninsular Italy, inner Yugoslavia, Morocco and Egypt, where not only have the newly-born industries brought much-needed revenue to the economy, but they have also given some relief to an overcrowded rural population.

The discovery of mineral oil in the Middle East and its use as an industrial fuel was a further help to the Mediterranean lands. At first, its impact was felt because pipelines were constructed to delivery points on the Levant coast, and refineries were built at Baniyas, Tripoli (Lebanon), Sidon and Haifa. Installations and maintenance brought engineers and technical experts from Western Europe and the U.S.A., and with them came a host of subsidiary industries and a new way of life. More recently, large deposits of mineral oil and natural gas have been found and exploited within the Mediterranean basin itself, chiefly in Italy and North Africa. Although as yet these have not led to many industries other than those connected with the extraction, transport and preparation for export of the products, the wealth they have brought to the regions concerned must have a beneficial effect on future industrial development.

Nuclear power stations are also beginning to make their appearance around the Mediterranean. Italy already has three, at Latina, Garigliano and Trino Vercellese. The last-named, known as the Enrico Fermi station, has an annual output of 2000 million kWh, and claims to be the largest nuclear power plant in the world using enriched uranium 235.

The Mediterranean lands would appear to be entering on a new period of prosperity. At the same time, a word of caution is necessary. Although the supremacy of coal as a source of industrial fuel and power has declined with the growing use of hydro-electricity, mineral oil, natural gas and nuclear power, a fact which seems to favour the Mediterranean lands, the industrial regions of Western Europe and North America have had the advantage of two centuries of progress, during which the Mediterranean lands were in a state of social torpor and economic backwardness. When neglect and inaction have been prominent over such a long period they produce regrettable effects which cannot be remedied quickly, and successful competition with older-established industrial regions is difficult to achieve. Moreover, as we shall see, the Mediterranean lands as a whole are poorly endowed with mineral resources other than petroleum and natural gas, and with a few possible exceptions have limited quantities of other raw materials which can serve as a basis for large-scale industrialisation.

The development of industry even on a small scale is dependent on various factors. In the remainder of this chapter these will be examined with special reference to the Mediterranean lands under the headings: Fuel and Power Resources; Minerals; Other Raw Materials; Communications and Transport; Labour and Markets; Industries and Manufactures.

FUEL AND POWER RESOURCES

COAL AND LIGNITE

The Mediterranean lands are sadly lacking in coal deposits. Geologically this is to be expected, since most Mediterranean countries were born of the Alpine orogenesis and have structures which were formed mainly since Carboniferous times. Only in Spain and Turkey are there any extensive seams of coal, and here they lie in extra-Mediterranean districts (see Fig. 33). Spain produces annually about 13 million tons of coal, principally from the Oviedo coalfield near the Biscayan coast. Turkey's fields, which extend 100 miles (160 km) along the Black Sea coast from Eregli to Zonguldak, yield 4 million tons a year. These totals pale into insignificance beside the 125 million tons annually from the Ruhr coalfield or the 120 million tons from the Upper Silesian field.

Portugal has a few seams of coal north-east of Oporto, and Spain has a further two fields of poor quality near Bélmez and Puertollano on the northern flanks of the Sierra Morena. Nearly all Italy's coal production is from a small field around Carbonia in Sardinia; Yugoslavia mines about 1 million tons in Serbia; and Albania has an output of about 250,000 tons a year. Morocco has a growing production of anthracite from a field at Djerada which is said to have reserves of 100 million tons; and Algeria has two fields, one at Kenadsa and one at Colomb Béchar, but their small size and remote location are great drawbacks to development. Kenadsa has an annual output of only about 120,000 tons, and the field at Colomb Béchar is as yet unexploited.

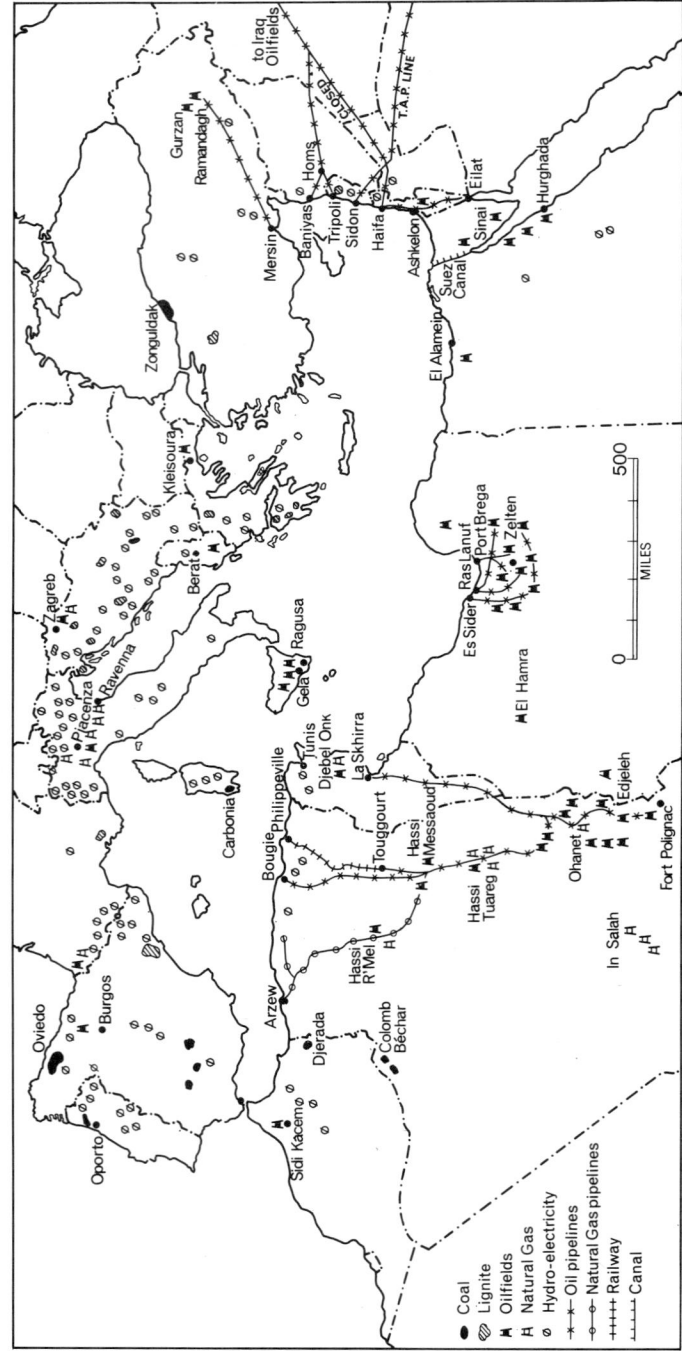

FIG. 33.—The Mediterranean lands: fuels and power. The chief oil and gas pipelines are named, and the ports marked are pipeline terminals. Compare with Fig. 38. A new pipeline to Port Harega in Libya is shown on Fig. 104.

Coal of the lowest rank is called lignite. It has not been as fully car-bonised as hard coal and anthracite, and usually vegetable structures can be seen in it. In some varieties, sometimes called *brown coal*, the woody tissues are not so plain. Lignites and brown coals are much younger than hard coals, and are commonly found in basins in Cretaceous and Tertiary formations. They are much more widely distributed and occur in greater quantities around the Mediterranean than hard coal. The largest output at present is in Yugoslavia, where four fields produce annually upwards of 23 million tons. Turkey has several deposits which yield a total of 2 mil-lion tons a year. Albania excavates roughly 300,000 tons per annum from surface workings; Lebanon mines a small amount; and Mediterranean France uses a deposit north-east of Marseille for the reduction of bauxite to alumina at La Barasse.

Greece has several lignite fields, not all of which are being exploited. A large deposit in Euboea is used mainly for the generation of thermal elec-tricity, and there are smaller fields not yet mined in the plains of Patras, Olympia and Messene. The greatest possibility is in western Macedonia, where deposits estimated to total more than 9000 million tons have been discovered; on these the Greeks have based the Ptolemaís scheme (*see* page 336).

PETROLEUM AND NATURAL GAS

The large accumulations of mineral oil and natural gas which are found in exploitable fields result from earth movements. The widely dispersed oil globules in the original sedimentary rocks can come together only if suitable reservoirs are formed by slight folding or by faulting; and if there are both an overlying layer of impermeable rock to prevent the oil reach-ing the surface and being lost by evaporation, and an underlying im-pervious stratum to act as a floor on which the oil can rest. Large-scale folding such as is found in the Alpine system is unfavourable to the pre-servation of oil; but where sedimentary strata are lying on a rigid platform of crystalline rock, as in North Africa and the Middle East, folding is re-duced in intensity, and long series of anticlines and synclines occur with a minimum of faulting. These provide conditions for the accumulation of oil; anticlines form the commonest form of petroleum reservoir. Mineral oil, however, may be preserved in other types of crustal structure (*see* Fig. 34).

Within the Mediterranean lands, the conditions which would seem most favourable to the formation and preservation of petroleum occur mainly on the northern edges of the Saharan region, in Morocco, Algeria, Libya and Egypt, in all of which oil is being exploited. It has also been found in Tunisia, but details are not yet available. The petroleum was formed in the Tethys geosyncline, in warm waters rich in organic life and over a long period of sedimentation; and during the ensuing Alpine earth movements a slight folding of the surface strata south and east of the Atlas mountain series produced suitable anticlinal reservoirs. The largest oil

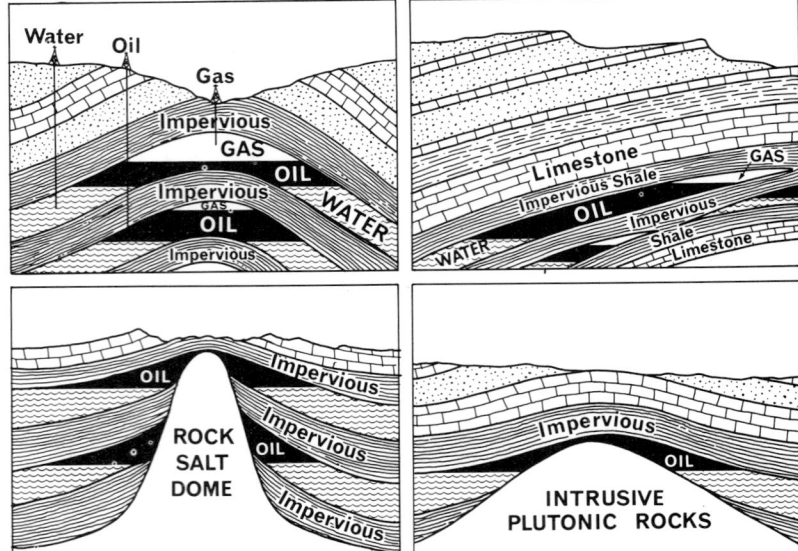

FIG. 34.—Sections to show some geological structures favourable to the accumulation of petroleum and natural gas. The most common oil-containing rock is sandstone and the most common cap-rock is shale.

deposits found so far are in Libya, which had an output in 1965 of 58·5 million tons of petroleum. In the same year two large fields in Algeria produced 26 million tons, Egypt had a total of 6·4 million tons from the Sinai peninsula and the area between the Nile and the Suez Canal, and Morocco had an output of 100,000 tons. Exploration for oil is continuing throughout the desert margins of North Africa; the discovery of a new and extensive field 12 miles (19 km) south of El Alamein in Egypt has recently been reported.

In 1940 oil was discovered in Turkey at Ramandagh, about 60 miles (96 km) east of Diyarbekir, and in 1951 a further strike was made not far away, at Gurzan, but hopes of a large production from either have not been realised. The total at present is about 1·5 million tons a year. Extensive prospecting is proceeding in the plains around Adana and Iskenderun, and between Diyarbekir and Mardin, where favourable geological formations offer greater promise of success. In the Middle East, the major oil deposits found so far lie east of the boundaries of the Levant lands. Good structural formations, similar to those in Turkey, occur in Syria and Lebanon, and exploration has taken place in the Bekaa and between Homs and Palmyra; up to the present, however, although there are signs of oil, no real flow has been obtained. In Israel, too, there has been no major strike; in 1965, there was a total output of 200,000 tons. It is thought, however, that oil in paying quantities exists in undiscovered fields southeast of Gaza.

On the European side of the Mediterranean, Italy has the biggest production of oil. There was already a small output from a field near Piacenza in north Italy when in 1953 a major deposit, said to be one of the largest in Europe, was discovered in Sicily around Ragusa, Gela and Fontanarossa. A second field has been discovered more recently around Caltanissetta and Enna, in the middle of the island. Italy's annual production is about 2·6 million tons and is increasing. An oilfield south-east of Zagreb in Yugoslavia yields over 2 million tons a year. In 1963 Greece struck oil at Kleisoura, and in 1964 oil was found in Spain about 40 miles north of the city of Burgos, but it is still too early to say if either deposit is at all substantial.

Natural gas or methane may also be found in association with petroleum. It is formed in the same way as mineral oil and is a direct result of organic decomposition. It may overlie or be dissolved in the upper layers of the oil, but occasionally deposits of natural gas occur without oil being present. Such is the case in north Italy, where in 1945 enormous deposits of methane were found at Caviaga, east of Milan. Subsequently it was discovered that natural gas underlies most of the plain south of the river Po as far east as Ravenna. The economic consequences of the exploitation of this resource as a power fuel and raw material are inestimable. The gas is distributed by pipeline for use in thermal electric stations, industrial plants and for household purposes, and it serves also as the basis of the manufactures of nitrogenous fertilisers, synthetic rubber and a large variety of other chemicals. Small quantities of natural gas are found near the Yugoslavian oil-field mentioned above.

Far surpassing the European deposits of methane are those discovered in 1961 in the Algerian Sahara, first at Hassi R'Mel, and later at Hassi Tuareg, Ohanet and the Ahnet district. In total the reserves of gas in these fields are estimated at 80 billion cubic feet (*see also* page 401). From the Hassi R'Mel deposit a 300-mile pipeline carries gas to Arzew, a port near Oran, where it is liquefied at a temperature of −258° F (−161° C), and exported in specially constructed ships. The world's first commercial cargo of liquefied methane was despatched from Arzew to Canvey Island, Essex, in October 1964. It is also being exported to Le Havre, and in March 1966 an agreement was signed by which Algeria is to supply Spain with methane for 15 years. The extent of the oilfields in Libya and Algeria has raised hopes that further exploration will lead to more finds of natural gas there and in the neighbouring countries of Morocco and Tunisia; mineral oil and methane were reported in 1964 to lie in association near Sfax.

WATER POWER

The mountainous character of so much of the Mediterranean lands suggests the possibility of a rich endowment of water power potential. We have to remember, however, that the incidence of severe summer drought over most of the region inevitably means that for the most part river levels drop sharply at that season; indeed, many of the smaller streams dry up altogether. Nevertheless it may be said that on the whole the Mediterranen lands have adequate and in some cases rich supplies of flowing water suitable for the generation of hydro-electricity. The Cantabrians, Pyrenees, Alps and Dinarics have rain or snow at all seasons, so that most of the rivers flowing from them can be used at all times. In summer, when the volume of these rivers would normally be reduced by evaporation, it is augmented by snow-melt. The mountains of Turkey, especially those which give birth to the headwaters of the Euphrates, are useful sources of water power, and so to a less degree are the Atlas ranges. The Apennines, Betic Cordillera and Spanish sierras are not so well endowed, for the summer drought is more keenly felt in these ranges, but reservoirs have been constructed and rivers diverted to them to ensure a flow of water to generating stations during the dry season.

One of the problems facing engineers responsible for the siting and building of hydro-electric power stations and retaining dams for reservoirs in many of the Mediterranean lands is that a very large proportion of the mountains is composed of limestone. Limestone is usually jointed and is permeable, so that most of the precipitation is absorbed. The surface of the rocks may be dry, but vast stores of subterranean water are built up, either percolating through the limestone or accumulated in natural underground reservoirs. These waters may escape to the surface at lower levels and help to maintain a regular river flow, even in periods of severe drought. This is notably the case in the Apennines, Dalmatia, parts of the Sierra Nevada, and the Middle Atlas of Morocco. It is an obvious advantage to have this constant water supply, but for the engineer the jointed character of the rock, especially in parts of the Alps, presents its own problems in dam construction. Under the great pressure exerted by large volumes of water in artificial reservoirs, the jointed limestones along the side walls may slip, with resultant huge overspills and floods, landslides and disastrous losses of property and possibly of life in the lower valley. At the least, in many reservoirs built in regions of severely jointed limestones there are wasteful losses of water through the permeable surface layers. These are reasons why, for instance, there is little or no development of water power along the river Durance and in the Maritime Alps in Mediterranean France.

Italy is outstanding in the Mediterranean lands as a generator of hydro-electricity, having an annual output of more than 46,000 million kWh, and claiming to be the largest generating country in Europe. Almost every suitable river in the Alps is utilised, and there are stations in the central Apennines along the rivers Nera and Valino, in the Lucanian Apennines and in Sardinia. A very recent construction is the Valmalenco Dam at Alpe Gera, completed in 1964. The dam, which lies at an altitude of 10,262 feet (3128 m), holds back a lake fed by waters from the southern slopes of the Bernina massif in the Bergamo Alps and, in turn, the lake feeds three power stations.

The development of hydro-electricity in Spain has been phenomenal. In the past quarter of a century over 1000 generating stations have been built, with a total output of more than 21,000 million kWh a year. The majority of the plants are in the Cantabrians and eastern Pyrenees; others are located along the coastal huertas and in the Central Sierras. In many cases the water from hydro-electric stations is used to feed irrigation systems; in others, the waters collected for irrigation have been used for small generators which supply power to very limited districts. The rivers of the Meseta are not very suitable for hydro-electricity generation. They flow in deeply entrenched valleys where dam construction would not be difficult, but their greatly reduced volume in summer is a serious drawback. Only near Madrid has there been much development.

Opportunities for the use of water power in Portugal are confined to the mountains of the north, especially in the provinces of Minho and Beira Baixa, where rainfall is more reliable. The schemes provide power principally to Oporto and Lisbon, the chief industrial cities, and they have also enabled new industries to take root in rapidly-growing towns in the Tagus basin. The latest development is a project known as the Douro River Scheme, situated on the frontier between Portugal and Spain and controlled jointly by the two countries. Three dams are being built to impound the river on the Portuguese side, the largest situated at Bemposta, and at Aldeavitla in Spain a power station is being built with an installed capacity of 855,000 kW. It will ultimately produce 2440 million kWh per annum, which is equal to 10% of Spain's present total hydro-electric power output. The project will allow irrigation of about 275,000 acres (111,100 ha) of the river basin, and it will make possible the exploitation of large iron ore deposits which have been discovered at Moncorvo, south-west of Bemposta. It is also estimated to increase Portugal's hydro-electric output to 8500 million kWh.

As already mentioned, the Alps of Mediterranean France are mostly unsuitable for the construction of hydro-power stations. The region, however, benefits from a large transmission of current from the harnessing of the Rhône, notably in the giant Donzère–Mondragon project near Montélimar. In the west of the region a series of small hydro-electric stations is centred on Sabart in the eastern Pyrenees and supplies power to Carcassonne and other towns in western Languedoc.

Yugoslavia is very rich in water-power possibilities, as might be expected from its relief and ample rainfall. From virtually no hydro-power development before the Second World War, the country now has an annual output of over 7000 million kWh, and this is only one-tenth of the estimated potential. The chief stations are in the Karawanken Alps, the Dinaric Alps draining to the Adriatic, and along the valleys of the Sava and its right-bank tributaries. In Greece the highlands, although extensive, have poorly distributed possibilities for hydro-electric development. There are few stations completed, and these are in the west of the peninsula, where population is poor and communications difficult (*see*

Fig. 33). The annual total output remains at less than 1 million kWh. Albania has good water-power resources. It claims to have four installations developing a total of 259 million kWh a year, but details are not to hand.

Hydro-electric power has made slow progress in Turkey, although there seems to be great potential along the Black Sea coast, the inner slopes of the Pontic ranges, the outer slopes of the Taurus and in the south-east of the country. The present annual output amounts to just over 100 million kWh, mainly from installations on the rivers Seyhan and Kizil Irmak. The former provides power to the Adana area, the latter to Ankara. In 1966 the foundation of the Keban Dam was laid near the confluence of the east and west branches of the river Euphrates in south-east Turkey. When complete, this project will generate 6 million kWh a year, and will transmit power to western Anatolia and Istanbul.

In the Levant lands the use of water power for the generation of electricity is only in its infancy, and stations which have been constructed are secondary to the irrigation systems of which they form a part. Swift-flowing and well-filled rivers are rare, and so the power installations are small and of low generating capacity. The Orontes river in Syria was harnessed at the Maharde Dam in 1962, for irrigation and hydro-electric purposes. In Lebanon a hydro-electric station has just been completed on the river Litani, and in Israel there is provision for generating stations on the Jordan Project which was due to be in full use in 1968. This spectacular scheme will dam Lake Tiberias to form a giant reservoir, and will carry water by pipeline to the south of the country, where irrigation channels will transform the semi-desert Negev. The project will also supplement irrigation systems *en route*. In 1966 Jordan commenced the Mukhaida Dam project on the Yarmuk river, near the Syrian border, about 125 miles (200 km) north of Amman. The primary object of the scheme is to divert the river Yarmuk into the East Ghor Canal and take its waters for irrigation to the shores of the Dead Sea, but it will also have power generating stations.

Similarly, the main purpose of the dams constructed along the river Nile in Egypt was to make perennial irrigation possible; the generation of hydro-electricity was secondary, and stations at the Sennar and Aswan Dams produce only a small amount of current. With the completion of the High Dam at Aswan, however, and with a generating station an intrinsic part of the scheme, Egypt is estimated to achieve a total of nearly 900 million kWh a year, which would place it high among the countries of North Africa as a producer of hydro-electric power. At present, Morocco has the greatest hydro-power development in North Africa, chiefly in the Middle Atlas; 92% of its electricity plants are water-driven and yield a total of over 1300 million kWh a year. Hydro-power prospects in Algeria are not as good as in Morocco; 1100 million kWh are produced annually, chiefly in Kabylia. Tunisia has several small stations with a total output of just over 3 million kWh, but Libya has no hydro-electric power.

MINERALS

The Mediterranean lands as a whole are poor in mineral ore resources. Nevertheless in some countries there are valuable deposits of iron, copper, lead, zinc, bauxite, tungsten, chrome and cobalt ores, together with large quantities of phosphates and potash; and to these may be added smaller amounts of manganese, tin, mercury, antimony, sulphur, silver, magnesite, nickel, uranium and asbestos. In this section a general account is given of the distribution and production of the chief minerals (*see* Fig. 35). More detail in respect of individual countries is left to later chapters.

The richest deposits of *iron ore* are situated in Spain, Algeria, Morocco and Yugoslavia. High-grade haematite occurs in the hinterland of Bilbao, Santander, Gijon and Vivero in Biscayan Spain, and lower-grade ores are found near Teruel, Badajos, Granada and Cartagena. In Algeria there are several fields of non-phosphoric iron ore in the Tell and near Tebessa; in Morocco there are workings near Melilla, with reserves around Essaouria, Casablanca, Kenifra and Meknes. The chief iron-field in Yugoslavia is near Ljubija; other deposits situated in the Sava valley have not as yet been fully exploited. Iron ore occurs also in Tunisia (at Djerissa), Egypt (near Aswan and in the Bahariya oasis), Italy (mainly in the isle of Elba), Portugal (at Moncorvo), Albania (in the eastern mountains), and Greece (around Phthiótis).

Included at this point because they are associated with iron in the manufacture of steel alloys are tungsten, manganese, chrome (chromium), cobalt and ilmenite. *Tungsten* (wolfram) is the chief mineral ore produced by Portugal, about 3000 tons per annum coming from deposits in the provinces of Minho and Beira Baixa. Since the annual world production of tungsten is not much more than 20,000 tons, Portugal's contribution is relatively large. There are also small deposits of tungsten in Spain. The Mediterranean lands rank high also in the output of *chrome ore*, producing roughly one-third of the world's supply. The bulk comes from Turkey, whose deposits at Güleman, Fethiye, Bursa and Eskişehir yield upwards of 500,000 tons a year, which is about 25% of the world total. Other deposits of chrome occur in Thessaly and near Phthiótis in Greece, in the eastern mountains of Albania and around Skopje in Yugoslavia.

Manganese deposits are widespread around the Mediterranean, but the total production, about 250,000 tons a year, is less than 5% of the world output of 5·3 million tons. Morocco (175,000 tons) is the chief Mediterranean producer, followed by Turkey (21,000 tons), Greece (16,000 tons), Spain (16,000 tons), Italy (13,000 tons) and Algeria (10,000 tons). Deposits of manganese in Yugoslav Macedonia are just beginning to be exploited. *Cobalt* has been found around the Mediterranean only in Morocco; the amount produced there, 1·3 million tons per annum, places the country fifth in the world for this ore. *Ilmenite* is iron-titanium oxide; it is mined chiefly for the *titanium* content, a mineral which is widely diffused but rarely found in abundance, and usually in association with iron

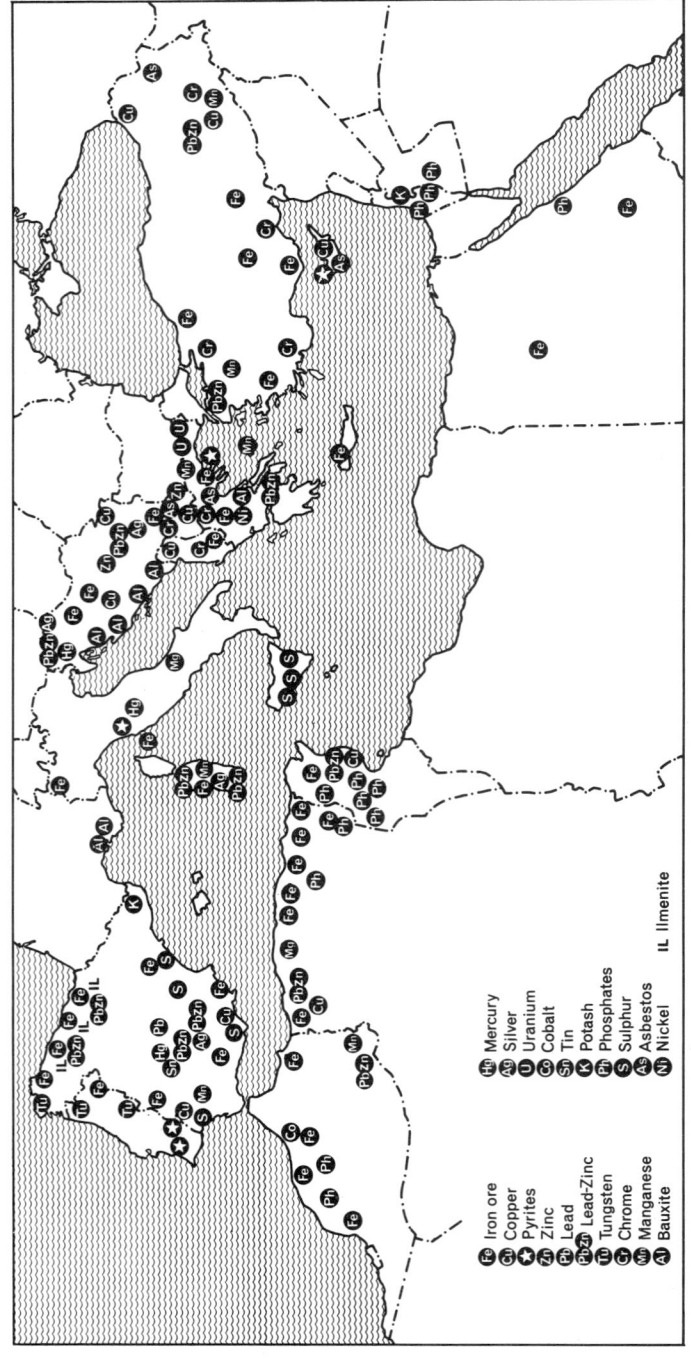

FIG. 35.—The Mediterranean lands: minerals (*see also* Fig. 33 for coal and mineral oil).

ore. The largest Mediterranean producer is Spain, with an annual output of over 40,000 tons.

Copper has been mined in the Mediterranean region since ancient times; in fact, its name comes from the island of Cyprus (Lat. *cyprium* or *cuprum*), the "land of copper." Copper is widely distributed in nature; it occurs in most soils, in ferruginous mineral waters and in association with many other mineral ores. It is found in all the Mediterranean lands, but usually not in sufficient quantities to warrant exploitation. The principal ores of copper are oxides, carbonates and sulphides. Some of the oxides and carbonates have a copper content of not more than 5%, but the sulphides, commonly known as *copper pyrites*, may yield anything from 30 to 80% pure copper. For this reason they are the most valuable from an economic point of view. Portugal, with an output in 1964 of 607,400 tons of cupriferous pyrites, is the chief Mediterranean producer. Cyprus in the same year exported 86,000 tons of pyrites and 61,000 tons of copper concentrates, mainly from mines in the Troödos mountains. There are extensive copper ore deposits around Bor in Yugoslavia, yielding annually about 90,000 tons. Turkey produces some 22,000 tons of copper per annum from Ergani Madeni, about 60 miles north-west of Diyarbekir, and at workings on the Black Sea coast near the Russian border. Spain, which at one time was a major producer from the Rio Tinto mines, now has only a small output (4000 tons). Copper ore has also been discovered in workable quantities in Albania, Tunisia and Algeria.

An important by-product in the reduction of copper pyrites is sulphur; *iron pyrites* (iron disulphide), however, which is usually found in the same areas as copper pyrites, is worked principally for its content of sulphur, which is used in the manufacture of sulphuric acid. Spain produces nearly 2 million tons of iron pyrites a year, and Cyprus 725,000 tons.

Lead and *zinc* are often found in association, sometimes with *silver* in addition. Morocco (96,000 tons) is the chief Mediterranean producer of lead, followed by Yugoslavia (91,000 tons), Spain (73,000 tons) and Italy (49,000 tons). Lead is also worked in small amounts in Greece, Tunisia and Turkey. The main zinc producers are Italy (135,000 tons), Spain (86,000 tons) and Yugoslavia (56,000 tons). Important quantities of *silver* come from Yugoslavia (94,000 tons), the largest producer in Europe, and from Spain (55,000 tons) and Italy (29,000 tons). *Bauxite*, the source of aluminium, is found in Mediterranean France, Yugoslavia, Italy and Greece. It was first discovered near Les Baux on the Rhône delta, hence its name. The deposits of Les Baux are now exhausted, and quarrying for the ore has moved to the river Argens basin in Provence, which produces more than 90% of France's total output of over 2 million tons. Yugoslavia's production (1 million tons) is from the Dinaric karstlands and Istria, Italy's from the central Apennines, and that of Greece from east of Mt Parnassus.

Many other metallic ores occur in small amounts in the Mediterranean lands. Sometimes, as in the case of *mercury*, they may be of significant economic value. Spain, around Almadén, is the world's leading producer of mercury, and substantial quantities come also from Tuscany in Italy and from the Julian Alps in Yugoslavia. A small quantity of *tin* (2200 tons) is mined in Spain, and deposits have been found in southern Algeria; *nickel* occurs in Greece (Phthiótis) and Algeria (Ahaggar plateau), *antimony* in Sardinia and Yugoslav Macedonia, and *uranium* in eastern Macedonia.

The chief non-metallic minerals found in the Mediterranean lands are phosphates, potash, sulphur, salt and asbestos. *Phosphates* are of outstanding importance as a raw material for the manufacture of fertilisers. They occur in vast deposits in the Maghrib countries. The phosphate fields of Morocco which lie east of Safi and around Kouribga produce annually over 10 million tons, which represents over 20% of the world total, and to this amount must be added the large exports from the Gafsa area of Tunisia and from deposits around Tebessa in Algeria. Phosphates are obtained also in Jordan (560,000 tons) and Egypt (near Qusseir). *Potash* is also used in the fertiliser industry. The chief deposits are in Catalonia in Spain, and it is obtained also in Israel and Jordan by solar evaporation of the waters of the Dead Sea. These waters also yield common salt, magnesium bromide and bromine, the last being an ingredient in the manufacture of explosives. *Sulphur* in the raw state occurs in the volcanic region of Sicily, and there are deposits, as yet unworked, east of the Gaza strip in Israel. In addition, there is the supply of sulphur obtained from pyrites (mentioned above). There are deposits of rock salt in Morocco and Libya, but most *salt* in the Mediterranean lands is obtained by evaporation and refining of sea water along the coasts, or by solution and precipitation in salt basins and saline flats. *Asbestos*, a fibrous rock capable of being woven into incombustible cloth, is found mainly near Skopje in Yugoslavia, around Kars in Turkey and in Cyprus.

OTHER RAW MATERIALS

Some raw materials other than minerals were dealt with in the previous chapter. They include wool, cotton, flax and hemp for the textile industries; sugar cane and sugar beet for refineries; tobacco for cigarette factories; and various fruits and vegetables for canning works. To these are added the raw materials used in the *paper-making* industry.

The art of making paper seems to have been known in China as early as the second century B.C. It did not become known in the Mediterranean lands until late in the eighth century, after Arabs had captured at Samarkand Chinese prisoners who were skilled in paper-making. The manufacture of paper in Europe was first established by the Moors in Spain in the middle of the twelfth century, the headquarters of the industry being Valencia and Toledo. Later the manufacture was introduced into Italy, no doubt through the Arab occupation of Sicily. Chinese paper was made by pulping cotton, but the Arabs learned to use flax, which grew abundantly in the Levant and North Africa, supplemented by linen rags and any vegetable fibre which would pulp. With the fall of the Moorish power the paper-making industry declined in Spain, but it had already spread from there to France late in the twelfth century and reached England a hundred years later. In Italy, however, the manufacture spread northwards to Florence, and then to Padua, Treviso, Venice, Parma, Bologna and Milan, in most of which it still continues to be a minor industry. Before the use of paper as a writing material, the Egyptian *papyrus*, from which paper takes its name, was employed widely in Italy, Greece, the Levant and North Africa; elsewhere in Europe, parchment, prepared from the skins of sheep, goats and calves, was in common use.

The rise of industry during the Industrial Revolution was accompanied by an increased consumption of paper and a search for new fibrous materials to cope with the demand. Linen and cotton rags began to be supplemented by esparto grass, hemp, wood and straw, and these today are the chief raw materials in the manufacture of paper. The main sources of *esparto grass* are the Spanish Meseta and the Plateau of the Shotts in Algeria and Morocco. Esparto is used in small paper works widely dispersed in southern Spain and along the coast of the Maghrib; the bulk of the grass is exported, chiefly to the United Kingdom, France and West Germany. Most kinds of *straw* can be utilised in paper-making; in the Mediterranean lands wheat, barley and maize straw, and in Egypt rice straw, are the most important varieties used. Paper works based on straw occur mainly in towns near large-scale cultivation of cereals, for instance in the north of the Spanish Meseta, the north Italian plain, eastern Sicily, the Danubian plains of Yugoslavia and the Nile delta. Biscayan Spain, Alpine Italy, Dinaric Yugoslavia and Anatolia are the regions which mainly use *wood pulp* as a material for paper-making. This is due to the large forest areas found there, and to the water power available. The development of hydro-electric power has stimulated the growth of many new paper works in the Cantabrians, the Italian Alpine provinces, Slovenia and Bosnia-Hercegovina.

COMMUNICATIONS AND TRANSPORT

In most Mediterranean lands inland communications have never been easy, either because of the relief or, in the Levant and North Africa, because of semi-desert and desert conditions. The Mediterranean Sea for centuries provided the chief means of transport and gave a certain unity to the region as a whole; indeed, if air transport be excluded, it still offers the easiest and most direct route from one end of the region to the other. Moreover the peninsular character of the European side means that seaborne traffic can approach most of the areas fit for human occupation and development, which in nearly all cases are on or not far from the coasts. In the Levant and North Africa, too, most people live in a narrow belt adjacent to the sea, so that maritime communication is more important than land transport. Egypt is an exception, for here a navigable river offers an extension inland of water communications (*see* page 458).

We have already noted that the farming and pastoral communities of the Mediterranean lands, and they include most of the people, had until very recently no thought of industrialisation. They were satisfied to depend on primitive techniques in their work, on local craftsmen for household and occupational requirements, and on local supplies of goods necessary for their way of life, which was simple and self-sufficient. In other words, they had little need for any modern development of land transport.

The growth of nationalism and the achievement of independence in so many countries, especially in this present century, changed things drastically. The new political and social conditions brought a realisation that in the modern world a proper and up-to-date utilisation of a country's resources is vital to the success of its economy, and that rich supplies of hydro-electric power and vast deposits of mineral oil and natural gas outweigh the disadvantage arising from the lack of coal in the region, a factor which previously had hindered the growth of industry. But the development of industry even on a small scale depends, not just on the presence of power resources but to a very large degree on lines of communication. In the past hundred years all Mediterranean countries have begun to look at their transport facilities.

Following the opening of the Suez Canal in 1869, railways were constructed from more northerly European countries to the chief Mediterranean ports, some of them making use of tunnels driven through the Alps; but no Mediterranean country had anything like a comprehensive railway system within its own boundaries. Even today, the only really good networks are in Mediterranean France, Italy and, to a less extent, Spain, Portugal and northern Yugoslavia, and of these the Spanish system during the civil war of 1936–39 and the Italian and Yugoslav railways during the Second World War were so severely damaged that some parts have still not been repaired. There are no railways at all in the west of peninsular Greece, and Albania has a total of less than 100 miles (160 km) of track, all built since 1947. The railways of Turkey are concentrated in the western half of the country, and in the Levant lands a skeletal system was constructed primarily for military needs and not for economic reasons. Egypt has a main-line railway from Alexandria up the Nile to Aswan, with branches from Cairo to Suez and Port Said, and a track follows the coast westwards from Alexandria to Salum near the Libyan border. This last was built for military purposes during the Second World War and is of little economic significance. Originally the coastal line ran to Tobruk in Cyrenaica, but in 1962 this extension, together with short tracks in Tripolitania, were closed permanently, partly because of shortage of money in Libya, partly because of the abundance of road transport. In the Maghrib most railways are short lines from the ports, running inland to tap mineral districts and mainly north–south in direction. They are connected from east to west by a series of tracks between Tunis and Casablanca.

There has been much railway construction during the past 25 years, especially in the Maghrib and in developing countries such as Yugoslavia. Several electric railways, too, have been built in Mediterranean France and the Italian Alps; in 1962, for instance, a new metre-gauge electric railway was completed, to connect Trento and Malè in the Adige valley in Italy. The tendency everywhere nowadays, however, is to provide roads rather than railways. In mountainous districts the expense involved in making cuttings, tunnels, bridges and viaducts so as to obtain suitable gradients for railways is very great, and most Mediterranean countries are too poor to embark on any large-scale construction. Roads are cheaper to build and maintain, are not so dependent on easy gradients, and can more readily be constructed in relatively remote areas, where local building materials are available and transport of heavy constituent parts and equipment is obviated, which would not be so in the case of railways. This is notably to be seen in the interior of North Africa and the Middle East, where railways are few and uneconomic, but where there are now many trans-desert roads carrying motor traffic which has largely supplanted camel transport.

The increased use of motor vehicles as a means of transport has led in all Mediterranean lands to the improvement of existing roads and the building of new ones. This in turn has helped the growth of industries not only in the more advanced countries but also in regions which hitherto were purely agricultural or pastoral, and even in parts of the North African desert where there was little human activity of any kind. As in Western Europe, some of the more developed lands are building roads of the motorway type, so as to speed up transport of raw materials and manufactured products.

In the Iberian peninsula, new roads are reducing the artificial nodality of Madrid and facilitating cross-country passage of commercial vehicles. The improved road network has been made easier in Spain by the reconstruction which was necessary after the destruction of bridges and viaducts during the civil war. In Mediterranean France the industrial growth of the Étang de Berre and Marseille districts was accompanied by a network of new and improved motor roads. Under construction at present is the last stage of the Paris–Mediterranean motorway, which will traverse the region and join up with the Estérel–Côte d'Azur motorway opened in 1961. A road tunnel is also projected through the western Pyrenees from Aragnouet (France) to Bielsa (Spain).

Italy has been noted since Roman times for its skill in road building, but in modern times its engineers are greatly indebted to lessons learnt from the makers of *autobahnen* in Western Europe, especially in West Germany and Benelux. A series of magnificent motorways, known in Italy as *autostrade* (sing. *autostrada*), was planned, and is still in course of construction. The first to be completed was the Milan–Turin autostrada (81 miles;

130 km), and this was followed by the Austostrada del Sole, which links Milan via Bologna and Florence to Rome and Naples. It is hoped that eventually this motorway will be continued to Reggio (Calabria), the ferry terminal for Sicily, and thus open up part of the poverty-stricken Mezzogiorno to much-needed industrial development. In north-east Italy the Autostrada del Brennero is a continuation of the Austrian Alpen Autobahn, which it meets at the Brenner Pass; when completed this motorway will connect with the Autostrada del Sole and give the whole of Italy easy access to Central Europe. There are already first-class roads along the east and west coasts of peninsular Italy. Now a new autostrada is planned across the difficult terrain of Abruzzi and Latium to link these two roads and to form a connection with the Autostrada del Sole.

Road and railway construction through the Alps has helped to make northern Italy one of the most highly industrialised regions in Europe and certainly the greatest in the Mediterranean lands. The latest help in this development is the Great St Bernard road tunnel, completed in March 1964. The road tunnel connects Aosta and Martigny, is open in winter, and effects a saving of 6·2 miles (9·9 km). The tunnel itself, the first road tunnel under the Alps, is 3·7 miles (5·9 km) long at an altitude of about 6000 feet (1800 m), and is approached at both ends by roads covered with protections against avalanches. On the Italian side the road is 8·1 miles (13 km) long and on the Swiss side 3·4 miles (5·5 km). Beneath the road surface a pipeline carries oil from Genoa to a refinery at Colombey, near Aigle, in Switzerland. A further mark of economic advance in northern Italy is the opening in 1965 of the first underground railway in Milan. The initial line, 10 miles (16 km) long, is in use; a second is in course of construction, and two more are planned to complete the network.

In Yugoslavia road and railway construction has formed part of every national economic programme since 1945. The great development of hydro-electricity demanded increased land communications, especially in Dalmatia and the Dinaric mountains. The railway from Belgrade to Dubrovnik was modernised and extended to Titograd. A motorway, the Adriatic Highway, most of which is now completed, will join Rijeka to Titograd; a road, opened in 1963 from Tuzla via Sarajevo to Mostar, is being extended to the Adriatic Highway, so giving a motor route from Belgrade across the southern Karst to the coast; and a highway is under construction from Ljubljana via Zagreb, Belgrade, Niš and Skopje to the Greek frontier at Gevgelija. Further road and railway developments are taking place in the valleys leading to the river Sava and in the Macedonian region centring on Skopje. A joint Yugoslav–Rumanian hydro-electric power and navigation scheme at the Iron Gate on the river Danube involves the building of new roads and railways on both banks. A lake, 90 miles long, will be impounded and will flood the present rapids and submerge a number of towns, among them Douji–Milanovac on the Yugoslav bank. This last will necessitate the resettlement of 25–30,000 people in a new town with a completely new system of communications.

There has been extensive road construction and modernisation in Greece, mainly along the eastern side of the peninsula and in Macedonia, where roads are planned to connect with those of Yugoslavia; but there remain large areas of the country, notably in the Pindus region, where communications are almost non-existent or at best are no more than ill-made tracks. Lack of facilities for modern transport over a big proportion of Greece is one of the greatest drawbacks in the development of its economy. Similarly in Albania, much road construction is required; less than 2000 miles (3200 km) of road are fit for motor traffic, and these are chiefly near the coast. The mountain districts of the north are still largely inaccessible to wheeled vehicles, and transport is by pack mules and donkeys.

Most of the railway network of Turkey has been reconstructed in the past 40 years, and extensions to the system form part of the current five-year economic plan; for instance, a through railway from Ankara to Moscow has been opened. Roads, too, are being built in the Taurus region of Anatolia and in the eastern end of the country, the object of both road and railway construction being to link isolated districts and to open up areas which so far are without transport facilities. But Turkey has many obstacles to the making of land communications. It is a large country with a very difficult topography; it has relatively few natural resources in much of its area; its population is badly distributed, being dense in parts of the west and very scanty in the east. Finally, the removal of capital functions from Istanbul to Ankara, followed by the re-orientation of road and rail systems on the new capital, has involved the country in such vast expenditure as to leave little money for the development of communications in the more remote districts, many of which are accessible at present only by tracks. Turkey, with a coastline approximately 3000 miles (4800 km) long, has for long regarded sea-borne traffic as almost as vital a part of its economy as communications by land.

A large proportion of the railways of the Levant is narrow gauge and single track. As already noted, much was constructed for military purposes during the two World Wars, and there has been little development since 1942. The emphasis in recent years has been on the improvement of road communications, especially those concerned with transit traffic between the ports of the Levant and the northern regions of Iraq and Persia. The age-old camel caravans still cross the desert, maintaining the prosperity of towns such as Aleppo, Homs, Damascus and Amman, their western termini, but increasingly they are giving way to motor traffic on new roads which reach the Mediterranean coast.

The opening up of the oilfields of Iraq and the Persian Gulf has had a big influence. Some of the Persian Gulf fields are connected by the Trans-Arabian Pipeline (TAP) from Abqaiq (Saudi Arabia) to Sidon (Lebanon), and although the road which follows its course for purposes of maintenance is not primarily a commercial route, it carries a considerable traffic. On the other hand, along the pipelines which run from the important group of oilfields around Kirkuk in northern Iraq to Baniyas (Syria) and Tripoli (Lebanon), there are major roads with branches to Baghdad which are first-class commercial highways. There are also networks of new roads surrounding all the Mediterranean oil terminal ports especially in Syria and Lebanon. Israel has an excellent road system, better than any other Levant country, but because the pipeline which connects Haifa to the Kirkuk fields has been closed as a consequence of the conflict between Israel and the Arab states, its roads are not used to their full capacity.

In North Africa the position is much as in the Levant. More attention is being given nowadays to land communications by road, thus railway construction, except here and there in the Maghrib, is virtually at a standstill. Roads in Egypt follow both banks of the Nile, and there are extensive developments in connection with the New Valley scheme. Roads also run westwards from the Nile valley to important oases such as Qattara, Bahariya and Dakhla, and eastwards to the Red Sea ports of Hurghada and Quseir. The coastal road between the last two is in process of being paved. A coastal road from Alexandria to the west is of poor quality, but those running towards the north-east from Cairo to Ismailia, Port Said and the Sinai peninsula are good motor roads.

In Libya, Tunisia and Algeria, the discovery of mineral resources at long distances from the coast has speeded the making of roads, sometimes along well-established trans-desert caravan routes. Today motor roads run hundreds of miles to link the deposits of mineral oil, natural gas and phosphates with the coast, and some of them are continued southwards to supplant the ancient caravan routes to Timbuktu, Niamey, Kano and Ft Lamy on the southern side of the Sahara. Pipeline and terminal construction has had the same effect near the coast as in the Levant. Road systems have developed throughout the Tell of Algeria and the Tunisian coastal region, and are especially noticeable around the gas ports of Arzew and Algiers, the oil ports of Bejaia (Bougie) and La Skhirra, and the phosphate ports of Skikda (Phillippeville) and Sousse.

Railways in Morocco were built mainly to tap the phosphate and mineral fields, but the only construction in recent years has been in the Kouribga region. Road systems, on the other hand, have been extended and multiplied as new deposits of useful minerals have been discovered. There are now good networks along the coast from Tangier in the north to Agadir in the south, and in the Meknes–Fez and Marrakesh regions. The lofty Atlas ranges present a formidable barrier to communication with the south-east of Morocco. The only good motor roads pass around their northern and southern ends from Melilla and Agadir respectively, and across their centre via difficult passes from Marrakesh.

Air transport has also had a tremendous impact on the Mediterranean lands. There are good airports for local traffic in every country, but in some there are important international airports. The airfields of Malaga, Rome, Surcin (Yugoslavia), Athens, Beirut, Heliopolis (Egypt), Algiers and Castel Benito (Tripoli, Libya), for example, lie at convenient stopping-points on long-distance routes from Western Europe to South America, West and South Africa, India, the Far East, Australia and New Zealand.

LABOUR AND MARKETS

LABOUR

The development of natural resources and the growth of industries in the Mediterranean lands are giving rise to a demand for labour on a hitherto unprecedented scale, but are also bringing social and economic problems. By far the largest proportion of the population of the region is engaged in agriculture and pasture, but there have always been large urban concentrations in all the Mediterranean lands. In these cities and towns the people were mainly craftsmen, merchants and labourers, but there were never sufficient occupations to absorb all the potential labour. In consequence many of the larger cities had considerable numbers of permanently unemployed vagrants and beggars, and the smaller towns fared little better. This is still the position in many Mediterranean countries, especially in the Levant and North Africa, but the changes resultant on the exploitation of natural resources and the introduction of manufacturing industries are to be seen nearly everywhere. A comparison might be made with the social and economic transformation which took place in Western Europe during the Industrial Revolution. However, it must be borne in mind that the Mediterranean lands are undergoing an industrial revolution so speeded up by modern knowledge and techniques that many of the peoples cannot cope with the problems involved, and that the process is complicated by power politics.

It must be remembered, too, that industrial development is being accompanied by a corresponding revolution in agriculture. As farming practice becomes more efficient and water resources for irrigation are used to better purpose, there is a surplus of labour in the countryside, and this tends to drift into the cities or into the regions of mineral exploitation where there is a demand for workers. Unfortunately most of this rural over-population has its roots deeply embedded in the soil and does not settle permanently to work in factories, mines, oilfields or on road and pipeline construction; at intervals large numbers return to look for employment in the fields. In any case, rural workers entering the cities are simply adding to the numbers of unemployed already there, and moreover have to adjust themselves to an urban way of life. This is often a long and disappointing process, especially in regions such as northern Italy, where industrialisation has reached a stage of labour saturation and offers few new opportunities. In the countries of North Africa rural migration into towns is a serious problem for the migrants almost invariably are poverty-stricken and live in wretched conditions.

In addition, in all the Mediterranean lands, as was noted in Chapter VI, there is a general increase of population occasioned by improved social conditions. In the Iberian, Italian and Balkan peninsulas, for example, total population in the past 25 years has risen from 104 to 120 millions; this growth, averaging two-thirds of a million a year, can be paralleled in other parts of the Mediterranean region. It is too great for available food resources, and as yet industrial development is too small to absorb it; indeed, it is doubtful if industrialisation will ever get rid of the surplus.

In the Mediterranean lands, then, it is obvious that labour is in plentiful supply; the amount and quality varies from country to country, and with the degree of industrial growth. Except where industry has been present for many years, it is essentially unskilled labour; where new industrial processes are being introduced, the executive and supervisory positions are held by experts brought from abroad. This is especially the case in the development of the oil and gas fields in North Africa and the Middle East. Even when account is taken of the numbers absorbed by enlarged services such as city transport, docks and harbour work, and in connection with tourism, there is still an unsatisfactory surplus of labour.

A possible outlet in the past was emigration. It has been estimated, for instance, that between 1864 and 1924 over 15 million people left Spain, Portugal and Italy to settle overseas, mostly in the U.S.A., Argentina, Brazil, Canada, Australia and New Zealand; and Greece, Lebanon and Turkish Armenia also provided considerable numbers. Emigration is officially encouraged today only in a few special cases, for example, from Italy to Australia; on the whole, most countries accepting immigrants have introduced the quota system and give preference to people with specialist qualifications rather than to displaced and uneducated peasants. The peoples of the Mediterranean lands are having to look more and more to their own resources.

The picture is not entirely black, however. Emigration in the old and accepted sense is no longer a safety valve, but in the years since the Second World War a modified type of emigration has emerged, in which more than a million workers move annually from the Mediterranean lands to Western Europe, to meet the labour needs of industrial countries, not permanently, but for limited periods. Up to 1961 about half were from Italy, but since then the Italian economy has increased its own needs and the numbers leaving that country have fallen. Nevertheless, Italy remains the greatest exporter of labour, having sent about 300,000 workers to West Germany and about the same number to Switzerland. Italians also go to France, which is another major importer of workers with an annual inward movement of an average 140,000 Spaniards, 60,000 Portuguese and many Moroccans and Tunisians. Greece and Turkey are also suppliers of labour to the west; 115,000 Greeks and 85,000 Turks are at present working in West Germany. The flow of emigrants from these two countries, however, is being discouraged by the home authorities—a welcome sign of the improvements planned in their own industrial and agricultural economies. Temporary emigration from the Levant and North Africa is insignificant, but note should be made of the exodus of French *colons* from Algeria after it achieved independence. This mass immigration into

Mediterranean France resulted in an unemployment crisis there. Against the losses of potential man-power caused by this seasonal or annual movement of peoples in the Mediterranean lands must be placed the return of hundreds of thousands after a couple of years abroad bringing back to their mother countries new industrial skills and capital which may be used to advance economic progress.

MARKETS

We have seen that with the onset of the Industrial Revolution the countries of Western Europe opened their markets to agricultural products and mineral ores from the Mediterranean lands. The growth of industry in these lands, however, is not having the same immediate impact abroad. The first objectives of nascent industry are to satisfy demands in the country of its birth, to improve local standards of living, and gradually seek to reach a satisfactory economic balance between agriculture and pasture on the one side and manufacturing industries and the use of natural resources on the other. Nearly all the Mediterranean countries are still in this stage of industrial development, although some are now beginning to move out of it and compete successfully with the older-established industrial lands to the north. The first moves towards industrial competence lie in the sphere of improved communications, light engineering and food processing. Heavy engineering, the production of heavy iron and steel goods, and the development of large-scale chemical works are signs that a country's industrial economy is reaching full stature and can face international competition.

Italy, for instance, mainly by virtue of industrial growth in its northern plain, is a member of the European Economic Community (E.E.C.: the Common Market), on a par with France, West Germany and Benelux. Portugal forms part of the European Free Trade Association (E.F.T.A.), in association with the United Kingdom, Norway, Sweden, Denmark, Austria and Switzerland. Since both E.E.C. and E.F.T.A. are in existence to promote close economic association for their constituent countries, membership of either denotes that industrial development is very far advanced. Greece, though much less industrialised, has been accepted as an associate member of E.E.C., and has important markets also in the United Kingdom and North America. Spain, too, has large trading interests with Western Europe and the U.S.A. Yugoslavia is a Communist country but with an ideology differing from that of Moscow; it has markets on both sides of the Iron Curtain. Albania, by its acceptance of the Chinese brand of Communism, has more or less shut itself off from trade with the Western world and East Europe, and is making slow economic progress. Israel is the most advanced country in the Levant and has good markets for its agricultural products and those of light industries.

Home markets for economic products such as food preparations, light engineering, textiles, chemicals and cement have been stimulated in the Arab countries, notably in Egypt, the Maghrib and Lebanon, although the last is strictly not "Arab." Attempts were made in 1964 to establish an Arab Common Market comprising Iraq, Jordan, Kuwait, Syria, Egypt and Algeria, but with only limited success. High costs of production, low standards of workmanship and political jealousies which led to the erection of discriminatory tariffs all militated against a large expansion of purely inter-Arab commerce. There are certainly large foreign markets for mineral oil, natural gas and other raw materials from the Middle East and North Africa, but there are few signs as yet that these products will lead to large-scale industrialisation in the countries of their origin.

INDUSTRIES AND MANUFACTURES

In the nineteenth century the only industrialised regions in the Mediterranean lands were around Barcelona, Marseille, Milan, Istanbul, Aleppo and Alexandria, and they were concerned mainly in the manufacture of silk, woollen and cotton textiles. Local supplies of raw material and the skill acquired by centuries of craftsmen led, for instance, to a large export of Turkey carpets, Syrian *crêpe-de-chine* and damask (the name comes from

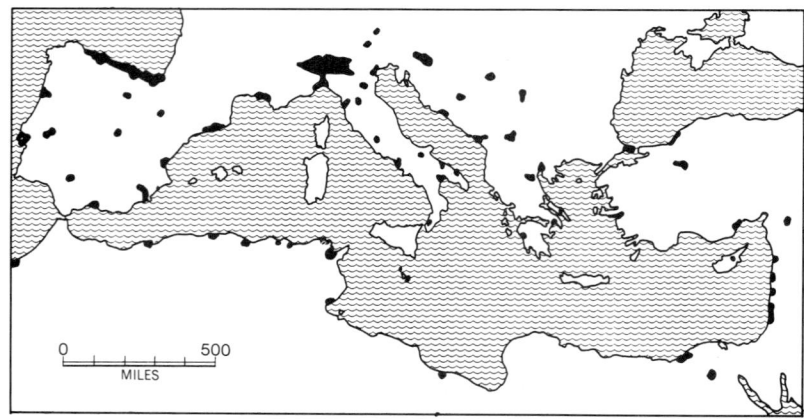

FIG. 36.—The Mediterranean lands: industrial areas.

Damascus), and Milanese silks. With the break-up of the Ottoman Empire in this present century, Syria, which was its chief manufacturing region, has declined in importance; with the exception of Aleppo, the cities mentioned are still among the most highly industrialised centres in the Mediterranean lands and indeed in Europe (*see* Fig. 36). The advent of hydro-electricity and mineral oil as motive power has been a decisive factor in their advance, and these fuels, so plentiful around the Mediterranean, have made possible also the dissemination of modern industries throughout the region, in some countries even in the most remote and unlikely places.

TEXTILES

Textiles are still the most valuable manufactures of the Mediterranean lands. The total amounts of woollen, worsted, cotton, silk and rayon tissues exported from Italy, Spain, Portugal, Egypt and Israel are so large and cheap as to cause great concern to the older industrial textile regions of the United Kingdom, West Germany, France and the U.S.A. Special fiscal arrangements have reduced the problem as between Italy, France and West Germany, for these countries form part of the European "Common Market"; but competition is having adverse results in Lancashire, the West Riding of Yorkshire, Rhode Island and Massachusetts, where many factories have had to be closed. Turkey has many new woollen, silk and cotton factories, but the craft industry producing hand-made carpets has declined in face of cheaper, machine-made products in Western Europe and the U.S.A. Nevertheless, there is still a big demand for Turkey carpets for the Bedouin and in the cities of the Levant. In Libya and the Maghrib the textile industry has hardly progressed beyond the craft stage; blankets and carpets are its chief products.

FOODSTUFFS

The processing and manufacture of foodstuffs were among the first industries in the Mediterranean lands to be modernised, notably where Government subsidies were made available and "co-operatives" were established. New techniques were introduced to the drying and packing of fruit, and canning factories built to deal with both fruit and vegetables. This has taken place in every Mediterranean country, but especially in Italy, Spain, Yugoslavia, Turkey, Israel, Algeria, Morocco and Portugal; the last two are noted for fish canning, mainly of sardines.

IRON AND STEEL

All Mediterranean countries with deposits of iron and other metallic ores are now keeping more and more of their output for use within their own boundaries. This has meant the building of smelting works and sometimes of steel mills. In northern Spain, for example, there are blast furnaces and steelworks at Bilbao, Oviedo and Avilés, the last having one of the largest integrated plants in the west of Europe. The iron and steel industries of Milan, Turin and Genoa were established early in the century, and new plants have been opened recently at Naples, Barletta and Taranto. Turkey has a steelworks at Karabuk north of Ankara, and in 1965 a second plant was opened at Eregli. This latter produces steel strip, rolled sheets and tinplate, and is said to be the largest integrated steelworks between Italy and India. The first fully integrated iron and steel works in Greece was brought into operation in 1963 near Eleusis; it is hoped, by using imported as well as local ore, to have an ultimate annual output of 500,000 tons of steel. Tunisia inaugurated its first steelworks in 1966 at Menzel-Bourguiba, near Bizerta; it is capable of producing 100,000 tons a year.

Algeria and Yugoslavia, both of which have deposits of iron ore, have as yet negligible supplies of home-produced steel, but plans have been made for substantial development in the future.

Aluminium smelting is very important in the hinterland of Marseille and along the Dalmatian coast of Yugoslavia; and there are *copper* smelters and concentrating plants at Huerta in Spain, Castro Verde in Portugal, Bor in Yugoslavia and Nicosia in Cyprus.

LIGHT ENGINEERING

Heavy engineering in the Mediterranean lands has not yet made much progress; it is concentrated mainly in the Milan–Turin–Genoa "industrial triangle" and the Spanish Biscayan states. Light engineering, however, is widespread, and new works are constantly being built. The industry is well established along the northern coastlands of Spain, in the north Italian plain and in most large cities, and new enterprises for the production of agricultural, electrical and textile machinery and for hardware of all kinds are springing up wherever hydro-electric power is available. For instance, there are modern light engineering workshops in Portugal at Fundão, Covilha and Santarém where none existed before the Zezere hydro-electricity scheme was inaugurated. Outside the Biscayan lands, Barcelona and Madrid, Spain has light engineering at Valencia, Alicante, Malaga, Seville, Zaragoza and most other towns of any size. In Italy, new works have been erected in the south of the peninsula at Taranto, Foggia, Caserta, Reggio and Catanzaro, and iron and steel works have commenced production at Bagnoli near Naples and at Taranto. Light engineering is prominent in the economic programme of Yugoslavia, especially in the towns in the river Sava and its tributary valleys, and along the Morava–Vardar "corridor"; and in Greece there are big developments in the Athens–Piraeus region, Euboea and western Macedonia.

Istanbul and Ankara have light engineering, and more plants are coming into existence in Turkey in the towns of the Black Sea coast. In the Levant, pipelines from the Middle East have given rise to light engineering in their terminal ports of Baniyas, Tripoli, Sidon and Haifa. The main light engineering centres in North Africa are Cairo, Alexandria, Tunis, Oran, Algiers and Casablanca. Elsewhere, the industry is dependent for its growth on the development of mineral resources and is located in districts of exploitation.

CHEMICALS

The manufacture of chemicals, especially of fertilisers, is increasing everywhere in the Mediterranean lands. The production of chemicals often accompanies iron smelting, steel making, coal coking, oil refining and the generation of hydro-electricity. The rich oil and hydro-power resources of the region offer great possibilities to the chemical industry, and there are in addition vast quantities of raw materials such as phosphates, potash and salt to help in its development.

Italy is already outstanding in its output of chemicals. Their manufacture is largely controlled by industrial giants such as the Montecatini and Edison combines, which amalgamated in 1966 to become the largest industrial group in the country. Between them they produce nearly 80% of Italy's chemicals, including 50% of the fertiliser output and 62% of the plastics and synthetic fibres. The activities of the group include a large oil refinery and petro-chemical complexes at Ravenna and Brindisi, in addition to several major chemical works in the "industrial triangle" of the north, and at Leghorn and Florence. In an effort to bring economic relief to the overcrowded south, the "Cassa" (*see* page 275) has financed chemical plants at Catanzaro, Caserta and Reggio, and more are planned. Hydro-power has led to the production of electro-chemicals at Bolzano and Trento, deep in the Dolomitic Alps.

Spain, too, has a long-established chemical industry. Barcelona is the chief centre of the manufacture, followed by the towns on the Biscayan coal and iron fields, notably Oviedo, Bilbao and Santander. There are large chemical works also in Valencia, Murcia, Burgos and Madrid, the last-named specialising in pharmaceutical goods. In Portugal the industry has not yet made much headway, the main region of production being around Lisbon, and then mostly for fertilisers. Mediterranean France has chemical manufactures at Marseille and at several places around the Étang de Berre; in the latter they are associated with oil refineries. Yugoslavia's chief chemical works are at Belgrade, Ljubljana and Sarajevo, and there are others near hydro-power stations in Dalmatia. Greece has chemical manufactures at Salonika, Piraeus, Volos (Thessaly) and Pírgos (Olympia); the recently developed Flórina–Ptolemaís–Kozáni "triangle" produces nitrogenous fertiliser on its lignite fields, and a major chemical industry is planned for the region. Albania has only a small chemical production, but it claims to have over 20 chemical and light engineering plants under construction, mostly with Chinese capital and technical assistance.

In the rest of the Mediterranean lands the chemical industry is still in embryo, but the potash of the Dead Sea, the vast deposits of phosphates in North Africa, and the growing number of oil refineries hold distinct promise for the future. Turkey's production of chemicals is associated mainly with a coking plant on the Zonguldak coalfield; there is a small chemical works at Tripoli in Lebanon; and in Israel and Jordan potash from the Dead Sea is a raw material for bromides and other chemical products. The oil refineries at Suez and Alexandria are said to supply all Egypt's domestic needs for chemicals, but in view of the increasing use of artificial fertilisers in the country, this may not be true. In the Maghrib the development of the phosphate fields has led to the manufacture of superphosphates (fertiliser) at Tunis in Tunisia, Algiers and Bone in Algeria, and Casablanca in Morocco. A new plant, inaugurated at Safi, a port on the Atlantic coast of Morocco, will use phosphates to produce chemicals ranging from sulphuric and phosphoric acids to phosphate fertiliser.

Soap manufacture is an important branch of the chemical industry. Soap is basically a combination of oils or fats and a powerful alkali such as potash or caustic soda. Two of the essential raw materials, olive oil and potash, which can be obtained from wood ash, are available in large quantities around the Mediterranean, and soap boiling and manufacture have a long history in some of its lands; Marseille, for instance, was making soap from olive oil and potash as early as the thirteenth century. Nowadays caustic soda and potash are usually provided for the soap boiler by separate branches of the chemical industry, so saving him one stage in his manufacture, and many other oils and fats are imported to augment olive oil. Marseille is the centre of soap-making in the Mediterranean, and imports ox and sheep tallow, palm oil, cottonseed oil and coconut oil in large quantities. Other regions producing soap in commercial amounts are southern Spain, southern Italy, Greece, Turkey and Syria. In most of these the soap factories would be regarded as primitive according to modern standards and practice, but there has been a considerable advance in recent years, both in manufacturing techniques and in the equipment used.

HARBOUR AND PORT DEVELOPMENT

Because the industrialisation of the Mediterranean lands is still very young, considerable alterations and improvements have been made urgently necessary in harbour and port facilities, to cope with the export of bulk products such as phosphates and other minerals. New wharves and loading equipment have been installed in some of the older ports, and in some cases completely new ports have been constructed. The harbour and docks of Avilés in northern Spain have been reorganised to meet the requirements of the iron and steel industry. The phosphates of Morocco have given rise to the port of Safi and to new warehouses and quays at Casablanca; and phosphates and iron ore have led to extensive improvements in all the Algerian ports. In Israel the port of Eilat, at the head of the Gulf of Aqaba, was inaugurated in 1965, with potash and phosphate warehouses and facilities for bulk loading.

The development of terminal ports for the export of mineral oil and natural gas has already been mentioned; in all of them special equipment for delivery to tankers has been installed, and refineries have been erected in some. To these exporting ports must be added ports with facilities for import. In Mediterranean France the Étang de Berre, which is connected by roads and canals to Marseille, is a convenient stopping-place for tankers from the Levant coast and from North Africa, and several refineries have been established there. A 470-mile (750 km) pipeline from Lavara, a small port near Marseille, to Karlsruhe in West Germany started operations in 1962, and now carries over 30 million tons of crude oil a year to two refineries near Strasbourg and two near Karlsruhe. In Italy, a recently completed pipeline runs 620 miles (990 km) from Genoa to Stuttgart in West Germany, and another is planned to link Trieste with a refinery at

Schwechat near Vienna. This latter will be 320 miles (512 km) long and will have an initial capacity of 1,300,000 tons of crude oil annually, rising gradually to 6 million tons.

All these specialised facilities to deal with bulk imports and exports are indications of the growing importance of the Mediterranean lands in international commerce, yet they do not present a full picture. We have seen that in almost every country the growth of modern industrial enterprises is being accompanied by improvements and enlargements of transport systems. Together, these have necessitated great alterations of wharves, warehouses and docking space at ports. In the older ports, such as Barcelona, Genoa, Naples, Venice, Salonika, Istanbul, Tunis, Algiers, Casablanca, Lisbon, Bilbao and Alexandria, increased accommodation has had to be provided because of the larger volume of trade and the greater size of ships, and on a smaller scale the same story may be told of many minor ports, notably in Yugoslavia, Syria, Israel and Libya. The harbour and docks at Rijeka and Split have been almost reconstructed; since 1952 a new port at Latakia has replaced the old one; Tripoli and Benghazi in Libya have been modernised; and Beirut in Lebanon has been greatly improved.

The ancient Biblical port of Jaffa in Israel, with its modern sister-port, Tel Aviv, was declared obsolete in October 1965, and all large vessels instructed to proceed to Haifa. Jaffa and Tel Aviv are poor harbours, and cargoes had to be discharged from liners into lighters. A new deep-water port is being built at Ashdod, about 20 miles (32 km) south of Tel Aviv. This is not yet complete, but in the section already in operation, the total volume of citrus fruits and Negev minerals being dealt with is greater than in Jaffa and Tel Aviv combined.

The former French naval dockyard at Bizerta in Tunisia was renamed in 1966 the Bizerta International Dockyard. With new docks and repair shops, it is now open to liners and other ships from any foreign country. It is managed by the Tampa Ship Repair Company (America), which provided most of the equipment and owns 49% of the stock, the remainder being controlled by the Tunisian Government. This is just one example of the way foreign capital and expert knowledge are being used in the effort to industrialise the Mediterranean lands. Other countries benefiting in the same way are Spain, Greece, Yugoslavia, Turkey, Israel, Libya, Algeria and Morocco.

TOURISM

No account of the economic geography of the Mediterranean lands would be complete without a consideration of the very real impact made on most of them by the phenomenal rise of the tourist industry. The genial temperatures and long periods of cloudless skies in winter have always attracted visitors to the more conveniently situated areas such as the French Riviera, but in general such visitors were confined to the wealthier classes. In recent years, however, the increased standards of living in the countries of Western Europe and the rapid development of fast air transport have brought the sunny shores of the Mediterranean within the scope of all, not only in winter but throughout the year, and holiday-makers began to flock to the older-established Cote d'Azur in France and the Riviera di Ponente in Italy. As a result of the increased demand, helped by the judicious advertisements of tourist agencies encouraging a flight from the gloomy skies of northern countries, the smaller "rivieras" in Spain, Portugal, and along the northern Adriatic began to reorganise their facilities and build new hotels and flats. The Costa Brava, Costa del Sol, and the Rivieras di Levante, Rimini, Pesaro, Split and Dubrovnik became popular resorts for Western European, including British, tourists, and the more venturesome travelled to Malta, the Levant, Turkey and North Africa. Today, visits to Majorca, Iviza and Morocco are commonplace, and holidays in Tunisia are by no means prohibitive in price; and when the political position in the Eastern Mediterranean becomes more settled, the flow of tourists to Egypt and the Holy Land, small at present, will be greatly augmented. An increase in tourism brings in its train great developments in service industries such as food processing, and in luxury trades, but a much more noteworthy result is the transformation in the landscape caused by the building of new hotels and blocks of flats, and by the construction of roads and systems of water supply, sewage and electrification in areas previously undeveloped. The tourist industry provides a welcome addition to the revenues of the more backward countries, and by its impact on their ways of life is bringing changes also in their social economies. Visiting tourists are interested in and enjoy the cultures they find in the Mediterranean lands, but they bring with them their own cultural ideas and demands, and these are having a significant effect on the whole Mediterranean economy—an effect which is bound to be felt in increasing degree; for it must be remembered that the Mediterranean lands have as neighbours some of the richest and most developed states in the world.

STUDY QUESTIONS

1. What conditions are required for the large-scale development of hydro-electric power and where are they found around the Mediterranean? To what extent has this form of power led to the growth of industry in the region?

2. With special reference to the Mediterranean lands, show the value of motor transport in the political and economic development of emergent states.

3. Write a short essay on *one* of the following: (*a*) the oilfields of the Mediterranean lands, (*b*) hydro-electricity in the Arab states of the Levant and North Africa, (*c*) the distribution of mineral ores in the Mediterranean lands.

4. One criterion in the growing industrialisation of a country is its production and consumption of chemicals. Where and how far can this test be applied in the Mediterranean lands?

5. Indicate the changes (political, social and economic) which the discovery and exploitation of petroleum and natural gas in the Mediterranean lands and the Middle East have caused in the ways of life of the inhabitants.

6. Write an account of the distribution and exploitation of non-metallic minerals around the Mediterranean.

7. Write a general account of industrialisation in the Mediterranean lands. Refer in your answer to problems relating to fuel and power supplies, communications and transport, and the supply of suitable labour.

8. "Roads are more important than railways in new and developing states." Criticise this statement with special reference to the Mediterranean lands.

PART TWO
REGIONAL GEOGRAPHY

Chapter IX

THE IBERIAN PENINSULA. SPAIN

INTRODUCTION: THE IBERIAN PENINSULA

CLINGING to the south-west of Europe is the Iberian peninsula, a rectangular land mass separated from the rest of the continent by the Pyrenees, a continuous chain of rugged, high-peaked mountains through which no more than ten passes allow of road communications. The Iberian peninsula has an area of 231,000 square miles (420,600 sq. km)—nearly twice that of the British Isles—and is divided into Spain and Portugal. Spain is almost six times as large as Portugal.

The peninsula is so shut off by the Pyrenees from its neighbour to the north that Louis XIV of France, towards the end of the seventeeth century, was led to declare that "Europe ends at the Pyrenees." Pedro Lain, a Spanish historian, called the peninsula "Marginal Europe." One would certainly disagree with the French king, but Lain's definition is very apt, since the Iberian peninsula is distinct from the rest of Europe in its climatic types, its geographical outlook and the development of its peoples—the last especially so in modern times.

PHYSICAL ASPECTS

STRUCTURAL DEVELOPMENT OF IBERIA

The complicated structure of the Iberian peninsula has led to much speculation about its development. It will be useful, therefore, to examine its geological history as a preliminary to the more detailed treatment of the structural divisions of Spain and Portugal.

In the north-west of the Iberian peninsula—in Galicia, north Portugal and much of the Central Sierras—there are rocks of pre-Cambrian age, similar in type to those in the Baltic Shield; and traces of Caledoni⸱n folding have been found. According to one hypothesis, these were folded in late Carboniferous times in high Hercynian mountain ranges, running from east to west across the present area of the peninsula. The ranges were then eroded almost to their stumps, and submerged and covered by Mesozoic and Tertiary deposits. Towards the end of the Tertiary period the Alpine orogenesis buckled the sedimentaries on the floor of the Tethys Sea, which covered the area, so lifting and folding the Betic Cordillera across the south and south-east of the present peninsula. At the same time the Pyrenees and Cantabrians were being uplifted in the north. Between the northern and southern systems the ancient Hercynian platform was forced upwards as a great horst, to form the plateau of the Meseta which now occupies most of the peninsula.

The Cantabrian mountains and Pyrenees are usually regarded as part of the Alpine system, but the presence in them of so many rocks of Carbo-Permian age suggests that strictly speaking they are Hercynian folds rejuvenated in the "Alpine storm." To the same period belong the Catalonian mountains and the ranges which fringe the Meseta in the north-east. It seems likely, too, that the Central Sierras, the Sierra Toledo and the Sierra Morena were uplifted across the surface of the

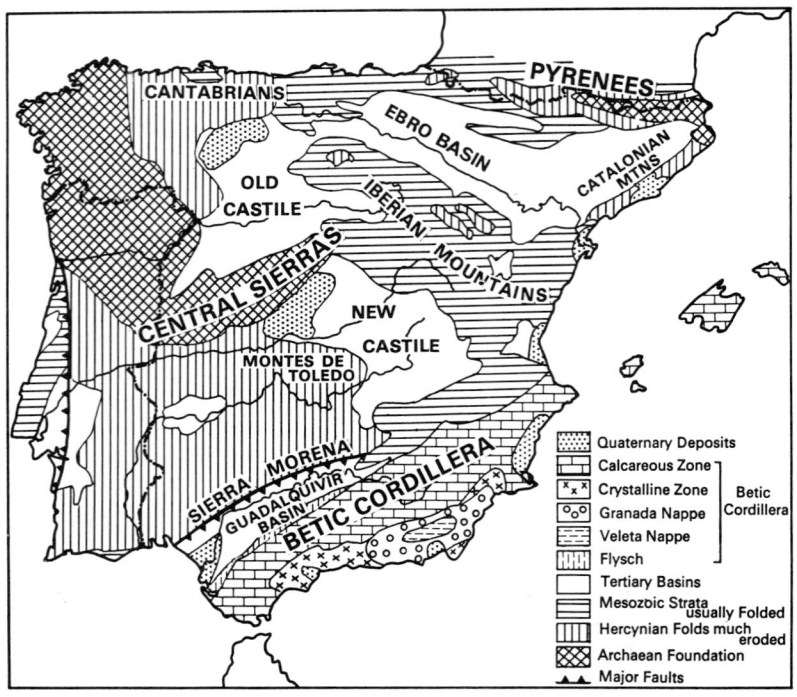

FIG. 37.—Iberian peninsula: structure. The boundary between Spain and Portugal is shown by a chain line. The Hercynian formations are continued under the Tertiary basins of Old and New Castile.

Meseta by thrusts from the south late in the Alpine-building period, and that they are the results, not of folding, but of faulting.

The Betic Cordillera, on the other hand, are true Alpine ranges in structure. To the north there is a narrow belt of flysch, similar to that north of the Alps in Central Europe. It is followed by an outer limestone zone. Nappe formation in Granada has resulted in the Sierra Nevada, the highest part of the Cordillera, in which crystalline rocks come to the surface in the Veleta "window." The southern ranges are mostly of limestone. There are only faint traces of nappe formation in the Pyrenees and none at all in the Cantabrians. Fundamentally, the greater part of the Iberian peninsula is of Hercynian rocks.

Pressures exerted on the horst of the Meseta caused faulting on its northern and southern margins. Between the Meseta and the Pyrenees was formed the trough of the Ebro basin, and in the south the Guadalquivir basin lies between the Meseta and the Betic Cordillera. The same pressures which resulted in the "horsts within a horst" of the plateau sierras caused down-faulting north and south of these block ranges and a series of transverse troughs or depressions. The northernmost includes the basins of Old Castile; south of the Central Sierras are the basins of New Castile and the middle Tagus, the latter in Portugal. The upper Guadiana basin in Extremadura is in a third series. All these depressions are floored by Tertiary sands, marls and clays. A great fault running from the mouth of the river Douro to Cape St Vincent resulted in the downthrow of the Meseta west of it, and produced the lowlands of Portugal.

The south-west of the Iberian peninsula is still unstable: in recent centuries Portugal has suffered many disastrous earthquakes, probably because of earth movement along the great fault. This fault may have been formed in an epeirogenic upheaval of Pliocene times, when the whole peninsula, except in the south-west, was uplifted, resulting in the steep edges of the Meseta, which make access to the interior difficult, except from Portugal. In the same uplift the rivers of the Meseta were rejuvenated. Their deeply-incised, gulley-like valleys constitute serious obstacles to north–south communications on the plateau.

There are few traces of the existence of the Ice Age in Iberia. The Pyrenees, Cantabrians and Sierra Nevada show signs of valley glaciation, such as U-shaped valleys, but nowhere in the peninsula was there an extensive ice sheet. Probably the climate was too dry.

STRUCTURAL DIVISIONS OF SPAIN

From the foregoing it is seen that Spain may be divided into the plateau of the Meseta, around which are the pseudo-Alpine ranges of the Pyrenees, Cantabrians and Galicia in the north, and the truly Alpine Betic Cordillera in the south, separated from the Meseta by the troughs of the Ebro and Guadalquivir. But this simple division into plateau, mountain ranges, and lowland river basins is not really satisfactory in examining Spain's geography. For besides being distinguished from each other by accidents of geology, the regions are further differentiated by climates which range from wet to very dry, and by peoples who in different parts of the country are so unlike each other in language, culture and economic development as almost to give the impression they belong to separate nations. Moreover, this "compartmentalism" of Spain (as it has been called) is encountered even within the major structural divisions, so that, to obtain a true picture of the country's geography, each must be sub-divided into minor regions. The whole country is better grouped according to physical, climatic and economic rather than purely structural considerations.

In this chapter, therefore, Spain is divided initially into: (1) the Atlantic coastlands, (2) the Mediterranean coastlands, and (3) the remainder of the country. These are further sub-divided into 1(*a*) Galicia, the Cantabrian mountains and the coastal plain of the Asturias, 1(*b*) the province of Santander, the Basque provinces and the western Pyrenees. The Mediterranean coastlands include 2(*a*) the eastern Pyrenees and the series of isolated coastal plains which occur along the east and south coasts of Spain, 2(*b*) the basin of the river Guadalquivir, which although outside the Mediterranean is related in its development to the coastal plains along it.

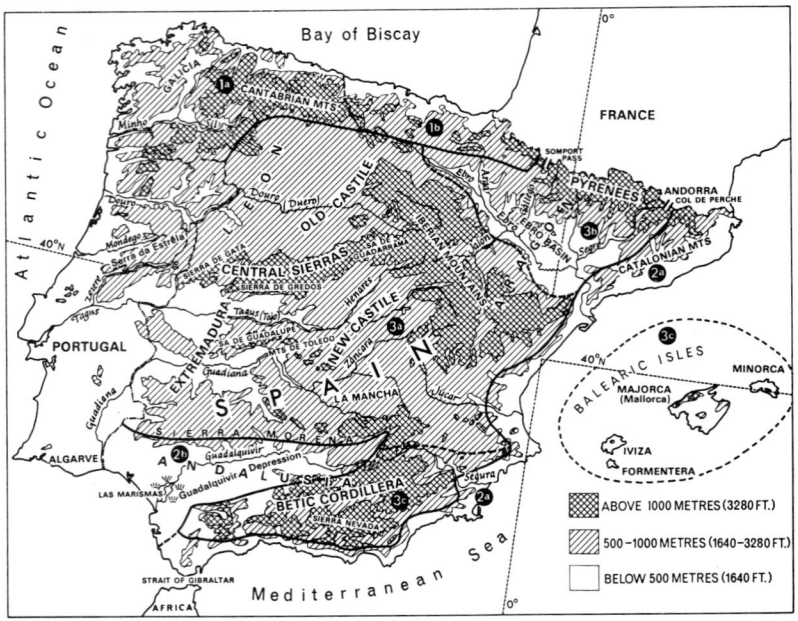

Fig. 38.—Iberian peninsula: physical features. The numbers correspond with the regional divisions of Spain used in the text.

The remaining regions are 3(*a*) the Meseta, 3(*b*) the central Pyrenees and the basin of the river Ebro, 3(*c*) the Betic Cordillera and the Balearic islands. The divisions are shown in Fig. 38.

1. The Atlantic coastlands

(a) *Galicia; the Cantabrian mountains; the Asturian plain.* Galicia, in the north-west of Spain, is a low undulating plateau of pre-Cambrian granites. The region was severely fractured when the Cantabrian mountains were being formed and, in the intervals between the resultant horsts, swift, short rivers have carved deep valleys. Slight sinking of their lower courses has led to invasion by the sea and the formation of a ria coastline, similar to that in Brittany and south-west England. The soils of Galicia, derived from igneous rocks, are poor.

East of Galicia, the quartzites and limestones of the Cantabrian mountains rise to over 7000 ft (2150 m). The range forms a high barrier between the coast and the interior, pierced by only one main road and one railway. From the southern slopes of the Galician and Cantabrian highlands flow the headwaters of the Minho (Miño), and of the Esla and its tributaries which flow to the Douro (Duero). These are important because of the hydro-electric power stations recently constructed on them. North of the Cantabrians is the narrow but well-developed coastal plain of the Asturias. Its soils are not much better than those of Galicia, but careful cultivation has made them very productive.

(b) *The province of Santander; the Basque provinces; the western Pyrenees.* The Cantabrian mountains east of Asturias decrease in height and the ranges are more broken. They are largely covered by Mesozoic sandstones and limestones. These have developed into good soils, so that the province of Santander and the rolling, hilly Basque provinces which succeed it eastwards are agriculturally the most favoured parts of Spain.

The undulating lowlands continue to the French boundary, and communications to the interior in this region, though not easy, are much better than farther west.

The western Pyrenees are included here because they have a population which is closely related to that of the Basque provinces. They form the lowest part of the Pyrenees, rarely rising to more than 7000 ft (2150 m). The western Pyrenees lie west of the Somport Pass (5310 ft, 1618 m), which is traversed by a road and railway. There are several other passes, notably that of Roncesvalles (3435 ft, 1047 m). On the French side the western Pyrenees have steep slopes, but in Spain they descend in steps to low sierras and intermontane basins floored by Mesozoic deposits similar to those of the Basque provinces.

2. The Mediterranean coastlands

(a) *The eastern Pyrenees; the coastal plains.* East of the Col de la Perche (5120 ft, 1551 m), the Pyrenees are broken into a number of ranges, the highest of which, with many peaks over 8000 ft (2440 m), are in France. On the Spanish side, although there are occasional high mountains, such as Puigmal (9460 ft, 2883 m), the ranges are lower and enclose several longitudinal depressions. The eastern Pyrenees are pierced by roads and railways. One road crosses by the Col de la Perche, another by an easier route nearer the coast. A railway from Barcelona to Toulouse makes use of the valley leading to the Col de la Perche, then tunnels under the Carlotta massif. Coastal roads and the railway between Spain and France pass along the narrow gap between the Pyrenees and the Mediterranean coast.

The eastern and southern coasts of Spain are rugged and often cliff-lined, and there is very little lowland. North of the river Ebro, the sub-Pyrenean sierras are flanked by narrow coastal plains; south of the river the lowlands are chiefly the result of delta formation by the short, swift streams flowing from the Meseta or the Betic Cordillera to the Mediterranean. North of the Ebro, the plains of Catalonia include those of Gerona, Barcelona and Tarragona, which have a flooring of Tertiary sands and river alluvium. They are separated from each other by granite outliers of the eastern Pyrenees, or by the Mesozoic formations of the Catalonian mountains. In between the ranges are further small lowlands, parallel to the coast.

Southwards along the coast are the plains of Castellón de la Plana and Valentia, completely isolated by the steep edge of the Meseta from western climatic influences. At the south-east corner of Spain, hemmed in by the Betic Cordillera, are the plains of Alicante and Murcia, which form a continuous lowland. Along the south coast the mountains are so near the sea there is little room for coastal plains. The only ones of any size lie behind Almería and Málaga, where water for irrigation is available. At the western end of the coast a tiny strip of lowland lies behind the narrow, rocky peninsula of Gibraltar. This small plain serves as a kind of "no man's land" between British and Spanish territory.

(b) *The basin of the river Guadalquivir.* The province of Andalusia includes the southern slopes of the Meseta—Sierra Morena—the basin of the river Guadalquivir, the Betic Cordillera and the southern coastal plains. Here attention is confined to the wedge-shaped lowland opening westwards to the Atlantic and drained by the Guadalquivir (Arab. *wadi al kabir*, "the great river"). It is a trough let down between the Meseta and the folded Cordilleran ranges, with limestone hills in its eastern section, Tertiary clays in the middle stretch, and alluvium and muds in the area nearer the sea. It is included with the Mediterranean coastlands because it has a Mediterranean climate; but because it is open to the west it receives oceanic winds which bring more rain than to the plains on the east and south of Spain.

3. *The Meseta; the central Pyrenees; the Ebro basin; the Betic Cordillera*

(a) *The Meseta.* Geologically the term "meseta" is applied to the whole of the region of Iberia and north-west Africa involved in pre-Cambrian flexing and Hercynian folding. In Iberia the Meseta is the vast tableland of Spain, which stretches from the Cantabrians in the north to the Guadalquivir basin in the south, and from the borders of Portugal to the Mediterranean coast. It is a horst, originally part of the Hercynian mountain system, peneplained, submerged beneath the water of the Tethys Sea, uplifted again in Tertiary times, and tilted downwards towards the west. The level of the tableland falls from about 3200 ft (975 m) in the east to less than 1500 ft (460 m) near Portugal, but it is traversed by three series of mountain ranges which in places exceed 8000 ft (2440 m).

The northern series, the Central Sierras, includes the Sierra de Guadarrama, Sierra de Gredos de Avila and Sierra de Gata. It continues into Portugal as the Serra da Estrêla. These ranges are composed largely of the granites and schists of the pre-Cambrian Meseta platform, broken into horsts and massifs packed tightly against one another, with rounded tops or high plateaus. They are a formidable barrier between the northern and southern Meseta.

The second series is known collectively as the Mountains of Toledo, and includes the Sierra de Guadalupe and Sierra de San Pedro. They are similar in origin and rock structure to the Central Sierras, but are neither as high nor as difficult to cross. The Sierra Morena, forming the southern margin of the Meseta, are the third series. Viewed from the plateau, they are not really mountains, but rather the warped edge of the Meseta. They fall steeply to the Andalusian basin of the Guadalquivir, but are not a serious obstacle to communications.

North of the Central Sierras is the basin of Old Castile (Castilla la Vieja) and León, at an average height of about 2500 ft (760 m). South of the ranges the depression of New Castile (Castilla la Nueva) is about 300 ft (90 m) lower. These hollows in the surface of the Meseta were once salt-water lakes, in which were deposited Tertiary and later sediments which now floor the basins. In the north-east of the Meseta are the Iberian mountains, a confused area of folded ranges. They are mainly of Mesozoic limestones formed in Tertiary times and greatly eroded, so that the region is more plateau-like than mountainous.

Before its final uplift the Meseta was covered by Tertiary sedimentaries. Large areas of these remain in the plateau basins and in the basin of the Ebro to the north. Over most of the plateau they have disappeared; where denudation has been extensive, the older and more resistant rocks thus disclosed have given rise to a broken relief. Differential erosion of the original Tertiaries has resulted in a great number of low, flat-topped plateaus rising above the general level of the Meseta, sometimes to a height of 4000 ft (1230 m). The flat tops of the *paramos*, as the low plateaus are called, represent the original level. Denudation has lowered the floor of the Meseta, leaving the paramos as cliff-lined blocks of limestone, fit only for poor sheep pasture.

The Meseta is crossed from east to west by the rivers Douro, Tagus (Tajo) and Guadiana. They flow in deeply entrenched valleys and, in Spain, are unnavigable. A marked seasonal régime makes them of little value for hydro-electric development, and their waters are too far below the general level of the plateau to be used for irrigation, except locally. The tributaries of the Tagus, for instance, fed by melting snows on the Central Sierras, are more valuable than the main stream: they are dammed for power, domestic water supplies for Madrid, and irrigation.

(b) *The central Pyrenees; the Ebro basin.* These two regions are taken together because historically they constitute the ancient kingdom of Aragon, and are geographically complementary.

The central Pyrenees, lying between the Somport Pass and the Col de la Perche, are a massive barrier of folded mountains, rarely falling below 5000 ft (1525 m) and rising in Maladetta to 11,174 ft (3406 m). In the main, they are composed of crystalline rocks. Most of the valleys leading into the mountains from the south finish blindly, and only three of them are continued by poor roads across the range. One road goes to Andorra, a tiny republic of 191 square miles (495 sq. km), which lies in interconnected valleys at an altitude of more than 6500 ft (2000 m). At the foot of the central Pyrenees is a broad belt of less elevated sierras which present scarp slopes to the Ebro lowlands south of them.

The river Ebro flows through a long, triangular basin, which is almost enclosed between the Pyrenees and the Meseta. The upper course of the river is in the Basque provinces, and it enters its plain tract below Miranda. The surface of the basin is far from being level. The almost horizontal Tertiary beds which floor it have been scored into deep valleys by the Ebro and its tributaries. Differential erosion has resulted in many flat-topped, isolated plateaus, not high enough to be called paramos nor to make much difference to the general monotony of the arid-looking landscape. The Ebro leaves its basin by a gorge through the Catalonian mountains and enters the Mediterranean by a delta. It is of negligible value for navigation. Its volume varies too much; its speed in the gorge is too great; and its delta channels are constantly in process of silting.

(c) *The Betic Cordillera; the Balearic islands.* The Betic Cordillera lie across southern Spain, with an east–north–east to west–south–west trend. The Cordillera are divided into two parallel belts of highland, separated by a narrow depression which widens into a number of distinct basins. The northern belt, the sub-Betic region, is composed (among other ranges) of the Sierra de Lucena, Sierra del Pozo, Sierra de Segura and Sierra de Tiabilla. They are all mainly of limestones, with clays and sandstones in the valleys. Their average height is less than 6500 ft (2000 m). The southern belt is largely of crystalline rocks, and reaches much greater altitudes. It runs from the Sierra Bermeja in the west to the Sierra de las Estancias in the east, and is highest in the centre in the Sierra Nevada, with the peak of Mulhacen (11,420 ft, 3482 m). The high basins strung along the central depression include Loja, Granada, Moreda, Braza and Lorca.

East of the Betic Cordillera, and separated by a channel about fifty miles wide (80 km), are the Balearic islands. Folds of Jurassic limestone, topped by Tertiary strata, suggest they are continuations of the northern belt of the Cordillera. The largest islands are Majorca (Mallorca), Minorca (Menorca) and Iviza (Ibiza). There are nearly twenty other islets, some too small to be inhabited.

CLIMATE AND VEGETATION

The Iberian peninsula, of which Spain forms the major portion, is situated between 36 and 43½ degrees N., *i.e.* in summer it falls within the normal anticyclonic belt of the Mediterranean, and in winter under the influence of the westerlies. The climate of the peninsula, however, shows great variations from the conditions which usually follow from this position. Although Iberia is almost surrounded by sea, maritime influences play only a minor part in determining its climate. The peninsula is like a miniature continent, in winter developing a high pressure system in its interior, with accompanying cold, frosty days and nights, and some snow. It is often possible to enjoy open-air skating in Madrid during January and February. In winter, when the Mediterranean region has its maximum precipitation, the interior and east of Iberia are still dry, so that much of the peninsula has little rain at any season. Parts of the Ebro basin, for instance, have only 12 in. a year.

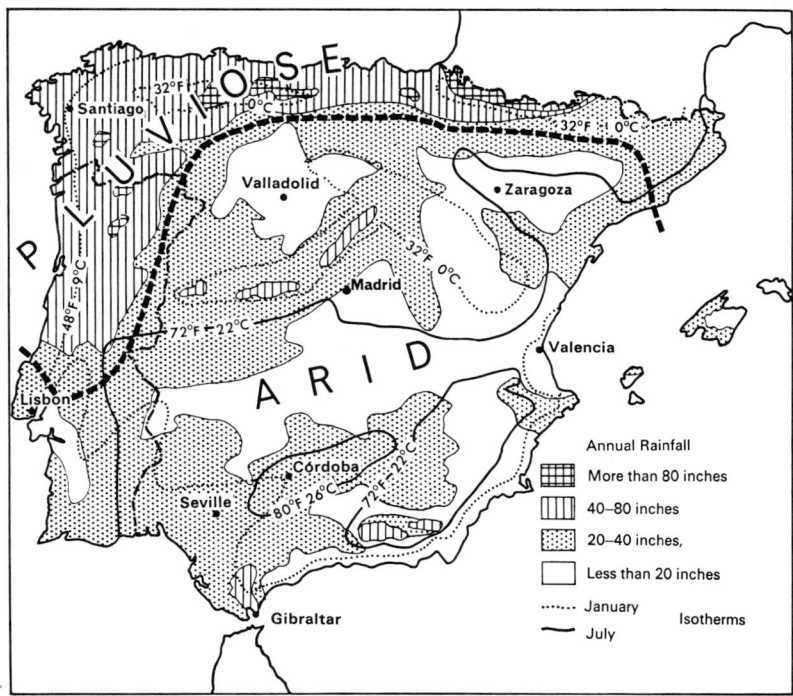

FIG. 39.—Iberian peninsula: climate, showing (a) the rapid fall of winter temperatures away from the coast, and the large area in the north of the Meseta below freezing-point (unique in western and southern Europe), (b) the extensive areas with less than 20 in. of rainfall annually, (c) the favourable climate of Portugal in comparison with that of Spain.

The depressions which move along the Mediterranean in winter bring rain to the north, north-west and west of Iberia, where the mountain ranges and the western edge of the Meseta form a screen, leaving the rest of the peninsula in their rain-shadow. The high Betic Cordillera is also well watered in winter. The outer slopes of the Cantabrians and the north-west corner of Iberia have maximum precipitation in winter, but they have sufficient rainfall in summer to justify their inclusion in the region of west European marginal climate. Santiago has an annual rainfall of 65 in., of which 23 in. fall in summer. This region is also the most equable in Spain, with mean temperatures ranging from 45° F (7·2° C) in January to 66° F (18·9° C) in July. Atlantic influences are felt farther south in Portugal, whose lowlands, open to the sea, may receive up to 30 in. rainfall annually (the climate of Portugal is treated more fully in the next chapter). The rocky peninsula of Gibraltar, at the western end of the Betic Cordillera, has an annual rainfall of 35 in. and, farther east, the Sierra Nevada may have up to 45 in., falling as snow in winter. The Sierra Nevada are among the few Mediterranean mountains which retain a capping of snow in summer.

Away from these highland regions, the peninsula's annual rainfall is low. Valladolid, in the north-west of the Meseta and under the lee of the mountains, receives only 13 in. a year; Zaragoza, in the Ebro basin, $11\frac{1}{2}$ in. Few districts of the Meseta have an annual precipitation of more than 20 in., and these are in the higher parts of the plateau sierras. Madrid, near the Sierra de Guadarrama and at an altitude of 2168 ft (660 m), has a yearly rainfall of $16\frac{1}{2}$ in.—rather more than the average on the plateau. One of the driest regions of the Meseta is La Mancha (Arab. al mancha, "the thirsty land") in New Castile. Rain on the Meseta comes in heavy showers of short duration but great erosive power. Before it has had time to soak into the surface or increase the volume of the plateau rivers to any extent, it is dried up by evaporation. Consequently the plateau has normally a scorched appearance. In the southern half it may approach semi-desert conditions.

The coastlands of the east and south have, in general, slightly more rain than the Meseta, with a definite winter maximum. The Mediterranean coastal plains in the north, owing to their proximity to the Pyrenees, have the highest precipitation, around 20 in. a year. Barcelona, however, only 69 ft (21 km) above sea-level, has a mere 15 in. The driest of the coastal plains are Murcia and Alicante, where, in the shelter of the Betic Cordillera, the annual rainfall is $14\frac{1}{2}$ in.

The annual rainfall is taken as a basis for dividing Spain into two regions, a *pluviose* (rainy) and an *arid* sector, using the 25-in. isohyet as the line of demarcation. The pluviose sector includes the north-west corner, the Biscayan coastlands and the Pyrenees; the arid sector, the rest of the country.

The anticyclonic conditions which obtain over arid Spain both in winter and summer tend to give continental extremes of temperature, annual and diurnal. Winter temperatures do not on average fall below freezing point for any considerable periods, although snow is not uncommon on the northern plateau and frost may be experienced for days on end. Night frosts are frequent in January and February. January mean temperatures increase from north to south, from 39° F (3·9° C) in Valladolid and 41° F (5° C) in Madrid, to 50° F (10° C) in Seville. Summer temperatures range from 66° F (18·9° C) in Valladolid to 84° F (28·9° C) in

Seville. Summers in the Guadalquivir valley are perhaps the hottest in Europe. Madrid's July average is 78°F (25·6 °C).

The coastal plains of the east and south are more typically Mediterranean in their temperatures. Barcelona ranges from a mean of 46° F (7·8° C) in January to 74° F (23·3° C) in July, Valencia from 51° F (10·6° C) to 76° F (24·4° C), and Murcia from 50° F (10° C) to 79° F (26·1° C).

From the foregoing, it will be seen that Spain offers two sets of climatic contrasts: (a) between the pluviose and arid sectors of the country, and (b) between the coastlands and the interior. These contrasts are evident also in the natural vegetation, which varies from the forested and verdant mountains of the north-west to the parched, arid plains of La Mancha.

North-west Spain has a natural cover of forests of oak and chestnut, with pines at higher levels, and these are continued into the western Pyrenees. The central and eastern Pyrenees are clothed with cork-oak and pine in the wetter parts, and Mediterranean shrubs such as gorse and broom in the drier, and on the limestone platforms at their base there is an extensive cover of garrigue. Forests of cork-oak and pine are found also in the Betic Cordillera, and on some of the plateau sierras. Over most of the Meseta and the coastal plains the natural vegetation is grass, richer in the wetter parts but descending to poor steppe in La Mancha, the Ebro basin and the eastern Guadalquivir basin. Much of the grass is esparto valuable for sheep rearing and as a raw material for paper.

HUMAN GEOGRAPHY

HISTORY AND PEOPLE

It is believed that human habitation of the Iberian peninsula began in the eleventh century B.C., when Cro-Magnon man migrated from Africa to settle in caves near Murcia and Andalusia, and along the Cantabrian coast. In the caves of Altamira, near Santander, he has left well-preserved red and black drawings of bison, horses, boar and deer. He was followed by the Iberians, who landed on the east coast and penetrated to the interior. In the sixth century B.C. the Celts came in by the same route as the Iberians, and after much fighting merged with them to form the Celtiberians. It was part of this Celtic migration which peopled the west of Ireland and Scotland.

Meanwhile the Phoenicians, seafaring merchants from the eastern Mediterranean, set up trading posts and small settlements on the south and west coasts. The chief of these was Agadir, where Cadiz now stands. The Greeks, too, had coastal trading stations. The Carthaginians were called in to help the Phoenicians repel the attacks of barbarians from the north; they moved inland and took over much of the interior, directing operations from their headquarters, New Carthage, now Cartagena.

In the third century B.C. the Romans invaded the peninsula, and retained control for more than 500 years. They called the peninsula Iberia and the eastern portion Hispania—hence the name of Spain. The region to the west, the present Portugal, was called Lusitania. The Romans introduced their language and culture, constructed roads, aqueducts and bridges, and built beautiful villas. The aqueducts of Segovia and Mérida, and the bridges at Alcantara, Salamanca and Mérida date from Roman times. The beneficent rule of the Romans, who met with little resistance from the inhabitants at any time, became very relaxed, so that when the Visigoths invaded the peninsula from the north in the fifth century A.D. they found it easy to conquer. Visigoth domination began in A.D. 414 and lasted 300 years, during which most of the benefits the Romans bestowed were lost. In the latter years of their rule, the country was threatened by Moorish inroads from the south.

The Moors landed from North Africa in 710. After a harsh and vigorous seven-year campaign they commanded the whole peninsula except for the wild, rugged highlands of the Asturias and north of the river Douro in Portugal. For seven centuries the Iberian peninsula was divided between the Muslim Moors and the Christian Visigoth-Iberians, and all the time the conquerors were harassed by guerilla bands from the north. Although they were cruel masters, the Moors introduced not only their religion but also laws and customs derived from the civilisations of Egypt and Persia, and there are still signs of the long period of occupation. Place-names derived from Arabic are very common in the south; much of the architecture has Muslim characteristics; irrigation systems like those in North Africa were constructed wherever possible; and plants such as citrus fruits, cotton and sugar cane were imported. Some of their laws of water usage are still in force.

By the eleventh century, easy conquest, luxury and internal squabbles were loosening the Moors' grip on the country. They were gradually driven from the north of the peninsula by the tough, mountain-bred, fanatical Christians. The little kingdom of the Asturias spread over the mountains to become the larger kingdom of León; Castile and Aragon became Christian again; by 1085 the Moors were compelled to retreat south of the Sierra Morena. This was the period of Spain's legendary hero, El Cid Campeador, whose name struck terror into the hearts of the Moors. It saw too the birth of Portugal as a separate country. By the beginning of the thirteenth century the Moors had lost Córdoba and Seville, and were encircled in Granada and the Portuguese Algarve. In 1474, the year the kingdoms of León, Castile and Aragon were united by the marriage of Isabella of Castile and Ferdinand of Aragon, the end of the long struggle was in sight. Granada, the last Moorish stronghold, was captured in 1492 and the hated occupiers finally expelled from the peninsula.

The reign of Ferdinand and Isabella marks a turning point in the history of Spain. In the same year that Granada surrendered, Christopher Columbus, a Genoese sailing in the service of Spain, discovered the New World. Spanish *conquistadores* soon followed in his wake. Adventurers such as Pizarro, Cortes and de Soto brought back from the Americas vast stores of gold and added new territories to the Spanish crown. Spain became a leading power in exploration and colonisation.

This "Golden Age," during which Spain was the richest and one of the most powerful states in Europe, lasted until the death of Philip II in 1598. Afterwards decline set in. Philip's father, Charles I, was an Austrian Hapsburg, who came to the throne of Spain by marriage and ruled from 1516 to 1556. He was elected Holy Roman Emperor in 1519 and Spain was immediately embroiled in the wars and politics of the rest of Europe. At the same time as the conquistadores were extending her empire in the New World, the country was dragged into wars with England, France and the Netherlands. Her increasing exhaustion at home was demonstrated in 1588 by the ruinous defeat of the great Armada, although it should be said that a contributory cause of this disaster was the inferiority of Spanish ship design, consequent on the reluctance of Spanish shipbuilders to accept new ideas and techniques. The Hapsburg successors of Philip II were ineffective rulers in Spain—they were more interested in Austria—and when the last of them died in 1700, the gold brought back from America had been squandered, and Spain was almost bankrupt. Dispute about who should succeed the Hapsburgs led to the War of the Spanish Succession, and when it ended in 1713 the Spanish throne was given to the Bourbons (Borbóns). With two short inter-missions they ruled Spain until 1931.

The Bourbon monarchy proved to be as effete as the later Hapsburgs. There were many uprisings by the Spanish peasants against the harshness of the aristocracy and the squalor in which they were forced to live. Matters became worse after 1833, when rival claimants to the throne precipitated the Carlist Wars, civil warfare which continued inter-mittently for forty-three years and left many parts of the country in ruins. General discontent and labour troubles were prolonged into the present century. In 1931 the king was dethroned, exiled and a republic proclaimed. Political and economic turmoil ensued; in 1936 civil war broke out again, and continued for three years. Armed forces under General Franco rose successfully against the official republican govern-ment in Madrid and seized power, but not before one of the bitterest con-flicts in history had been fought. In 1939 Franco became Chief of State and ruler of Spain, a position he still holds today.

Under his leadership the country has made considerable social and economic advances. It has even returned to its monarchist traditions. In 1947 a public referendum ratified the Act of Succession, which proclaimed Spain a kingdom, with Franco (Francisco Franco Bahamonde) Chief of State. On his death he is to be succeeded by a person of royal blood, but up to the present the Council of the Realm has not designated an heir. Spain, therefore, has a peculiar political status; it is a kingdom without a king.

History offers few contrasts so striking as between Spain during the sixteenth century and at the present time. Less than four hundred years ago Spain was a great power, claiming dominion over a large portion of the world and drawing vast riches from the exploits of its seamen and exploring adventurers. Today it is economically backward and politically unstable. Only the Canary Islands and the two tiny African enclaves of Rio de Oro and Rio Muni remain of its empire. Much of its decline was undoubtedly due to the ineptitude or indifference of its rulers during the past three centuries, but this is only part of the explanation. We must search in geography for other important reasons.

In the first place Spain, unlike Portugal, is not really a maritime nation. Its coasts, except at the entrance to the Guadalquivir basin, are shut off from the interior of the country by the wall-like edges of the Meseta; it is noteworthy that Cádiz, its greatest port in past times, is near the mouth of the Guadalquivir. It is a reasonable supposition that Spain was encouraged to maritime adventure by the successful exploits of Portugal; her own victory over the Moors had aroused feelings of national pride and confidence. But as we have seen, the "Golden Age" lasted only a hundred years, and in any case it brought little benefit to the great mass of the people. Wealth and land ownership were concentrated in the hands of the Crown, the Church and the nobility, and the position is only slightly changed today.

A second factor was Spain's isolation from the rest of Europe by the barrier of the Pyrenees. It was underlined by the adoption of a broad gauge for the railways which approached the French frontier. With the memory of several invasions still fresh, Spain deliberately chose a different gauge from its neighbour in order to restrict the easy passage of troops, but it just as effectively slowed down commercial transport and hindered industrial development.

Spain's present internal political troubles also have geographical causes. At the beginning of the century the country had virtually no industrial activity, except the mining and export of mineral ores, the iron and steel production of the Biscayan region and the textile manufactures of Barcelona. A very large proportion of this was in the hands of Basques and Catalans—peoples who lived in "compartments" outside the main mass of the country and were different in ethnic origin, language, culture and ways of thinking, as well as material well-being. Catalonia and the Basque provinces became increasingly separatist in politics and demanded self-determination. Their demands precipitated the civil war of 1936–39, in which the rebels were joined by many of the working classes of the plateau, whose condition, especially after the world economic crisis of 1929, was wretched in the extreme.

The civil war destroyed whatever economic advance had been made in the early part of the century. In addition to heavy loss of life, the transport system was crippled, the industries in Catalonia and the Basque lands were brought to a standstill, livestock was decimated, and a large proportion of the best agricultural land in the country was laid waste.

During the Second World War, Spain was unable to take advantage of her uneasy neutrality to improve her trading position with any of the combatants. She was much too occupied in attempting to rebuild her own shattered economy. Moreover, because the opposing sides in the civil war had been helped by Fascist, Nazi and Communist men and arms the country was ostracised by the Western powers after the Second World War, and excluded from the help given to other countries of Western Europe to rehabilitate themselves. Not until 1954 was any assistance given to Spain, and then the U.S.A. came to her aid. Only since that date has she shown signs of real economic advance; even now it is very slow and laboured.

The people of Spain are the result of invasion and settlement from the south, east and north. The true Spaniard, if any one type can be regarded as such, is found in Old Castile, and Castilian is the basis of the present Spanish language. There are, however, in Galicia, the Basque provinces and Catalonia, peoples who differ markedly in origin and tongue from the Castilians and have their own culture and traditions. In the south, too, the long occupation by the Moors has left its mark on the physical characteristics and temperament of the people of Andalusia. Their dialect is tempered with a large number of Arabic derivatives. It will be noted that the inhabitants of the Meseta seem to be the descendants of the original Spanish people, and that the various sub-peoples are around its edges. The Basques live at the eastern end of the Biscay coastlands, and are found also in south-western France. The Catalans live in north-eastern Spain and appear to be the same people as the Provençals of southern France, the dialects being very much akin. The Galicians are of the same racial stock as the old inhabitants of Brittany, south-west Ireland and some parts of west Scotland. They may be offshoots of a Celtic migration.

POPULATION

Spain, with a population of 31,339,500, has an average density of 160 persons per square mile, which is low compared with its neighbour Portugal's 255 per square mile. It must be remembered, however, that a far larger proportion of Spain is mountain or dry plateau, whereas Portugal has wide plains open to the sea.

The greatest concentration of population, outside the Meseta, is in the north. Catalonia and the Biscayan lands are the regions of industrial development, with a total of 10·5 million inhabitants: more than a third of the population in less than a quarter of the country's surface area. Catalonia has 262 persons a square mile, and some provinces along the Bay of Biscay 218. The density of 232 in the province of Galicia is noteworthy, for the region is one of fishermen-farmers and has little industry. The coastal plain of Valencia has a density of 252 but Murcia, the largest of the other coastal lowlands, has only 114. Away from the north, the greatest density is in the lowlands of Andalusia, where it is 166 a square mile.

The most densely peopled region of the Meseta is New Castile, with an

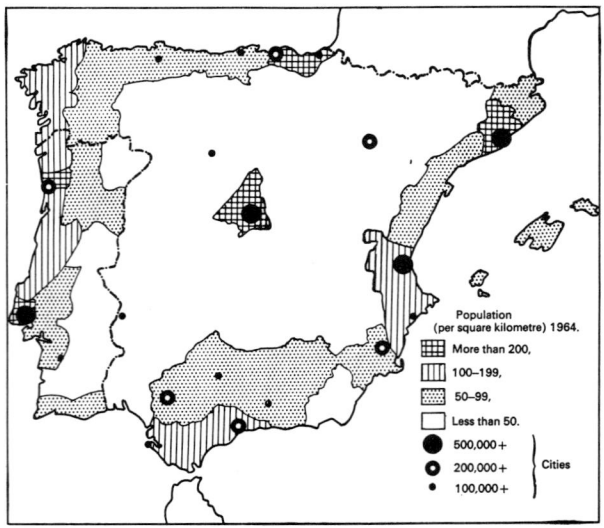

Fɪɢ. 40.—Iberian peninsula: population density (per sq. kilo-
metre). Of the cities shown, Madrid has more than 2
million inhabitants, and Barcelona and Lisbon 1 million
each. The figures in the text give density per sq. mile.

average of 123 persons a square mile; but this includes well over 2 millions
in Madrid alone, and the average distribution outside the city is around 80.
Over the plateau as a whole the average density never exceeds 85 and in
some areas, such as La Mancha and Extremadura, there are very few
inhabitants. The sparsest population is in Aragon, which includes the
central Pyrenees, the Ebro basin and the mountains of the north-east
Meseta. Here the average is 57 persons a square mile.

THE ECONOMY

GENERAL FEATURES

Spain is one of the best endowed of all Mediterranean countries in
agricultural potential and mineral resources, but so far she has lacked the
national unity essential for their full development.

Agriculture, which employs at least half the working population, is
backward and often at subsistence level. The outstanding characteristic of
the rural population is its poverty. Conditions along the north coast and
in the Mediterranean *huertas* are somewhat better, but rarely are there
signs of true agricultural prosperity. A much more serious policy of
agrarian reform is needed. The large *latifundia* of southern Spain must be
split into smaller and more productive units, and the uneconomic "patch-
farming" of the north and north-west requires the stimulus of co-operative
methods. In all parts of the country there is a woeful lack of farm machinery, fertilisers and knowledge of modern techniques.

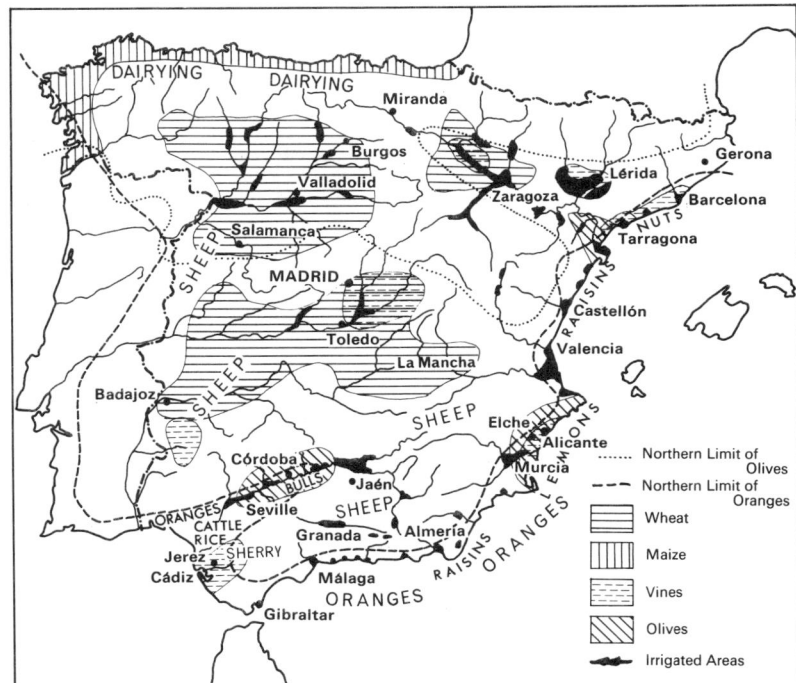

Fig. 41.—Spain: agriculture. The northern limit of olive cultivation is often taken as the boundary of the Mediterranean type of climate in Europe, but there are large areas of the southern Meseta in which the climate is not typically Mediterranean.

Wheat is the most important field crop and covers large areas of the Meseta. The total output varies considerably from year to year, according to the vagaries of the weather, and in some years Spain has had to import wheat. It is doubtful, too, whether the area under *secano* wheat can be increased, again for reasons of climate. In other parts of the country, however, where irrigation can be further developed, larger acreages are already being devoted to sugar beet (in the north) and to sugar cane, tobacco, cotton and tomatoes (in the south). Equally important, yields per acre are increasing. Spain already ranks first in the world in the production of olive oil and cork, and in exports of oranges and orange juice, and she is third in output of wine.

Spain is one of the most important European producers of lead, copper, mercury, silver, zinc, manganese and iron ores. In each case the output could be greater, but the Spanish peasant, with his long tradition of work on the land, regards labour in the mines as degrading. The Oviedo coalfields, for instance, are always short of miners. The minerals so essential to the development of the country's own industries are largely exported, though during the last decade home consumption has been growing, helped by a phenomenal increase in the generation of hydro-electricity.

Developed hydro-electric power has risen from about 5 million kWh annually in 1940 to 27,300 million kWh in 1966. mainly in State-owned schemes. Not only has it enabled the industrial regions of Barcelona and the northern coastlands to extend their activities, but it has also made possible the dispersal of manufacturing industry to regions previously without any. Coal production amounts to about 13 million tons a year, but as far as the interior of the country is concerned the coalfields are badly situated, and the coal is mostly of poor quality.

Communications are another weak point in Spain's economy. Both road and railway systems were constructed so as to centre on Madrid. This concentration on the capital city has made the development of manufacturing industries in the rest of the plateau very difficult. Any improvement is hampered by the deep valleys which cut across the Meseta; and as time goes on, Madrid's predominance tends to become more permanent. Three-quarters of the railways are broad gauge, the remainder narrow gauge—another disadvantage—and much of the track and rolling stock was damaged or destroyed during the civil war. It has not yet been fully repaired or restored, and the same is true of the roads; but reconstruction and development of the whole system of communications rank high in the present economic development programme. The growth of tourism, which has been phenomenal in Spain, has helped. From a mere handful of visitors in 1950, numbers have grown to 10·1 million in 1965 and 17·3 million in 1966.

In many ways it appears that Spain is only just awakening after centuries of lethargy and mismanagement by its rulers, centuries in which its ordinary people, hard-working, frugal and fanatically attached to their country and religion, were given little or no opportunity to improve their lot. Today things are changing. The conservative Castilian, the energetic Basque and the progressive Catalan are being brought together. Slowly and often reluctantly they are beginning to appreciate that Spain's complete economic recovery will be achieved, not through internal jealousies and conflict, but by unity.

REGIONAL ECONOMY

1. *The Atlantic coastlands*

(a) *Galicia; the Cantabrian mountains; the Asturian plain.* The mountainous north-west of Spain has the highest rainfall in the country. On its rivers, the Minho (Miño) and Sil in Galicia, and the Esla from the western Cantabrians, hydro-electric power stations have recently been constructed. The current generated amounts to about one-tenth of Spain's total hydro-electricity, and it may lead to the development of industry in this otherwise poorly endowed region. Already there are fertiliser factories at Puenteareas and a pulp and paper mill at Pontevedra, the latter making use of timber from the forest-clad mountains. Probably of greater immediate importance, however, is the water made available for irrigation on the Meseta south of the Cantabrians.

The soils of Galicia are poor, and those of the Asturias not much better, but by dint of careful cultivation good crops of maize, vegetables and orchard fruit are obtained. The wet grasslands have made north-west Spain the country's most important cattle-rearing region, supplying milk and dairy produce to the towns of the Biscay coast. The farms of Galicia have been so fragmented by the laws of inheritance that they are too small to support a family reasonably, and there has been constant emigration to the towns of the Basque country. The farms of the Asturias are larger and more prosperous. In both Galicia and the plain of Asturias the coastal districts have more people than the interior, for many farmers there are fishermen too and thus can supplement their income.

The chief fishing ports are Corunna (La Coruña) (182,211), Vigo (165,671) in Galicia, and Gijón (134,011) in the Asturias. A fifth of Spain's catch comes into these ports, principally sardines from near the coast and cod from the Newfoundland Grand Banks. The value of the Galician ports is reduced by their distance from the more developed parts of Spain and by the fact that there is no railway to connect them directly with the rest of the Biscayan coast. In spite of this, they have important sardine-canning and cod-drying factories.

Galicia has no mineral resources, but the coastal plain of Asturias is the most highly mineralised part of Spain. Between Gijón and Oviedo is the largest coalfield in the country, producing bituminous and anthracite coal, though not of the best quality. South-west of Avilés are extensive deposits of iron ore which have led to smelting and steelworks at Oviedo and Avilés. Zinc occurs near Avilés, mercury a few miles south of Oviedo. Industrial activity is increasing in the region, and less of the mineral ores is being exported in the raw state than was the case only a few years ago. Oviedo (133,953), the largest town, has iron and steel, chemical and glass works, coke ovens and zinc smelting. Some of its power supplies come from the hydro-electric stations on the south side of the Cantabrian mountains. The industrial development of Asturias is proceeding so rapidly that there is a labour shortage despite the influx of surplus population from Galicia.

(b) *Santander; the Basque provinces; the western Pyrenees.* The coastal plains and the wide valleys of the rivers that flow to the Bay of Biscay are agriculturally the most favoured part of Spain. Maize, fruit, vegetables and dairy products find ready markets in the numerous towns of Santander and the Basque provinces. Vineyards are found on many southward-facing slopes.

Santander is historically a part of the kingdom of Old Castile, and its people are Castilian, but its economic development is so bound up with that of the Basque provinces that it is always included with them. The Basques are a virile mountain people; they accepted industrialism earlier than the more easy-going Castilians. The Basque provinces are Vizcaya, Alava and Guipúzcoa, known collectively as Vascongadas. With Santander they form the most extensive industrial region in Spain.

Industrialisation was helped by the existence in the hinterland of Santander and Bilbao of the largest deposits of hematite iron ore in the
country. Santander is also the chief producer of zinc ore, and lead and
lignite occur in minor quantities. Until recent years most of the iron ore
was exported via Santander and Bilbao to South Wales, which in return
sent coking coal for a smelting and iron and steel industry at Bilbao.
Today this reciprocal trade is very small, although it continues; more
and more of the mineral output is being smelted and processed locally.

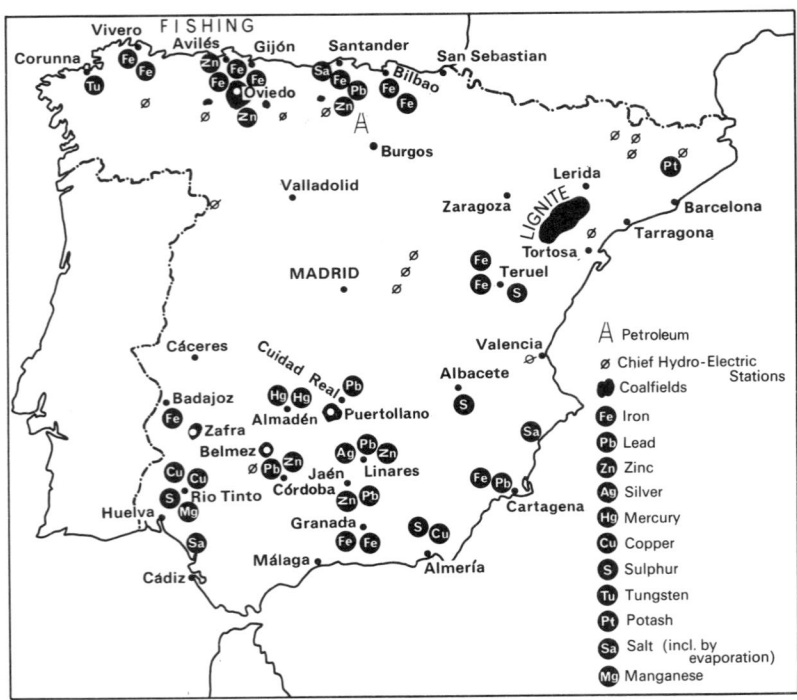

FIG. 42.—Spain: minerals. Although Spain is richly endowed with mineral resources
the only real industrial development is in the north of the country.

Bilbao (350,884) is the largest city on the Atlantic coast and the chief
industrial centre. It is a port situated at the head of a ria, but large ships
must use its outport of Portugalete. The iron and steel industry is paramount: the province of Vizcaya produces about 60% of Spain's total, in
spite of the new and larger steelworks being built at Avilés in Asturias.
Based on the steel industry are shipbuilding, engineering, boiler works
and the making of machinery. There are coke ovens, cement works,
chemicals and glass manufacture and paper mills. The raw material for
the paper comes from the pine forests of the Cantabrians. Bilbao is also
a commercial and fishing port, with sardine and tunny canneries.

Santander (128,452) has industries like those of Bilbao, but on a smaller scale. Both towns smelt lead, zinc and copper, and both give comparatively easy access from the coast to the interior. Reinosa, a small town in the mountains, near the source of the Ebro, has important hydro-electricity works. With electro-smelting, glass manufacture and a school of naval architecture, it is a growing industrial centre. It is also in the middle of a dairy cattle region and has a dairying industry which uses electrical power. San Sebastian (148,644), at the eastern end of the Biscayan coast, is not only a port and industrial centre, but a major holiday resort—the most popular in Spain. It has food processing, textile and paper industries; in its hinterland are many small towns with metallurgical, chemical, glass and engineering works. It has also some strategic importance, commanding as it does the narrow lowland route from France, west of the Pyrenees.

The western Pyrenees, though well-watered on their outer slopes, are poorly peopled. The inhabitants, largely Basque in origin, are engaged in lumbering in the pine forests, which clothe the mountains in the wetter parts or in poor transhumant farming and pasture in the valleys. Dairy cattle are reared in forest clearings and maize is the chief food crop. Rainfall decreases rapidly eastwards in the sub-Pyrenean zone and, with the greater aridity, wheat takes the place of maize and olive groves begin to appear. This sub-Pyrenean area presents a great contrast in fruitfulness to the lands facing the Bay of Biscay.

The largest towns of the western Pyrenees region are Pamplona (115,044) and Jaca. Both are market towns. Pamplona has textile factories and Jaca is a crossroads, commanding the Somport Pass.

2. The Mediterranean coastlands

(a) *The eastern Pyrenees; the Mediterranean coastal plains.* The eastern Pyrenees are a valuable source of hydro-electric power (*see* Fig. 42). The Segre, a tributary of the Ebro, and the Ter, which flows directly to the Mediterranean, have been harnessed and current is sent to the industrial region of Catalonia to the south. The economy of the eastern Pyrenees is pastoral, but with sheep rather than cattle. In the valleys and depressions, wheat is the chief crop. Population is scanty, though with the general increase of industry in the district north of Barcelona, and with larger numbers of people using the eastern route from France into Spain, villages at the foot of the mountains are growing in size, especially near the power stations.

The best developed of the Mediterranean coastal plains are those of Catalonia and Valencia. The Catalonian plains include Gerona, Barcelona and Tarragona, which are separated by the northern ranges of the Catalonian mountains and well watered by streams from the eastern Pyrenees. Much of the mountain area is forested, while the lower slopes are terraced for vines, olives, and nut-trees. Cork from the forests north of Barcelona is sent out from the small ports of Palamos and San Felíu.

[*Courtesy of the Spanish Ministry of Information.*

FIG. 43.—Spain: harvesting rice in the delta of the Ebro, nearly one quarter of which is now given to rice. The bundled sheaves lying in the water, the stumps of rice stalks protruding from its surface, and the harvester's sickle are typical.

The plain of Gerona in the north, with more rainfall, has mixed farming—maize, wheat, fodder crops, dairying and pig rearing. Farther south there are market-gardens supplying the city of Barcelona with fruit and vegetables. In the plain of Tarragona the vine is dominant. Throughout the Catalonian lowlands there are irrigation networks, so that every piece of potentially productive land is used. Even on the Ebro delta, until recent years a marsh in winter and a dried-up plain in summer, rice is grown in exportable quantities by means of a carefully regulated system of drainage and irrigation canals.

The Catalans are much more businesslike than the Castilian Spaniards, and had developed trading and industrial activities while the rest of Spain was still fighting the Moors. The Catalan language seems to be a debased version of the French Languedoc dialect, and in many ways the culture is more closely related to southern France than to Spain. The people of Catalonia have also been greatly influenced by long-continued contacts with merchants from the eastern Mediterranean. Very early in history Barcelona became a major trading port.

Barcelona (1,696,008) is the second city and foremost port of Spain. On an excellent harbour, and facing the trade routes of the Mediterranean, it was a focus of shipping and commerce as early as the fifteenth century. With the Industrial Revolution, it developed cotton and silk manufactures, using imported raw materials and fuel. Today it is overwhelmingly the textile capital of Spain, manufacturing woollens, linen, jute and synthetic fibres. The textile industry, encouraged by hydroelectricity, has spread into the north of the plain. Barcelona has the largest paper mills in Spain, and is the chief engineering city as well; it specialises in marine engines, railway locomotives and rolling stock, motor cars, heavy machinery, electrical apparatus and shipbuilding. In its northern suburbs is a heavy chemical industry, using pyrites from other parts of Spain, phosphates from North Africa and potash salts from large deposits in the interior valleys of the province. Barcelona's food-processing industry rivals that of Madrid.

Tarragona (42,100) is the market and outlet for the wine trade of the northern region. It exports hazel nuts, medlars, almonds and other fruit. Maize and rice are the main cereals; and in the *huertas* (kitchen gardens or irrigated lands) peas, beans, lentils, onions and other vegetables are grown. Along the coast of Catalonia is a growing tourist and holiday industry, especially north and south of the city of Barcelona. The resorts of the Costa de Levante and Costa Brava are now competing with those of the French Riviera.

Southwards along the coast are the plains of Castellón de la Plana and Valencia. Sheltered by the Meseta behind them, they have scorchingly hot summers and low winter rainfall, but by sinking wells and making use of the waters of the numerous streams flowing from the plateau rim they have been transformed into huertas of the highest fertility. Maize and rice are again of first importance, with wheat and barley as secondary crops. Valencia is the chief rice-growing province in Spain. Olive groves and vineyards occur everywhere, and in the best irrigated areas are orange and lemon groves, apricots, carob beans, peaches, pomegranates and fig trees. The province of Valencia provides the finest example of huerta cultivation in the country. It supports Spain's third largest city, Valencia (583,151), and one of the densest populations in the country. On a good harbour at the mouth of the river Guadalaviar, Valencia is the chief port for raisins (sun-dried grapes). It is also a manufacturing city, with textiles and engineering, chemicals and shipbuilding.

Lying at the south-east corner of Spain, hemmed in by the ranges of the Betic Cordillera, are the plains of Alicante and Murcia, forming a continuous stretch. This is the driest part of the Mediterranean coastlands, and water for irrigation is brought by a complex canal system from the mountains. On lands too high to be watered in this way there are vines, olives, fig trees and almonds, which can withstand drought because of their long roots. On the irrigated areas crops can be grown without intermission, for the winters are warm enough for the cultivation of onions, peas, beans and tomatoes. Wheat is grown side by side with subtropical produce such as cotton and groundnuts; and along with the usual Mediterranean fruits may be seen bananas and sugar cane. At Elche there are groves of date palms more reminiscent of an African oasis than of Europe. On the inner edges of the plains sheep rearing is the chief occupation, the animals being taken on to the Meseta during the winter, when the rains come.

Alicante (132,809) is the chief port for grapes, and is the outlet for the industries of Murcia (255,933), which manufactures linen, paper and explosives. The province of Murcia has deposits of iron ore and lead in the Sierra de Cartagena; there are smaller amounts of zinc, copper and tin. These minerals are all exported raw from Alicante and Cartagena. Salt is evaporated from lagoons along the coast south of the town of Alicante.

The south coast of Spain is backed so closely by the Betic Cordillera that there is little room for lowlands. The only plains are behind Almería and Málaga, where water is available for irrigation. Here are grown citrus fruits, cotton, tobacco, figs, vines and early vegetables, especially potatoes. Sugar cane and dates show the nearness of Africa. Almería (88,852) exports table grapes, iron ore, lead, silver, esparto grass, citrus fruits and salt. Málaga (324,949) has an important wine trade, sugar refineries, soapworks, textiles and engineering. After Barcelona, it is the main exporter of Spain's Mediterranean produce.

At the western end of south Spain is the narrow, rocky peninsula of Gibraltar which, though territorially a part of Spain, belongs to Great Britain (*see* separate section at end of chapter).

The Mediterranean coastlands of Spain, though they occupy in total area only a small part of the country, contain a large proportion of the population, with one city of over 1,500,000 people and another with more than 500,000. The fact that every one of the lowlands strung along the Mediterranean littoral supports a large concentration of people gives ample proof of their collective agricultural productivity. Two points are worthy of note: the value and success of irrigation throughout the region, and the growth of industry in the northern portion, based largely on the development of hydro-electric power in the Pyrenees. Industry is now spreading southwards from the Barcelona area, helped by the new power stations constructed on the lower river Ebro where it passes through a gorge near the southern end of the Catalonian mountains.

(b) *The Guadalquivir basin*. This river basin is included with the Mediterranean coastlands because it has a Mediterranean climate; but because it lies open to the west it receives more rain than the south and east coasts. Even so, the total precipitation in the eastern basin is scanty, and much of the surface there is esparto steppe.

Andalusia, which includes the Guadalquivir basin, was the last part of Spain to be reconquered from the Moors. It shows the most obvious signs of their long occupation—in place-names, architecture, aqueducts, irrigation systems, etc., and in the variety of plants they introduced, some of which, such as citrus fruits, sugar cane and cotton, have already been noted in the coastal huertas. Under Moorish rule, Andalusia was the most productive region in Spain; when the Moors were driven out, the province declined.

For this the aristocracy and the Church were largely to blame. As a reward for their assistance in the reconquest they were given large grants of land. The dispossessed peasants were forced to work on the extensive estates (Sp. *latifundia*) as labourers or to become share-croppers on small-holdings. In the course of time the latifundia passed into the hands of landlords who lived in Madrid or Seville. They left the running of their estates in the hands of managers and in a majority of cases this is still done. The absentee landlords are little interested in new, scientific methods of farming; large areas are left fallow every third year; implements are primitive and machinery rarely seen; and too much land is devoted to wheat and olives, which, in the climate of Andalusia, require a minimum of labour but give a good cash return. There is little doubt that with reforms in land ownership and farming techniques, and better use of water which flows down both sides of the Guadalquivir valley, the basin would become a vast huerta. Measures for improvement have been decided upon by the Government, but so far few have been put into operation.

The exceptions are in the alluvial valleys and on the irrigated clay soils of the region between Seville and Córdoba, where sugar cane, tobacco, cotton, groundnuts, rice and vegetables are successfully cultivated, as well as the ubiquitous wheat and olives. But the yields are small compared with those of the east coast huertas. The best conditions are in the Seville district, where irrigation enables enormous quantities of bitter oranges to be produced for export, to be used in making marmalade.

The growing of vines is of greatest importance around Jerez and Jaén, but viticulture is found on all hill slopes. Jerez has been noted for centuries for the production of sherry: the wine takes its name from the town. Young bulls are bred south of Córdoba and sent to the Marismas, below Seville, to be prepared for use in bullfights (Sp. *corridas*) all over the country. The Marismas are a marshy wilderness on both sides of the Guadalquivir below Seville. On the north side are vast water meadows where the bulls are reared; on the south, where there has been some reclamation, rice is grown.

The Sierra Morena, which form the northern boundary of the Andalusian basin, are rich in minerals. On their gentle slopes are wheatfields and cork-oak forests, with maquis in the poorer parts. Goat rearing is part of the economy, as it is throughout Andalusia. Copper and cupriferous pyrites are mined at Rio Tinto and exported through Huelva. Mercury, of which Spain is the world's leading producer, is found at Almadén. Lead–zinc–silver ores occur at Linares and near Jaén on the south side of the river valley. Spain comes ninth in the world for lead output, twelfth for zinc and twelfth for silver. Near Bélmez and Puertollano are two small coalfields of poor quality. The many streams which flow from the Sierra Morena to the Guadalquivir have been dammed for irrigation and power, but the irrigation systems could be greatly improved, and the power generated is at present negligible.

Seville (531,571) is the largest town of the basin. It is situated at the head of navigation and lowest bridge point of the Guadalquivir; the river, which is tidal, is kept open only by dredging. Seville has textile manufactures and light engineering, but its chief function is as the collecting centre and exporting port for the wine, oranges, minerals and olive oil of the basin. It is the regional capital. Córdoba (215,454) was once a stronghold of the Moors and contains many examples of their architecture. In the centre of wheatlands and cattle farms, it is a market and has fast-developing electrical and light engineering industries too. Cádiz (128,460), on a narrow harbour south of the Guadalquivir mouth, exports sherry and olive oil. It was once the chief port of Spain but has declined considerably in importance. It can accommodate larger ships than Seville and competes for trade to the Canaries and South America, besides being a naval dockyard.

3. *The Meseta, central Pyrenees, Ebro basin and Betic Cordillera*

(a) *The Meseta.* In consequence of its elevated, isolated character and continental climate, the Meseta has a backward economy (*see* Fig. 44). The northern Meseta, that is, north of the Central Sierras, is the basin of Old Castile. It is slightly more favoured than the south as far as rainfall is concerned, and large areas are devoted to the growth of wheat without irrigation—a method known as *secano* (Sp. "non-irrigated land"). In the better-watered districts, fodder crops, peas and beans are grown in rotation with secano wheat and, in the poorer districts, potatoes and rye. Where irrigation is possible, flax and hemp are cultivated, and vines appear on the lower slopes of valleys. Where the soil is too porous for agriculture the basin of Old Castile is covered by garrigue and steppe, on which sheep are reared, mainly on the flat tops of the *paramos*. Old Castile was the original home of the Merino sheep, which was taken to South Africa and Australia, and produces the finest-quality wools. The amount of wool exported from Spain is, however, small.

The basin of Old Castile is thinly populated. There are only two towns of any size, Valladolid and Burgos. Both are railway foci for the northern half of Spain, and wheat markets for the basin, which is the granary of the country. Valladolid (172,239) is a flour-milling centre and has railway and automobile engineering; and Burgos (88,825), nearer to the Basque industrial region and with easy access to it, has paper, chemical and agricultural engineering industries. It is also a tourist centre.

[*Courtesy of the Spanish Ministry of Information.*

FIG. 44.—Spain: a view across the Meseta near Belmonte in the province of Cuenca. This arid region provides winter pasture for sheep, but except for a few olive groves is otherwise unproductive. The tree at the road junction serves as a direction post.

South of the Central Sierras lies the basin of New Castile. It is not so obviously a basin as Old Castile: the western portion is broken by the mountains of Toledo and the granite plateaus of Extremadura, across which flow the Tagus and Guadiana. Extremadura and New Castile are drier than the northern basin and have more "Mediterranean" characteristics; the olive, absent in Old Castile, makes its appearance. Secano wheat is again the main crop (*see* Fig. 27), but aridity and poor facilities for irrigation make sheep rearing the chief occupation, especially in

Extremadura, which has the largest flocks of Merino sheep in the country. Here and over large areas in the south-east of the New Castile basin, transhumance is common, the sheep being driven up the mountains in summer and brought down to the plateau level in winter. In the south-east is the basin of La Mancha (Arab. *al mancha*, "the thirsty land"), a vast, arid plain covered with drought-resisting shrubs (Sp. *matorral* "undergrowth") or esparto grass, which is used for paper-making as well as fodder. The southern basin is more scantily peopled than north of the Sierras. Only Badajos (102,499) and Toledo (46,500) are of any size. Toledo at one time had a reputation for the quality of the steel swords made there, but this ancient craft has completely disappeared.

Although the basins of the Meseta are poorly populated, the southern foot of the Sierra de Guadarrama holds the largest concentration of people in Spain, in Madrid, the capital. Madrid (2,558,583) is an artificial creation: the site was chosen solely because it is geographically in the centre of the country. It has nothing else to commend it, since the region is arid and unproductive. Nor is it in easy communication with all parts of the country, except by dint of heavy engineering projects. Although it has been made the focus of Spain's road and railway systems, and great efforts have been made to increase industrial activity, it is hard pressed to compete with Barcelona and the Basque coast, where there are more raw materials and better facilities for overseas trade.

Madrid is the administrative and commercial centre of Spain, and its industries are mainly concerned with consumer goods, such as foodstuffs, furniture, clothing, footwear and leather goods, glassware and pottery, and pharmaceutical chemicals. In the past twenty years its population has grown by over half a million, and new industries connected with electricity, gas, cement and machinery have been helped by hydro-electric power; but it appears unlikely that Madrid will ever become a great industrial city. Its water supply comes from streams to the north, as already noted, and from the huge reservoirs of Buendia and Alocén, impounded in the upper Tagus basin. Some miles north of Madrid is the famous palace of the Escorial, part of which has now been turned into a monastery.

(b) *The central Pyrenees; the Ebro basin.* The high central Pyrenees have only slight economic value. There is a little lumbering, and sheep are reared in clearings up to 5000 ft (1525 m). In a few high valleys approached by a difficult road is the tiny republic of Andorra (191 sq. miles, 495 sq. km), whose 15,500 inhabitants live by a precarious subsistence agriculture of rye, potatoes and vegetables, by transhumant pasture of cattle and sheep, and—more recently—by tourism. This last, however, has been developed more by entry from the French side of the Pyrenees than from Spain. Andorra is a remarkable example in modern times of how a mountain people can preserve its independence. At the foot of the central Pyrenees a series of low limestone sierras is too dry for any vegetation except garrigue, on which sheep are reared. Wheat, rye and vines are cultivated very near the rivers, but considerable areas are "badland," of no use at all.

Shut off from rain-bearing winds, the Ebro basin is one of the driest regions of Spain. Its winters, too, are decidedly cool for a Mediterranean land. Zaragoza, for instance, in the middle of the basin, has an average January temperature of 42° F (5·6° C) and an annual precipitation of 11½ in. During the winter, when cold air drains down the slopes of the central Pyrenees, the basin may experience frost at night. Away from the river Ebro and its tributary valleys, vegetation is maquis or garrigue on hills and steppe on lowlands. East of Zaragoza, the district of Los Mane-gros is by nature almost semi-desert, but irrigation has succeeded in making parts of it productive. The middle section of the river basin has occasional surface encrustations of salt or gypsum; in such places irriga-tion is either useless or too expensive. On the garrigue and steppe the chief occupation is sheep-rearing.

Below Logroño the river Ebro has been tapped for irrigation, and from there to Zaragoza two major canals—the Canal Imperial de Aragon along the left bank and the Canal de Tauste along the right—provide water to a narrow belt of land. South of the Ebro, the valleys of the Jalon and Guadalope are partially irrigated. Further east the left-bank tributaries, notably the Cinca, Esera, Noguera Ribagorzana, Noguera Pallaresa and Segre, are more completely controlled, so that a large portion of the eastern basin north of the parent river is fully irrigated. This includes the Llanos (Sp. "plains") de Urgel and part of Los Manegros. In the upper Segre valley, hydro-electricity is generated and sent to the Barcelona district and to Lérida, lower down the valley. The irrigated areas are the only parts of the Ebro basin which are more than scantily populated. Large crops of wheat and sugar beet are grown in them and onions, vines, olives and tree crops such as almonds, apricots, peaches and plums are cultivated. Peas, beans, tomatoes, pimento and alfalfa (grass) are other crops. In the western end of the basin, nearer to the wetter Cantabrian sierras, cattle rearing is important.

The chief town in the Ebro basin is Zaragoza (Saragossa) (377,412). It is well placed in the centre of the basin, where the Ebro can be bridged and where routes round both ends of the Pyrenees converge towards the Jalon Gap, which leads through the Iberian mountains to Madrid. Its industries are concerned mainly with the products of the irrigated lands— flour milling, sugar refining, oil pressing, wine-making and jam manu-facture—but it has also modern iron and steel works, railway and electrical engineering, cement manufacture and machine tool making. After Madrid, it is the largest city in "arid" Spain. Lerida (72,115) has grown rapidly in the eastern irrigated region, benefiting from the hydro-electric power developed on the river Segre. Logroño (69,279) is the market for the western basin, where irrigation is less necessary.

The Ebro is of little value for navigation, as its volume is too va-riable and its speed too great in the gorge by which it passes to its delta.

Hydro-electric power stations have been built in the gorge, above Tortosa, and current is sent to the towns of the coastal plain.

(c) *The Betic Cordillera; the Balearic islands.* In the west of the Betic Cordillera the rainfall is sufficient for secano cultivation of cereals, vines and olives, and the mountain slopes have forests of cork-oak. Farther east the landscape becomes increasingly barren and there are large areas of esparto grass, which supports transhumant sheep-rearing. Only in the basins between the northern and southern mountain belts is there any considerable population, for only here is it possible to harness the numerous mountain streams for irrigation.

The chief basin, around Granada, is watered by snow-melt from the Sierra Nevada and has been transformed into a *vega*, the name given in southern Spain to fertile lowland plains—although these mountain basins are only low in comparison to the surrounding heights. In the Granada basin the chief products are maize, wheat, sugar beet and fodder crops, with vines and olives climbing up the lower slopes. Granada (161,851) has flour mills, sugar refineries, paper mills and a woollen industry. It is also a tourist centre, for it contains the Alhambra, a magnificent castle and palace built by the Moors, typifying the high degree of civilisation they reached in their last stronghold in Spain. The other intermontane basins, Loja, Moreda, Lorca and Braza, have similar agricultural products to Granada.

In the Balearic islands, agriculture is possible only by irrigation. This is well developed, and the same crops are grown as in the huertas of the east coast of the mainland. Fishing for sardines and anchovies occupies many of the coastal population but is of only local importance. The largest islands—Majorca, Minorca and Iviza—have become favourite holiday resorts, largely because of the reliable Mediterranean climate, which here is tempered by the surrounding sea. The chief towns are Palma (170,740) on Majorca, and Mahon (19,000) on Minorca.

GIBRALTAR

STRUCTURE AND RELIEF

At the western end of south Spain is the narrow, rocky peninsula of Gibraltar which, although territorially a part of Spain, belongs to Britain. The whole territory is rather less than 3 miles (4·8 km) in length from north to south and varies in width from $\frac{1}{4}$ to $\frac{3}{4}$ mile (0·4 to 1·2 km). The Rock, as it is called, is about $2\frac{1}{2}$ miles (4 km) long, and at its northern end rises almost perpendicularly from a strip of flat, sandy ground which connects it with the Spanish mainland. The highest point of the Rock towers 1398 ft (426 m) above the sea. Southwards it is terminated by steep slopes leading to Windmill Hill Flats, which fall from 400 to 300 ft (122 to 91 m) above sea-level. Windmill Hill terminates abruptly along its southern face in a wall-like cliff nearly 200 feet (61 m) in height, at the bottom of which lie the Europa Flats. These Flats slope on three sides to coastal cliffs 50 ft (15 m) high which plunge straight down into deep water. The southern terminal is Europa Point, nearly 13¼ miles (21 km) from the opposite African coast. On the eastern side the Rock is almost as steep and inaccessible as it is from the north, but on the west side the slopes are more gradual as they near the sea, and here are the town, the barracks, the dockyards and the harbour.

The Rock of Gibraltar consists chiefly of pale grey limestone overlain by blue-grey shales, both of Lower Jurassic age. The limestone is usually compact and stratified, but in places it is amorphous and crystalline in structure. The overlying shales are intercalated with beds of grit, mudstone and limestone. There are also superficial deposits of limestone breccias, bone breccias and calcareous sandstone of Pleistocene age. The oldest of these superficial formations is the limestone breccia of Buena Vista, devoid of fossils and apparently formed under the stress of hard frosts, indicating very severe climatic conditions. To account for such frosts, it is suggested that the Rock at that period must have been raised to a great altitude. In that case Europe and Africa would have been connected by a land bridge near the present Strait, and there would have been a wider strip of lowland at the base of the Rock than there is today. The low ground had a rich vegetative cover, as is shown by the wealth of animal remains discovered in several caves in the Rock.

This uplift was followed by a subsidence to a depth of 700 ft (210 m) below the existing level. This would account for the ledges and platforms (raised beaches) eroded by the sea high above the present sea-level, and for the deposits of calcareous sandstones rich in sea shells of existing Mediterranean species. The extent of some of these eroded ledges shows that pauses of long duration intervened between the periods of depression. After this the Rock was again uplifted considerably and Europe and Africa united once more; and at a later date there was a new subsidence to the present level of the Rock.

There are many caves in the Rock, some of them of great extent. The best known are the Genista and St Michael's caves. In the Genista have been found the remains of a bear, a hyena, several species of the wild cat family, a pygmy rhinoceros and two forms of ibex. The St Michael's cave, about 1100 ft (335 m) above sea-level at its mouth, slopes sharply downwards and extends by a series of chambers connected by narrow, tortuous passages over 400 ft (122 m) into the Rock; its further limits are still unexplored.

CLIMATE AND VEGETATION

The climate of Gibraltar is pleasant and healthy, mild in winter and only moderately hot in summer. The heat, though not excessive, is lasting; from April to October the mean temperature does not fall below 61° F (16·1° C). The coolest month is January, with an average of 54° F (12·2° C), and the hottest is August with 74° F (23·3° C). The average *maximum* in summer is about 84° F (28·9° C); only very rarely does the thermometer register 90° F (32·2° C) in the shade. The average annual rainfall is 35·1 in., over 40% of which falls in December, January and February. The summer months of June, July and August are almost rainless, with only 2% of the yearly total. The winter rainfall comes in sharp, heavy showers, with long intervening periods of sunshine; spells of bad weather are seldom of more than a few days' duration.

Water supply for drinking and cooking purposes is almost wholly derived from rainwater stored chiefly in underground tanks; there are very few good wells. Large storage tanks have been constructed in the interior of the Rock, with specially prepared catchment areas at a high altitude (see Fig. 45). The collecting areas cover 38 acres (15 ha), and the storage tanks have a capacity of over 6 million gallons. In addition, establishments of the armed forces and some of the larger houses have their own rainwater tanks. A large quantity of brackish water for baths and flushing purposes is pumped from the sandy flats north of the Rock.

The upper part of the Rock in summer is scorched and bare, but after the first autumn rains it abounds in wild flowers and shrubs, many of which are peculiar to Gibraltar. At lower altitudes, where there is a greater depth of soil, the vegetation is luxuriant and is limited only by the amount of water available for summer irrigation. Hardly any land, however, is used for cultivation, except in small vegetable plots attached to houses. The stone-pine and wild olive are among the few trees growing in a natural state, but in the public and private gardens there is a wide variety of trees, including the orange, lemon, fig, almond and pomegranate. On the eastern side of the Rock the palmito or dwarf palm is abundant.

The only wild animals found in Gibraltar are Barbary apes and a few rabbits and foxes. The apes are said to be the sole representatives of the monkey family living wild in Europe. They occur on the upper part of the Rock and are carefully conserved, for the story goes that if they disappear from Gibraltar the stronghold will fall into other hands.

HISTORY AND PEOPLE

Gibraltar was known to the ancient Greek and Roman geographers as Calpe, and with an eminence designated as Abyla, near Ceuta on the African coast, formed the renowned Pillars of Hercules which until Phoenician times were the limits beyond which the seafaring peoples of the Mediterranean did not venture. The military history of the Rock begins with its capture and fortification in 711 by Moors and Berbers under Tariq ben Zaid. Gibraltar is called after Tariq, the name being a corruption of Jebel Tariq (Mount Tariq). During the Muslim occupation of Spain the fortress was besieged at least seven times by Christian forces, but not until 1462 did it pass once more into Spanish hands. It was heavily fortified by the Spaniards and for two centuries was looked upon as impregnable. In 1704, however, during the War of the Spanish Succession, it was besieged and captured by naval forces under Admiral Sir George

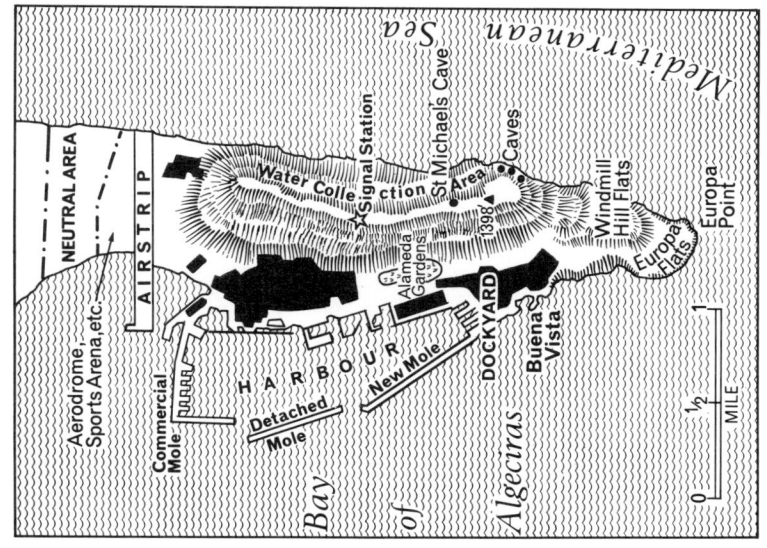

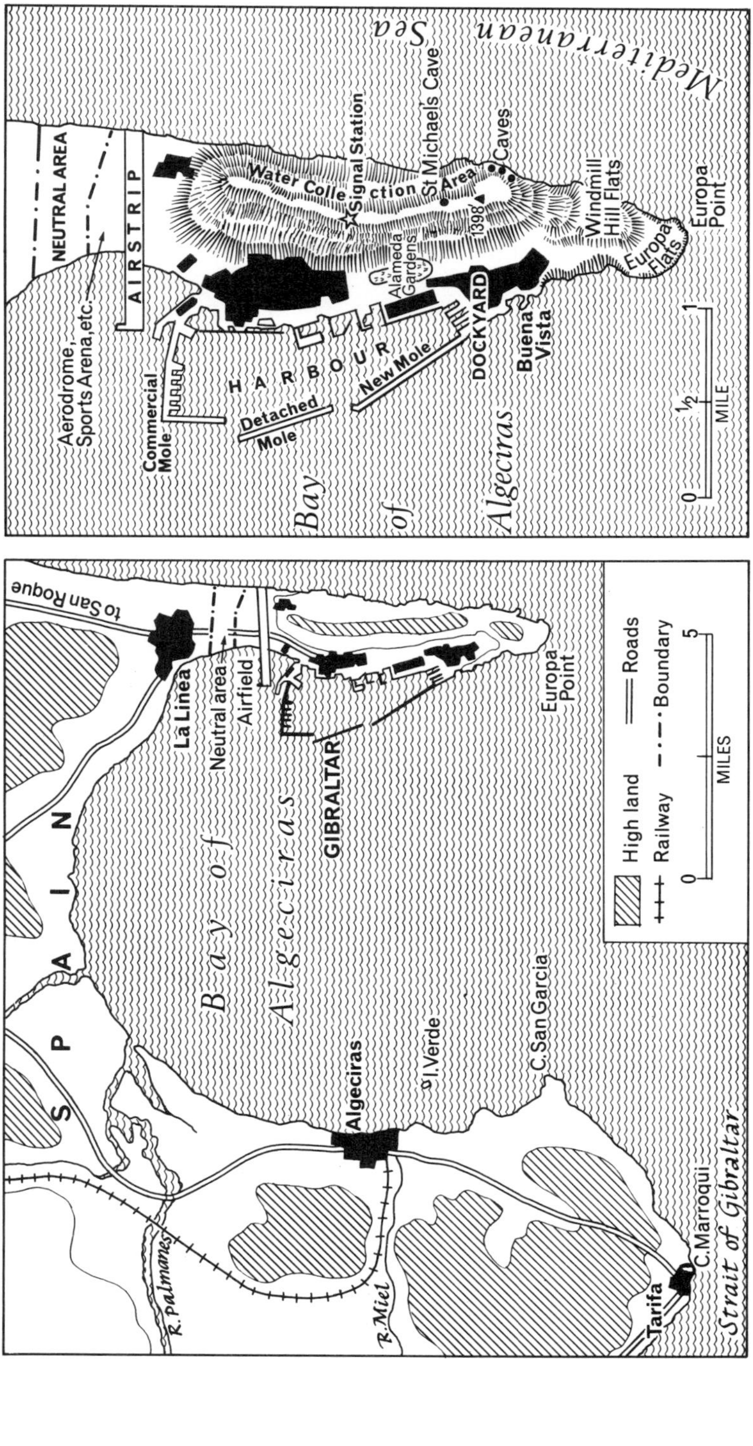

Fig. 45.—Gibraltar: situation.

Rooke, who caused the British flag to be hoisted although the war was being fought in the interests of Austria. Since that date Gibraltar has formed part of Britain's territory, and its people take great pride in their association with the homeland and the Commonwealth. Unlike so many former colonies, Gibraltar does not desire independence in the familiar sense; as recently as 1967 a vote taken by referendum decided overwhelmingly against decolonisation. The strategic value of the Rock to Britain has declined, especially since the control of the Suez Canal has passed to Egypt, but it is still of importance as a bastion against the growing ambitions of the Arab nations and the political penetration of the Soviet Union into Mediterranean affairs. For these reasons the Spanish claim to have Gibraltar restored to their jurisdiction has been denied.

The population of Gibraltar numbers about 25,000, made up partly of permanent dwellers and partly of temporary armed forces, tourists and visiting seamen. The native Gibraltarians are of mixed race, but with very little Spanish blood; after the British capture of the Rock in 1704 almost all the Spanish population left the peninsula and founded the little town of San Roque six miles to the north. The present people are mostly of Italian descent, with a fair admixture of Maltese and Jews. The size of the population is limited by the area available for occupation and by security reasons. Surplus numbers caused by natural increase cannot be accommodated, and during the past century more and more of the poorer classes have been pushed across the frontier into the neighbouring Spanish town of La Linea de la Concepcion. This is really a suburb of Gibraltar, but it has a population more than twice that of the parent city. A large army of workers comes daily from La Linea into Gibraltar, returning shortly after sunset, at which time the gates are closed and locked for the night. Aliens are not allowed to reside in Gibraltar without a permit, and immigration, even of British, is forbidden.

THE ECONOMY

The economy of Gibraltar is based almost entirely on its function as a military fortress and base. It may not be as impregnable as formerly, but it still has a strategic position at the entrance to the Mediterranean, it is easy to reach by sea and air, it has deep-water harbours, and there is a large pool of local labour. Gibraltar relies heavily on the presence and upkeep of military personnel, and upon development schemes financed by the British Government. The most important of the latter is the adaptation of the harbour to civil as well as military purposes, and the facilities provided for the repair of passing ships. The Rock has no agriculture or minerals, and its industries are confined to fruit and fish canning, tobacco processing and coffee blending for most of which the raw materials have to be imported and in which Britain has been most helpful. The daily migration from La Linea provides the labour for these industries and helps to cater for the requirements of the military garrisons and of tourists, for in recent years the tourist industry has developed enormously.

STUDY QUESTIONS

1. Make a division of Spain into geographical regions. Describe the relief and drainage of each region and show how these have influenced communications through the whole area of the country. (O. & C.)

2. Contrast the climate of the Meseta with that of the south coast of Spain and that of the northern coastal region. (O. & C.)

3. Account for the regional differences in economic development to be found in Spain. (J.M.B.)

4. Discuss the bearing of physical factors upon the economic development of two contrasted regions in Spain.

5. Outline the geographical background of the main politico-economic problems of Spain. (J.M.B.)

6. Write a comprehensive account of the Meseta of Spain. (J.M.B.)

7. Discuss the characteristic features of agriculture in the Mediterranean coast-lands of Spain. (J.M.B.)

8. Describe the distribution of population in Spain, pointing out reasons for variations in regional densities.

9. Write an account of the fuel and power resources of Spain.

Chapter X

PORTUGAL

PHYSICAL ASPECTS

PORTUGAL, on the western side of the Iberian peninsula, is rectangular in shape, about 300 miles (480 km) from north to south and rarely more than 100 miles (160 km) wide. Most of the country lies outside the Meseta and is at a lower elevation. Because its surface is broken in such a way as to form extensive coastal plains penetrating the interior, the whole of Portugal is open to the sea, allowing the free entry of rain-bearing, cooling winds from the Atlantic. To the north and east it is bounded by Spain, but the frontier is historic rather than physical.

Portugal was born in the land immediately to the south of the river Minho, which was given originally to the Count of Portugal. Its boundaries were extended southwards during the drive to expel the Moors from the west of the peninsula. This campaign was accompanied by a parallel movement southwards of the Spanish forces, but the two Christian armies did not mix. The regions they took by conquest were settled, on the west by the Portuguese, on the east by the Spaniards; so that gradually, by the process of occupation, the line of demarcation between the two peoples became the frontier. As it passed through a region which even today has a scanty population, there have been singularly few arguments about its position. In fact, with one minor exception, it has remained unaltered since the thirteenth century. It is also a natural linguistic frontier, for Portuguese, though akin to Castilian, is a separate Romance language.

Physically the Portuguese are much like the Spaniards, though on average slightly taller. But there are ethnic differences between the peoples of north and south Portugal. In the north they resemble their Galician neighbours; south of the Serra de Estrêla they are a mixture of Iberian with Moorish, Berber, Jewish and Negro strains. This last is found mainly in the south of the Algarve, and is attributed variously to a prehistoric negroid population and to imported slave labour in the days of colonial expansion.

East of the fault-zone which runs southwards from the mouth of the river Douro is the worn-down western edge of the Meseta, composed of ancient granites and other crystalline rocks. The plateau ranges of the Meseta in Spain are continued into Portugal, and the lowlands are extensions of the down-warpings in the Spanish plateau (*see* Fig. 37). The Central Sierras of Spain have their counterpart in the Serra de Estrêla and Serra da Guardunha; the Sierra de Guadalupe is continued into the Serra d'Ossa; and the Serra do Caldeirão and Serra de Monchique, which run towards the rocky Cape St Vincent, are extensions of the Sierra Morena. West of the fault-zone the Serra da Estrêla is continued into hill ranges of Mesozoic age. These are chiefly of limestone, and form the northern slopes of the lower Tagus basin, finishing in the cliffs of Cape Roca. Similar Mesozoic limestones occur also in the extreme south of the Algarve. The first of the lowlands stretches to the north and south of the river Mondego, and represents the westernmost part of the basin of Old Castile. It is at a much lower level, however, and is floored by Tertiary sands and clays, with alluvium near the rivers. The more extensive plain in the lower Tagus and Sado basins may be regarded as an extension of the Spanish Estremadura or Badajoz basin. In this plain of central Portugal the Tertiaries conceal the line of faults and extend on to the ancient platform in the east.

STRUCTURAL DIVISIONS

Portugal may be divided physically (and economically) into (1) the north, (2) the centre, and (3) the south (see Fig. 46). Northern Portugal—the provinces of Minho, Douro, Tras os Montes, Beira Alta, Beira Baixa and Beira Litoral—is predominantly mountainous or hilly, and extends from the northern boundary southwards, to include the Serra de Estrêla. Central Portugal comprises the hilly country of Estremadura, the plain of the Tagus in Ribatejo (riba Tejo, "bank of the Tagus"), the plain of the Sado and the hilly basin of the Guadiana in Alentejo. Southern Portugal is the Algarve, a small province shut off by mountains from the rest of the country and turned geographically more towards Africa.

1. Northern Portugal

The northern provinces of Portugal consist of a number of small horsts separated by steep-sided valleys, so arranged that oceanic influences penetrate inland. The highland massifs, such as the Serra da Cabreira, Serra de Villarelha, Serra de Nogueira, and Serra da Lapa, are parts of the ancient Meseta platform, broken by severe fracturing in Tertiary times. Two series of intersecting faults split the region into horsts, which are about 4000 ft (1220 m) high in the west, in Minho, and somewhat lower in the east, in Tras os Montes. Along the fault valleys flow the rivers Minho, Limia, Cavado, and the right-bank tributaries of the lower Douro. North of the Douro the highlands approach the coast, and some of them terminate in cliffs. The coastline is straight, a contrast to the rias of Galicia to the north. Between the mouths of the Limia and Douro there is a narrow coastal plain of alluvial silts brought down by the rivers.

In the south of northern Portugal the granite massifs of the Serra da Estrêla rise to over 6500 ft (2000 m). They are an extension of the Central Sierras of Spain. As in the more northern highlands, they are split into a number of horsts, among which are the Serra de Lousa, Serra Guardunha and Serra do Moradal. Along the northern and southern flanks of the

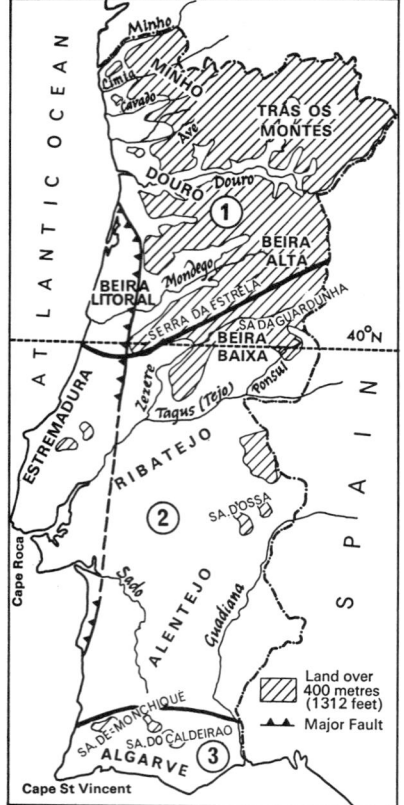

FIG. 46.—Portugal: physical features and divisions. The numbers refer to sections in the text, and the names of provinces are shown. *See also* Figs. 37 and 39.

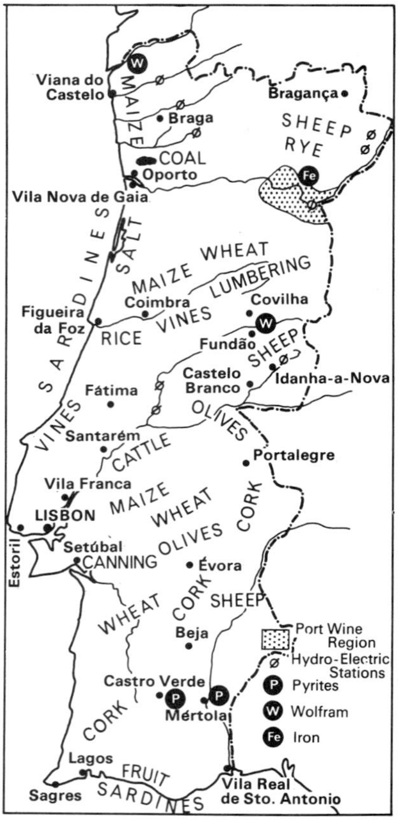

FIG. 47.—Portugal: economic. Correlate with the distribution of population shown in Fig. 40.

Serra da Estrêla flow the rivers Mondego and Zezere. The Zezere has been harnessed for hydro-electricity at Castelo do Bode, Cabril and Bouca to supply Lisbon with power. West of the highlands of northern Portugal a major fault, stretching north–south from the mouth of the Douro to Cape St Vincent, has allowed the land to subside on the seaward side, to form a low coastal plain backed by low hills. The coast of this lowland is straight and lined with sand-hills, behind which are lagoons and swamps.

2. Central Portugal

Central Portugal may be taken as comprising the provinces of Estremadura, Ribatejo and Alentejo. Estremadura lies along the coast north and south of the river Tagus (Tejo). The northern portion has a backbone of folded Mesozoic and Tertiary hills, in which Jurassic limestones and sandstones predominate. The limestone exposures are dry and karst-like, the sandstones fertile and productive. Ribatejo consists of plains which encompass the lower Tagus; these lowlands widen south of the river, and continue southwards into western Alentejo. The central Portuguese lowlands are covered by Tertiary marls and loams, with alluvium near the rivers. The latter flood annually in winter. Eastwards the plains rise to a series of low horsts, of which the Serra d'Ossa is the highest. These horsts are similar in origin to those of northern Portugal, being derived from the fracturing of the Meseta margins, and having soils which are not very fertile.

The plains of Alentejo are drained by the river Sado. The highlands in the east of the province (known collectively as the Alentejo plateau) form the lower basin of the Guadiana, which in parts acts as the boundary with Spain.

3. Southern Portugal

South of Alentejo a series of barren mountain ranges of crystalline rock, such as the Serra de Monchique, Serra da Mezquita and Serra do Caldeirão, form the northern boundary of the Algarve, a province unlike any other in Portugal. The mountains are a continuation of the Sierra Morena in Spain. South of the mountain rim, the Algarve slopes towards the coast as lowlands, which are composed of Mesozoic sandstones. The slope to the south and east gives the region a definite southern or "African" aspect. This region was the last part of the country to be reconquered from the Moors. Its long occupation is reflected in the lower stature, the dark skins and dark eyes of its inhabitants, many of whom have inherited Moorish blood.

CLIMATE

Much about the climate of Portugal may be gathered from what has already been noted about that of Spain (see Fig. 39). No part of Portugal, however, has less than 25 in. of rainfall annually, since the country is more open than Spain to the moist westerlies. Temperatures, too, are tempered by nearness to the sea, so that annual ranges are less than in the neighbouring country. Lisbon, for instance, ranges from an average of 51° F (10·6° C) in January to 71° F (21·7° C) in August—the hottest month—and has an annual rainfall of 27 in., three-quarters of which comes in the winter half of the year. The southern aspect of the Algarve produces higher temperatures, average ranges being from 55° F (12·8° C) in January to 75° F (23·9° C) in July. Rainfall in the Algarve is about 26 in. annually.

The mountains of northern Portugal are the wettest part of the country, annual precipitation of 50 in. being common in the Minho province; and over most of the region there is rarely less than 40 in. In northern Portugal a larger proportion of the precipitation comes in summer than in the rest of the country, but there is still a winter maximum. In that season there may be snow on the Serra da Estrêla and some of the northern-most horsts. A notable feature of the climate of northern Portugal is the very high temperatures experienced in summer in the deep, sheltered valleys of Tras os Montes, where the thermometer occasionally registers 104° F (40° C) in the shade.

HUMAN GEOGRAPHY

HISTORICAL OUTLINE

Until the middle of the eleventh century the history of the area now covered by Portugal was common with that of Spain, except that there was always some difference between the peoples of Lusitania, as the western portion of the peninsula was called, and those of Iberia. During the Moorish occupation, the entire population of the Iberian peninsula was united against the heathens, and the inhabitants of the first Spanish kingdom of León included both Lusitanians and Iberians.

At the beginning of the eleventh century a young Burgundian count so distinguished himself in the service of the king of León that he was given in marriage a princess whose dowry was the land between the rivers Minho and Douro. His son, Afonso (Alfonso) Henriques, rebelled against the Leonese and proclaimed his little domain a kingdom. He routed the Leonese army sent to subdue him, then advanced to the south, driving the Moors before him. He added to his kingdom all the territory as far as Évora, in Alentejo. In the following centuries the Moors were pushed farther south, and encircled in the Algarve, which they held only with difficulty. In the early fifteenth century the last Moor was expelled from the south-west of the peninsula, and Portugal assumed almost its present shape.

The country's land boundaries were more or less fortuitous. The Portuguese and Spanish forces followed the retreating Moors southwards, but remained distinct from each other, separated by a belt of rough country. Through this inhospitable region, which even now is sparsely peopled, the frontier between the two countries was tacitly recognised from the very first and, with only slight changes in the upper Douro and Tagus basins in Portugal, it retains its original shape.

Prominent among the early rulers of Portugal was John (João) I, who in 1385 made an alliance with England which has never been broken; in 1387 he married Philippa of Lancaster, daughter of John of Gaunt, thus cementing the alliance. One of John's sons was Prince Henry, called the Navigator, who from his school of navigation at Sagres sent out expeditions which discovered Madeira, the Azores and the Canary Islands, and made extended reconnaissance of the west coast of Africa. It was largely as a result of Prince Henry's enthusiasm that Portugal was responsible in later years for opening up many parts of the world as yet unknown.

In 1487 Bartholomew Diaz rounded the Cape of Good Hope and in 1498 Vasco da Gama reached India. In 1500 Cabral discovered Brazil, in

1501 Corte Real landed in Greenland; in 1541 Cabrillo explored the coast of California, and Martins the coast of Alaska. The Portuguese were the first to land in the Moluccas, China, Japan and Australia. In 1520, Magellan was the first to circumnavigate the globe. Portugal laid claim to an enormous empire; and because of the gold, precious stones, silks and spices brought back by its ships it became fabulously rich.

The wealth which came from distant lands proved in the long run to be the country's undoing. Its rulers became corrupt and incompetent until, about the middle of the sixteenth century, Philip II of Spain invaded Portugal and added the country to his crown. For sixty years it was ruled by Spain. Drawn into wars with France and England, Portugal, like Spain, lost much of its overseas empire. In the following century the Portuguese rose against Spain and, with English help, regained their independence in 1640. To reinforce the English alliance, the new king, John IV, gave his daughter in marriage to Charles II.

Portugal now began to exploit Brazil more fully, and a period of renewed prosperity commenced. But it was apparent rather than real, for it was based not on trade, but on plunder and looting. So although many beautiful churches and palaces were built and furnished with magnificent ornaments of gold, silver and precious stones, the ordinary people of Portugal—especially in overcrowded Lisbon—were wretchedly poor. Throughout the country, agriculture was of the most primitive type and industry virtually non-existent. To make matters worse, an earthquake shook the country in 1755 and destroyed most of the capital. During the Napoleonic wars Portugal was invaded three times and its countryside laid waste. Such were the conditions when the king abdicated, to become Emperor of Brazil. By so doing, he cut the motherland off from the wealth of this colony.

Throughout the nineteenth century there was discontent among the people. Successive kings were blamed for the poverty-stricken state of the country and the monarchy became increasingly unpopular. Peasant uprisings were frequent. In 1908 they culminated in the assassination of King Carlos and his heir. The new king, Manuel, was dethroned in 1910 and Portugal proclaimed a republic.

Since then, the country has had to face constant internal difficulties, principally concerned with the condition of its working classes. After the First World War, civil strife so convulsed the country that the military took charge of the Government in order to restore peace. Oliveira Salazar, professor of economics at Coimbra University, was made President of the Council in 1928, and given a free hand to reorganise the country's economy. Salazar remained in power until 1968, and under his beneficent dictatorship Portugal made substantial industrial and agricultural advance.

POPULATION

Portugal has a population of 8,889,000 and an average density of 255 persons per square mile. Its people are unevenly distributed, the greatest concentrations being around Lisbon and Oporto (*see* Fig. 40). In general, the density of population decreases with distance from the coast. The large estates of Alentejo, especially in the east of the province, are sparsely peopled, but mountainous northern Portugal, with its tiny farm-holdings, is severely overcrowded. The whole country may be said to be over-populated, and the pressure of too many people has led to large-scale emigration, mainly to Brazil. Unfortunately for Portugal, the emigrants include many of the more progressive and better educated of its people.

THE ECONOMY

Portugal's economy is almost entirely agricultural and forestal, plus an important contribution from sardine fishing. Only a quarter of the working population is engaged in industry, and this concerned mainly with the preparation for export of the products of field, forest and sea. Manufacturing industries were already expanding around Lisbon and Oporto before 1928; since then, under Salazar's wise if somewhat autocratic administration, they are spreading to other parts of the country. But shortage of fuel, poor supplies of minerals, insufficient capital and the very low standard of literacy are great drawbacks. The fact that Portugal's chief products—cork, wine, sardines, olive oil—have only minor significance in world commerce has been another factor in her slow industrial advance.

MINERALS AND POWER

Mineral wealth consists mainly of wolfram and pyrites. The chief wolfram deposits, yielding about 3000 tons of ore a year, are in the Fundão district of the upper Zezere basin, and in the lower Minho valley. Cupriferous pyrites occur around Mértola and Castro Verde, in southern Alentejo. Small amounts of iron ore are mined near Moncorvo, in the upper Douro basin; and there are a few seams of poor coal east of Oporto.

Away from the larger towns, charcoal is used for domestic heating and cooking. Coal for industrial purposes and for the railways must be imported. In the past few years, however, there has been a notable development of hydro-electric power. The greatest scope for this is in northern Portugal, with its mountains, its more reliable rainfall and swift rivers. Power stations have been constructed in three areas: in Beira Baixa along the river Zezere; in the Minho province on the rivers Lima, Cavado and Ave; and on the Douro near the Spanish frontier. These schemes serve respectively Lisbon and Oporto, where most of Portugal's industry is concentrated, but they also give power to new and modernised factories and workshops in Fundão, Covilha, Coimbra and Santarém. The Zezere scheme in addition provides irrigation water to the Tagus plains. The Douro Project, which is shared by Spain, is planned to have the greatest output capacity of any hydro-electricity plant in west Europe (*see* page 169).

AGRICULTURE

Improvement in Portugal's agricultural economy has been slower than in industry. The chief problems are connected with irrigation and education. In the south of the country there are large areas still virtually unproductive because of lack of water, but irrigation schemes are slowed down by difficulties of level. Most of the rivers flow in narrow valleys, whose floors are far below the surface of the surrounding plateau; the Guadiana, for instance, because of its gorge-like valley, is so far of little

[*Courtesy of Portuguese State Office*

FIG. 48.—Portugal: Oporto, the new Arrábida bridge over the Douro. Part of a huge programme of motorway (*auto-estrada*) and bridge construction throughout the country. The recent President Salazar bridge at Lisbon is the most remarkable example.

value for irrigation. This part of Portugal too—and in fact the whole of the eastern half of the country—needs a good road system.

Perhaps the greatest need in Portugal today is for a revolution in agricultural methods, which are often primitive. Knowledge of fertilisers and modern scientific farming is scanty and difficult to improve, for the greatest degree of illiteracy occurs among the rural population. The small farmers of the north, living from hand to mouth, have neither the time nor the capital necessary for improvement; the absentee landlords of the south are satisfied with present conditions and their tenants are given little opportunity to improve themselves. Nevertheless, the economic measures introduced by Salazar are slowly bearing fruit and, if the advance Portugal has made in the last thirty years has been slow, it is on sound lines.

REGIONAL ECONOMY

1. *Northern Portugal*

The mountainous region of northern Portugal is better watered than the rest of the country, and for the most part has a denser population. Every available square inch of cultivable land is utilised, yet despite considerable emigration to other parts of Portugal and overseas there are too many people for its meagre resources. Farms are so small and fragmented that some families have to exist on a piece of land hardly large enough to produce cabbages for their soup or maize for their bread—these being their staple foodstuffs.

In the valleys of the provinces of Minho and coastal Douro, with an adequate rainfall assisted by irrigation from wells, maize is the chief crop; cattle and oxen are reared for dairy produce and as draught animals. Flax is grown in lower, wetter areas near rivers. In the uplands, rye is the chief food crop, and sheep and goats are reared for wool, hair, milk and cheese. The higher slopes are clothed with edible-chestnut trees; in the tiny fields which cling to the mountains, potatoes are grown.

In the provinces of Tras os Montes ("the region beyond the mountains") and Douro Alto is the most difficult part of northern Portugal, with its people concentrated into isolated villages. Here wheat is commoner than maize, but rye is the chief cereal and black bread is the staple food. In Beira the mountain dwellers in the Serra da Estrêla work as shepherds, charcoal burners or lumberers in the chestnut and oak forests which cover the slopes; and in the wild region of Beira Baixa (Lower Beira), the foothills of the desolate *serras* support olive trees, especially around Castelo Branco, which is noted for olive oil. In Beira Alta (Upper Beira) and Beira Baixa there is still a domestic woollen industry, using local supplies of wool; but as a result of hydro-electric power developed on the rivers Zezere and Ponsul, tributaries of the Tagus, factories for woollens and linen have been built at Covilha, Fundão and Idanha-a-Nova.

The vine is cultivated throughout northern Portugal, but except in the Douro valley in Tras os Montes, the grapes do not ripen properly, and produce a rather acid *vinho verde* ("green wine") which is drunk locally. In the Upper Douro, however, are the vines that yield port wine. Here, in a soil which is more like rubble broken down from the granites and mica schists of the steep valley slopes, the long-rooted vine thrives. The summer heat—in gulleys as much as 104° F (40° C)—gives an excellent balance of alcohol and sugar, as is required in the best wines. The vineyards climb up 120 miles (192 km) of valleys, on terraces supported by low, dry walls, to the limit where the grape runs the risk of drying up before it ripens. Work in the vineyard region is restricted to growing the grapes and producing the *must*, that is, unfermented juice. This is carried in casks on flat-bottomed boats along the Douro to storehouses in Vila Nova de Gaia (45,739), a small town opposite Oporto, near the mouth of the river. Here by careful fermentation the wine is made ready for export.

The vines for port wine were introduced from Burgundy early in Portugal's history, but not until 1703 did an increasing demand from England cause a rapid extension of the vineyards. Since that date, when English exporters began to settle in Oporto, much of the trade has remained in English hands, and many of the inhabitants of the Lower Douro have English-sounding names. The export of port wine is today Portugal's main source of income, and Great Britain the chief customer.

South of the Douro estuary is a low coastal plain backed by hilly country. The coast itself is straight and lined with sandhills, behind which are lagoons and swamps. The inhabitants of this littoral zone are often fishermen-farmers, the chief catch off the coast being sardines. Salt is obtained by evaporation in salt pans. Inland, in Beira Litoral, the area is fertile, especially in the flood-plain of the river Mondego, where maize and rice are grown. Higher up the valley are wheatfields and vineyards; in the hills to the east, olive oil is an important product.

The chief town of northern Portugal, and the second in the country, is Oporto (310,000), on the river Douro where it cuts through the hills and begins to widen to its estuary. Access to its harbour is impeded for ocean-going vessels by a bar across the mouth of the river. Most large ships now use the outport of Leixões, an artificial port 3 miles (5 km) north of the estuary. Oporto is the centre of the wine trade; it also has flour mills, food industries, fish canning, iron and steel works, engineering, and wool textile and silk industries. It is helped by hydro-electric power developed in the river valleys to the north. Other towns in northern Portugal are small and are chiefly agricultural markets. They include Coimbra (45,508) and Braga (41,043), both ancient regional capitals; Viana do Castelo, a naval dockyard; Figueria da Foz, a market for fish; and Fátima, a hill village in the south of the region. Fátima is growing rapidly as a religious pilgrimage centre.

2. Central Portugal

This region consists of the hill province of Estremadura, the plains of Ribatejo, and the large province of Alentejo; this last is divided into lowlands near the coast, and the broken horst country of the Alentejo plateau further inland. The valleys among the hills of Estremadura have fertile soils, and so have the alluvial Ribatejo flood-plains. The soils of Baixo Alentejo are fertile too but are not well used; those of the highlands of Alto Alentejo, derived from crystalline rocks, are infertile.

The plains of central Portugal, especially in Estremadura and Ribatejo, produce heavy crops of maize, wheat, rice and fodder. Between Santarém and Vila Franca, cattle-rearing is outstanding. Here and farther up the

Tagus plain are bred the bulls used in Portugal's special type of bull-fighting, in which the animals are not killed. Vines are grown extensively, and olive groves appear on the drier sides of hills. Farms in the Alentejo lowlands, in contrast to those in northern Portugal, are large—some of them up to 1300 acres (520 ha); in fact, some might be called villages. They are very like the *latifundia* of southern Spain. Around the owner's and steward's houses are store rooms, wine presses, oil presses, barns, silos, cheese dairies, bakeries, carpenters' and wheelwrights' workshops and the smaller houses of the employees, as well as dormitories for seasonal workers. Near by there are roofed shelters for the piles of cork awaiting transport to Lisbon. The owner, a rich man, is often an absentee land-lord who leaves the running of the estate in the hands of the steward.

[*Courtesy of Portuguese State Office.*

FIG. 49.—Portugal: a view of Palmela, a small town in the Setúbal peninsula. It originated as a Moorish citadel on a height above the very flat plain, and the modern town is on a shoulder of the hill. Tree crops grow near the town.

The mountains of inner Alentejo are clothed with cultivated forests of cork-oak (*see* Fig. 31). The region is the main source of cork, which, after pine (used for pit-props and for its resin), is the most important forest product of Portugal. The cork-oak forests occupy roughly a quarter of the forested area of the country. They are carefully tended; the cork, which is the bark of the tree, is stripped off at intervals of nine years, the time taken to grow new layers. The chief centres for cork collection are Portalegre, Évora (24,144) and Beja. Lisbon is the port of export. The cork-oak also yields tannin, used in the leather-tanning industry; and large numbers of pigs are reared in the forests, where they feed on acorns.

In eastern Alentejo, agriculture is at subsistence level and confined to small areas. The wide, flat stretches between the horsts, the *campos*, are used more for sheep rearing than for arable farming.

Situated on hills on the north banks of the Tagus, about 8 miles from the sea, is Lisbon (Lisboa), the capital of Portugal, with a population of 1,397,000. Here the river widens into a basin which forms one of the best harbours in the world (*see* Fig. 50). The earthquake of 1755, which destroyed the old city, enabled Lisbon to be replanned and rebuilt in grandiose style; and the more modern additions of the present century have been equally well planned. Lisbon has doubled in size in the past twenty years, but eighteenth- and twentieth-century architectural styles have blended in a most harmonious and satisfying way.

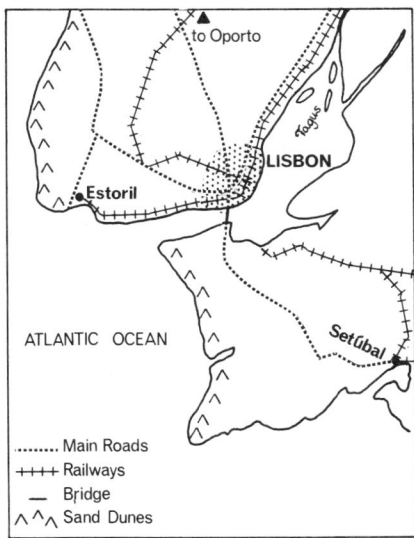

FIG. 50.—Portugal: Lisbon. The bottle-necked estuary of the Tagus encloses one of the best harbours in the world, 12 miles (19 km) long and 7 miles (12 km) wide. The southern margins are naturally swampy, but are being reclaimed and settled. The new President Salazar Bridge links Lisbon directly with southern Portugal; the next bridge-point is nearly 40 miles (64 km) up the Tagus.

As the outlet of fertile central Portugal, and being on the best harbour in western Iberia, Lisbon has developed a large variety of industries, in addition to its entrepôt trade and to being a port of call for ships. To the old industries connected with wine, cork, sardines and olive oil have been added shipbuilding, textiles (mainly cottons), oil refining, oilseed crushing and chemical manufacture (chiefly of fertilisers). It is also the headquarters of the Portuguese long-distance cod-fishing fleet and of steamship lines to Africa and South America. It is an important airport; and last, but not least, it has extended along the banks of the Tagus in a series of holiday resorts among which Estoril has reached international fame. Lisbon is connected to south Portugal by a suspension bridge, the Salazar Bridge, which was opened to road traffic in 1966.

South of the mouth of the Tagus, is the peninsula of Setúbal, largely pine- or heath-covered (see Fig. 49). In the south of the peninsula, on the wide estuary of the river Sado and protected by a long sandspit, is the town of Setúbal (44,605), the chief sardine-canning centre, and one of the ports for the pyrites of south Alentejo. In the Sado lowlands south of the peninsula, rice growing is important.

In the mountains which separate central Portugal from the Algarve in the south, a mineralised area produces pyrites containing copper. The deposits are similar to those of the Rio Tinto in the Sierra Morena. The chief fields are around Mértola and Castro Verde.

3. Southern Portugal

The Algarve is potentially a rich land of wheat, vines, olives, figs, almonds and even sugar cane and sweet potatoes; but its farmers, though hardworking, are handicapped by lack of surface water. They inherited from the Moors a knowledge of irrigation, but it is employed only on a small scale. A big extension of the irrigation system is needed before full measure can be taken of the Algarve's agricultural potential.

Off the coasts are the richest fishing grounds of Portugal, the chief catch being sardines and tunny, which are canned at Vila Real de Santo Antonio and Lagos. Most of the fishermen are also part-time workers in the canning factories. Lagos was the starting point for the seafaring explorers sent out by Henry the Navigator; today it has an airport on some of the European routes to West Africa and South America. Sagres, on the south-western tip of Europe, is a fishing port; here was situated Prince Henry's school of navigation. Tourism is developing rapidly along the coasts of the Algarve.

STUDY QUESTIONS

1. From the points of view of (a) climate, (b) natural resources, (c) economic development, contrast the regions of Portugal which lie north and south of Lisbon.

2. Illustrate the influence of relief and climate upon the lives of the people of Portugal.

3. Show how geographical conditions have influenced the location and importance of Lisbon and Oporto.

4. Describe the distribution of population in Portugal and analyse the chief factors upon which this distribution depends.

Chapter XI

MEDITERRANEAN FRANCE

MEDITERRANEAN France cannot be delineated precisely. It is that part of France which has the winter rain and summer drought associated with the Mediterranean climate; but climatic boundaries are rarely exact, and here the landward boundary of the region is taken as approximately the

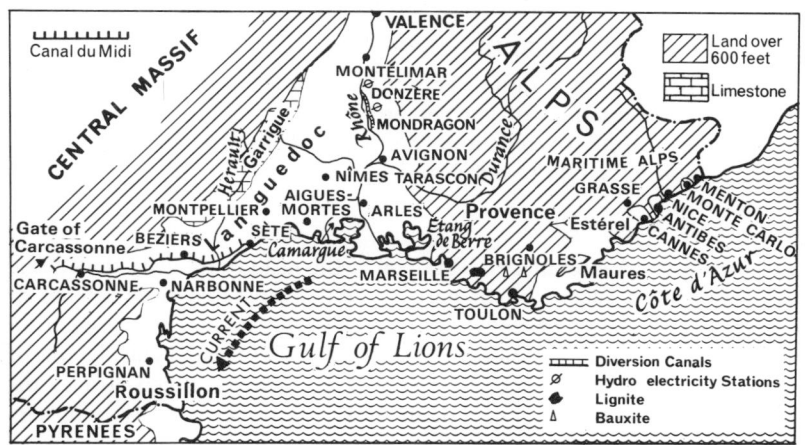

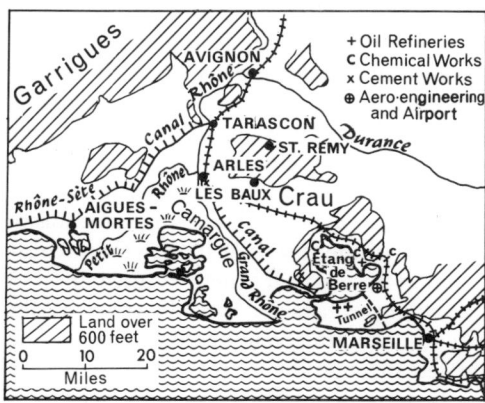

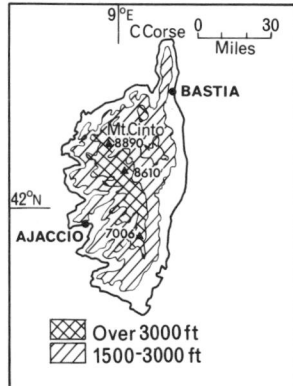

FIG. 51.—France: Mediterranean region. Although the Garrigue is the only area marked as lime-stone, most of the Alpine region shown is composed of similar rock. The smaller map shows the Rhône delta and Marseille in more detail.

FIG. 52.—Corsica.

northern limit of olive cultivation in the Rhône valley. As this more or less coincides in the region with the limit of the holm oak, a characteristically Mediterranean tree, it may also be regarded as delimiting the typical Mediterranean climate. In this case, Mediterranean France forms a rough triangle, with the coast from near Narbonne in the west to the Italian frontier in the east as its base, and Valence near the southern end of the Rhône "corridor" as the apex, and with a southern extension in the west to the Spanish frontier (see Fig. 51); and to this must be added the large island of Corsica (see Fig. 52). The whole region covers an area of around 24,000 sq. miles (62,400 sq. km), roughly one-ninth of France.

PHYSICAL ASPECTS

STRUCTURE AND RELIEF

The Mediterranean region of France, also known as the Midi, is divided according to the names of ancient provinces; the whole region is here divided into (1) the lower Rhône valley, (2) Roussillon and Languedoc, (3) the Rhône delta, (4) Provence, and (5) Corsica.

1. The lower Rhône valley

From above Montélimar to Tarascon at the head of its delta the Rhône flows through a succession of narrow defiles separated by stretches of alluvial plains. West of the river a series of limestone terraces climbs gradually towards the south-west of the Massif Centrale. Near the massif they are known as *garrigues* (Fr. waste land), a name given also to the scanty vegetation which covers them; nearer the river the low-lying terraces may be covered by alluvium. East of the Rhône the plains are of alluvium overlying coarse gravels. After the Tertiary mountain-building movements which resulted in the formation of the Rhône corridor, the valley was subjected to eustatic movements (changes in sea-level) associated with the Quaternary Ice Age. At the period of maximum glaciation, when sea-level was reaching its lowest, the river cut down through the limestones to produce erosion platforms represented by the garrigues (see Fig. 53). At the same time, torrential outpourings from the glaciers on the Alps washed down vast quantities of rock débris to build huge plateaus of pebbles and gravel on the eastern side of the river. With the rises in sea-level in the inter-glacial phases and in post-glacial times, sedimentation of a more normal character buried the gravel fans and spread a cover of silts over the neighbouring limestone terraces. In recent geological times, the changing velocity of the Rhône, fast through the narrow defiles and slow in the intervening plains, has resulted in a deposition of its load in the lowlands, blocking its course and causing braiding and shifting sandbanks, and reducing its navigability to a minimum. This has now been improved; diversion canals south of Montélimar and between Donzère and Mondragon, constructed in connection with the building of hydro-electricity power stations, are intended also to form a part of the complete canalisation of the river at some time in the future.

South of the Rhône corridor and stretching from the eastern end of the Pyrenees to the Italian border is a region which offers many contrasts. High, rugged mountains stand next door to flat, deltaic plains; winters are wet and summers dry: winds may be warm from the sea or bitterly cold from the Alps; low-lying shores are succeeded by cliff-girt coasts; and areas of dense population stand cheek by jowl with others almost deserted.

2. Roussillon and Languedoc

Along the coasts of Roussillon and Languedoc, longshore drift from east to west in an almost tideless sea, plus the effect of wind, has built up a fringe of sand dunes and offshore bars. Some of the latter have enclosed lagoons (*étangs*) and marshes (*see* Fig. 54). Behind these is a broad zone of undulating plains, with soils varying from fertile river alluvium, Tertiary and marine clays, and decayed basalt, to less fertile limestones and gravels. North of the plains is a continuation of the garrigues of the lower Rhône, low limestone ridges which flank the southern edge of the Massif Centrale.

3. The Rhône delta

The Rhône delta may be said to begin at Tarascon and covers an area of approximately 240 sq. miles (625 sq. km). It is traversed by two main distributaries, the Grand Rhône and the Petit Rhône, which diverge south-east and south-west near Arles. At the seaward end of the delta the Grand Rhône is the more active and its deposited load is extending the delta south-eastwards. The load carried by the Petit Rhône is much less—only about one-tenth that of the larger distributary—and delta building at the western end is almost at a standstill. The delta is becoming lopsided. The western portion of the delta, drained by the Petit Rhône, is known as the Camargue; in the south it is a monotonous stretch of salt flats, with a sparse cover of halophilous vegetation, but much of the north has been reclaimed for agriculture. East of the Grand Rhône is the Crau, a large fan of water-worn stones and coarse gravels swept there in post-glacial times by the river Durance, which then abandoned its course and became a tributary of the Rhône. The southern Crau provides poor pasture for herds of transhumant sheep; the north has been irrigated from the Durance and cultivated wherever possible. The Crau is traversed by several canals which connect the Rhône with the Durance, the Étang de Berre and Marseille.

4. Provence

The coastlands east of the Rhône delta are made up first of east–west limestone ranges as far as Toulon; then of Maures and Estérel, two low plateaus of ancient rocks; and finally of more limestone ranges, the Maritime Alps, this time with a north–south trend. The western ranges, the

Alps of Provence, rise to over 3500 ft (1070 m) and are separated by wide valleys and basins, notably along the river Durance and its tributaries. A subsidence of the land at their western extremity gave rise to the Gulf of Marseille and the Étang de Berre, a large lake which is often mistakenly regarded as a part of the Rhône delta. The massifs of Maures and Estérel are fragments of an ancient continental mass, probably of Hercynian age, which foundered during the Tertiary orogenesis. They are composed of pre-Cambrian gneisses, schists and granites, and are just over 2500 ft (760 m) at their highest point. They have given rise to a steep, rocky coast with few inlets. The eastern coastlands are the Côte d'Azur, a succession of small plains and, where the coast cuts across the grain of the Maritime Alps, of limestone cliffs. The largest plain is the valley of the Var, behind Cannes. The Côte d'Azur, facing the south and sheltered from the mistral, is known also as the French Riviera.

5. Corsica

South-east of the Côte d'Azur is the island of Corsica, 3367 square miles (8750 sq. km) in area. Most of it is composed of the same granites and schists as Maures and Estérel, and together with Sardinia probably formed part of the same ancient land mass. In the north-east and east there are slightly folded hills which are separated from the higher west by a depression. These represent strata which were directly involved in the Alpine folding movements. Most of Corsica lies above 1500 ft (460 m) and is extensively covered by well-developed maquis. The western side of the island rises to 8890 ft (2710 m).

CLIMATE

The Mediterranean coastlands of France are under the influence of off-shore north-easterly prevailing winds in summer and have anticyclonic conditions. In winter the westerlies are the dominant winds, bringing depressions, often via the gap between the Pyrenees and the Massif Centrale. The results are the usual hot, dry summers and mild, wet winters which characterise the Mediterranean climate. In the winter the western half of the region has temperatures lower than in the east. The January mean temperature of Montpellier is 41° F (5·0° C) and of Marseille 43·3° F (6·3° C), as compared with 46·4° F (8·0° C) at Nice. This is because the first two are affected in winter by the mistral, a strong, cold wind which blows southward along the Rhône valley from the snow-clad Alps, whereas Nice lies in the lee of the Maritime Alps. Summer temperatures are uniformly high: in July they average 72·9° F (22·8° C) in Montpellier, 72·1° F (22·2° C) in Marseille and 73·8° F (23·2° C) in Nice. Both Montpellier and Nice have average annual rainfalls of 30·9 in., approximately one-third of the total falling in October and November. Marseille has a mean annual precipitation of 22·6 in., nearly 40% of which falls from October to December.

HISTORICAL OUTLINE

The ancient provinces which make up Mediterranean France did not become genuinely united with France until comparatively late in their histories. Languedoc became French in 1420 and Provence was annexed in 1486; Roussillon was incorporated in 1659 and Corsica in 1786. Avignon, in the Vaucluse district of Provence, was chosen as his residence by Pope Clement V in 1309, and the town and the surrounding territory remained in Papal hands until 1791, when they were annexed by the French National Assembly. In 1860, Savoy and the area around Nice were ceded by Italy. In 1790 the names Languedoc and Provence disappeared from the official map of France and were replaced by those of *départements* (similar to English counties), but the provincial names soon reappeared and are now in general use. The name Languedoc dates from the end of the thirteenth century and refers to the region in whose tongue (*langue*) the word for "yes" was *oc*, as opposed to the centre and north of France which at that time used the *langue d'oil*, from which is derived the *oui* of today. The Romans conquered southern France after 125 B.C., and called the lands east of the Rhône *Provincia Romana*, from which comes the name of Provence.

The Greeks founded colonies at Marseille (Gr. *Massalia*, Lat. *Massilia*), Antibes and Nice as early as 600 B.C., and it is thought that the Phoenicians may have preceded them, for it is suggested that the name Massalia is derived from the Phoenician word for "settlement." In 118 B.C. the Romans founded the colony and seaport of Narbonne, which is interesting since this town is now about five miles inland, shut off from the sea by silts carried from the Rhône. Nîmes, Béziers, Narbonne and Toulouse were flourishing Roman towns until the fifth century, when Mediterranean France fell into the hands of the Visigoths, who ruled there for two hundred years. In the eighth century the Franks moved southwards and Languedoc and Provence were conquered and became part of the empire of Charlemagne, but after his death in 843 most of Languedoc was joined to the kingdom of the West Franks, and Provence to Lotharingia.

The history of both provinces for five centuries after this partition is one of disorganisation and disorder. Languedoc was ruled by warlike counts and petty barons who ignored the distant King of France and maintained a constant state of civil war, in which the peasantry was cruelly oppressed. This lasted until 1420, when the administration of the province was reformed and Languedoc became a real part of the French kingdom. Provence after the partition passed into the hands of Burgundy and then of Germanic kings, and after 1112 was juggled between the Spanish rulers of Barcelona and Aragon, until in 1486 it was finally annexed by France. From that date the history of the Midi is included with that of France.

The people of the south are independent, dignified, proud, and at the same time pleasure-loving, light-hearted and chivalrous. In their medieval history there appeared the troubadours (wandering lyric poets) who sang of the joys of life, of love and chivalry, and demonstrated very clearly the characteristics which mark off the people of Languedoc and Provence from those of other parts of France. Their ways of thought have been coloured, too, by the succession of religious rebels—Albigensians, Manicheans, Huguenot Protestants, Calvinists—who have at various times found refuge in the Midi, and by the doctrines of the French Revolution in which Provence played a prominent part. The *Marseillaise* was the marching song of the Provençal rebels of Marseille before it was adopted as the French national anthem.

Roussillon was included in the Roman province of Gallia Narbonensis until A.D. 462, when it passed, like Languedoc, to the Visigoths and then to the Franks. But it suffered the usual fate of border regions, and was shuttlecocked backwards and forwards between French counts and the houses of Barcelona and Aragon until 1258, when Spanish rule became permanent. In 1659, with the decay of the power of Spain, Roussillon was ceded to France.

Corsica was inhabited in early times first by the Ligurians and then by the Etruscans. It was colonised by the Carthaginians, who were driven out by the Romans in 201 B.C. The island remained in Roman hands until A.D. 469, and then the Vandals took possession. With their disappearance from the historic scene early in the sixth century, Corsica was occupied successively by the forces of the East Roman Empire, by the Franks under Charlemagne, and by the Muslim Moors. The island was dominated by the Moors from 810 to 930, and they were succeeded in the next four centuries by the Tuscans, the Holy See, the Pisans, Aragonese and Genoese. The powerful commercial republic of Genoa ruled from 1347 until 1768. In the latter part of this period, however, Corsica was often in a state approaching anarchy, its people were taxed to the limit of their resources, its rulers were frequently petty tyrants, and its coasts were ravaged by Barbary pirates; so that when its inhabitants staged a massive rebellion it came as no surprise. The republic of Genoa had become decrepit and was unable to regain control of Corsica and in 1786 it sold the sovereignty of the island to France. During the Napoleonic wars (Napoleon was a native of Corsica) the island was occupied in 1814 by the British, but in 1815 it was restored to France.

From this short summary it is clear that the Corsicans have had a very chequered history; and if in modern times they became distinguished by a certain wild intractability and ferocity, the cause must be sought in their unhappy past, especially in the centuries when they lay under the yoke of the Genoese. They are an extremely independent people and even in the early part of this century had little regard for the rule of law. It is not many years since brigandage and the vendetta formed part of their normal way of life, and the law-breaker found a safe refuge in the almost impenetrable maquis which covers much of the island.

THE ECONOMY

1. *The lower Rhône valley*

According to an old French jingle, *À Valence le Midi commence*—the Midi begins at Valence—so for our purposes we shall regard this thriving market town as the northern limit of Mediterranean France. Market gardens on both sides of the Rhône south of Valence are succeeded below Montélimar by mulberry trees in groves or lining the roads; they supply leaves for the rearing of silkworms which are cultivated as a cottage industry to produce silk for its manufacture in Lyon, to the north. From Montélimar, where the Rhône valley begins to open to the plain of Avignon, both banks of the river are lined with orchards of peaches, apricots, cherries and pears. Olives make their appearance, and wheat and vines are important. The main cultivation is of early vegetables and table grapes, which are sent to the markets of Lyon, Paris and Marseille. Excellent wine (Château neuf du Pape) is produced near Avignon; its name reminds us that the town was once the home of the Popes. On the west the plain rises to the limestone foothills at the base of the Central Massif. These have scanty grasses and lime-loving shrubs on which sheep are reared; such landscape is known as garrigue (Fr. *garigue*).

The many small towns and villages along this section of the Rhône have been overshadowed by Lyon. Valence (55,023), Montélimar and Avignon (75,181) are the largest; all have silk manufacture and food processing, Montélimar is noted for nougat, and Avignon is the centre of a vegetable-canning industry. All, too, are helped by plentiful hydro-electric power. The Donzère–Mondragon scheme, not far from Montélimar, has one of France's largest generating stations, and is integrated with the Genissiat scheme in the north of the Rhône valley. The scheme, which is intended also to regulate the flow of the Rhône and to provide water for irrigation, diverts some of the river into canals and power dams on the eastern banks, whence it passes through power stations and is returned to the main stream. Four similar plants are planned for the lower Rhône, one at Montélimar (almost completed) and three downstream from Mondragon, the final one at Tarascon. The Rhône scheme is intended primarily to supply power to the national grid, but it is bound to have a revitalising effect throughout Mediterranean France and especially in the reclamation and development of the delta.

2. *Roussillon and Languedoc*

West of the delta of the Rhône, a dune-lined coast is backed by the small plain of Roussillon near the Spanish border and by the larger plains of Languedoc north of the Pyrenees. The Roussillon lowland is floored with débris washed down from the Pyrenees; the area is well watered by several small rivers; and there is intensive cultivation of orchard fruits and early vegetables. Vines are important and there is an export of wine. The chief market is Perpignan (83,025), a road and railway junction with good communications round and through the eastern Pyrenees to Spain. Port Vendres, a small port, has packet steamer lines to Marseille, Barcelona and North Africa.

[*Courtesy of French Government Tourist Office.*

FIG. 53.—Mediterranean France: Languedoc, typical Mediterranean vegetation. The view is of one end of the Étang du Ponant, one of the many lagoons along the coast. In the background are tall umbrella pines rising above clumps of holm oak. In the foreground and round the lagoon is a discontinuous cover of maquis or garrigue—stunted, thorny bushes and xerophilous shrubs. The parched vegetation suggests the picture was taken in the summer.

East of Roussillon there is little agricultural activity in the coastal belt, and the only town of any account is Sète (Cette) (38,000). It is a port at the terminus of the Canal du Midi, which runs via the Gate of Carcassonne to Toulouse, but until recently its importance was declining, mainly because the harbour was silting up. Its main trade is in wine and petroleum, and the latter has given the port new life. Oil refineries have been built at Frontignac, a suburb on the edge of an étang, and the harbour has been dredged and modernised. Tunny, sardines and anchovies are caught off the coast, but the fishing industry is of minor importance.

The plains of Languedoc were one of the granaries of imperial Rome, but the cultivation of wheat is now largely confined to the west, towards

Carcassonne. Here there is mixed farming, with wheat, maize, fruit, cattle and pigs. Carcassonne (37,000), the chief town in this western area, was sited on a hill commanding the passage between the Pyrenees and the Central Massif. The old town, surrounded by impressive walls, has been supplanted by a new one at the foot of the hill, and important food processing and textile (woollen, cotton, rayon) industries have developed there. The old town remains as a tourist attraction.

Most of the rest of Languedoc is given over to viticulture. Vines are to be seen everywhere, in one of the best examples of monoculture in Europe. Languedoc is the world's greatest producer of wine, accounting for nearly half the total output of France. The wine is almost entirely *vin ordinaire*, which is distributed throughout the country via the Rhône–Saône corridor, the Gate of Carcassonne, or by sea from Marseille.

Monoculture, *i.e.*, dependence on a single crop, as in Languedoc, has its dangers. Winds like the mistral may do great seasonal damage; but far more serious are the virus diseases which may destroy the vines and poison the soil. In the years before 1880, for instance, a type of aphides, *phylloxera*, destroyed four-fifths of all the vineyards. The disease was ultimately conquered by the use of newly-discovered sprays and by the introduction of resistant stock from the vineyards of California. The revived industry adopted co-operative methods of cultivation, harvesting, wine-making and marketing. New threats to Languedoc's monoculture came from the great increases in the amount of land devoted to viticulture in Algeria— although for the time being this threat has receded—and from the French Government's campaign against excessive wine-drinking which is alleged to be rampant in France. Consequently nearly all the farmers in Languedoc now devote some of their land to the cultivation of maize, wheat, vegetables, and fruits such as peaches and apricots. The chief centres of wine production in co-operative factories are Montpellier (123,367), Nîmes (105,199), Béziers (78,544) and Narbonne (38,000), around all of which monoculture is giving way to mixed farming. Nîmes is a route centre, and has railway repair works and wool textile manufacture.

North of the plain is a continuation of the garrigue country of the lower Rhône. The limestone ridges flanking the Central Massif are here more extensive, and support a xerophytic scrub in which aromatic shrubs such as thyme and lavender are mixed with short grasses. Sheep-rearing is important in these hills and transhumance is normal, the sheep being moved to the higher Central Massif in summer. The flocks are reared for wool, skins and cheese. In some of the valleys between the ridges are Government-sponsored plantations of pine trees.

3. *The Rhône delta*

The western part of the Rhône delta is the Camargue, drained by the Petit Rhône and bounded in the east by the Grand Rhône, the main distributaries. The southern Camargue is an expanse of salt marsh, useless except for the production of salt in evaporating pans at Aigues-Mortes

FIG. 54—Mediterranean France:: Languedoc, the harbour of La Grande Motte. The Mediterranean Sea is in the foreground. The spits enclosing the lagoons are being reclaimed and developed in many places. La Grande Motte, south of Montpellier, encloses the Étang du Ponant. The plants shown are mainly cluster pines with poplars and oaks near the eastern edge of the picture. The harbour works, which are entirely artificial, are not yet completed.

and chemicals at Les Salins-de-Giraud, both tiny settlements near the seaward ends of the two Rhônes. An interesting feature of the southern Camargue is the herd of horses which roam wild, feeding on scanty grasses near the coast. The middle Camargue supports herds of half-wild cattle in the care of cowboys, and transhumant flocks of sheep, but the grazing area is gradually being reduced. Reclamation of the northern Camargue is being extended southwards, and pastoralism replaced by mixed farming, with wheat, vines, vegetables and dairy cattle. About 100,000 tons of rice are also produced annually in this part of the delta.

East of the Grand Rhône is the stony Crau, a large fan deposited by the Durance. The Crau, dry on the surface, scorched in summer and swept by the mistral in winter, is for the most part a desolate area. Sheep are taken there in winter, to feed on the garrigue and scanty grasses which root between the stones. In the east of the Crau, irrigation using the waters of the Durance has made possible the cultivation of early vegetables, hay, vines and olives. Near a low limestone ridge which crosses the Crau is the "ghost town" of Les Baux, which gave bauxite its name; the deposits are now exhausted. St Rémy is a small market town in the irrigated region.

4. *Provence*

The French coast immediately east of the Rhône delta is very broken and has several good harbours which an east–west current keeps relatively free from the silts brought down by the Rhône. Behind the coast the highland areas of the limestone Basse Alpes and Maritime Alps and the crystalline Maures and Estérel have little economic value except for sheep-rearing, but their valleys are important. In the valleys of the upper Argens and its tributaries deposits of bauxite are quarried; the bauxite is reduced to alumina (aluminium oxide) near Marseille, using lignite from a near-by field as fuel, and the alumina is sent for final smelting to electro-metallurgical stations in the High Alps and along the Pyrenees. In the valleys between the Maures and Estérel massifs there are forests of cork-oak, which provide corks for the wine industry. In the valleys of the Côte d'Azur flowers are cultivated for the cut-flower trade and the manufacture of perfumes; and early vegetables and peaches are also grown. The centre of the perfume industry is Grasse, north-east of Cannes.

It was inevitable that a major port should grow on one of the excellent harbours at the southern end of the Rhône–Saône corridor, and the development of Marseille in modern times can be attributed primarily to its position. Excellent roads and railways have been constructed from the city through the corridor, and it has become the centre of an industrial region which extends to the shores of the Étang de Berre. It imports oilseeds, sugar, timber, wheat, rice and tropical produce, processing them and exporting the finished products. Water communications inland are relatively poor; barge canals connect the port to the Durance, the Étang de Berre and the lower Rhône, but no further. Plans have been made, however, to improve navigation of the Rhône and enable large barges to traverse the river to Lyon.

Marseille (783,738; conurbation 807,500) is the second city of France, with one of the most cosmopolitan populations in the world. Its products include vegetable-oil refining, the making of soap, margarine and chemicals, flour milling, sugar refining, marine engineering and ship-building in the city area. The new developments around the Étang de Berre are also within its industrial boundaries. Marseille lies in a good position on the tanker route from the oilfields of the Middle East, and the Étang de Berre, connected by canals to the port, offers convenient sites for oil refineries. Already there are three large ones on its shores, with associated petro-chemical industries including the manufacture of explosives. Marseille's hinterland covers the whole of France, parts of Switzerland and Belgium, and even—for passengers and mails *en route* to the Far East—extends to the British Isles; thus it is one of the chief liner and passenger ports of Europe.

Toulon (172,586), on a good harbour backed by fortified limestone hills, is France's Mediterranean naval base with naval and civil dockyards. It exports bauxite from the quarries of Brignoles, to the north. The chief towns of the Côte d'Azur are holiday and tourist resorts. They are in four groups centred on Cannes, Nice (295,000), Monte Carlo and Menton. With its sun-drenched beaches, casinos, luxury trades and near-by mountain scenery, the region, known also as the Riviera, has become the "playground of Europe." Monte Carlo lies in the sovereign principality of Monaco, which has an area of only a few hundred acres. The little state accepts most French laws and customs, but in many ways is independent. It has been in the hands of the Grimaldi family since the tenth century, when they came from Genoa. Since 1860 the principality has been under French protection.

5. Corsica

The island of Corsica is the most under-developed part of France. Most of the surface lies more than 1500 ft (460 m) above sea-level and is extensively covered by thick maquis, among which only sheep and goats can find sustenance. The forests of holm oak, cork-oak, chestnut and pine, which throughout history have provided valuable exports of timber, have been sorely depleted by ruthless cutting and now cover less than one-quarter of the island. The main lowlands along the east coast are malarial. The small population of this side of Corsica lives in dirty, neglected villages in the valleys which run from the coastal plains into the plateau. The most habitable parts of the island are the strips of lowland at the heads of rias on the west coast. Farming is primitive, and subsistence crops of wheat, maize, potatoes and vegetables are supplemented by edible chestnuts gathered from the forests. Olive groves and vineyards are common along all the coasts; Cap Corse, a wine produced in the extreme north, has a high reputation. Ajaccio (40,000), the chief town, is situated on a ria and, like Bastia (51,000), a packet station in the north-east, has tunny and sardine fisheries. In recent years, sea and air communications with the mainland have been improved, and efforts made to develop a tourist industry in the north of Corsica, as an extension of the tourism of the French and Italian Rivieras.

STUDY QUESTIONS

1. Write a geographical account of Mediterranean France and comment on the importance of this region to the rest of the country.

2. Marseille has been an important settlement since the dawn of history. How far have geographical conditions affected its position and growth, especially in modern times?

3. Write short explanatory notes on the following: (*a*) the French Riviera, (*b*) the natural vegetation of Corsica, (*c*) the Camargue, (*d*) viticulture in Languedoc

Chapter XII

ITALY

ITALY is physically a well-defined geographical entity, centrally situated in the Mediterranean Sea, which it divides into two basins, east and west. The country has been described as a long pier jutting into the sea, or as a leg, terminating in a heel and toe, but descriptions of this kind are incomplete. Besides the familiar peninsula, Italy includes in the north a continental portion. This comprises a share of the Alpine arc of mountains, and the alluvial Plain of Lombardy, which is the most extensive continuous stretch of lowland in Mediterranean Europe. In addition the large islands of Sicily and Sardinia are part of Italy.

PHYSICAL ASPECTS

STRUCTURAL DIVISIONS

The major physical features of Italy are the Alps and the Plain of Lombardy in the north; and the Apennines, which run the length of the peninsula. For purposes of study, however, it is more convenient to divide the country into: (1) northern, (2) central, (3) southern and (4) insular Italy (see Fig. 55). Northern Italy is taken as that part of the country north of 44 degrees latitude; a second line drawn across the peninsula south of Rome and the Abruzzi mountains marks off central Italy; and southern Italy is the remainder of the peninsula. Insular Italy is self-explanatory. One advantage of dividing Italy in this way is that each division differs in structure, climate, and economic and cultural development. Northern Italy includes two of the major physical features; and the Apennines, running through northern, central and southern Italy, fall naturally by the above divisions into three distinct parts.

1. Northern Italy

The region may be subdivided into (a) the Italian Alps, (b) the Plain of Lombardy and (c) the northern Apennines. The plains of Venetia are regarded as part of the Plain of Lombardy, and the coastal plain of Liguria is included with the Apennines (see Fig. 56).

(a) *The Italian Alps.* Across the north of Italy, rising like a wall above the valley of the river Po, stands the arc of the Alps. The ranges may be divided into: the western Alps, from the coast to the Valle d'Aosta; the central Alps to the river Oglio and Lake d'Iseo; and the eastern Alps to the Julian Alps on the eastern border.

The western Alps rise to over 10,000 ft (3050 m), but just across the French border the ranges reach over 14,000 ft (4250 m). The valleys are

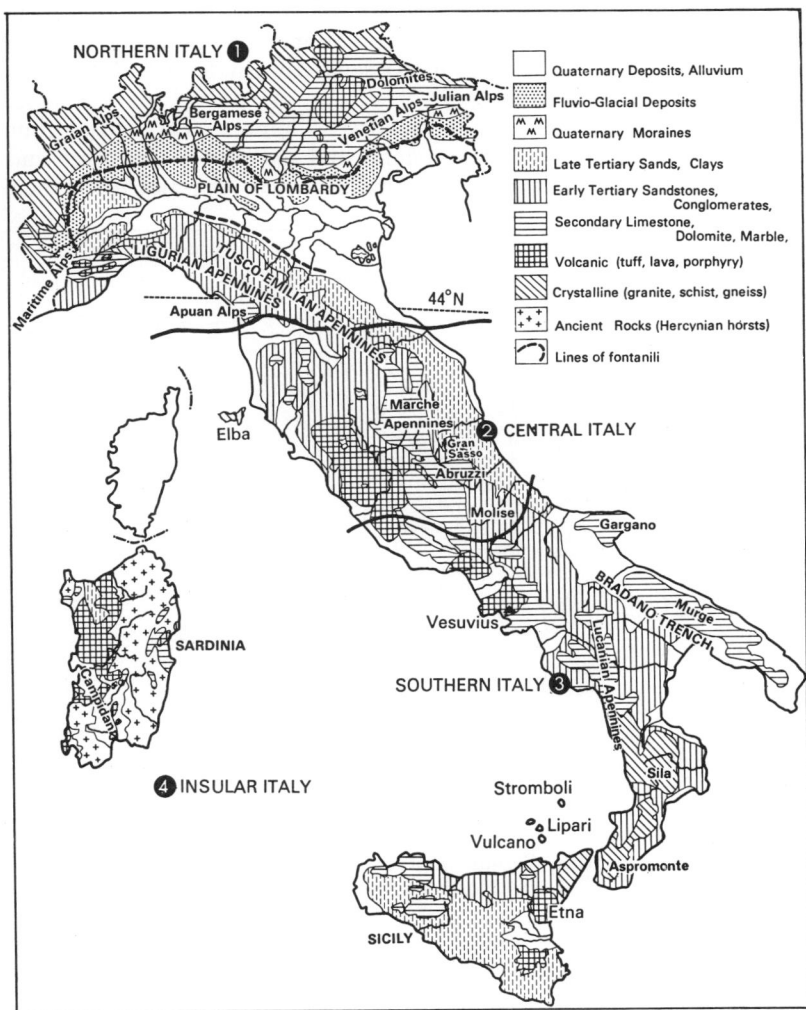

FIG. 55.—Italy: structure (much simplified). The numbers refer to sections in the text.

orientated mainly in an east–west direction and provide good routes to the Mont Cenis, Little St Bernard and de Tende passes. The valleys of the headwaters of the Po—the Dora Riparia and the Dora Baltea—are followed by roads and railways to France. The western Alps fall eastwards to the Plain of Lombardy by the series of low ranges of Piedmont.

The central Alps are narrow in Italy and, along the Swiss border, have the highest peaks, such as Monte Rosa (15,217 ft, 4638 m). The valleys through the crystalline mountains of this section are deep and narrow, but towards the south some of them widen and contain lakes dammed back by moraines. The largest lakes are Maggiore, Lugano, Como and d'Iseo. The central Alps are pierced by the important Simplon, St Gotthard, Splügen and Majola passes. The St Gotthard's southern exit leads to Milan and Genoa.

The central Alps continue beyond Lake Como to Lake d'Iseo, but crystalline rocks give way to limestone, and the ranges are lower and wider. East of d'Iseo, the eastern Alps are lower still and reach their

FIG. 56.—Italy: northern. Sub-divisions are (a) Alps, (b) Plain of Lombardy, (c) Northern Apennines.

widest, extending up to 100 miles (160 km) from north to south. They are cut by many broad valleys in this direction, and these in turn are crossed by longitudinal valleys giving east–west connections, so that the mountain mass does not form a serious obstacle. The river Adige leads to the Brenner Pass (4495 ft, 1370 m) on the boundary between Italy and Austria, the Piave gives access to the Comelico Pass, and the Tagliamento to the Carnico Pass. All these river valleys are followed by roads and railways. Lake Garda, almost 1000 ft (300 m) deep, in the west of the region, lies in a fault valley which was dammed by a moraine.

One of the eastern ranges, the Dolomites, is composed of dolomitic or magnesian limestone and has been eroded into fantastic shapes. Dolomite is the double carbonate of magnesium and calcium. The calcium carbonate is dissolved by rainwater and washed away, leaving the insoluble magnesium carbonate behind, sometimes in strange, twisted shapes, sometimes in step-like terraces. The Dolomites have become a great attraction to tourists.

The easternmost ranges of the Italian Alps—the Venetian and Julian Alps—are plateaus rather than mountains, and in parts have all the characteristics of karst. The area they cover was at one time known as "Italia Irredenta" and was a subject of dispute between Italy and Austria (which claimed it because it was German-speaking). It was finally given to Italy in 1919. The boundary between Italy and Yugoslavia, which runs through the Julian Alps, was also for long in dispute until its present position was agreed.

The Italian Alps have never been a serious obstacle to communication. The many passes mentioned, to which should be added the Great St Bernard and the Stelvio, have been used for commerce since the Middle Ages. Through most of them invaders have entered Italy, but not since Roman times have Italians been very successful in penetrating northwards. This is largely because the passes converge on the Plain of Lombardy, allowing invading armies to concentrate, whereas forces moving to the north become widely dispersed. Easy movement through the passes has also resulted in similar peoples being found on both sides of the mountains. Italian-speaking cantons occur on the Swiss side of the boundary north of Lombardy; and in the north-west in Piedmont, there is a French-speaking population on the Italian side.

(b) *The Plain of Lombardy.* Between the Alps and the northern Apennines is a great triangular depression known as the Plain of Lombardy, although its eastern portion lies in Venetia. It was originally an arm of the Adriatic Sea, but it was filled in by alluvial deposits washed down mainly from the Alps. The surface of the plain slopes gently from the north and south towards the river Po, which has been forced to the south of the depression by the greater quantity of silts brought from the Alps as compared with those from the northern Apennines. The plain of Lombardy is, in consequence, a huge asymmetrical valley.

The deposits north of the Po have been "sorted" so as to form three belts lying roughly east–west. At the foot of the sub-Alpine moraines is a belt of coarse sands and gravel, in a series of fans. This belt is too porous for much surface water and therefore is of minor importance for agriculture, except where irrigation is possible. From the southern face of the gravel zone, water issues in a line of springs (*fontanili*) to flow across the second belt, which is composed of fertile alluvium. Nearer the Po, the third belt consists of muddy marshland with occasional patches of drier alluvium. There are similar belts, including fontanili, south of the Po, but they are narrower and less well defined.

The Po enters the Adriatic by a large delta, which is growing rapidly. The town of Adria, a coastal port in Roman times, is now nearly 15 miles inland. South of the delta a number of lagoons (Valli di Comacchio) have been shut off from the sea by extensive sandbanks.

With the Plain of Lombardy are usually included the narrow, coastal

FIG. 57.—Italy: hauling marble at Carrara. The quarries here and at Massa, on the edge of the Apuan Alps, are famous for their pure, white marble. The picture shows blocks weighing several tons being hauled up from the bottom of the quarry. This marble is mainly used for statuary.

lowlands which lie between the Ligurian Apennines and the Gulf of Genoa. They are connected to the Lombardian plain by the easy Bochetta and Altare passes.

(c) *The northern Apennines.* The dominant feature of the Italian peninsula is the Apennine mountains, which extend in a great curve from the Ligurian Apennines in the north to the Strait of Messina in the south, trending first from north-west to south-east towards the Adriatic coast, and then turning back to form the "toe" of Italy. The Apennines fall naturally into three sections: the northern Apennines extend from the Maritime Alps nearly to Ancona and include the Ligurian, Etruscan and Emilian Apennines; the central Apennines are composed of the highest parts of the mountain range, in the provinces of Marche, Abruzzi and Molise; and the southern Apennines continue southwards in lower and less distinct ranges, terminating in the massifs of Calabria.

The northern Apennines—which form the southern boundary of the Plain of Lombardy—are a series of short ranges composed of easily eroded sandstones, chalky marls and clays, very much dissected by narrow, deep valleys and troubled by landslides. In the west the Ligurian Apennines are linked to the Maritime Alps and, like them, are close to the sea. The Ligurian Apennines, which are nowhere very high (Mount

Ebro, 5581 ft (1701 m), is the highest peak), are pierced by several passes, of which the chief are the Bochetta (Giovi) and the Altare (Cadibona), leading from the coast to Milan and Turin respectively.

The eastern ranges of the northern Apennines, the Etruscan-Emilian Apennines, are higher than those of Liguria (Mount Cimone, 7095 ft (2163 m)), but in general are not difficult to cross. They are pierced by several roads but few railways, for the passes are high and necessitate expensive tunnels. Between Bologna and Florence, for instance, the railway runs under the mountains by a tunnel 11½ miles (18·4 km) long. West of the main ranges of the northern Apennines are the Apuan Alps, composed of metamorphosed limestone. Quarries on their lower slopes produce the famous white marble of Carrara and Massa (see Fig. 57).

2. Central Italy

This region is the northern half of the Italian peninsula; it extends from the northern Apennines to a line drawn south of the city of Rome and curving round the southern end of the mountains of Abruzzi to the mouth of the river Sangro. Central Italy may be divided into (a) the central Apennines, (b) the plains and hills of Tuscany and Umbria, and (c) the basin of the lower Tiber (see Fig. 58).

(a) The central Apennines, higher and wider than those of the north, are composed predominantly of limestones, which in places have been eroded to steep-sided peaks, in others to flat-topped, barren plateaus. The Gran Sasso d'Italia, which rises in Monte Corno to 9584 ft (2921 m), is the highest part of the Apennines; it is a broad plateau, from which rise jagged peaks. Much of the limestone of the central Apennines, especially in Abruzzi and Molise, is karst, with little surface drainage. At best, except in a few faulted basins, it supports only a scanty sheep-rearing population. Here and there among the ranges are longitudinal depressions, caused by faulting. Some of them are ill-drained and marshy; others have a flooring of alluvium. The chief of these basin depressions are drained by the rivers Aquila and Sulmona to the Adriatic Sea. On the eastern side of the central Apennines, the Adriatic coastlands are made up of sands and clays washed from the mountains to the floor of the sea, and later uplifted. These narrow coastal lowlands are greatly dissected by the mountain torrents which cross them. The Adriatic coast is of recent emergence and very straight, with few harbours.

(b) Tuscany and Umbria. Within the curve of the central Apennines, and bounded on the west by the Ligurian and Tyrrhenian Seas, is a region of plateaus and low hills, with intervening alluvial basins and valleys which are drained mainly by the rivers Arno and upper Tiber. The northern portion is Tuscany, which comprises the Arno basin and the adjacent coastal lowlands. The Arno rises in the northern Apennines and when it leaves the mountains flows through the Plain of Tuscany, an undulating lowland broken by low hills. Near the river the plain is flat and liable to flooding, but successful control and drainage have made it productive.

The coast of Tuscany, in common with the whole of the western coast of central and southern Italy as far south as Naples, is being silted. The blockage of drainage to the Tyrrhenian Sea has resulted in coastal marshes in several places. The most extensive in central Italy are the Maremma marshes, south of the mouth of the Arno.

South of the Arno basin are the hills and valleys of south Tuscany and of Umbria. This is a region of Tertiary sands and clays in the valleys, above which rise sandstone plateaus and the cones and calderas of an ancient and extinct vulcanicity. The most impressive of the extinct cones

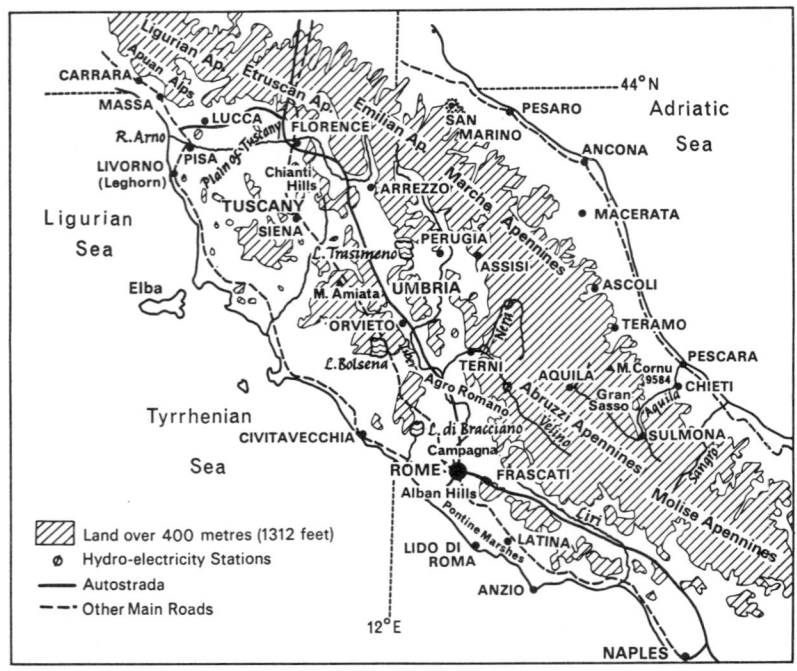

FIG. 58.—Italy: central. The region may be sub-divided into (*a*) central Apennines and Adriatic coastlands, (*b*) hills and plains of Tuscany and Umbria, (*c*) lower Tiber basin.

is Monte Amiata (5687 ft, 1734 m). Many of the calderas contain lakes, the largest of which is Lake Bolsena. Nearer to the central Apennines and north of Lake Bolsena is situated Lake Trasimeno, which by association might erroneously be taken to be a crater lake. It lies in a limestone hollow and has no surface outlet; its waters escape to the river Tiber by an underground channel.

(c) *The Tiber basin.* South of the Umbrian hill country, the river Tiber flows through the Agro Romano, a lowland which opens to the Campagna, the name given to the coastal plains and the Tiber delta. The Agro

Romano, although predominantly a plain, is dotted with many low hills of volcanic origin. The Alban Hills, for example, which run along the south of the Agro Romano and the Campagna, are composed of volcanic rocks that have weathered into very fertile soils. Until fifty years ago the plains of the lower Tiber were a stretch of rough pasture or malarial swamp. The swamps were continued south of the Tiber delta in the Pontine marshes. Most of the marshy area has now been reclaimed.

3. Southern Italy

Southern Italy consists of (a) the southern Apennines, with which are included the plains of Apulia, and (b) Campania (see Fig. 59).

(a) *The southern Apennines* may be said to begin south of the river Sangro, where the mountains swing from the Adriatic littoral to form the "toe" of Italy. They lose their folded character and, instead of lying in well-defined ranges, are faulted and dislocated into isolated blocks separated by lowlands. During the Tertiary period these lowlands were invaded by the sea. Most of the blocks are of Cretaceous limestone, covered in places by Pliocene clays, marls and sands, which are found also in the lowlands and valleys. Vertical displacement has lifted some of the limestone platforms to over 3000 ft (900 m); in the Lucanian Apennines, Monte Pollino rises to 7448 ft (2270 m), Monte Cervati to 6228 ft (1899 m) and Volturino to 6022 ft (1836 m).

Farther south, the limestone Apennines give place in Calabria to a succession of ancient crystalline horsts of Hercynian age, the chief of which are the Sila and Aspromonte massifs. The Sila is an immense granite plateau, rising to 6327 ft (1929 m). For most of the year it has a fairly heavy precipitation, with snow in winter. In hollows in its surface, large reservoirs (Lake di Cécita, Lake Arvo, Lake Ampollino) have been constructed for hydro-electric power. Aspromonte, in the extreme south of the peninsula, is composed of schists.

On the Adriatic side of south Italy, in Apulia, there are two limestone plateaus, Monte Gargano and the Murge; the former is separated from the Campanian Apennines by the Plain of Apulia (Tavoliere di Puglia), and the latter from the Lucanian Apennines by the trench of the river Bradano. Both plateaus, which rarely rise to more than the 2000 ft (610 m) of Monte Gargano or the 1200 ft (365 m) of the Murge, are karst and usually without surface water: the water-table is too low, except in hollows eroded in the limestone. Here, and in valleys, there are deposits of terra rossa, which is fertile if water is available.

(b) *Campania.* Southwards from Gaeta, where the spurs of the Apennines reach the coast of the Tyrrhenian Sea, is the plain of Campania, the name also of the province, and not to be confused with the Campagna of central Italy. Campania is divided by the rocky Sorrento peninsula into the Plain of Naples in the north, and the Plain of Salerno in the south.

The Plain of Naples, with its extensions into the lower valleys of the rivers Volturno and Liri, is the result of subsidence and of subsequent

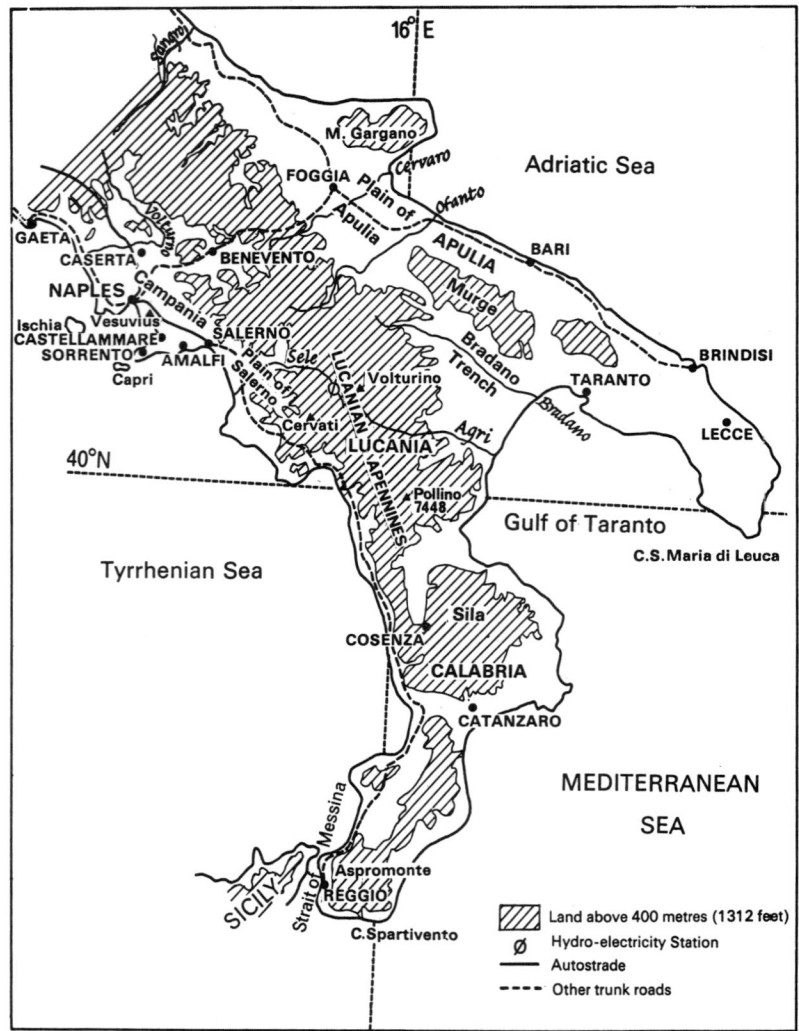

FIG. 59.—Italy: southern. The region may be sub-divided into (a) southern Apennines, (b) plains of Apulia, (c) massifs and lowlands of Calabria, (d) Campania.

infilling by volcanic activity, which still continues. In the north of the plain is the extinct cone of Roccamonfina, and at the southern end, towering over Naples, is Vesuvius, an active volcano. North-west of Naples are the Phlegraean Fields (Campi Flegrei), the wreck of an immense volcano, where hot, sulphurous springs (*solfatare*) are still active and molten lava occasionally spurts through the surface in places. In historic times the eruptions of Vesuvius have been very destructive. The most violent was in A.D. 79, when the Roman town of Pompeii was covered by mud washed from the slopes of the volcano and Herculaneum (Ercolano) was buried in hot ash.

All the soils of the Plain of Naples are derived from basaltic lavas, basic tuffs, or alluvium deposited by the rivers—especially the Volturno—but their productivity varies with their age. In a belt on the eastern side, from the Volturno southwards to Nocera and extending up the slopes of the hills enclosing the plain on that side, the soils are old, well developed and very fertile. In the areas more recently covered by volcanic activity, the decomposition of the surface deposits is not yet sufficiently advanced to give the maximum results, and agriculture is limited to wheat, maize, sugar beet and hemp. The delta of the Volturno has marshes built up in the same way as the Maremma and Pontine marshes; they are now largely reclaimed.

To the south of the Plain of Naples, and separating it from the Plain of Salerno, is the Sorrento peninsula, a spur of the southern Apennines composed of limestone. The isle of Capri is a broken-off piece of the peninsula. The Plain of Salerno is made up of Tertiary clays and sandstones covered by alluvium brought down by the river Sele, which drains it.

4. Insular Italy

The name "insular" should strictly include all the islands around the coasts of Italy, but is usually confined to the large islands of Sicily and Sardinia. Small islands, such as Elba, Ischia, Capri, the Lipari islands, etc., are included with the regions nearest to them.

(a) Sicily. Separated from the "toe" of Italy by the narrow Strait of Messina is the island of Sicily (9925 sq. miles, 25,805 sq. km). The north of Sicily is mountainous. The ranges, a continuation of the Apennines, rise in the Madonie to 6484 ft (1976 m). Nearer to the Strait of Messina,

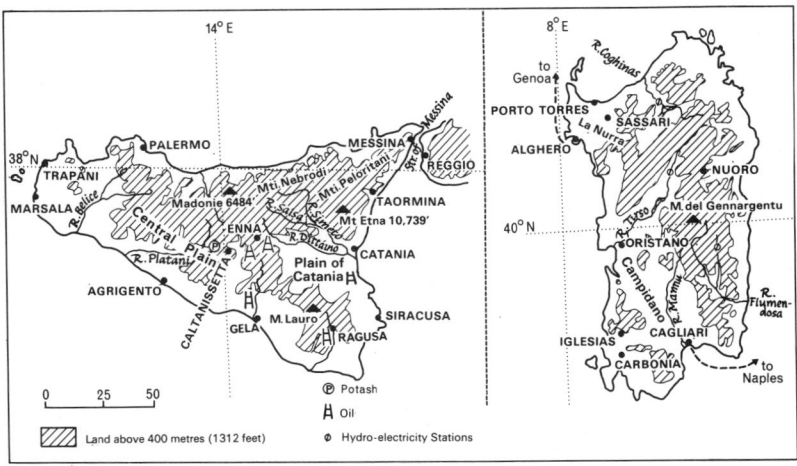

FIG. 60.—Sicily and Sardinia. Together these are known as insular Italy, and economically they are regarded as part of Italy's Mezzogiorno.

the Monti Peloritani have horsts of gneisses and schists similar to those in Calabria; westwards the ranges are of Mesozoic limestones and Tertiary sandstones. To the south of the Monti Peloritani is Mount Etna (10,739 ft, 3273 m), an active volcano. Most of the remainder of Sicily consists of high, rolling plains of Tertiary marls, clays and sandstones, at an average height of more than 600 ft (180 m). These rise in the south-east and south-west to low limestone plateaus, the one in the south-east having a cover of basic lavas and tuffs. The only real lowland is the Plain of Catania, in the east of the island.

(b) *Sardinia*. Roughly 200 miles (320 km) west of central Italy is the island of Sardinia (9300 sq. miles, 24,180 sq. km), nearly as large as Sicily.

In structure Sardinia is very like Corsica, from which it is separated by a narrow strait; it is mainly a horst of Hercynian age, uplifted, tilted and fractured during the Alpine orogeny. Most of the eastern half of Sardinia is a plateau of granites and quartzites, at an average elevation of over 3000 ft (910 m) and rising to 6000 ft (1830 m) in the Monti del Gennargentu. In the north-west of the plateau there is a cover of Tertiary lavas and tuffs, extruded when the island was uplifted and faulted. The plateau slopes towards the west, terminating in low cliffs along the west and south-west. The western part of the plateau has patches of Mesozoic limestones and Tertiary sedimentaries. These originally covered the entire surface of crystalline rocks but have been eroded except in hollows and valleys. Cutting across the south-west of the plateau is the wide low-lying depression of the Campidano, a plain floored with alluvium; there are other alluvial deposits at intervals around the coast.

CLIMATE

There are great climatic differences between the continental portion of the country and the remainder. In the north, the Alps and the Plain of Lombardy have a climate classed as continental; the peninsula and the islands have a Mediterranean climate. This broad classification, however, has to be modified because of (a) the shelter given by the Alps to the Plain of Lombardy, which is also shut off from most Mediterranean influences by the Maritime Alps and northern Apennines, and (b) the north–south trend of the peninsula, lying athwart the depression tracks of the westerlies and acting as a rain-barrier. The western side of the peninsula is protected against cold northerly winds by the Apennines; the eastern side is in the rain-shadow of the mountain backbone.

Climate in the Alps, as might be expected, varies with altitude and aspect. Precipitation is heavy, and greater in summer than in winter. But no season is dry, and snow lies on the peaks of the western ranges all the year. During the winter, when depressions move from west to east in the north of the Mediterranean, cold air may be drawn from the Alpine region to affect the lands to the south. The violent, icy winds which as a result blow over the Ligurian Sea to Corsica and Sardinia are the *maestrale* (*cf. mistral* in France); those in the north of the Adriatic, affecting the

Italian coastlands as far south as Ancona, are the *bora* (*see also* Chapters III and XIII).

The southward-facing valleys and foothills along the southern flanks of the Alps are sheltered and have summers in which the mean temperature for the hottest month is from 70° F to 75° F (21·1° C to 23·9° C). The winters are cool, ranging in January from 35° F to 38° F (1·7° C to 3·3° C). Annual precipitation is heavy—Como, for instance, having 66 in.

The Plain of Lombardy has a climate best described as continental, with cool winters, hot summers and rainfall mainly in summer; but south of the river Po, and in the northern Apennines, such Mediterranean characteristics as milder winters and less summer rainfall begin to appear. Winters in the Plain of Lombardy are generally short but sometimes severe, especially when cold air drains from the Alps and settles in hollows (temperature inversion). Frosts are common and foggy weather frequent. The mean January temperature for Milan is 32° F (0° C), for Piacenza the same, and for Alessandria 31° F (−0·6° C). Venice, more open to Mediterranean influences, has a January mean temperature of 39° F (3·9° C) and Bologna, in the south of the Plain, 36° F (2·2° C). July temperatures everywhere are around 75° F (23·9° C).

Rainfall in the Plain of Lombardy decreases from west to east and from north to south, but on an average is over 20 in. annually. Milan has an annual precipitation of 33·9 in., well distributed throughout the year but with a slight summer maximum. Eastwards the amount decreases to 29·3 in. in Venice; southwards, to 25·5 in. in Alessandria, and 22 in. in Bologna. Most of the rain in Bologna comes in the winter half of the year.

The climate of the Italian peninsula varies with position west or east of the Apennines, and there are considerable differences between the north and south. In the north of the western side, the coastal plain of Liguria, sheltered by mountains and open to the warm Ligurian Sea, has very mild winters and hot summers. Genoa, for example, has a mean in January of 47° F (8·3° C), and in August (the hottest month) of 77° F (25° C). Its annual rainfall amounts to 44 in., of which over 30 in. falls in the six months of winter.

In the coastlands west of the Apennines, south of Liguria, winter temperatures are lower than might be expected: the January mean for Leghorn is 45° F (7·2° C) and for Viterbo 42° F (5·6° C). This is largely due to the influence of the depressions which pass over them in that season. From Naples southwards, January temperatures are higher—usually over 47° F (8·3° C). Summers along the coast are hot: Leghorn 76° F (24·4° C), Naples 75° F (23·9° C) and Viterbo, slightly inland, 73° F (22·8° C). Annual rainfall, with a definite winter maximum, ranges from 35 in. in Florence and 33 in. in Rome to 32 in. in Naples. These totals contrast with those on the eastern side of the peninsula.

The Adriatic coastlands lie in the rain-shadow of the Apennines and are open to cold winds in winter from the north-east. Rainfall at Foggia amounts to 19 in. a year, and the January mean temperature is 43° F

(6·1° C). The January mean for Ancona is 42° F (5·6° C) and for Chieti 39° F (3·9° C). July temperatures on the whole are higher than on the west coast, Foggia having in that month an average of 80° F (26·7° C), Ancona 78° F (25·6° C) and Chieti 73° F (22·8° C). The Apennines have mountain variants of the east and west coast climates, according to altitude and aspect. Winters in the Abruzzi are severe, with heavy snowfall; temperatures are below freezing point for over a month on the high plateaus, and are not much above it even in the low valleys enclosed by the mountains. Aquila, for instance, at a height of 2390 ft (728 m), has a January average of 36° F (2·2° C). July temperatures at high levels are around 60° F (15·6° C) and in valleys 70° F (21·1° C).

The "toe" of Italy, and Sicily, are distinguished by an almost complete absence of frost; a long, sunny and droughty summer; a short period of rainfall in winter, and high average temperatures in that season. Reggio, in Calabria, ranges from 53° F (11·7° C) in January to 79° F (26·1° C) in July and has an annual rainfall of 29·5 in. The Calabrian massifs have rain-falls of over 40 in. but some of the valleys between them receive less than 20 in. Rainfall comes in short but heavy showers, and large areas are gullied by soil erosion. Winter temperatures in Sicily are much the same as in Calabria, i.e. around 53° F (11·7° C), and summers about 77° F (25° C); rainfall varies from 30 in. in the mountains in the north of the island to 25 in. in the south. The months from May to August are virtually rainless. Much of the rainfall in both Calabria and Sicily is lost by rapid run-off in the crystalline areas and by evaporation. Sicily is affected in summer by the *sirocco*, a dry sand-laden wind from the Sahara, which results in scorchingly hot days.

The climate of Sardinia is Mediterranean, tempered by altitude, but, as is so often the case around the Mediterranean basin, there are big differences in temperature and annual rainfall between regions very close together. The exposed western side of the island has an annual precipita-tion of 25–30 in. and on the highest plateaus it reaches 45 in.; but the sheltered east coast may have less than 20 in. and around Cape Monte Santo only 16 in. All these totals are average amounts, but the rainfall in Sardinia is unreliable, and in some years the island suffers from prolonged droughts. Sassari, in the north-west of Sardinia, ranges from 47° F (8·3° C) in January to 77° F (25° C) in July, and has an annual rainfall of 24 in. Caltanissetta, in the south, has means of 44° F (6·7° C) in January and 76° F (24·4° C) in July, with 24 in. of rainfall. The effectiveness of the precipitation in Sardinia is reduced by the sirocco in summer and the maestrale in winter, which cause rapid evaporation.

HUMAN GEOGRAPHY

HISTORICAL OUTLINE

The first "cities" in Italy were undoubtedly founded by Greeks and Etruscans, but the history of the country may be said to date from the settlement of groups of Latins on the Palatine Hill, which is within the walls of present-day Rome. By the end of the second century B.C., Rome was a state of soldiers and farmers. It had become master of the Italian peninsula and most of the Po basin, with dominion over territory stretching from Spain to Greece and Asia Minor, and along the north coast of Africa. Further successful invasions of France, Belgium, Britain and part of Germany took place under such famous soldiers as Marius, Sulla, Julius Caesar, Pompey, Antony and Octavian. In 44 B.C. the last-named was elected Emperor of the newly proclaimed Roman Empire. The Empire lasted four centuries before it finally disintegrated; then it took 1500 years for Italy to emerge once more as a unified and sovereign state.

During the Middle Ages, Italy was invaded by barbarians from the north. The invaders were rarely strong enough to defend their conquered territories, so for several centuries the country lay at the mercy of first one and then another set of marauders. This was especially the case with southern Italy and Sicily. First the Byzantines, then the Arabs and finally the Normans controlled southern Italy without serious opposition. In northern Italy the Lombards, a fierce Germanic tribe, reigned for two centuries, with Pavia as their capital. Meanwhile, other parts of the country began to emerge as separate states under individual rulers. These were all united under Charlemagne, who in A.D. 800 was crowned in Rome as the first Emperor of the Holy Roman Empire. It looked as though Imperial Rome was being re-born, but after his death Italy began to divide again. In Rome the Papal State was created, and Berengarius became king of the "Kingdom of Italy," which was composed of Lombardy, Tuscany and Umbria. The kingdom was short-lived, and in the tenth century northern Italy was invaded and subjugated by the German Holy Roman Emperor. The final phase of the Middle Ages saw a struggle for power between the Papacy and German or Austrian Emperors. One of the latter, Frederick II, was born in Italy and had his court at Palermo in Sicily.

During this period of strife, many Italian cities took the opportunity of organising themselves into small independent states. They lay in the more vigorous north; and under democratic administrations, the arts, law and education began to flourish and foreign trade grew in strength. The Scaligeri family in Verona, the Gonzagas in Mantua, the Estes in Emilia and the Medici in Florence became rulers of city states. Pisa, Genoa and Venice were the headquarters of successful seafaring and trading republics, and grew extremely prosperous. The great Italian authors, Dante, Petrarch and Boccaccio, belong to this period; Marco Polo, a Venetian, at the end of the thirteenth century travelled through central Asia to China and Tibet, returning to Venice via India and Persia.

Two centuries later, in 1492, Christopher Colombus, a Genoese sailing in the service of Spain, discovered the Americas anew. A few years later Amerigo Vespucci, a Florentine, made further voyages and gave his name to the new lands. These explorations turned the course of history, for the Mediterranean ceased to be the centre of the civilised world. The countries with direct contact with the Atlantic Ocean—Spain, Portugal, France, England and the Netherlands—acquired new power and overseas possessions. The Mediterranean became a political and economic backwater, and Italy a weak, disunited country. In 1559, Naples, Sicily, Sardinia and the Duchy of Milan passed under Spanish rule; they remained so for 150 years. By the eighteenth century two other foreign dynasties were ruling in Italy—the Hapsburgs in Tuscany, and French Bourbons in Parma and Piacenza. Towards the end of the period, the Duke of Savoy, ruler of a mountain-girt province which had early proclaimed its independence, took possession of Sardinia.

The possibility of a free and united Italy, so long an apparently unattainable ideal, emerged after the Napoleonic wars (Napoleon himself had been King of Italy for a short time after 1805). In 1820 there arose a movement known as the Risorgimento, or "re-arising," aimed at uniting all Italy under one government. Its leaders were great statesmen or soldiers—Cavour, Mazzini, Garibaldi. In 1861 the Duke of Savoy, head of the oldest ruling house in Italy, became king, with the "Mezzogiorno" (southern Italy, Sicily and Sardinia) and Lombardy part of his kingdom. Venetia was annexed in 1866. In 1870 the Pope, giving up his political power in Rome and Latium, retired to the Vatican Palace, and Rome was made capital of the new Italy. The northern provinces of the Trentino, Trieste, Venetia Giulia and Istria, which had remained in Austrian hands, were joined to Italy after the First World War; and for the first time in fifteen centuries the country was restored to the sovereign dignity of Roman times.

But unification did not bring prosperity. The country was divided into a progressive and rapidly developing north, and an over-populated, illiterate, poverty-stricken south. During the years 1924–39 Mussolini's Fascist régime tried to remedy the imbalance, but the economic and social problems of the Mezzogiorno persist to this day. Fascist policy aimed at putting Italy on equal terms with the world's great political and economic powers, by building up industrial output, improving communications, draining swamps, increasing agricultural production and acquiring an overseas empire. It laid the foundations of future development, but proved too aggressive, causing hardship to the people it purported to benefit. It tried to move too fast in a country whose climate and topography demand slow progress, and whose people, in the Mezzogiorno, were far behind Western Europe in standard of living, education and ways of thought. In southern Italy, too, the limit placed on emigration by the Fascist Government accentuated the problem of over-population.

In the years 1943–45, Italy was a huge battlefield and most of the Fascist achievements were destroyed. Railways, bridges, viaducts, hydro-electric power stations and harbour works were blown up, the countryside devastated and many of the cities left in ruins. After the Second World

War and the defeat of Fascism, Italy was faced with the task of rebuilding the country and feeding its population, which in 1951 amounted to 47 million people. But industrial incentive and agricultural hopes were at a low ebb; the standard of living declined; and there was a steady rise in unemployment. In 1948 Italy ceased to be a kingdom and voted for a republic.

Since then the worst problems of industrial stagnation and hunger have been mitigated and most of the war damage repaired, so that the political and economic position is better today than at any time before 1939. The population has risen to 53 millions; and in spite of the still unsolved problem of the depressed areas of the south, the general standard of living has improved.

POPULATION

The population of Italy at the last census (October 1961) was 50,464,000; but as it is increasing by 400,000 a year the current population would be over 53 million, which would give an approximate average density of 455 persons a square mile. Italy is not a rich country. It is relatively poor in raw materials and mineral resources, and its agriculture is limited by lack of rainfall and the mountainous character of much of its surface, so that it cannot support this large population at a reasonable standard of living. In other words, it is heavily over-populated.

The greatest concentrations of people are in the better-endowed industrial regions of northern Italy. Most parts of the Plain of Lombardy have densities of over 400 per square mile; in the Milan conurbation and along the Ligurian Plain there are more than 650 persons per square mile. Similar densities are found in the Agro Romano and the Plain of Naples, where there are fewer opportunities for industrial development and where, in consequence, the cities contain large numbers of unemployed. The Plain of Lombardy has a textile industry which ranks fifth in the world for the production of cotton and woollen fabrics; in it are located world-famous firms such as Vespa and Lambretta (motor scooters), Alfa Romeo, Ferrari and Maserati (motor cars), Guzzi and Gilera (motor cycles); and its engineering firms provide experts in the construction of roads, bridges and dams. The Kariba Dam in Africa is an achievement of northern Italy. The south of the country has no openings for industrial employment in any way comparable, and its universally poverty-stricken appearance presents a sad contrast to the north.

South of Rome, including Sicily and Sardinia, lies the Mezzogiorno, whose dense population is Italy's most serious problem. This is accentuated by the high reproduction rate, i.e. the excess of births over deaths per 1000 of the population. In southern Italy it averages 15 and in Sicily 13, as compared with less than 5 in northern Italy. The "toe" and "heel" of Italy—Calabria and Apulia—have population densities of 520 per square mile; in pockets in Campania there are over 900 per square mile in rural areas, a density which in northern Italy would be found only in

Fig. 61.—Italy: distribution of population, 1961 (by provinces). Maps showing distribution and density of population should be read with due regard to relief and the existence of very large cities. Lombardy, for instance, has an average density of 787 persons per sq. mile, but a large proportion of it is Alpine and scantily populated. Its lowlands, which include the large city of Milan, have an average density of over 900 persons per sq. mile. Similarly Lucania, with a relatively small density, is actually over-populated.

the cities. There are few possibilities for extensive absorption of surplus population by industrialisation of the Mezzogiorno, and the solution to over-population for the immediate future seems to lie either in emigration or in some policy of birth restriction. The first is not easy; Italy has no overseas possessions, most other countries have restricting quota systems for immigrants, and industrial northern Italy has reached saturation point. Birth restriction, too, presents religious difficulties, for the people of the

Mezzogiorno are fervent Roman Catholics and thus forbidden at present to use artificial means of birth prevention.

The least populated regions in Italy are in the Alps, central Apennines, volcanic hills of Umbria, the limestone massifs of Lucania, and Sardinia; but even here only the northern ranges of the Alps, the caldera region of Umbria, and the high plateaus of northern Sardinia have less than 120 persons per square mile.

THE ECONOMY

THE PROBLEM OF THE MEZZOGIORNO

Before examining the regional economy of Italy, it is well to look further at the contrasts that exist between the north and south of the country. The native peoples of the Plain of Lombardy have a long history of achievement and prosperity, engendered to some degree by the more stimulating climate experienced there, in spite of resources which are really only meagre. In the past forty years industrial advance has been phenomenal. Large numbers of immigrants have come from the south to share the new prosperity and to swell the population. Northern Italy has now 21 million inhabitants in an area which—including the sparsely populated Alps—is less than a quarter of the whole country. Both industrially and agriculturally, saturation point has been reached; yet the flood of immigrants continues, and unemployment is increasing. Nevertheless to southern Italians the north is a picture of wealth and opportunity, in contrast to the poverty, overcrowding and under-development they see around them.

The economic geography of southern Italy is most depressing. Although there has been some amelioration in recent years, centuries of struggle in an adverse environment have reduced the spirit of enterprise or the desire to rise above the generally low standard of living. The same applies to Sicily and Sardinia, though to a lesser extent. The reasons for this backwardness must be sought in both history and geography.

Geographically a large proportion of southern Italy is mountainous. Much of it is composed of soft limestones, easily eroded and liable to landslides. Valleys and coastal plains are blocked by mud and pebbles washed from the highlands, and may turn into marshes. Soil erosion is a common feature of a landscape which is often bare and dry, and many hill slopes have no soil at all. Southern Italy is subject to destructive earthquakes, and vulcanicity in the Campania is still active. It should be noted, however, that the fertile soils of the volcanic district support the densest rural population in the country. Farms are found far up the slopes of Vesuvius, where streams of lava may destroy their fields and crops. South of Rome, the summers become hotter and more arid, and many of the streams dry up; the karst areas are without surface water at any season.

Much of Sicily is porous limestone and poorly watered on the surface;

and the rain which falls on the crystalline mountains in the north runs off too quickly or is dried up. Sardinia is composed largely of crystalline plateaus with thin soils which cannot support a dense population and offer only a scanty living to shepherds and subsistence farmers. Sicily is far more productive than Sardinia and has over three times as many people. This number, however, is too great for its economic capacity, and both islands will remain badly over-populated unless industry can be increased and agriculture improved.

Historical factors in the deterioration of southern Italy are possibly of greater importance than geography, although in some cases it is hard to distinguish between them. They date from the third century B.C., when Greek and Carthaginian trading stations and colonies flourished on the coasts of southern Italy and Sicily. The traders and colonists were expelled by the Romans, their agricultural settlements depopulated, and the land was split into large parcels and given to Roman patricians. These wide estates (*latifundia*), supervised by stewards and worked by slaves, produced the wheat and wool required by Rome. They formed the pattern of farming in southern Italy for the next two thousand years. Even in the nineteenth century, over most of the region, the peasants (*braccianti*) were landless or at best had insufficient land to support a family and had to supplement their income by working for a landlord at extremely low wages.

The latifundia system continued until the 1930s, when the *latifondi* (the modern equivalent) were appropriated by the Government, split into small farms and leased to peasants. At the same time, the grazing rights of the "sheep barons" of the Apulian Plain, which had been reduced late in the nineteenth century, were terminated and much of the better-watered grasslands ploughed up. There are still a few wheat-producing latifondi in Calabria and Sicily, but they will disappear soon. Agrarian reforms are being introduced, but the standard of life in much of the rural Mezzogiorno has not yet shown any striking change, chiefly because of inadequate water supplies and the enormous cost of improving them.

Other adverse historical factors have included war, piracy and maladministration. The Mezzogiorno's central position in the Mediterranean and the vulnerability of its coastal plains invited invasion by Goths, Vandals, Arabs, Byzantines, Lombards, Franks and Aragonese. None, except the last, remained for long, but all left a trail of devastation in the most fertile parts. The coasts, too, were harassed by pirates from Barbary, Tripoli and Turkey, who forced the southern Italians into the mountains so that the neglected lowlands became still more marshy and malarial.

In 1559 southern Italy, Sicily, Sardinia and the Duchy of Milan passed into the hands of the Spanish Bourbons, to become the "Kingdom of the Two Sicilies." It remained in their possession for 150 years; one short intermission aside, it was a period of misrule, corruption and oppression, with the latifondi system at its worst. The court of Naples presented all the signs of prosperity and grandiose magnificence, but the city itself and the rest of the Mezzogiorno were reduced to misery and abject poverty.

The psychological effects of centuries of oppression have been lasting. The people, especially the rural population, are distrustful of officials who seek to introduce reforms. They have little use for education, and resent interference with their old-fashioned and inefficient farming methods, appearing content with a way of life that perpetuates their poverty. In Sicily, especially, the succession of foreign overlords engendered a resistance to authority and legislation which is reflected today in the corruption of officials and the power of lawless secret societies such as the Mafia. The problem is made worse by the dense populations in those regions least able to support them and by the rate at which they are increasing (*see* p. 271).

The "Cassa." Such was the alarming position the Republican Government faced when it came to power after the Second World War. To try to find a solution it inaugurated in 1950 the *Cassa per il Mezzogiorno*, the Fund for the Development of the South, usually known as the "Cassa." Its purpose is to undertake or encourage public works like land reclamation, flood and erosion control, the provision of aqueducts, sewers, roads, railways and ferry boats; it gives help in the building of vocational schools, fosters tourism and provides additional capital for the setting up of private industry. Before the war the Fascist Government had begun to tackle the problem with schemes of reclamation and agrarian improvement, and had tried to relieve the pressure of population by planned settlement of colonists in North Africa. Its efforts met with little success, however, and the Cassa of 1950 appears to have wider vision and more promise.

In southern Italy the results are decidedly encouraging, although it must be said that up to the present the Cassa's endeavours have been concerned rather with laying the foundations of future progress than with immediate returns. Priority has been given to water control, land reclamation and road-making; but at the same time factories have been built for food processing and manufacturing paper, cement, tyres and textiles. Iron and steel works are already in existence. Thousands of people in the Mezzogiorno are now employed on the new Cassa schemes, electricity and water have been made available for new industries, soil erosion and flooding are being combated, and co-operative farming introduced. But the problem of overcrowding still remains!

REGIONAL ECONOMY

1. *Northern Italy*

(a) *The Italian Alps.* Precipitation throughout the Alps is heavy and comes at all seasons. In the western Alps, the northern sides of the valleys receive the most sunshine. They have vineyards on the lower slopes and oats, barley and hay above, up to about 3500 ft (1070 m). Higher still, and on the north-facing slopes, there are forests of pines. In the valleys, maize is the chief crop and dairying the main occupation. The Piedmont is the most important region in Italy for dairy cattle, and produces butter and cheese.

FIG. 62.—Italy: economic. Hydro-electric power stations and resources of oil and natural gas are omitted to avoid overcrowding. They will be found on the regional maps, Figs. 56, 58, 59, 60.

The greatest asset of the western Alps is their water power, which is gradually changing the economy of the region (*see* Fig. 62). The rivers have been harnessed to provide a fifth of Italy's hydro-electricity, princi- pally for the Turin district, but it is also helping the development of light engineering industries far up the valleys. Near Aosta, in the Dora Baltea valley, are a small coalfield and some deposits of magnetite; these, helped by hydro-electricity and imports of scrap iron, are the basis of steel and chemical industries in the town. The people of Valle d'Aosta are mostly French-speaking. The tourist industry is also developing in the western Alps, not so much because of the Italian resorts but because the northern passes lead to well-known French winter sports centres such as Chamonix.

The winter climate in the wider valleys and around the lakes of the central Alps is mild because of their sheltered position. Maize, vines, peaches, apricots and fodder crops are grown. The occasional appearance of olives here and around the lakes of the eastern Alps is evidence of the favourable climatic conditions. The mild winters and hot summers tempered by the waters of the lakes have made the southern margins of the region a favourite with holiday-makers, especially around lakes Lugano and Como.

The first hydro-electric power station in Italy was built in the Val Tellina, in the central Alps. Today almost every suitable river is harnessed, so that more than half Italy's hydro-electricity comes from this region. The Alps as a whole produce three-quarters of Italy's total current. With an output of over 46,000 million kWh annually, the country is Europe's largest generator of hydro-electricity, 70% of the potential resources being used. An important result of the construction of dams is that water is made available for irrigation in the dry limestone sub-Alpine zone.

The eastern Alpine region is more forested and has more summer mountain pastures than the central and western Alps. Lumbering is important, and transhumant cattle-rearing occupies many of the people in the higher valleys, where agriculture is confined mainly to fodder, potatoes, rye and barley. In the more open valleys, and especially around Lake Garda, maize, tobacco, vines and fruit are grown; along the western shores of the lake there are olive and lemon groves. Lemons are particularly susceptible to frost, and special protective measures are taken when temperatures are low. Many of the people of the eastern Alps are German-speaking, for the ease with which the mountains are penetrated has led to occupation at various times by Austrians, Swiss and Yugoslavs, as well as Italians.

On the whole, the Alps of Italy are poorly peopled compared with the rest of the country. Except in the eastern Alps, industry has hardly penetrated the mountains; and the hydro-electric power stations, unlike those of France, lie mostly in areas of scanty population. The eastern Alps have power stations in the upper valleys of the Adige, Piave and Tagliamento, generating roughly as much current as the western Alps. The more open character of the region has encouraged the growth of electro-chemical, electro-metallurgical, engineering and paper industries in the Adige valley at Bolzano (88,000) and Trento (75,000), the largest towns in the interior of the Italian Alps. The Dolomites, which lie between the Adige and Piave valleys, have a prosperous tourist industry.

The greatest concentrations of people in the Alpine zone are along the southern flanks of the mountains, and more and more they are becoming centres of industry, helped by hydro-electricity. Varese (67,000), Como

(82,000), Bergamo (122,271) and Brescia (197,501) have wool textile and engineering industries. Como and Trento are major tourist centres. Much of the raw wool for the textile industry comes from sheep reared in the sub-Alpine hills, where transhumance, once common, has largely disappeared.

(b) *The Plain of Lombardy*, south of the Alpine region, has a belt from east to west of sandy, gravelly outwash, followed by another of alluvial fans. Between the two is a line of springs (*fontanili*) from waters which have soaked through the gravels. There are similar but narrower zones north of the Apennines. The northern and southern gravelly zones are generally too dry for agriculture, and sheep-rearing is important, but a highly organised system of irrigation both there and in the alluvial belts has led to a great variety of crops, including maize, wheat, clover and other fodder crops, sugar beet, rice, flax, and hemp (*see* Fig. 63). Scattered through the north of the Plain of Lombardy are groves of mulberry trees, on the leaves of which silk-worms are reared; but sericulture is a declining occupation, most raw silk now being imported. Vineyards producing the well-known Asti wines cover the slopes at the western end of the plain, and in the east the terra rossa of Venetia supports olive groves. The Plain of Lombardy is the most important agricultural region in Italy.

The marshy riverine belt, where the river Po has built its banks higher than the level of the plain, is subject to flooding, so that extensive and costly reclamation has been necessary. Most farmers are engaged in dairying and rice cultivation. Because of the flood danger there are few towns on the banks of the river. The Po enters the Adriatic by a delta, where there are dyked fields reminiscent of the Dutch polders.

Most of the towns of the agricultural belt lie in two lines, north and south of the river. The northern line includes Pavia (74,000), Cremona (73,000), Mantua (62,000), Verona (248,945), Padua (219,579), Treviso (75,000) and Udine (86,000). They are all essentially market towns, but with the growth of industry in northern Italy they have shared in the development of modern food processing, textile manufactures, engineering and chemical industries. The southern line of towns contains Alessandria (92,000), Parma (165,315), Reggio (124,943), Modena (158,955), Bologna (481,740) and Forli (91,000). The road connecting these southern towns is known as the Emilian Way. They are larger than the northern towns, for in addition to having the industries already mentioned their sites command routes through the northern Apennines. The only large town of the plain actually on the river Po is Piacenza (88,000), to the west, where flooding is uncommon. Ferrara (157,625) and Ravenna (127,638) lie in the middle of the plain, in a hemp-producing and manufacturing district.

In the west of the Plain of Lombardy the greatest supplies of hydro-electric power are available from the Alps, and in 1945 enormous deposits of methane gas were discovered at Caviaga, east of Milan. Hence it is the most highly industrialised region in Italy. Further deposits of methane gas have been found underlying most of the plain south of the Po, as far east as Ravenna, where the gas is used as a raw material in the making of synthetic rubber.

The focus of the industrial region is Milan (Milano), the second city of Italy, with a population of 1,677,013. Situated at the convergence of Alpine routes, it was already a trading and craft centre in the Middle Ages. Today it is the chief industrial and commercial city in the country, the centre of most of the great manufacturing groups. It has all kinds of

[*Courtesy of Italian State Tourist Office.*

Fig. 63.—Italy: harvesting hemp on a farm on the Po plain. Approximately 22,000 acres of the plain are under hemp, mostly in the west. The annual production is about 5250 tons. Italian hemp is noted for its length and toughness.

engineering, and it manufactures cottons, woollens and worsteds, silk and man-made fibres. It is the focus of the most intensive railway network in Italy. Around it are a number of satellite towns, such as Monza and Saronno, which have chemical, metallurgical and textile industries, for which Milan is the market.

Turin (Torino, 1,112,182), the second city of the Plain, is at the meeting point of routes through the western Alps with the west–east route of the Po, on which the city stands. The Dora Baltea leads to the St Bernard

Pass, the Dora Riparia to the Mont Cenis Pass and tunnel, the Col de Tende to Mediterranean France, and the Altare Pass to the coast. Turin has cotton and rayon industries, but these are giving way to motor engineering; the giant Fiat works and the smaller Lancia plant are world famous. Turin also has railway and aeronautical engineering; and sheet steel is produced in electric furnaces, using imported scrap. Novara (87,000), midway between Milan and Turin, and Cuneo (46,000), in the south-west of the Piedmont, are overgrown market towns, with textile, chemical, engineering and food industries.

Lying outside the Plain of Lombardy, but linked to its industrial and commercial life by gaps through the Ligurian Alps, is a narrow and discontinuous coastal plain which enjoys a Mediterranean climate, in contrast to the continental characteristics of Lombardy. In the west along the Riviera di Ponente are the holiday resorts of San Remo, Santa Margherita and Rapallo. The amount of lowland available for cultivation is limited, as the mountains are near the coast, which in places is cliff-lined. On the small plains, oranges, pomegranates, flowers, and early vegetables are cultivated. The surrounding slopes are terraced for vines, olives and figs. Only small amounts of cereals are grown; and in general the people of Liguria are concerned with tourism or with industry and commerce in the ports.

The chief of these is Genoa (Genova, 846,292), the second port of Italy, situated on a good harbour. Behind it the Bochetta Pass leads to Milan and, via the St Gotthard tunnel, to Switzerland and West Germany, for which countries Genoa has become the Mediterranean outlet. Besides its function as a port, Genoa has shipyards, steelworks, engineering and chemical manufactures, soapworks and textile industries. Helped by hydro-electricity from the Alps and methane gas piped from the Plain of Lombardy, and using imported scrap iron, a large integrated iron and steel works has been established west of the city. There are oil refineries too. Since 1945, Genoa has more than doubled its population, and its industries have grown fourfold. It is at the southern tip of Italy's "industrial triangle," with Milan and Turin at the other two corners. Savona (72,000), to the west of Genoa, is the port for Turin and the western Piedmont; it has industries similar to Genoa but on a much smaller scale. Spezia (129,551) is a naval base and dockyard, with jute manufacture and oil refineries.

The eastern outlet of the Plain of Lombardy is the port of Venice (Venezia, 365,748). Built on a number of islands in lagoons north of the Po delta and shut off from the Adriatic by the Lido, a line of sand dunes which have become a holiday resort, Venice was originally simply a refuge against the attacks of the Huns. Gradually it developed into a trading centre and one of the richest cities of Europe. Its commercial importance was greatly reduced after the discovery of the Cape route to India and the Far East, and the advent of long-distance ocean-borne traffic, and it declined still further with the opening of the Suez Canal, when the

Adriatic became little more than a backwater; but its picturesque position and the romantic association of canals, gondolas, and beautiful buildings encouraged a tourist industry, on which the city still largely depends. Here its craft industries, such as the making of lace, silk, glassware and silver filigree, have been of great assistance. In recent years, the increase of industry in northern Italy has given Venice new life. In its mainland suburbs of Mestre and Porto Marghera there are shipyards, oil refineries, chemical works, zinc and bauxite processing plants and engineering works. With the improvements of its harbour facilities, Venice is once again a premier port in the Mediterranean. Trieste (281,110), the northernmost major port in the Adriatic, has shipbuilding, steel and paper works, and oil refining; and it serves as a transit port for Austria and Yugoslavia rather than as an outlet of the Plain of Lombardy, for it lies on the extreme eastern edge of the lowland.

(c) *The northern Apennines.* These form the southern boundary of the Plain of Lombardy. They have considerable forest cover, with oak, beech and chestnut at lower levels, and scattered conifers above. The higher parts are used mainly for grazing sheep and goats. The valleys are cultivated for wheat, maize and vegetables, while vineyards and olive groves cover the terraced slopes. Cattle are reared on the northern slopes overlooking the Plain, providing the cities of the Emilian Way with milk, butter, cheese and meat. The northern Apennines are the best-developed part of the mountain backbone of Italy.

With its large cities, high agricultural yields, hydro-electric power and methane gas, northern Italy is economically the most important part of the country. The big industrial concerns are found there. Montecatini is a chemical, mining, metallurgical and electrical giant. Fiat is Italy's largest company, best known perhaps for its cars but with equally important naval, aircraft and electro-chemical branches. The Italian Edison company is responsible for a third of all electrical power. Snia Viscosa produces about two-thirds of the country's man-made fibres and tissues. Pirelli and Michelin's Italian subsidiary make high-tension cables and rubber products as well as the tyres for which they are best known.

The Plain of Lombardy is also one of the most densely peopled regions in Italy (*see* Fig. 61). Its phenomenal industrial growth during the past forty years has attracted a flood of immigrants from the Mezzogiorno. The better social and economic conditions have proved such a magnet that there is now a surplus of labour and consequent unemployment, notably in the "industrial triangle." It is imperative that the flow of population from the south be halted, possibly by removing some of the industrial "bulge" to the Mezzogiorno.

2. *Central Italy*

(a) *The central Apennines*, composed mainly of limestone, are high and karst-like, with little surface water except in depressions and valleys. They support only a sparse population, which is engaged principally in sheep rearing and subsistence agriculture. The larger depressions are drained by the rivers Aquila and Sulmona; in them, assisted by irrigation, wheat, sugar beet and almonds are cash crops. The upper Nera and Velino rivers have been harnessed for hydro-electric power, which is supplied to Rome (*see* Fig. 58). Most of the people of the central Apennines live in villages built high up the mountain slopes and approached by difficult and winding roads. The village sites were chosen mainly for defence, but sometimes merely to avoid building on cultivable land in the valleys below. The best known of these hillside villages is Assisi, a pilgrimage centre associated with St Francis.

In the north-eastern corner of the central Apennines is the tiny independent republic of San Marino, only 24·1 square miles (63 sq. km) in area and with a population of 17,760. It has managed to preserve its independence partly by political expediency, partly because of its position on the slopes of Monte Titano, an isolated mountain, 2437 ft (750 m) high, which has little attraction for outsiders. The Sammarinesi, as the people of the republic are called, live by subsistence agriculture, quarrying, olive-oil pressing, cheese making, and the tourist industry. San Marino (4000) is the only town. It has a small silk industry. It is interesting that there are more citizens of San Marino living in Italy and elsewhere than in the tiny state itself. Up to 20,000 Sammarinesi living abroad help its economy by their remittances to families at home.

The eastern slopes of the central Apennines have been deforested and the land is cut by deep gullies, the result of soil erosion. The better alluvial areas have been reclaimed and on them cereals and olives are the chief products. In the wider parts of the coastal plain are the market towns of Macerata (38,340), Ascoli (50,000), Teramo (41,000) and Chieti (47,000)—all surprisingly large in view of the comparative poverty of the region. The Adriatic coast is straight, with few harbours. Most of the coastal towns are fishing ports which, in the north, are developing also a tourist trade. The chief are Ancona (100,000), Pesaro (66,000) and Pescara (87,000), which serve in addition as markets for their agricultural hinterlands.

(b) *Tuscany and Umbria.* In its rich polyculture and way of life, the region which lies within the curve of the central Apennines and the Ligurian and Tyrrhenian seas presents a marked contrast to the harsh landscape of the neighbouring mountain ranges. In the north, the Plain of Tuscany, *i.e.* of the lower Arno, is intensely cultivated, with wheat, maize, sugar beet and fodder crops. Dairy cattle are reared in the middle of the Plain, and all the hill slopes are covered with vineyards and olive groves. The Chianti hills in the east are famous for their wines. Lucca (88,000), the chief town of the olive-growing district, has oil-crushing mills.

At the point where the river Arno enters the Plain of Tuscany stands the city of Florence (Firenze, 454,708). Situated on the Flaminian Way from

Rome and commanding routes through the northern Apennines, Florence has a strong strategic position. Under the powerful Medici family it became the capital of Tuscany and a centre of Renaissance art and architecture. It still retains its craft industries—leather and metal working, lace making and jewellery—and its museums and cathedral draw thousands of tourists annually; but it is more important today as an industrial city. There are chemical and machine tool works, railway and electrical engineering, woollen manufacturing and food-processing, the last concerned principally with making macaroni and other *pasta*.

The main routes of the Tuscan Plain are the ports of Leghorn (170,884) and Pisa (90,000). Leghorn (Livorno), on a good harbour, is the more important and has shipbuilding and heavy engineering. Pisa, on the Arno eight miles from the sea, was the chief port in medieval times but the river silted and Leghorn took over its port functions. During the past twenty years, navigation of the Arno has been improved by dredging and Pisa is once more a major port, with chemical and iron and steel industries. Iron ore is imported from the island of Elba, which lies off the Tuscan coast. The Leaning Tower is of course the city's best-known feature.

The coast of Tuscany, in common with the whole coastline as far south as Naples, is being silted and the blockage of drainage to the Tyrrhenian Sea has resulted in coastal marshes at several points. The most extensive are the Maremma marshes, south of the mouth of the Arno. Until 1950 they could be used only as winter pasture for sheep, but since that date large-scale drainage and reclamation under State supervision have transformed the area into small-holdings which are leased to landless peasants and farmed as co-operatives. The Maremma, once a malarial swamp, is a fine example of the merits of reclamation and re-settlement. The crops produced and marketed are principally wheat, maize and vegetables, especially tomatoes. There are as yet no large towns in this part of Tuscany. The rocky isle of Elba produces iron ore, which is sent to Genoa, Pisa and Civitavecchia.

South of the Arno plain, the hills and valleys of Tuscany and Umbria are covered with soils derived either from sandstones or, in south Tuscany, from volcanic extrusions. Farmlands cover the Tuscan valleys and extend even to the tops of some of the hills. Everywhere fields of wheat, barley and maize mingle with orchards of peaches and apricots. Olives, vines and mulberries are grown throughout the region. In the less fertile parts sheep are reared, especially in Umbria, where there are considerable areas of macchia. On the upper slopes of the higher cones are patchy forests of oak and chestnut.

The largest town of the Tuscan hill country is Siena (61,000), a market, tourist and route centre. Farther east, in basins or troughs between the Tuscan and Umbrian hills and the high central Apennines, the towns are larger, for they lie along the Flaminian Way, the route along the Tiber valley from Rome to Florence and the north, and each commands a road through the mountains. The chief of these focal points are Arezzo (75,000),

Perugia (112,000) and Terni (95,000). All have wool textile manufactures, and at Terni are a hydro-electric power station, and chemical and engineering works. Orvieto, on a more direct route from Rome to the north, is the centre of a wine-producing district.

(c) *The Lower Tiber basin.* Until fifty years ago the plains of the lower Tiber were a stretch of rough pasture or malarial swamp. The landlords of the vast estates into which the plain was divided were content with the income from sheep-rearing, and did little to improve the land. Irrigation was almost non-existent. Agrarian reform was imposed on them by the Fascist Government, especially after 1928. Today, irrigation schemes feed wheatfields, dairy farms and vineyards in most of the Agro Romano, and the malarial swamps of the Campagna have been drained and made into

[*Courtesy of Italian State Tourist Department.*

FIG. 64.—Italy: a farm near Rome. The machinery used for threshing is comparatively old-fashioned. In the background cattle are grazing on the hill slopes. Cattle yoked in pairs for draught purposes are also to be found in Portugal, southern Spain and Greece.

smallholdings. On the rich, volcanic soils of the Alban hills, south of the Campagna, the vineyards around Frascati are noted for their wines.

The reclamation of the Pontine marshes, which lie south of the Tiber delta, was part of the same scheme. Many attempts to reclaim these swamps had been made in the past two centuries, for they were a barrier to communications and a source of disease. The name "malaria," it should be noted, is derived from the Italian *mal'aria*, which means "bad air," for early medical science blamed the disease on the stench of rotting vegetation in the marshes. In the years 1926–32 the marshlands were cut by intersecting canals, whose waters were pumped into the Mussolini

Canal and carried to the sea, thus draining the stagnant pools cut off by coastal silting. The Pontine marshes became an area of re-settlement, farms of 20–60 acres being leased to peasants. The small-holdings, separated from the sea by salt lagoons and a line of sand dunes, extend in a belt 60 miles (96 km) long and 20 miles (32 km) wide. Among them are several settlements with agricultural schools and depots, commenced by the Government. Some of them have developed into large towns; Latina, founded only in 1932, now has over 200,000 inhabitants. The erstwhile Pontine marshes are today a major producer of cereals, vegetables, vines and tree crops.

Along the coast have grown holiday resorts for the people of Rome. Civitavecchia, a small port north of the coastal plain, serves the capital, though only to a minor extent; it is becoming better known for its steelworks. Anzio is a fishing port and the maritime outlet for the produce of the reclaimed Pontine area.

Dominating the whole of the lower Tiber region is the city of Rome, built on seven volcanic hills on the left bank of the river and in the middle of the Campagna. Its central position in the Italian peninsula—and indeed in the Mediterranean basin—made it an excellent capital for the Roman Empire, for to it were easily brought from conquered territories the food and other products the metropolitan region could not supply. With the fall of the Roman Empire, and after the partial disintegration of the Holy Roman Empire, the Popes became rulers of Rome and the city lost much of its political and military importance. At no time, however, did it cease to be a metropolis; it merely exchanged secular for ecclesiastical leadership, for the Pope is the head of the Roman Catholic Church. The city retained this status in a disunited Italy until 1870, when the country once more became a sovereign state and Rome was chosen as capital.

Rome has grown from a population of 244,000 in 1870 to 2,573,551 in 1966. Despite its size, it is not a great industrial city. It has railway, electrical and various branches of light engineering, and some textile, clothing and chemical works. But its main industrial activities are connected with food processing, luxury goods, camera and cinematograph manufactures, radio and television, furniture and the assembly of machinery from components provided by the Lombardy industrial region. Rome derives its chief source of income from the ruins of its ancient civilisation and from being the greatest religious centre in the world, drawing millions of pilgrims and tourists annually. Within its walls the ruins of the Coliseum, the Forum, the arches of Titus and Constantine stand side by side with the magnificent statuary of the Renaissance and hundreds of churches and basilicas, of which St Peter's is the most famous. As the political capital, it is the administrative centre of Italy. It is the chief railway focus in the peninsula, and its airport is an international route centre.

Vatican City, or the Vatican State, is an independent political unit, covering 109 acres in the south of Rome. When the Papal States were incorporated in 1870 into the Italian state, the Pope retired to the Vatican Palace. There he and his successors remained, virtually in house custody, until 1929. In that year, by treaty, the Pope was given sovereignty over the newly-defined Vatican City, which included some other buildings in Rome, and a summer villa and estate at Castel Gondolfo on the shores of Lake Albano. The Vatican City has its own administration, postage system, coinage, and radio and television station.

3. Southern Italy

(a) *The southern Apennines and plains of Apulia.* The southern Apennines have already been described as a series of limestone or crystalline horsts separated by areas of subsidence. In general, the limestone heights are karst, and in spite of higher rainfall have little surface water. At best they are suitable only for sheep-rearing. In solution hollows and on benches on their slopes, where Tertiary clays and marls have been preserved and springs provide water, subsistence farming is carried on. The crystalline horsts of the Sila and Aspromonte have similar occupations, but their impervious rocks provide an excellent catchment area for the heavy winter rainfall; several lakes on the surface of the Sila have been transformed into reservoirs for hydro-electric power stations and for irrigation in the valleys and coastal plains (*see* Fig. 59). All the horsts have a scattered cover of forests of beech and Mediterranean pine, but deforestation in the past has caused widespread soil erosion. The limestone is easily worn away, and in winter torrential showers, often of hail, cause landslides when the protecting forest cover is removed. Piles of mud and pebbles are swept from the highlands into the deep, narrow valleys and on to the coastal plains, leaving the upper surfaces bare and sterile. The transported sediments block the drainage, and turn the coastal plains into swamps, which become malarial and able to support only a sprinkling of inhabitants.

The provinces of Lucania (Basilicata) and Calabria, which are composed almost entirely of the Apennine highlands, are the poorest in Italy, yet they contain nearly 3 million people. Most of these, however, live in the small coastal plains of Calabria. The plains are intensively cultivated for wheat and vegetables, and have olives, vines, figs, oranges and lemons in irrigated huertas. Citrus fruits are the main wealth of Calabria; orange and lemon groves cover much of the area around Reggio (161,272), Cosenza (78,000) and Catanzaro (74,000). The crystalline plateaus in the interior of Calabria supply water for irrigation, and their power stations generate about 3% of Italy's hydro-electric power, but the development of industry in the "toe" of Italy is not commensurate with this total. Calabria remains the most over-populated province in the country.

Textile, chemical and iron and steel works have been established in Reggio, Cosenza and Catanzaro, with the help of the Cassa, and the harbour facilities of Reggio, the ferry port to Sicily, have been improved, but these can absorb only a tiny fraction of the ever-growing mass of people along the coasts. In the mountainous interior of Lucania and Calabria the position is even worse, for there are fewer resources and the birth-rate is among the highest in the world. Here Italy's "Problem of the Mezzogiorno" is at its worst.

On the eastern side of southern Italy is the province of Apulia (Puglia), with two areas of lowland fringing the Adriatic Sea. The first is the Plain of Apulia, between the Campanian Apennines and the limestone plateau of the Murge. It is a plain of recent emergence, and has a thin cover of marine clays and sands overlying impure limestone. In some parts the limestone has dissolved and its residual deposits have formed a thick, impermeable layer below the surface silts, producing malarial swamps; in other places the limestone is very porous, making irrigation difficult. The Apulian Plain is watered by streams from the base of the limestone Apennines; but in summer it is the hottest part of Italy, average July temperatures being 85° F (29·4° C). The rivers dry up and there is a shortage of water for household purposes.

In these conditions, the plain was given over to sheep-rearing. The wretchedly poor shepherds were employed by landowners who lived in Naples or Rome and who resisted any use of the plain for arable farming. In the 1930s the grazing rights of the sheep barons were terminated, and sheep-rearing confined to the worst parts of the plain. In 1939 the Apulian Aqueduct was completed after 30 years' work, to feed water to the plain. The westward-flowing river Sele was diverted through tunnels pierced in the Apennines to an aqueduct over 150 miles (240 km) long, and its waters directed to irrigation channels in the Apulian Plain, and to supply systems in the towns. The Cassa is increasing the scope of the aqueduct, so that more land is constantly brought into use, chiefly for wheat and vegetable production. In the middle of the plain is Foggia (134,581), which has grown rapidly because of the aqueduct; in it the Cassa has built new dairies, grain warehouses and a co-operative olive-oil processing works.

In the "heel" of Italy is another plain, with a cover of terra rossa, and here, as in the Apulian Plain, the provision and control of water supplies is the chief problem. The principal products are olives and olive oil, of which Apulia is a major exporter. The chief towns are Brindisi (70,000), Taranto (212,503) and Lecce (75,000), each surrounded by irrigation systems and rich agriculture, and acting as markets for olive oil, wine and fruit. Brindisi, on a good harbour, was a growing mail port for the East until the advent of air travel, but has now declined in importance. Taranto's functions as a naval, shipbuilding and fishing port have been augmented by new iron and steel works.

In contrast to the dry plains, the narrow coastal plain and terraced slopes north and south of Bari, on the east coast, are one vast orchard. The soil, enriched by phosphatic deposits and irrigated by streams from the Murge plateau, supports vines, olives, figs, oranges, lemons and almonds. Bari (340,614), the centre of this fruitful huerta, is the chief Adriatic port south of Venice. It exports olive oil, wine and fruit. New industries started by the Cassa include rubber, metal pipe and marble works. Elsewhere on the Apulian coasts, the Cassa is building new aqueducts for the better distribution of irrigation waters to the huertas, and improving the roads on the difficult slopes.

(b) *Campania*. The Plain of Naples, in the north of Campania, is the most fertile of the Tyrrhenian lowlands, its productivity being attributable in a large degree to the breakdown of basaltic lavas and volcanic tuffs, especially in the east of the plain. The rich soils have long supported a full range of Mediterranean polyculture, with crops of wheat, maize, vegetables, flax, hemp and tree crops such as peaches, apricots, mulberries

Fig. 65.—Italy: Naples. The plain of Naples is the most intensively cultivated region in Italy, with vines, peaches, apricots, olives, figs and mulberries on hill slopes, and wheat, maize, vegetables, flax, hemp and oranges at lower levels.

and vines, all on small farms. On hill slopes are more vineyards, olive groves and fig trees; at their feet are orange groves. On the limestone hills bounding the eastern plain, sheep are reared. In the west and north there were coastal swamps around the river mouths, but most of them have been reclaimed and re-settled, as in the Pontine and Maremma marshes; the land now produces wheat, vegetables, flax and hemp. The Campanian lowlands, after the Plain of Lombardy, are the most productive part of Italy, yet many of the inhabitants live in a state of dire poverty belied by the rich landscape, and the pressure of rural population is great.

The largest city of Campania is Naples (Napoli), with a population of 1,251,445. It is a major port on a first-class harbour, with good routes through its agricultural hinterland to Rome and, via Benevento, to the Adriatic coast. Its importance as a port is increased by the absence of good harbours on the Tyrrhenian coast until Leghorn is reached in the north. Naples is in a position of great scenic beauty—"See Naples and die!"—but within the city itself, although there are magnificent buildings and a prosperous industrial area, parts are filthy overcrowded slums, teeming with hordes of immigrants from the poverty-stricken rural areas of southern Italy and with the city's own surplus of unemployed.

Naples is Italy's greatest industrial city outside the north. It has ship-building, chemical, leather, cotton and rayon manufactures, railway engineering and food processing; as part of the Cassa developments, light industries of all kinds are being introduced. At Bagnoli, a southern suburb, is a new iron and steel works using imported fuel and raw materials.

Among other Cassa projects scattered through the plain are hotels—for Pompeii, Capri, etc., attract many tourists—tobacco works, paper and cardboard factories, and food-processing plants, especially for the making of macaroni. At Caserta (50,000) there are glass, paper and plastics factories. In the Phlegraean Fields region, new thermo-electric stations supply power to motor, electrical and mechanical engineering works.

South of the Plain of Naples, a spur of the Apennines forms the rocky Sorrento peninsula. In little bays at the foot of its cliffs there are holiday resorts such as Sorrento and Amalfi; Castellammare is a naval base. Capri, a beautiful island off this picturesque coast, attracts thousands of tourists from Naples.

The southern part of Campania is the Plain of Salerno, through which flows the river Sele. Its products are the same as those of the Plain of Naples, but farming methods are more primitive and yields smaller. The chief town is Salerno (140,402), whose industries are concerned mainly with the agricultural products of the Sele basin. Hydro-electricity generated in the upper Sele valley has led to electrical engineering in Salerno and is helping Cassa projects—macaroni making, tobacco and paper works—throughout the plain.

4. Insular Italy

(a) *Sicily*. The economy is essentially agricultural, and its industries are mainly connected with farm products. It has a population of 4,712,000 and the very high density of 475 persons per square mile, which is far beyond the island's capacity to support. Much of the area is over-populated, and large numbers emigrate to northern Italy. The climate is typically Mediterranean, with rainfall chiefly in winter. But the total precipitation is not great—Palermo has 25 in. a year—and much is lost by rapid run-off and by evaporation. Sicily needs a complete reorganisation of its water supplies, so as to increase its agricultural yields and reduce the pressure of population. This is one of the objects of the Cassa, which has already brought into operation the Palermo Aqueduct to distribute irrigation water to the central plain. Other dams have been constructed in the upper valleys of the Salso and Simeto rivers to feed the extended irrigation systems of the Plain of Catania.

The richest farming areas are the small coastal plains along the north coast, which are watered by streams from the limestone heights behind (*see* Fig. 60). Their chief crop is lemons, followed by oranges and tangerines, and there is a big output of vegetables, which can be grown all the year round. The plains of the centre and south are wheat-lands, with olive groves and sheep on the higher areas. The Plain of Catania, thanks to the new irrigation systems, is the most improved region of Sicily, producing all the crops of the northern huertas, together with vines, olives and almonds. One of the most fruitful districts is on the lower slopes of Etna, which have fertile volcanic soils in places; other parts of the mountain are covered with a mass of broken lavas and pumice.

Sicily has deposits of sulphur near Caltanissetta, Agrigento and Catania (*see* Fig. 62), but the competition of larger and more easily exploited supplies from Louisiana has robbed it of its former pre-eminence in the export of this mineral. Of far greater significance is the discovery of mineral oil in several places in the eastern half of the island. The first deposits were found in 1953 near Ragusa and Gela, and since then oil has been struck in large quantities at Caltanissetta and Enna, and offshore drilling at Gela has given good results. Potash occurs at San Cataldo, a few miles west of Caltanissetta, and is processed for fertiliser in the near-by small town of Serradifalco. This is another Cassa project (*see* Fig. 14).

In view of the absence of any outstanding manufacturing industries, the cities of Sicily are surprisingly large—an indication of the island's over-population. Palermo, the capital, has a population of 643,455. Situated on a good harbour and in the centre of a rich huerta, it is Sicily's chief port. Its industries include shipbuilding, chemical works, mechanical and naval engineering, and food processing. Catania (401,489) exports the products of its hinterland, and has glass and pottery works, and paper mills. Messina (267,017), on the strait, exports oranges from the groves which surround it and is the ferry port for Reggio, on the mainland. Taormina, a small town on a limestone bluff overlooking the Mediterranean, is a holiday resort famous for its ruins of a Greek theatre and for its view of Mount Etna. Other large towns of Sicily are Siracusa (90,000), Agrigento (48,000) and Trapani (77,000), all in fertile huertas, and Caltanissetta (63,000), a wheat and sulphur market in the central plain. Trapani exports the wine of Marsala. On the whole Sicily is better endowed with resources than most of southern Italy, but much further attention by the Cassa is needed.

To the north of Sicily are the volcanic Lipari isles, with Stromboli, a volcano in constant activity and known as the "lighthouse of the Mediterranean." Another of the group is Vulcano, which has given its name to all volcanoes.

Centrally situated in the Mediterranean, Sicily has attracted a succession of invaders during its history, nearly every southern European and north African people having attempted to occupy and govern it at one time or another. Each invasion in turn left its mark. The Greeks developed city states and trading colonies; the Romans used the island as a granary and left a legacy of latifondi; the Arabs introduced irrigation, citrus fruits and cotton; the Bourbons exploited it and left it in a state of destitution. Under this succession of foreign overlords, the Sicilians—hard-working, frugal, clannish, hot-blooded, fiery—developed a resistance to authority and legislation which has made the work of the Cassa very difficult. Past experience of corruption among Government officials has made them suspicious of the Cassa experts; but the reforms and improvements of the past ten years have done much, not only to increase the economic capacity of Sicily, but to convert its people to an acceptance of outside interference and an acquiescence to agrarian reforms.

(b) *Sardinia*. Although Sardinia is not much smaller than Sicily, its population, 1,413,300, is less than one-third of the larger island's. The density is 152 persons a square mile; although this is small compared with other parts of the Mezzogiorno, Sardinia is overcrowded and is one of the poorest provinces in Italy. The plateaus are largely unproductive, with bare rocks dotted with patches of macchia and occasional cork-oaks, but they serve as catchment areas for the water needed in the lower-lying areas. The Cassa has constructed dams in the upper valleys of the rivers Coghinas, Tirso and Flumendosa, and the impounded waters are used for hydro-electricity and to feed irrigation systems (*see* Fig. 60). The Cassa has been responsible too for the drainage of malarial swamps which dotted the coasts, and for the reafforestation of some of the plateau slopes. The rearing of sheep and goats is the chief occupation throughout the highlands of Sardinia, and wool and cheese are staple products.

The best agricultural areas lie at the two ends of the Campidano, where, with irrigation, the chief crops are wheat, maize, rice, tobacco, beans and sugar beet. Olives, vines and almonds grow on slopes, and there is some sheep-rearing. In the centre of the plain there are large wheat farms. The largest town in Sardinia, Cagliari (211,126), is situated at the southern end of the Campidano. It is the island's chief port, trading mainly with Naples; it has salt pans, woollen manufacture and cement works. At the northern end of the plain is Oristano, a small market town.

The crystalline rocks of the south-western plateau are highly mineralised, yielding lead and zinc near Iglesias and coal at Carbonia (*see* Fig. 62). The peninsula of La Nurra in the west of Sardinia has deposits of lead, zinc, iron and antimony. Sassari (90,000) concentrates the minerals of the La Nurra district, and is in the chief olive-growing region. The concentrated ores are exported to Italy through Alghero and Porto Tórres, which are also small tunny- and sardine-fishing ports. The coal of Carbonia is sent to Italy from Cagliari; nearly all Italy's coal comes from Sardinia.

The poverty of Sardinia is visible in most parts of the island. Although the Cassa is very active in its schemes of reconstruction and rehabilitation, many years must elapse before Sardinia has a standard of living comparable even with that of the southern Apennines.

STUDY QUESTIONS

1. Make a division of peninsular Italy into geographical regions. Describe the relief and drainage of each region and show how these have influenced communications through the whole peninsula. (O. & C.)

2. Compare the agriculture of the Lombardy Plain with that of Italy south of Naples. (O. & C.)

3. Write a concise geographical account of *either* Sicily *or* Sardinia. (O. & C.)

4. Account for regional contrasts in economic development in Italy. (J.M.B.)

5. Suggest a division of Italy into natural regions. Discuss the bearing of physical factors upon economic activities in any *two* of the regions recognised. (J.M.B.)

6. Poverty is more prevalent among the rural population of southern Italy and Sicily than among the rural population of the Plain of Lombardy. Discuss the influence of geographical conditions on this state of affairs. (J.M.B.)

7. Describe the position, chief manufactures and commercial activities of *either* Milan *or* Naples.

8. Compare the industrial activities of Italy with those of the Iberian peninsula.

9. Describe the distribution of population in Italy and account for any regional differences in density you may note.

10. Give an account of the fuel and power resources of Italy, and indicate their importance in the economy of the country.

Chapter XIII

YUGOSLAVIA

THE Socialist Federal Republic of Yugoslavia came into existence in 1919 as a confederation of six small states: Serbia (with its autonomous provinces of Vojvodina and Kosovo-Metohija), Croatia, Slovenia, Bosnia-Hercegovina, Macedonia and Montenegro.

PHYSICAL ASPECTS

STRUCTURAL DIVISIONS

Three-quarters of Yugoslavia is mountainous, the highest ranges lying along the western, southern and eastern margins. In the north is the only extensive stretch of lowland in the country. The chief river of Yugoslavia is the Danube, which flows for 945 miles (1512 km) either across the northern plain or to form the boundary with Rumania. Its longest tributaries are the Sava, Drava and Morava. The Drava forms part of the Yugoslav–Hungarian boundary. Nearly 70% of the surface of Yugoslavia is drained to the Danube. The only important southward-flowing river is the Vardar, which passes through Greece to the Aegean Sea.

The physical—and mainly structural—divisions which may be distinguished in Yugoslavia are: (1) the Alpine zone, (2) the Dinaric ranges, (3) the Morava–Vardar "corridor" lands, and (4) the Danubian plains (*see* Fig. 66).

1. The Alpine zone

In the north-west of Yugoslavia the Karawanken Alps and the Julian Alps are continuations of the Alpine ranges of Austria. Mount Triglav (9393 ft, 2863 m), in the Julian Alps, is the highest peak in Yugoslavia. Away from the mountains the region is a high plateau cut by deep valleys, such as that of the Sava, which rises in the Karawanken Alps. In places the valleys have widened into extensive basins, the most important of which is around Ljubljana. This north-western Alpine zone constituted the old state and present republic of Slovenia.

2. The Dinaric ranges

The Dinaric Alps, the most extensive mountainous area in Yugoslavia, stretch from the Alpine zone in Slovenia to the river Drim and Lake Skadar in the south, spreading eastwards, south of the Sava valley, to the West Morava river and the Field (or *polje*) of Kosovo. This mass of mountains and plateaus, one of the most rugged in Europe, comprises the

293

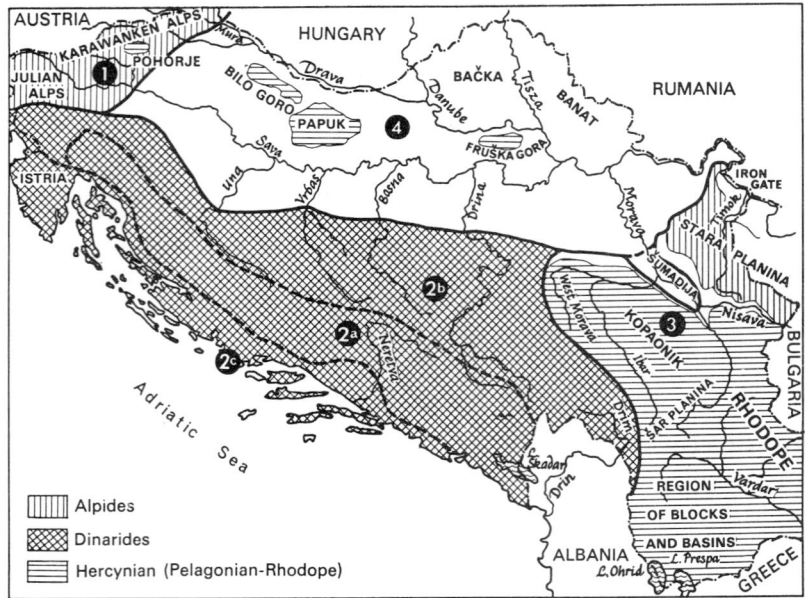

Fig. 66.—Yugoslavia: structural and physical divisions. The numbers correspond with sections in the text. The Pelagonian-Rhodope massifs are sometimes regarded as a median mass of the Alpides system, and, although composed of similar crystalline rocks, are strictly not part of the Hercynian (Carbo-Permian) system.

republics of Bosnia-Hercegovina, Montenegro, and the southern part of Croatia. The region may be sub-divided into three belts: (a) a central plateau dominated on its western edge by mountains which rise to over 8000 ft (2440 m), (b) an eastern series of lower and less difficult ranges, with river valleys opening northwards, and (c) a still lower belt along the Adriatic Sea, known as Dalmatia.

(a) *The plateau and mountains* which fill western Bosnia-Hercegovina and the whole of Montenegro are composed of very permeable and soluble limestone. They are known as the Karst or High Karst. Although it has one of the heaviest precipitations in Europe, the surface of the region is dry, bare and inhospitable, for it allows rain and melting snows to soak or flow quickly through the outer strata to form underground streams and lakes. The Neretva is the only river to have its course entirely on the surface. This is because it has cut a very deep canyon, which takes its valley floor below the level of the water-table.

The peneplained platforms on the plateau are deeply grooved where solution has widened the joints in the limestone into narrow gorge-like apertures known as *clints* or wider ones called *grykes*. There are many depressions or basins where the roofs of underground caverns have collapsed or where surface rocks of relatively greater solubility have been dissolved. The larger basins are known as *polja* (Serb. *polje*, "plain"), and may be many miles in diameter; smaller ones, *dolina* (Serb. *doline*, "hollow"), vary in diameter from hundreds of yards to a few feet. Polja and dolina are often floored with red earth, terra rossa, the insoluble quartz and clay impurities left as a residue by the dissolved limestone. The red colour derives from a long accumulation of minute traces of insoluble iron hydroxides. In some of the dolina there are fresh-water Tertiary deposits, suggesting that the area experienced epeirogenic uplift before the surface collapsed to form the depressions. Limestone regions in other parts of the world which, like the Karst, have a topography with grykes, sink-holes and broken river drainage with underground streams and caverns are said to have "karst" characteristics.

The High Karst, *i.e.* the mountainous western rim of the plateau, is a range high enough to form a climatic divide between the Mediterranean and continental influences. It is also a most difficult barrier to communications. There are only four passes through the High Karst, and all are at high altitudes. The highest peak in the range is Durmitor (8294 ft, 2538 m).

(b) *The mountain ranges east of the Karst*, though lower, are still rugged. They are composed partly of very soluble limestone similar to that of the Karst, partly of sandstones and crystalline rocks. The limestones, although in places they have dissolved to form polja, are not dry on the surface as in the Karst, and the whole of this sub-region usually has enough soil cover to support tree growth. The mountain ranges are traversed by numerous rivers whose deep, gorge-like valleys make communications difficult. The chief rivers are the Una, Vrbas, Bosna and Drina, which cut through the mountains on their way to the Sava in the north. Along their northern margin the mountain ranges decrease in height and the valleys widen, to form southern extensions of the plains of the Sava.

(c) *Dalmatia.* On the western side of the Dinaric region, the land falls in steep terraces from the High Karst to the cliff-lined Adriatic coast. On some of the lower terraces there are outcrops of flysch, with good soils; in the lower valleys of rivers which emerge from the base of the Karst there are alluvial flats and terra rossa. North of Sibenik a slight sinking of the land has resulted in a more continuous coastal plain. Southwards, the only lowlands are the river valleys mentioned above, and the narrow strip cut by the Neretva. The coast of Dalmatia is lined with strings of long, low, narrow islands, the remains of concordant limestone ranges which have subsided, and been drowned and partly dissolved by the sea. Parts of the Dalmatian mainland have long, branching, rectangular inlets where depressions have been similarly invaded.

3. *The Morava–Vardar "corridor" lands*

East of the Dinaric region, Yugoslavia consists of a series of rugged, crystalline mountain blocks and enclosed basins, different in origin from the folded ranges of the west. They are parts of the Rhodope-Pelagonian massif, probably of Hercynian age, which was fractured and dislocated in mid-Tertiary times, the down-faulted areas being inundated by the waters of the Aegean Sea to form the "Aegean Lake." Later uplift broke the "Aegean Lake" into a number of separate small lakes, most of which have dried up, leaving basins floored with Tertiary rocks and a surface cover of lacustrine silts and alluvium. Two lakes which remain are Ohrid and Prespansço, on the Yugoslav–Albanian–Greek border.

The movements of uplift and subsidence were greatest in the south in Macedonia. Here the mountain blocks rise to over 8500 ft (2590 m) in the massifs of Korab, Šar Planina and Borislaec, and several others have an altitude of 7000 ft (2130 m). Between them are the basins of Bitola, Tetovo, Skopje and Strumica, interconnected by narrow defiles. The Macedonian mountains form the water-parting between the Danubian tributaries and the rivers flowing to the south. In the north of the region, where the uplift was not so great, the highest block, the Kapaonik, does not reach 5000 ft (1520 m). The basins of Kosovo and Metohija, connected by a wide opening, are sufficiently extensive to form together an autonomous province of the republic of Serbia. In the north, the river valleys widen to form plains. The largest is along the lower Morava and called the Šumadija.

Some of the valleys of rivers flowing northwards to the Danubian plain and of those flowing southwards to the Aegean Sea are connected at their heads by low cols, and form continuous—if somewhat difficult— routes through the mountains. In the west, one of these "corridors" leads from the Ibar valley to the upper Vardar and the Tetovo and Skopje basins. East of this, the Morava and Vardar valleys are continuous and are known as the "Diagonal Furrow," the most important north–south "corridor" in the Balkans. A third route utilises the Struma valley, in Bulgaria. This is connected to the valley of the Nisava, a tributary of the Morava, which provides a passage eastwards from the Diagonal Furrow to the Sofia basin and thence to the Maritsa valley and Istanbul. This is the route taken by the Orient Express line. The two western corridors converge at their northern ends on Belgrade, and southwards they lead through Greece to the port of Salonica.

East of the Morava–Vardar corridor, the mountains in the south are the western edges of the Rhodope massif. North of the river Nisava are the Alpine folds of the western Balkan mountains, which swing northwards to the Danube, where they are separated from the Transylvanian Alps of Rumania by the Iron Gate. The Yugoslav Rhodope is split into several blocks; the highest is Plackovica (5763 ft, 1757 m). The Balkan mountains in Yugoslavia have a few lofty peaks in the south, such as Midzor (7172 ft, 2186 m), but towards the Danube they decrease in height to little more than hills. East of the Balkans, and shut off by them from the rest of the country, the Timok valley widens to the plain of Kladovo, near the Danube.

The "corridor" lands draining south to the Vardar form the republic of

Macedonia. The first kingdom of Serbia grew in the western Ibar–Kosovo corridor, but the heart of the present republic is the Morava valley, the Šumadija.

4. The Danubian plain

Northern Yugoslavia forms part of the Pannonian basin, and is low-land. The eastern portion is a flat, monotonous plain, very similar to the adjoining Hungarian region. Through it flow the river Danube and the lower reaches of its tributaries, the Drava, Sava and Tisza. The Drava and Sava drain the western plain; the Tisza cuts the eastern portion in two. The rivers are flanked by broad belts of fertile alluvium, and east of the Danube there are extensive areas covered with loess. The western Danubian plain is undulating and broken by ancient crystalline rock masses which have been upthrust to form the forested hills of the Pohorje, Bilo Goro, Papuk and Fruška Gora, between the rivers Drava and Sava.

This hilly western region is Slavonia, a part of the republic of Croatia. The eastern plain, south of the Danube, is northern Serbia. Vojvodina, an autonomous province of Serbia, lies north of the Danube and is divided by the Tisza into the plains of the Bačka to the west, and of the Banat to the east. The latter are a continuation of the Banat of Rumania.

CLIMATE AND VEGETATION

The High Karst on the west and the mountain blocks of Macedonia in the south form a barrier between the Mediterranean and continental climates experienced in Yugoslavia. The Adriatic coastlands and the southern Vardar valley have the hot, dry summers and mild, wet winters associated with a Mediterranean climate, and occasionally these conditions penetrate to the interior of the country via the gaps in the mountains or along the valleys. The average January temperature for these "Mediterranean" areas is 41·5° F (5·3° C), and in July it is 79·5° F (26·4° C), with an annual rainfall of about 25 in.

The rest of the country has a continental climate—hot summers, cold winters and precipitation which falls mainly in summer. Temperatures range from January averages of 29° F (−1·7° C) to 73·5° F (23·1° C) in July. Annual precipitation varies considerably according to elevation, aspect or rain-shadow effects. Mostar, for instance, in the valley of the Neretva, in the Dinaric Alps, has 55 in. annually, whereas Belgrade, in the northern plain, has only 18·5 in. Niš and Skopje, in sheltered valleys, have 17 in.

Precipitation in the Dinaric ranges overlooking the Adriatic Sea is strikingly high for a region so far removed from Atlantic influences. The district north of Titograd has registered 183 inches in a year, and Titograd itself has an annual precipitation of 52 in. The north-west Alpine region has about 70 inches in the mountains, and the Ljubljana basin 54 in. a year.

The Dalmatian coastlands are sometimes affected in winter by the *bora*, a cold wind blowing from the High Karst. During anticyclonic calms, cold air accumulates in the high valleys and when a depression passes along the Adriatic it is drawn down the coastlands as violent, icy winds which are a danger to shipping and greatly feared by fishermen. The high velocity of these winds is due to the steep thermal gradient caused by the presence of cold, high mountains near a warm sea (*see also* page 38).

A tenth of the surface of Yugoslavia consists of bare, high mountains or barren Karst. Of the remainder, the vegetation is almost equally divided between forests, pasture and arable land. Most of the mountains are forested, mainly with deciduous trees such as oak and walnut up to about 5000 ft (1520 m), and with conifers, chiefly pines, at higher levels. Pasture land is found in the basins among the mountains or as Alpine pastures above the tree line. In the Bačka and Banat there remain areas of steppe vegetation which have not been ploughed for agriculture. The chief arable lands are in the Šumadija and the Danubian plain west of the Danube. The river valleys are cultivated, and in some of them two, or even three, successive harvests in the same year are not unusual.

HUMAN GEOGRAPHY

HISTORY AND PEOPLE

The people of Yugoslavia are classified as South Slavs. In the westward migrations of the early Slavs, various tribes at different times penetrated the mountains of Yugoslavia and settled in this most difficult environment. The Slovenes occupied the Alpine region, near the present Austrian and Italian borders. The Croats settled in the valley of the Sava and the hill ranges south of it. The Montenegrins and Macedonians took possession of the southern Dinarics and the southern "corridor" lands. The Serbs—the most powerful tribe—first occupied the eastern Dinarics, then spread towards the Morava valley and the eastern Danubian plain. These were the principal peoples, but there were in addition smaller communities in the fastnesses of Bosnia, Hercegovina and Pelagonia.

From the middle of the fifteenth century the whole of the Balkan peninsula was overrun by the Ottoman Turks, who spread their empire to the gates of Vienna. They were gradually driven back by the armies of the Holy Roman Emperor, and in 1699 Slovenia and Croatia became part of the Austrian possessions. In the course of time the inhabitants of these regions adopted a more Westernised culture than the other South Slavs. For nearly 400 years the Serbs and other mountain peoples lived under the domination of the Turks, who ruled with savage cruelty. The South Slavs, scattered in separate communities and isolated from each other by high mountain ranges, were unable to unite effectively against their oppressors. Their only defence against the armed retribution which invariably followed their refusal to pay the exorbitant taxes levied upon them was to withdraw to their mountain fastnesses and defy all Turkish attempts to crush them. There, living from hand to mouth, they developed an intense local patriotism and an unquenchable yearning for independence.

The first real chance of liberation came in the first part of the nineteenth century, when the Serbs rebelled against the hated Turks and achieved an uneasy kind of independence. Complete freedom came a step nearer after 1878, when the Ottoman Empire was defeated in a war with Russia. In 1881 the Niš region rebelled successfully, and all the rest of the mountain peoples became free when the Turks withdrew from southeastern Europe in 1912, keeping for themselves only a small area behind Constantinople (Istanbul). Freedom did not last long, however, for the Treaty of Bucharest in 1913, which terminated the Turkish war, gave Macedonia to Bulgaria and so precipitated the Second Balkan War. The result was that Macedonia was partitioned between Greece and Serbia, with the larger portion allotted to Serbia.

In the meantime, the Austrian-owned regions of Slovenia and Croatia were becoming restive and demanding independence; nationalist groups in the two provinces were fostering revolution, aided and abetted by Bosnia and Hercegovina, which had been annexed by Austria in 1908.

The assassination in 1914 of the Crown Prince of Austria in Sarajevo led to the invasion of Serbia by the Austro-Hungarian forces, and this campaign in turn precipitated the First World War.

In 1918, at the end of the war, the heterogeneous peoples of the northern Balkans became united as the Kingdom of the Serbs, Croats and Slovenes, under the King of Serbia. In 1929 the name of the new country was changed to Yugoslavia, as being the "land of the South Slavs." The frontiers, as fixed in 1919, included all the highlands to the east of the important Morava–Vardar corridor, and took from Bulgaria a portion of Macedonia it had retained.

In 1941, during the Second World War, Yugoslavia was invaded by the Italians and Germans. The country was partitioned between Germany, Italy, Hungary and Bulgaria. More than 10% of the population was killed, newly established industrial plants were left in ruins, towns and railways were destroyed and the countryside was a scene of desolation. In this period of tribulation the people of Yugoslavia ceased to be Serb, or Croat, or Bosnian, or Macedonian, and banded themselves into an "underground" Liberation Army to fight against the occupying forces; so that when, in 1945, the country was free again, Yugoslavia's peoples were more closely united than ever before. In 1947 a portion of Venezia Giulia was taken from Italy and added to Yugoslavia, and the fragments of Macedonia still in Bulgarian hands were annexed.

At the end of the war Yugoslavia was under Soviet domination, with Marshal Tito, a leader of the wartime resistance against the Germans, in charge of government. Yugoslavia was proclaimed a Communist federal republic, within the Soviet zone of influence, which now stretched without a break from the Black Sea to the Adriatic. Tito, however, did not wholly accept the Soviet interpretation of Marxist Communism, and withdrew his country from the domination of Moscow. Yugoslavia is still Communist, but with differences from the ideology of the Soviet Union. The country is still friendly with Moscow; but, seeing itself in a position of balance between East and West, it maintains open relations with the Western powers, and is not behind the Iron Curtain. The Western powers, for their part, welcome the split in the Communist ranks, for it means that the Soviet Union is once more denied an easy land passage to the Mediterranean.

POPULATION

The population of Yugoslavia totalled 19,741,000 in 1966, with an average density of 193 persons per square mile. The population is unevenly distributed. Some parts of the mountains in the west are almost uninhabited, whereas the agricultural plains of the north, especially the Vojvodina, are comparatively densely peopled. The greatest concentrations are around Belgrade and Zagreb and in the Alpine region of Slovenia. The average numbers of people per square mile in the republics which comprise Yugoslavia are: Serbia 223, Slovenia 203, Croatia 190, Bosnia-Hercegovina 166, Macedonia 141 and Montenegro 88. With the increased mechanisation of agriculture in the northern plains, overpopulation is beginning to make itself felt, and the Government has introduced measures to attract surplus labour from the plains to the infant industries in the valleys of Bosnia-Hercegovina, Montenegro and Macedonia. Present trends show a distinct increase in Yugoslavia's population south of a line drawn across the country through Sarajevo and Skopje.

There are three official languages in Yugoslavia—Serbo-Croat, Slovene and Macedonian. In addition there are at least six other "minority" languages, each spoken by considerable numbers. This assemblage of different tongues hindered the initial federation of Yugoslavia, and there are still political and economic tensions due to linguistic differences and the varying standards of cultural and living conditions found in the different republics. On the whole, however, the peoples of Yugoslavia have been united very effectively. The material advances made since 1919 have helped by raising the standard of living and increasing the general prosperity, but probably the tragic experiences of the Second World War had more effect.

THE ECONOMY

GENERAL CHARACTERISTICS

Before 1939, both industry and agriculture were backward. About 80% of the working population was engaged in inefficient or subsistence agriculture and only 7% in industry. At the present time, the number of agricultural workers has fallen to 52% of the total, yet production has increased, and the proportion of industrial workers has risen to 13%. The biggest increases are in the numbers engaged in building construction, transport and commerce. Moreover, the contribution of industry to the national income in the same period has risen from a paltry 9·5% to 47%.

Most of the advance came from developments in the Danubian plain and Slovenia, but the policy of the Government is to spread industry through the mountainous regions of the south, using the hydro-electric potential and the mineral deposits so abundant there. Since 1945, hundreds of factories have been built to produce goods such as diesel engines, automobiles, railway rolling stock, telephone exchanges, etc., which used to be imported. New agricultural techniques are releasing workers, not only for the factories, but for building roads and railways, the lack of which in some districts is a tremendous handicap.

Yugoslavia may be a Communist country, but it looks to the Western powers for capital and technical advice rather than to the Soviet Union. Its exports, mainly of foodstuffs, mineral ores and tobacco, go to Italy, West Germany, the U.S.A., the United Kingdom and the Soviet Union, in that order. Its imports of fuel (coal and petroleum), machinery and transport equipment, raw materials and foodstuffs come mainly from the U.S.A., Italy, West Germany, the Soviet Union and the United Kingdom.

Post-war reconstruction, inaugurated and encouraged by the U.S.S.R., was taken over by the Western powers until Yugoslavia was able to continue independently. Today, the country shows promise of becoming a strong and progressive Mediterranean power.

MINERALS AND POWER

Yugoslavia ranks high among the countries of Europe in wealth of water power, as might be expected from its relief and ample rainfall in the higher regions. Yet the volume of hydro-electric power before 1945 was small. In 1946 it amounted to 478 million kWh, but by 1962 had increased phenomally to 6851 million kWh; and this was still only a tenth of the estimated hydro-electric potential of the country. Hydro-electric power production far surpasses the total of thermally generated energy, which in 1962 was 4424 kWh, and new hydro-electric stations continue to be built.

The chief hydro-electric power plants are in the wetter parts of the Dinaric Alps draining to the Adriatic Sea, at Split, Dubrovnik and Jablanica. There is another large station at Maribor, in the Karawanken Alps. A large proportion of Yugoslavia's hydro-electric power potential is in the area drained by the right-bank tributaries of the Sava, and there are many stations along the valleys of the Vrbas, Bosna, Drina and Ibar (see Fig. 67).

Yugoslavia possesses considerable deposits of useful minerals. Hard coal is mined in the Timok and Ibar valleys in Serbia, but output amounts to only a million tons a year. Lignite and brown coal are more plentiful and widespread, the annual output being upwards of 23 million tons. The chief producing areas are in the Bosna valley near Sarajevo, around Ljubljana in Slovenia, north-west of Belgrade, and in the Istrian peninsula.

A small oilfield south-east of Zagreb yields $1\frac{1}{2}$ million tons of petroleum a year, and there are deposits of natural gas in the same region.

Iron ore occurs in large quantities at Ljubija and in the Sava valley near Sisak, but is not yet fully exploited. Bauxite is found in the Dinaric karstlands and Istria. With an annual output of over a million tons, Yugoslavia is a major producer. Lead–zinc–silver ores occur in the Kara-wanken Alps, the Drina valley and at the southern end of the Kopaonik mountains. The yearly output of lead amounts to 98,000 tons, of zinc

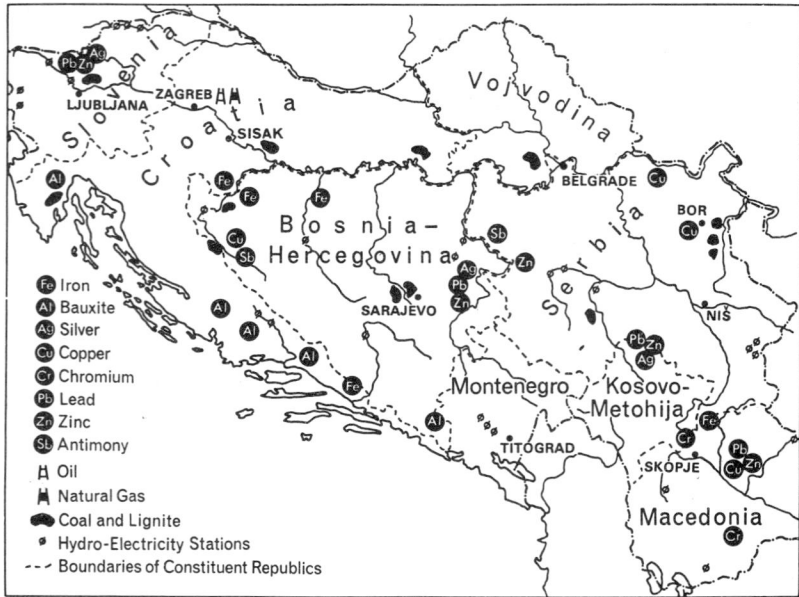

Fig. 67.—Yugoslavia: minerals and power. The map also shows the six republics—Bosnia-Hercegovina, Croatia, Macedonia, Montenegro, Serbia and Slovenia—which make up the federal state of Yugoslavia. In the republic of Serbia there are two autonomous provinces, Vojvodina, with a large Hungarian minority population, and Kosovo-Metohija, with a population predominantly Albanian.

39,000 tons and of silver 94 tons. There are extensive deposits of copper around Bor, in eastern Serbia, yielding annually 92,000 tons. Workable supplies of chromium and asbestos occur near Skopje, and there is mercury in the Julian Alps. The output of manganese and antimony in the Macedonian mountains is increasing, and uranium has been discovered in eastern Macedonia.

REGIONAL ECONOMY

1. The Alpine zone

The Julian and Karawanken Alps to the west and north of this region have deciduous forests far up their slopes, with conifers above. These have led to a lumbering industry, and to pulp and paper works in the Mura valley, where one of the largest hydro-electric power stations in Yugoslavia is situated. The plateau at the foot of the mountains, especially in the basins and along the rivers which cut its surface, has fertile soils and good farmland, producing wheat, maize and potatoes. Fodder crops are grown for cattle and pigs, and there is some transhumance to the mountain pastures in the Julian Alps. Vineyards and fruit orchards are found on all the lower slopes.

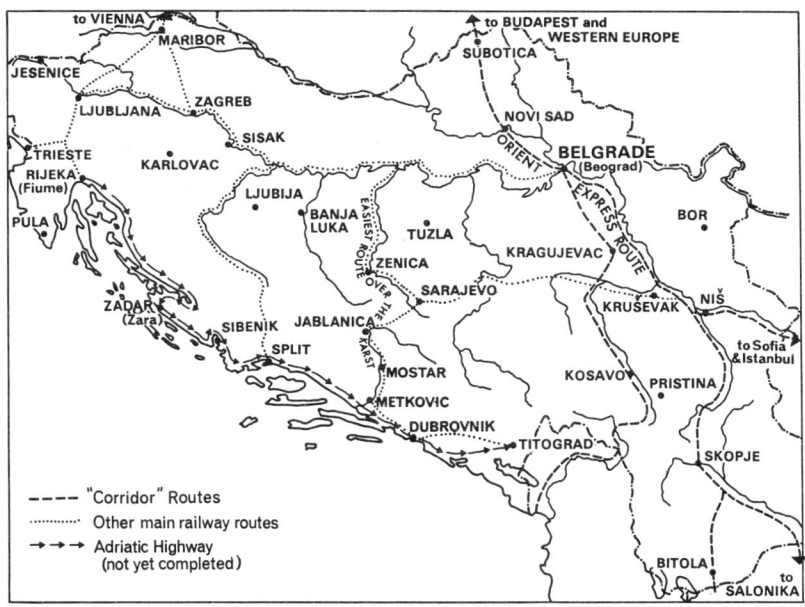

FIG. 68.—Yugoslavia: chief towns, and main railway routes through the mountains. Correlate this map with Figs. 66 and 67.

There are deposits of lead, zinc and mercury in the mountains, lignite in the plateau basins, petroleum and natural gas in the Mura valley. Along with the forest products and the hydro-electricity, they have made Slovenia (as this Alpine zone is called) an important industrial region, with a population density nearly as great as that of Serbia. Its towns have benefited, too, by the fact that the plateau is not difficult to cross, so that roads and railways from Austria lead through it to the ports of Trieste and Rijeka (Fiume).

Slovenia was for centuries under the rule of Austria, and its towns show little of the oriental architecture seen in most other parts of Yugoslavia. The chief city is Ljubljana (182,000) in the centre of a fertile basin. It is a road and railway centre, with electrical engineering, wool textile factories, chemical and aluminium works. Maribor (89,000), in the north-east of

Slovenia at the foot of the Karawanken Alps, supplies hydro-electric power to most of the plateau and has an oil refinery and light engineering works. Jesenice (18,000) until a few years ago was a tiny hamlet far up the Sava valley; newly constructed blast furnaces, steel works and rolling mills are encouraging a very rapid growth.

2. The Dinaric ranges

(a) *The plateau and mountains.* The mountains which fringe the western Karst are almost uninhabited, and the plateau itself has little use except for sheep- and goat-rearing on scattered patches of poor vegetation. Some of the polja, however, have fertile soils watered by streams flowing from the base of the slopes enclosing the depressions; and the Neretva valley is floored by alluvial deposits. The chief crops grown in the polja are wheat and maize, and there are tobacco fields, vineyards and plum orchards. Mostar (51,000) is the largest town in the Karst region. It is situated in the Neretva valley, which leads to the easiest route across the High Karst, and it serves as a market for the low-lying plains which surround the lower Neretva. In the south, lying astride the Yugoslav–Albanian frontier, is Lake Skadar, the flooded portion of a large polje. North of the lake, Titograd (35,000), the capital of Montenegro, has new light engineering works. Tobacco is an important cash crop in all the polja.

Yields of all crops are lower in the Karst region than elsewhere in Yugoslavia. Until recently there was a constant stream of emigrants to Serbia and abroad. This has been checked by the growth of industries, such as those of Titograd, and by work provided in the construction of new roads and improved railways in the region.

(b) *The mountains east of the Karst.* The mountainous region of central Yugoslavia is the most important source of timber in the country. More than half the area is forested, mainly with beech and pine. In the valleys which open to the north and in the basins in the interior, wheat, maize and potatoes are the principal crops, though the cultivation of sugar beet and hemp is increasing. Cattle are reared in the lowlands and sheep in the mountains. Bosnia-Hercegovina is the chief sheep-rearing part of Yugoslavia, with a current total of 2·3 million sheep. The manufacture of homespun and hand-loom woven woollen cloth is carried on in many of the mountain villages.

Central Yugoslavia is rich in minerals. In its middle course the river Bosna flows through a wide basin which, besides being a progressive agricultural district, contains several deposits of lignite, manganese and iron ore. Centred on Sarajevo, this basin is becoming an industrial region. Sarajevo (227,000), the capital of Bosnia-Hercegovina, has heavy engineering and a thriving chemical industry, encouraged by hydro-electricity developed at Jablanica, on the river Neretva. It is a busy commercial centre, and the third largest city in Yugoslavia. The architecture of Sarajevo and of most of the settlements in the mountains presents great contrasts to that of Slovenia, and shows the influence of centuries of Turkish domination. Flat-roofed houses of sun-dried mud bricks are common, and disused mòsques and minarets stand side by side with Greek Orthodox churches.

Iron ore occurs in the valleys of the Una and Vrbas where they begin to widen in the north, and there are deposits of zinc and antimony in the Drina valley. These mineral resources and the richer soils of the valley lowlands have given rise to a line of small towns along the northern margins of the central mountain region. Most of them are markets for the minerals and agricultural produce, but Banya Luka (53,000) has engineering works, using iron and steel from the blast furnaces and steel-rolling mills of Ljubija, which only fifteen years ago was a village.

Yugoslavia is making great efforts to improve the economy of its central mountain region, which for so long was the most backward part of the country. Mineral deposits previously neglected are being exploited, and new ones sought. Forest industries are being developed with the help of hydro-electricity. And, as already noted, numbers of power stations are being constructed along the valleys. In all this, communications are a paramount need. The railway from Belgrade to Dubrovnik, on the Adriatic, has been modernised. This line runs up the Morava valley to Stalac, turns west into the valleys of the Zap Morava (West Morava) and Drina to Sarajevo, then cuts through the Karst barrier via the upper Bosna and Neretva to Mostar and the coast. Recently it was extended to Titograd. In 1963, a new road was completed from Tuzla, in the lower Drina valley, to Mostar, passing through Sarajevo. This will be extended to join the Titograd–Dubrovnik section of the Adriatic Highway, and will give a much-needed motor transport route across the southern Karst.

(c) *Dalmatia*. The discontinuous lowlands of Dalmatia, on the western side of the High Karst and fringing the Adriatic coast, have long offered attractions for settlement. At various times they have been occupied by Greeks, Romans, Venetians and Italians. Today the great majority of the inhabitants are Yugoslav. The region has a Mediterranean climate, and the landscape is characteristic of the coastlands of that sea—terraced hillsides clothed with olive groves, vineyards and fig orchards; lime-washed cottages and hamlets clinging to the slopes; fields of wheat and maize, and irrigated groves of citrus fruits in the lowlands. Many of the inhabitants are fishermen-farmers: the Adriatic Sea provides seasonal catches of mackerel, sardines and lobsters (*see* Fig. 69).

The growth of towns is limited in Dalmatia to the occasional lowlands, so that each settlement developed as the centre of an agricultural district, isolated from its neighbours except by sea. Larger towns grew where there were good harbours backed by passages through the mountains behind, as at Rijeka, Sibenik, Split, Metkovic and Dubrovnik. In modern times the region has been helped by the discovery of large deposits of bauxite in the hinterlands of Split, Metkovic and Dubrovnik, and by hydro-electricity generated near Split, Jablanica and Rijeka. Salt, obtained by solar evaporation along the coast, has led to an electro-chemical industry at Sibenik.

The largest town in the region is Rijeka (Fiume, 106,000). Because of its easier connections across the Dinaric region with Slovenia and Austria to the north, and with the Danubian plain to the east, it is being developed as Yugoslavia's chief port, displacing Split (101,000), for centuries the centre of Dalmatian trade. Split remains the market for olive oil, grain

[Courtesy of the Yugoslav Embassy.

FIG. 69.—Yugoslavia: Hvar, a fishing port on the island of Hvar in the Adriatic Sea. The harbour is sheltered by an offshore string of limestone islands (the Infernal Isles), a characteristic feature of the Dalmatian coast.

and bauxite, and a large nylon factory has been built there. The two ports share most of Yugoslavia's shipbuilding industry. At places along the coast, near the hydro-electric plants, there are recently-built aluminium, ferro-alloy, cement and electro-chemical works.

The sheltered position of the Dalmatian lowlands, in the lee of the Dinaric Karst, has made them a holiday playground, especially in the north, where the more extensive and accessible stretches of beach are lined with small resorts. The tourist industry and the general industrial activity of Dalmatia will be further increased by the Adriatic Highway, a motor road from Rijeka to Titograd, which is nearing completion. When finished, it will link up with new motor roads to the interior. The growing towns of the Dalmatian coast, with their new industrial establishments and housing estates, have a decidedly "Western" appearance, but all contain areas of older buildings which in their Italianate and baroque architecture are quite different from the oriental appearance of settlements on the other side of the Dinaric Alps.

In the north of the Adriatic, the Istrian peninsula is a dry, limestone platform on which the chief occupation is sheep-rearing. Lignite and bauxite occur in small deposits, and are sent either to Rijeka or to Karlovac, in Croatia. Pula (38,000), at the southern tip of the peninsula, is Yugoslavia's naval port and dockyard. In the north-west is the Italian port of Trieste, which was claimed by Yugoslavia in 1945 but was made a Free Territory instead, together with a narrow coastal strip on each side of the port. Gradually the eastern coastal strip was taken over by Yugoslavia, and the *fait accompli* was confirmed in 1954. Despite vigorous objections from Yugoslavia and the Soviet Union, the port and the western coastal strip were restored at the same time to Italy. Yugoslavia continues to use the port facilities of Trieste, but to a decreasing extent as Rijeka is further developed.

3. The Morava–Vardar "corridor" lands

The south of the region, draining to the river Vardar, is the republic of Macedonia. These southern "corridor" lands are more open to Mediterranean influences than the north, and most of their precipitation falls in winter. Macedonia consists of high massifs, separated by basins and valleys. The highlands are poorly forested; in fact, less than 4% of the total area of Macedonia is forest-clad, as compared with over 40% of Bosnia-Hercegovina, and 25% of Serbia. Sheep-rearing is the chief occupation on the massifs, and there is domestic woollen industry in the mountain villages. The valleys and basins have fertile soils and an agricultural economy, but Macedonia, lacking mineral resources, remains under-developed. The lowlands, because of their approach to Mediterranean climatic conditions, grow more wheat than maize, and in the higher basins rye is cultivated. Tobacco is an important crop, and is the region's chief export. In some of the valleys, irrigation is necessary and where it has been introduced, as in the lower Vardar valley, there is production of citrus fruits, plums, cotton and rice.

An exception to the general backwardness of Macedonia is around Skopje (228,000), situated at the convergence of the Ibar and Morava–Vardar corridors. It is the largest town in southern Yugoslavia, a road and railway centre, with food, leather and wool textile industries. The other main towns in the south are Bitola (50,000) and Pristina (41,000), both collecting centres in basins.

Macedonia is a melting-pot of peoples, and is becoming more so as malarial swamps are drained, irrigation systems improved, new crops introduced and settlers invited from other parts of Yugoslavia. Most of its inhabitants are Macedonians, but in the course of history its "corridors" have been penetrated and settled by Romans, Greeks, Serbians, Vlachs, Albanians, Bulgars, and Turks. Skopje still has an important Turkish and Bulgar minority and, with its bazaars and mosques, presents a definitely .

oriental appearance. Macedonia remains an area of dispute between Yugoslavia and Bulgaria; its present allocation to Yugoslavia was mainly intended to deny to Bulgaria the use of the southern end of the very important Morava–Vardar corridor.

North of Macedonia the corridor lands fall within the republic of Serbia, which had its birth in the Ibar valley and the Kosovo basin. When the region was invaded by the Turks, the Serbs withdrew into the mountains of this central region. After the expulsion of the Turks the Serbs moved into the lower valley of the Morava, leaving their original home virtually uninhabited. Since 1912, however, it has begun to develop again. In the highlands live transhumant shepherds, and the valleys produce maize, wheat, hemp and potatoes. Industry has as yet scarcely appeared in the small market towns of the region, and the population, though increasing, remains sparse. The Ibar corridor, which traverses the mountains of western Serbia, is continued by the valley of the Drim. The lower course of this river (Alb. Drin) is in Albania, and so the corridor to the Adriatic is not much used by Yugoslavia.

The Morava, which rises near the Skopje basin, has a valley which widens towards the north, where it is known as Šumadija. Fertile soil and a humid climate support a dense agricultural population, but there are few large towns. Maize, wheat, sugar beet and hemp are the chief crops; and here are the largest mulberry groves (sericulture) and plum orchards in Yugoslavia. Plums are made into jam, dried as prunes or used for the manufacture of plum brandy (*slivovitz*), the Serbian national beverage.

The largest town in the Morava valley is Niš (81,250), at the confluence of the river with the Nisava. It is a commercial and route centre, where the Nisava valley leads from the main north–south corridor to the Bulgarian depression and Istanbul. It is a junction for railways from the north to Salonika, and eastwards to the Bosphorus. Kruševak is a small town near the confluence of the Morava and West Morava; it has lead and zinc smelters, using ores from the near-by Kapaonik mountains. Kragujevac (55,000), at the northern end of the Ibar valley, manufactures cottons and silk, and has an engineering industry.

East of the Morava, the corridor lands are little developed. South of Niš the Rhodope has very few people, and north of the town the western ranges of the Balkan mountains support sheep-rearing and a little lumbering. To the west of the Timok, which cuts through the Balkan mountains to join the Danube, there are important deposits of copper and pyrites at Bor. At the northern end of the mountains the Danube runs through a narrow gorge, the Iron Gate (Fig. 70), and its swiftly-flowing waters are a hindrance to up-river shipping. A deep channel has been blasted to improve navigation, and although the swift current remains a disadvantage, the Danube is a main artery of Yugoslavia's foreign trade to eastern Europe. A hydro-electric power station is being completed on the Iron Gate, its construction being financed jointly by Yugoslavia and Rumania. The plain of the lower Timok, isolated from the rest of Yugo-

FIG. 70.—Yugoslavia: the Iron Gate. A gorge cut by the Danube between the Transylvanian Alps and the Balkan mountains. A main road cuts across the base of the cliffs on the far side of the river.

slavia by the mountains, has little share in the general economic advance of the country, and depends on primitive agriculture and sheep rearing. Its outlet is the small river port of Kladovo.

4. *The Danubian plain*

The northern plains of Yugoslavia have the richest farms in the country, and co-operative methods are showing impressive increases in the yields of maize—the chief crop—wheat, sugar beet and potatoes. The rearing of fat cattle and pigs is an important part of the rural economy. Croatia and northern Serbia, including Vojvodina, have the highest density of population in Yugoslavia, and many parts of the purely agricultural areas have more than 200 persons per square mile. Sugar refineries, flour mills and distilleries are scattered throughout the region, and there are leather, tobacco and food-processing factories in all the large towns.

The Danubian plain is also the most industrialised part of Yugoslavia. It is the seat of the textile industry and has rapidly developing heavy engineering and chemical works. The largest industrial concentrations are around Belgrade and Zagreb, at the eastern and western ends of the plain. Belgrade (Serb. Beograd) is built on a hill site overlooking the confluence of the Danube and Sava, where the two western corridors to the south converge and enter the plain. Easy routes in every direction make the city a good commercial focus. It was originally the market for the

agricultural produce of Šumadija, and when the rich farmlands of Vojvodina were added to Serbia it became an agricultural engineering
centre. As the capital of Serbia, Belgrade was only a small town, with a
population in 1918 of 112,000. As capital of the federated Yugoslavia, it
grew rapidly to 240,000 by 1931, 470,000 by 1953 and 697,000 today.
More and more industries were attracted to it. The chief are food processing, tobacco manufacture, electrical engineering, chemical and cotton
textile industries.

At the western end of the plain is Zagreb (503,000), the capital of
Croatia and the second city of Yugoslavia. It is the textile metropolis,
manufacturing wool, cotton, silk and rayon. Zagreb has heavy engineering and machine tool works, makes electrical apparatus, paper, glass and
chinaware, and is a banking centre. In the plains of Vojvodina, north of
the Danube, the economy is based on farming produce in the Bačka,
and pasture in the Banat. Throughout the western part of the region
there are flour mills, sugar refineries and agricultural engineering works
and repair shops. The Bačka is densely peopled, but with only two large
towns, Novi Sad (102,469), at a bridge point over the Danube, and Subo-
tica (78,000) serving the north. Both are collecting centres and markets,
with light industries. The Banat has large areas of steppe, with sheep
rearing. Its market is Zrenjanin, in the middle of arable farms.

STUDY QUESTIONS

1. Write an account of the natural resources of Yugoslavia. (O. & C.)

2. Examine the economic and political consequences of the fact that the Adriatic
coast of Yugoslavia is bordered by a range of high and in parts impassable mountains. (O. & C.)

3. Make a comparative study of Belgrade and Madrid as the capital cities of their
respective countries.

4. Examine the extent to which Yugoslavia possesses resources for the development of manufacturing industries. (J.M.B.)

5. Discuss the physical character of the coastlands of Yugoslavia. (J.M.B.)

6. Divide Yugoslavia into natural regions and give an account of the division
you consider the most important in the country's economy.

Chapter XIV
ALBANIA

ALBANIA is a small republic which extends along the western littoral of the Balkan peninsula between Yugoslavia to the north and Greece to the south, and has an area of some 11,101 square miles (28,863 sq. km). Yet in spite of its small size it is still the least-known part of Europe, and many of its geographical and geological problems remain unsolved. There are several reasons for this. The wild and inaccessible character of the mountainous country to the north and east, the fierce and lawless disposition of the highland people, and the difficulties presented by their language were almost complete obstacles before the opening of the present century. From 1913, when Albania became a separate independent state, to 1945, the country passed through periods of anarchy, political chaos and warfare, during which any comprehensive survey of the natural phenomena and resources was wellnigh impossible. Since 1945, when Albania was proclaimed a Communist republic, it was first an ally of Yugoslavia, then a satellite of the Soviet Union and enclosed by the Iron Curtain, and after 1964 shifted its political and economic allegiance to Communist China. Almost completely isolated from the countries of the West since the Second World War, Albania by this latest move has reduced friendly relations with the Soviet Union to a minimum; but she continues to trade with the rest of the European Communist bloc. At the present time about 50% of Albania's import and export trade is with Communist China, 42% with European Communist countries, and only 8% with Western countries. It remains not only the least-known but also the least-developed and most backward country in Europe.

PHYSICAL ASPECTS

The surface of Albania may be divided essentially into a coastal plain backed by a mass of high, rugged mountain ranges. The highlands may be sub-divided longitudinally into two regions, an eastern section near the boundary with Yugoslavia and Greece which is almost impassable, and a western section which is penetrated by wide river valleys. It is convenient, therefore, to divide Albania physically into (1) the coastal plain, (2) the western mountains, and (3) the eastern mountains (see Fig. 71 (a)).

STRUCTURAL DIVISIONS

1. *The coastal plain*

The plain is narrow in the north and widens southwards to its termination near Vlonë (Valona). At its widest, along the valley of the river

Shkumbi, it is about 30 miles (48 km). The plain is crossed by low limestone ridges running from the western mountains to the coast, where they
form steep headlands. The surface of the plain is consequently a series of
depressions separated by spurs and traversed by roughly parallel rivers. In
the east of the plain the rivers have built alluvial fans; nearer the coast there

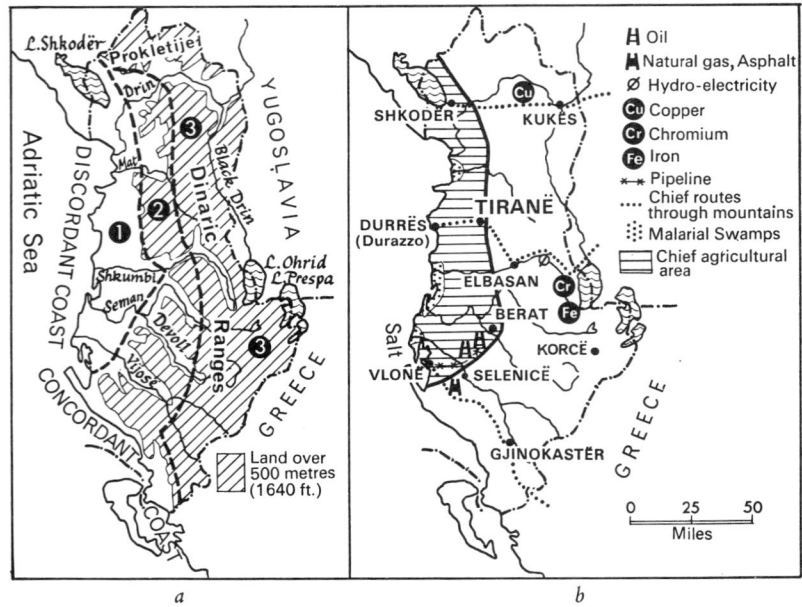

FIG. 71.—Albania: (a) physical features and divisions, (b) economic. The numbers in
   (a) refer to sections in the text. For continuations of the main routes through the
   mountains, see Fig. 68.

are swamps. The coastline from the river Drin in the north to the gulf of
Vlonë is discordant, presenting a contrast to the concordant coasts usually
found along the eastern Adriatic.

2. The western mountains

These mountains rise like a wall behind the coastal plain, but they are
deeply dissected and not so impenetrable as the ranges further east. They
are split from north to south into several blocks by the rivers Drin, Mat,
Shkumbi, Seman, Devoll and Vijosë. The alluvial valleys of the rivers
have encouraged settlement, but the intervening mountain blocks have
resulted in the isolation from each other of many of Albania's rural communities, in a compartmentalism which is undoubtedly one of the roots
of the country's backwardness. All the mountain blocks are high and inhospitable, and some of Albania's loftiest peaks are found in them; the
principal summit is Mount Tomor (7916 ft, 2413 m), which overhangs the
town of Berat. The southernmost block skirts the coast from the gulf of

Vlonë southwards, and resumes a concordant character; it reaches a height of 6986 ft (2129 m) in Mount Griba and terminates north-westwards in the lofty promontory of Cape Gjuhëzes (Glossa, Linguetta).

3. The eastern mountains

These are a continuation of the extremely complex Dinaric system of western Yugoslavia, and form part of the watershed between the Adriatic and Aegean seas. In the south of Albania they consist of four, and in one area five, parallel ranges which may rise to over 7000 ft (2130 m); Mount Jablanitza, which forms part of the boundary with Yugoslavia, is 7425 ft (2260 m) high. In the north the number of ranges is reduced to two, but they are higher and more impenetrable. The Prokletije range, the Accursed Mountains, has peaks of over 8000 ft (2440 m) and is an almost impassable barrier between Albania and the neighbouring Montenegrin districts of Yugoslavia. Between the southern ranges are longitudinal valleys, in one of which are lakes Ohrid (Okhrida) (107 sq. miles, 278 sq. km) and Prespa (Prespansço), lying astride the international boundary. There are very few routes across the eastern mountain wall; the only ones suitable for vehicular traffic are: a road from Shkoder which makes use of the White Drin valley to reach Niš and Skopje in Yugoslavia; another which traverses the Shkumbi valley and skirts Lake Ohrid, also to Skopje; and a third which climbs the Vijosë valley and leads to Yannina (Ioannina) in Greece.

CLIMATE AND VEGETATION

The climate of the coastal plain may be regarded as typically Mediterranean, but with the heavier winter rainfall associated with the eastern Adriatic littoral. Temperatures along the coast range from about 48° F (8·9° C) in January to 77° F (25·0° C) in July; inland in the river valleys winters are slightly colder and summers hotter. Rainfall averages about 60 in. a year, two-thirds falling in the months from October to March. During the spring the coast may be affected by the *bora*, a fierce, cold wind from the northern Adriatic. In the mountains the climate is greatly modified by altitude and rain-shadow effects. During the summer, temperatures during the day may be high, falling at night almost to freezing point. Winters are short but exceedingly cold; total precipitation may amount in the north to 90 in. or more, and snow may remain on the Prokletije and other mountains until August.

Most of the mountain slopes of Albania are covered by splendid forests; in fact, about half the total surface of the country is forested. The principal trees are the oak, valonia oak, beech, ash, elm, poplar and walnut, which give way in the higher regions to the pine, birch and fir. The acorns of the valonia oak are used as a tanning material. The chestnut, wild pear and wild olive are also plentiful. The limestone spurs in the coastal lowlands are covered by garrigue. In the alluvial plains there are stretches of permanent pasture and water-meadows, but an increasing acreage is being ploughed for agriculture; about 26% of the country is given over to pastoral occupations. Arable land, olive groves, vineyards and fruit orchards account for 18% of the surface; the remaining 6% is waste land and swamp, much of the latter being malarial.

PEOPLE AND HISTORY

The Albanians are apparently the most ancient race in south-eastern Europe. There is no record, even in legend, of their arrival in the Balkan peninsula. They are probably the descendants of the earliest Aryan immigrants, who were represented in historical times by the Illyrians, Macedonians and Epirots. The Illyrians, it is thought, were the progenitors of the *Ghegs*, or northern Albanians, and the Epirots of the *Tosks*, or southern Albanians. The great Greek geographer, Strabo, writing in the first century A.D., describes the Via Egnatia as the boundary between the Illyrians and Epirots. This Roman route, which joined Durrës (Dyrrhachium) and Salonika, followed much of the course of the river Shkumbi, which now separates the Ghegs from the Tosks. The name Gheg is not adopted by the Ghegs themselves, who regard it as a nickname; the name Tosk is possibly cognate with *Tuscus*, *Etruscus*, while the form *Tyrrhenus* perhaps survives in Tiranë. The Albanians call themselves Shküpetar, and their language has the same name or, more commonly, Skipetar. The language is derived from Thraco-Illyrian—the original tongue of the Balkans—and has borrowed extensively from Latin, Greek, Slav and Turkish. There was no written Albanian language until late in the nineteenth century. The Albanians call their land Shküpenia or Shküperia, the former the Gheg, the latter the Tosk form of the word.

Most of the primitive peoples of the Balkan peninsula were either hellenised or latinised, or were subsequently absorbed by Slavonic immigration, but the Albanians remained largely unaffected by foreign influences. Incursions by the Greeks, Romans, Slavs, Turks and Italians, and subsequent intermarriage with the Ghegs and Tosks, has produced a people of mixed blood; nevertheless the Albanians, preserving their original language and with customs and tribal organisations of great antiquity, are a distinct ethnic type, quite different from their neighbours, and Ghegs and Tosks are the most characteristic representatives.

The Ghegs are taller, fiercer and more lawless than the Tosks, more superstitious and backward, and until very recent years these wild mountaineers devoted themselves almost exclusively to fighting, robbery and pastoral pursuits. The Tosks are equally warlike, but their disposition has been modified by intercourse with the Greeks and Vlachs, and they are more ready to occupy themselves with commercial, industrial and agricultural activities. The natural antipathy between the two sections of the Albanian people, although less than formerly, has been an obstacle throughout history to any really satisfactory co-operation between them. It led to the *vendetta* or blood-feud, the primitive *lex talionis*, in which the duty of revenge was a sacred tradition handed down to successive generations in the family, the village and the tribe. The vendetta is now forbidden by law, but for centuries it was an established usage in cases of homicide, robbery and trespass in isolated communities or clans in the mountains. It is estimated that at one time because of vendetta only one-quarter of the population of certain mountainous districts died natural deaths.

The population of Albania is estimated (1966) to be 1,914,000, with an average density of 172 persons per square mile. There is a natural increase annually of 33 per 1000 persons, one of the biggest in Europe, so that Albania, in common with most Mediterranean countries, is facing the problem of over-population. Two-thirds of the Albanians are Muslims of an unorthodox type; they seem to have been converted to Islam during the Turkish invasions of the sixteenth and seventeenth centuries, but retained many Christian traditions and customs. About 370,000 profess the Christian Orthodox faith, especially in the south where the Tosks were more open to Greek influences. Roman Catholics number about 220,000, mainly in the north of the country; the Ghegs to the north and east of Shkodër are nearly all Roman Catholics.

The very early history of Albania is only imperfectly known, but the remains of structures of the classical period attest the influence of Roman rather than of Greek culture. The Romans ruled the region until the middle of the fourth century when it became a province of the Byzantine Empire. In A.D. 640 northern Albania was invaded by the Serbo-Croats and with some interruptions continued under Serbian rule until 1360. In 861 southern Albania was conquered by the Bulgarians, who remained in power until 1014, when the region reverted to Byzantine rule. The southern Albanians, however, helped by the Serbs from the north, maintained a constant warfare against the Byzantine emperors, and ultimately Stefan Dushan (1331–58), the greatest of the Serbian kings, included the whole of Albania in a short-lived Serbian empire. After his death the empire broke up and Albania entered a period of rule by native chieftains which continued until the advent of the Ottoman Turks. The Turks advanced into Albania in 1431 and occupied the Tosk territory of Ioannina; and in spite of valiant opposition led by the Albanian hero Skanderbeg, they were in possession of the whole country by 1502 and held most of it until they were expelled from the Balkans in 1912.

During the period of Ottoman rule the authority of the sultans was never effectively established, and some mountain fastnesses held by the Ghegs in the north were never really subjugated. The abandonment of Christianity by the majority of the people and their acceptance of Islam did not denote their submission to the Turks. In the centuries which followed the conquest of Albania there were interminable conflicts between tribesmen and Turks, and also between Christian and Mohammedan Albanians, between Ghegs and Tosks; and there was constant opposition, both passive and active, to the demands for taxes and levies made by the sultans and their representatives. In fact, during this period many of the mountain peoples, in particular the Ghegs, became almost autonomous. They would pay no taxes to the Turks; they refused to accept conscription into the Ottoman armies; and they accepted no law except their own unwritten criminal and civil *Kanun* or code. In this period, too, the vendetta became a recognised part of the social pattern and the Albanians earned a reputation for inhospitality and banditry which they have hardly lost today.

The eighteenth and nineteenth centuries, which saw the crumbling of the Ottoman Empire, were marked in Albania by increasing anarchy and lawlessness, and even after 1913, when the country was recognised as a separate political entity, it remained in a state of chaotic disunity. In 1925, however, Albania was proclaimed a republic under Zog, who later had himself elected king. He attempted to introduce economic and social reforms, but before his efforts could bear fruit, the Second World War broke out and his country was invaded and occupied by Italy. In 1945, at the end of the war, Albania became an independent state once more, but now the Communists among its people took control and named it a People's Republic, a status which it holds today.

Worn out by war and financially exhausted, the Albanians were in no position to develop their country's resources without outside help, so they turned to Yugoslavia, their Communist neighbour, in the hope of obtaining economic assistance; but when in 1948 Yugoslavia abandoned the Stalinist Communist ideology and substituted one of its own, Albania transferred its friendship and requests for help to Moscow. The Soviet Union, anxious to gain a foothold in the Mediterranean, was very willing to co-operate, and began to build naval strongpoints and bases along the Albanian coast and to assist in agricultural and industrial development. The exports of mineral oil, grain and timber which they demanded in return from Albania, however, proved to be so exorbitant as to foster intense resentment; in any case the Albanian people, especially in the mountainous districts, are unsatisfactory co-operators. They have never at any time in history been completely united; there are intense local rivalries and jealousies which in the past led to the vendetta and still cause political disruption; religious differences are a source of friction; and an adherence to ancient customs and traditions maintains a backward look and obstructs progress.

Yet a nationalistic concept seems to be slowly emerging, with a realisation by many that economic development must be accelerated if the country is to survive. When, therefore, in the early 1960s the Albanian Government decided that the Soviet Union's assistance was having only negligible results, especially in agriculture, it invited aid from Communist China. In consequence of the new alignment, the Soviet Union abandoned its building schemes in Albania and withdrew its experts and financial assistance; and the current five-year development plan (1961–65) was cut short. In the present five-year plan (1966–70) Chinese help has been substantial, but details of its results so far are only imperfectly known. We are told that a copper-smelting plant being built by the Soviet Union at Kukës was completed and opened in 1965; 25 chemical and engineering works are being constructed with Chinese aid; the area and output of land under the plough have been increased; and the number of tractors, always a useful index in emergent countries, is now over 8000, far more than when the Soviet Union was a partner. The assistance of China is undoubtedly having beneficial results in Albania. Of far greater significance to the Soviet Union and the Western world is the advent of Communist China to the sphere of European politics and to the Mediterranean, an event which is a source of anxiety and may have far-reaching and unforeseen effects.

THE ECONOMY

Over 80% of Albania's population is engaged in some form of land use, and of these the great majority are occupied with animal husbandry. Sheep (1·6 million) and goats (1·1 million) are the chief animals, and there are 400,000 cattle and 112,000 pigs, the last being kept mainly by Christian communities. Transhumance, mostly of sheep and goats, is common, especially in the mountainous areas, the animals being driven to high pastures for the summer months. Albania has also 122,000 asses and mules. Pasture land covers about 26% of the country's area. Wool, hair, skins and cheese are products of the pastoral industry and account for a small proportion of the country's exports.

The area under cultivation in Albania amounts to nearly 1 million acres, that is, about 18% of the surface; this is one-third greater than it was 25 years ago. Upwards of 360,000 people are directly dependent on the production of field and tree crops. The standard of agriculture varies enormously. In the mountain valleys there is primitive subsistence farming, and wooden ploughs and harvesting by sickle are common. In the more extensive mountain basins around Korcë, Kukës and Gjinokastër, however, and in most of the coastal plain (see Fig. 71 (b)), modern techniques are being introduced; between Durrës and Tiranë the agricultural economy is comparatively well advanced. The amount of cultivable land is being increased by ploughing meadows in the alluvial lowlands and by reclaiming coastal swamps, which has the further result of reducing the numbers of malaria-carrying mosquitoes. Nine-tenths of the arable land is now under State control in State farms, co-operatives and "local agricultural enterprises"; the remainder, mostly in the more inaccessible districts, is privately held in lots of up to 25 acres.

The chief grain crops are maize, wheat, barley and rice. With the exception of rice, which is cultivated in reclaimed swampland, the best cereal regions are in the alluvial valleys and on the slopes near the margin of the coastal plain. The output of maize is more than three times that of other cereals. Of commercial crops large quantities of sugar beet, cotton and tobacco are grown. In the foothills which border the mountains, especially near Shkodër, Tiranë, Elbasan and Berat, there are vineyards, olive and orange groves, and apricot, plum and cherry orchards. Forest industries in the mountains are growing; there is lumbering for oak, walnut and coniferous woods, and a policy of reafforestation and conservation has been adopted by the Government.

Albania has considerable mineral resources which may lead to future industrial activity, but most of them have as yet been little exploited (see Fig. 71 (b)). There is a lignite field south of Tiranë which yields about 300,000 tons annually, and two small oilfields at Qytet Stalin, near Berat, produce 500,000 tons of oil a year. The output is sent by pipeline to Vlonë, where there is a refinery. The total is more than sufficient for Albania's small requirements; most of the surplus is exported to China. There is a considerable water-power potential in the mountains, and before they left the country the Russians had completed four hydro-electricity stations, with a total production of nearly 300 million kWh annually. Two of them, near Tiranë, and on the Mat (Mati) river, were constructed to provide power to the capital; the others are at Shkopeti and Bistrice. Copper is mined (144,000 tons a year) in the Pukë district of the Drin valley and smelted in a new plant at Kukës; chrome ore (294,000 tons) is extracted near Lake Ohrid, and in the same region a large field of hematite iron ore is being exploited (260,000 tons annually). There are natural gas and asphalt deposits at Selenicë, and salt is obtained by evaporation at Vlonë. There are believed to be deposits of lead–silver and antimony in the northern mountains, but gold mines which were worked in antiquity in the Drin valley and silver mines in the Prokletije range, which were known to the Venetians in the Middle Ages, are no longer in existence.

An improvement in communications is sorely needed in Albania. There are at present only about 2000 miles (3200 km) of roads fit for motor traffic, and large sections of the mountain regions, especially in the north, are inaccessible for wheeled vehicles. Communications there are still by pack mules or donkeys. There are in total less than 100 miles (160 km) of railway, and these are in short stretches from Durrës and Vlonë to neighbouring market towns; the most extensive connects Durrës to Tiranë, a distance of less than 20 miles (32 km).

The industries of Albania are still in their infancy. They are concerned with oil refining, the extraction and marketing of mineral ores, food processing, sugar refining and the upkeep of hydro-electric plant. More recently, as already noted, light engineering and chemical works have been established in many towns, notably in Tiranë, Shkodër, Elbasan, Durrës and Vlonë. Textile factories using home supplies of wool and cotton have been built in Tiranë and Shkodër, but textile manufacture is still mainly a domestic industry carried on in homes throughout the country.

Most of the larger towns of Albania are situated near the junction of mountains and plain. The chief are Tiranë (156,950), the capital, Shkodër

(47,040), Elbasan (35,330) and Berat. Korcë (43,745), situated in a fertile basin, is the largest town in the mountain belt. Along the coast Durrës (47,870), the chief port, lies on a mediocre harbour which was greatly improved, first by the Italians and later by the Russians. The only other good port, Vlonë (46,905), is the chief outlet for the oil and minerals of southern Albania.

STUDY QUESTIONS

1. Make a geographical study of the Adriatic coastlands of the Balkan peninsula. (J.M.B.)

2. Discuss the influence of the position and relief of Albania on the life and trade of its inhabitants.

3. Write a concise account of the geography of Albania.

Chapter XV

GREECE

PHYSICAL ASPECTS

GREECE has been described variously as "a bare country with all its ribs showing" and "the skeleton of a worn-out country from which all the good land has been stripped." The southern part, with its long finger-like projections southwards into the Mediterranean Sea and its thousands of islands, certainly gives this impression, but it must be remembered that there is also a continental portion of Greece which is quite different from the rest of the country.

STRUCTURAL DIVISIONS

The heart of Greece lies in the southern part of the Balkan peninsula and is a peninsula itself. It is almost divided in two by the Gulf of Corinth, so that the southern third of the area forms a separate peninsula, the Pelo-ponnesus or Morea, usually treated as a distinct region; the northern two-thirds of the peninsula is called peninsular Greece. Northwards, the country widens to the hills and plains of Macedonia and Thrace, which extend eastwards to the border of European Turkey. Around the coasts are several archipelagoes containing islands which range in size from mere dots to hundreds of square miles. Greece can thus be divided into: (1) peninsular Greece, (2) Peloponnesus, (3) Macedonia and Thrace, and (4) insular Greece (see Fig. 72).

1. Peninsular Greece

The middle of peninsular Greece is a mass of high mountain ranges, to the east and west of which the country, though still mountainous, is more open. It is convenient, therefore, to divide the region into (a) western, (b) central, and (c) eastern peninsular Greece.

(a) *Western peninsular Greece.* This is the region generally known as Epirus (Ipiros). It consists of a number of folded ranges running parallel to the coast and rarely rising to more than 4500 ft (1370 m), the highest point being Psili Korifí (5187 ft, 1581 m). There is less limestone and more sandstone than in the central peninsular ranges, and in the valleys and small plains the soil is productive. The most extensive plain is that of Árta, around the shallow Gulf of Amvrakia. Elsewhere the west coast has steep, rocky shores, with few openings (see Fig. 73). The Ionian islands, of which the largest are Corfu (Kérkira), Levkás, Cephalonia (Kefallinía) and Zante (Zákinthos), form a festoon archipelago; they are the upstand-ing portions of a foundered mountain range. The Ionian islands are usual-ly included with western peninsular Greece rather than with insular

Greece, since they are more closely associated with the economy of the mainland than are the archipelagoes of the Aegean Sea.

(b) *Central peninsular Greece.* The centre of peninsular Greece is occupied by a series of folded mountain ranges, which are a continuation of the Dinaric Alps of Albania and Yugoslavia. In the north, near those countries, the ranges are broken into high, rugged blocks, separated by depressions containing lakes. The highest of the blocks are Smólikas (8636 ft, 2633 m), and Timfi Ovos (8140 ft, 2480 m), the largest lake is Prespa

FIG. 72.—Greece: physical features and divisions. The numbers refer to sections in the text.

(Prespansço) (104 sq. miles, 270 sq. km). Most of the lake lies within the Yugoslav and Albanian frontiers. Southwards the Pindus mountains are a high and more continuous range, in which several peaks are more than 7000 ft (2130 m), above sea-level. The highest are Tzoumérka (7851 ft, 2429 m), Timfristós (7609 ft, 2319 m) and Peristéri (7530 ft, 2295 m). The Pindus form a difficult barrier between the east and west of peninsular

[*Courtesy of Spyros Meletzis, Athens.*

FIG. 73.—Greece: Parga on the west coast, south of Plataria. The village in a
small lowland, the monastery on the hilltop and the bare limestone islets are
typical. This is karst limestone.

Greece; there is no railway across them and only two good roads, one of
which rises at the Métsovon Pass to 5087 ft (1551 m).

At the southern end of the Pindus, east–west ranges cut across the main
mountain mass. In one of them, Mount Parnassus rises to 8064 ft (2458 m).
Along their southern flanks, bordering the Gulf of Corinth, are the small
plains of Agrínion and Phokís. All the central mountains are composed
mainly of limestones, which are often karst, barren and reminiscent of the
Karst of Yugoslavia.

(c) *Eastern peninsular Greece.* East of the central mountains a number of
ranges run towards the Aegean Sea, and between them are alluvial lowlands. There are some high peaks in the ranges but, on the whole,
eastern Greece is lower than the remainder of the peninsula; the lowlands
are more extensive and the coast more broken, with many good harbours.
The chief lowlands are the plains of Thessaly, Boeotia and Attica. The
Plain of Thessaly is mainly the basin of the river Piniós. It is overlooked
by Mounts Olympus (9571 ft, 2917 m), Ossa (6409 ft, 1953 m) and Pelion
(Pilíon, 5308 ft, 1618 m), all famous in Greek history and mythology. The
Plain of Boeotia at one time contained Lake Copais (Kopaís), but this has
now been drained and its bed is rich farmland. The Plain of Attica lies
behind Athens. Boeotia and Attica, with the citadels of Thebes (Thívai)

and Athens, were the heart of Ancient Greece. Another productive low-land in the east is the lower valley of the river Sperkhiós, known as the Plain of Phthiótis (Fthíótis). Off the coast is the long, narrow island of Euboea (Évvoia), separated from the mainland by a shallow strait; it is usually included for study purposes with the mainland, of which it is structurally a part.

2. *The Peloponnesus*

Southern Greece is the peninsula of Peloponnesus or Morea, joined to peninsular Greece by the Isthmus of Corinth. Peloponnesus is entirely mountainous: folded ranges follow the north–south Dinaric trend and splay out at their extremities into four "fiigers," with intervening deep gulfs. The mountains rise in places to over 6000 ft (1830 m), *e.g.* Sikionía (7789 ft, 2374 m), Párnon (6855 ft, 2087 m) and Ponakhaïkón (6322 ft, 1927 m). Within the mountains are several enclosed basins of good soil, such as those around Trípolis and Megalópolis. Around the coasts, and more especially at the heads of the southern gulfs, are small alluvial plains isolated from each other by high mountain ridges. The gulf plains are Argos, Sparta (Spárti) and Messene (Messíni); on the west coast, in the lower basin of the river Ládhon, is the Plain of Olympia. On these plains grew the original city states of Ancient Greece. On the north-east and north-west corners of Peloponnesus are narrow coastal plains around Corinth and Patras (Pátrai).

3. *Macedonia and Thrace*

North of peninsular Greece is western Macedonia, known also as High Macedonia to distinguish it from eastern Macedonia, which is mostly lowland. High Macedonia lies among mountain blocks which seem to run from the Pindus to the Aegean shores but are in fact similar to the faulted and dislocated Pelagonian massifs of Yugoslav Macedonia. In Greek Macedonia they are rarely more than 4000 ft (1220 m) high. Within the mountains are two large basins, a northern one which contains Lake Vegorrítis (Ostrovo) and extends southwards to Ptolemaïs, and one in the south around the upper Aliákmon river.

The north-east of Greece is a region of coastal plains and low hills, bordering the northern Aegean Sea and backed by the foothills of the Rhodope massif. It is divided by the river Néstos (Mesta) into eastern Macedonia to the west and Thrace to the east. Here are the most extensive lowlands in Greece. They are widest in the west in the Plain of Thes-saloníki (Salonica), across which flows the lower river Vardar. The western end of the plain, Campania, was once occupied by Lake Yiannitsá but is now completely drained.

East of the Plain of Thessaloníki is the limestone plateau of Chalcidice (Khalkidhikí), a peninsula which terminates in three cliff-girt prongs. Beyond are the Plain of Seres in the lower Struma valley, and the Plain of Philippi west of the Néstos. All these plains have alluvial soils and are

[*Courtesy of the Greek Embassy.*

FIG. 74.—Greece: the harbour of Firra on the island of Thira in the Cyclades. Many of the islands, which are hard crystalline rock, rise to over 2500 ft. Steep, winding, stepped mule-tracks climb from the harbour to the villages above. The Cyclades have little economic importance except for the emery and wine of Náxos, and a small output of iron ore in Sériphos and four other islands.

the most fertile in Greece. Lake Tachinos, which lay in the Struma valley, has now been drained like Yiannitsá and is rich farmland. Farther east, the plains of Thrace are narrower and more hilly than those of Macedonia, and they rise gradually to the foothills of the crystalline Rhodope. Only a tiny portion of this massif is in Greece, but it contains Mount Koulá (7143 ft, 2177 m), one of the highest points in the Rhodope.

No part of the mainland of Greece is more than 60 miles (96 km) from the sea, and so there are no long rivers with their courses entirely Greek. In the north, only the lowest parts of the courses of the Vardar (Axios), Struma, Néstos, and Maritsa (Évros) are in Greece. The Maritsa forms part of the boundary between Greece and Turkey. The longest entirely Greek river is the Aliákmon in High Macedonia. None of the rivers is navigable, and their volume varies so much that opportunities for hydro-power development are limited. They may, however, be useful for irrigation.

4. Insular Greece

The islands which are considered under this heading lie on the eastern side of Greece, in what is usually called the Aegean Sea but which in the south is known also as the Mirtoan Sea and the Sea of Crete. The islands may be grouped as follows:

(a) A northern group includes the Northern Sporadhes (Voríai Spo-rádhes), an archipelago of small islands off the coast of peninsular Greece, and the larger islands of Thásos, Samothrace (Samothráki) and Lemnos (Límnos). Thásos is an outlier of the Rhodope massif; Samothrace and Lemnos are composed mainly of limestone.

(b) In the south of the Aegean are the Cyclades (Kikládhes), fragments of a fractured crustal block which was topped by limestone and pierced by volcanoes, all of which are now extinct. Signs of former volcanic activity are to be seen in the crater harbour of Mílos and the lava soils of Thíra.

(c) In the east, and structurally a part of Asia Minor, are the islands of Lesbos (Lésvos), Chios (Khíos), Sámos and the Dodecanese (Southern Sporádhes) archipelago, which includes the larger islands of Rhodes (Ródhos) and Kárpathos.

(d) Crete, over 150 miles (240 km) long, 8–20 miles (13–32 km) wide and with an area of 3000 square miles (7800 sq. km), is the largest island in the Aegean. It appears to be a continuation of the Dinarides of the Pelo-ponnesus, but with an east–west trend. It has a mountainous backbone which rises to 8193 ft (2497 m) in Mount Idhi, 7904 ft (2410 m) in the Iévka Ori and 7166 ft (2184 m) in Áyios Nikólaus. The range, which is composed of limestone, is broken into three distinct blocks. On the south of the island the mountains are so close to the sea that there is little room for lowland, and most of the coast has steep, bare cliffs. On the north there are small coastal plains in the centre and west.

CLIMATE

Although the situation of Greece is truly Mediterranean, its climate varies from the Mediterranean norm. Three distinct climatic types may be distinguished, and they can be further divided into local sub-types.

(i) The true Mediterranean climate is found in the coastal regions of the peninsula and in the islands. Here the summers are hot and dry; the winters mild, wet and windy. Temperatures range from 45° F (7·2° C) in January to 80° F (26·7° C) in July. Rainfall, however, is much greater on the west coast than on the more sheltered east. Corfu, for instance, has an annual precipitation of 50·4 in., 39·7 in. of which falls in the six winter months; whereas Athens has an annual rainfall of only 15·4 in., 12 in. of it in winter.

(ii) Away from the coast, the mountainous peninsula has a climate which is basically Mediterranean but is much affected by altitude. Summer temperatures, except in valleys, rarely rise above 60° F (15·6° C) and the winters may be severe, with snow lying for several months. Precipitation may amount to 70 or 80 in. annually and, although most comes in winter, there is sufficient in summer to keep a constant flow in the rivers.

(iii) The third climatic type is found in Macedonia and Thrace, where there is a definite tendency to continental conditions in the seasonal distribution of rainfall and in the occurrence of winter frosts on the plains. Salonica, for example, ranges from an average of 40·6° F (4·7° C) in January to 78·6° F (25·8° C) in July; its annual precipitation amounts to 21·5 in., which falls at all seasons but with maxima in May and November.

Temperature on all the Aegean coasts may rise on occasions to over 100° F (37·8° C) in the shade, setting up strong sea breezes which temper the sultriness. Noteworthy, too, are the winds which blow in winter from the north-west. They are pulled from the high-pressure regions of eastern Europe to the lower-pressure areas in the Mediterranean and affect the northern Aegean Sea and its adjacent lands. They are invigorating winds, but they may bring spells of cold weather with frost, and as they advance to the south may reach gale force.

NATURAL VEGETATION

Of the total area of Greece, 17% consists of bare mountains or uncultivated marshland, 15% of forest, 39% of pasture and 27% of cultivated land. The remaining 2% includes lakes, towns and roads.

The forests, which occur mainly in the Pindus mountains and the Arcadian Highlands (in Peloponnesus), are of pines and oaks at higher levels and of wild olives on the lower slopes. Olives are not found where frosts are at all frequent. Much of the forest was cut down when the country was ruled by Turkey. The result was soil erosion and the formation of coastal swamps, which became malarial. At least a quarter of the remaining forest was destroyed during the Second World War. Since 1945, serious efforts have been made to re-forest the country; but, since rural Greece depends to a large extent on firewood as fuel, the authorities in some parts are fighting a losing battle. Much of the deforested areas are covered with maquis or garrigue, on which goats find a meagre sustenance; and a large proportion of the pastoral lands consists of Mediterranean shrubs and patchy grasses which are green only in winter.

The beauty of the Greek landscape lies more in the craggy, limestone heights, often brilliantly white, which rise along the Aegean Sea and in the islands from an azure blue sea, than from the vegetation which may clothe them.

HUMAN GEOGRAPHY

HISTORICAL OUTLINE

The Homeric age may be regarded as the starting point of Greek history. There were earlier civilisations in the region—the Minoan in Crete and the Mycenaean in the Peloponnesus—but not much is known about them and they seem to have come to a sudden end. How much the civilisation of the ancient Greeks owes to Crete and Mycenae, and who were the indigenous inhabitants of the country, are still open questions.

Ancient Greece as it was known to Homer some 3000 years ago lay south of a line drawn roughly from the mouth of the river Piniós to the Gulf of Amvrakía (Árta). From the shores of this small and difficult mountain country spread a civilisation that has had a lasting influence on the whole world. Around its southern peninsulas grew city states, each on a coastal plain enclosed by mountains. Their inhabitants, although essentially agriculturists, developed also a love of city life and showed it by erecting magnificent buildings and temples, and by depicting it in literature and philosophic discussions. Ancient Greece was swallowed by the Roman Empire, but not before it had spread its civilisation to all parts of the Mediterranean. Even in those far-off times, Greece was sadly over-peopled and colonies were founded in Asia Minor, Sicily, Italy, Libya, southern France and Iberia, each based on the city state pattern. Greek influences penetrated Rome, which became "hellenised" (Hellas, " Eλλας, is the name of the country in Greek, and the people are Hellenes). As the bounds of the Roman Empire were extended, Greek-style architecture, temples and sports arenas were imposed on the conquered territories and the Greek language, rather than Latin, was the usual means of communication in the eastern Mediterranean.

The glories of classical Greece were eclipsed on the fall of the Roman Empire. The history of the country for several centuries is more a record of barbarian invasions, occasional plagues (chiefly malaria) and frequent earthquakes, all of which helped to undermine the prosperity of the late Roman Empire. Sporadic raids by Vandal and Ostrogoth pirates in the fifth century had little lasting effect, but in the sixth century Slavonic tribes (Wends, Slovenes) invaded from the north and occupied the mountainous inland; after 1084 nomad Vlachs took possession of Thessaly. The dissolution in 1204 of the Byzantine empire—of which Greece formed part—brought in its train a series of invasions by Frankish barons and Venetian and Catalan merchant adventurers, eager for new territory. For over two centuries Greece consisted of a number of small states, many of them governed by "despots" (rulers with absolute power). From the beginning of the fourteenth century the mutual quarrels of these petty princes led to conquest by the Turks. Some of the despots had employed Turkish pirates as auxiliaries, and these, augmented by Ottoman Turkish forces, took over the lands they conquered and then turned on their employers. By 1460 the Turks had complete control of the country, having conquered it piecemeal, and they remained in power until the nineteenth century. Hellas sank into the poverty and wretchedness which have lasted to the present time.

The people of Ancient and medieval Greece generally lived near the coasts, and much of their prosperity depended on the sea. With the advent of the Turkish invaders, they were driven inland, to meet with opposition from the mountain dwellers. The lowlands they vacated became malarial. Decimated by wars, weakend by disease and malnutrition, and living in a mountain environment where hardship was a constant companion, the Greeks nevertheless looked to a return of the days of ancient glory, and after centuries of oppression they were among the first to welcome the liberal ideas which developed in Europe during the eighteenth and nineteenth centuries.

In the years 1821–29 they rose against the Turks, and in 1830 the Greeks were the first Balkan people to become independent of the Sultanate. This was the rebellion in which Lord Byron, the English poet, fought for Greek liberation; it resulted in the Kingdom of the Hellenes. It was the beginning of modern Greece, but the country was small in area, being confined to the region south of the river Sperkhiós.

With the gradual expulsion of the Turks from the Balkans, the little kingdom acquired more territory. The Ionian islands became Greek in 1863 and Thessaly in 1881; in 1913, with the final downfall of the Turks, Epirus, Macedonia, western Thrace, Crete and most of the larger Aegean islands were added. In 1918, eastern Thrace was occupied and in 1947 Greek ownership of Kárpathos, Rhodes and the Dodecanese islands was confirmed.

Greece attempted in 1920 to occupy all the eastern shores of the Aegean so as to make it an entirely Hellenic sea. Their reasons were that over a million Greeks lived in the coastlands of Asia Minor and that Smyrna (now called İzmír) was overwhelmingly Greek in population. The Turks, however, had recovered from their defeat in the First World War and, inspired by Kemal Ataturk, they drove the Greeks from the mainland of Asia Minor. To obviate further incursion by either country into the other's territory, Greece and Turkey agreed, by the Treaty of Lausanne in 1924, to the present boundaries and arranged for an exchange of peoples. Upwards of 1,300,000 Greeks were expatriated from Asia Minor; about half that number of Turks living in Greece, mainly in eastern Thrace, were moved to Turkey. The huge incursion of Greeks, especially into Macedonia and Thrace, upset the economy of the country and caused much poverty and suffering. But it had the effect of making the population of Greece more homogeneous than it had been for centuries and of introducing much-needed new blood. One less desirable result was that many of the immigrants who could not find land to settle on moved into the cities, adding to already overcrowded slums.

During the Second World War, Greece was torn asunder once again, first by the Italians and later by the Germans, yet despite the ravages of war, famine and disease, the country has made remarkable progress since 1945. It is still very poor, and living conditions in the mountains near the Yugoslav border are so miserable that many of the inhabitants are attracted to Communism as a cure for their troubles. In the cities, too, in the slums which grew inevitably as a result of overcrowing and unemployment, Communism has gained a foothold.

Since 1960, relations between Greece and Turkey have become strained once more, largely because of conditions in Cyprus (see Chapter XXIII). Most of the inhabitants of this island, which is independent, are Greek Cypriots. The minority are Turkish Cypriots. Many Greek Cypriots desire *Enosis*, that is, complete union with Greece, and all of them demand a larger share in the government of their island than the Turkish Cypriots are willing to admit. The two people's mutual distrust led to a sporadic and bitter civil war, and to attempts first by Great Britain and later by the United Nations to restore peace and tranquillity. The quarrel was taken up by Greece and Turkey; Turkey is alleged to have introduced economic sanctions against Greece. Among them was a new expulsion of Greeks who still lived in European Turkey. In 1964, 2346 Greeks were expelled across the river Évros (Maritsa), whereas Greece claims that no action has been taken against Turkish nationals living in Greek territory. The position of Cyprus in the economy of Greece, and the future relations of Greece and Turkey, remain to be settled, but for the time being there is an uneasy peace.

POPULATION

The population of Greece is 8,388,500, with an average density of 163 persons a square mile. As four-fifths of the surface of the country is mountainous and can support only a very sparse population, densities in most of the lowlands are high—too high, indeed, for their food-producing capacity.

The greatest numbers of people live in the plains of Attica and Boeotia (see Fig. 75), with the largest concentration around Athens–Piraeus. Here the density rises to nearly 450 persons a square mile. It is the most industrialised part of the country. In the remainder of Greece only the plains of Thessaloníki and the island of Corfu have more than 100 persons per square mile, and many of these are gathered in the towns of Thessaloníki (Salonica) and Kérkira. A map showing distribution of population in Greece is often misleading, for in many of the lowlands there are pockets of dense population surrounded by poorly peopled farming areas. The Pindus mountains, the limestone prongs of Chalcidice, and the high blocks near the Albanian border have very few inhabitants. Some of the mountainous regions of western and eastern peninsular Greece, south-eastern Peneloponnesus, and eastern Crete are not much better.

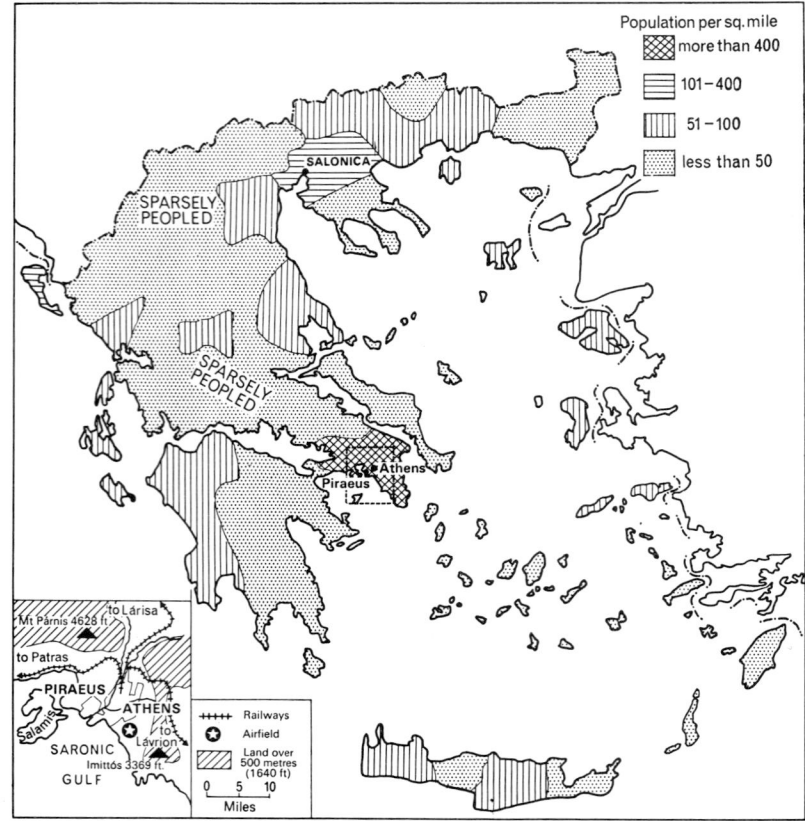

FIG. 75.—Greece: population. The rural and semi-urban population (living in com-
munes of less than 10,000 people) is 4,747,000 (1961 census), 56% of the total.
The metropolitan area of Athens, which includes a number of boroughs under
their own mayors, has a population of 1,900,000 (*see* inset map), nearly one-fifth
of the country's total.

THE ECONOMY

GENERAL CHARACTERISTICS

Greece is an agricultural country. Just under half the working population is engaged on the land and responsible for the chief exports (currants,
olives, olive oil, tobacco, grapes, citrus fruits, cotton) of the country.
Of these, tobacco is the most important. Greece is a country of small
farms. Over 90% are less than 10 acres in size, and their owners cannot
afford modern machinery or fertilisers, so that yields are low. The
Government is encouraging co-operation, with good results on the larger
plains, but many of the farms in the interior are too tiny and too scattered
among the mountains to benefit from agrarian reforms. The rural
population is increasing rapidly; although the pressure is relieved some-

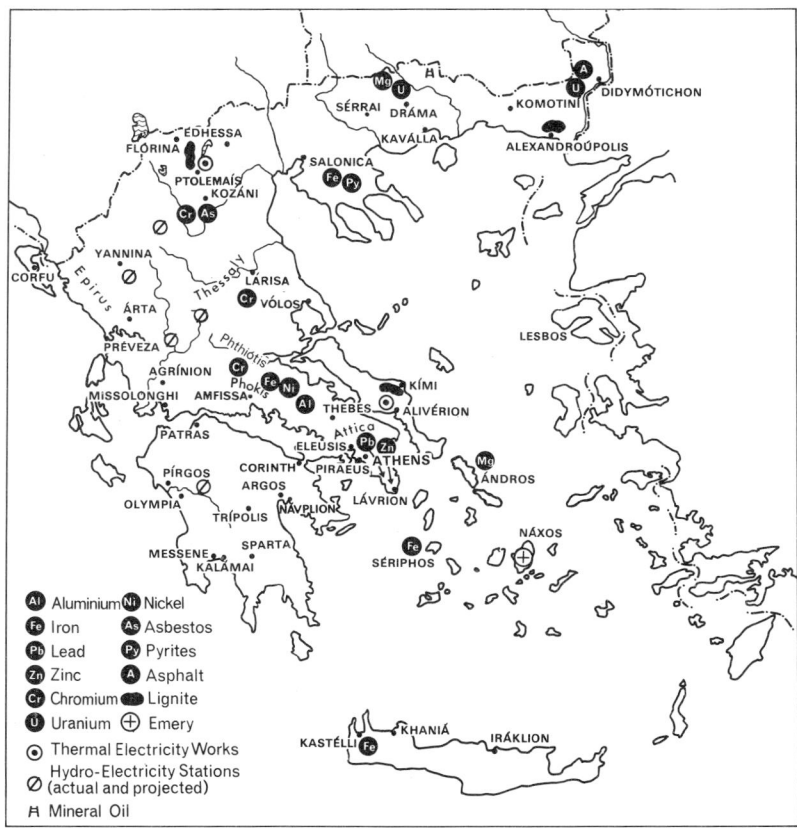

Fig. 76.—Greece: chief towns and minerals. Greece's mineral resources are limited but varied. Output (in thousand metric tons) of main ores amounts annually to: lignite, 2550; bauxite (aluminium), 884; iron, 297; pyrites, 164; manganese, 126. Mineral oil has been discovered north-east of Dráma.

what by emigration, the small farms are constantly adding to the over-population of the countryside. There is no easy solution to this problem, but it is obvious that if Greece is to achieve a more balanced economy than it has at present, there must be a great development of industry to attract the surplus workers from the land.

The Government is conscious of this problem but is handicapped by lack of capital and natural resources. The extensive highlands have poorly distributed and inadequate possibilities for hydro-electric power develop-ments; soil erosion is serious, in spite of the great efforts made to combat it; minerals are present in large variety but rarely in sufficient quantity for successful exploitation; and communications over large areas, especially of central peninsular Greece, are almost non-existent. Some so-called main roads are little more than rough, boulder-strewn tracks. Great numbers of the inhabitants are illiterate, and one of the major elements in the Government's social policy is an educational programme aimed at improving the cultural standards of the people and raising the quality of the labour force.

Industrial development is slow, but it is proceeding along well-planned lines. Existing food processing, textile, chemical and light engineering industries are being extended and modernised, notably in the regions of densest population, and new industrial areas are growing in western Macedonia and Euboea. The export of mineral ores has fallen, since they are used more and more at home. In agriculture, the policy is to reduce the cultivation of wheat in favour of cotton, animal feeding stuffs, fruit, vegetables, meat and dairy produce. Extensive investment is under way in irrigation and land reclamation projects. The tourist industry is under review, and new hotels and better facilities are being provided. The merchant fleet, especially passenger liners, has been increased enormously. In the period 1950–63 the average annual rate of growth of the gross national product, that is, of all branches of Greek economy, was 6·4%, one of the highest in the world. In 1964, industrial production alone increased by over 12%. Official figures show also that today Greece ranks fifth as a world passenger shipping owner, after Great Britain, Italy, France and the U.S.A.

These great efforts to bring Greece's economy more in line with that of Western countries have attracted enormous amounts of capital and material assistance from abroad, in particular from the U.S.A. But the motives of the Western powers are not entirely altruistic. Greece forms a natural barrier or buffer between the Western world and the Soviet Communist bloc. The Western countries hope that, by building up the Greek economy and helping the country to develop its resources, Communist influence and infiltration will be minimised. So far their efforts have been effective, and official Greek political sympathies lie with the West.

1. Peninsular Greece

(a) *Western peninsular Greece.* In general, Epirus is a poor, highland region. Agriculture occupies 82% of its population, of whom the vast majority live in the coastal plains of Árta and Yannina (Ioánnina). The chief crops in the lowlands and valleys are maize, barley, rye, tobacco and a little wheat. Walnuts, chestnuts and figs are grown everywhere in Epirus, and the Plain of Árta has citrus fruits and olives. There is as yet no industrial development. The largest towns, Yannina (35,000), Árta (16,900) and Préveza (11,200) are little more than straggling villages. The Loúros hydro-electricity station, which generates 10 million kWh annually, may lead to the growth of industry in Yannina.

Off the coast are the Ionian islands of which the chief are Corfu (Kérkira), Sta Maura (Levkás), Cephalonia (Kefallinía) and Zante (Zákinthos). The largest and most important island is Corfu, which has fertile soils and one of the densest populations of all the Greek islands. Two-thirds of its area is cultivated for vines, olives, citrus fruits, vegetables and maize. Similar crops are found in the other islands of the group. The Ionian islands are noted for their olive oil, reputed to be the best in Greece; and grapes, as well as being used for wine, are dried as raisins. Corfu (27,000) is the chief port and the centre of a growing tourist trade.

(b) *Central peninsular Greece.* The Pindus and other mountains in the centre of peninsular Greece are well wooded, but have only a very sparse population and no towns. Some lumbering is carried on, and the making of charcoal and gathering of acorns have local importance. The chief occupation is sheep-rearing, especially in the north, where Vlach shepherds live almost isolated from the rest of Greece. At the southern end of the central region, lying along the coast of the Gulf of Corinth, are the small plains of Agrínion and Phokís, which grow good crops of wheat, maize and tobacco. Both plains have extensive vineyards, and Phokís is noted for olives and olive oil.

(c) *Eastern peninsular Greece.* The eastern side of the Greek peninsula contains a large proportion of the richest agricultural land and almost all the industry of Greece. From the north to south there is a succession of coastal plains, some only very small. The largest are the Plain of Thessaly, which is broken by hills into the basins of Tríkkala, Kardhítsa and Lárisa; the Plain of Phthiótis, which is really the river Sperkhiós valley; and the Plains of Boeotia and Attica. All the plains grow wheat, maize, tobacco, vines and olives. The Plain of Thessaly has mulberry groves and cotton fields, and the latter cover an increasing area in Boeotia. Sericulture in Thessaly gives promise of a future silk industry, but at present most of the crop is exported. In Thessaly, too, cattle-rearing and cheese-making are prominent. The Plain of Attica has large market gardens and fruit orchards, to supply the demands of Athens.

In the east of the peninsula there is a varied, though as yet small, mineral production. Large deposits of lignite occur on the island of Euboea, around Kími and Alivérion. In the latter town is the largest thermo-electric power plant in Greece, supplying half the current used in Athens–Piraeus. Lignite occurs also outside Athens. Iron ore and nickel are mined in Phthiótis, and lead and zinc at Lávrion, in Attica. Chromium occurs in Phthiótis and Thessaly, and widespread deposits of bauxite have been found eastwards from Mount Parnassus.

In Thessaly, a power station on the Mégdhova, a tributary of the Achelóos, generates 250 million kWh per annum. Plans are well advanced for another station on the Achelóos itself. The impounded waters will serve irrigation systems in the Plains of Agrínion and Thessaly.

Small industries, such as cigarette making in Agrínion and Lárisa (55,400), olive oil processing at Eleusís and many other towns, and fish drying and salting at Missolonghi (Mesolóngion), are scattered through eastern Greece and along the plains north of the Gulf of Corinth; but there are only two real industrial regions: a small one in the Plain of Thessaly, and a much larger one around Athens and Piraeus. The capital of Thessaly is Lárisa, which makes textiles, farm implements and matches, but the centre of industry is Vólos (49,200), its chief port, which has growing shipbuilding and chemical industries.

Athens was sited nearly 1000 years B.C. on the slopes of a hill in Attica where it could be protected by the Acropolis, a citadel built on the summit. In the course of time Athens spread to the surrounding plain, and was linked by roads to the port of Piraeus. Today the capital and port form one city, with a population of 1,852,700. Prior to 1830, when Greece became an independent kingdom, Athens was only a small town but, like Rome, when it was made capital of the country it grew at a phenomenal rate. It is in consequence a modern city and only a few fragments, such as the Acropolis, tell of its antiquity. (*See* inset, Fig. 75.)

Athens itself is concerned mainly with administration, commerce, banking and tourism. Its chief industrial area lies south-west of the city and extends to Piraeus. Here are food processing, chemical and textile manufactures, agricultural and railway engineering, and the making of electrical apparatus. Piraeus has shipbuilding and oil refining. It is the chief port of Greece, dealing with 44% of its exports and 66% of its imports.

2. *The Peloponnesus*

The name Peloponnesus means "the island of Pelops," because the ancient Greeks thought this southern peninsula was an island. The Peloponnesus, also called Morea, is joined to peninsular Greece by the narrow Isthmus of Corinth, which has been pierced by a canal. The Corinth Canal, constructed in the nineteenth century, is too narrow and shallow for modern vessels and it is planned to deepen and widen it in the near future. The Peloponnesus has played a most important role in the history of Greece, for in it grew the famous city states of Corinth, Sparta, Argos, Messene and Olympia. Set well back from the sea in fertile, sheltered lowlands, they were safe from attack by sea-rovers and were clear of the malarial swamps which fringed the river mouths. From them sailed the Greek traders and pioneers who carried the influence of Greece to all parts of the Mediterranean basin.

The mountains which cover most of the Peloponnesus run in four finger-like ranges from north to south. They enclose several plains, some in high hollows in the interior of the peninsula, others along the south coast. On the west coast, in the lower basin of the river Ládhon, is the Plain of Olympia. The highlands have forests of pine, oak, cedar and wild olive, but there has been much wasteful cutting, and large areas are covered with garrigue, on which sheep and goats are reared. The largest of the enclosed basins is around Trípolis (18,500), which lies in a kind of polje, with no outlet for surface waters. The marshes that used to cover the basin have been drained; wheat and maize are grown on its floor, vines and fruit on the surrounding slopes. The absence of olive groves denotes a variation from the typical Mediterranean climate.

As in peninsular Greece, the chief products of the lowlands of Peloponnesus are wheat, maize, rice, barley, grapes and olives. The coastal plains of Argos and Messene are noted for citrus fruits, figs and vegetables, while cotton and tobacco are of increasing importance. In recent years, large irrigation and drainage schemes in all the plains have increased the cultivable area, almost eliminating malaria; and the hydro-electric power station on the river Ládhon, besides providing current for the growing industries of Patras and Pírgos, serves as flood control for the Olympian plain, where an extensive coastal marsh has been reclaimed and then irrigated.

Deposits of lignite have been found in the plains of Patras, Olympia and Messene. South-west of Corinth, iron ore has been discovered, and iron pyrites south of the city, but there has been little exploitation as yet. Red and yellow marble is quarried in the easternmost mountain ridge.

The outstanding product of the Peloponnesus is currants, the dried fruit of vines which produce small, black grapes. The vineyards cover the narrow plain of Patras and all the surrounding slopes. The word "currant" derives from "Corinth," which was once the chief exporter but has been superseded by Patras. Currants are still known in France as *raisins de Corinthe, i.e.* dried grapes from Corinth. Today Corinth is a decayed port with 15,900 inhabitants, and Patras (95,400) has become not only the chief port of the Peloponnesus but the third largest in Greece. Its industries include the making of machinery, cotton goods, paper and wine.

Other towns in the Peloponnesus are Kalámai (38,200), the outlet of the Messene plain, with machinery and soap works, olive oil presses, and cigarette and tile manufacturing; Pírgos (20,500), in Olympia, with flour mills, soap and chemical works; and Argos and Návplion, little more than villages, with flour milling and fruit and vegetable canning.

3. Macedonia and Thrace

These are the newest additions to Greece, having been acquired in 1913 and 1919 respectively. Before then they were most backward in their economies. Only since 1922, when the Greeks expelled from Turkey were settled in the region in exchange for repatriated Turks, has there been any considerable industrial and agricultural advance. Thrace is still completely agricultural, except for a small metallurgical industry which has developed near Didymótichon (Dimotika) as a result of asphalt deposits and a few veins of uranium and thorium. Macedonia, with better soils and resources, has become one of the most prosperous parts of Greece.

Western (or High) Macedonia lies among mountain ranges running from the Pindus towards the Aegean Sea. Within the mountains are two large basins, around the upper Aliákmon river in the south, and a more northerly one which contains Lake Vegorrítis (Ostrovo) and extends southwards to Ptolemaís. Only a few years ago these basins were almost deserted, the only inhabitants a few Vlach herdsmen tending their sheep. They were then developed in much the same way as the intermontane basins of Yugoslavia, being drained and re-settled. Today they support wheat, maize, plums and vines. Kozáni (21,500) has become the market for an important wheat region and has a leather industry based on local hides. Édhessa (15,500), in the northern basin, has a flourishing textile industry.

Western Macedonia is undergoing an industrial transformation. In 1954 the construction of dams began on the Aliákmon river. When completed they will supply water to thousands of acres of new cultivable land in the Kozáni basin. The Agra hydro-electric scheme, using the waters of a tributary of the Aliákmon, is already in operation and the Ptolemaís thermo-electric power station, the most ambitious of its kind in Greece, was opened in 1959. The Ptolemaís scheme is based on deposits of lignite found within the Flórina–Ptolemaís–Kozáni triangle, estimated to total upwards of 9000 million tons. The coalfield, besides supplying fuel for the power station, will provide processed lignite for the railways, and for industrial and domestic use throughout Greece. Already there is an output of nitrogenous products, especially fertilisers, and there are plans for a major chemical industry.

In eastern Macedonia, the plains of Campania (the lower Vardar), Seres (the lower Struma) and Philippi are among the most fertile in Greece, especially since rivers have been controlled, reservoirs constructed, irrigation and drainage schemes well advanced, and delta swamps minimised. Lake Yiannitsá in the Vardar flood-plain and Lake Tachinos in the Struma valley have been completely drained, and their beds turned into rich farmland. The lowlands of eastern Macedonia have been transformed within the past twenty years and are producing ever-increasing crops of wheat, maize, rice, sesame, tobacco and cotton. In the older lowlands—that is, those already under cultivation before 1913—there are mulberry trees (for sericulture), vines and orchards, but in the reclaimed areas there is a notable absence of trees. Except in the limestone peninsula of Chalcidice, the olive is rarely found in Macedonia.

The number of areas growing cotton should be noted. Greece is the only country in Europe which can grow and export a surplus of raw cotton, and it is the policy of the Government to increase output at the expense of the ubiquitous wheat and maize. Dairy farming, too, for which the Macedonian plains are well suited, is being encouraged.

Besides the lignite in western Macedonia there are deposits of iron ore and pyrites in Chalcidice, chromite and asbestos in Kozáni and manganese and uranium in Dráma.

The plains of Thrace grow the same products as the Macedonian plains, but methods are still often primitive. The chief crop is tobacco of the "oriental" variety, of which Thrace has almost a monopoly; there are olive groves and cotton fields near the coast. Behind Alexandroúpolis

(Dedéagach) is a small lignite deposit, and in north-west Thrace borings are being made for oil.

The chief city of Macedonia is Salonica (Thessaloníki), the second port of Greece, with a population of 251,000. Situated near the mouth of the river Vardar, it is also the outlet for southern Yugoslavia, and its hinterland extends northwards beyond Belgrade. Its function as an international port was reduced for some years following the Second World War because of political claims and counter-claims but, with the easing of tension between Greece and Yugoslavia, Salonika is recovering its former role as the chief port of the northern Aegean. It is also the most important industrial centre in Greece, after Athens–Piraeus. Its activities in food processing, cotton and silk textiles, agricultural engineering, chemicals, leather, soap and shipbuilding are likely to be increased with the development of the Ptolemaís scheme.

Dráma (32,200) and the port of Kaválla (44,500) are the chief towns of the Plain of Philippi, and are markets for the Macedonian tobacco crop. The largest towns in Thrace are Komotiní (28,350) and Alexandroúpolis (18,700), its port.

4. *Insular Greece*

Although the Greek islands are noted for their scenic beauty, they are with few exceptions backward in their economy, poorly peopled and of minor importance.

(i) The islands of the northern Aegean—Thásos, Samothrace, Lemnos and the Northern Sporádhes—are all unproductive.

(ii) The eastern group of islands includes Lesbos, Chios, Sámos and the Dodecanese. The first three are mountainous but they include stretches of fertile lowland, which produce cereals, tobacco, cotton, citrus fruits, vegetables and olives. Lesbos produces one-fifth of Greece's olive oil and Mytilene (Mitilíni) (25,750), its chief town, has oil pressing, soap and cotton thread factories.

The Dodecanese, known also as the Southern Sporádhes, were Italian possessions until 1945. Since that date, land reclamation projects on a large scale have resulted in marked agricultural progress, especially in the yield of wheat, cotton, water-melons, sesame and fruit. Sponge diving is important off the islands of Kálimnos and Sími: an average of 60 tons of sponges is gathered yearly.

(iii) Life in the high, limestone islands of the Cyclades (Kikládhes) in the south of the Aegean is difficult and backward, and many of the people emigrate. The chief occupations outside subsistence farming are the production of wine and mineral ores. Emery is mined in Náxos, iron ore in Sériphos and manganese in Andros, but the total output is small.

(iv) *Crete*. The mountainous backbone of Crete (Kríti) has been largely deforested. In the cleared areas and on the upper slopes there is much garrigue, on which sheep and goats are reared by transhumant shepherds. In the forests there is some lumbering and, as in the Peloponnesus, reafforestation schemes are helping to preserve timber resources, at the same time combating soil erosion and reducing the encroaching garrigue. Crete is often quoted as the type example of Mediterranean climate and polyculture, but the importance of its production of wheat, maize, vines, olives, tobacco and citrus fruits in the economy of Greece is easily exaggerated. Cattle are reared in the coastal lowlands, and a dairying industry, subsidised by the Government, is developing. The only mineral exploited in Crete is iron ore, which occurs at Kastélli.

Crete has a population of about half a million, mostly crowded into the plains in the centre and west of the north coast. The largest towns and ports are Iráklion (Candia) (63,500) and Khaniá (Canea) (38,500). Both have industries dependent on agricultural activities, e.g. olive oil processing, tanning, soap manufacture and wine production. Crete is the south-eastern outpost of Europe, and its strategic position in the eastern Mediterranean has given the island a stormy history. In ancient days it was the home of the little-known Minoan civilisation. Before it became part of Greece in 1913, it had been successively under Arab, Venetian and Turkish domination. In the Second World War it was invaded by Germany, which hoped to use it as a stepping-stone to the Middle East. The devastation which resulted has only recently been repaired.

STUDY QUESTIONS

1. Make a geographical comparison between the Adriatic and Aegean Seas. (O. & C.)

2. Only a small proportion of the land area of Greece is capable of cultivation. What are the main restrictions on agriculture in this region and what are the main products of the farming carried on there?   (O. & C.)

3. Divide Greece into its natural regions and give an account of *two* of them. (O. & C.)

4. Give a reasoned comparative account of economic development in Greece and Peninsular Italy.

5. Comment upon the salient differences between the human geography of Greece and Mediterranean France.

6. What are the geographical factors which have contributed to the growth of Athens and Salonica?

7. Describe, and suggest reasons for, the distribution of population in Greece.

Chapter XVI

THE MALTESE ISLANDS

The Maltese Islands are centrally situated in the Mediterranean, about 60 miles (96 km) south of Sicily and 180 miles (288 km) east of Tunisia. The group comprises Malta (95 sq. miles, 247 sq. km), Gozo (26 sq. miles, 68 sq. km), Comino (1 sq. mile, 2·6 sq. km), and two uninhabited rocky islets, Cominotto and Filfla. From the dawn of maritime trade the possession of Malta has been important to the nation strongest on the sea for the time being. The group is a member of the British Commonwealth.

PHYSICAL ASPECTS

STRUCTURE AND RELIEF

The Maltese Islands rise from a submarine shelf which extends southwards from Sicily. The surface of Malta consists mainly of flat-topped undulations, highest in the south-west of the island, where the coast in places has cliffs climbing abruptly 400 ft (120 m) from deep water. Here are the Bingemma Hills, rising to 788 ft (240 m), the highest point in the islands; they run nearly at right angles to the main axis of Malta. The west coasts of all the islands are cliff-girt and inhospitable, but the east coasts are lower and have several good harbours. Outstanding among these is the Grand Harbour of Valletta, the capital of Malta. Valletta is built on a precipitous promontory, Mount Sceberras, about 1 mile (1·6 km) long, pointing north-east. Well-sheltered creeks with deep water indent the opposite shores on both sides of the promontory, so that there are two harbours, the Grand Harbour to the south and the Marsamuscetto (or Quarantine) Harbour to the north (see inset, Fig. 77). The surface of Gozo resembles that of Malta, but the general altitude is less and there are many conical rather than flat-topped hills.

The Maltese Islands consist largely of Tertiary limestones, with somewhat variable beds of sandstone, Greensand and Blue Clay. The series may be correlated with similar formations at Tripoli in Africa, and Cagliari in Sardinia, and this, together with the numerous faults found in the islands, suggests that the group are fragments of a former extensive plateau. The geological "Great Fault" stretches from coast to coast at the foot of the Bingemma Hills, and to the north of it a system of lesser parallel faults has divided the island into blocks of uneven altitude. Occasional Pleistocene (Quaternary) deposits are of interest, for they contain fossils of hippopotamus, pygmy elephant and a gigantic dormouse.

The Blue Clay forms a stratum impervious to water and holds up the rainwater which soaks through the overlying spongy coralline limestone. Where the clay is at higher levels, as in the west of the islands, perennial springs flow from its surface and many have been collected into gravitational water supplies and carried by aqueducts to irrigation systems. The larger part of the water supply, however, is derived by pumping from strata at about sea-level. These strata are generally impregnated with salt water, which, being denser than fresh water, acts as a barrier and prevents the escape further downwards of the rainwater. Movement to the sea is retarded by the honeycomb character of the limestone and by capillary

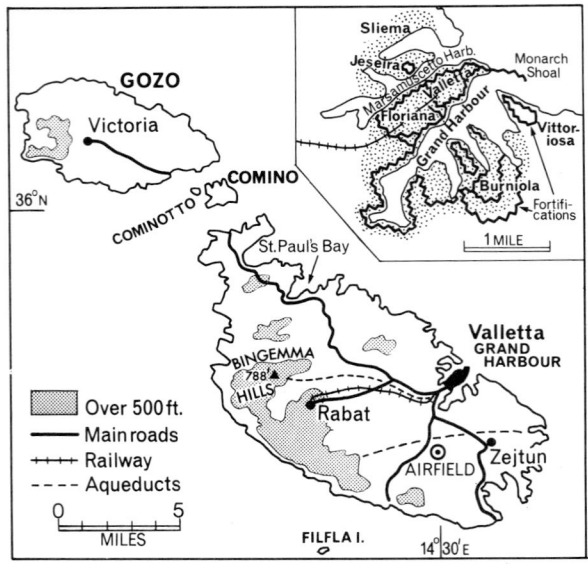

Fig. 77.—The Maltese Islands: inset, Valletta and the Grand Harbour, with the industrial region shown by a dotted area.

action, so that the soakage from rain must move horizontally, seeking outlets near sea-level. At this stage the rainwater is intercepted by wells and by tunnels hewn for miles in the water-bearing rock. Large reservoirs assist in the storage of the water after it is raised, and help to equalise its distribution. Underground water is of paramount importance to the Maltese Islands, for there are no permanent rivers or lakes on the surface.

CLIMATE AND VEGETATION

The climate of the Maltese Islands is typically Mediterranean. Temperatures range from averages of 55° F (12·8° C) in January and February to 82° F (27·8° C) in August. Maximum temperatures of over 90° F (32·2° C) are common from June to September. The mean annual rainfall is 21 in., with an almost complete drought in the summer months.

This figure, however, is somewhat misleading, for long-continued droughts, sometimes for two or three years, may reduce the actual precipitation in some years to not more than 10 in. The prevailing winds are north-easterlies, which blow on an average of 150 days a year and are mild and pleasant. The north-west *gregale* blows around the autumnal equinox and sometimes in the winter months. It is a strong, blustery wind which may reach hurricane force for periods of up to three days. It is a menace to shipping at anchor; the breakwater on the Monarch Shoal was designed to resist its ravages (*see* inset, Fig. 77). The regular tides around Malta are hardly discernible, but under the influence of low barometric pressure and the gregale, the tidal range may be increased to 2 ft.

A thin soil and the absence of surface water have resulted in a natural vegetation of a poor garrigue type—stunted broom, tough grasses, bulbous plants and an occasional dwarfed carob tree. For most of the year the land looks parched and bare, but with the onset of the winter rains it becomes green and fresh, and speckled with anemones, gladioli, irises, geraniums and violets. The fauna of Malta is very restricted in numbers and varieties. It is limited to hedgehogs, weasels, rats, mice, lizards and non-venomous snakes, and to migratory birds, in addition to the usual domestic animals. Of these last, goats (29,000) are the most numerous, followed by sheep and pigs.

HISTORY AND PEOPLE

In very early times the Maltese Islands were inhabited by a people, possibly originating in North Africa, who left a legacy of megalithic monuments such as the Hagar Qim in Malta and the Gigantia in Gozo. No less than 7000 skeletons of these neolithic people were found in one cemetery, the rock-cut hypogeum (underground chamber) of Hal Saflieni in Malta. From 1800 B.C. the Phoenicians founded colonies in Malta (Melita) and Gozo (Gaulos) and they were joined in the sixth century B.C. by the Carthaginians. It was from Carthage that the islands inherited the earliest form of their language. When Carthage surrendered to the Romans in 216 B.C., the victors did not treat the Maltese as conquered enemies, but rather as *socii*, allies, who were expected to do little more than contribute supplies of wheat to Rome. During this period Malta was converted to Christianity by St Paul, who in A.D. 58 was shipwrecked off the coast (Acts xxvii. 7), by tradition in St Paul's Bay.

The advance of Islam along the southern shores of the Mediterranean led in A.D. 870 to the invasion of the Maltese Islands by the Arabs, but although they remained until 1090, they did not establish their religion there; indeed, they left few lasting impressions except on the Maltese language, where their Arabic dialect was blended in a minor way with the earlier Punic tongue to give the basis of modern Maltese. The Arabs were expelled by Roger the Norman, Count of Sicily, and until the sixteenth century the Maltese Islands were administered by the rulers of Sicily, who in succession were Normans, Angevins, Aragonese and Castilians.

In 1530 the islands were given to the Order of St John and remained under their guardianship until the end of the eighteenth century. The Order of St John was founded in Jerusalem in the eleventh century as a nursing brotherhood, but it gradually became an association of militant knights dedicated to the eradication of Islam, with its headquarters in Rhodes. Driven from Rhodes by the Turks in 1523, the Knights were offered a home in Malta by Charles I of Spain, on condition they opposed the westward advance of the Turks in the Mediterranean. The Knights were eminently successful, for in 1565, although outnumbered by five to one, they defeated a Turkish fleet which had besieged Malta for five months and ended for ever the Muslim threat to Western Europe by sea. With this victory came the realisation that Malta was the "key to the Mediterranean." La Vallette, the Grand Master of the Knights, built Valletta and endowed it with fortifications unrivalled anywhere at that time; and such was the reputation of the strength of the fortress that for 200 years no foreign power made an attempt to challenge it.

During this time, however, the martial spirit of the Order began to wane, and so too did its friendly relations with the Maltese people, who were called on to provide money for the building of magnificent churches and palaces, and services for their feudal overlords. When, therefore, the French under Napoleon landed at Valletta in 1798, they met with no resistance. But the Maltese, who at first welcomed the French, soon found their new masters worse than the old; and when they saw their churches pillaged, their monasteries and convents destroyed, and their ancient customs and Catholic practice replaced by atheistic republican ideas and way of life, they rose in rebellion and, helped by the British, forced the French to vacate the islands after a stay of only two years. In 1802 the Maltese petitioned Britain to accept the sovereignty of the islands, and this was confirmed in 1814 by the Treaty of Paris.

When the British took over the administration the economy of Malta was at a very low ebb. The feudal government of the Knights had become unbearable; nevertheless, under their rule great quantities of grain, vegetable oils, timber and luxury goods had been imported into the islands to support the members of the Order and their garrisons, and the islanders had profited by this wealth. None of this was now available; and since the Maltese could not grow sufficient food for themselves and there were no natural resources which they could develop, their prospect looked bleak. It was in these circumstances that Britain began to look for new ways to restore the economy. In the next 20 years the defences of Valletta were further strengthened, the harbour improved, a garrison of 20,000 men provided a source of income, Valletta was made a free port, and all British trade with the eastern Mediterranean was carried on through Valletta. By 1839 the British fleet was based on Malta, the Admiralty had inaugurated a packet service, and several shipping companies were using Malta as a regular calling place on their runs to Egypt and the Levant.

Port services provided employment for traders and carriers, and with increasing internal prosperity Maltese farmers began to grow more grain and other foods, and women to spin and weave cotton. With the opening of the Suez Canal in 1869, the economy improved enormously. The Mediterranean became a world highway and an increasingly large number of ships called at Malta for coal and other supplies on their way to and from the Indian Ocean and the Far East. From 1871 to 1881, 8000 additional workers found employment in the dockyards; in the towns new bankers, merchants and shopkeepers were constantly demanding additional labour; and in the countryside farms became larger and more prosperous. By 1882 about 80% of the recorded tonnage of shipping calling at Malta had cargoes for ports outside the Mediterranean, and the islands were at the height of prosperity.

The boom did not last, however. By the end of the century it was already evident that the economy was once more on the decline, and by 1945 Malta's economic position had reached a crisis. In the first place, as ships increased in size—and more so when they became oil-fired—they had less need to call at Valletta to refuel; and as Europe began to turn more to the New World for its supplies of grain and other commodities, fewer vessels sailed through the Mediterranean. The British Government came to the rescue by extending the naval dockyard and augmenting the military garrison with the unfortunate result that in time the money earned by working in the dockyard or spent by the Services in the towns became the main source of Malta's livelihood. Unfortunate, because by the end of the Second World War it was obvious that Malta's importance as a naval base and strategic bastion had reached vanishing point; air warfare and the advent of the atomic bomb had changed defensive values. For this reason and because of the changed political and military situation at the eastern end of the Mediterranean, including the loss of control of the Suez Canal, the British Government decided to withdraw from the naval dockyard and transfer it to a civilian firm for commercial shipbuilding and repairing.

This was a serious blow to the economy, for most of Malta's workers were dependent directly or indirectly on the defence services, and there was no immediate alternative demand for labour. Moreover, there was a growing problem of over-population. When the British took over the islands at the beginning of the nineteenth century the Maltese people numbered 80,000. Since then the population has increased to over 330,000, with an average density of more than 2600 persons per square mile, and this in a small country which has no possibility of supporting more than a fraction of that number. Since 1959, the year of the transfer, however, much progress along new lines has been made, and this is considered in the next section. In 1964 Malta was given its independence within the British Commonwealth, but the political situation within the islands remains somewhat unsettled. A minority of its leaders wish to create a republic outside the Commonwealth, but in face of the desire of the majority of the people and of the Church to maintain the *status quo*, they are making little headway. The Church in Malta is powerful, for the majority of the inhabitants are staunch Roman Catholics.

The people of Malta may be differentiated into those who live in the country districts and those who form a cosmopolitan fringe in the towns along the coasts. In spite of long centuries of foreign rule, the people of the interior and the west of the islands show evidence in their language and their Semitic facial characteristics of their Phoenician descent. They have certainly been affected in blood, speech and customs by the endless succession of invaders and allies, but to a far less degree than might be expected. Most of the townsfolk, on the other hand, are of mixed origin, with blood from Normans, Greeks, Spaniards, Sicilians, and English mingling in their veins with that of their Punic ancestors. Maltese is the ordinary language outside the towns, but English is the official language and is understood by all but a few. A small minority, known as the Italian party, speaks Italian.

THE ECONOMY

Away from the industrial region which has developed around Valletta, the chief occupation everywhere is agriculture; but the area suitable for cultivation is small, probably not more than one-half of the islands' surface. This is due to the porosity of the limestone cover, the absence of surface water, and the paucity of fertile soils. Wherever irrigation is possible from wells and springs, cultivation is intensive, two and often three crops being raised in a year. The average farm is small, usually not more than five acres, composed of tiny fields walled up in terraces with enormous labour to prevent the soil being washed away. Shortage of soil is a problem; it has even been imported from Sicily. Viewed from the sea, the top of one terrace wall appearing above the next produces a barren effect; but the aspect of the land from a hill in early spring may be one of luxuriant verdure. It is estimated that there are 16,000 farmers in Malta, and as a rule they live away from their lands in some neighbouring nucleated village or town.

The chief grain crops are wheat, barley and maize, and the principal fodder crops green barley and a tall clover called "sulla." Vegetables of all sorts are easily grown on the irrigated lands, and potatoes and onions are exported when they are scarce in northern Europe. Great efforts, too, are being made to encourage the growing and export of flowers. There is a considerable area under vines and wine is produced, but it is generally more profitable to sell the fruit as grapes than to convert it into wine. Figs, apricots, nectarines, peaches and oranges are grown to perfection, and some, especially blood oranges, are exported. Carobs and prickly pear are extensively cultivated, and some cotton is raised as a rotation crop. There are large numbers of goats and sheep which graze on the garrigue; and oxen are used for ploughing, for the small terraced fields are unsuited to modern machinery. With the exceptions mentioned above, the farm crops are consumed locally, and the total production falls far below the requirements of the islands. About three-quarters of the wheat consumed comes from abroad, and considerable quantities of vegetables and fruit are imported from Sicily. A small amount of fish, such as tunny, sardine, anchovy, and mackerel, is caught off the coasts.

The bulk of the working population of Malta, as already noted, was until recently dependent for its livelihood on the naval dockyard and harbours, and in catering for the needs of Service personnel. For more than 150 years Malta's means of paying its way was provided by a high rate of British defence expenditure, amounting in the years before withdrawal to about £20 million annually, used mainly in the development of the island's economic heart, the Grand Harbour. This large import of money, men and goods resulted in a lop-sided economy, with imports far exceeding exports. By 1962 Malta's combined exports and re-exports brought in just over £4 million, but the value of imports was over £28 million. This imbalance became clearly visible in 1959, when long-term changes in Britain's defence policy resulted in the transference of the naval dockyard, which alone employed over 7000, to a civilian firm; and it necessitated the preparation of far-reaching plans for a new Malta, with new industries and other sources of employment.

The transition period between the function as a naval base and stronghold and that of a purely commercial port of call is being covered by a series of development plans, financed largely by Britain. While the former naval dockyard is being converted for commercial ship-repairing, the civil harbour has been modernised, and electricity, water and power supplies expanded to meet the needs of new industries. Already twenty new factories have been established, producing a wide range of goods including synthetic fibres, textiles, paint, furniture, plastics and spring mattresses; and car assembly and light engineering are providing new sources of employment in addition to the longer-established food processing works, breweries, cigarette and tomato paste factories. Craft industries, such as the making of gloves, pottery and lace, are being encouraged to expand; it should be noted that at the beginning of this century 5000 females were engaged in the making of Maltese lace in their homes, but that these numbers had fallen in recent years to less than 1000. Further industries are expected to be attracted to Malta by the special terms they are being offered, which include ten years free from income tax, ready-built factories at nominal rents, and freedom from customs duties. Malta's location of itself brings the growing markets in the Mediterranean, Africa and the Middle East within easy reach, but the success of Malta's new ventures will depend on how far they can compete in the world market with rivals already well established. Tourism is increasing rapidly. In 1959 some 12,000 tourists went to Malta; in 1968 the number had grown to 50,000, and new hotels and amenities are being provided to attract more. In this development rapid air transport is a big advantage.

Malta has always suffered from over-population. Even in the

nineteenth century the surplus population migrated, chiefly to countries bordering the Mediterranean, notably along the African coast from Egypt to Morocco. In the twentieth century emigration is definitely encouraged. In 1920 the British Government introduced vocational training for intending emigrants, but the world economic depression of the 1930s reduced the capacity of other countries to accept them. After the Second World War, with a further increase in the pressure of population, passages for emigrants were paid by various governments, and between 1948 and 1962 over 80,000 Maltese went overseas, mostly to settle in Australia, Canada and England.

The chief town and capital of the Maltese Islands is Valletta (17,725), on the Grand Harbour. Originally built as a fortress it became a naval base and dockyard, and now it is in process of being transformed into an entrepôt port and ship-repairing centre. Besides the export of agricultural produce and the products of craft industries, it has light engineering, iron pipe manufacture and food processing, and is a centre for banking and insurance. In the interior of the island of Malta the largest town is Rabat, situated where springs from the Bingemma Hills provide water for irrigation; it is a very colourful tomato market and has a light engineering industry. Adjoining Rabat is Medina, an ancient and most picturesque walled settlement with a cathedral. The island of Gozo has proportionately more good soil than Malta. Its largest town is Victoria (previously called Rabato), many of whose inhabitants are farmers owning land outside its boundaries.

STUDY QUESTIONS

1. Write a short essay on the position and strategic importance of the Maltese Islands.

2. Describe the position and trade of the following ports: Naples, Valletta, Trieste. Sketch maps are essential. (O. & C.)

3. Examine the possible results on the economy of the Maltese Islands of (a) their achievement of independent status, (b) the uncertain future of the Suez Canal.

Chapter XVII

WESTERN BASIN SOUTH. MOROCCO

INTRODUCTION: THE MAGHRIB

On the south side of the Western basin of the Mediterranean, the Atlas lands form a region so distinctive as to set it apart from the main body of the African continent. Politically, the region comprises Morocco, Tunisia and the northern parts of Algeria, the area to which the term "The Barbary States" is often applied. The southern, and larger, part of Algeria is occupied by the Sahara Desert, and is not "Mediterranean" by most standards; it will, however, be included in the regional treatment of Algeria chiefly because of its political and economic importance.

In addition to the larger states already mentioned, the region with which we are concerned also includes the small Spanish enclave of Ifni, which opens to the Atlantic coast, and the Spanish possessions (mainly Ceuta and Melilla) on the Mediterranean coast of Morocco. The Arabs have for long referred to the Atlas lands as *Djezira el Maghrib*—the Western Isle—and the designation is useful as it reminds us of the isolation of the region, an isolation produced by the Atlantic Ocean to the west, the Mediterranean Sea to the north and east, and the Sahara Desert to the south. In some ways the desert barrier is the greatest of all. There are two physical characteristics which serve to make this region unique in the continent—its relief and its climate—and we now turn to these two topics.

PHYSICAL ASPECTS

STRUCTURE AND RELIEF

The major physical feature (or group of features) of the Maghrib consists of the series of mountain ranges generally known as the Atlas mountains. Structurally, these are quite distinct from the main mass of the African continent as they are fold mountains which were thrust up, like the Alps of Europe, during the Alpine mountain-building period of late Mesozoic and Tertiary times, and they therefore form a comparatively late addition to Africa, a continent which includes few fold mountains. The degree of folding involved was often not great, so that the sedimentary rocks which were affected usually retain their original characteristics; they have rarely been subjected to the metamorphism which sometimes accompanies the formation of fold mountains. Limestones, for instance, are widespread as they are in the Mediterranean lands of Europe. In some of the more intensely folded areas which do exist, however, notably in parts of the High Atlas, formerly deep-seated crystalline rocks which

originally may have been part of the basement plateau were thrust upwards during the folding, and these rocks now appear at the surface in
places where the limestones which earlier covered them have been worn
away (*see* Fig. 78). The Rif Atlas are exceptional in this region because
nappes have developed as a result of intense folding, while parts of the
crystalline basement are also exposed at the surface.

[*Courtesy of Hulton Press Ltd.*

FIG. 78.—View in the High Atlas. The gorge in the foreground runs through the
    sedimentary rocks, which remain fairly horizontal. In the background tower
    up higher crystalline massifs formed of basement rock, snow covered. The
    spurs near the upper right-hand side of the picture are truncated; this suggests
    faulting.

The general pattern of physical features is shown on Fig. 79. This pattern will be discussed in some detail in the regional sections which follow;
for the moment it is sufficient to observe that the predominantly east–west
trend of the grain of the land had its origin in the "squeezing" of thick
masses of sediments which were laid down between the main African
Shield to the south and the Tyrrhenian Shield to the north. In the Maghrib many of the sediments, such as those forming the High Atlas and
Saharan Atlas, lie actually on the African Shield. Substantial earth movements seem to have begun in late Mesozoic times, though the main folding
took place in the Tertiary when there was renewed compression with
more pronounced thrusting coming from southward movements of the
Tyrrhenian Shield—that is, from the north. The High Atlas which had

undergone prolonged denudation after earlier Mesozoic folding were up-lifted epeirogenically during the Tertiary "storm," and crystalline rocks were exposed in the main ranges. The Rif Atlas came into existence near the Moroccan coast (as it now is), nappes—the only ones in the Atlas system—being caused by the sharp thrusts from the north. The more southerly ranges have no nappe structures, partly because they lie on the African Shield. It is likely that the Moroccan Meseta (*see* p. 355 below) was raised to its present elevation at this period and that the Tyrrhenian Shield was fragmented, leaving only upstanding horsts such as are found

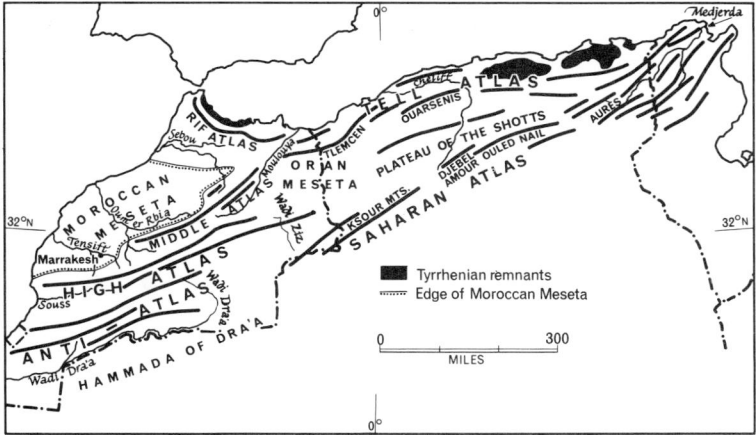

FIG. 79.—The Maghrib: morphology.

in Corsica, Sardinia, Calabria and the Sahels of the North Africa coast (*see* Fig. 91). Complete crustal stability has not been attained even today in the Maghrib, as is shown by such terrifyingly destructive earthquakes as those at El Asnam (Orléansville) in 1954 and at Agadir in 1960.

CLIMATE

The climate of the Maghrib reflects the location of the region, which lies near the western side of a major land mass, roughly between latitudes 27 degrees N. and 37 degrees N.; that means that the Maghrib is located near the southern limits of the Mediterranean type of climate. Seasonal alternation is experienced between westerly winds with accompanying depressions during the winter months and the northerly winds of summer (*see* Chapter III). It is interesting to notice that while some of the easterly moving winter depressions enter the region via the Strait of Gibraltar, some move south-eastwards having passed from the Bay of Biscay via the Gate of Carcassonne. The latter group of depressions begins to influence the climate of the coastal areas about midway between Oran and Algiers, and this accounts for the fact that the rainfall of the Tell (*see* p. 377 below) is greater in the eastern parts of Algeria than in the western (*see* Fig. 80).

On the whole it is true to say that winters are rainy in the Maghrib and summers dry, and also that rainfall on the whole decreases in amount with increasing distance southwards; the northerly parts of the region experience three or four months of summer drought, while the steppes farther south suffer intense drought for about six months of the year. It is also important to note that very wide rainfall differences can exist within quite small areas as a result of rain-shadow effects caused by the various mountain ranges (*see also* p. 407). It is true in summary to say that only a small part of the Maghrib experiences a genuinely Mediterranean type of climate. This is partly because the region overlaps into the deserts of the south, and partly because the east–west sub-parallel ranges of the Atlas restrict the Mediterranean type of climate to the coastal areas.

NATURAL VEGETATION

The natural vegetation of the Maghrib varies considerably from place to place, chiefly in accordance with variations in rainfall and relief (*see also* Chapter V). For instance, forests of conifers and oaks on the moister hill slopes of the Atlas give place to scrub and grassland of a semi-desert type

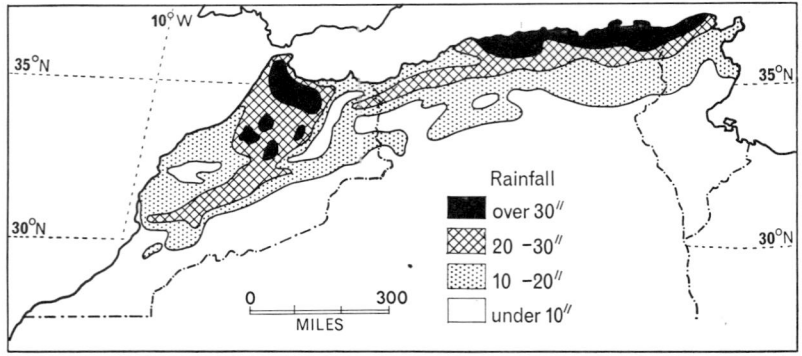

FIG. 80.—The Maghrib: annual rainfall.

on the Plateau of the Shotts (*see* Fig. 80) and in central Tunisia. On the whole, vegetation becomes poorer with increasing distance southwards from the Mediterranean Sea, and also with increasing distance inland from the Atlantic Ocean.

Along the Mediterranean coastal zone (the Tell) we find a typical Mediterranean vegetation of the maquis type, with evergreen bushes, stunted oaks and flowering heath plants; typical shrubs include laurel, myrtle, oleander, rosemary, juniper and broom, together with creepers and thorny plants. This can be very dense in the wetter areas. On the wetter mountain slopes forests of oaks and conifers originally occupied wide areas, but large parts of the forests have been destroyed partly by farmers clearing for cultivation (often using fire), and partly because of the damage caused by nomadic flocks, especially by goats. The well-known

Forest of Mamora, for example, lies to the north-east of Rabat on the well-watered edge of the Moroccan Meseta (*see* Fig. 79), but here losses from fire and from deliberate destruction have in part been made good by re-afforestation with pines and eucalyptus. The Forest of Cedars on the Middle Atlas is also a famous beauty spot. On the other hand, where extensive limestone outcrops lie near the surface and where water supply for plant growth is therefore strictly limited, the maquis degenerates into garrigue, vegetation made up of heath and poor scrub. In garrigue areas patches of such shrubs as gorse, lavender, thyme, sage and small thorny shrubs are normally not sufficient to provide a full vegetation cover, and exposures of bare rocks and soils are widespread.

As conditions become drier over the crests of the Atlas, vegetation becomes sparse and poor. The maquis becomes very open and stunted, and grass, often of a coarse type, appears; to the south of the Anti-Atlas and the Saharan Atlas mountains this semi-desert type of vegetation merges into desert, much of which is barren *erg* (sandy desert). Numerous oases such as Tafilelt, Figig and Biskra lie near the foot of the mountains, while others such as Touggourt and Ghardaia lie farther south in the Sahara (*see* Fig. 81).

HUMAN GEOGRAPHY

PEOPLE OF THE MAGHRIB

The original population of the Maghrib was probably Hamitic, and belonged to that branch of the Hamites known as the Berbers; this is why the region has been termed the Barbary States. The word *Berber* came from the Latin *barbari* which was generally applied to all non-Romans. Berbers today are only a minority (though an important one) of the total population, hence the preference for the term *Maghrib* rather than Barbary States. The Berbers form for the most part a branch of the Mediterranean race (*see* p. 90), and they closely resemble some of the peoples of southern Europe such as the Spaniards and Italians, being fairly lightly built, fairly tall and dark. They have black wavy hair and usually brown eyes. Most are agriculturalists, though many have been forced by the semi-arid conditions under which they live to become nomadic or semi-nomadic pastoralists. One interesting sub-group is that of the Kabyles, who inhabit the picturesque Kabyle and Djurdjura massifs to the south-east of Algiers. These people are remarkable, as many of them have fair hair and blue eyes, characteristics of northern rather than southern Europe. There have been many speculations as to the origins of the Kabyles, and one conjecture is that they may be descendants of the Vandals who invaded North Africa in the fifth century (*see* p. 95); they may be said to be Nordic in type.

Berber society is based upon the village; each village is autonomous and is democratically ruled by a kind of council of adult male citizens. Sometimes villages will come together in a loose kind of federation to administer some particular social service such as education or road building, but the autonomy of each village is always respected. Each group of villages owes allegiance to its Kaid, who is in turn responsible to the King (the Sultan of Morocco changed his title to "King" in 1957).

The Berber is a fighting man; there is, indeed, a saying that the Tunisian is a woman, the Algerian a man, and the Moroccan (meaning in this context a Berber) a warrior. His folk-lore is of battle and he is brought up in a warlike tradition. Before the pacification by the French, there was often ruthless fighting between tribes, villages and even between neighbours.

A later group of immigrants than the Hamitic Berbers is that generally known as the Arabs or Moors, a Semitic people who came in a series of invasions during the spread of Islam from the seventh century onwards. Since then a considerable amount of intermixture between Berber and Arab has gone on, and since both peoples belong mainly to the Mediterranean race and have close physical resemblances, it is not now always easy to distinguish between them. The Arabs came originally from the east, and this is reflected in the fact that there are today almost no Berbers in Tunisia, while more than half the inhabitants of Morocco speak the Berber language. Moreover, the Arab horsemen failed effectively to penetrate the more remote Atlas areas (especially the mountainous Aurès, Kabyle and Rif districts) and also the cul de sac of southern Morocco, all of which remain predominantly Berber (see Fig. 81). While Arabs do not differ greatly from Berbers in physical appearance, they speak a different language and are pastoralists rather than agriculturalists. Their form of government is completely despotic; the sheikh is the undisputed leader of the community and he enjoys a religious as well as a social status. Unlike the Berber, the Arab is sometimes described as a pleasure-loving, greedy person, often slothful.

The fourteenth century saw the rise to power of another state—Turkey

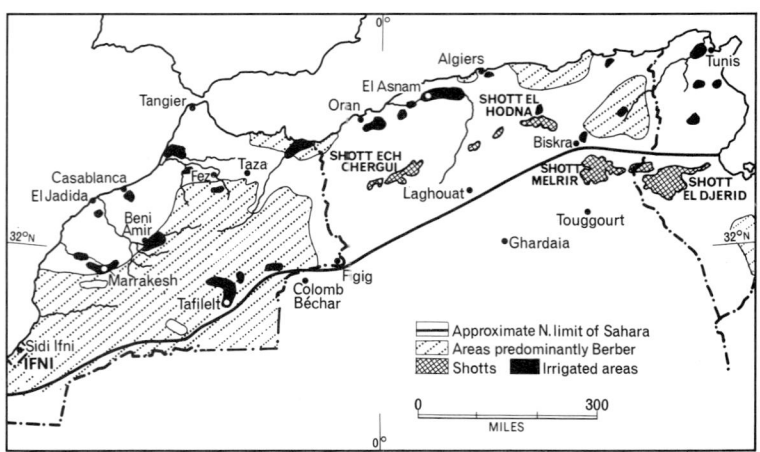

Fig. 81.—The Maghrib: some general features. For names of rivers see Fig. 79.

—and the Turks in 1453 captured Constantinople, the key fortress in the eastern Mediterranean. During the next century the Turks subdued most of North Africa, beginning in 1517 with Egypt; shortly afterwards Tripoli was conquered and Tunis and Algiers became vassals of Turkey. As a result by 1574 the formerly powerful Arab–Berber empire had virtually disappeared. Turkish control over the Maghrib, which became notorious as the base of the infamous Barbary pirates, was always tenuous, however, and it never existed at all in Morocco, which remained an independent state until 1912 when France established a protectorate. In 1830, France (ostensibly exasperated by the activities of the Barbary corsairs) sent a military expedition to Algeria and after four years claimed suzerainty over the Algerian coastlands, though fighting continued until 1847 when the Tell was subjugated and dissidents driven inland to the mountains. In 1883 Tunisia became a French protectorate. After the declaration of the Moroccan protectorate in 1912, the domination of France was extended throughout the Maghrib with the exception of some Spanish enclaves in Morocco.

During the period of French rule many Europeans made their homes in the Maghrib, especially French farmers (colonists or *colons*) in Morocco, Algeria and Tunisia, and Italians in Tunisia. In addition many Frenchmen took up residence and work permanently in the towns, notably in Casablanca and Algiers. The farmers settled for the most part in the Mediterranean coastal areas, and they did much to develop the territories. Their farming was of a high standard and the importance of the Maghrib as an exporter of agricultural produce has been due in the main to their efforts; following the granting of independence to the three larger territories, however, their numbers have been sharply reduced in recent years mainly by emigration to France. Between 1956 and 1963 it is estimated that the numbers of Europeans in Morocco fell from 400,000 to 140,000; in Algeria from 1,500,000 to 140,000; and in Tunisia from 255,000 to 40,000. In Algeria the exodus was hastened by the confiscation after independence of property owned by non-nationals, while a decree published in Tunisia in 1964 also ordered expropriation of lands owned by settlers. Although such measures bring some immediate benefit to local populations, they have resulted in the Maghrib in crippling losses of skilled workers, administrators and capital resources, while valuable French markets have also been lost.

GENERAL SUMMARY

There are marked contrasts in human geography between the Maghrib (which is predominantly Muslim) and Mediterranean Europe (which for the most part is Christian). Nowhere on the European side is there the concern with the rearing of livestock, especially the nomadic and semi-nomadic grazing of sheep and goats, on the scale met with in the Maghrib. This contrast can probably be attributed fundamentally to climatic differences. Furthermore, the indigenous peoples of the Maghrib show a greater relative dependence upon a subsistence form of agriculture, especially upon the production of wheat and barley, with the help of primitive methods of farming; as a result there is far more poverty in the Maghrib even than in Mediterranean Europe.

At the same time, however, there are similarities to be discerned between agriculture in the two regions. Hence, in *The Geography of Modern Africa*, recognises three types of crops which are common to both sides of the Mediterranean Sea:

1. Rain crops which depend upon winter precipitation for their water needs. Pre-eminent among these are wheat and barley, which between them account easily for the largest part of the cultivated area in the Maghrib. Indeed, in the Mediterranean lands generally cereal crops occupy almost as much cultivated land as all other crops put together; this point is illustrated by the following figures which are typical of the region:

Percentage of Cultivated Land Under Cereals

	Wheat	*Barley*	*All cereals*
Algeria	25	17	46
Italy	25	15	49
Morocco	22	23	51
Spain	22	7	31
Tunisia	26	15	45

2. Crops which are equipped by nature in some way to withstand the summer drought which is often intense. These include the olive, fig, certain types of nut (including the edible chestnut) and cork (from the cork-oak). They are very distinctive Mediterranean crops.

3. Crops which depend upon irrigation; they are grown mainly along or just above valley floors. Some of these such as grapes, citrus fruits and deciduous fruits are perennials (grapes are not always grown under irrigation). Some, such as vegetables and flowers, are annuals. These crops are grown in the Maghrib not only for domestic use but also for export, particularly to France. It is true that the proportion of the total cultivated area devoted to them is comparatively small, but the value of the products accounts for a large part of all agricultural exports by value.

One feature of the human geography of the Maghrib, which it shares with all Mediterranean lands, is the large number of its towns and cities. In a region so predominantly pastoral and with crop production at a generally low level, such urban growth is unexpected; yet 20% of the population of the Maghrib may be classified as urban. Some of the urban growths, such as Fez and Marrakesh in Morocco, are of ancient lineage, while others (*e.g.* Casablanca and Oran) are of recent development. It is noteworthy, however, that despite this feature the Maghrib has never developed a capital city for the whole region; Morocco alone during the course of its history has had no fewer than four capitals (Rabat, Fez, Meknes and Marrakesh). This can partly be attributed to the broken physical character of a region which is divided into well-marked sub-regions by its accidented topography, and partly to its troubled history.

As a final observation it should be emphasised that the Maghrib is a large region; it extends from east to west for a maximum distance of almost 1500 miles (2400 km) (almost as far as from London to Moscow) and from north to south for distances varying between 120 and 400 miles (190–640 km). It covers a total area of just over 300,000 square miles (780,000 sq. km) which is about as large as France and the Federal Republic of Germany combined.

MOROCCO

The Kingdom of Morocco extends from the Peninsula of Ceuta in the north to beyond the Wadi Dra'a in the south; it covers an area of 171,300 square miles. The southernmost part, known as Southern Morocco or Tarfaya (*see* Fig. 82), used to be a Spanish protectorate which was governed as part of Spanish Sahara before it was ceded to Morocco, and it has a population of only about 21,000. The Atlantic Ocean forms the western boundary of the territory, while on the east Morocco is bounded by Algeria, though the boundary to the north-west of the Wadi Dra'a in the desert is rather indefinite. Morocco does, in fact, lay claim to much of the western Sahara, including Spanish Sahara, Mauritania and parts of Algeria, and these claims have at times resulted in considerable ill-feeling between the country and her neighbours.

PHYSICAL ASPECTS

STRUCTURE AND RELIEF

Figure 79 shows the general arrangement of relief in Morocco. Two major series of mountain ranges—a northern and a southern—partially enclose a triangular plateau which has its base along the coast between Rabat and Essaouria (Mogador) and which is sometimes known as the Moroccan Meseta. This originally formed part of the ancient platform upon which most of Africa stands, and though most of its surface is now covered by younger (mainly Cretaceous, Tertiary and Quaternary) rocks, most of which are limestones, the old crystalline rocks are exposed in some places, notably along the sides of river gorges. It was the resistance of this ancient block which caused the Atlas ranges to be forced apart into the northern and southern systems.

To the south and south-east of the Meseta the most prominent feature is the High Atlas range, the highest and the most impressive of all the Atlas mountains, which extends north-eastwards from the coast near Agadir. The ranges are cut off sharply at the coast, giving rise to very impressive cliffs and headlands. It is in the central parts of this range that crystalline rocks have been thrust up and now appear at the surface (*see* Fig. 78). The highest parts of the mountains, large segments of which consist of high plateaus, developed as a result of the uplift of the peneplanes formed after the initial folding in Cretaceous times and subsequent erosion referred to on p. 349 above. These plateaus lie over 10,000 ft (3000 m) above sea-level, while many of the peaks which rise above them are over 13,000 ft (3960 m) high: Jebel Toubkal, the highest point in Morocco, rises to 13,665 ft (4165 m). Towards the north-east of the range the crystalline rocks disappear, as they are covered by massive limestones which are gashed by wild, picturesque gorges.

To the south of the High Atlas the Anti-Atlas, a massif with a broad plateau-like surface which is really the slightly up-turned edge of the main African basement plateau, is separated from the main system by the triangular depression of the Souss. Through this depression flows the Wadi Souss which reaches the Atlantic just south of Agadir. To the south of the Anti-Atlas lies the broad valley of the Wadi Dra'a, the longest river of this sub-Saharan region and the only one which reaches the sea, though its flow is intermittent. For much of its course the Wadi Dra'a forms part of the southern boundary of Morocco. Eastwards from the upper valley of the Wadi Dra'a lie the valleys of the Wadi Ziz, which irrigates the well-known oasis of Tafilelt, and the Wadi Saoura, which waters a string of oases including that of Beni Abbès.

To the north of the High Atlas the Middle Atlas branches off to form the western boundary of the plain through which flows the Moulouya on its way towards the Mediterranean coast east of Melilla. The Middle Atlas consists mainly of gently folded limestones and the ranges of this system have been compared in this respect to those of the Jura, though towards the north there has been much fracturing and some volcanic activity. The Rif Atlas runs roughly from east to west from the lower Moulouya valley, keeping parallel with the coast and curving northwards near longitude 5° W towards the Strait of Gibraltar. The system is separated from the Middle Atlas by a broad corridor which connects the lower Moulouya plain with the Rharb, a roughly triangular-shaped lowland across which flows the Wadi Sebou. The corridor is commanded by the old towns of Fez and Taza, and it forms the main route between Morocco and Algeria.

The fertile Rharb Plain has its corners near the towns of Fez, Rabat and Larache. For a very long time this area was a gulf of the Atlantic, and thick layers of marls and clays were deposited on the floor of the large embayment; these deposits now form the basis for fertile agricultural land.

To the south of the Rharb the Moroccan Meseta lies with an average elevation of about 1000 ft (300 m) above sea-level. During Mesozoic and Tertiary times, when it was subjected to great strains caused by the folding of the Atlas ranges near by, it was fractured, particularly in the southern part where the resulting subsidence was responsible for the down-faulting of the Plain of Marrakesh, sometimes known as the Haouz. A zone of piedmont plains known as the Dir, formed of alluvial deposits washed down from the mountains, extends over the eastern region at the foot of the High and Middle Atlas, while rivers nourished by precipitation including winter snow) on the Atlas cross the plateau, often in incised valleys. Such rivers include the Oum er Rbia and the Tensift.

In the eastern parts of Morocco the broad valley in which the Moulouya flows separates the Rif Atlas and the Middle Atlas on the west from the eastern plateau; this plateau is a westward continuation of that part of the high plateaus of Algeria called the Oran Meseta (*see* p. 379 below). Farther south the line of the High Atlas is continued eastwards (though with a break near Bou Arfa) by the Ksour mountains (which form part of the Saharan Atlas) in Algeria.

CLIMATE

The climate of the western parts of Morocco differs from that of the other parts of the Maghrib because it is affected primarily by Atlantic rather than by Mediterranean influences. The vast mountain arc of the Rif Atlas, the Middle Atlas and the High Atlas shelters the "core" area of the country (the Rharb and the Meseta) both from Mediterranean and from Saharan influences, and the result is that this largely enclosed region is by Maghrib standards well watered. It is not surprising that more than half the total population of the whole country lives in this area, across which flow the Tensift, the Oum er Rbia and the Sebou, three of the five perennial rivers of the Maghrib; the other two are the Cheliff of Algeria and the Medjerda of Tunisia.

During the summer, the position of Morocco with regard to the Azores high pressure system is responsible for the dominance of north-easterly winds over the greater part of the country; these winds are strengthened by the low pressure complex which develops over the Sahara at this season. In the winter, however, a series of depressions associated with the belt of westerly winds which extends over most of the territory at this seasons moves from the Atlantic to the Mediterranean, and these depressions bring rain, particularly to the windward slopes of the mountain ranges and to the slightly elevated edges of the Meseta. On the other hand, leeward slopes commonly suffer from a marked rain-shadow effect, an effect which is noticeable also in the down-faulted Haouz region where Marrakesh records a yearly average of only 9·3 in. (compare Essaouria, 13·2 in.). In a general way rainfall decreases from north to south; thus, Tangier has an annual average of 32·5 in. as opposed to the 13·2 in. of Essaouria; the diminution of rainfall along the Atlantic coast is more rapid between Tangier and Rabat than it is farther south. The Taza corridor and the Rharb which together open westwards to the Atlantic have about 24 in. a year, while the Meseta generally records between 12 and 16 in. except in the drier Haouz. The Atlas mountains probably receive over 30 in. but they cast sharp rain shadows; the Mediterranean coast, for example, which lies in the rain shadow of the Rif Atlas, has only about 10 in. (compare the figure for Tangier given above), while the southern and south-eastern parts of the country have less than this. These southerly areas form part of the Saharan fringe.

Summer is everywhere dry except on the Middle and High Atlas where the considerable elevation produces some summer rainfall. Elsewhere, however, about 80% of the total precipitation occurs during the passage of depressions during the winter. The general pattern of rainfall is shown on Fig. 80.

It will be reasonable to expect considerable temperature variations in a country extending over about nine degrees of latitude and encompassing such marked variations in relief. To these points should be added the fact that seasonal inequalities become pronounced with increasing distance from the Atlantic, largely because of the increasing dryness of the air. Thus, the temperature range at Essaouria on the coast is 12° F (6·6° C) (57° F (13·9° C) January to 69° F (20·6° C) September), while at Marrakesh it is 33° F (18·3° C) (52° F (11·1° C) January to 85° F (29·4° C) September). On the higher parts of the Atlas ranges winter temperatures are well below freezing point and snow is widespread.

Another factor which markedly affects temperature along the Atlantic littoral is the cool Canaries Current which flows southwards off the coast. This current, allied with the land and sea breezes which are very well developed in this area, produces a comparatively chilly and damp climate in the coastal zone where mists and even fogs are prevalent. The Canaries Current has the unexpected effect of lowering temperature (particularly in summer) in the coastal strip with increasing distance *southwards*; summer temperatures at Essaouria are lower than those at Tangier, though inland the effect of the current is quickly lost and summer temperatures rise rapidly (compare the figures for Essaouria and Marrakesh given in the preceding paragraph). The climate is not more unpleasant inland than on the coast, despite the higher summer temperatures, because of the uncomfortably high relative humidity and the mists and fogs produced along the coast by the cool current. Inland the air is much drier, which makes for pleasant conditions, while the sunnier conditions away from the coast are more advantageous to farmers than the chill mists of the littoral. We might observe, however, that while the Canaries Current makes life less pleasant and easy in the coastal zone, it carries the great advantage that it supports very large numbers of fish which provide the basis for sizeable fishing and canning industries; this will be examined later.

NATURAL REGIONS

We can now recognise a number of natural regions (*see* Fig. 82) as a preliminary to a study of the human and economic geography of Morocco.

1. *The Atlantic coastal plain* is up to 30 miles (48 km) broad. The coast itself is not generally hospitable, as parts are rocky and there are few sheltered bays to protect shipping against the strong swell which rolls in from the ocean. Most river mouths are partially blocked by sand bars so that their value for navigation is very limited. Immediately inland from the coast is a sandy zone known as the Sahel which is not very fertile, but between the Sahel and the Meseta lies a zone of clay supporting a black

fertile soil called *tir* which is suitable for cereals. The coastal plain is well watered in the north by the rains of winter, and the parts called the Chaouia, which is the tir area near Casablanca, and the Doukkala, are very productive, but the southern part, the Abda, tends to suffer from insufficient rainfall. (These areas are so called from the tribes which have made their homes in them.) Wheat, barley and maize are the traditional crops on the tir, while more recently sugar beet has been grown on an increasing scale. Early vegetables are produced for the urban markets and there is a considerable amount of market gardening.

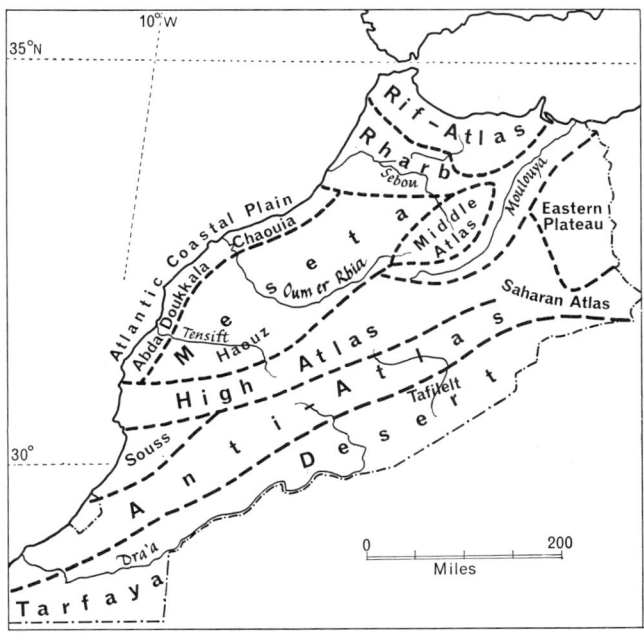

FIG. 82.—Morocco: natural regions.

2. *The Moroccan Meseta*, which occupies the west central part of the territory, lies at an average height of about 1000 ft (300 m) above sea-level. The north-western edge is fairly well watered as it catches a reasonable amount of rainfall from the winter depressions, and this region, which includes the area around Meknes, is very productive, raising large crops of cereals and grapes. The central parts of the Meseta, however, are rather arid, especially the down-faulted Haouz which suffers from a rain-shadow effect (*see* p. 52 above). On the plateau generally the prevailing steppe type of vegetation assists sheep-rearing, but irrigation is widely practised in the Haouz where fruits, especially dates, olives, citrus fruits and grapes, are extensively grown. In the piedmont areas of the east (the Dir) where alluvial plains occur (p. 356 above) many small watercourses descend from the mountains, providing water for irrigation. Thanks to the comparative

abundance of water, therefore, and to the variety of soils, sedentary, prosperous communities based upon the cultivation of irrigated gardens and orchards have developed on the Dir. Larger rivers such as the Oum er Rbia and the Tensift cross the Meseta from the Atlas, often flowing in deeply incised valleys. They, too, are used for irrigation, especially near Marrakesh (the Tensift), while the Oum er Rbia and its tributaries have been dammed to the north-east of Marrakesh and the south-east of El Jadida (formerly Mazagan, *see* Figs. 81 and 85).

3. *The Atlas ranges.* These ranges, particularly the High Atlas and the Anti-Atlas, act as marked climatic and human divides between the generally moister west and north-west on the one hand, and the desert and semi-desert of the south-east on the other. Although the High Atlas are deeply gashed by many gorges and valleys, they are not easy to cross because the valleys are usually too much like ravines to offer reasonable routes. The northern and western slopes are generally well watered and forested, and in the broader valleys the Berbers grow cereals and fruit with the help of irrigation, while olives are grown on the lower slopes of the High Atlas. Many of the men of the villages leave their homes seasonally to work in the towns and on the farms of the lowlands. The inward-facing slopes, on the other hand, are notably dry and barren. The few inhabitants are pastoral rather than agricultural, for a sedentary life is possible only near the small streams which flow from the mountains but which quickly lose themselves in the desert once they reach the plains. Snow is widespread on the higher slopes during the winter when life almost stops as the deep drifts pile up. At this season many of the men have gone south to find grazing for their animals near the desert borders.

On the Middle Atlas stock-rearing is of greater importance than on the High Atlas, for mountain pastures are of better quality and are more widespread. The semi-nomadic Berbers migrate seasonally to the heights in the summer to take advantage of the pastures uncovered by the melting of the snow, and they move down to the plains in the winter. The typical Berber village in this region lies in the zone where cultivation is possible midway along the migration routes. The melting snows provide valuable supplies of moisture for the lowlands below, while the massive limestones of the region soak up much of the snow-melt and the precipitation. The water later issues from the rock in springs which gush out near the base of the mountains.

4. *The south-eastern desert.* The Anti-Atlas and the High Atlas slope steeply down to the valley of the Dra'a and towards the Sahara in an area where the population is virtually confined to oases. Even the Wadi Dra'a which looks impressive on a map, flows only intermittently in its lower courses; apart from oasis dwellers this is a land of nomads who tend their flocks and herds. The best-known oasis is that of Tafilelt, watered by the Wadi Ziz which flows southwards from the High Atlas through deep gorges. About 100,000 people live in or near this oasis which is roughly 11 miles (18 km) long and up to 10 miles (16 km) across. This famous

palmerie, which also manufactures ornamental tiles and pottery, has lost much of its earlier importance. Figig, too, has an extensive *palmerie*.

5. *The eastern plateaus* lie between the High Atlas and the Moulouya depression to the west and the Algerian border to the east. They are remote and scantily populated, and are of little agricultural importance at present. Their chief value is their mineral wealth, to which we shall turn later.

6. *The depressions and lowlands.* These restricted areas provide the bulk of the most valuable farm land in the whole country. The areas concerned are the Souss, the Rharb, and the Moulouya Depression, though in a sense the Haouz might be included. The Souss, with its sub-arid climate, is too dry to be very productive without irrigation; Tarouddant, for example, has average temperatures of 81° F (27·2° C) in January and 113° F (45·0° C) in August, yet gets an annual average rainfall of only 8 in. The naturally bare landscape, broken by clumps of coarse grasses and thorn trees, hardly provides enough grazing for the flocks of sheep and goats which form the main means of subsistence apart from the agriculture which is carried on with the help of irrigation, water being secured from the Souss and its tributaries. In the irrigated orchards and gardens (which are often protected by cactus hedges) citrus fruits, almonds, figs and pomegranates are grown, as well as bananas, tomatoes and cereals.

The Haouz is also rather dry for agriculture except where irrigation has transformed the landscape; olives are increasing in importance in the area, while the Marrakesh *palmerie* is famous. Grapes and citrus fruits are grown and market gardening is carried on.

The more northerly lowlands, the Rharb and the Moulouya, are better watered and are very productive, especially the Rharb which benefits from the oceanic influences which penetrate inland. The Sebou waters the Rharb Plain which it enters near Fez; it floods extensively during the winter but shrinks considerably in the summer, when the swampy riverine lands are used to provide pasture for flocks of sheep and goats. Very large crops of wheat and barley are grown, especially near Fez, while the extensive olive groves near Fez and Meknes are said to yield the best-quality olives in the world; oranges are also widely grown. Between Meknes and Rabat lies the cork-oak forest of Mamora which has suffered from over-exploitation and clearing; population is rather sparse in the forest region.

The upper Moulouya valley suffers because it lies in the rain shadow of the Middle Atlas, and it receives less than 8 in. of rain a year on the average; it is also very remote and inhospitable, and not surprisingly is sparsely populated. The lower part of the valley, however, which is really an extension of the Algerian Tell, is fertile, and produces heavy crops of cereals and fruits, including grapes.

Notice how the Rharb and the lower Moulouya valley are linked by the corridor of Taza which provides the easiest route between Morocco and Algeria. The main railway linking Rabat, Fez, Algiers and Tunis passes through this corridor, and also the main trunk road between the two territories.

HUMAN GEOGRAPHY

HISTORY AND PEOPLE

As already noted, most of the people of Morocco are either Hamites (Berbers) or Semites (Arabs or Moors) and the Berbers were probably the original inhabitants. The Arabs came later (near the end of the seventh century and onwards) as a result of the Islamic conquests. Fig. 81 shows the parts of Morocco which remain predominantly Berber, though much intermixture has blurred the original line of division between the two groups.

The history of Morocco was until recent years largely a story of inter-necine warfare between Berber and Arab, between tribes, between vil-lages, and even between neighbours. The tribe in Morocco is a more integrated and cohesive unit than it is in either Algeria or Tunisia, and inter-tribal fighting was common before the French pacified the territory; all groups, however, owe allegiance to the King (formerly the Sultan). Despite this cohesion personal animosities within the tribe can reach ex-treme proportions, and bitter quarrels are common. It is not surprising, therefore, that the history of Morocco has been turbulent in the extreme and the advent of law and order was delayed for a very long time—until, in fact, the arrival of the French, who signed a treaty (the Treaty of Fez) with the rulers of Morocco in 1912, after which most of the country became a Protectorate of France. French control was exercised through a Resident-General who acted in collaboration with the Sultan. Legislation was effected through proclamations which required the signatures of both Moroccan and French authorities. The chief area outside the protectorate was the former Spanish Zone which comprised a narrow strip west of the Moulouya along the Mediterranean coast (the Rif country).

Much could be written about the follies and the injustices of colonial rule, but it is only fair to say that Morocco, in common with many other ex-colonial territories, has much for which to thank her former colonial administrators. Under French rule (1912–56) peace was brought to the country for the first time, although complete pacification was not finally achieved until 1934 (see Fig. 83). Roads and railways were constructed, the output of agricultural products leapt up, a new activity, mining, took firm root and became a major industry, and modern ports and cities (Casablanca is the most notable) were established. The country was ex-ceedingly fortunate in its outstanding first Resident-General, Marshal Lyautey (1912–25), who pacified most of the country and then devoted himself to furthering economic development. The population of Morocco more than trebled itself under French rule, while many French settlers moved in and began agricultural development of a modern type. Such developments inevitably gave rise to new divisions and stresses; for example, the new industrial life and interests of the towns contrasted sharply with the tribal form of culture which often persisted unchanged in the countryside, while tensions also arose between the settlers and the *évolués* (Moroccans who followed the French pattern of farming and way of life) on the one hand and traditionally-minded Moroccans on the other.

It is not surprising that the ferment which affected the whole of the colonial world after the Second World War was sharply felt in Morocco, where nationalistic elements, especially in the urban areas, rebelled against foreign rule. The situation was complicated in 1953 by the exile of the

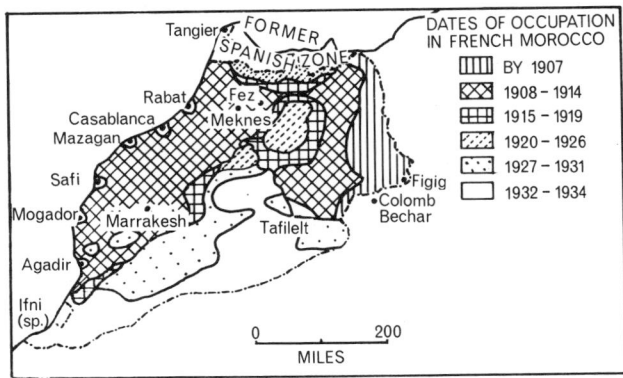

FIG. 83.—Morocco: political development. The enclaves around the Atlantic ports were occupied by 1907.

Sultan, who refused to co-operate with French officials. After a sad period of bloodshed and atrocities, independence came to the country in 1956, and in 1957 the Sultan changed his title to "King."

Unfortunately for Morocco, independence has brought losses as well as gains. Most of the progressive French farmers, uncertain as to their future status and safety in an independent territory, left for France; it is estimated that the numbers of Europeans in Morocco between 1956 and 1967 fell from 400,000 to 98,000. The loss of a large proportion of its skilled and progressive citizens which this exodus entailed has dealt the economy a severe blow. Even today, only a small proportion of Moroccans partici-pate in a money economy: most of the people still exist on a subsistence basis, a mode of life characterised by stagnation, which can offer no goods to sell, and which generates no purchasing power or resources for invest-ment. It will take many years of effort before the country can equip itself with the capital resources necessary for the emergence of a healthy, mod-ern type of society, despite the start which has been made.

POPULATION AND SETTLEMENT

The population of Morocco in 1967 was 13,323,000, and about three-quarters of these inhabitants were rural, though the urban population is

rapidly increasing as a result of modern economic and social developments. Most of the people live to the north-west and west of the main
Atlas ranges, especially in the foothill and piedmont zones which are comparatively well watered, on the Rharb, and along the Atlantic coastal plain
(*see* p. 358 above). Population density generally exceeds 100 persons per
square mile in these areas, a marked contrast to the situation in areas such
as those south of the High Atlas where population is extremely sparse and
where most of the inhabitants are concentrated in oases and along wadis.

Houses in the rural parts of Morocco are normally humble affairs, consisting generally of single-roomed, single-storeyed structures of sun-dried
clay roofed with clay tiles. They are typically built closely together, a
relic of the days when the need for defence was paramount. Quite often
(and for the same reason) houses are huddled round the *kasbah*, the fortress
of the local chief. In most villages houses are customarily situated with
little regard for orderly arrangement, and in the mountain areas, where the
groups of houses seem often to cling precariously to the steep slopes, it is
frequently possible to step out of the door of one house directly on to the
roof of its neighbour!

A prominent characteristic of rural life is the weekly market, or *suq*,
normally held at a traditional site which is deserted except for the duration of the *suq*. The markets are normally located about 20–30 miles apart
so that tribesmen can visit the nearest one and return home within any
single day. The traditional means of travel to the *suq* is on foot, but in
these days it is becoming usual to go by bus or by car. Local produce is
exchanged for imported or manufactured commodities such as household
hardware, tea, coffee and cloth, while the services of tradesmen and skilled
workers such as cobblers, bakers, tinkers and blacksmiths are available.
Minor ailments are also prescribed for and treated by the intinerant
"doctor."

Native Moroccan towns (*i.e.* towns not established by the French) are
generally simply overgrown villages, and three distinct functional sectors
are commonly discernible: the *medina* (the traditional huddle of
houses comparable to that of the villages), the *ghetto* or *mellah* (mainly
occupied by Jews who have for long been very active in the commercial
life of Morocco, indeed of the whole of the Maghrib), and the *kasbah*, or
Arab quarter. To these in some cases may be added the *European Quarter*,
which is commonly situated a short distance from the main town and
which is more graciously laid out. These points are illustrated in the cases
of two towns, Essaouria and Taza, in Fig. 84.

CHIEF TOWNS AND CITIES

Fig. 85 shows the location of the more important towns and cities of
Morocco, and their disposition accords well with that of the population
generally which lies mainly to the north-west and west of the main Atlas
ranges Oujda, located on the main railway linking Morocco and Algeria
and the centre for a lead and zinc mining area, is the most notable exception

to this rule. Of the other towns we might take special note of Rabat, Fez, Meknes, Marrakesh, Casablanca and Tangier.

The capital of Morocco, though it is not the largest settlement, is the port of Rabat (228,000), a very elegant and charming town which, with its twin town Salé, lies astride the estuary of the Bou Regreg. As a port it has been overshadowed by Casablanca and Kenitra. There has been some development of industry in the capital, however, the setting up of the steel works at Skrirat near by providing an example of this. Rabat is one of the four capitals which Morocco has had, the other three being Fez, Meknes and Marrakesh.

Fez (220,000), commanding the eastern Rharb and the western approach to the corridor of Taza, lies at the crossing of two traditional routes: (a) the north–south caravan route linking Tangier with Marrakesh and

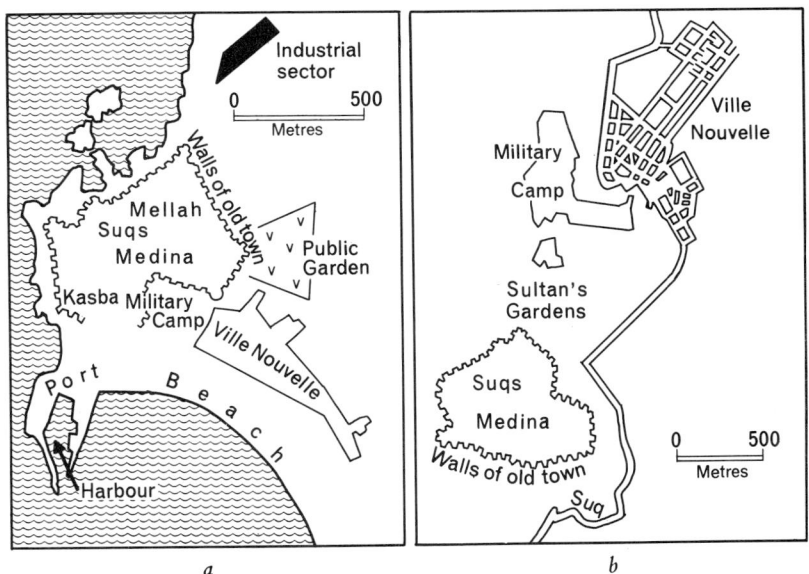

FIG. 84.—Town structure in Morocco: (a) Essaouria, (b) Taza.

with the Sahara (via the Atlas), and (b) the east–west route from the Atlantic coast to Algeria (via the corridor of Taza). It is thus not surprising that Fez has developed a famous market, while it greatly benefits from the copious water supply derived from many Atlas streams. It is better supplied with water than any other inland town of Morocco. Its prestige in the world of Islam has stood higher than that of any other city of the Maghrib; it has in fact been called the "Mecca of the West" though its importance as a religious centre of international significance has now declined. Even so, it remains the religious capital of Morocco, while its university confers prestige in intellectual affairs. It is a leading centre of native crafts in addition to its commercial interests, and its carpets and leather work are widely known.

Meknes (180,000) has never achieved the importance of Fez, although it is the centre of a very productive agricultural region for which it has become a leading market. Like Fez, it is prominent for craft work and its activities include the production of brasswork, jewellery, carpets and leather goods.

The largest inland town of Morocco is Marrakesh (250,000), easily the chief city of the south. It was established during the eleventh century near the Tensift, in a convenient position to command the Haouz Plain, yet within 40 miles of the foothills of the High Atlas at an intersection of traditional routes. It is set in its vast *palmerie*, which in appearance resembles a Saharan oasis where vineyards and orchards of oranges, olives and other fruits abound; it is a great market centre where the cereals and fruits of the moister north and west, together with imports from overseas, are exchanged for the dates, hides and skins of the dry south and south-east. Native crafts and industries flourish, and include the manufacture of pot-

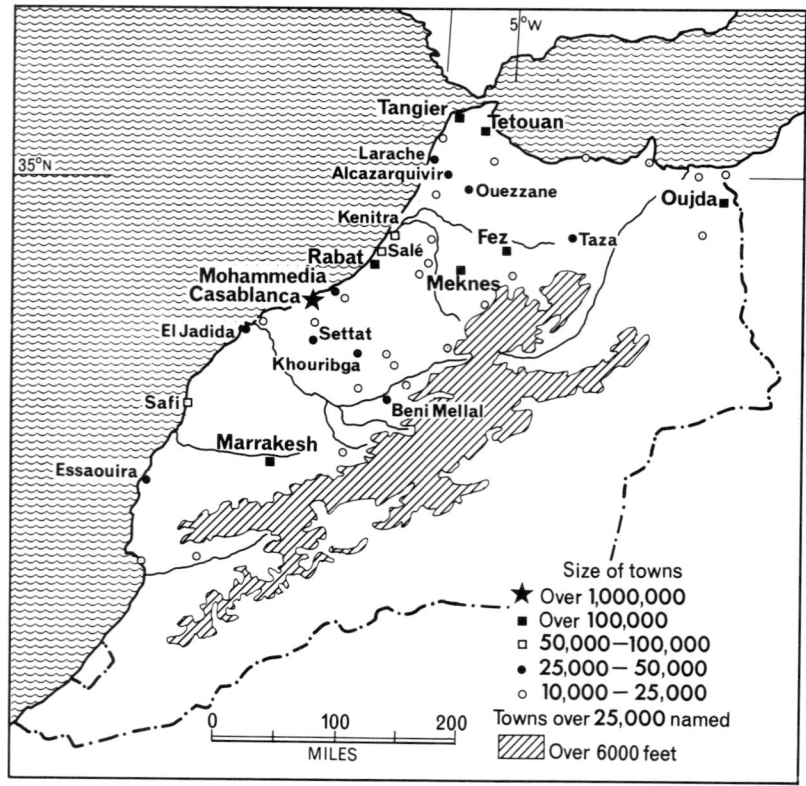

FIG. 85.—Morocco: chief towns. *Based partly on Awad.*

tery, carpets and jewellery. The town was traditionally a bastion of defence against the warlike tribesmen of the Atlas and the Saharan fringes.

The chief port and the largest town of Morocco is Casablanca (just over 1 million inhabitants), which has developed from a modest port of about 10,000 souls in 1907 to become one of the leading ports of Africa today. It handles about three-quarters of the total overseas trade of Morocco, one important reason for this being its location comparatively near the main mineral areas; phosphates from Khouribga comprise a substantial proportion of its exports (*see* p. 372 below). The natural shelter originally available for shipping was not very good, but the water in the harbour is deep and there is no trouble from silting. The port is now well provided with wharves and modern port facilities, and the town is the chief centre of industry in the whole country; in fact, about 70% of the modern factories of Morocco are situated in Casablanca. Superphosphates are manufactured; cereals are processed into flour, semolina and macaroni; and olives are used in the manufacture of olive oil, some of which in turn is used in the preparation of soap. Cement is also an important product, and the demand for it in this rapidly expanding city is very great. As well as busying itself with overseas trade, Casablanca is the leading fishing port in Morocco, and fish are preserved and canned ready for export as well as for sale within the country. Its airport is of international importance, and the city has become a focus for roads and railways. Near by is the growing industrial centre of Fedhala. Casablanca far overshadows Kenitra (Port Lyautey), the chief outlet for the Rharb, which is handicapped by the constant deposition of silt by the Sebou on which the town stands. Continual dredging is necessary to keep open the port which large vessels cannot enter.

The port of Tangier, which faces Spain and Gibraltar 14 miles away across the Strait of Gibraltar, gains some importance from the calling of ocean liners and from the tourist trade which it attracts. It is one of the oldest towns in Morocco (*see* Fig. 86), and possibly dates back to Phoenician times, while it was the leading port of the country until the Second World War. Since that time, however, consequent upon the rapid increase in importance of Casablanca, its trade has declined. Between 1925 and 1959 Tangier was administered as a demilitarised International Zone, but this arrangement came to an end when the town became part of Morocco in 1960. The population is about 142,000.

Smaller Moroccan ports include Safi, second in importance to Casablanca, which handles phosphates and which is the leading port for landing sardines; El Jadida, also with interests in fish canning; Essaouria, formerly known as Mogador; and Agadir, the port for the Souss.

THE ECONOMY

Enough has been said to show that Morocco is a country which has very considerable possibilities for agriculture, despite the handicap of aridity in some areas and despite pests such as the locust which ravage the crops from time to time, and it is not surprising that farming is the chief occupation, giving employment to almost three-quarters of the total working population. Cereals easily comprise the most important group of crops grown,

[*Courtesy of B.E.A.*

FIG. 86.—Morocco: a market in Tangier. The geometrical patterns on the mosque are characteristic of Moslem architecture, as are the baskets made from esparto grass and palm-leaf fibre.

particularly barley, followed by wheat, though yields per acre are generally low. It is estimated that about 20% of the surface area of Morocco is suitable for arable farming and a further 25% for pastoral activities, while a further 10% is forested. At the same time the general economic situation is constantly being modified as mining and manufacture are steadily increasing in importance. According to a United Nations survey published in 1962, primary production (which includes both agriculture and mining) accounts for 41% of the gross national product, services for 35%, and industry for 16%. The last two figures are high, judging by African standards.

AGRICULTURE

Barbour points out that there are two types of agriculture in Morocco—capitalistic and subsistence. The first type is practised by French settlers, who have opened up land particularly in the Rharb, Chaouia, Doukkala and Abda areas, and by the more progressive Moroccan farmers, known generally as *évolués*, and it takes the form of a mechanised agriculture involving crop rotation and the use of mineral fertilisers. Large crops of citrus fruit, tobacco and grapes, together with barley and wheat, are produced by the settlers and the *évolués*; progressive farmers of this type account for about half of the total commercial production of all crops in the country. The other type of farming is the traditional subsistence agriculture on small, sub-divided holdings carried on with the help of primitive methods and appliances. Wooden, horse-drawn ploughs are normally used, while much cultivation is carried on by hand. Fertilisers are hardly used, crop rotation is rarely practised and yields are poor. The chief crops grown are cereals (85% of the cropland is under cereals, mainly wheat and barley), but the small farms are particularly vulnerable to the uncertain climate. Rainfall, for example, is very irregular, and if the rains come late in the year the *fellahin* (Arabic *fellah*, a tiller) are not able at the right time to plough soils hardened by four or five months of summer drought, because their wooden ploughs are not keen enough to turn the packed and indurated soil, while the scorching *sirocco* (often known in Morocco as the *shergui*) does much damage, especially in inland areas away from moderating maritime influences. Houston points out that in any five-year sequence farmers may expect one very good harvest, one bad or disastrous, and three ranging between poor and good.

About 80% of the agricultural land in the country is owned and worked by Moroccan cultivators, but about 10% of these own about 60% of the land. These are the large landowners (*évolués*) who make extensive use of hired labour. About 40% of the cultivators are small-scale farmers who, with their families, work on their own farms, sometimes with the help of paid workers. The remaining 50% of the farming population are the landless workers or share-croppers who receive about one-fifth of the harvest as their share of the proceeds. It is not surprising under these circumstances that very great inequalities in wealth exist: it is estimated that 60% of Moroccans may be classified as undernourished and needy. A start has been made, however, to deal with this situation by a careful programme of land reform. In the Rharb, for example, 8000 hectares (nearly 20,000 acres) of farm land were in 1966 apportioned to 691 farmers, while in October of the same year King Hassan announced that foreign settlers who had bought land would be required in future either to cultivate it or to "give it up for other people." Such measures can increasingly be expected after the severe measures taken against settlers in Algeria and Tunisia (*see* p. 391 and 416).

Morocco is well placed for the growing of vegetables because, thanks to her southerly position and to her maritime climate with its early spring, she can have spring crops ready for market a fortnight before the Algerian Tell. Olives are increasing in importance in some areas, as has been emphasised, and they are well suited to the drier southern parts of the Meseta, while vine cultivation is increasing in the Chaouia.

In a country of uncertain rainfall like Morocco, irrigation can play a very important role; less than a quarter of the country receives on an average 24 in. of rain or more yearly, while another quarter receives bebetween 12 and 24 in. and must be classed as semi-arid. About a half of the entire country consists of steppe and desert. In these unfavourable circumstances the Moroccan farmer has shown considerable ingenuity in

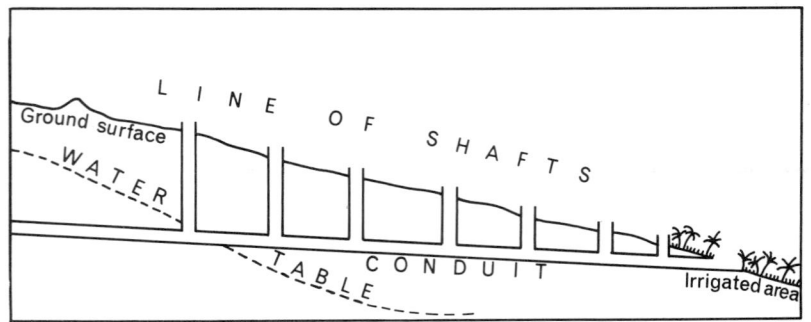

FIG. 87.—Diagram of a foggara. The line of shafts, of which the upper ends project 4 or 5 ft above ground level, is a characteristic feature of a foggara. Not infrequently such a line may be seen running down the centre of the main street in a settlement. The shafts are dug initially as a means of "levelling" the course of the conduit and to expedite the removal of excavated material, and they are subsequently kept in good repair to facilitate maintenance work on the conduit and to provide ventilation. *Based partly on Highsmith.*

tapping such water reserves as there are. Particularly notable are the *foggara* of Tafilelt (*see* Fig. 87) and the similar *rhettara* of Marrakesh: these are subterranean tunnels which channel underground water from high ground to adjacent plains. Some of these tunnel systems are astonishing; for instance, the network of 400 rhettara which serve the Marrakesh area has a total length of 430 miles (as far as from Paris to the Spanish frontier). Similar works have been constructed in the valleys of the Souss and the Dra'a. In addition, considerable supplies of underground water exist beneath many of the lowlands, including the Rharb, Haouz, Souss and Tafilelt, and these are tapped by means of wells.

Schemes are now being worked out to develop large-scale irrigation projects, such as that at Beni Amir on the Oum er Rbia (*see* Fig. 79). In this region lived originally a semi-nomadic population of about 100,000 pastoralists who wrested a precarious living from the poorly watered steppe. These inhabitants were at first hostile to the new way of life required on the irrigation area, but after initial difficulties the scheme has proved very successful. Crop growing is conducted according to a strict rotational pattern involving alfalfa, wheat, cotton, vegetables and a fallow year, and both the output and the value of the land have very greatly increased since 1937 when the scheme was inaugurated. The population of the irrigated zone quadrupled between 1937 and 1954. Various comparable schemes are in operation (*see* Fig. 81) and others are planned; for instance, a dam is now under construction on the river Tessaout, 80 kilometres (about 50 miles) north-east of Marrakesh, while construction of a dam across the Wadi Ziz began in 1967.

Houston emphasises the importance that such schemes could have in helping to enrich an economy which at the moment is conspicuous for its general poverty. Estimates suggest that if all the potential water resources were fully used they could support an additional population of 4 million people at a higher standard of living than that which is normal today, while other schemes involving better land use (such as the modernisation of dry farming methods) could support a further 20 million people. To this should be added other advantages such as the development of hydro-electric power from irrigation dams. It is clear that, if ever the resources of Morocco are utilised to anything like their full extent, the country will have taken many strides forward from its present low standards of living.

STOCK-REARING

The dominance of stock-rearing in the economy of Morocco is a natural response to a climate which is so often hostile to cultivators. Sheep and goats are reared almost everywhere and together may number nearly 30 million animals; indeed, in the Middle and High Atlas entire tribes are almost wholly occupied with sheep-rearing on a nomadic basis. Any increase in cultivation on the lowlands, however, is bound to restrict the area available for pasture to the nomads, and this is a problem which must be closely watched in the future. More intensive cultivation of fodder crops might help the pastoralists, but it will not be easy for the nomads to adjust themselves to this new way of life. Pastoral farming is of predominant importance on the plains of the north-east, on the Meseta, on the Plain of Souss and in most sub-arid areas. Raw wool forms an important export.

In many areas, while stock-rearing is a dominant way of life, the production of crops is carried on as a supplementary activity. This is the case, for instance, in parts of the Atlas regions and in parts of the steppe country, where thin soils in natural hollows and on the flat floors of wadis are simply scratched on the surface with the help of the light ploughs, which are the only cultivating appliances available. Cereals are the main crops grown under these conditions. In the Middle Atlas life is transhumant rather than nomadic. Sheep and goats are moved to lowland pastures for the winter, particularly to the Moulouya valley, to the Rharb and to the plain of the upper Oum er Rbia, most of the inhabitants of the villages accompanying the stock. In spring everyone returns to villages in the valleys of the Middle Atlas, where the soils are tilled preparatory to the summer cultivation of wheat, barley and maize. Most of the villagers remain in these valleys throughout the summer, tending crops and fruit trees, though some of the stock is taken to high mountain pastures where grazing is possible for a short period around mid-summer.

FISHING

The fishing industry of Morocco is steadily increasing in importance, for many different kinds of fish abound in the cold waters of the Canaries Current. Sardines, bonito, anchovy and tunny are the fish mostly caught. The canning of sardines has become an important industry at ports such as Casablanca, Safi and El Jadida (Mazagan), and both tinned and preserved fish form notable exports. Morocco ranks second only to Portugal as a world producer of sardines. Other fishing ports include Agadir and Rabat.

MINING

The mineral reserves of Morocco are of great note, and many railways have been built to help their development (see Fig. 88). Particularly important are the deposits of phosphates which occur in a broad limestone zone running roughly parallel to the coast some miles inland from the ports of Casablanca, El Jadida and Safi. The Moroccan output of this valuable raw material, from which fertilisers are manufactured, accounts for about one-fifth of the total world production. Morocco ranks as the second world producer after the U.S.A. and as the leading world exporter. In 1965, phosphates accounted for 27% by value of the total exports from Morocco, and nearly 15,000 workers were engaged in the Moroccan phosphate industry. Over 8 million tons are despatched overseas each year, and it is planned to exceed that figure in the future as the new plant is being installed at the producing centres. Phosphates form the leading export from Casablanca in terms of tonnage, while the port of Safi would never have existed without the phosphate export. The largest deposits are tapped at Kouribga by the railway which branches off the Casablanca–Marrakesh line to Oued Zem (see Fig. 88), and at Louis Gentil on the railway from Safi to Ben Guerir. Electric trains now quickly transport the Kouribga phosphates to Casablanca where there are factories for the manufacture of superphosphates, valuable as fertilisers. Both phosphates and superphosphates are leading exports.

An important feature of the mining industry is that it provides a considerable stimulus to other economic activities. For instance, the mines provide a ready market for large amounts of electricity, while the railways earn considerable profits from transporting minerals from the mines to the ports.

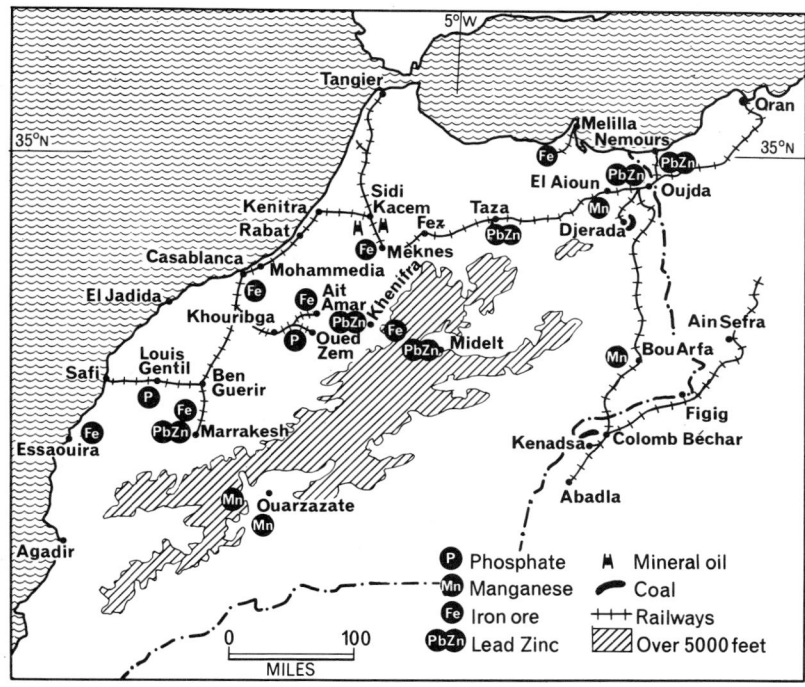

Fig. 88.—Morocco: minerals and railways. The railway running north-eastwards from Colomb Béchar through Ain Sefra is of narrow gauge; other railways are all of standard gauge.

In earlier years eastern Morocco was one of the poorest parts of the country, and while this is still largely true, some prosperity has been brought to the region by the discovery of useful deposits of coal, lead, zinc and manganese. Reserves of approximately 100 million tons of anthracite exist at Djerada, and production is now going ahead (about half of the output is exported), while lead deposits near the Algerian border at Bou Arfa, and in the upper valley of the Moulouya near Midelt are being exploited for export.

Iron ore deposits are worked mainly in the former Spanish zone near Melilla, while reserves also exist near Essaouria, Casablanca, Khenifra and Meknes. Manganese is worked at El Aioun west of Oujda and at Bou Arfa near the Algerian border; these latter deposits are tapped by the railway which runs southwards from Oujda to Colomb Béchar in Algeria. There is a small output of petroleum which is refined at Sidi Kacem (formerly Petitjean) near the southern edge of the Rharb, and at Mohammedia near Casablanca. A start has also been made on a large-scale prospecting scheme for natural gas and mineral oil, and natural gas was in fact discovered in some quantity near Douar in 1966; the extent of these deposits is not yet known.

MANUFACTURING INDUSTRY

Although Morocco is still primarily an agricultural country, the development of industry has gone rapidly ahead since the close of the Second World War, and references to various industrial activities have been made in earlier sections of this chapter. Probably about one-half of all industrial workers are occupied in small-scale handicraft industries which turn out such goods as textiles (including embroidery and carpets), leather goods, ornamental brasswork and jewellery; while these industries are especially important in the large towns of Morocco, they are carried on to some degree in most parts of the country.

We have previously noted that about 70% of all the modern-type factories of Morocco are concentrated in or near Casablanca, and the Chaouia is easily the leading industrial region in the country; this concentration of industry has been encouraged by the fact that three-quarters of the total sea-borne trade of Morocco passes through Casablanca, while it is also significant that the Chaouia lies near the centre of the most densely populated part of the country. Processing of primary domestic produce is the most important form of industrial enterprise, and this includes the manufacture of superphosphates, brewing, flour milling, the refining of vegetable oils and the subsequent manufacture of soap and candles, tobacco processing and sugar refining. New sugar refineries have been opened and another is under construction; these will produce sugar from domestic supplies of sugar cane and beet. Sugar production has greatly increased since 1963, and Morocco now supplies about 75% of her requirements. The manufacture of cement has been greatly expanded in recent years, encouraged by the great scale of building and the construction of dams. The canning of vegetables has also greatly increased in importance, while it is interesting to note that the most important manufactured product *exported* from Morocco is tinned fish. Fish canning is carried on in 200 factories (most of them have been established by European enterprise) in Casablanca, Safi, Essaouria, Agadir and El Jadida. Interesting recent developments include the start which has been made in the assembly of motor vehicles using imported components parts,[*] and a sugar refining plant which is to be established with the help of a West German firm, while an Italian company is to build an electro-chemical plant. While details of these proposals are not yet available, there are clear indications that Morocco is seeking to diversify her industrial base.

Further industrial expansion in Morocco is hindered by two outstanding difficulties—lack of power resources and lack of markets, Only limited amounts of coal and mineral oil are so far known to exist in the country,

---

[*] This could prove to be a very significant development indeed, for in some other countries such an assembly industry has paved the way for the full-scale manufacture of motor vehicles. This in its turn can lead to the establishment of heavy industry as has happened in Australia and Mexico. See JARRETT, H. R., *A Geography of Manufacturing*, Macdonald & Evans, 1969, chapters X and XII.

though this situation may well change as a result of the intensive search for natural gas and mineral oil now being undertaken. So far, however, the main form of power has been hydro-electricity. A considerable number of fairly small and medium-sized hydro-electric power plants have been established in the Middle and High Atlas, though the output of power needs to be supplemented during periods of low water by the thermal-electric plants which are located in most of the larger towns.

The lack of markets referred to above is a disability which Morocco shares with other developing territories. In theory, Morocco has two groups of markets open to her—overseas and domestic—but in a highly competitive world dominated by established industrial giants the prospects for breaking into overseas markets must be regarded as slight. The main difficulty on the domestic front arises from the fact that as so many Moroccans rely chiefly on subsistence forms of economy they have little money to spend on manufactured goods, and this means that the market available for such goods is very limited. It is fairly clear that until a substantial proportion of the two-thirds of the population who at present rely on traditional forms of livelihood is induced to modify its way of life, there is little chance of increasing notably the size of the domestic market, and this in turn must discourage further industrial expansion.

SPANISH NORTH AFRICA

Spanish North Africa comprises a number of tiny territorial enclaves which have somewhat precarious political and economic bases. Their total population amounts to about 155,000 persons, of whom about 79,000 live in Melilla and 73,000 live in Ceuta. As these small possessions between them have a total area of only about 82 square miles (213 sq. km), they record the unusually high population density of 1890 persons per square miles. This is an indication that the territories have an economic and strategic value out of all proportion to their size, despite the fact that fishing and mining are the only activities stemming from natural resources. Canned and salted fish are exported, together with iron ore mined near Uixan in the Rif, but the main importance of the territories arises from the great use made of the ports by coastal vessels which call to take on supplies of fuel oil, coal, ice and drinking water.

Apart from the main centres of Ceuta and Melilla, other detached parts of Spanish North Africa include Alhucemas, the Chafarinas Islands and Peñon de la Gomera. These are small garrison centres.

IFNI

Ifni is an enclave, a Spanish possession of rather less than 1000 square miles (2600 sq. km) in area, which thrusts itself into southern Morocco. Its cliffed coast is about 50 miles (80 km) in length and it extends from the mouth of the Bou Sedia in the north to the river Assaka which forms the south-western boundary. Inland, a narrow coastal plain rises to a mountain ridge, about 4000 ft (1240 m) in elevation, which is one of the southern branches of the Anti-Atlas. Rainfall is very limited, and the resources of the territory are not in themselves enough to maintain the population; many of the men are forced to seek work in southern Morocco. Most of the inhabitants, about 50,000, are Berbers (*see* Fig. 81) and considerably more than half of these live in the northern part of the enclave.

The chief activities include the cultivation under irrigation of wheat and barley, stock-rearing (mainly sheep and goats), date production, the growing of vegetables (also under irrigation) and fishing along the coast. Sidi Ifni, the capital, with a population of 13,000, is the only town of any size.

STUDY QUESTIONS

1. To what extent do you consider the Maghrib to be a geographical unit?
2. How far is it true to say that the Maghrib has a Mediterranean climate?
3. What are the main characteristics of the physical geography of the Maghrib?
4. Write an explanatory account of the distribution of population in Morocco.
5. Discuss the need for irrigation in Morocco. Illustrate your answer with actual examples.
6. Write an essay on farming in Morocco. Discuss the changes which are taking place today in farming practices.
7. Write an essay on the towns of Morocco.

Chapter XVIII

ALGERIA

ALGERIA, which extends for a distance of 620 miles along the Mediterranean coast between Morocco and Tunisia, and which has a total estimated area of 856,000 square miles, is easily the largest of the territories of north-west Africa. Yet it is in a way misleading to talk of it as a Maghrib country, for the greater part of its area (about 730,000 square miles) lies in the Sahara Desert. A substantial part actually lies to the south of the Tropic of Cancer and is therefore in inter-tropical latitudes; the habitable part of northern Algeria is limited to an area of about 80,000 square miles. Only the northern seventh part of the territory, which covers about 125,000 square miles and extends for distances varying between 120 and 210 miles from the coast, can properly be said to belong to the Maghrib. It is with this northernmost part that we are chiefly concerned in this chapter, though we cannot entirely overlook the importance of the Saharan region, for the contribution made by this extensive area to the national output has risen sharply in recent years, largely as a result of mineral developments.

PHYSICAL ASPECTS

STRUCTURE AND RELIEF

The Atlas zone generally in Algeria is narrower than it is in Morocco, and there is a more simple overall pattern of relief. This pattern takes the form of a series of zones running from west to east (see Figs. 79 and 89). In order from north to south we can distinguish the coastal zone, the Tell Atlas, Constantine Uplands Zone, the Plateau of the Shotts, the Saharan Atlas–Aurès Zone and the Sahara Desert; broadly, the Plateau of the Shotts is bordered by Atlas ranges to the north and to the south, the Tell Atlas falling away towards the coast to the north and the Saharan Atlas reaching down towards the desert to the south. This very general picture, however, needs elaboration and modification.

The coastal zone is narrow, and consists for the most part of a series of steps, each rising up steeply from a terrace below; sometimes the lowest step plunges directly into the sea as a high cliff. In some areas, notably near Oran and Algiers, a distinct coastal range occurs, the most impressive being the Dahra range which lies between the Wadi Cheliff (the longest river in Algeria) and the sea to the west of Algiers. These coastal ranges are sometimes known as Sahels and they include some of the remnants of the former Tyrrhenian Shield (see p. 348). The whole coastal zone is known as the Tell, which is possibly a linguistic survival from the Latin *tellus*, the fertile earth, though Barbour includes the mountains of the

377

Constantine region and the Aurès massif as parts of the Tell because these uplands enclose fertile valleys and enjoy a Mediterranean type of rainfall, two features which together permit agriculture.

We have previously seen that coastal plains and lowlands are very restricted in area in the Maghrib generally, but where they do occur they are of great importance as they are often fertile and productive (compare the case of Morocco in the previous chapter). In the Algerian Tell the most important lowlands are the Cheliff valley, the Mitidja (between the isolated Sahel near Algiers and the Tell Atlas; the town of Blida lies near its

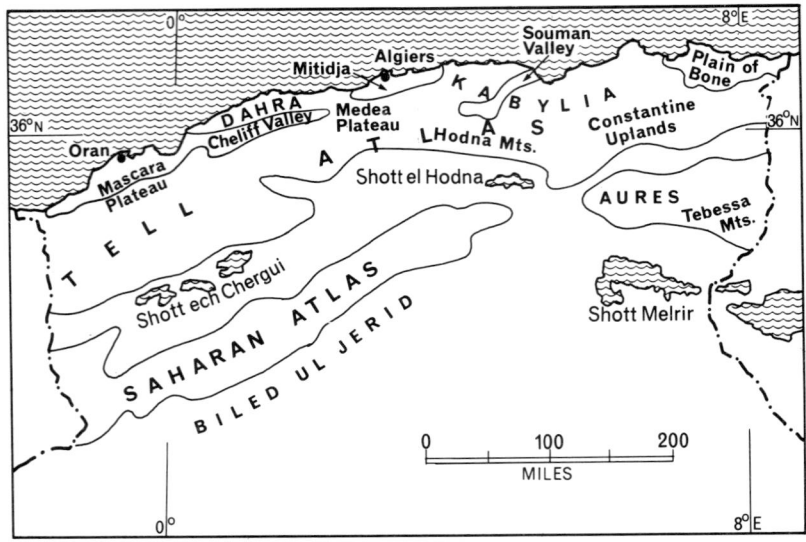

FIG. 89.—Northern Algeria: natural regions.

southern limit), and the Plain of Bone. There are also smaller ones. These plains were turned into productive farm lands by former French colonists.

To the south of the immediate coastal zone, the Tell Atlas continues the line of the Rif Atlas of Morocco, though the two sets of ranges are separated by the lower Moulouya valley. The Tell Atlas is not as high as the Moroccan ranges and is more broken, comprising as it does discontinuous uplands separated by valleys and plains. Notable ranges within the line of the Tell Atlas include the Tlemcen and the Ouarsenis. Farther to the south, the Saharan Atlas which roughly continues the line of the High Atlas is even less continuous, and consists simply of a series of disconnected ridges of which the best known are the Ksour mountains, the Djebel Amour and the Ouled-Nail mountains. These ranges have been heavily eroded, and when viewed from the air they appear to be largely buried in masses of their own débris; they appear low and almost insignificant when viewed from plateaus to the north, but they form an impressive series of features when sighted from the south as they fall steeply away towards the desert by as much as 5000 ft (1500 m) or sometimes 6000 ft (1800 m). To the east of the Ouled-Nail mountains there is a marked break in the line of uplands as a kind of lowland embayment breaks through from the south to include the Shott el Hodna depression.

Both the Tell Atlas and the Saharan Atlas are deeply gashed by gorges cut by streams which become raging torrents during the rainy season though they may dry up almost completely during the summer; this is a typical feature of Maghrib rivers. Notice that the two sets of ranges approach each other more closely with increasing distance eastwards as far as the Shott el Hodna depression, while at the same time they become lower and more broken. In the eastern third of the Atlas region, however, the mountains are higher, more impressive and more confused in arrangement. The line of the Tell Atlas is continued in the southern part of the mountains of Kabylia; the northern part is a comparatively large fragment of the former Tyrrhenian Shield, but the southern parts of the crystalline rocks forming this fragment are covered with great thicknesses of Jurassic limestones, which have been thrust up to form the highest mountain range in Algeria, the Djurdjura. The Tell Atlas is also continued in the mountains of Constantine, while the Saharan Atlas continues in the Aurès massif and the Tebessa mountains. The mountains of Kabylia are heavily dissected and rugged, narrow ridges sharply alternating with steep-sided and deeply incised gorges. The whole region is difficult of access even today, and it remains a centre of Berber language and culture (*see* Fig. 81). The Aurès massif, too, is an almost inaccessible highland region characterised by great ridges and deep valleys.

Between the Tell Atlas and the Saharan Atlas series of ranges lies the Plateau of the Shotts, an upland plain with an average elevation of between 3000 and 4000 ft (900–1200 m) above sea-level though the general height decreases from west to east. The plateau is broadest in the west and gradually narrows eastwards and it is of generally subdued relief. The western part is known as the Oran Meseta and this is comparable in origin with the Moroccan Meseta, except that it has been thrust up to a greater elevation. The plateau generally takes its name from the many shotts (depressions containing shallow saline lakes) which occur on its surface. The lakes, which are sometimes known as "sebkras," increase in size during the winter as they are fed by the rains, but they may dry up completely during the summer. The best known of the shotts include the Shott ech Chergui and the Shott el Hodna (*see* Fig. 89). Notice the Hodna mountains which break the even character of the surface of the plateau to the north of the shott of the same name. Between the mountains of Constantine and the Aurès massif the Plateau of the Shotts is very narrow, and the shotts which stud its surface (for example in the Aïn Beida area) are small.

To the north of a line running roughly between the oases of Colomb Béchar, Figig, Laghouat and Biskra, the Saharan Atlas fall sharply down towards the desert in the region known as the Biled-ul-jerid (the land of

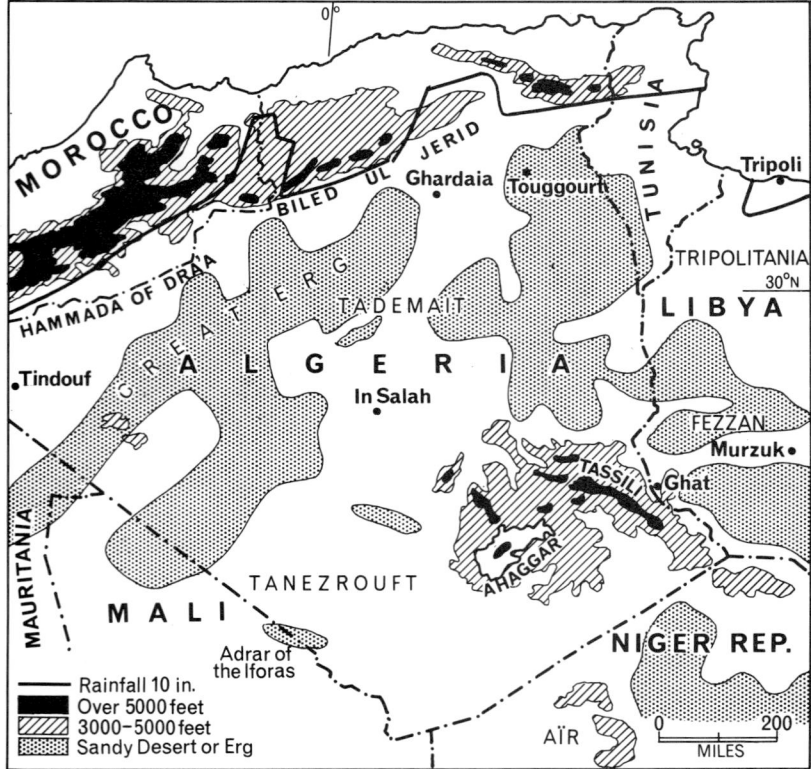

FIG. 90.—The central Sahara.

dates). Although this survey is concerned mainly with northern Algeria,
it will be appropriate to say something about the vast Saharan part of the
country, and the general features are shown on Fig. 90.

From the physical point of view the most prominent series of features
in the Algerian deserts are the extensive plateaus of Ahaggar and Tassili
which lie towards the south-eastern parts of the country, while a lower
plateau links Ahaggar with the Adrar of the Iforas, a dissected upland
which extends across the southern border into Mali. These plateaus include areas developed on massive sedimentary rocks (especially sandstones),
volcanic areas and residual uplands which form part of the ancient African
basement; the general result emerges in a series of landscapes bewildering
in complexity and in beauty. Diolé, for instance, says of Tassili that when
seen from a distance it appears to be only a massive block, but the traveller
who penetrates it perceives the complexity, the systems of ramparts, the
corridors and the crenellated walls which together make it a "well-
defended and incredibly ramified domain."★ Other writers have com-

★ In *The Most Beautiful Desert of All*, London, 1959, which can be recommended
for its descriptions of desert scenes and life.

mented on the "theatrical" and "dreamlike" qualities of these highlands, which are often rendered more impressive by the astonishing range of colours presented by the crystalline rocks and the volcanic rocks which in places have been thrust into them.

In an enormous horseshoe-like pattern around these central uplands lies a series of depressions which sweep across Algeria between the central plateaus and the Atlas regions; parts of these depressions such as Reggan and the north-east lie below 500 ft (150 m) above sea-level. Shott Melrir is actually below sea-level while other parts such as Tanezrouft, Tademait and the Hammada of Dra'a (*see* Figs. 79 and 90) lie at higher elevations. Some of this extensive area consists of *erg* (sandy desert), some of *reg* (stony desert), and some of *hammada* (rocky desert), and these different types of desert originate from the weathering of the surface rocks and the subsequent dispersal of the finer products of erosion. Much dispersal takes the form of dust storms, and the movement of dust which accompanies these storms can affect very wide areas. Travellers have recorded, for instance, flying through almost unbroken clouds of dust for as far as 400 miles—about the same distance as that from the coast of southern England to the estuary of the Forth in central Scotland. The extent of erg is shown on Fig. 90, and while this is the desert of popular imagination it forms a comparatively limited part of the desert as a whole. Wide expanses of reg lie between the erg and the Ahaggar and Tassili plateaus, particularly in Tanezrouft and Tademait. Sometimes the surface of the reg is strewn with gravel which is quite flat, as though it had been raked smooth, while in other places it is as though slabs and boulders have been carelessly thrown down by a giant hand with no form or order; such an area has been aptly described by Diolé as a "mere chaos of stones."[*]

On the whole the central highlands of the Sahara are rocky, so that they fall into the category of hammada desert. Enormous cliff-like eminences often tower upwards for many hundreds of feet, and these sometimes afford evidence of geologically recent uplift or of volcanic outpourings. Often great gorges with almost vertical sides tear through these highlands —gorges which may have originated during an earlier period when the climate of the Sahara was moister than it is now. On the other hand, some hammadas such as the Hammada of Dra'a are very much lower and flatter, and they lack the grandeur of the more southerly plateaus. However, many questions remain unanswered about the nature of desert erosion and the consequent formation of land forms.[†]

There are, of course, no true rivers in the Algerian Sahara, but we have mentioned the steep-sided gorges known as *wadis* which scar the high plateaus, and which can be traced in some cases (in a less incised form) for hundreds of miles even across the lower-lying areas. The Wadi Saoura, for example, has on occasion actually flowed along a well-defined course

[*] *Op. cit.*
[†] These are summarised in a sister book in this series, JARRETT, H. R., *Africa*, Macdonald & Evans, 1966 (Second Edition), pp. 173 *ff.*

for as far as 500 miles southwards from the Atlas, and it supports an almost continuous line of date palms pointing towards the heart of the desert. At places such as Beni Abbès and Adrar along its course, where water is more abundant than usual, notable oases have developed.

The wadis which extend outwards from the Ahaggar Plateau are of the gorge-like form and from time to time they are invaded by raging torrents of water following the storms which occasionally burst, especially over high ground. Such torrents sweep masses of finely weathered material along towards lower ground until finally the water is lost as, released from the containing walls of the wadi, it spreads out over the desert floor before being swallowed up—perhaps by the very sand it has brought down with it from the upper reaches of the wadi. These watercourses are thought to have originated during an earlier period when the climate of the Sahara was considerably moister than it is today.

CLIMATE

It is not easy to give a summary account of the climate of Algeria because of the complex pattern involved. This complexity arises partly from the general location of this large country which extends from Mediterranean into inter-tropical latitudes, and partly from the complicated pattern of relief. It will probably be least confusing to deal first with the Maghrib section, and after that to give a brief account of the climate of the desert region.

Temperature patterns in the Maghrib are affected by the following chief factors:

(1) latitude;
(2) distance from the sea;
(3) altitude and aspect;
(4) prevailing weather patterns.

The general effect of latitude is, of course, to produce higher temperatures with increasing distance southwards; thus, the average temperature of the hottest month (August) in Algiers is 74·7° F (23·6° C), while for Biskra (July) it is 89° F (31·7° C). It would be wrong to conclude, however, that the higher temperature experienced at Biskra stems entirely from a lower latitude. The fact is that Biskra is sharply cut off from maritime influences by the Atlas system, and the high summer temperature owes more to continental influences than to any difference in latitude. This point can be better appreciated from a consideration of the winter temperatures of the two places, for whereas the coolest month at Algiers (January) records an average temperature of 53° F (11·7° C), at Biskra the comparable figure (also for January) is 51° F (10·6° C). It is clear that any effects of latitude are masked by the effects derived from distance from the sea.

Even this is not the whole story, however, for the question of aspect cannot be ignored. Whereas Algiers is sheltered from the south by the Atlas ranges and is therefore affected mainly by influences which come from the Mediterranean, Biskra is sheltered from the north, and lies fully open to Sahara influences. These two towns have been chosen as examples because they illustrate contrasts of temperature which occur widely between the coasts of Algeria and the Biled-ul-jerid.

Within the Atlas system itself, other factors come into play, though the effect of the higher altitude is very much what we might suppose. The Atlas zone is markedly cooler, on the average, than the lowlands, though on the Plateau of the Shotts this is often not the case in summer as the rarefied, clear air permits a high degree of insolation, and this produces temperatures which are often higher than those of the coastal region; compare, for instance, the August figure for Algiers given above with the July figure (July is the hottest month in this case) for Constantine, 79° F (26·1° C). In winter, on the other hand, there is great loss of heat on the plateau through strong radiation, and temperatures are correspondingly low (at Constantine the average January figure is 43° F, 6·1° C), while the region is often swept by northerly winds which bring temperatures down below freezing point; severe snowstorms are not uncommon at this season. Such conditions do not occur along the coastal lowlands where frost is of rare occurrence and where the mean January temperature is about 55° F (12·8° C). Winter conditions are in general rather cooler than this in the Biled-ul-jerid, but the very severe weather typical of the Atlas system is not experienced.

The importance of prevailing weather patterns was mentioned earlier, and we should say a word about this. A typical weather pattern experienced in the Maghrib during the winter half of the year is the depression, and the passage of a depression brings with it associated winds which markedly affect temperatures. For instance, it is the northerly winds typical of the rear of depressions which account for the blizzards encountered on the Plateau of the Shotts in winter to which reference has been made. In spring and early summer, on the other hand, the southerly winds which blow in the front of a depression can be uncomfortable and even dangerous as they blow from the Sahara. Not only are these winds scorchingly hot, often causing crops to wither, but they frequently sweep along masses of fine desert dust; these conditions are typical of the *sirocco* at its worst (*see* p. 38).

The pattern of rainfall in Algeria is shown on Fig. 80. The main point which should be made is clear enough—that rainfall in general decreases away from the Mediterranean coast. This bare statement, however, needs qualification. It is noteworthy, for example, how the coastal areas east of El Asnam (Orléansville) receive notably more rain than those farther west, and the reason for this has already been given (p. 349). The western parts of the Tell record on an average about 16 in. of rain a year, while in the eastern parts the comparable figure rises to 30 in. or even more. Inland, the Tell Atlas ranges are on the whole well watered, but the Plateau of the

Shotts suffers from a marked rain-shadow effect; the rainfall it enjoys rarely exceeds 20 in. and is often as low as 10 in. The northern slopes of the Saharan Atlas receive in general between 10 and 15 in., but the figure decreases sharply southwards; Biskra, for example, records a mean annual total of only 6·3 in. The effect of the contrast between the Atlas and the Biled-ul-jerid is perhaps most noticeable in the spring, near the end of the rains, when from the crest of the Saharan Atlas it is possible to look northwards over the green, grassy steppes of the Plateau of the Shotts, while to the south the desert stretches away from the foot of the Atlas towards the erg with its dunes and yellow sand.

The seasonal distribution of rainfall has already been emphasised, and little more need be said on this point; it might be useful for the reader to refer back to what was said above on pp. 48 ff. One marked effect of this seasonal distribution is to be seen in the watercourses of northern Algeria; the Cheliff is the only perennial river of any size in the whole country, and most streams are intermittent, storming down from the highlands after rain but dry during the summer drought. Another effect which should be noted is the violence of many of the rainstorms, for this violence produces heavy run-off which causes severe soil erosion. Barbour has estimated that no less than 250 acres *per day* are on an *average* lost to Algeria as a result of soil erosion.

It is not necessary to say very much about the climate of the extensive desert parts of Algeria, for these cannot be classed as Mediterranean in any real sense; the reader who needs more information on this point is referred to other books.* We may, however, mention the aridity which is the most prominent feature, and this, coupled with an interior location, produces very marked variations in temperature, both diurnal and seasonal. Dust storms known as *simoons*, during which the air is filled with whirling clouds of dust, form a very unpleasant feature of the climate of the Sahara. The term *simoon*, used here because it is widely known, is rarely used in the Sahara itself. In the northern desert hot dusty winds are called *cheheli*, and in the central areas the name is *ouahdj*.

The small amount of rain which does fall over the Algerian Sahara falls mainly in the winter half-year, and it is associated with the depressions which bring rain to the Maghrib and which sometimes extend their influence southwards into the desert. Trailing fronts from winter depressions can on occasion extend surprisingly far south. The writer recalls one which reached as far south as Gambia, West Africa, on one occasion when he was resident there, and the resulting thunderstorm in February, at the height of the dry season, caused great alarm among the populace. Very extensive areas, however, receive no rain at all for years, and then a storm may break and bring a torrential downpour—perhaps as much as 2 in. of rain may fall in a single storm, and it is then that the wadis become raging torrents. The highlands of Tassili and Ahaggar are comparatively well watered, for storms of great violence bring enough rain to support a

*E.g., JARRETT, H. R., *op. cit.*

sparse population on the natural pastures. The highest summits of these massifs carry snow in winter.

NATURAL REGIONS

The simplest and most satisfactory sub-division of Algeria is one based upon physical geography; four chief zones can be recognised on this basis in the northern part of the country, and these are the Tell coastal zones, the Tell Atlas, the Plateau of the Shotts, and the Saharan Atlas. The Sahara Desert will also receive brief attention.

1. *The coastal zone of the Tells.* This extends all along the 620 miles of Mediterranean coast and is narrow and broken. Discontinuous coastal ranges (Sahels, Fig. 91), parts of which are remnants of the Tyrrhenian Shield, act as barriers between the restricted areas of lowland and rise up as a series of steps often directly from the sea, especially in the Kabyle area. One of the most notable of these coastal ranges is the Dahra. A few bays along the coast offer some shelter to shipping, and the best of these (which are not necessarily very good) have given rise to the leading ports of Algiers, Mers-el-Kebir (Oran), Bejaia (formerly Bougie) and Bone. The Tell is the best-watered part of Algeria and has an annual rainfall of about 16 in. (which permits the growing of cereal crops) in the western parts, and up to 30 in. farther east, though the seasonal distribution is irregular. The natural vegetation is mainly woodland and considerable areas on the Sahels are still forested, the oak and the pine being of widespread occurrence.

The Tell is more reminiscent of southern France than any other part of Algeria, with its characteristic Mediterranean climate and its geological similarities, and it is not surprising that this region became the chief area of French settlement and the most productive part of the whole country. This is particularly the case in the segment west of Algiers, where before the arrival of the French the semi-nomadic inhabitants cultivated unreliable crops of cereals and tended their stock. This situation was changed, however, by the advent of immigrants (Spanish as well as French) and by the general suitability of the region for viticulture. The warm, humid climate of the coastal Tell proved ideal also for the production of early spring vegetables and fruit, both of which command high prices in Paris markets. Rainfall decreases towards the west, as we have seen, and more attention must therefore be paid to water supply. As well as the vine, fruit, vegetables and cereals (wheat and barley) are widely grown.

The lowlands of the Tell were originally marshy and unhealthy, for free drainage was impeded by the Sahels which often lie between the lowlands and the sea. A tremendous amount of labour, however, has been expended in the carrying out of drainage schemes, and wide areas now form prosperous farm lands producing good crops of cereals, vegetables, cotton, tobacco, grapes, citrus fruits and olives. The vineyards of the Plain of Mitidja have been described as the most magnificent in the entire African continent. Oddly enough, in view of the original marshy tendency, most parts of the lowlands benefit from irrigation as the winter rainfall is not great (*see* p. 387 below), while the summers are hot and dry.

The Mitidja, with its level surface, its deep and rich soils, and its adequate water supply, is today one of the most productive parts of North Africa, despite the fact that it was once an unhealthy marsh. Most farmers in the area devote the greater part of their land to the cultivation of vines which demand a considerable amount of attention (regular pruning, spraying, weeding and manuring, as well as the harvesting of the grapes in late summer) though much of the work is now carried on with the help of machines. Even during the hot, dry summer the vine with its long tap-root does not need irrigation, and water derived from streams and artesian wells is used to irrigate citrus orchards (mainly orange and lemon) and tobacco fields. During the winter—the rainy season—only vegetables are grown (peas, beans, potatoes, carrots and lettuces), and these find a market in France in the early spring. Other crops include olives and flowers (which are grown for the perfume which can be extracted from them). The produce is sent to market towns such as Blida, and some of it is then sent on to Algiers for export, while some is processed in local factories—for example, tobacco is cured, olive oil is extracted and refined, perfume is manufactured and wine is produced.

2. *The Tell Atlas.* The coastal zone is bounded to the south by the Tell or Maritime Atlas, which consists of a series of long, narrow ridges such as the Tlemcen and the Ouarsenis, separated by depressions, some of which are low enough to permit the construction through them of roads and railways on to the Plateau of the Shotts. The ranges have been worn down so that their upper surfaces are plateau-like, while many of the valleys which cut through them are very deep and picturesque, a notable example being that of the gorge of the Rhumel, which runs north-east-wards from Constantine to the coast.

The moister slopes of the Tell Atlas are forested; there is a great deal of cork-oak on the mountains of Constantine, and the traveller by rail through these mountains can see piles of bark torn from the cork-oak trees lying alongside the track; the bark is awaiting transport prior to treatment for the manufacture of cork. Also crops of cereals and fruit are produced where water supply and terrain permit. For example, the uplands of Kabylia are well watered and fruit growing is a major concern, figs and olives being especially important. The Grande Kabylie highland mass is, in fact, one of the most densely populated parts of Algeria, but the Berbers whose homeland this is live under conditions of great poverty. Their mountain strongholds and the villages which cluster along the ridges of the region have always been difficult for the invader to subdue, and it is here that the language and customs of the Berbers have been least affected by outside influences. Sheep and goats are reared generally on the mountain slopes.

Most of the villages of the Tell Atlas region west of Algiers lie in sheltered positions in the steep-sided valleys. These valleys were once wooded, but much of the forest has now been destroyed, the wood being used for building purposes or for firewood; often the hillsides have been terraced to prevent soil erosion, while some re-afforestation has been carried out with the same end in view. The farms belonging to the villagers are usually small, cereals (mainly wheat and barley) forming the main crops, but where hill streams bring additional supplies of water orchards of orange, lemon and almond trees are found. In drier parts, orchards of fig and olive predominate and cereal and vegetable crops are grown between the trees. High up on the mountain slopes forests of Aleppo pine, cork-oak and cedar still flourish.

At intermediate heights lie alluvial plains such as those of Tlemcen and Sidi bel Abbès, which originally depended upon stock-rearing and the extensive cultivation of cereals, until immigrant *colons* established extensive vineyards. Higher still in elevation, the plateaus of Medea and Mascara (*see* Fig. 89) are also favourable for vine growing—indeed, the best vintages of Algeria come from these areas.

There is thus a considerable diversity of landscape and land use in the Tell region as a whole, a diversity ranging from damp and forested mountain areas such as Ouarsenis and the Blida Atlas on the one hand, to low-lying areas such as the Cheliff valley on the other. The Cheliff valley experiences a marked rain-shadow effect because of its enclosed position between the Dahra and the Ouarsenis massifs, and summers are uncomfortably hot. At El Asnam (Orléansville), for example, the mean daily temperature maximum in July and August is no less than 99° F (37·2° C), while the mean annual rainfall is only 16·3 in. Vines are, however, grown along the valley, together with tree crops (olives, figs and apricots) and cereals (wheat and barley). Herds of sheep and goats graze on the maquis which covers the hill sides. Small-scale irrigation and hydro-electric projects have been undertaken in recent years.

3. *The Plateau of the Shotts.* This lies to the south of the Tell Atlas. It is highest and broadest in the west where the Shott ech Chergui occupies a depression about 100 miles (160 km) long and about 20 miles (32 km) across at its widest point. The lowest part of the plateau lies to the south-east of Algiers, in the extensive depression occupied by the Shott el Hodna; this depression continues south-eastwards towards the Shott Melrir, so breaking through the Saharan Atlas. To the north of the Shott el Hodna the Hodna mountains rise sharply up. In its eastern section, between the mountains of Constantine to the north and the Aurès massif to the south, the plateau is very narrow, and the shotts in this area, such as those near Aïn Beida, are small.

The plateau is semi-arid, and during the summer its surface takes on a desert-like appearance, but even so flocks of sheep and goats are widely pastured by the nomadic inhabitants on what is really a steppe-like form of vegetation. Cultivation is very restricted owing to the lack of water; indeed, in some areas supplies of water are so restricted that even irrigation is not practicable, though this is not the case in the moister areas bordering the Tell Atlas where limited crops of cereals are produced. Alfalfa, or esparto grass, with its deep roots, has been successfully planted, especially in the west; this grass is used for the manufacture of high-grade paper, and it has become an important commercial product. The monotonous aspect of high plains extensively planted with this grass has given rise to the expression *mer d'alfa*.

4. *The Saharan Atlas.* This consists for the most part of a number of discontinuous ranges which are generally only a few hundred feet higher than the Plateau of the Shotts; prominent among these ranges are the Ksour, the Djebel Amour and the Ouled-Nail. To the east of the Hodna–Melrir depression, however, the line of the Atlas is continued in the prominent Aurès massif, a heavily dissected plateau of a general elevation of about 4000 ft (1200 m) above sea-level, though the highest peaks which are snow-covered in winter rise above 7000 ft (2100 m). The scenery is varied and often magnificent, stony and sandy desert-like tracts alternating with fertile forested hill slopes, while wooded and productive valleys cut through the uplands; impressive ravines cut across the plateau surface and seam the limestone ranges. Many of the high slopes are covered with forests of cedar, while below these forests of oaks and pines flourish; these woodlands slowly give place at lower levels to pastures and maquis. Along the slopes of the valleys in the centre and north of the ranges are grown crops of cereals (especially barley and wheat), while along the valley floors there are orchards of peaches, plums, apples and olives, and olive oil is produced on a large scale. In addition, in the moister north, walnuts, pomegranates and apricots are especially important and form a source of considerable revenue. In the south conditions are drier and favour date palms in the valley oases, between which extend scanty pastures. The rugged relief has helped to keep the Aurès rather isolated, and the Berber inhabitants remain exclusive as in the case of Kabylia.

5. *The Sahara Desert.* This extensive region is not Mediterranean in any true sense, but it is included here for the sake of completeness. We shall moreover see later that the region which was thought to be almost worthless not so many years ago now makes a very substantial contribution to the wealth of Algeria.

Southern Algeria has within its boundaries various types of desert, including the *erg* of the west and north, the *hammada* of the south-east (notably the Tassili and Ahaggar massifs) and the north-west (the Hammada of Dra'a), and the *reg* of the south-west and centre in Tanezrouft and Tademait respectively, though these physical divisions are not altogether clear cut. Oases are fairly widely scattered, especially in the north and west, though the best-watered areas as far as surface supplies are concerned comprise the Tassili and Ahaggar plateaus where the density of population is slightly higher than it is elsewhere (*see* p. 403). Well-known oases include In Salah in Tuat and Tamanrasset in the Ahaggar, both on the road linking Algiers with Kano (the Hoggar route, *see* Fig. 91); the Wadi Saoura group including Beni Abbès and Adrar on the road between

Colomb Béchar and the river Niger; the group strung out along the line near the lowest slopes of the Atlas in the Biled-ul-jerid region (Colomb Béchar, Figig, Laghouat and Biskra); and the group in the north-east (Ghardaia, Touggourt and Ouargla).

Quite different in character and appearance are the oases of the east. In one of the remote valleys of the eastern Tassili, for example, lies the Djanet oasis which has been described as the "most beautiful oasis in the world." Even today it is scarcely touched by outside influences in a direct way, though indirectly a great change has come over the inhabitants as they have been freed from the fears of past centuries, when they had to suffer raids and pillaging from desert marauders. As if to emphasise the fact that

FIG. 91.—View up the Arak gorge in the Hoggar highlands of the central Sahara. Sparse vegetation is visible along the floor of the gorge and the steep valley sides mantled with rock débris (scree).

three major regions converge in this area, we find in the oasis three distinct settlements, one peopled by Senussi who have come from eastern Libya via Fezzan, one by Tibu, an Hamitic-Negroid group from mountainous Tibesti, and the third by Tuareg, nomads from Tassili and Ahaggar. The isolation may not, however, last much longer. The Government has already decided "in principle" to set up small industrial enterprises in the south and to erect 200-bed hotels in Djanet, Tamanrasset and Ghardaia.

Rain may fall in Djanet only once every four years or so, and the water upon which settlement depends is obtained from deep wells with the aid of ropes, pulleys and donkeys (*cf.* the Mzab, *see* p. 404). Between the white houses, small "fields" no larger than gardens are bordered by palms which enclose the growing crops of wheat, barley and vegetables. Life is still self-contained in this remote spot.

HUMAN GEOGRAPHY

HISTORY AND PEOPLE

A fundamental feature of the human geography of Algeria, one which applies generally throughout the Maghrib, is the distinction between Berber and Arab. This has already been explained, and reference has been made to the special case of the Kabyles. The reader might find it useful at this point to refresh his memory from the details regarding the people of the Maghrib and their early history already given on pages 351–353.

The modern period in Algerian history may be said to have begun in 1830, when France invaded the territory avowedly to suppress the activities of the notorious Barbary pirates. The town of Algiers fell that same year, but less accessible parts of the country such as Kabylia were not subdued until 1857. In 1870 the policy of assimilation was adopted; according to this form of government the overseas territory concerned became officially part of the metropolitan country, and any citizen of the territory who could satisfy certain educational requirements could become a full voting citizen of France. Movement of people and goods between France and *la France d'outre-mer* was entirely free and without control. In the case of Algeria the *départements* which lay within the Maghrib were recognised as parts of metropolitan France, while the Saharan areas remained under military rule. This administrative framework remained substantially unchanged until 1959, when additional *départements* were established.

After the Second World War nationalistic feeling rose high in Algeria, though officially the nationalist movement was outlawed. In 1947 a popularly elected Algerian Assembly was set up, half of the members representing Europeans and half Muslims, though this was only an advisory body. Nationalistic feeling steadily mounted, however; in 1955 a state of emergency was proclaimed, military reinforcements were despatched, and Algeria was virtually at war with France, which remained for long firmly opposed to the granting of full independence to the territory. This opposition arose partly from economic reasons (the discovery of mineral oil was important in this respect) and partly because according to the prevailing French political conceptions Algeria was part of the mother country, and the question of independence could not therefore arise. This position proved untenable, however, and after a costly and barbarous struggle Algeria became independent in 1962.

One notable result of the pacification of the territory by the French had been a dramatic increase in population. In 1836 there were about $2\frac{1}{2}$ million Muslims in Algeria, but by 1960 the figure was over 10 million. A high birth-rate was partly responsible for this, but equally important was the decline in mortality which developed as a result of better standards of hygiene encouraged by the French. Numbers of European settlers also made their homes in Algeria during the colonial period, and we have said something about the valuable contributions to economic progress made by these *colons*. In 1956 there were about 1½ million Europeans in Algeria, though only about half of these were French; the remainder came mainly from Spain, Italy, Corsica and Malta. Four-fifths of these Europeans lived in the towns. As a *colonie de peuplement* Algeria did not prove the success which the French expected, and since the granting of independence the number of Europeans has fallen to less than 100,000. Since 1962 the Algerian Government has enacted measures dispossessing European farmers of their land; the situation remains confused and troubled.

POPULATION AND SETTLEMENT

The population of Algeria in 1966, in the first census to be held after independence, was recorded as 12,093,203, of whom just over half a million lived in the two Saharan *départements* of Saoura and the Oases. The remainder of the people live in the northern parts of the country, especially in the coastal Tell and in parts of the Tell Atlas. The five largest towns and cities of Algeria are also in these same regions; these towns are Algiers, Oran, Constantine, Bone and Sidi bel Abbès. Something will be said later about these important centres.

Population density in northern Algeria works out at about 15 persons per square mile, but this overall figure masks wide variations. On the steppes of the Plateau of the Shotts, for example, the density is often less than 2 persons per square mile, while in areas where stock-rearing is combined with cereal production, as on the High Plains of Constantine, it may reach 7 persons. On the other hand, there are smaller productive regions which carry over 30 persons per square mile; these regions include areas intensively cultivated by *colons* such as the Mitidja and the Plain of Bone, the various towns and cities and their immediate environments, and even parts of apparently unpromising uplands like the Kabylia massif, which shelters surprisingly large populations who remain intensely conscious of their racial and cultural separateness from the main body of inhabitants (*see* p. 351).

The information given regarding the form of settlements in Morocco (*see* p. 364) could apply with very little modification to conditions in Algeria. The same clay-walled, flat-roofed houses, which are often strengthened with stone or with palm timbers, huddle together (a relic of the need for protection in earlier days) in small villages around the *ksour* (fortress); sometimes the houses rise in tiers on scarcely accessible slopes, while above the village in some areas such as the Aurès towers the *guelaa*, a combination of village granary and defensible redoubt. Kimble has called the *guelaa* the "architectural *pièce de résistance* of Barbary." It is built of mud, strengthened by stone and date palm timbers, and it may be three or four storeys high. It stands on the most easily defended site in or near the village and is often accessible only by scrambling up a rope ladder or by scaling a hazardous cliff face. Some *guelaas* include approximately one separate chamber for each family of the village, and in these chambers the year's harvest of fruit and grain is stored, together with household goods which cannot easily be carried when the villagers migrate to their summer pastures. Traditional towns in Algeria show the same general layout as their counterparts in Morocco. The old *medinas*, with their narrow streets, enclosed courtyards, and bustling shops typically form the centre of town life, and sometimes a *European Quarter* with a gridiron street plan stands in sharp contrast to the *kasbah*, the Arab quarter with its narrow streets and houses crowded closely together. On the whole it is true to say that towns which have received an injection of European life and vigour have prospered, while other towns such as Tlemcen have tended to stagnate.

Unfortunately, it seems that life in the *medinas* is changing, not entirely for the better. In earlier years these centres were the homes of artisans and craftsmen who produced their goods for sale in the *suqs* (*see* Fig. 84); it was customary for these producers to segregate themselves in separate streets according to their craft. Thus, booksellers, goldsmiths, *parfumeurs*, and the manufacturers of incense often were grouped in their separate streets in the central parts of the *medina*, while metal workers, tanners, leather workers and others who plied the dirtier and noisier crafts were to be found nearer the fringes. In these days, however, all these craftsmen and artisans are feeling the strain of competition from imported, mass-produced European goods; their numbers therefore are tending to decrease while their goods are being replaced in the *suqs* by shoddy imported articles. Another unfortunate feature of contemporary town life is the often appalling degree of overcrowding. In Algeria, as in many other countries today, there is a considerable movement of people away from the countryside into the towns, though there is not sufficient work available for them all. The result is that many of these new arrivals are crowded into *bidonvilles*, sordid "tin-pan towns" notable for their squalid shanties of sheet-iron (often flattened-out metal containers) and wood. These *bidonvilles*, not surprisingly, form natural centres of poverty, social unrest and disease. We may add that the features of town life described in these paragraphs are also to be seen in Morocco and Tunisia.

CHIEF TOWNS AND CITIES

It might at this stage be useful to say something about the more important towns and cities of Algeria. The largest and most important of these are Algiers (population 884,000), Oran (393,000), Constantine (223,000), Bone (165,000) and Sidi bel Abbès (105,000).

Algiers has been a port since before Roman times, though during the long period of Turkish suzerainty it was little more than an anchorage for pirates which was protected by a jetty built out from some tiny islets. After the French occupation, however, the port and town grew rapidly in size to cope with the demands of modern commercial development, and today Algiers is one of the most important ports in the Mediterranean; it has nearly 900,000 inhabitants and is easily the leading port of Algeria, while it is also the capital of the territory. Most of its trade is with Marseille. Even so, the bay on which it stands does not offer very much natural shelter, and it has been necessary to construct an extensive artificial harbour. As well as dealing with about one-third of the total trade of Algeria, it is a bunkering station and a well-known and popular tourist centre, while it is the chief commercial and manufacturing town in the country. Factories in or near Algiers which process local raw materials include flour mills, tobacco and cigarette factories, olive oil refineries, tanneries and distilleries, while an oil-refining plant is now in operation at Masison Carrée near by. Algiers is a collecting centre for wine, vegetables, fruit, cereals and olive oil of the Mitidja, while through the port also pass esparto grass, wool and hides from the Plateau of the Shotts together with dates from much of the Biled-ul-jerid. Iron ore and phosphates are also exported. The panoramic view of the capital obtained from the sea is impressive and beautiful, with white buildings climbing steeply up the lower slopes of the small massif of Bouzarea which rises directly up from the coast.

The second port is Oran, with about 400,000 inhabitants, which deals with almost as great a percentage of the overseas trade as Algiers though its harbour is entirely artificial (*see* Fig. 92). It is linked by rail with the iron

[*Courtesy of Ewing Galloway, N.Y.*

Fig. 92.—Algeria: Oran, a typical Sahel (ridge) rising up from the Mediterranean coast. The old fort stands over 1300 ft (396 m) above the port which lies on the flat ground at the foot of the Sahel. On the hill slopes the bush and tree growth is typical of Mediterranean lands, though the date palms in the lower left-hand corner show that the desert is not so very far away. What signs does the picture show of the importance of the port?

mines in the Tell, while its hinterland also includes part of Morocco. Chief exports include wine, cereals, esparto grass and sheep, while manufactured goods are imported. It was originally a small market town serving the port of Mers-el-Kebir (formerly a pirate lair, Mers-el-Kebir later became a naval base, though it has lost much of its earlier importance); its importance now, however, exceeds that of the older port. Industries such as glass making, cotton spinning, soap manufacture, iron smelting and the processing of food (especially fish canning and flour milling) are all carried on in the town. Oran competes for the overseas trade of western Algeria with

[*Courtesy of Ewing Galloway, N.Y.*

Fig. 93.—Algeria: Constantine. The old town was built on a meander cove almost surrounded by the wild gorge of the Rhumel, part of which can be seen in the picture.

Nemours (which exports mainly coal), Beni Saf (iron ore) and Mostaganem (agricultural produce).

Constantine (*see* Fig. 93), located 40 miles inland from the port of Skikda (Philippeville), has a population of about 250,000. In earlier days it was a fortified town, but it is now a centre for administration and for the eastern end of the Plateau of the Shotts. The town has spread on to the neighbouring plateau from its original strategic position within a meander of the tremendous gorge of the Rhumel, as the question of defence is not now an important one. While the newer suburbs lie to the south-west of the old town, the older city remains little disturbed, with the tortuous, narrow streets of the *medina* given over to various native crafts and industries (*see* p. 392). Constantine attracts a considerable tourist trade.

Bone is the largest port of eastern Algeria, the third port of Algeria, and an important industrial centre. It exports mainly the phosphates and iron ore mined near the Tunisian border near Tebessa (*see* Fig. 94) with which it is linked by electrified railway. The main industries include the process-ing of local produce (flour milling, cork manufacture, fish canning and tobacco processing), the manufacture of chemicals, and general engineer-ing. It is planned to build an oil refinery and an iron and steel plant near the town, and when these projects are completed its importance will be considerably enhanced. Between Bone and Algiers, the port of Bejaia specialises in the export of mineral oil (it forms the seaward terminus of the oil pipeline from the oilfields of the interior—*see* Fig. 95) and also iron ore.

Sidi bel Abbès is an old Moorish town which lies in a fertile alluvial basin. It was for many years the headquarters of the famous French Foreign Legion.

THE ECONOMY

Agriculture and stock-rearing are by far the chief occupations of the people of Algeria—agriculture where availability of water and terrain permit and stock-rearing elsewhere; there is a great contrast between, on the one hand, the landscape and the economy of the cultivated parts of the Tell, and, on the other hand, the interior steppes which are given over for the most part to sheep-rearing. Fishing is of less importance than in Morocco, but mining is today of tremendous significance, while the con-tribution to the national income due to manufacturing is increasing fairly rapidly.

AGRICULTURE

Most of the original Berber inhabitants of Algeria lived in the Tell regions, in areas where rainfall permitted the growing of crops and where pasture was sufficient in amount for their stock. Even so, the swampy and unhealthy lowlands of the coastal zone (including the Cheliff valley and the Mitidja) were almost uninhabited, though today these lowlands form some of the most productive parts of the country, where large crops of cereals, fruit and vegetables are grown; a large part of this produce finds its way to the markets of France. Until recently the same contrast in farm-ing methods existed in Algeria as in Morocco between the European farms, which were concentrated mainly in the better-watered northern parts of the country, and the native farms on which traditional methods of cultivation were followed. Techniques employed on the more pro-gressive farms were advanced, and yields of grain were usually double those obtained on native holdings. As in Morocco, some agricultural workers were landowners (about 42%), some were landless labourers (about 47%), and some could be classed as share-croppers (11%). This situation has now been modified by the wholesale departure of Europeans and by the expropriation of their lands.

The chief agricultural activity on the larger farms is the cultivation of the vine, and the value of the wine shipped overseas has for long greatly exceeded that of any other agricultural export; it is despatched in large quantities to France, and also to the former French territories of West Africa. Following the departure of the French, however, many vineyards have been abandoned, partly because French growers persuaded their Government to restrict the import of Algerian wines. The restriction was lifted in 1967. It is also true that the devout Muslim is forbidden by his religion to drink alcohol. Fig. 94 shows the chief wine-producing areas; vines are grown more particularly on the lower slopes of the Tell Atlas, on certain plateaus within the Tell Atlas zone (*see* p. 387), on the coastal plains and on the Sahels where they are protected both from frost and from the desiccating sirocco.

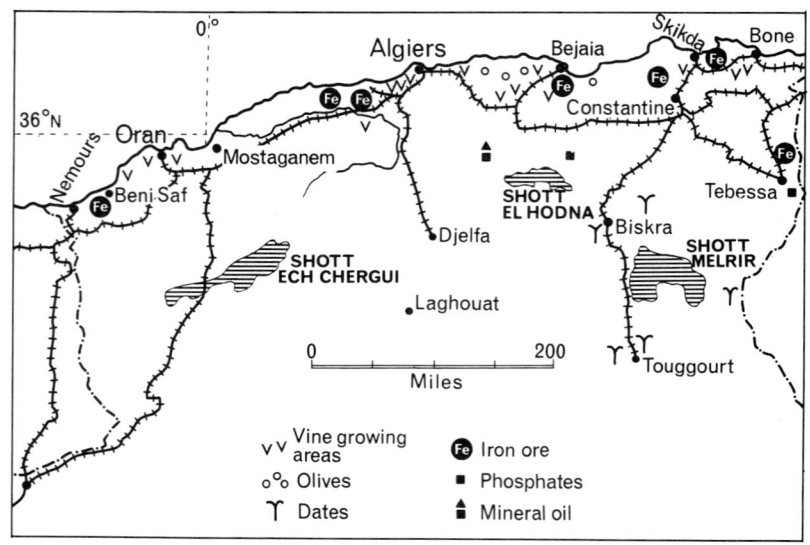

Fig. 94.—Northern Algeria: some economic features. *See also* Fig. 95.

A crop of increasing importance is tobacco, which is grown especially near Constantine. It forms the basis of a flourishing manufacturing industry, and cigarettes, cigars and pipe tobacco are all produced for domestic use and for export. Other crops which have previously been mentioned include vegetables and fruit (especially olives, citrus fruits, figs, apricots and dates), which are grown along valleys and on lowlands where supplies of moisture permit, and esparto grass which is grown extensively on the Plateau of the Shotts. Cereals (wheat and barley) form the chief crops grown by the Algerian peasants.

The fact remains, however, that the Algerians are not able to produce enough foodstuffs to supply their own needs. Algeria generally is a poor country, despite the wealth formerly accumulated by some *colons* (though the number of wealthy settlers was much smaller than generally believed). European farmers before independence produced more than half of the entire domestic crop of Algeria, and since most of the *colons* have now gone the future is perhaps more uncertain than ever before. Barbour reminds us that as long ago as 1936 about 400,000 cwt of flour were distributed to the needy within the country, and in more recent years nearly one-fifth of the commercial harvest of cereal crops has been laid by, as an insurance against future emergencies. The total population increased tremendously during the period of French rule and has more than trebled itself in the past hundred years. The result of all this is that the food situation is desperate. The underlying physical reason is, of course, lack of water, and there is no doubt of the great need for well-planned irrigation schemes, while hand in hand with such schemes should march an increasing struggle against soil erosion (*see* p. 384). Irrigation in parts of the Plateau of the Shotts alone could produce many thousands of acres of cultivable land, and land even to the south of the Aurès massif was cultivated in Roman times and could be brought under the plough once again.

Another possibility of increasing food production lies in the realm of agrarian reform, but this would necessitate a preliminary careful mapping of the areas likely to be affected and it would also require a complete overhaul of the systems of land tenure. The Berber people, for example, in accordance with their democratic way of life, share any inheritance, so that a single fruit tree may come to be shared among several families while land units become steadily smaller. The Arabs, on the other hand, keep an inheritance intact, though it is not always easy to determine exactly to whom a particular piece of property belongs. But these are problems which must engage the attention of the government of independent Algeria for many years to come if a full-scale disaster is to be avoided.

STOCK-REARING

Pastoralism is easily the most important occupation away from the cultivated areas, and it is a way of life well suited to the extensive areas of steppe and the seasonal pastures of the interior. Sheep are far more numerous than any other animal, and it is estimated that there may be 5 million between the coast and the desert margins. A general semi-nomadic movement of sheep northwards takes place throughout the summer, and in autumn, when the flocks have reached the coastal Tell, many of these animals are sold to farmers along the littoral for fattening prior to export. The quality of the mutton, like that of the wool which forms a minor export, could be greatly improved.

Second to the sheep in numbers is the goat; there may be 2 million goats in Algeria, most of them owned by members of the indigenous population. They graze on natural pastures and need a minimum of attention. Goat-skins are exported to France, mainly for use in the glove manufacturing industry, while the milk and meat of the animal provide valuable dietary supplements. The hair and skins are also used locally.

Cattle are reared in appreciable numbers in Algeria, though there are fewer of them than of sheep or goats. Most cattle are to be found in the Tell, for they need larger and more assured supplies of water than either sheep or goats. Even in this region they suffer from a lack of good-quality fodder during the summer. The eastern parts of the Tell, which are better watered than the west, carry larger numbers, and while the animals yield useful quantities of milk and beef they are most prized as draught animals.

MINING

It is now generally realised that Algeria has very considerable reserves of mineral wealth, and mineral exports, especially mineral oil, natural gas (methane), iron ore and phosphates, are of great importance at the present time. Rich non-phosphoric iron ore is mined in many parts of the Tell in places linked by rail to a convenient port; such places occur near Beni Saf, in the Cheliff valley, and in a zone extending eastwards from a location south of Bejaia. Iron ore is exported from Beni Saf, Oran, Algiers, Bejaia (formely Bougie), Skikda (formerly Philipeville) and Bone, most of it going to Britain and Western Germany, with smaller amounts finding their way to Belgium and the Netherlands (France has large domestic reserves). A more important producing area lies north of the railway terminus of Tebessa, near the Tunisian border to the south-east of Constantine, where the Ouenza Bou Khadra mine produces 86% of all iron ore mined in Algeria. Phosphates are also mined near Tebessa, in a region which is really a continuation of the larger Tunisian phosphate belt, while some is produced on the Plateau of the Shotts to the north of the Shott el Hodna. About half a million tons are produced each year, and most of the output is exported via Bone.

There is a small coalfield at Kenadsa, about 20 miles (32 km) west of Colomb Béchar. Total production, however, about 120,000 tons per annum, is not sufficient to supply the needs of the country, and Algeria needs to import each year about three times as much coal as she produces herself.

Mineral oil has for some time been produced on the Plateau of the Shotts to the north-west of the Shott el Hodna, but in recent years spectacular discoveries of both mineral oil and natural gas (methane) have been made in the Algerian Sahara. These discoveries markedly affect the economy of northern Algeria, since it is through Algerian ports that export of these products takes place, particularly through Arzew and Bejaia. The discovery of large-scale oil reserves in North Africa has been one of the most astonishing economic achievements in post-war years; before this time it was generally believed that the continent of Africa was devoid of any substantial reserves of mineral oil. The table below shows how inaccurate this belief has proved to be.

The story of the spectacular developments in mineral oil production in Algeria is a post-war one. Between 1951 and 1961 some £300 million were spent on the search for oil, and the first reward came in 1956 with the discovery of oil deposits in the Polignac Basin (at Edjeleh) and at Hassi Messaoud (*see* Fig. 95). The Edjeleh deposits lie at depths between 1400 and

Oil Production in Africa
(Metric tons, 'ooos)

Territory	1956	1961	1966
Libya . . .	0	850	72,290
Algeria . . .	40	15,660	33,770
Nigeria . . .	0	2,290	20,690
Egypt . . .	1,830	3,320	7,075
Gabon/Congo . .	0	880	1,550
Tunisia . . .	0	0	810
Angola . . .	0	100	650
Morocco . . .	100	80	100

5000 ft (430–1520 m) below the surface, while the Hassi Messaoud reserves lie between 11,000 and 13,000 ft (3300–4000 m). Other oilfields have since been located as shown on Fig. 95. The first area to be brought into production was that near Hassi Messaoud, from where oil was first despatched in 1957 by pipeline to Touggourt and thence by rail to Philippeville (now Skikda). Despatch is now by direct pipeline to Bejaia, and it is proposed to tap this direct route by constructing a branch pipe to Algiers; this new pipeline will leave the present one at Beni Mansour, and it will mean that oil will be able to flow directly to Algiers instead of, as at present, being shipped from Bejaia. A new 24-inch pipeline is also being constructed from Hassi Messaoud to Arzew (see below) in an attempt to speed up the output of Saharan oil, for at the moment output is limited by the pipeline capacity.

There were at least two good reasons why development of oil reserves first took place at Hassi Messaoud, the first being that the centre lies very much nearer the Mediterranean coastline (especially the Algerian part of it) than does Edjeleh. Transport could therefore be established much more speedily. The second point is that Hassi Messaoud lies in the area underlain by a subterranean reservoir of water fed from the Atlas, of which we shall have more to say later. Water supply, therefore, has never been a difficulty. The new town of Hassi Messaoud (which means "the blessed well") is a garden city of air-conditioned houses, its beauty enhanced by lawns, flowering shrubs and bushes, and newly planted trees. It even has two swimming pools! Crops are grown for local use.

The second area to be developed was the Fort Polignac Basin, particularly the part near Edjeleh. Two difficulties met with here were the greater distance from the Mediterranean coast and the fact that the part of the littoral nearest to the oilfield lies in another territory (Tunisia). The first pipeline to be constructed ran northwards from Edjeleh to the Tunisian port of La Skhirra (see Fig. 98), but the field is now linked with Bejaia via Ohanet and Hassi Messaoud so that an all-Algerian route is available.

Very considerable reserves of natural gas (methane) have now been discovered at Hassi R'Mel, which lies a few miles north of Ghardaia, and a methane pipeline has now been constructed to the Mediterranean port of

Arzew, 295 miles away, with extensions to Algiers and Oran. The first commercial exports of natural gas pumped along this route were despatched in 1964. On arrival at Arzew the gas is liquefied in a special plant by cooling it to a temperature of $-258°$ F $(-161 \cdot 1°$ C$)$, and this liquefied gas is then shipped in specially insulated tankers. The main export at present is to Britain, where the gas is mixed with home-produced coal gas

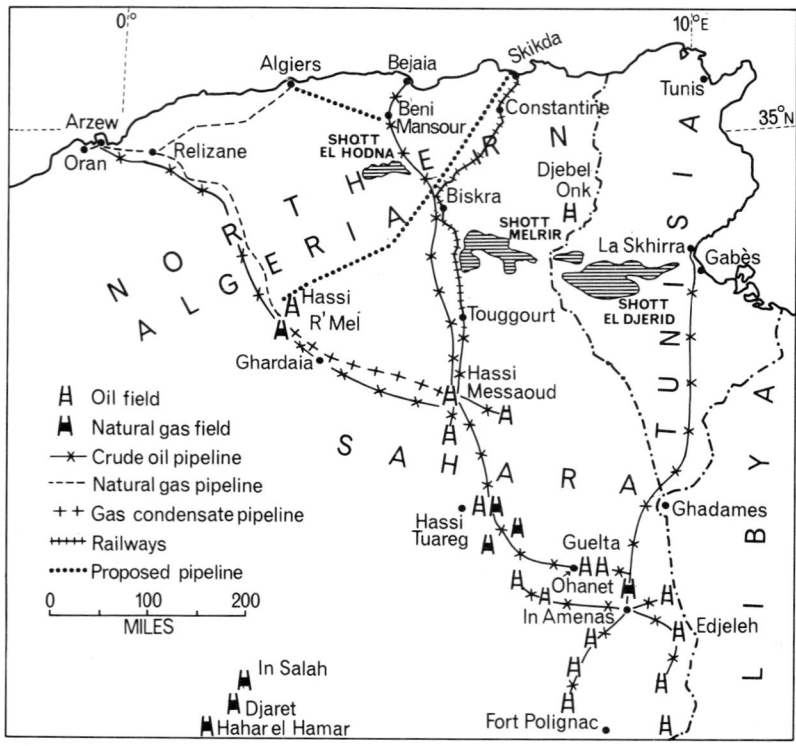

FIG. 95.—Algeria: mineral oil and natural gas.

to increase both the volume and the quality of gas made available to consumers.

Fig. 96 shows the effects which these developments are having on the small port of Arzew, which used to be a pleasant coastal resort depending partly on the summer tourist trade, partly on the export of locally grown alfalfa, and partly on a small fishing industry. There was also a small naval jetty. New jetties have now considerably enlarged the harbour, and these provide safe anchorage for gas tankers; they will also accommodate oil tankers when the need arises. Between the new jetties lies the gas liquefaction plant, and an interesting point about this is that it has been constructed on land built up from what was part of the sea floor; by this means any disturbance of existing land tenure was avoided.

Large supplies of natural gas are also being tapped at present on the El Biod Plateau near Hassi Tuareg, while oil deposits have been located below the gas. The original discovery of the gas in 1961 was rendered spectacular by the fact that the well caught fire eleven days after gas was struck, probably through the action of static electricity, and the biggest oil-well fire in history roared skywards for 166 days to a height of 450 feet (135 m), consuming 550 million cubic feet of gas and 840,000 gallons of petrol *each day*. A natural gas pipeline is now being built to the port of

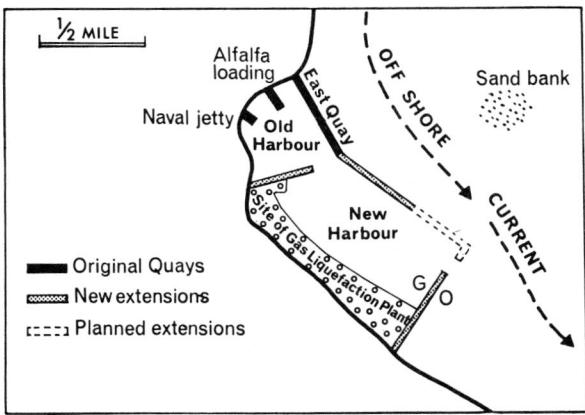

Fig. 96.—Algeria: the port of Arzew. G= wharfage for gas tankers; O= possible wharfage for oil tankers.

Skikda; this is part of a plan to supply natural gas to southern and eastern Europe. Methane-carrying ships will ply between Algeria and the European ports of Genoa and Koper (Yugoslavia), from where pipelines will run inland. Markets for natural gas are being sought in France and Italy.

At the present time the total proven reserves of the Algerian Sahara are said to amount to about 1500 million tons of oil and 80 million million cubic feet of natural gas. The distribution of these reserves is shown in the following table.

Area	Mineral Oil (million tons)	Natural Gas (million cubic feet)
Fort Polignac Basin	451	17,600,000
Hassi Messaoud Region	480	
Hassi R'Mel	400	35,200,000
Ohanet Region	15	
El Biod Plateau	85	26,000,000
Ahnet Region*		1,800,000
Total	1,431	80,600,000

*Shown on Fig. 95 as the In Salah group.

Export of oil from Algeria has leapt up since 1956 as is shown on the table on page 399, but this spectacular development does not mean that this new major producing region does not have its problems. One point is that world oil production was adequate to meet all demands even before the region became a producer, and it is fairly certain that the increase in output would not have been so rapid had not France been so anxious to become independent of Middle East supplies after the Suez incident of 1956. The difficulties attending production in a wild desert terrain far removed from the service ports need not be laboured, while another problem arises from the quality of the oil which is exceptionally light in type, thereby contrasting markedly with the Middle East product. Crude oil from Hassi Messaoud yields only about 20% of fuel oil, whereas oil from Kuwait yields 50%, and this is unfortunate for North Africa, as the pattern of oil consumption in Western Europe shows a high demand for fuel oils and other heavy products, and a correspondingly smaller demand for the lighter products such as petrol. Some Algerian oil has been exported to the U.S.A. where the demand for petrol is proportionately greater, but the U.S. market, with its import restrictions, home production and its established connections with Venezuela and the Middle East is not an easy one to break into.

It is clear, however, that exports of mineral oil and natural gas are greatly adding to the economic strength of Algeria which has for so long been far too dependent upon her exports of wine. Even so, the situation is not entirely straightforward. Political troubles have hindered development of the oilfields, and there may be difficulties with the government of an independent Algeria; early in 1967, for example, a serious rupture between the Government and some of the producing companies over royalty payments was only narrowly avoided.

MANUFACTURING INDUSTRY

Algeria has for long been a supplier of primary goods, and this role was officially encouraged until the Second World War, for France did not wish to stimulate the development of industries which might become competitors to metropolitan companies. She rather regarded Algeria as a useful outlet for her own manufactured goods, and, in return, the greater part of the Algerian export of agricultural products and minerals was taken by France. A further hindrance to industrial development lay in the very limited availability of industrial fuels; we have seen that the only coalfield in the country is remote and of small potential, while the presence of mineral oil and natural gas on a large scale was unsuspected. Prospects for the generation of hydro-electric power are markedly less promising than in Morocco. In addition an overall shortage of industrial capital acted as a marked deterrent to industrial expansion.

Since the Second World War, however, the situation has drastically changed. Even during the war, the isolation of North Africa from France encouraged the beginnings of industrial development, while the dramatic discoveries of mineral oil and natural gas have transformed the situation with regard to fuel and the hydro-carbon type of raw materials. In addition, there is of course a wide range of agricultural and mineral raw materials locally available for processing prior to export.

It is not surprising under these circumstances that industrial development in Algeria is at present concerned mainly with the treatment of domestically produced primary raw materials, especially of agricultural produce. Flour milling, wine production, olive oil manufacture, and the production of jams, tobacco, textiles and cork have now taken root in varying degrees in most of the ports, in particular in the port areas of Algiers, Oran and Bone. Fish curing and canning are also important, together with the processing and canning of fruit and vegetables.

A start has also been made with the processing of minerals, for instance in the fertiliser factories which use supplies of domestic phosphate at Oran, Maison Carrée and Bone, as well as in the oil refinery at Maison Carrée. In 1966 this refinery processed 1·6 million tons of crude oil, about half a million tons being destined for export, but it is likely that this figure will increase when the new pipeline from Beni Mansour is in operation (*see* p. 399). Further plans include the development of chemical industries near Arzew and Maison Carrée, and an iron and steel works at Annaba. This plant is already in partial production, and it is expected that it will be fully operational in 1969. It is in addition likely that consumer goods industries will develop, especially near Algiers which provides the biggest market in the country, now that supplies of industrial fuel in the form of natural gas are readily available. Similar developments may take place at Arzew and Oran.

SOUTHERN ALGERIA

We have referred in this chapter to certain aspects of the life and economy of southern Algeria, because of the increasing impact which developments in the Sahara are having upon the situation in the north. It might be useful to conclude with a few more systematic observations regarding life in this extensive region.

LIFE AND WATER

On the whole it is true to say that life exists in the Sahara wherever water supplies make it possible. For instance, perhaps the best known of all the desert inhabitants are the Tuareg, who for long held sway over the central parts of the Sahara, robbing caravans passing between North and West Africa and terrorising other inhabitants. They were subjugated by the French during the early years of this century only with considerable difficulty. The home regions of the Tuareg lie in the highlands of Tassili and Ahaggar, wild and rugged areas, but areas which receive a scanty rainfall—enough to nourish pasture on which camels may be grazed. In many of the gorge-like valleys of these massifs, moreover, lie pools of deep water known as *gueltas* which result in unexpected local areas of fertility. The Tuareg are often known as the "People of the Veil," for the men always wear a veil over their faces which are entirely covered except for an eye slit.

Brunhes has described the way of life of some of the Saharan oasis dwellers, particularly in the Souf and the Mzab. The Mzab group of oases lies west of Touggourt, and supports about 30,000 people; the largest town is Ghardaia (Figs. 81 and 95), with about 8000 inhabitants. The area lies on a dissected limestone plateau at an elevation of about 2000 ft (600 m) above sea-level, and water is obtained from deep wells with the help of donkeys. A water-skin which holds about 10 gallons of water is tied to one end of a long piece of rope, the other end being attached to the donkey; as the donkey approaches the well, therefore, the bucket is lowered into it and as he walks away the water is drawn upwards. The whole process is made easier as a ramp is built towards the well so that the donkey walks downhill as he draws up the full bucket of water, while the rope itself is passed over a pulley supported on a frame at the well-head. Under these unpromising conditions groves of date palms are irrigated, while crops of fruit (figs, pomegranates, grapes and peaches), cereals (mainly barley) and vegetables are grown between the palms or round the edges of the groves.

The *palmeries* of El Oued (one of the Souf group of oases which lie to the south of the Shott Melrir, *see* Fig. 89) are quite remarkable, for they resemble sunken gardens. The dry surface sand has been laboriously dug away to expose the moist sand beneath, and in the hollows so formed groves of date palms are tended. Dry surface sand from the areas immediately around the gardens continuously blows into the *palmeries*, and this must be removed. This is done with great effort, by shovelling it into baskets which are then carried on the backs of the workers up the steep slopes bordering the gardens, to be dumped on the desert floor outside. This work goes on unceasingly, especially after sand storms, for otherwise the palms would be buried beneath the blown sand. The gardens are so deep that only the tops of the tall palms can be seen at ground level as they protrude above the excavations. In recent years the discovery of artesian water has made it possible to establish new *palmeries* and agricultural plots.

Until recently, most people tended to think of the Sahara as a region almost entirely without water, but it has now been proved that there are vast quantities of water there—but they lie often hundreds of feet below ground. Water from Ahaggar, for instance, spreads laterally outwards underground from the flanks of the massif, while water from the Atlas is now known to move south-eastwards and southwards beneath the great erg deserts of Algeria and Mauritania (*see* Figs. 90 and 97). It has also been shown that an enormous aquifer extends from the Atlas at depth eastwards under southern Tunisia and into Libya, south-westwards into Mauritania, and southwards under the Great Erg of Algeria and under the barren reg of Tanezrouft, and when this aquifer is tapped by boring, great gushes of sweet water are forced up by the subterranean pressures. When the first bore was put down near Ghardaia in 1950, for instance, this water was found at a depth of 4000 feet (1220 m) below the surface, yet the artesian water gushed up in an enormous fountain 600 feet (180 m) high. This vast store of underground water has been accumulating for very many centuries, and it is being constantly replenished and added to by water derived from the Atlas winter rains. The average yearly intake from this source has been computed, and care is taken not to deplete the underground reservoir by drawing off in any one year more than is received from the rains. At the moment there is no danger of this happening, but as more water is used for future projects a more careful watch will have to be kept.

[*Courtesy of Ewing Galloway, N.Y.*

Fig. 97.—View of the erg (sandy desert) of Algeria. The dress of the Berbers is a protection against the glare of the sun and blown sand. The shape of the load on the left-hand camel suggests the figure of a women in purdah.

Oases which were threatened with extinction are now being saved, and new ones opened up for settlement and for cultivation. The old oases of Ouargla and El Oued, for example, were being threatened with decay partly because sand was moving over them on too large a scale to be held back, and partly because available water supplies were insufficient to keep them alive. Limited surface irrigation was possible, but this only had the effect of causing the accumulation near the surface of the ground of salts harmful to plant growth; this accumulation of salts was slowly destroying the *palmeries* and was making impossible the growing of crops. The increased supplies of water now available make it possible to leach out these noxious salts and to provide sweet water for plant growth, so that the date *palmeries* are receiving a new lease of life, while these and other oases are developing into market gardens and agricultural centres. It is even thought that the reg (the gravelly desert) of Tanezrouft may be developed, for just beneath the surface gravel there are fossil soils, and it may be possible to cultivate these when the subterranean water is made available. The total area which may be affected is not far off the total area of Great Britain.

ECONOMIC SUMMARY

The resources of southern Algeria are very limited, despite recent discoveries, and this is why the overall density of population is low (it works out at about 0·8 persons per square mile). The region will increasingly benefit, however, from the natural gas and mineral oil supplies which we have discussed, while extensive deposits of iron ore are reported from Tindouf, near the Moroccan border in the western part of the country, and of manganese to the south of Colomb Béchar. These deposits are now being examined by experts, and it has even been suggested that some industrial development may take place in these remote areas. Difficulties of transport, however, are very great. Other minerals are also known to exist, and supplies of nickel, wolfram and tin have been located in the Ahaggar massif.

It is also possible that we may see some degree of agricultural development in oases and elsewhere, as it becomes practicable to make use of the supplies of artesian water beneath the desert floor. If there is to be any commercial development, however, the question of providing communications will be a vital one, for at the moment the only railways are those which run northwards from Beni Abbès and Colomb Béchar in the north-west and from Touggourt in the north-east. Roads are very few and of generally poor quality. The interior position of the territory will for long remain a great handicap to development.

STUDY QUESTIONS

1. What are the main features of the physical geography of Algeria?
2. Write an account of the climate of Algeria.
3. Write an explanatory account of the distribution of population of Algeria.
4. Write an essay on village and town life in Algeria.
5. What were the chief contributions made by the *colons* to the economic development of Algeria?
6. Attempt an assessment of the importance of mineral developments to the present-day economic strength of Algeria.
7. What chief geographical contrasts would you notice along a transect extending southwards from Algiers to the southern borders of Algeria?

Chapter XIX

TUNISIA. SOME PROBLEMS OF THE MAGHRIB

TUNISIA is by far the smallest of the three main territories of the Maghrib, with a total area of 63,000 square miles (163,800 sq. km); this is slightly more than that of England, 50,332 square miles (130,310 sq. km). About half of this area is desert, or at least semi-desert, which occurs largely as a result of the location of the territory in the rain shadow of the Atlas. Whereas, for example, the annual rainfall at Casablanca is almost 16 in. a year, at Gabès, which lies in approximately the same latitude, the corresponding figure is just over 6½ in. Despite these apparently adverse circumstances, however, the history of Tunisia has been at least as eventful as that of her larger neighbours, and this can probably be accounted for in large measure by the location of the territory near the south-eastern limit of the "Western Basin" facing the important water link (the Sicilian Channel) between the western and the eastern parts of the Mediterranean Sea. Indeed, the Cape Bon Peninsula thrusts itself forward to within 90 miles (144 km) of the Sicilian coast at Marsala. Tunisia also lies comparatively open towards the east by land, and during the invasions of the seventh and the eleventh to twelfth centuries the Arabs were able to penetrate into the country with comparative ease from the east along the Jefara (the coastal plain of the south). Since Tunisia was inevitably the first of the Maghrib territories to feel the onslaught of the invader, it has become more predominantly Arab than either Algeria or Morocco.

PHYSICAL ASPECTS

STRUCTURE AND RELIEF

There is no well-defined natural boundary between Algeria and Tunisia, and the various physical divisions which we met in the larger country extend without interruption into the smaller. In the north, for example, the line of the Tell Atlas is continued in the Kroumirie Range, extensions of which continue north-eastwards and terminate abruptly at Cape Blanc; this upland zone is composed for the most part of sandstone ranges which in some places reach the north coast and give rise to rugged cliffs, but lowland areas of small extent open to the sea between the cliffs. Farther to the south, the line of the Saharan Atlas and the Tebessa mountains (see p. 379) is continued in Tunisia in a fairly narrow upland zone which is known as the High Tell or Dorsale (Fr. "backbone"), most of which lies at elevations of more than 2000 ft (600 m) above sea-level, though the highest parts attain heights of 5000 ft (1500 m). The structure of the High Tell is complex, for sandstones and limestones were folded into anticlines and synclines during the Alpine orogeny, and these formations were later faulted and fractured. Between the present ranges the floors of former lakes appear as valleys and enclosed basins. The line of the High Tell is continued in the Cape Bon Peninsula.

Between these two upland zones lies the Medjerda valley. This is really the Tunisian extension of the narrow section of the Plateau of the Shotts met with in eastern Algeria, and it opens eastwards to the Plains of Tunis and Bizerta; between these plains lies the delta built up by the river. Although the Medjerda is a perennial river (the only one in Tunisia), the seasonal nature of the rainfall causes dangerous flooding in the winter, and sometimes the whole of the flood-plain is submerged for a distance of 25 miles (40 km) from the sea. The plains (especially the delta of the Medjerda) were formerly malarial, but the black alluvial soils, of which they and the flood-plains higher up the valley are composed, provide excellent farm land and produce the finest harvests in the whole country. Bizerta, with its fine natural harbour, became a powerful naval base during the period of French rule.

To the south of the High Tell an elevated plateau extends across the border from Algeria in the region known as the High Steppe which varies in altitude between 1000 and 2500 ft (300–750 m) above sea-level. The High Steppe gives place eastwards and southwards to the Low Steppe, an undulating region marked by low rocky ridges, wide shallow basins and by extensive exposures of limestone. Watercourses extend from the High Tell across the steppes, and sometimes during the winter flood waters storm down from the high ground, occasionally even reaching the sea. More usually, however, the flood waters spread out and are lost by evaporation in the many *sebkras* (salt marshes) which occur on the surface of the steppe country. On its eastern margins the Low Steppe merges into a coastal lowland known as the Sahel where the underlying rock is covered by fairly recent sandy deposits. The landscape of the Sahel is diversified in parts by low, undulating hills.

Southwards from the steppe and the Sahel the extensive depression in which lie the Shott el Djerid and the smaller Shott el Rharsa extends eastwards from the Algerian border. The lowest parts of this depression are actually below sea-level. The depression narrows towards the east and it finally reaches the coast between La Skhirra and Gabès. Most of the area to the south of this depression consists of semi-desert and desert. To the east the coastal plain known as the Jefara is overlooked by an escarpment known in general as the Ksour mountains, and the rocky nature of the surface in these areas is characteristic of an hammada type of desert. The Ksour escarpment dips away westwards and southwards beneath the Great Eastern Erg which occupies the south-western and southern parts of the country.

CLIMATE

The main feature of the climate of Tunisia is the contrast which exists between the Mediterranean north and the Saharan and sub-Saharan south;

we have earlier noticed similar contrasts in both Morocco and Algeria. Conditions in the northern parts of the country are illustrated by the following climatic statistics for Tunis.

	J	F	M	A	M	J	Jy	A	S	O	N	D	Range	Total
°C	10	11·1	12·2	15·6	18·9	23·3	26·1	26·7	26·4	20	15	11·7	16·7	
°F	50	52	54	60	66	74	79	80	76	68	59	53	30	
in.:	2·2	2·0	2·4	1·9	0·9	0·6	0·3	0·4	0·9	1·6	2·3	2·5		18·0

The markedly Mediterranean character of the climate is seen in both the temperature and the rainfall régimes. Mild winters alternate with fairly hot summers, while the winter rainfall maximum is clearly shown. The comparatively low annual rainfall is suggestive of a location in a rain shadow (see p. 407). Temperatures on the mountains of the northern parts of the country are lower than those shown above, and rainfall totals for the same areas are substantially higher; over 35 in. of rain a year are recorded on the Kroumirie Range and over much of the High Tell, while the figure rises to 60 in. in the wettest areas. On the other hand, the valley of the Medjerda suffers from a rain-shadow effect and parts of it receive only about 15 in. per annum. The High Tell, partly because of its central position and partly because of its comparatively high rainfall, has not inaptly been referred to as the "water tower of Tunisia," for it sends water northwards to the rivers Mellègue, Medjerda and their tributaries, and southwards to the steppes.

Marked contrasts to the foregoing climatic pattern exist in those parts of Tunisia which lie to the south of the High Tell. Temperature ranges become noticeably greater, for instance, and summer temperatures away from the coast average 82° F (27·7° C) or more as opposed to the 79°F (26·1° C) typical of the northern coastal areas, while winter average figures fall to 42° F (5·6° C) rather than 50° F (10° C) (compare the case of Biskra, p. 382). Along the coasts of the south, winters are considerably milder than this, however, and mean January figures are 51° F (10·6° C) or even slightly higher.

Rainfall is markedly less to the south of the High Tell than it is in most areas farther north. On the steppes, for example, yearly rainfall averages vary between 20 in. in the northern parts to 8 in. in the south, while figures are little higher along the coastal Sahel. Along the Jefara 5½–7 in. a year are recorded on an average, while the Ksour mountains average 10 in.; in the Shott el Djerid depression the figure is about 6 in., but in the Great Eastern Erg yearly totals fall from 4 in. in the northern parts to 1 inch in the far south. In common with most parts of Morocco and Algeria, the force of the sirocco is felt in Tunisia, and considerable damage to crops from this cause is not infrequently reported.

NATURAL REGIONS

Although Tunisia is the smallest of the Maghrib territories it includes a wide variety of landscapes and regions. For the purposes of this study we can recognise seven distinct natural regions—the northern Tell; the valley of the Medjerda and the coastlands of the Gulf of Tunis; the High Tell; the Sahel; the steppes; the central depression; and the south which really forms part of the margins of the Sahara Desert.

1. *The northern Tell*. This region comprises two distinct parts: (*a*) the disconnected lowlands along the Mediterranean coast, and (*b*) the Kroumirie Range and its extensions which terminate abruptly at Cape Blanc. The coastal lowlands provide pockets of fertile ground where cereals, fruits, citrus and olives are all grown. Only one small port, Tabarka, has developed, however, for the lowlands are too restricted in area and too

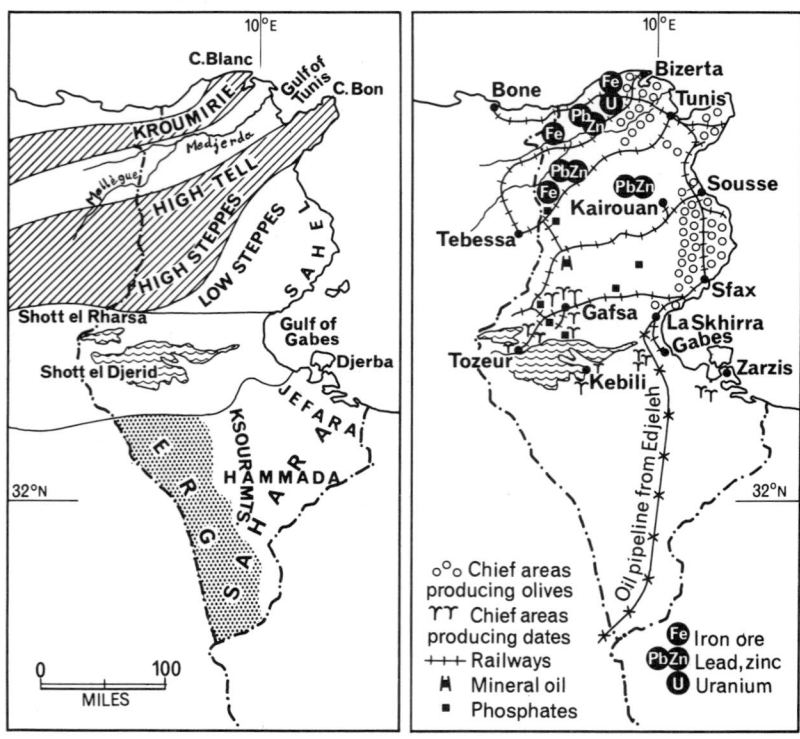

FIG. 98.—Tunisia: natural regions. FIG. 99.—Tunisia: some economic features.

isolated to become of more than limited importance. On the other hand, the valleys and small plains in the Kroumirie Range together form one of the main areas of cereal production in Tunisia, and wheat and barley are widely grown. The higher parts of the range (which often has precipitous flanks) are well watered, and they carry the most important forest stands in the country. Cork-oak, Aleppo pine and cedar are all well represented, and debarked cork-oaks and piles of bark awaiting transport are familiar sights in this region. Stock (cattle and sheep for the most part) are reared, and cereals (mainly barley) are grown in forest clearings on the lower parts of the uplands, but the population is on the whole sparse.

2. *The valley of the Medjerda* and that of its main tributary, the Mellègue, decrease in elevation eastwards to include the marshy coastlands of the Gulf of Tunis (including the Plain of Tunis); these valleys together form the eastern continuation of the Plateau of the Shotts. The valleys consist in their upper and middle courses of a succession of basins separated by rocky divides; the basins formerly contained lakes, and the silt which was deposited on the lake floors now provides rich alluvial soils for the cultivator. It is not surprising, therefore, that the whole region has developed into the leading agricultural area in Tunisia, and the valleys themselves, together with the fertile bordering hill country, produce heavy crops of cereals (mainly wheat and barley) and citrus fruits. Olive groves are prominent in the Medjerda valley while vegetables and tobacco are also grown. The Plain of Tunis forms a natural extension of this agricultural region, and vines and olives are intensively produced, especially in the southern parts of the plain; the growing of vegetables and tobacco, together with market gardening and the rearing of cattle, is also of considerable importance. The Plain of Bizerta is another productive subregion, and the area around the main settlement has for centuries been famous for its orchards. Unfortunately, the plains suffer from the effects of the desiccating sirocco, and considerable damage arises from this from time to time.

The region as a whole was the scene of considerable settlement by Europeans during the period of French rule, but the former large-scale European farms have now been for the most part expropriated and are to-day run mainly on a co-operative basis (*see*, however, p. 420). Major works now being undertaken to promote flood control (affecting 130,000 acres, 52,000 ha), land reclamation (130,000 acres, 52,000 ha), soil conservation (300,000 acres, 120,000 ha) and irrigation (125,000 acres, 50,000 ha), will further increase the productivity of this important region.

3. *The High Tell.* To the south of the Medjerda valley lies the High Tell, an upland area which becomes steadily narrower eastwards until it ends at Cape Bon. This forested region suffers from its isolated interior position, though railways have been built to tap reserves of minerals which occur there (*see* Fig. 98). The northern parts of the High Tell are well watered and are characterised by sedentary farming communities which produce crops of fruit and cereals: sheep and goats are also reared. The southern parts are drier and have traditionally supported a semi-nomadic stock-rearing population, but, largely as a result of the security which resulted from French administration, permanent settlements are now more commonly seen. This upland belt is notable as it forms a climatic divide between the Mediterranean north of the country and the sub-Saharan areas to the south.

4. *The Sahel region,* which comprises the eastern coastal lands of Tunisia between Hammamet (a small town near the southern root of the Cape

Bon Peninsula) and the region south of Sfax, is a very important one. It has the form of a sandy plain of variable width which is for the most part flat, though gently undulating hills occur quite frequently. The Sahel is broadest in the area between Sousse and Sfax. Rainfall varies between about 20 in. in the north and 8 in. in the south. Despite the generally low rainfall, however, it is possible to produce useful cereal crops on the Sahel because the sandy soils are retentive of moisture, while supplies of artesian water are also available. The very heavy dews in this coastal strip provide valuable additional supplies of moisture.

The Sahel is one of the most important regions in the world for the production of olives, a development which began following grants of extensive areas to French land companies during the later part of last century. Early experiments with vine growing were not very successful, but it was quickly realised that the olive is able to withstand longer periods of drought than the vine even without irrigation, and very large numbers of olive trees were planted on the new estates. The most important producing areas are those near Sousse and Sfax, where there may well be over 10 million olive trees, while a further half a million are normally planted each year. The olives are planted in long straight rows on the large estates, and the trees extend over the gently undulating landscape right away to the horizon. Most of the work involved in olive production is carried out by Arabs; each worker undertakes to take care of a specified number of trees, and he receives a proportion of the crop as his payment. The olive trees, which can tolerate surprisingly dry conditions, now extend from the coast on to the fringes of the dusty steppes (see Fig. 99). It is significant that the prospect of permanent employment on the olive plantations is inducing many formerly semi-nomadic groups to take up a sedentary way of life.

Although the olive tree can tolerate dry conditions, the amount of oil produced depends very much on the year's rainfall and is therefore variable: for instance, while some 80,000 hectolitres of olive oil were produced in 1965, the figure for 1966, a year of severe drought, was no more than 25,000 hectolitres. The olive tree bears fruit every two years, and this is a further reason why output is variable from year to year. Almonds are also widely grown in the Sahel. Good quality olive oil is exported from Sfax, mostly to France and Italy, while phosphates from Gafsa, esparto grass from the steppes and dates from the Shott el Djerid region are also shipped from the same port. Sfax is also the headquarters for the Greek boats which collect sponges from the sea floor in the area.

5. *The Steppes and High Steppes.* Between the Sahel and the interior uplands (the High Tell) lie the Steppes and the High Steppes, the locations of which are shown on Fig. 98. The Steppes are developed mainly on a low limestone plateau on the surface of which lie extensive shallow basins (many of which carry *sebkras* in their lower parts) separated by fairly low rocky ridges. Unfortunately, water supply is an urgent problem, for the average rainfall is low (6–12 in.), largely because of a rain-shadow effect produced by the Atlas zone generally and by the Aurès massif in particular

(*see* p. 388). This is not the only reason for the difficulty of providing an adequate water supply, however; the limestone of which the plateau is composed is of course porous, so that much of the scanty rainfall soaks away before it can be put to any useful purpose. Most of the northern and central parts of the steppe region is given over to the production of esparto grass, very extensive areas being under this crop, and to the nomadic rearing of sheep and camels, but in the south of the region the landscape becomes distinctly barren. Crops of cereals are grown generally in the depressions, but in the absence of irrigation yields are sparse. Cultivation of olives and almonds is continually pressing westwards from the Sahel, while dates are produced in the oases of the drier south particularly near Gafsa; the quality of the dates is, however, inferior to that of fruit produced farther south.

Towards the west and north the Steppe gives place to the High Steppe, a more elevated region which on the whole receives slightly more rainfall than the Steppe; yearly average totals rise to about 20 in. in the northern parts from about 12 in. along the southern margins. The chief way of life on the High Steppe is pastoral nomadism; the custom is for the nomads to pasture their animals on the steppes during the winter and to migrate northwards each summer to the moister Tell region, but this pattern of livelihood is becoming increasingly difficult to maintain as more of the pastures of the Tell are being brought under cultivation. Many of the nomads help with the harvest in the Tell during the period of their residence there.

6. *The central depression.* To the south of the Sahel and the steppes is situated the depression in which lies the Shott el Djerid. Parts of this depression near the Algerian border are below sea level, while farther to the east the line of the depression is continued by the Gulf of Gabès. The oasis of the Shott el Djerid and the oases near Gabès are important producers of dates, but the area generally is too dry to be of much value for cultivation, though in some places irrigation is now possible. The wells, which have been sunk to permit this, depend for their water upon the rains which soak into the limestone plateau of the steppe farther north.

Most of the date export comes from the Tozeur district between the Shott el Rharsa and the Shott el Djerid, where it is estimated that almost a million date palms are distributed among a number of oases, while a further half a million palms stand in the area around Kebili, to the south-east of the Shott el Djerid. Care has to be taken to stop encroachment of desert sand from the Great Eastern Erg in the latter region.

The town of Gabès lies at the seaward end of an oasis set in a region which is green for two or three months after the scanty winter rains; it is, however, brown and dusty for the remainder of the year. From a distance the oasis looks like a forest of date palms (there may be a quarter of a million of them) and these provide the main source of wealth. Between the palms are small cultivated patches in which are grown early vegetables (potatoes, carrots and lettuces, for example), fruits (pomegranates, melons, oranges and figs), flowers and fodder crops for the donkeys which provide the chief form of transport.

7. *The Saharan regions.* To the south of the Djerid depression the ground rises to a series of plateaus which form part of the Sahara Desert and its margins. The coastal plain of the Jefara to the east of the region is fringed with lagoons and salt marshes, and it supports only a sparse population. Most of the inhabitants live along the actual coast though semi-nomadic peoples pasture their herds in the interior (*see* p. 417). The most prosperous part of this region is the peninsula on which stands the town of Zarzis, for here the cultivation of the olive is the leading occupation. There is some cultivation in the slightly better-watered Ksour district (*see* p. 416) while a few spring-line oases near the foot of the escarpment provide centres for settlement based upon cultivation and stock-rearing. In general, however, the hammada of the west, like the Great Eastern Erg between the Ksour escarpment and the Algerian frontier, supports only a poor type of scrub pasture which provides a scanty sustenance for the herds of goats and camels which are raised on a semi-nomadic basis.

The island of Djerba (the island of Tennyson's Lotos Eaters) in the Gulf of Gabès forms a detached part of this region and is well known for its energetic inhabitants and for its dates. It is fast becoming popular as a tourist centre.

HUMAN GEOGRAPHY

HISTORY AND PEOPLE

Tunisia stands in such a position that she is far more open to outside influences than Algeria or even Morocco. It is not surprising, therefore, that many different groups of people have had a share in her cultural, social and economic development, and after the original Berber inhabitants a long succession of invaders entered the country from Phoenicia, Rome, the Levant (the Arabs), Turkey and France; all of these have left some impress upon the human geography of the country. There have also been substantial numbers of immigrants from Spain, Italy and Malta, while many Jews are also numbered among the population. Yet it is an apparent paradox that despite these diverse cultural roots, Tunisia has developed a strong national consciousness and vitality, and she has won for herself an influence in international affairs which is far stronger than might be expected simply from considerations of her size and population. One is reminded in this respect of England, another country whose people stem from very diverse cultural roots.

After the populating of Tunisia by the Berbers, the first outside contacts were those brought by the Phoenicians between the thirteenth and the second centuries B.C., the focus of Phoenician activity being the well-known city of Carthage which was located on the shore of the Gulf of Tunis a few miles away from the present capital. The Phoenicians, however, were traders rather than colonists, though they did initiate certain improvements in the cultivation of the olive. After the sack of Carthage in the second century B.C. Rome became the dominant power. The Romans introduced far-reaching changes, including new irrigation and dry farming methods; the development of trade, mainly with the Imperial City (North Africa was for long regarded as the chief granary of the Roman Empire); and the foundation of cities and the construction of roads and aqueducts. They generally stamped an impress on the country which has not been entirely lost even today. There is no doubt, however, that the Roman innovation which has most profoundly affected life in Tunisia and the Maghrib generally was the introduction of the camel, first "imported" by the African Emperor Septimius Severus about the year A.D. 200, though more than a century was to elapse before the animal was in fairly general use. E. F. Gautier, the distinguished French geographer, has argued that the introduction of the camel initiated an economic revolution comparable in importance to that caused by the inventions of the steam engine, the motor car and the aeroplane.

The political influence of Rome finally came to an end with the Arab (Muslim) invasions of the seventh century, while further waves of Arab invaders came in the eleventh century. These warlike nomads, it has been said, swarmed into the Maghrib like clouds of locusts, and cultivators had perforce to retreat to mountain strongholds and remote areas, where even today the fortified granaries which they had to establish (*guelaas* and *ksours*) still exist as picturesque survivals of a turbulent past (*see* pp. 391 and 416). Widespread destruction of the works set up by the Romans followed the footsteps of the advancing Arabs, who poured into Tunisia via the Jefara. Tunisia, which perforce bore the brunt of the Arab invasions, was almost completely overrun by the invaders, and today Berbers are confined mainly to parts of the inhospitable southern segment of the country; they account for barely 1% of the total population (contrast the case of Morocco, p. 352).

Although the coming of the Arabs ushered in a long period marked by much anarchy and piracy, which also lasted through the years of Turkish suzerainty, it is not correct simply to evaluate this long era as one of unrelieved barbarity. In the thirteenth century, for example, immigrants entered the country from Spain following the recapture by the Spanish of Cordoba and Seville from the Moors. These immigrants, generally known as Andalusians, introduced irrigation and improved farming methods, while they also served with distinction in the government and stimulated renewed interest in art. Turkish influence was first felt in the Maghrib in the sixteenth century (*see* p. 353), and from that time Tunisia was governed as part of the Ottoman Empire by quasi-independent Beys. The country fell under French influence in 1881, and was administered as a French Protectorate until 1956; in that year, following a troubled period after the Second World War, Tunisia became an independent state.

We have previously mentioned the immigration especially from Italy and France which took place during the period of colonial rule, and as in Morocco and Algeria the *colons*, with their comparatively sophisticated farming techniques, made great contributions to the economic strength of the country. Post-independence departures of Europeans and expropriation of their land has now drastically reduced their numbers (*see* p. 353), and has drained the country of many skills which it could ill afford to lose.

POPULATION AND WAYS OF LIFE

The total population of Tunisia in 1966 was 4,457,466, and as in the other Maghrib territories it is increasing rapidly. The annual rate of increase is reckoned to be just under 2%, and one important result of this is that just over half the inhabitants are under 20 years old. The first census taken in Tunisia was taken in 1921, when 2,093,000 inhabitants were recorded. The latest figures therefore show an increase of 2,344,466 persons, a rise of 114% in 45 years. This rate of increase is great enough, if it continues, to double the existing population in the next 35 years. The numbers of non-indigenous people have decreased sharply since independence in 1956; for instance, the Jewish population alone fell from 58,000 to 30,000 in 1963.

About two-thirds of the inhabitants of Tunisia depend upon the land for their livelihood, and the remaining one-third live in the various towns and cities. Urban life in Tunisia is of long standing, and goes right back to the foundation and development of Carthage; the modern successor to Carthage, Tunis, together with its suburbs and adjoining settlements, carries about one-fifth of the total population.

Fig. 102 shows broadly the dominant ways of life met with in Tunisia. In the northern third of the country and on the Sahel, settlement is for the most part sedentary. In the mountainous regions of the north, villages, often located in forest clearings and protected by hedges of prickly pear, are sparsely scattered, but on the lower-lying areas villages and small towns which have developed into market centres and administrative foci are more closely spaced. Older settlements are typically located on strongly defensible sites, but newer villages are more widely scattered.

In the southern two-thirds of the country conditions are quite different, for on the steppes and in the regions near the Ksour escarpment seminomadism has traditionally been practised, but there are signs that this situation is changing, especially on the steppes. Among the reasons for this is the fact that northern summer pastures are diminishing in extent because of increased cultivation, and there is also the point that the expansion of olive growing along the Sahel and on the eastern steppes offers prospects of more permanent employment.

Clarke has given an interesting account of the way of life of the Ouderna, about 40,000 in number, whose lands include the eastern parts of the Ksour escarpment and adjacent parts of the Jefara. On the uplands land is individually owned, and olives and figs are grown near the *ksours*

(fortified granaries), while in a zone near the foot of the hills are plantations of figs, olives and date palms. The Jefara offers winter grazing on the
scrub pasture, while at this season cultivation is sometimes possible on the
lowlands along the lines of wadis and in depressions which temporarily
hold supplies of moisture. The Ouderna begin to leave the uplands near
the end of October after the fig and date harvest; some of the group, however, may not leave until after the olive harvest in December, while some
of those who left in October or November may return to help with the
gathering of the olives. The onset of the sparse winter rains on the Jefara
(*see* p. 409) promotes a rush to the best cultivation basins where the first
comers secure the best land; there is no individual ownership there. After
the ploughing and sowing the flocks are grazed on the winter scrub pasture; all the people have by this time left the upland villages to enjoy the
ample supplies of milk and the comparatively good living in this "blessed
season." Milk becomes less plentiful in April, however, as the pastures
begin to wither under the strengthening sun, and herdsmen are left to
tend the grazing herds while the wheat and barley are harvested; the harvest may be good or meagre according to the season. After the harvest
is trodden and winnowed, the grain and straw are taken by camel to the
uplands where they are stored in the *ksours* or are stacked in underground
silos, and the people remain on the uplands for the fig harvest which commences in July; the various fruit harvests last through much of the summer, after which the downhill migration begins again.

Other groups of semi-nomads wander over the area to the south of the
Djerid depression, spending a few weeks in October or November at an
oasis. Even here, however, the more copious supplies of water now being
secured from artesian sources are encouraging more and more nomads to
turn to a sedentary form of life. Despite this, many nomads cling to their
traditional ways, and nomadism will disappear very slowly if at all in the
foreseeable future, especially in the Great Eastern Erg.

CHIEF TOWNS AND CITIES

Although, as has been emphasised, Tunisia is a comparatively urbanised
country, few towns of any great size exist. Easily the largest city is Tunis,
while other important centres include Sfax, Sousse, Bizerta and Kairouan.

Tunis, with a population of 410,000, is the capital of Tunisia. It stands
for the most part on an isthmus between an inland marshy lake (a *sebkha*)
and the Lake of Tunis (*see* Fig. 100), and it is well placed for collecting the
produce of the Tell (including the Medjerda valley) and the northern
parts of the steppes and the Sahel. These areas, of course, are the most productive of the country. Tunis only became a port in 1893 following the
construction of the sea canal, 6 miles (9·6 km) long, which now links the
town with its outport of La Goulette—with which it is also connected by
rail; Tunis and La Goulette together form easily the leading port of
Tunisia. The main goods handled for export include wine, olive oil, fruit,
vegetables, iron ore and phosphates.

As shown in Fig. 100 the picturesque old Arab town (the Medina) is flanked by an attractive and well-laid-out European Quarter, though not far distant drab and squalid *bidonvilles* (*see* p. 392) form a depressing contrast. It is unfortunately true that the comparatively limited development of industry in the capital makes it impossible to offer employment to all the inhabitants seeking work, and unemployment presents a very real problem.

The second port is Sfax (population 70,000) on the Gulf of Gabès. Sfax has developed largely for the export of phosphates, though it also handles olive oil from the Sahel and dates from the Shott el Djerid, a trade which is shared by Gabès, a much smaller port. Sousse (48,000) is a mineral port

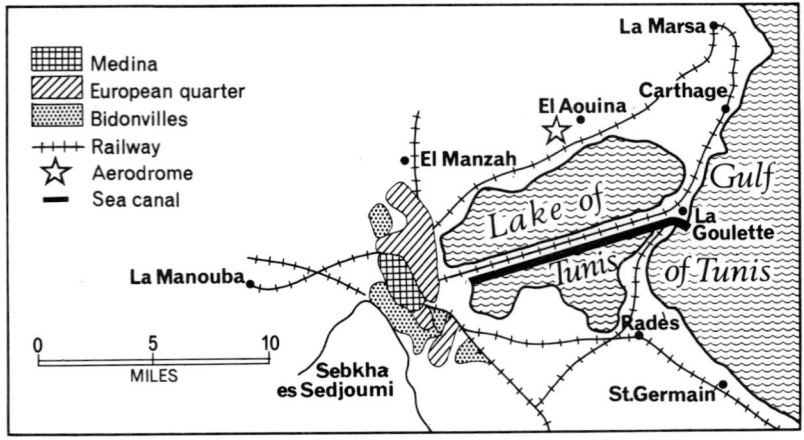

FIG. 100.—Tunis.

which also handles some of the produce of the Sahel, while Bizerta (46,000), like Tunis but on a smaller scale, exports minerals and agricultural produce from the northern parts of the country. Bizerta was developed by the French as a naval base because of its excellent sheltered harbour— a rare feature in the Maghrib. It now has an oil refinery. The loading port of La Skhirra, near Gabès, is linked by means of a 24-inch oil pipeline to the mineral oil producing fields near Edjeleh.

The largest inland town is Kairouan, with about 35,000 inhabitants. It is interesting to note that the Phoenicians and to a lesser extent the Romans were both seafaring peoples, and both developed capitals (Carthage and Tunis) near the Tunisian coast. The Arabs, on the other hand, were landsmen, unfamiliar with the sea. It was probably natural, under these circumstances, that the Arabs should establish an inland city as their capital, and the choice fell upon Kairouan which developed into a notable Islamic centre, famous as a holy city which was second in the Maghrib only to Fez, and even today remarkable for its monuments of the past. It is now

[*Courtesy of the Tunisian Embassy.*

FIG. 101.—Tunisia: an old street in Tunis. The capital is the only large town. The street, though narrow and undrained, is lit by electricity, with the "bazaar" type of shop open to the street.

the centre of an iron, lead and zinc producing region with some manufacturing and commercial importance, while it also produces blankets and carpets from local supplies of wool.

THE ECONOMY

The natural resources of Tunisia are limited, but even so the full development of the potential of the country has by no means been achieved. Only about one-eighth of the surface area of the country is under cultivation, and only about 1% of the cultivated area is irrigated, despite the crying need for water in this, the least well watered of the Maghrib territories. Over most of Tunisia agriculture is still primitive, and constitutes simply a supplementary activity to stock-rearing (as with the Ouderna, *see* p. 416). Probably two-thirds of the total population still seek a precarious livelihood in traditional ways, producing from the land and from their stock barely enough to satisfy their own requirements, engaging in barter to secure a few essentials but rarely taking part in any monetary transactions (*see* Fig. 102). It is true that this situation is changing; one factor which is helping to bring this about has been the securing for Tunisian ownership of the large-scale, formerly European farms. Some of these farms have been parcelled up into smaller holdings, some are being worked co-operatively and some are now State-owned. Another factor is the speeding up of industrial development, while the extension of aboriculture is also persuading many workers to take up paid employment. While all

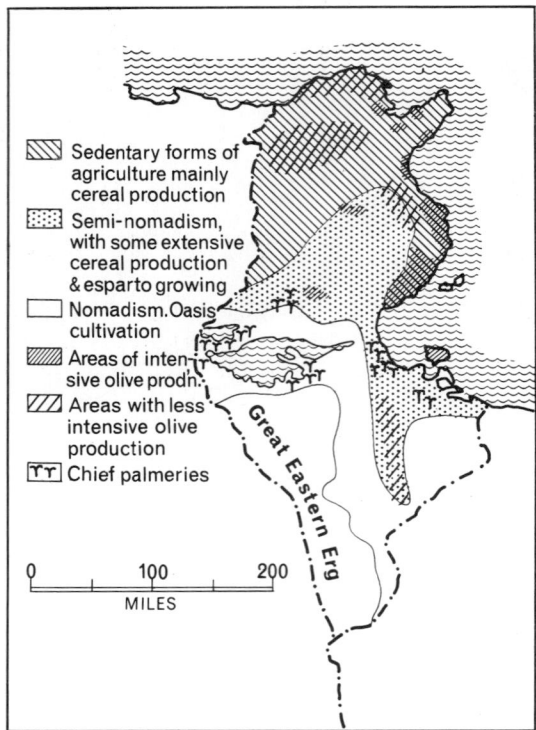

FIG. 102.—Tunisia: forms of land use.

this is true, however, only a minority of the people as yet are affected by these changes, though the number will certainly rise sharply within the next decade.

AGRICULTURE AND STOCK-REARING

The general pattern of agriculture has been described above. Although agriculture is responsible for about half the national income, much of the country is agriculturally unproductive; this is particularly the case in the centre and south where rainfall is inadequate and too unreliable to permit successful crop farming. As yet there are few irrigation schemes in operation, and most of the ones which are working are in the Medjerda valley; there is also one near Kasserine which secures its water from a wadi draining south-eastwards from the Tebessa mountains. However, boreholes have been sunk to tap supplies of artesian water in the Djerid depression. The discovery has recently been announced of underground supplies of water near El Hamma in the Djerid depression. The supplies are described as "inexhaustible" and they could have significant repercussions on the future economy of the region. In many areas small retaining walls have been built across valleys to conserve water supplies, but these small-scale projects are of value for providing water for stock rather than for irrigation, as the amounts of water retained are comparatively small. Progress so far has not measured up to the needs of the country, and it is slow, though a new water supply project in the upper Medjerda valley, completed in 1967, is making possible considerably increased crop production (*see* p. 411 and Fig. 103).

About half of the cultivated land of Tunisia produces cereals, especially wheat and barley, with some oats, though yields per acre are low, especially in the south. Apart from cereals, the chief agricultural products are olive oil, wine, citrus fruit and dates, most of which have traditionally been exported to France though some of the olive oil goes to Italy. Tunisia is, in fact, the world's largest producer of olive oil. The grape and citrus output comes mainly from the lowlands adjacent to the Gulf of Tunis and from the Cape Bon Peninsula, the olives mainly from the Sahel and adjoining parts of the steppes and the Medjerda valley, and the dates from the sub-Saharan zone in the south.

The export trade of Tunisia has suffered considerably since 1964 when French–Tunisian trade agreements were blocked by France because of the expropriation of European-owned farms. It was only near the end of 1966 that the French Government permitted wine exports to France to to begin again, though on a limited scale, except for supplies despatched as partial compensation for the nationalisation of land formerly owned by French farmers in Tunisia. Free wine imports into France were again permitted in 1967. Similarly, the export of citrus fruits received a sharp setback after the closing of the French market, but in 1965 exports had so far recovered that the citrus export accounted for 5% by value of all exports in that year. This recovery was made possible by the opening up of new markets, mainly in European countries other than France. There has also been difficulty with Italy because of the expropriation of lands formerly owned by Italian farmers, but the Tunisian Government in 1967 concluded an agreement with the Italian Government under the terms of which it is to pay compensation to the Italians whose farms were taken over in 1964.

Enough has been said to indicate the importance in Tunisia of stock-rearing, which is carried on for the most part on a nomadic or semi-nomadic basis. We have also explained that there is a tendency today for many nomads to forsake their traditional ways of life, and reasons for this have been given. It is estimated that stock-rearing accounts for about one-fifth of the total income from agricultural sources in Tunisia, and that it is dominant over about two-fifths of the productive parts of the country.

[*Courtesy of the Tunisian Embassy.*

FIG. 103.—Tunisia: new methods and machinery in the Medjerda valley. The
Medjerda scheme, begun by the French, includes land reclamation, irrigation
and protection against floods and soil erosion. From this valley comes a very
large percentage of Tunisia's food.

It is further estimated that there may be over 5 million sheep and goats in
the country, 600,000 cattle, 334,000 horses, mules and asses, and 217,000
camels. Cattle are reared in the moister north, while large flocks of sheep
and goats are supported in the Medjerda valley and also on the steppes,
where the broad-tailed sheep outnumbers all other animals reared, and
where attempts are being made to reduce the numbers of goats because
they ravage vegetation so thoroughly that there is a great danger of soil
erosion. Animal products, including wool, hides and skins have an important place in the domestic economy as they form raw materials for
many handicrafts industries. To the south of the steppes the camel is the
most important animal reared.

FISHING

The fishing industry in Tunisia is an important one, for a wide variety
of fish is taken in coastal waters. Tunny, sardines and mackerel are the
chief catches, while crayfish are also important. Sponge fishing is carried
on largely by Greeks in the south, Djerba and Sfax being the main centres
of this activity. A new fishing port was opened in 1967 at Mahdia, between Sousse and Sfax. This is a well-equipped port which can accommodate ocean-going trawlers, while refrigeration and cold storage facilities
are also available. As a result of increased training and better handling
facilities the output of fish in 1966 was more than double that of 1965—
25,832 as against 11,265 tons.

MINING AND MANUFACTURING

The mineral output of Tunisia is of considerable importance, and mineral exports include phosphates, iron ore, lead and zinc. Most of the phosphates come from the Gafsa area to the north of the Shott el Djerid, and a railway has been built from Sfax across the southern Sahel and steppe to tap these supplies. This railway has, in fact, been extended to the *palmeries* of Tozeur. Smaller phosphate deposits, also reached by rail, lie on the interior plateau near the Algerian border (*see* Fig. 98); these deposits form the eastward continuation of the Algerian reserves. Iron ore occurs fairly widely in the northern parts of the country, but mining depends mainly upon rail access: the most important mining areas lie in the Tebessa mountains and the Medjerda hills. Output is not as great as in Algeria; the largest mine in the country at Djebel-Djerissa, for instance, produces just under 1 million tons a year (891,000 tons in the first eleven months of 1966) as opposed to the 3 million tons output in Algeria.

Deposits of lead and zinc are also fairly widely located over northern and central Tunisia, and mining is carried on near Kairouan and in a zone roughly parallel to the Algerian border to the north of the Tebessa mountains. Prospecting for mineral oil has been carried on for some years, and in 1964 it was reported that oil had been discovered in economic quantities near El Borma, in the south of the country, while natural gas and small amounts of oil have been located near Sfax. More recently, in 1966, oil has been discovered near Kasserine, while another recent discovery is that of uranium reserves near Beja, in the north of the country. Production of mineral oil has now begun, and in 1967 the El Borma field produced 2,234,000 tons of crude petroleum, while an oil refinery is now in operation at Bizerta.

Development of industry in Tunisia has made rapid strides since the close of the Second World War, but even so the level of manufacturing output is low. Handicaps to increasing industrial development include a lack of domestic fuel resources, lack of capital and a very restricted market. Industrial expansion is proceeding, however, and work has now started on what will be Africa's largest chemical industrial complex at Ghannouche, near Gabès. This will include a fertiliser factory, a cement works and a new port to handle expected trade expansion. Industries now being established near Sfax include a glove factory, a metal grille factory and a rubber processing plant. These are all signs of a new and progressive spirit in economic affairs. The leading industrial region in the country is that based upon Tunis and Bizerta, where a new ceramics factory was recently opened (1967). In 1966 Tunisia's first iron and steel works began production near Bizerta at Menzel-Bourguiba. Production of motor vehicles (300 Ford lorries a year) has recently started.

At the same time, traditional handicrafts and native industries are carried on in most towns (*see* p. 392). Examples include the manufacture of woollen, cotton and silk textiles, pottery, perfumes, leather and small metal goods. Some of these are produced on a considerable scale for a wider market, an example being the manufacture for export of carpets and blankets at Kairouan.

THE MAGHRIB: PRESENT-DAY PROBLEMS

The following is a general summary of the main problems of the Maghrib, dealt with for convenience under three headings:

(a) problems stemming directly from the physical environment;
(b) social problems;
(c) economic problems.

PROBLEMS STEMMING DIRECTLY FROM THE PHYSICAL ENVIRONMENT

The most obvious problem is that of water supply and water control. This comes about partly because of the seasonal nature of the rainfall and partly because the rainfall is often deficient in amount and unreliable: streams in the Maghrib are often raging torrents for a time during the winter while they dry up completely during the summer. Considerable sums of money have been spent, especially in Morocco and Algeria, on water control and irrigation schemes, and other projects are actively under consideration. For instance, the U.S.S.R. is extending technical and financial aid to Algeria to help in the construction of two dams in Great Kabylia. These will make possible the irrigation of 5250 acres (2100 ha) of land, and it is proposed at a later date to construct 26 further dams in the same region. The result of this ambitious scheme will be to bring 70,000 acres (28,000 ha) of crop land under irrigation. A comprehensive programme of drilling for water in remote parts of the Algerian Sahara will also shortly be commenced; it is expected that each of the 30 wells to be drilled will supply 70 litres of fresh water a second, and this will make possible substantial developments in agriculture in the areas selected (*see also* p. 421).

A further problem to which reference had been made is that of soil erosion, another result in part of the torrential rains. Re-afforestation schemes are projected to combat this menace, while controlled grazing of stock (*see* p. 422) is being attempted in some areas.

SOCIAL PROBLEMS

The most pressing problem is undoubtedly the tremendous increase in population which was experienced in all three of the Maghrib countries during the period of French rule and which is still continuing. A rate of population increase of the order of 2% per annum doubles any given population in just over 30 years; this is, in fact, the situation confronting the Maghrib today, and it means that in order to maintain living standards even at their present levels (and these are pitiably low for most of the inhabitants) a very marked increase in productivity is called for. For territories of resource deficiency such as Tunisia this presents a tremendous problem, and even for under-developed territories which are more favourably endowed by nature the difficulties are very great.

Other problems which arise are typical of those generally encountered when traditional societies are faced with new and changing situations. At first, there is likely to be hostility to any change among the people, and only slowly does the realisation dawn that the old ways are not always the best. Typical of a new situation facing many of the inhabitants of the Maghrib is the necessity for some at least of the nomadic peoples to adopt more sedentary forms of life. We have examined instances where this is happening in Morocco (*see* p. 370) and in Tunisia (*see* p. 413), and the reader might also refer back to p. 417 for further comment on this point.

A problem which is partly social and partly economic has to do with the development in large towns of *bidonvilles* into which crowd numbers of hopeful would-be workers, many of them coming from the country-side. These people live of necessity in squalor and poverty, and a real social problem is created as these settlements become natural hotbeds of disease, dissension and unrest. At bottom, the problem is an economic one, that of finding enough work to occupy the people concerned, but there is little likelihood that industry can develop at a sufficient rate to provide jobs to meet the demand in the near future, despite the efforts which are being made. This is a problem of widespread occurrence in developing territories.

ECONOMIC PROBLEMS

For agriculture probably the most pressing need in the Maghrib is that of improving farming techniques, but, as remarked above, this immediately brings to the fore the difficulty of the inherent opposition so often felt towards change, in this case by cultivators who are accustomed to the traditional methods of their fathers. As in the Moroccan example (*see* p. 371) the best way of overcoming this difficulty is by active demonstration of the superiority of modern methods, for as soon as farmers begin to see for themselves the advantages to be gained they will be quick enough to change their ways of working. Neither can the question of expense be overlooked, for the equipping of a farm with modern appliances can be an expensive business, and it will be a long time before even a majority of farms in the Maghrib are properly equipped for modern methods of working. The successful performance of the mechanised European farms before independence, however, clearly demonstrates the superiority of scientific methods of farming over traditional ones. Expenses on capital equipment are naturally considerably higher where irrigation needs to be developed, and it is likely that farms in the drier parts of the Maghrib may not be modernised within the foreseeable future.

Attempts to develop industry bring to the fore problems of a different nature: shortage of capital, limited markets, limited expertise are all factors to be reckoned with, and these points have all received attention in earlier pages. The only short-term answer to the problem of shortage of capital is to "import" capital from other countries, and this means creating a social and political atmosphere which will attract foreign investors and not frighten them away. One possible way of securing extended markets for the industries of the Maghrib would be for the three countries to set up a free trading association—a sort of Maghrib Common Market—though such an association would require careful planning. This should, however, be a possible development, and the first steps towards it are in fact already being taken. With regard to the third point mentioned above, there are two main ways to overcome the problem of limited expertise, and these are (1) to afford the labour which is available (and unskilled labour is abundant) the chance of becoming expert by actually working in industrial establishments, and (2) by setting up training facilities. This, however, is more easily said than done; industrial skills are not acquired overnight, and years of effort and experience are required before a pool of skilled labour can be created in a formerly non-industrial society.

One final point might be considered here. Before many parts of the Maghrib territories can be developed it will be necessary to provide more adequate communications; this is particularly true of those parts of the territories which lie in or near the Sahara Desert. The importance of this fact is being increasingly realised, and a great deal of attention is now being paid to the problem. A proposal, for instance, is now under active consideration for the construction of a trans-Saharan highway, 1750 miles (2800 km) in length, linking Fort Flatters in the north of the desert with Tamanrasset in the centre, and with Gao (Mali) and Agadès (Niger) in the south. It is now realised that such a road would benefit the Maghrib proper as well as the Sahara; for example, it would make it possible for Algeria to export petroleum products at economic prices to the countries of the Guinea Coast, while a survey has shown that the cost of transporting one ton of goods from Algiers to Agadès could be cut from the present £75 to about £35, and if return cargoes were assured costs could be reduced still further.

Typical of the efforts now being made to stimulate economic development in the Maghrib is Tunisia's four-year plan, first set in motion in 1964. At the end of the first year (1965) of effort, the following were the major achievements under the plan:

(a) a 3% increase in agricultural production;
(b) a 5·8% increase in power consumption "in all sectors";
(c) a 6·8% increase in industrial activity (this takes account of the service industries);
(d) a 10% increase in savings in the country; and
(e) an increase of 33% in foreign aid.

It is also significant that the level of imports remained the same as it was in 1964, despite increases in the purchase of capital equipment for the various projects in hand under the plan. If this kind of progress can be

maintained in Tunisia and emulated in Morocco and Algeria, the future
for the territories of the Maghrib will indeed be bright.

STUDY QUESTIONS

1. Attempt a division of Tunisia into natural regions, justifying your division.
2. Write an essay on the relationship between climate and agriculture in Tunisia.
3. Give an account of nomadism in Tunisia.
4. To what extent can regional variations in ways of life be ascribed to variations in climate in Tunisia?
5. Analyse the problems of future industrial expansion in the Maghrib.
6. Write an account of urban development in the Maghrib.
7. Attempt an assessment of the importance of irrigation to the territories of the Maghrib.

Chapter XX

LIBYA

It is proper to include the United Kingdom of Libya in this survey for one reason only—the territory has a Mediterranean coastline. Libya is almost entirely a Saharan country, and only along the coastal strip does a dry variation of the Mediterranean type of climate occur. Although the country is large, covering an area of 679,358 square miles (1,758,858 sq. km), the total population is only about 1¼ million, an indication of the general poverty of the territory until very recent times. The Kingdom, which became in 1951 the first independent state to be created be the United Nations Organisation, comprises the three major divisions of Tripolitania in the north-west, Fezzan in the south-west, and Cyrenaica in the east.

PHYSICAL ASPECTS

STRUCTURE AND RELIEF

By far the greater part of Libya lies on the main African basement plateau, and this is interrupted only in parts of the centre of the country by extensive lava extrusions which give rise to upland plains (see Fig. 104). Near the northern coasts the edges of the main plateau take the form of a series of escarpments which plunge down stepped scarp faces towards the north; the scarps are, in fact, often fault scarps. In the north-west of Libya the crest of the escarpment, which is very prominent in this region, has the name of the Jebel Nefusa, and the scarp face, which in some parts falls as much as 1000 ft (300 m) from crest to foot, overlooks a triangular sandy plain known as the Jefara; this plain is a direct continuation of the Tunisian Jefara. In Cyrenaica, the corresponding crest, also very prominent, is called the Jebel el Akhdar (the Green Mountain); the highest parts of this Jebel reach heights of 2700 ft (820 m) above sea-level, while the Cyrenian mountains which also form part of this upland region attain an elevation of 3500 ft (1060 m). The Jebel el Akhdar consists essentially of a limestone plateau broken by three faults, each of which has given rise to a northward-facing scarp; the most northerly of these scarps plunges directly into the sea in many places. The whole area is subject to destructive earthquakes. There is one fairly small upland plain suitable for cultivation, the Plain of El Marj (formerly Barce,) while a number of isolated lowlands of very limited extent lie between the Jebel and the sea.

The coastline of Libya is a remarkably smooth one, the two most prominent features being the Gulf of Sirte (or Sidra) which thrusts southwards almost to latitude 30° N., and the Barce Peninsula which sweeps northwards to the east of the gulf around the Jebel el Akhdar. There are

few good natural harbours along the coast which in some parts (such as
along much of the Barce Peninsula) is very rocky and steep, while in other
parts it is low and swampy. This is especially true of the coastal strip to
the south of Misurata, where the Sebkha di Tauorga extends southwards
for about 75 miles (120 km); indeed, the whole of the western part of the
coast almost as far east as Sirte comprises a broken line of lagoons and
oases which are interrupted by sand dunes. In Cyrenaica, the coastal lowlands north of the Jebel el Akhdar, such as those of Derna and Appolonia,
are narrow and salty.

The greater part of the surface of the main plateau of Libya carries
deserts of the varying types which we have described earlier (*see* p. 381),
with hammada, reg (which is often known in Libya as *serir*), and erg all

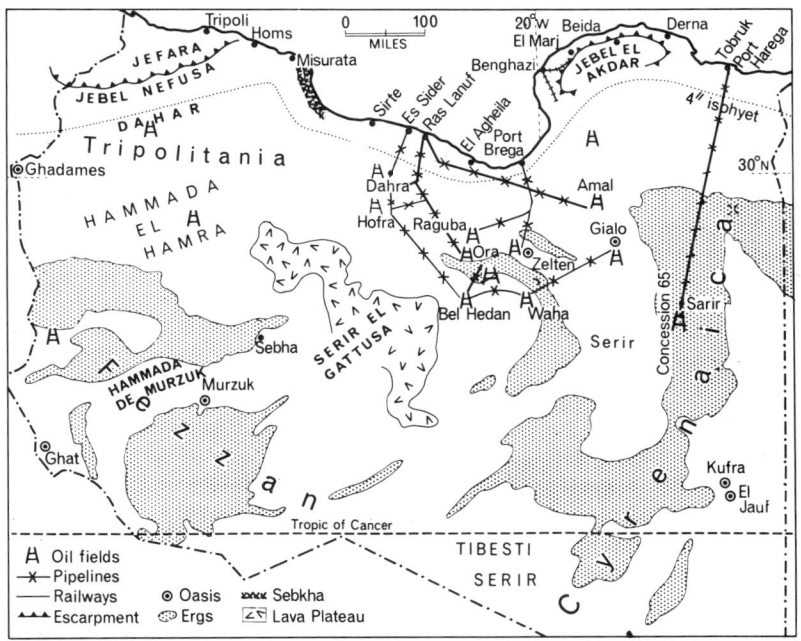

FIG. 104.—Libya: some economic features.

represented. Fig. 104 shows the location of the better known of the various types of desert. There are some notable oases in Libya, especially
Ghadames and Ghat in the Fezzan, and the Kufra group, headquarters of
the once powerful Senussi tribe, which lies across the main trans-Saharan
route from Benghazi on the coast to Abeshr in the Chad Republic. This
group lies in Cyrenaica.

There are no permanent rivers in Libya, though many wadis in the
north run from the Jebels towards the coasts; occasionally, water flowing
from the Jebel Nefusa will actually reach the coast, while in Cyrenaica a

number of wadis bite deeply into the Jebel el Akhdar on their way north-wards. Some wadis lead southwards from the Jebels, and they finally peter out in salt lakes and marshes which are known in Cyrenaica as *baltes*.

CLIMATE

Only the northernmost coastal districts, which lie respectively to the west and east of the Gulf of Sirte, together with the Jebels which overlook them, receive sufficient rainfall to permit sedentary occupation based on cultivation. The drier western parts of the Jefara receive less than 5 in. of rain a year on the average, but this figure increases to over 8 in. along the coast, to over 14 in. in the district around Tripoli (Tripoli itself registers 16·3 in.), and to over 12 in. on the moister parts of the Jebel Nefusa. The coastal lowlands of the Barce Peninsula receive about 10 in. a year in the west (11 in. at Benghazi) and this figure rises somewhat in the northern-most parts of the peninsula before dropping again to about 11 in. at Derna. The highest areas of the Jebel el Akhdar and the Cyrenian mountains receive about 25 in. in their wetter parts.

The coastlands of the Gulf of Sirte enjoy considerably less rainfall than the more elevated areas to the west and east which have been discussed. The small settlement of Sirte itself, for example, records about 7 in. per annum, while El Agheila near the southernmost reach of the Gulf receives 4 in. The Gulf coastlands, from the climatic point of view, are little more than marginal lands of the Sahara Desert, though it is worth pointing out that the coastal areas generally receive noticeable contributions of moisture in the form of dew. (Compare the Tunisian Sahel, *see* p. 412.) In general it may be said that the desert extends southwards from the areas just south of the Jebels (areas which receive roughly 10 in. of rain) over the remainder of this extensive territory, most of which records an average rainfall of less than 1 in. a year. In fact, the term "average" has little significance under these conditions, for individual storms may be separated by years in which no rain falls at all.

Temperatures, as may be expected in this generally arid kingdom which extends across the Tropic of Cancer near its southern limits, are extreme and at times very high. During the winter night temperatures frequently fall below freezing point, and a figure as low as 23° F (50° C) has been re-corded in the northern part of the desert. On the other hand, day tem-peratures in the summer are among the highest known anywhere on the earth's surface; the highest shade temperature ever recorded under stand-ard conditions was noted in September, 1922, at El Azizia, 25 miles (40 km) south of Tripoli—no less than 136·4° F (58° C)! On the northward-facing slopes of the Jebels, however, conditions are much more pleasant; this is particularly the case on the Jebel el Akhdar where the stifling heat of the desert is not experienced. Summers on the Jebel Nefusa are hotter than on the Jebel el Akhdar, and the region suffers from a violent hot wind known as the *ghibli*, which blows from the desert (the *ghibli* is comparable to the *sirocco* of Algeria and the *khamsin* of Egypt). At Tripoli, though the mean annual range of temperature is comparatively small (26° F or 14·4° C), actual temperatures of over 100° F (39° C) are frequently recorded during the summer months.

NATURAL REGIONS

For the purposes of this brief study it will be sufficient to recognise three natural regions: the north-west, the north-east, and the desert.

1. *The north-west region.* This region lies in the north-western part of Tripolitania, and on the whole it is the best-favoured and the most prosperous part of the whole country, especially the eastern section which is known generally as the Garian–Homs–Tripoli triangle (*see* Fig. 104). The core of the region is the sandy plain of the Jefara, bounded on the north by the low marshy coast commented upon earlier, and to the south by the purplish cliff of the Jebel Nefusa. Cultivation, in general, is possible along much of the coastal strip, in the Garian–Homs–Tripoli triangle in the east, and along the crest of the Jebel; in these areas as Fig. 104 (*a*) shows, rainfall is comparatively high. The remainder of the Jefara is semi-desert where esparto grass is grown and where semi-nomadic grazing is carried on. As in the neighbouring Tunisian Jefara, the nomads grow catch crops of cereals in depressions and along the wadis.

Cultivation by Libyan farmers both in the coastal oases which lie between Zuara to the west and Misurata to the east, and in the Garian–Homs–Tripoli triangle, depends partly upon winter rain and partly upon water drawn from wells, especially in summer. Olives, citrus fruits, almonds, vegetables and barley are produced, mainly on a subsistence basis, for crops are not large enough to be very significant commercially. The chief product, however, is the date, but although date palms abound the fruit is generally too poor in quality to be acceptable for export. In the areas between the coastal oases some dry farming is carried on, and olives, figs, grapes and barley are produced, while in near-by irrigable parts of the Jefara crops of wheat, barley and tobacco are grown.

Clarke has demonstrated that a typical small native farm (such a farm is known as a *sanyah*) situated in an oasis near Tripoli covers $3\frac{3}{4}$ acres (1·5 ha), and can be irrigated throughout. It carries about 80 date palms, 40 olive trees, 15 pomegranate trees, 4 apricot trees and 2 fig trees. About one-third of the land between the trees lies fallow at any given time, while on the remaining two-thirds a crop rotation system taking $2\frac{1}{2}$ years to work through is practised. A crop of alfalfa in one summer is followed the next winter by wheat; the following summer groundnuts or tobacco are grown, while a crop of vegetables in the second winter brings the rotation to a close.

A fair proportion of the coastal strip and the "triangle" was developed during the colonial period by Italian farmers, who were able to make use of more sophisticated farming methods than the native Libyans and who were frequently assisted by subsidies and loans from the Italian Government. One of the most important of their techniques involved the use of artesian water; this made possible a considerable increase in the production of groundnuts which have become the leading agricultural export. The subterranean water used by Libyan cultivators and drawn from wells comes as near to the surface as 15 ft (4·5 m) in places; the artesian water lies at depths of over 50 ft (15 m). Other crops grown are similar to those of the Libyan oasis farmers, especially olives (olive oil ranks second in value to groundnuts as an agricultural export), citrus fruits, almonds and grapes; cereals (wheat and barley) and groundnuts are rotated on the open ground between the trees (see also p. 438). It is hoped that the growing of sugar beet will shortly become a leading activity, and if it does Libya will have no further need of imported sugar.

Passing over the semi-arid Jefara, to which reference has been made above, we find that a second, though narrow, zone of cultivation extends along the comparatively well-watered crest of the Jebel, where crops of cereals and fruit are produced by the Berber inhabitants. The Jebel has possibilities for the extension of tree crops, though arboriculture has so far been carried on chiefly by a limited number of Italians, most of whom have now left the area. A market gardening scheme is shortly to be introduced with the idea of supplying Tripoli with fresh fruit and vegetables. To the south of the cultivated zone, on the dip slope of the Jebel escarpment (the Dahar), rainfall rapidly decreases in amount (see Fig. 104) and cultivators are replaced in the steppe areas by semi-nomads; the only commercial activity, and one of very limited significance, is the gathering of esparto grass. Farther south again, the steppe steadily gives place to desert.

2. *The north-east region.* This region lies within the northerly bulge of Cyrenaica (the Barce Peninsula) in which lies the Jebel el Akhdar; indeed, the Jebel and the associated coastal strip form the main parts of the region. On the Jebel, forests of cypress, ilex and juniper are broken by clearings characterised by reddish soils which contrast vividly with white outcrops of limestone. Valleys typically terminate in caverns and swallow holes where surface streams disappear underground. Farther south the forests give place first to a sort of garrigue and then to steppe. The area is not as a whole as prosperous as the north-western region for reasons which we shall examine shortly, but a rainfall well above the average for Libya makes possible closer settlement and a more variable land use than is generally met with in the territory.

Cultivation generally in the region is rendered difficult by the very limited extent of level land, by the accidented nature of a region deeply gashed by wadis and broken by faults, by the inaccessibility of so many of the more important watercourses, and by the difficulties of storing water behind dams in limestone country. It is also true that most of the inhabitants are Arabs rather than Berbers, and Arabs are by tradition herdsmen rather than cultivators. Many water controls built by the Romans have, in fact, been left unused by the Arabs, or even permitted to fall into decay. It is not surprising, under these circumstances, that there was very little cultivation in the region until Italian farmers began to settle in the 1930s;

livestock rearing was the main occupation of the Semitic inhabitants. The Italian settlers, however, greatly helped by grants and credits from the Italian Government, grew crops of cereals (wheat and barley), grapes and vegetables, while the production of tree crops (olives and apricots, for example) was begun. After the Italians fled before the Allied forces their farms were taken over by Libyans, who had not generally the skill or the capital to farm them efficiently, while the trees and vines (which are abhorrent to strict Muslims who touch no alcohol) were generally not cared for. Most of the land was given over to the cultivation of cereals and to pasture.

While goats and cattle are not uncommonly reared in the moister, well-wooded northern parts of the region, sheep and camels are more usual on the steppe and semi-desert areas farther south. A semi-nomadic way of life is customary, the flocks and herds wintering on the steppe and semi-desert areas which receive limited rainfall at this season, while they move northwards to the cooler surroundings of the Jebel for the summer. Attempts have been made in recent years to persuade farmers to reduce their large and destructive herds of goats and to concentrate instead on cultivation; as part of this programme many ancient works such as reservoirs and cisterns have been cleaned out and repaired, while new wells have been drilled. Plantations of juniper and eucalyptus, which are closed to all grazing, are being established near the coast, while local sheep have been crossed with imported strains in an effort to improve the quality of both wool and mutton.

Cultivation is carried on upon the coastal lowlands, but the oases which develop where springs gush out at the foot of the limestone scarp are hemmed in by rocky uplands, and are generally too small to become of more than local importance. The oasis of Derna, however, is larger than normal, and it produces bananas on a comparatively large scale, as well as the more usual cereals, fruits (mainly olives and peaches) and vegetable crops. The terraced limestone slopes overlooking the sea help to produce a landscape which is very typical of parts of the Mediterranean, particularly of Greece.

To the south of Benghazi lies a semi-arid coastal plain which is really a continuation of the dry coastlands of the Gulf of Sirte and which is the home of nomadic pastoralists. On the other side of the Barce Peninsula, to the east of Derna, the region known as Marmarica extends as far as the Egyptian border. This area is low but rugged, and since it lies in a rain shadow produced by the Jebel el Akhdar it, too, is semi-arid and carries little settlement.

3. *The desert.* Ninety-five per cent of Libya may be classified as desert, ranging from hammada developed on limestones and sandstones to the barren lava plateaus of the centre and the extensive sand seas (erg) of Fezzan and southern Cyrenaica. Until the recent discoveries of mineral oil this vast region contributed little to the general economy of the country. The mineral deposits will be examined later.

Apart from these mineral developments, the economic life of this region is almost entirely confined to the oases, though in some areas, such as the region to the south of the Gulf of Sirte, a sparse scrub vegetation along the beds of the various wadis provides some pasture for nomadic groups. In the oases the production of dates is the main activity—it is said that date palms occupy about 300,000 acres (120,000 ha) in central and southern Libya. Total production of dates is, however, not great and the amount available for export is small. Other tree crops include figs and apricots, while cereals (mainly wheat and barley), and vegetables are also grown for local use; in the southern oases the place of barley is taken by millet. Cultivation is a small-scale affair and the various fields in which the crops are grown are extremely small.

The main oases include the Kufra group, Gialo and Jarabub in Cyrenaica, and Murzuk, Ghat and Ghadames in Fezzan. Most of these appear from a distance as fairly large groups of date palms set in a surrounding immensity of sandy or rocky desert.

HUMAN GEOGRAPHY

HISTORY AND PEOPLE

The original inhabitants of Libya, as in the neighbouring Maghrib, were Hamitic Berbers. The area has experienced, however, a long series of invasions: foreign domination began in early times when Phoenician, Greek and Roman influences (*see* Fig. 105) in turn were strongly felt in the northern parts of the territory. In these areas spectacular ruins such as those of the Phoenician trading settlement of Leptis Magna and those of the Greek city of Cyrene are still to be seen. The Romans, with their customary brilliant skill in engineering, constructed reservoirs, cisterns and other water control works in Cyrenaica, and they also began the production of tree crops such as the olive. Tripolitania was administered by Rome as part of the province of Africa (the Maghrib formed the main part of this province), and Cyrenaica as part of the province of Crete.

As in Tunisia, Roman political influence was finally brought to a close with the arrival of the Semitic invaders (the Arabs) who entered the country in a succession of waves, particularly in the seventh, ninth and eleventh centuries. The economic and cultural heritage of the past was neglected, pastoralism as a way of life became dominant, and urban life was restricted to Tripoli, a barbaric settlement and the lair of pirates. After the period of Arab domination Libya became part of the Ottoman Empire (*see* p. 353), and this comparatively barren land remained nominally under Turkish control until 1911, by which time the more prosperous lands of the Maghrib and Egypt to west and east had fallen under the influence of France and Britain respectively. In practice, Turkish rule amounted to little more than a superficial control over some of the coastal settlements and the collecting of as much tax as possible; nothing constructive was done for the country. In 1911, an Italy hungry for colonies to satisfy her

FIG. 105.—Libya: ruins of a Roman theatre. This ruin at Leptis Magna near Tripoli is only one of the many signs of the Roman occupation and development of North Africa.

late-developing sense of nationalism discovered that the only parts of Africa open to her were economically unattractive areas, of which Libya was one. Her sphere of influence in North Africa was restricted to the area between Tunisia and Egypt, but she pushed southwards into the Sahara Desert and occupied much of that worthless area (as it then was) for reasons of prestige. Tripoli was occupied in 1911, and Turkey recognised her conquest of the area in 1912, though Italian rule was not completely effective in Cyrenaica until 1921, and in the desert regions until 1935.

Between 1912 and the loss of the colony during the Second World War, over 100,000 Italians settled in Libya, many in the cities and many in the countryside, the latter often with the help of loans and subsidies, which in all ran into many thousands of pounds, from the metropolitan government. Two types of farm holding were established: (1) private allotments of up to 75 acres (30 ha) which were developed with the help of private capital and unskilled Arab labour; and (2) the generally slightly larger *demographic settlements* which usually occupied poorer land and which therefore needed greater capital investment. This was supplied from Government sources and was repaid by the farmers over fairly lengthy periods. In addition to this form of investment, money was also spent by the Italians on the building of towns, roads, railways and harbours. The consequent influx of settlers, much as it may be deplored on other grounds, undoubtedly did a very great deal to stimulate economic production in Libya. Even today the greatly reduced numbers of Italians (there are now rather more than 30,000 in the country, most of them in Tripoli) play a far more important part in economic affairs than their numbers alone would suggest.

After the close of the Second World War, Libya, as a former Italian colony, became the responsibility of the United Nations, which (after much discussion and disagreement) granted independence to the territory in 1951. The differences between Tripolitania (mainly Berber and agricultural), Cyrenaica (chiefly Arab and pastoralist), and Fezzan (comprising scattered oases set in a matrix of desert nomadism) were recognised by the establishment of a federal form of government under the King; three provinces and two federal capitals (Tripoli and Benghazi) were set up in the "United Kingdom of Libya." The Federal Government alternated between the two capitals seasonally! In 1962 this wasteful and burdensome system was abolished, ten administrative districts replaced the three provinces, and a unitary form of central government was established with its headquarters in a new capital, Beida, in Cyrenaica. Today, of course, the outlook for this formerly poverty-stricken state has been completely changed by the discoveries of enormous amounts of mineral oil (see p. 439).

The population of Libya is estimated at 1,244,000, which works out at the very low density of fewer than 2 persons per square mile. Most of the inhabitants (830,000) live in Tripolitania, and about 350,000 in Cyrenaica, the remainder (about 60,000) occupying the desert province of Fezzan. About a quarter of the people live in the former capitals of Tripoli and Benghazi. Just over 30,000 Italians still live in Libya, most of them in the towns of Tripolitania, especially Tripoli. In Tripolitania about two-thirds of the rural inhabitants are agriculturalists and one-third nomads, while in Cyrenaica nomads and semi-nomads number about one-half of the total population. In Fezzan there are no towns; even Sebha, the capital, is no more than a large village. The oases do, however, carry a mainly sedentary population, though nomads probably number no more than one-quarter of the total.

The distinction between Tripolitania, which is chiefly Berber, and Cyrenaica, which is mainly Arab, has been stressed. Today, about two-thirds of the total population are Arab. The other one-third comprises Berbers and smaller groups such as the Italians and some Greeks, while in the southern parts of the country most of the inhabitants of Fezzan are Tibu, a people with an admixture of Negro blood who speak a Negro language. In earlier days the Tibu were renowned as marauders who possessed very great physical stamina and extraordinary skill in tracking. Today they are nomadic pastoralists for the most part, though in some mountainous areas of Tibesti (in the Chad Republic) they own land along the valley floors which is tilled by Negro serfs.

SETTLEMENT

Settlement in most parts of Libya is sparse, so sparse, indeed, as to be non-existent in many areas. It is estimated that about one-quarter of the total population is urban and that the remaining three-quarters in rural areas comprise roughly 40% sedentary cultivators and 35% nomads and semi-nomads. Most of the sedentary inhabitants live in the cultivated parts of Tripolitania and Cyrenaica, while oasis settlements also carry sedentary populations.

Easily the two most important towns are the former capitals of Tripoli and Benghazi, both of which are rapidly increasing in size largely as a result of the oil boom. The old medina of Tripoli (population 191,000) lies on a peninsula, and the large and elegant modern city and the port are legacies of Italian rule. There is still a considerable Italian element in the population, and Italians are employed as traders, merchants, clerks and tradesmen—positions for which a measure of education is essential. Industry in the city is very limited in scale, and is for the most part concerned with the processing of agricultural produce and fish and with traditional handicrafts such as the production of textiles and leather goods. Unfortunately, there are large numbers of unemployed workers in Tripoli—a common feature in North African towns. The harbour is to be considerably extended in the near future and a special wharf for trawlers is to be built.

Other towns in Tripolitania are small and are located for the most part either along the coast (for example Zuara, Homs and Misurata) or in the moister parts of the Jefara (El Azizia, Garian and Zawiyah are instances). These are market towns and local administrative centres, while Misurata is a small port.

Benghazi, with a population of 120,000, is the chief town and port of Cyrenaica, and two short railways with a total length of 115 miles (184 km) run from the town to Sulok and El Marj (formerly Barce), both small settlements of local importance. The town holds over one-third of the inhabitants of Cyrenaica, though industrial development is even more limited than it is in Tripoli. The town and the port have been largely rebuilt since the close of the Second World War. Derna (16,000) is an attractive small settlement and port which suffers from its isolated position, while Tobruk is a port formerly of local importance only, which is now springing into significance as a result of the oil export from the near-by shipping point of Port Harega (see p. 440). The new federal capital of Beida is situated on the heights of the Jebel el Akhdar.

THE ECONOMY

AGRICULTURE AND STOCK-REARING

It is estimated that no more than one-half of 1% of the total surface area of Libya is permanently cultivated, and it is unlikely that it will ever be possible to extend this area very greatly because of the rigorous climatic conditions. Catch crops are, however, grown in many parts of the north, the success (or otherwise) of the harvest depending upon the rainfall in any particular season. The most productive parts of the country are to be found in the north-west, where an above-average rainfall, supplies of

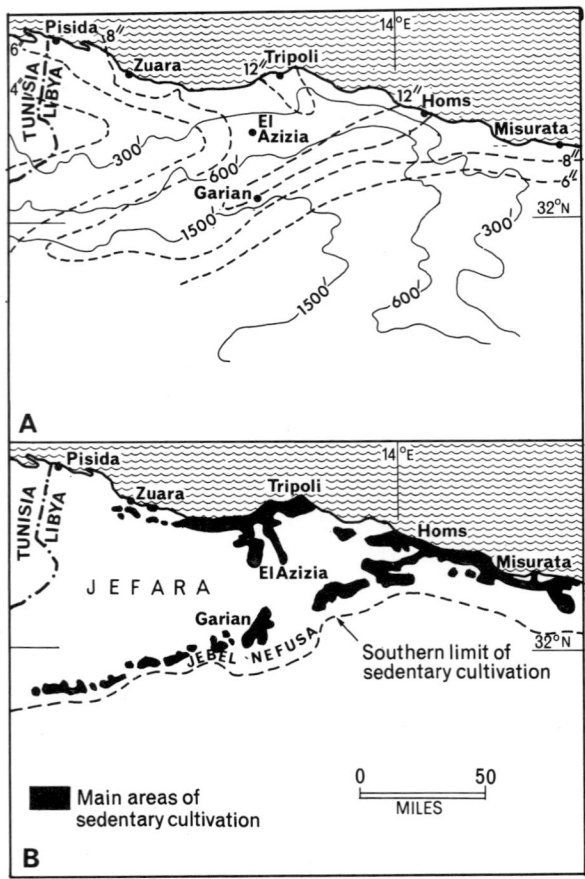

Fig. 106.—Northern Tripolitania (*based partly on Clarke and Hance*). (A) Relief and rainfall. (B) Towns and cultivation.

artesian water and the application of more efficient farming methods have permitted Italian farmers to produce crops on a sufficient scale to allow a limited export (*see* p. 431). In general, the most important crops grown in the north of Libya are cereals (barley and wheat) and groundnuts, while large numbers of olive and almond trees have been planted in the coastal oases; figs and citrus fruits are also produced, especially near the larger coastal settlements. In the south, the date is widely grown in the oases and forms a staple food, while millet and wheat are the most important cereal crops.

As has previously been mentioned, esparto grass is widely collected, especially on the Jefara and on the Jebel Nefusa, and is exported.

In some areas, notably in Cyrenaica, groups of semi-nomads sow cereals at the beginning of winter to take advantage of the meagre winter rains, and immediately afterwards they move southwards with their stock for winter grazing. They return for the spring harvest, and again move southwards, though for shorter distances, during the summer. While a few cattle and some goats are reared in the northern parts of the country, particularly in Cyrenaica, the sheep is easily the most important animal and it outnumbers all other forms of stock put together. The sheep provide their Arab owners with wool, meat and milk. The camel is widely reared, especially in the steppe and semi-desert areas.

One of the features of contemporary life in Libya, as in other comparable territories, is the drift of many inhabitants away from a nomadic to a more settled form of life. For example, along parts of the coast of Cyrenaica the Italians established a demographic settlement comprising nearly 2000 small farms. These have now been taken over by former nomads who are farming them with moderate success, and are producing crops of olives, figs and peaches. One particularly good feature of this experiment is that the farmers are reducing the numbers of their stock, especially of the goats which in the past have severely damaged protective vegetation by their voracious grazing (*see* p. 433). In other areas, however, the present situation is less happy. Clarke points out, for instance, that Fezzan, with an area of 213,000 sq. miles (553,800 sq. km), has a population of only about 60,000 and a cultivated area of barely 1250 acres (500 ha), and that the economy is dominated by a decaying oasis cultivation and pastoral nomadism. There is a small but steady movement of people northwards towards the towns of the coastal zone and to the oil centres, and while the numbers concerned are not great, it is a serious loss to the region because it is normally the young and able-bodied who are lost in this way.

MINING AND MANUFACTURING

Mention has previously been made of the recent spectacular discoveries of mineral oil in Libya, and the position early in 1967 is illustrated on Fig. 104. Exports of mineral oil have leapt up from nothing in 1956 to 850,000 metric tons in 1961 and to 72,290,000 metric tons in 1966; this makes Libya the largest mineral oil exporter in Africa. Oil was first struck in 1957 in Fezzan at a spot near the Algerian border about 50 miles to the south-east of Edjeleh (*see* Fig. 95), but the strike was not a large one and the great distance from the coast discouraged immediate development. Later discoveries have been numerous in Fezzan, Tripolitania and Cyrenaica, but most of them have been too small for exploitation at present.

Some very large strikes of oil and natural gas have been made, however, and the most important are shown on Fig. 104. The earliest fields to be developed were those of Zelten and Raguba, both of which are connected by pipeline to the shipping point at Port Brega; giant super tankers can use this port which has a small oil refinery. Both places have gas liquefaction plants under construction. The second major producing area was near Dahra and Hofra, now linked to Es Sider (Sidra) by pipeline; this line has been extended well beyond Hofra as far as Gialo, another productive area. Other discoveries of mineral oil and natural gas can be expected. In 1968, for example, it was announced that a further oilfield at Sarir (Concession 65) in the Sahara had commenced production with a shipment to Britain from Port Harega near Tobruk, while a new oil port is to be constructed west of Benghazi. It is expected that exports from Sarir will cause Britain to take the place of Western Germany as Libya's biggest oil customer. The difficulties surmounted before the Sarir field began production were considerable. The distance from Tobruk is 320 miles (512 km), a formidable distance, and the 34-inch pipeline had to be laid in arid country, scorched by the Saharan sun and crossing very accidented terrain which includes rocky, stony and sandy deserts. The oilfield itself lies in very difficult sand dune country. A further difficulty was that the Sarir oil has a high wax content and it solidifies at temperatures below 65° F(18·3° C)— and desert temperatures in this area fall considerably below that figure during the night (see p. 430). Specially designed heating devices had therefore to be installed in the pipeline. One fortunate feature, however, has been the discovery of artesian water beneath the oilfield, and an adequate water supply for present operations is therefore assured. Further plans to deal with the natural gas now being produced include the construction of a port to accommodate gas tankers at Al-Burayqah, while what will be the largest gas liquefaction plant in the world is under construction at Port Brega. The gas will be exported to Italy and Spain.

Mineral oil now accounts for about 99% by value of all exports from Libya; in the first half of 1966 the figure was 99·5%—£163 million out of a total export value of £163,796,482. Libya is now Britain's largest supplier of crude oil (10% of British imports in 1963). Western Germany, however, is Libya's largest customer, taking about 42% of the exports as against Britain's 20%, though this position may shortly change. An important point in this connection is that Libya lies much nearer to northwestern Europe than do the Middle East oilfields. For example, the distance from Port Brega to Britain is about 2500 miles (4000 km), whereas from the head of the Persian Gulf it is almost 6500 miles (10,400 km). While this means that considerably more mineral oil can be shipped from Libya to north-west Europe than from the Persian Gulf in any given time, it should be recalled that the two types of crude oil concerned are not entirely interchangeable; the situation is comparable to that which has arisen in the case of Algerian oil (see p. 402). One important result of the new oil wealth is that for the first time since independence the country is self-supporting. For some time after independence in 1951 Libya was able to survive only with the help of generous foreign aid (mainly from the U.S.A. and the United Kingdom) which was given in part exchange for permission to maintain military bases in the country. Libya, which is an Arab state attracted to Egypt rather than to the Maghrib, has never been happy about these bases, and it is no accident that she is asking for the agreement permitting them to be annulled now that she is feeling more secure financially.

It is not surprising that between 1958 and 1965 the national output of Libya increased in value about eightfold, from £52 million to about £408 million. In 1958 mining and quarrying activities together accounted for an output valued at £3·6 million; in 1965 the corresponding figure was £217 million—more than all other forms of economic activity put together. In 1965 agriculture accounted for £26 million (£14 million in 1958) and manufacturing for £13 million (£6 million in 1958). It is almost certain that there will be further developments in mineral oil production (for instance, the first large-scale offshore strike of natural gas in the Gulf of Sirte has already been announced), while a new mining industry altogether is presaged by the discovery at Pisida, which lies on the coast near the Tunisian border (see Fig. 104), of a deposit of household salt estimated to contain 250 million tons. The salt is about 3 ft (9 m) thick and is easy to reach, while it is said to be of such quality that it will need little more than grinding and packaging before it can be sold. This deposit could possibly become the basis of a chemical industry.

Manufacturing in Libya is extremely limited in scope and scale, and is mainly concerned with the processing of agricultural produce and with traditional handicrafts (see p. 437). Tripoli is easily the leading industrial centre, and enterprises recently opened include factories for the manufacture of foam rubber, of soap and of biscuits, while a plant is being erected for the refining and canning of vegetable oil. When completed, this factory will be able to deal with the entire local output of vegetable oils. The small oil refinery at Port Brega has been mentioned (it is interesting to note that it was prefabricated in Belgium and towed by sea to its present location!), and it is planned shortly to construct a gas liquefying plant at Zelten. This will produce liquefied gas for export to Spain and Italy. Other off-shoots of the mineral oil industry can be expected.

GENERAL SUMMARY

Although the future for Libya is more promising today than it has ever been before, thanks to the discoveries of mineral oil and natural gas, it must be borne in mind that the territory still has many problems to face. Except in this one sector, the economy remains impoverished and is likely to be so for a very long time to come. It may perhaps be argued that problems of four different categories face this country—physical, social, political and economic.

The fundamental physical problem is the overall lack of water in a country which receives a meagre rainfall and in which evaporation is intense; as a result, surface water supplies are few and undependable and there are no permanent streams. In a good year it is estimated that the cereal crop may be as much as 150,000 tons of grain but in a poor year it may be hardly one-tenth as much. Before any improvement in this situation can be expected much more use must be made of the subterranean water resources which exist in many parts of the country, many of which have been mentioned, though the danger of over-pumping with consequent depletion of reserves must always be borne in mind. More provision must also be made for the storage of surface water supplies; the Romans showed many years ago in Cyrenaica that this is a practical possibility. Agriculture on the Jebel el Akhdar could be greatly expanded if the admittedly deeply lying subterranean water present could be pumped to the surface, and tree crops (olives, citrus fruits and almonds, for example) could all be produced. There is, also, the possibility in the future that desalinated sea water might be used on a considerable scale for irrigation, particularly in the coastal zone.

The social problems are in part closely connected with the foregoing. While it is true, for instance, that a great increase in cultivation could take place in certain areas with the extended use of irrigation, it is also true that such an extension would of necessity considerably curtail the movements of nomads and semi-nomads. This is a situation of a kind met with elsewhere in North Africa (*see* pp. 371 and 413). If semi-nomads in Cyrenaica, to take a case in point, lost their "catch crop areas" near the Jebel el Akhdar, their whole way of life would have to be changed. We have earlier noticed that the decay of rural life in Fezzan is leading to social difficulties (*see* p. 439) in that area. There is no easy answer to these problems of social change; they must be met by a process of adjustment and adaptation which may sometimes appear to be unbearably slow. Such an adjustment is, in fact, already in progress, as nomadic people are taking up cultivation and as they are attracted by the prospect of paid employment in the oil industry and in the towns; many, indeed, are now working as labourers, truck drivers, and in various indoor occupations (as unskilled assistants in hotels and offices, for example). This is a trend which will continue and increase.

The internal political problems facing the country arise in large measure from the varied physical scene and from the isolation engendered by distance. Libya, unlike Tunisia, has never developed a sense of unity or a feeling of national self-consciousness, and there is still conflict of interest and viewpoint between Tripolitania and Cyrenaica, areas separated by extensive wastes of desert and scrub. The problems of Fezzan are different again, but this is hardly as yet a pressing political problem as Fezzan is economically a weak province. Regional conflicts of interest such as those which we have mentioned in this chapter are not easily reconciled, especially if the interests of one region or group appear to be winning a favoured place as against those of another. Regional antagonisms were rife over the location of Beida, the new capital, which appeared to favour Cyrenaica, while they could again erupt dangerously if the apportionment of the massive oil royalties appears in the future to favour one region to the disadvantage of the others.

We have already made mention of some of the problems which must be solved, if economic output in Libya is to be increased. We have seen, for example, that water supplies must be improved if agriculture is to expand, while improvements in farming techniques generally are badly needed. It is also true that the pastoralist desperately needs changes in outlook and technique. Essential needs, if the standard of living of the pastoralist is to be improved, include improvements in stock breeding, the establishment of veterinary services, the provision of more adequate supplies of fodder, better processing facilities for produce, and better marketing arrangements.

These are not the only forms of economic problem facing the country, however. As an example of a different type of problem there is the situation presented by the possible uses of the oil royalties now being received, for we must bear in mind that the sudden accession of wealth on a large scale brings many problems in train. Many observers of the Libyan scene are pointing to the affluence now being enjoyed by many contractors, merchants, hotel proprietors, property owners, oil men and Government officials, while at the same time, most of the people continue to live under conditions of extreme poverty; this poverty is thrown into gruesome relief by the new wealth of the few. Outward signs of the new affluence are to be seen in the boom in the building trades and in the rapid growth and development especially of Tripoli and Benghazi (with, unhappily, concomitant overcrowding and an extensive sprawling of new slums) and also in Beida. It will take time for the new wealth to work through to the ordinary workers and townsfolk and to the rural sector of the economy on a broad front. In a way a vicious circle develops as workers are attracted from the countryside by the prospect of paid employment, for one serious result is that there is a consequent scarcity of labour on the farms and many foodstuffs which Libyans should be producing themselves such as meat, milk, vegetables, fruit and wheat have to be imported. Prices of foodstuffs therefore rise, especially in the towns, and many workers (to say nothing of the unemployed) are hard put to it to purchase even basic necessities in this inflationary situation. The problem of revitalising the rural economy of Libya and of stopping the drift to the towns is one of the most pressing now facing the country.

STUDY QUESTIONS

1. Attempt a division of Libya into natural regions, justifying your division.
2. Explain the relationship between land use and climate in Libya.
3. What is the importance of mining to the present-day economy of Libya?
4. Write an essay on the problems of modern Libya.
5. What is the importance of nomadism in Libya today?

Chapter XXI

EGYPT (THE UNITED ARAB REPUBLIC)

EGYPT, officially known today as the United Arab Republic, has many claims to importance. The country was the cradle of one of the earliest civilisations in the long history of the human race; it is very large (386,000 sq. miles, 1,003,600 sq. km, though the inhabited area extends over only about 15,000 sq. miles, 39,000 sq. km); it is easily the most populous country of North Africa (30,083,419 inhabitants, 1966 census. Compare Switzerland, which has an area of 15,941 sq. miles (41,447 sq. km) and a total population of 5,565,000; even this works out at the considerable density of about 350 persons per square mile). It is the second most advanced territory from the industrial point of view in the whole of Africa, ranking only after the Republic of South Africa in industrial development; and it occupies an enormously important strategic position in the north-eastern corner of Africa. This last point was first recognised in the modern era by Napoleon, and it has since been emphasised by the cutting of the Suez Canal across the comparatively narrow isthmus of Suez. Although the importance of Egypt, therefore, cannot be in doubt, we are dealing with a country which is classed as Mediterranean for the single reason that it has a Mediterranean coastline. It does not experience a truly Mediterranean type of climate and its crops and economy generally are not typically Mediterranean.

PHYSICAL ASPECTS

STRUCTURE AND RELIEF

In broad outline the story of the geological and structural development of Egypt is comparatively simple, and can be understood with the help of Fig. 107. The first point to notice is that a finger-like protrusion of ancient basement rocks extends northwards from the borders of the Sudan Republic in the eastern part of the country, where it gives rise to the Red Sea Highlands. A detached part of this ancient block occurs in the south of the Sinai Peninsula. The platform developed on these basement rocks also extends westwards, but west of the Nile valley it is generally masked by later deposits; it does, however, come to the surface in isolated places (the outcrops are generally small and are not shown on Fig. 107), and also in the extreme south-west where it gives rise to the Gebel Uweinat.

A long period of weathering of the basement rocks from Carboniferous times onwards produced widespread masses of detritus which slowly accumulated in the form of sedimentary rocks of varying thicknesses; the most prominent and widespread of these rocks is the Nubian Sandstone which was formed between Carboniferous and Cretaceous times. These sandstones cover almost one-third of the total area of Egypt and in places they attain thicknesses of over 1500 ft (450 m). For the most part the Nubian Sandstone lies south of the latitude of Isna, though these deposits also occur in some areas farther north, for instance in a small rift valley which runs westwards from the Gulf of Suez. One very useful attribute

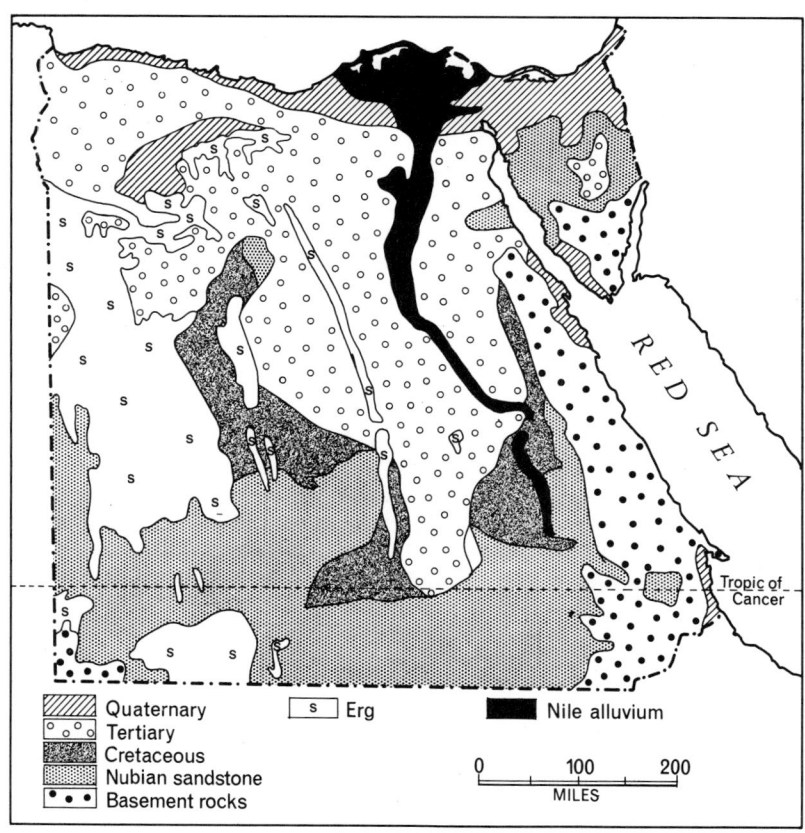

Quaternary
Tertiary
Cretaceous
Nubian sandstone
Basement rocks

Erg

Nile alluvium

0   100   200
MILES

FIG. 107.—Egypt: geology (simplified).

of these sandstones is that they are aquiferous; since they conduct north-wards water which falls as rain on the uplands extending from Dar Fur in the Sudan to Tibesti in the northern part of the Chad Republic, they are responsible for the formation of many oases and waterholes in the deserts west of the Nile. To the north of the Nubian Sandstone the receding seas of Cretaceous times left behind deposits of chalk and shale, and these de-posits occupy the area shown as underlain by Cretaceous rocks on Fig. 107.

Farther north again the widespread deposits of Cretaceous and earlier times give place to rocks of Tertiary age, and easily the most widespread of these later deposits are the limestones which extend under most of the Western Desert and the northern parts of the Eastern Desert, and which thrust themselves southwards in a great promontory as far south as the Tropic of Cancer. This promontory occupies a long shallow depression or warp in the underlying platform into which the Tertiary Sea flowed. It is this series of limestones which form the prominent plateau into which the Nile has cut its trench-like valley between Isna and Cairo, and it has provided most of the building stone so strikingly employed by the earlier inhabitants of Middle and Lower Egypt. In the north-west of the country these limestones are overlain by later deposits of limestone, shale and gypsum which extend over the Libyan Plateau and which include the whole region around the Qattara Depression. These deposits terminate in a series of low cliffs near the Mediterranean coast.

A series of depressions bordered by steep edges occurs in the limestone areas of the Western Desert, and in places where underground water lies near the floors of these depressions oases occur; prominent among these are Siwa, Bahariya, Farafra, Dakhla and El Kharga. The oasis of Siwa is noticeably saline, and the same is true of the extensive Qattara Depression which has been formed as a result of faulting and subsidence. Both of these oases are below sea-level, the lowest point on the generally swampy floor of Qattara lying at minus 440 ft (130 m).

The northernmost strip of Egypt is formed of Quaternary rocks which are varied in nature, comprising as they do gravels, sands and limestones, while more recent deposits include the alluvium of the Nile valley and the sands of the sandy deserts (erg). Most of the alluvium is derived from areas as far away as the Ethiopian Highlands, while the origins of the sandy desert deposits remain in doubt; much of it may have originated from weathering of the Nubian Sandstone.

The main features of the structure of Egypt include a fractured anticline in the east and a synclinal trough immediately to the west of this. The up-arching and fracturing in the eastern part of the country has produced the Red Sea Highlands on the one hand and the down-faulting of the Red Sea trough on the other, and it seems likely that these movements took place in mid-Tertiary times at the same times as the Alpine mountain-building movements farther north. During the same period the Gulf of Suez was formed, together with the small rift valley to the west which has already been referred to. The syncline to the west contains the valley of the Nile which is fault-guided in parts. The north-easterly "bulge" near Qena, for example, owes its form to faulting.

CLIMATE

Two types of climate can be distinguished in Egypt, for the hot desert which extends over almost the whole country gives place in the extreme north to a dry variation of the Mediterranean climate. Rain is almost entirely lacking in the desert region except for occasional storms. No precipitation at all may be experienced for a number of years, and then a

sudden storm may hurl down anything up to 2 in. of rainfall in a very
short time: the Red Sea Highlands receive slightly more rainfall than the
rest of the desert owing to their increased elevation.

The general pattern of rainfall and temperature is illustrated in the
following table.

	Coolest month		Hottest month		Annual temperature range		Annual average rainfall
	°F	°C	°F	°C	°F	°C	(in.)
Wadi Halfa . . .	58	14·4	89	31·7	31	7·2	0
Asyut	53	11·7	85	29·4	32	17·7	0
Cairo	53	11·7	81	27·2	28	15·5	1·3

The figures show that the amount of winter rainfall even in the north is
small, not enough to permit the carrying on of any kind of agricultural
activities without the help of irrigation. The rain at Cairo is distributed
over about five months of the year, though the "wettest" month, January, records an average of only 0·4 in., while Alexandria on the coast
registers 8·1 in. a year, with 2·6 in. falling in December and 2·2 in. in
January.

Temperature ranges in Egypt, both seasonal and diurnal, are great.
Winter temperatures in general are pleasant, with monthly averages
generally between 53° F and 60° F (11·7° C–15·6° C). Frosts are not experienced in the Nile valley as they are over much of the desert plateaus.
Summer conditions, however, become unpleasantly hot, especially inland; the figure for Wadi Halfa shown in the table above is a very high
one indeed, and the figure for Asyut is far too high for comfort. Even
these figures, however, mask the extremely uncomfortable noon temperatures of high summer which are commonly well above 100° F (37·8
C)—Aswan records a mean daily maximum in June of 107° (41·7° C).
During the night temperatures regularly fall by as much as 30° F (16·7° C)
in many areas, largely because of the low relative humidity of the air. At
Cairo the diurnal range of temperature in January is 53·6° F (29·8° C), and
in August 57·2° F (41·8° C). It is worth noting that the seas bordering
Egypt do not exercise as much of a moderating effect as is met with else-
where, especially in the summer, because they are so warm (*see* p. 18).

An unpleasant feature of the climate of Egypt is the *khamsin*, a southerly
wind similar in type to the *sirocco* of Barbary. It blows in the front sectors
of depressions which move eastwards along the Mediterranean, and it can
be scorchingly hot especially in the spring and early summer, while it
often carries large amounts of dust and at times even sand along with it,
so that the sun is obscured and living conditions are made very unpleasant.
The khamsin may blow for two or three days together. It is probably fair,
in summary, to say that Egypt in general experiences two seasons. A cool
and on the whole pleasant winter which lasts from November until April
gives place in May to an uncomfortably hot summer which lasts for the
rest of the year, while the advent of summer is marked by the onset of the
khamsin.

NATURAL REGIONS

We shall distinguish four main natural regions in this survey: the
Eastern Desert, the Sinai Peninsula, the Western Desert, and the Nile
valley, the last mentioned being by far the most important.

1. *The Eastern Desert* occupies the comparatively long and narrow
region lying between the Nile valley and the Red Sea, and the core of the
region consists of a relatively narrow highland belt composed of basement
crystalline and volcanic rocks (*see* Fig. 107) which is known generally as

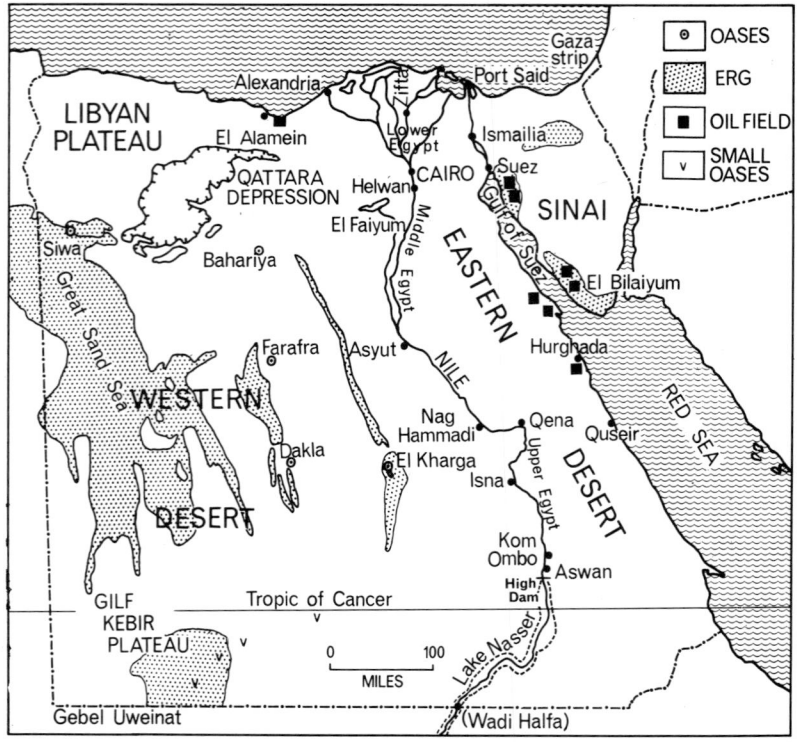

FIG. 108.—Egypt.

the Red Sea Highlands. The surface of these highlands is dissected, often
rugged, and the wadis which flow intermittently have cut a close network
of deep valleys; the large numbers of wadis and the depth to which many
of them have been cut are witnesses to the existence of more pluvial
periods in the past. Most of the wadis run generally in an east–west direction, the outstanding exception being the unusually long Wadi Qena.
The general level of these very accidented uplands lies roughly 2000 ft
(600 m) above sea-level, but many of the peaks reach heights of between
4000 ft (1200 m) and 5000 ft (1520 m) (Gebel Nugrus, 4934 ft (1504 m),

and G. Mishbish, 4439 ft (1353 m), for example), while a few are even higher (G. Hamata, 6486 ft (1977 m), and G. Shayib, 7175 ft (2187 m).

To the north and west the basement rocks are overlain by sandstone and limestone plateaus which are also greatly dissected. The Red Sea coast is rugged and dangerous, for there are few sheltered harbours, while the inshore waters are rendered dangerous for shipping by extensive coral reefs.

The high ground of the region has the effect of causing a limited amount of rainfall which produces temporary flows of water in the wadis. Water is retained in the alluvium on the floors of the wadis, and this feeds the wells sunk by the nomadic inhabitants, who are very few in number. Some precarious agriculture is carried on in sheltered depressions and in the valleys by the nomadic herdsmen who wander over the uplands; no permanent villages are to be found on the highlands. A few small settlements are located along the Red Sea coast, however, the most important being those associated with mining developments. Examples include Quseir, which is linked by a caravan trail with Qena, and which therefore is associated with a tenuous hinterland extending into the interior, Safaga and Hurghada.

2. *The Sinai Peninsula* comprises two distinct sub-regions, one of which occupies the northern two-thirds of the peninsula and the other the southernmost third. In the north a markedly dissected limestone plateau descends fairly gently to a broad coastal plain, the surface of which is largely covered by sand dunes. Shallow but broad wadis drain northwards from the plateau to the coastal plain which is fringed to the north by salt water lagoons, the largest of these being the Sabkhet el Bardawil. The southern third of the peninsula is developed mainly on a detached block of ancient basement rocks (*see* Fig. 107) which reaches a maximum height of 8652 ft (2637 m) above sea-level in the Gebel Katherina (Mount Sinai). This massif is bounded by fault scarps; to the east it plunges directly into the waters of the Gulf of Aqaba, while in the west a narrow coastal plain lies between the lowest scarp and the Gulf of Suez.

While the peninsula as a whole is not well watered, the northern areas receive rather more rainfall (about 6 in.) than the southern (just over $2\frac{1}{2}$ in.). Most of the few inhabitants are therefore found in the north, and while the nomadic way of life generally prevails, small areas around wells and springs are cultivated, wheat and barley being the main crops grown. Mining developments will be referred to later. The Sinai area has for many centuries been a zone of movement between Egypt on the west and the countries of south-western Asia (for instance Assyria, Syria and Palestine) on the east. The political situation in this region is obscure. Up to 1967 Sinai formed part of Egypt, but during the Arab–Israeli war of mid-1967 the area was occupied by Israeli troops and is now under Israeli control. Until the situation is clarified it seems better to continue to treat the area as part of Egypt, but the student should bear in mind the conditions obtaining when he is studying the area.

3. *The Western Desert* covers almost three-quarters of the total area of Egypt, and it has been described as the most "desert-like" desert in the world. It extends westwards from the Nile valley to the Libyan border, and southwards from the Mediterranean coast, through the Libyan Plateau, as far as the Sudanese frontier. Much of the south-west and south-east lies at altitudes of over 1000 ft (300 m) above sea-level, but most of the centre and north is lower than that. The region includes on the one hand the Qattara depression, the lowest part of which lies 440 ft (130 m) below sea-level, and on the other hand, in the south-west, the sandstone table-land of the Gilf Kebir Plateau which reaches a maximum elevation of 3550 ft (1082 m), and the ancient massif of the Gebel Uweinat which rises to 6256 ft (1906 m). The general geology of the region and its effect upon the relief has been examined earlier.

The Western Desert is characterised by wide expanses of desolate erg (*see* Fig. 107), between which lie extensive areas of rocky and stony deserts. Only a few nomads live in these wastes. Fortunately, however, the various sedimentary strata which underlie the region rest on an impervious basement floor, and they also tilt gently downwards towards the north. These features make it possible for rainwater falling on high ground to the south to percolate northwards in the form of artesian water. Where this water comes near to the surface oases develop (*see* p. 445), and this is particularly the case in the broad trough-like depression which runs from the Libyan border just to the south of the Libyan Plateau, south-eastwards in the direction of Aswan: in this depression lie some of the more extensive oases such as Siwa, Farafra, Dakhla and El Kharga. Some thousands of people live in these oases, and El Kharga is linked by rail with the Nile valley in order to facilitate the transport of dates, an important commercial product, while Siwa, which exports olive oil (a reflection of its more northerly location nearer the Mediterranean), is linked by road to Matruh which lies on the coastal railway to Alexandria. The sedentary communities in the oases are in the main self-supporting; they grow crops of cereals, fruit and vegetables, while dates are produced as a cash crop as well as for domestic consumption. With the proceeds of the sale of dates, goods can be purchased from the outside world. The total cultivated area in the oases, however, is only of the order of 30,000 feddans (one feddan = 1·038 acres). Outside the oases, the only cultivation carried on in the Western Desert is the growing of catch crops by nomads along the coastal strip, which, like much of the coastal strip of northern Libya, was a productive region in Roman times when water control works were constructed. Today, many of these works are being repaired and dry farming methods are being adopted; barley is grown and some settlement of nomadic groups is taking place.

An interesting and unusual area is that of the Faiyum, a depression in the Libyan Desert about 700 sq. miles (1820 sq. km) in area. The lowest parts lie below sea-level. Since Lake Qarun is saline the Faiyum is watered from the Nile by the Bahr el Yusuf, an ancient canal which many people believe was constructed by the Joseph of the Old Testament. The Faiyum has a total population of over half a million people, some of whom live in the towns of which Medinet El Faiyum is the largest. Local handicraft flourishes, and baskets and pottery are exported, while, in addition to the normal crops of the Nile valley, the growing of fruit is particularly important; citrus fruits, figs, apricots, grapes and olives are all grown. Rice growing has greatly increased in importance in recent years.

An ambitious plan is now being implemented to make further use of the artesian water of the oases of El Kharga and Dakhla and to extend the cultivated areas by as much as 190,000 feddans. It is hoped that this reclamation will be complete by 1970; the whole plan is generally known as the New Valley Project.

4. *The Nile valley* is a region probably unique in the world, while the Nile itself is a remarkable river, its source lying on the East African Plateau at the headwaters of the Kagera river, which flows into Lake Victoria. The river flows in a generally northerly direction for a total length

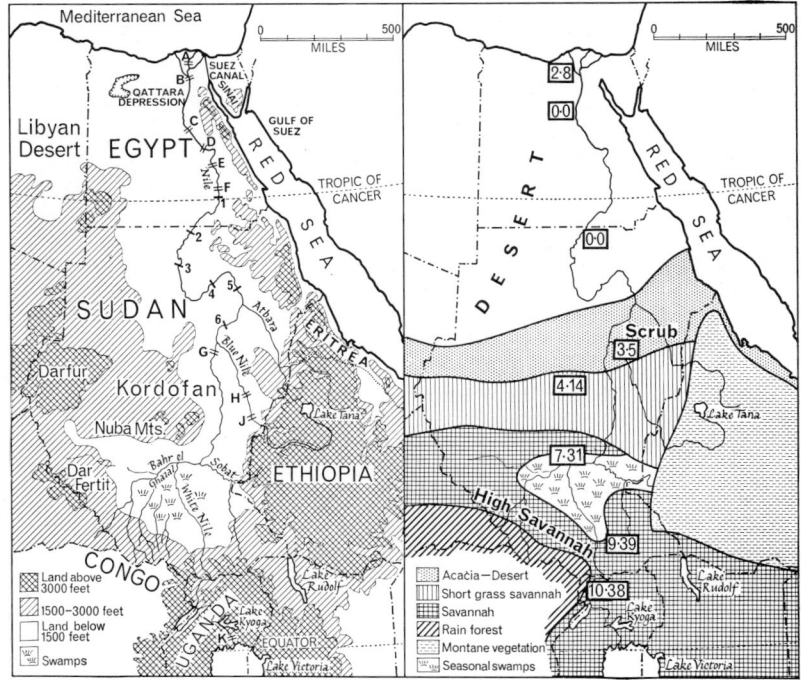

FIG. 109.—The Nile basin: relief. Cataracts are numbered 1 to 6. Dams and barrages: A, Zifta; B, Delta; C, Asyut; D, Nag Hammadi; E, Isna; F, Aswan; G, Jebel Aulia; H, Sennar; J, Roseires, K, Owen Falls.

FIG. 110.—The Nile basin: climate and vegetation. The first figure inside each panel gives the length of the rainy season in months; the second gives the average rainfall in inches.

of 4160 miles (6656 km) and over 35 degrees of latitude, from 3 degrees S. to 32 degrees N. It finally enters the Mediterranean in almost the same longitude as that in which it took its source (*see* Fig. 109).

In Upper Egypt the river has deeply entrenched itself into a gorge-like valley cut into the Nubian Sandstone which extends almost as far north as Isna, beyond which the sandstone is replaced by limestones. The gorge, flanked by precipitous cliffs on the eastern side and by a fairly low escarpment on the west, remains narrow as far north as Aswan; in parts it is only

[*Courtesy of Aerofilms Ltd.*

Fig. 111.—The Nile near the northern boundary of the Sudan. The valley is extremely rocky (near the second cataract just above Wadi Halfa) and the desert is flat beyond the granite outcrops. Inselberge (isolated, steep-sided hills) rise above the desert floor. This part of the valley is now flooded by the enlarged reservoirs up-stream from Aswan.

220 yards (200 m) across (*see* Fig. 111), but to the north of Aswan the valley opens out. The river tends to keep to the eastern side of the valley floor which below Isna winds between cliffs of white limestone on either side. Although the valley broadens downstream until it is about 10 miles across just below Nag Hammadi, it consists essentially of a number of small basins, like beads on a string, separated by narrower gorge-like reaches. These basins are floored with alluvium and are amazingly fertile and productive, a good example being the Basin of Thebes, a few miles up-river from Qena, with its spectacular ruins at Thebes, Karnack and Luxor to testify to its past prosperity and importance.

Below Cairo the valley opens out very widely into the Nile delta, which has been built up as a result of the repeated deposition of silt washed down by the river for the most part from the Ethiopian Highlands. Indeed, deposition is still proceeding in the delta, though at a very slow rate, because the river deposits such large amounts of material along its flood-plain that the amount still carried in suspension by the time it reaches the delta is very small. It will in future be even less than in the past because the lake which has now formed as part of the new High Dam project (*see* p. 456) will act as a gigantic silt trap, and very little silt will continue on its way below the High Dam. The delta has a maximum width of just over 150 miles (240 km) from Alexandria to Port Said, and a maximum north–south extension of 100 miles (160 km) (*see* Fig. 112).

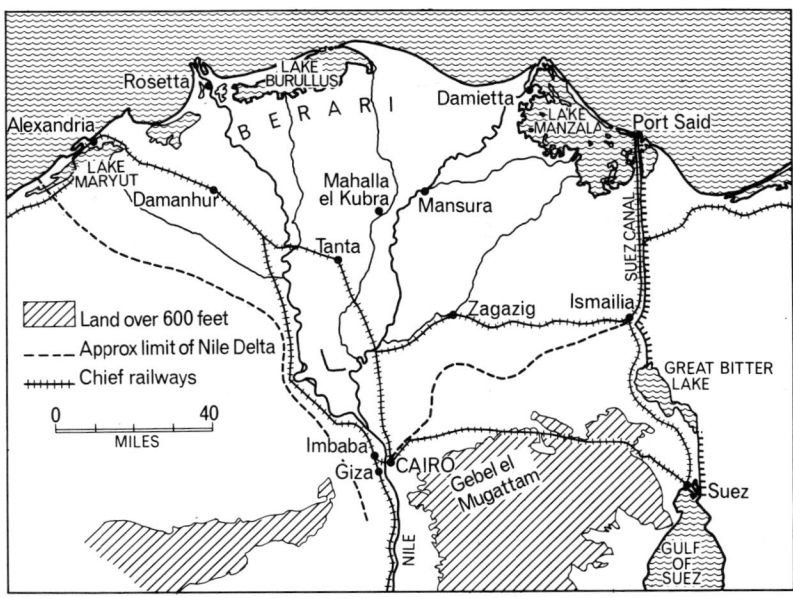

FIG. 112.—Lower Egypt. All but two of the largest towns of Egypt are in this region; the two exceptions are Asyut and Medinet El Faiyum.

The surface of the delta slopes very gently northwards towards the Mediterranean, and the northern parts are so little above sea-level that pumping is necessary to drain the water to the sea. At the present time, therefore, most of the northern part of the delta is too marshy for culti-vation, and future land reclamation in the *Berari* (barren lands) depends upon improved pumping and draining facilities, while it will also be necessary to leach the salt out of the soil. The coast is marked by shallow, brackish lagoons and salt marshes, some of which are very extensive. Two of the largest are Lakes Burullus and Manzala (*see* Fig. 112), the latter being about 800 square miles (2040 sq. km) in area. In earlier years the main river broke up into several distributaries in the delta, but today, because of greatly increased water control, there are two main outlets, a western (the Rosetta) and an eastern (the Damietta).

The total area of the Egyptian section of the Nile valley works out at about 13,500 square miles (35,100 sq. km), about 3% of the total area of the Republic. Yet on this 3% is crowded more than 99% of the total population! About 30,000,000 people jostle each other on this fertile ribbon of land, as opposed to the meagre total of about 80,000 inhabitants of the deserts, including the oases. An examination of the reasons for this astonishing imbalance of population and the chief problem arising from it will occupy us for most of the rest of this chapter.

THE RÉGIME OF THE RIVER NILE

The river Nile is one of the great rivers of the world, and its importance to Egypt can hardly be over-emphasised, but we cannot deal with the river as a whole since most of it lies outside the area with which we are concerned. The reader who is interested in the whole subject of the Nile may care to study the topic elsewhere.* It is clear enough, however, that the great value of the river arises from two simple facts: (1) that it carries water through the heart of the desert, and (2) that it floods every summer.

The summer flooding in the lower reaches of the Nile was an object of wonder in ancient times, and one which the people of those days were at a loss to understand. One traveller in Egypt in the year 60 B.C. wrote:

> The rising of the Nile is a phenomenon which astounds those who see it and appears quite incredible to those who hear of it. For whereas other rivers shrink about the summer solstice and grow smaller and smaller from that point onwards, the Nile alone begins to swell, and its waters rise day by day until in the end they overflow almost the whole of Egypt.

It is now well known that this summer flooding is derived from the summer rains of the Ethiopian Highlands, which cause the "swelling" of the Sobat, the Blue Nile and the Atbara, and of these tributaries the Blue Nile is easily the most important.

The Sobat begins to rise late in May, but in the lower reaches of the tributary the flood maximum is delayed until November. Flooding continues, however, until January as the water is slow in percolating through the swamps which are characteristic of the middle and lower river; there is much delaying sudd, even on the Sobat. When the river is in full flood its rushing water ponds back the more sluggishly moving water of the White Nile, so that discharge from the Bahr el Ghazal swamps is restricted and a great deal of water is lost through evaporation.

The Blue Nile flows throughout the year as it rises in Lake Tana, which is a permanent lake, but its flow is very restricted during the early part of the year. It begins to rise in June, and it continues to rise very rapidly

*For example JARRETT, H. R. (*Africa*, 2nd ed., 1966).

throughout July and August to reach a maximum early in September; during this time the White Nile above Khartoum is ponded back by its flood waters in a manner comparable to the case of the Sobat. The waters subside in November and December. It is this Blue Nile water upon which Egypt chiefly relies for the summer flooding of the main river, while another allied factor of importance is the vast amount of silt which is carried down from the Ethiopian Highlands by the early flood waters and deposited on the flood-plain in Egypt. This annual deposition has greatly helped in maintaining the fertility of the Nile valley throughout the centuries, though careful land use by the Egyptian farmer has helped as well.

The Atbara floods in summer and early autumn and reinforces the Blue Nile flood, but during the winter the river ceases to flow, and its course is marked simply by a series of pools along its bed.

Below the Atbara the Nile receives no further tributary; in fact, it loses much water through evaporation and seepage. The summer flood passes downstream reaching Khartoum in June, though the maximum does not occur until September, while at Cairo the maximum is delayed until October. By January the Blue Nile flood is exhausted, though the Sobat, as we have seen, is still contributing water, but from the end of January until June 80% of the water in the main river comes from the White Nile.

It will be clear that without the Nile life as we know it today in Egypt would be quite impossible. For centuries it has been said that "Egypt is the gift of the Nile," and this is as true today as ever it was. It is not surprising, therefore, that every effort has been made to use the water of the Nile to the best advantage, and this has led to the development of various forms of irrigation which will receive attention later in this chapter. Egypt is still primarily an agricultural country, despite some development of industry which has taken place.

WATER CONTROL ON THE NILE

While it is true that the annual flooding of the Nile is the feature which renders the river so valuable to the economy of Egypt, it is equally true that the yearly rise and fall of the Nile needs to be controlled if a large population is to provide for itself along the flood-plain. It is not surprising, therefore, that attempts have been made since very early times to achieve some measure of control over the flood waters of the Nile, and in fact the remains of the oldest dam ever constructed (as far as is known) can still be seen in the Wadi el Garawi, 7 miles (10 km) to the south-east of Helwan. The dam was built across the wadi at some time between the years 2950 and 2750 B.C., but owing to faulty construction it collapsed— possibly during the first flooding which tested it. The resulting catastrophe was so great that no further experiments were conducted along these lines for more than 3000 years.

The earliest barrage to be built across the Nile was completed early last century at the head of the delta by Muhammad Ali Pasha, while later barrages were constructed at Zifta (in 1901), Asyut (1902), Isna (1908) and Nag Hammadi (1930) (*see* Fig. 109). These barrages raise the level of the flood waters upstream and so make it possible for water to flow into the distributary canals. The old Muhammad Ali barrage has now been replaced by a newer, larger structure, as it had become inadequate to meet modern demands upon it. The Asyut barrage makes available additional water for the ancient Bahr el Yusuf which carries water to the Faiyum depression, while the delta barrage is important as it controls extensive irrigation on the fertile delta lands. No water is allowed to escape from the river into the Mediterranean at the time of Low Nile (from the end of February until the end of July); it is all retained for irrigation.

The greatest engineering feat of all, however, is the great dam at Aswan, which has twice been enlarged (in 1912 and 1934) since it was originally constructed in 1903. (The Aswan water storage is supplemented by the storage at Jebel, in the Sudan.) Very considerable care has to be taken in operating the dam (*see* p. 463). As the floods recede in November the sluices are closed and the vast reservoir begins to fill. It is full by January, by which time the last of the flood waters (which are derived from the Sobat) are moving downstream. The water is then available for use later in the year before the next flood, the first waters of which are allowed to pass unhindered. This great dam, however, will shortly be superseded by the New High Dam which is now being built on a site 4 miles (6·2 km) south of the original structure (*see* Fig. 108). The new dam was almost complete by the end of 1968 and the recent completion of the coffer dam means that the projected scheme is already to some extent in operation. The enlarged storage reservoir (the Egyptian part of which is known as Lake Nasser) has a high-water mark 200 ft (60 m) higher than that of the former one; when full it is 250 miles (400 km) in length (180 miles within Egypt and 70 miles into the Sudan; 288 and 112 km), while it varies in width between 5 and 10 miles (8–16 km). Although large amounts of silt will be trapped in Lake Nasser, the capacity of the lake is so large that many centuries should pass before a significant loss of storage capacity will result. It will also be possible to hold back surplus water from years of above average floods to supplement water replenishments in years of poor floods, and this "over-year" storage will therefore provide flood protection below the dam as well as evening out flood levels year by year. It is hoped that 776,000 feddans around the shores of the lake will become available for cultivation as water is now available for irrigation, and it is thought that tea, pineapples and timber may be produced and a livestock industry encouraged. It is estimated that the area of cultivable land in Egypt will be increased by 30% as a result of this enterprise, while the construction of hydro-electric stations at the dam site will supply power for the industries and homes of Upper Egypt.

An inevitable result of the flooding of so much riparian land has been the enforced moving of the former inhabitants, including the 10,000 townsfolk of Wadi Halfa which is now under water. The thousands of date palms which formerly constituted such a striking feature of the land-scape and which provided the basis for the economy of this part of Nubia are now all destroyed by the rising water.

The effects on the people on the Egyptian side of the border have not been too drastic, for these folk have simply been moved northwards to a 50-mile stretch of the river near Kom Ombo, a sugar-refining town. The basic crop produced in this region is sugar cane, while traditional crops are also cultivated. A scheme is in hand to increase the area of cultivated land near Kom Ombo by 250,000 feddans. This is to be done with in-creased irrigation, the water to be drawn from Lake Nasser. It is antici-pated that 200,000 of the 250,000 feddans will be devoted to sugar cane (at present about 26,000 feddans are producing this crop), so that there will be a marked increase in the output of sugar, molasses and fibre board. There will also be increased cotton production.

In the case of the Sudanese people involved, however (there were about 50,000 of them), a bigger move was necessary, and they have been re-settled about 60 miles (96 km) to the south-east near Khasm el Ghirba on the Atbara river in a different climatic zone. Here, a dam has been built which will provide cultivable land through irrigation and also hydro-electric power. It has been shown that the traditional crops of the Wadi Halfa area can be grown in this region.

The High Dam Scheme, spectacular as it is, has been criticised on several grounds. One criticism arises from the fact that Lake Nasser will serve as a very efficient silt trap, and the consequent loss to Egypt of fertilising silt and the resulting cost of essential fertilisers will be very great. Another point has reference to the fact that water losses to be extracted from the surface of Lake Nasser because of the intense evaporation in this hot, sunny and arid region will be immense, and the argument has been put forward that a far more efficient water conservation scheme could have been developed farther south, in the Sudan. Such a scheme was, in fact, worked out in the form of the abortive Jonglei Project. One of the main features of this scheme was to have been the construction of the Jonglei Canal between Bor and Malakal, which would have provided a shorter passage for Nile water and one unencumbered by swamp and sudd. It was hoped in this way to avoid much of the tremendous loss of water which at present occurs through evaporation in the swamps of the Bahr el Ghazal region.

The scheme did present certain difficulties, particularly in the Sudan, where the change in régime of the Nile which was envisaged would have affected the way of life of pastoralists of the Bahr el Ghazal such as the Shilluk, Dinka and the Baggara Arabs. At present the economy of these semi-nomads is governed by the seasonal rise and fall of the Nile, but this rise and fall would have disappeared with the system of control envisaged in the scheme. Despite this difficulty, however, the Sudanese Govern-ment was willing for the scheme to go ahead, but Egypt was not willing to agree to a scheme which would be in operation outside her own borders. Instead, she has pressed ahead with the more expensive and less effective High Dam scheme at Aswan which has caused large-scale displacement of Nile dwellers and the flooding of archaeological treasures. In fact, the extra amount of water which could have been available to Egypt as a result of the saving in evaporation expected through the Jonglei project would have been more than she will gain through the High Dam scheme, but the Jonglei project would have been less spectacular and would have contributed much less than the High Dam to the nationalistic emotions of the Egyptians.*

HUMAN GEOGRAPHY

HISTORY AND PEOPLE

The early history of Egypt is shrouded in mystery because of its antiquity, but it is suggested that agriculture began about 5000 years ago and permanent settlement about 2000 years before that. It is not easy to account for this early flowering of civilisation, but the suggestion has been made that the comparative isolation of the Nile valley on the one hand and the yearly gifts of water and of fertilising silt contributed by the river on the other were among the main causes. The "longish strip of market garden" as Kipling called it, was protected from foreign intervention on the east and west by deserts; on the south by the desert and by the Nile cataracts which halted navigation; and on the north by a Mediterranean Sea which was apt to become turbulent and storm-tossed with little warning and which was generally shunned by sailors 5000 years ago. The annual flooding and siltation enabled the Egyptians to secure two, and sometimes three, harvests a year, while the river itself acted as a unifying link. Vessels could sail downstream with the current and upstream with the help of the prevailing northerly winds.

Until roughly 3100 B.C., Egypt remained a disparate region of feuding tribes and villages, but at that time a southern king, Menes, organised the beginnings of law and order, and a feeling of national unity, which has never since completely disappeared, began to develop. By 2700 B.C. Egypt had emerged as an organised unitary state, with a written language, considerable technological skill, characteristic styles of art and architecture, and the beginnings of scientific knowledge. There seems little doubt that this early burgeoning of civilisation owed much to geographical considerations; it was essential, for instance, to know just when to expect the annual flooding in order that farming activities might be put in hand at the right time (this circumstance led to the compilation of the world's first solar calendar), and the foundations of mathematics were laid because of the need to lay out equitably strips of land near the river which would benefit from the Nile flood.

Unfortunately, after a very long period of prosperity, Egypt, in common with other parts of North Africa, underwent several centuries of

*For further details, see JARRETT, H. R., op. cit.

foreign domination and neglect. During the early part of modern historical times Egypt was a neglected part of the Ottoman Empire, a state
of affairs which stands in marked contrast with the glories of ancient times.
In 1798 came Napoleon's abortive attempt to conquer the country, and
this had the effect of bringing Egypt into closer touch with Europe and
awakening an appreciation of its economic and strategic possibilities.
Although the territory remained nominally within the Ottoman Empire,
the links with Constantinople grew weaker during the nineteenth century,
and after the Suez Canal was opened in 1869 Britain took an ever-increasing interest in the affairs of the country. In 1882 British troops were
stationed in the country to maintain order and to protect the Suez Canal,
and Egypt virtually became a British Protectorate, an arrangement which
was explicitly recognised in 1914 when Britain found herself at war with
Turkey in the First World War. The Protectorate came to an end in 1922
when the Sultan of Egypt became king, and since that time Egypt has
been an independent state. In 1952 came the revolution led by a group of
army officers who were sickened by the corruption of the ruling classes,
and this was quickly followed by the abdication of King Farouk and the
assumption of leadership by Colonel (later President) Nasser. Privileges
granted to overseas Powers gradually disappeared, and in 1956 the last
privilege was cancelled when British troops were withdrawn from the
Suez Canal zone, the responsibility for guarding which was vested in the
Egyptians themselves; Egypt fairly soon after this assumed entire control
over the Canal. In 1958 Egypt became the dominant partner in the United
Arab Republic, the other partner being Syria. This union, however, was
disolved after three years, for Syria, after a *coup d'état* in 1961, immediately
seceded from the Federation. Nevertheless, Egypt continues to refer to
herself as the United Arab Republic.

The most pressing and intractable problems facing Egypt today arise
from the size of the population; this is the dominating feature of the contemporary economic, political and social life of the country. Although the
average overall density of population is 64 persons per square mile, by no
means an excessive figure, it rises along the closely settled strip of Nile
alluvium to almost 1900 persons; in parts of Upper Egypt it is over 2500.
And an even more frightening feature is the high rate of increase in a
population which has grown from about $2\frac{1}{2}$ million in 1800, to $4\frac{1}{2}$ million
by the middle of last century, and to cover 30 million today, while the
annual rate of increase (about 2·4%) is about 600,000. This has come about
as a result of the maintenance of a high birth-rate (40–45 per thousand)
linked with a sharp fall in the death-rate (27 per thousand before the
Second World War, 16 per thousand today), as a result of improving
standards of hygiene, and because of better medical services. The net
result of this is that the population has almost doubled itself over the past
30 years and may double itself again during the next 30. Just over two-
thirds of the inhabitants live in the delta and the Canal zone.

Unfortunately, it has not been possible for agricultural output to keep pace with this increase in population: the amount of cultivated land per head of the population has actually declined, while the yearly consumption of maize, the main food crop, dropped from 209 lb per capita in 1938 to 154 lb in 1950. That of wheat also fell during the same period (163 to 132 lb) though that of rice increased (48 to 68 lb). Among the undernourished inhabitants disease is rife, malaria, trachoma, bilharzia and ankylostoma being especially prevalent.

While the tremendous overall pressure of population is the prime cause of the widespread poverty met with in Egypt, an important contributory reason is the grossly inequitable apportionment of land. Before the agrarian reform initiated by the revolutionary government in 1952, 95% of all landowners owned between them only 35% of the cultivated land, 70% of these having less than 1 feddan each, while the remaining 65% of land was in the hands of a small but exceedingly wealthy group. In addition, almost 2 million landless peasants were seeking employment on a day-to-day basis, but rarely managing to find work for more than 120 days each year. Between 1952 and 1959 about 295,000 feddans (much of the land coming from the former royal estates) were redistributed, but only about 200,000 landless peasants benefited—a good beginning but a small number among so many needy ones. In 1961 more stringent laws were enacted, the main provision being to reduce the maximum permitted size of a family holding from the 300 feddans laid down in 1952 to 100. The real need, however, is the provision of far more cultivable land, and this is likely to remain unsatisfied.

SETTLEMENT

The typical Egyptian *fellah* (*see* p. 369) is a hard-working farmer whose land is often less than 1 acre (0·4 ha) in extent and rarely is more than 5 (2 ha). He lives in a house made of mud bricks which have been hardened in the sun, while a flat roof serves as a store in this dry climate. The village in which he lives is likely to be situated on a mound formed from the ruins of earlier villages, and such a location is to some extent a safeguard against floods. He may possess a buffalo to pull his iron-shod plough or a donkey to help carry his goods to market, while a few hens provide eggs—a welcome variation in a generally monotonous diet of bread and vegetables, though some will have to be sold. His main cash crop is cotton, while a crop of *berseem* (Egyptian clover), which grows quickly and can be cut perhaps five times in a single season, provides fodder for his stock. In addition, he grows other crops, especially vegetables (onions are actually exported from Egypt). Almost two-thirds of the people of Egypt live in hamlets or small villages of the type just described, while most of the remaining one-third live in towns and cities of over 25,000 inhabitants.

CHIEF TOWNS AND CITIES

The urban population of Egypt is growing at a very rapid rate, and there are now fifteen towns and cities each with a population of over

100,000 inhabitants. In the first 60 years of the present century the proportion of the urban population rose from 13% to 25% of the rapidly expanding total. The development of new industries, of trade and of commercial and administrative functions has all helped to increase the populations of the various towns, the chief of which are Cairo and Alexandria. These two far outstrip all others in size and importance, though others worthy of note include Port Said (245,000), Ismailia (116,000) and Suez (203,000), three cosmopolitan towns which lie along the Suez Canal. An interesting feature about Port Said is that it is situated on land artificially built up above water level by making use of the sand which was dug out from the desert during the original construction of the Canal. We might observe that of the fifteen towns in Egypt each with a population of over 100,000 only one (Asyut) is in Upper Egypt, while one (Medinet El Faiyum) is situated away from the Nile valley. The importance of the delta (Lower Egypt) is thus emphasised (see Fig. 112). Five other towns which have populations of more than 100,000 (Tanta, 184,000; Mahalla el Kubra, 178,000; Mansura, 151,000; Damanhur, 126,000; and Zagazig, 124,000) are industrial centres in the delta.

Cairo, the capital, with a population of over 4 million people, is well placed between Upper and Lower Egypt to act as an administrative centre (see Fig. 112). It lies near a spur of the Mokattam hills (the Gebel el Mugattam—really a limestone plateau) which offers a firm building site near the Nile, while the presence of islands in the river makes crossing to the west bank comparatively easy at this point. Its position between the delta to the north and the main valley of the Nile to the south makes it a natural route centre, while its airport is one of international importance, and it is not surprising that it has grown to be the largest city in the continent of Africa. Areas of swamp along the present banks of the river have been reclaimed, and an elegant new city has been established on the floodplain between the river and the old city which closely resembles the medinas of the Maghrib towns with its narrow alleys, its bazaars and its old mud-brick houses. Traditional crafts such as the production of gold and copper ware, leather goods and pottery are still carried on. Satellite towns and dormitory towns have grown up to the north and west, the latter being linked by bridges across the Nile to the main part of the city. Many industries have been established, including the manufacture of textiles, particularly in the industrial satellite town of Giza (population 262,000). Cairo was selected as the capital of the United Arab Republic and is now the administrative, commercial and industrial capital of Egypt.

Alexandria, an important port with a sheltered harbour and the leading commercial centre of Egypt, has over $1\frac{1}{2}$ million inhabitants, and lies between the brackish Lake Maryut and the Mediterranean coast, near the western tip of the delta. This is important, as the offshore currents carry the silt brought down by the river eastwards from its mouth, so that silting is not a problem at Alexandria. It has grown to be the chief port of the country, and no other port even approaches it in importance, the only others of any account being Port Said and Suez. Raw cotton forms easily the most important export, both from Alexandria and from Egypt as a whole, and accounts by value for about 70% of the total export trade. Other exports include rice, vegetables and manufactured goods. Cotton ginning and rice milling, together with the manufacture of textiles and cigarettes, are notable activities, while an oil refinery has been established.

THE ECONOMY

AGRICULTURE

Life in Egypt is still based upon agriculture, and it is as true today as it was in the time of Herodotus (*c.* 440 B.C.) that "Egypt is an acquired country, the gift of the Nile." Irrigation has become of over-riding importance in order that the cultivated area may be extended and additional crops produced to support the dense population. The primitive *shaduf*, a bucket on one end of a lever weighted to balance the weight of the water, and the *sakia*, a kind of waterwheel, have been used for centuries, but their value is limited as only small amounts of water can be transferred over short distances with their help. They have for centuries, however, permitted the irrigation of land just above flood level which otherwise would be unused.

An early development in the use of the Nile lands was the ancient "basin" system of irrigation. The "basins," which are separated from the Nile by high embankments and from each other by lower banks, are very extensive, ranging up to 40,000 acres (16,000 ha) in area. As the Nile rises the flood water is admitted to the basins to a depth of up to 6 ft (1·8 m) via canals leading from the river, and the water lies on the land for between one and a half and two months. Fertile silt is deposited by the flood and the ground is thoroughly soaked, before the water is allowed to drain back to the river as the sluices are opened when the level of the flood is falling. Each *fellah* then cultivates his own small part of the basin (or he may be employed by a landowner); seeds are sown in the mud and the ensuing crops reach maturity in a comparatively short time although it is the winter season. Crops are harvested between March and May after which the ground lies fallow, cracked and aerated by the hot summer sun, until the floods of the following season. Extensive autumn and winter crops of wheat, barley, rice, millet, vegetables and even sugar cane are grown in this way. Important vegetable crops include onions (an export crop) and pulses (beans and peas); clover is grown as a fodder crop. Crop yields in Egypt are among the highest recorded anywhere in the world. Fruit crops, with the exception of dates, are not widely grown, though citrus fruits are produced near Cairo, vines and figs near the north coast, and olives in Faiyum.

These, then, are autumn and winter crops grown on flood land after the floods have subsided, but at the time of High Nile flood water is carried by shaduf and sakia to higher ground which would otherwise have no water, and this permits the growing of additional crops which ripen in the autumn. The chief crop grown in this way is maize, which requires considerable heat as well as moisture. In recent years increasing use of small diesel-powered pumps has made possible the irrigation of land formerly beyond the range of the shaduf and the sakia.

Until the last century the agricultural possibilities of the Nile valley were limited to those just noted, but there was the serious disability that farmers were very much at the mercy of annual fluctuations in the size of the flood. These fluctuations can be very considerable; for example, at Aswan the river flow in September can vary in different years between 4700 and 11,500 cubic metres per second. Although years when the level of flooding was well below average had a disastrous effect on crops, years of very high flood were also catastrophic as earth dykes were broken, land flooded too deeply for too long and crops "drowned." As the population of the country grew it was increasingly necessary to bring about a greater measure of control over the flood waters, and this first became possible with the introduction by Muhammad Ali of perennial irrigation, which is dependent upon the construction of dams to hold back flood water in the main river. The advantages of perennial irrigation are so great that the traditional basin system has almost disappeared along the lower reaches of the Nile and is now widespread only in Upper Egypt, but with the increased water control that the High Dam will bring perennial irrigation will replace the basin system everywhere. Perennial irrigation represents a very great advance because flood water is held back from one year's flood until the following spring, and is then slowly released for use during the summer, when additional crops can be grown before the flood waters rise again. Care has to be taken in working this system; for instance, the early flood waters with their load of silt are permitted to pass through the dams freely, otherwise the silt would be deposited behind the dams which would thereby be rendered useless after a few years. The later flood waters however, are relatively free from silt, and it is these which are held back. It is also necessary to control the amounts of irrigation water used on the land carefully, for too much watering can be as harmful to crops as too little. In addition adequate drainage of the irrigation water is essential to prevent the concentration of salts on the fields, for this renders them sterile and useless.

Over three-quarters of the total agricultural land in Egypt today is served by perennial irrigation, and the main summer crop grown as a result (which has revolutionised the economy of the country) is cotton, originally introduced by Muhammad Ali after the construction of the delta barrage. Cotton (which in any given year is likely to occupy between 20 and 25% of the cultivated area) and cotton products together account for about 70% by value of all exports. Cotton is chiefly a crop of the delta, largely because of the pressing need to grow food crops for the dense population in Upper Egypt. The success of cotton cultivation was largely assured by the outbreak of the American Civil War, which cut off American supplies of this raw material from Britain and north-western Europe, and when these markets were once secured the high quality of the crop ensured a steady sale for Egyptian cotton overseas. For many years the famous long staple (about $1\frac{1}{2}$ in.) Sakellarides (Sakel) was the main variety produced, a type of cotton acknowledged during the inter-war years to be second in quality only to the well-known Sea Island cotton, but in the years before the Second World War heavier yielding varieties such as Giza and Malaki were introduced. Development of other varieties is still proceeding at agricultural research stations. A shorter staple known as Ashmouni was important for many years, both in the delta and in Middle Egypt, but this has now largely been replaced by Menoufi.

Another necessary feature for the successful large-scale growing of cotton is a labour supply which is both plentiful and cheap. Such a supply is available in Egypt. There is the further point that the under-nourished peasants can themselves make no direct use of the cotton which they harvest (for instance they cannot eat it), and losses to landowners on this account are therefore negligible.

The cotton seed is sown in February, and regular watering and weeding of the cotton fields is needed during the following months. The harvest takes place in September in Lower Egypt (early rains in this region sometimes interfere with the picking and cause losses), and in August in Upper Egypt where the "basins" cannot be flooded until the cotton picking is completed.

Yields of cotton per acre in Egypt are very high (nearly $7\frac{1}{2}$ bushels to the acre), and are almost double the average American yield, but cotton is a very exhausting crop and great care has to be taken not to grow it too often on any one plot of ground, owing to the danger of soil exhaustion. As there is a clear temptation to the farmer to grow such a profitable crop at the expense of essential food crops, the Government controls very carefully the growing of cotton to preserve the balance between cash and food crops. It is, however, unfortunately true that in recent years cotton yields have been greatly reduced by various pests, and in some years one-third of the total crop is lost for this reason.

The crop with the highest acreage of cultivated land after cotton is *berseem* (Egyptian clover), which provides fodder for stock and improves soils from the fixation of nitrogen on its roots. Wheat is grown widely except in the northern parts of the delta, while barley is important along the coastal fringe and in Upper Egypt. The importance of rice is increasing, and this crop is grown especially in the Faiyum and in the seaward parts of the delta. Rice can tolerate a certain amount of salt in the soil, and it is therefore commonly grown for a year or two on reclaimed land while the salt is being leached away. In later years its place may be taken by clover and cotton. Maize is grown widely, though the best yields are recorded in the delta where the higher relative humidity of the atmosphere is beneficial, while in Upper Egypt it is to some extent replaced by sorghums and millets. Another crop which has become very important thanks to the development of perennial irrigation is sugar cane, which has received particular attention in the Thebes Basin. The extraction of sugar from the cane has become an important industry in Middle and Upper Egypt. Production of sugar is likely to increase as plans are announced to double the acreage under this crop near Qena and Sohag and greatly to increase it near Kom Ombo (*see* p. 457). Cultivation of vegetables (for example tomatoes, beans and cabbages) increases as the urban markets expand.

By way of summary we may note that it is possible to recognise three overlapping seasons in the agricultural year in Egypt:

Autumn to spring (*chetui*) crops, November–June: wheat, barley, clover, vegetables, etc.

Summer (*sefi*) crops (Low Nile), February–October: cotton, sugar cane.

Nili (High Nile) crops, July–October: maize, rice.

This pattern is typical of the delta, but in Upper Egypt where flooding is more widespread the scheme is rather different. Autumn crops such as maize, millet, rice and vegetables are grown above flood level. Winter crops such as wheat, barley, clover, pulses, maize and vegetables are grown on land from which the flood waters have receded, while summer crops include cotton and sugar cane, but harvesting is earlier than in the delta.

It is only fair to emphasise that certain difficulties have arisen in recent years as a result of the extension of perennial irrigation. One reason is that farmers have been induced to put too much land under cash crops and not enough under food crops. Over-cropping is also a very real danger, especially when there is such a desperate need to produce as much as possible to sustain the dense population. As a result there are signs of soil exhaustion. Another problem is that of increasing soil salinity, which is due to the wrong use of irrigation water, especially to over-watering and to inadequate drainage, while deposition of the fertilising Nile silt is impeded by the various dams and barrages. This last difficulty will greatly increase after the construction of the High Dam. The original Aswan Dam had numerous sluice gates through which the silt-laden waters of the first flood were permitted to pour, but the new dam will have no sluices; the water will be diverted round its extremities for the generation of hydro-electricity. Large-scale siltation will therefore occur in Lake Nasser to the great detriment of the cultivated land downstream.

Livestock are reared almost everywhere as part of the mixed farming system of the Egyptians, and cattle, sheep and other animals are to be seen in all parts. A rotation of crops is generally practised, which helps to maintain the fertility of the soil and which also provides for the growing of fodder crops such as berseem. This crop enriches the soil as do all leguminous crops, and it provides food for the animals, which in their turn help to fertilise the soil and to provide a limited amount of power for pulling the plough and for other domestic needs. Most of the "farms" in

Egypt are very small, over 70% of them being less than 1 acre (0·4 ha) in extent, and it is necessary, therefore, to use every square inch wisely.

MINING AND MANUFACTURE

Until recently it was believed that Egypt was not very rich in mineral wealth, with the exception of building stone, of which there is plenty, but today we are coming to think differently. Mineral oil has been produced in commercial quantities since 1908, and output has greatly increased in recent years; it has risen, for example, from 1,830,000 metric tons in 1958 to 7,075,895 tons in 1966. The output is derived from small oilfields near the Gulf of Suez (see Fig. 108), the best known of which is that near Hurghada, though the most productive is the newer field near El Bilaiyum (see p. 166). Further prospecting for mineral oil is taking place, and more oil has recently been found near the Gulf of Suez, while the first oil strike has now been made in the Western Desert, 12 miles (19 km) south of El Alamein. This field is expected to come into production in 1968, and it is forecast that output in Egypt by 1970 as a result may be as much as 30 million tons per annum. A strike of natural gas in the delta is also reported, and one at Abu Senan near El Faiyum, but details are not yet available.

Iron ore is mined a few miles to the east of Aswan and is used in the iron and steel plant at Helwan (see p. 467); the ore is of reasonable quality (50% iron) and the total reserves may amount to 23 million tons. Even larger reserves are now known to exist in the Bahariya Oasis which lies closer to Helwan, and exploitation of these reserves can be expected. The only other important mineral product is phosphate rock which is mined near Quseir; very large deposits of phosphate exist, while very large reserves of bauxite are reported in the Eastern Desert.

The generation of electricity is increasing (thermal electricity in towns such as Cairo and Alexandria, hydro-electricity at Aswan) and will expand rapidly as the High Dam scheme is completed. Already the first turbines at Aswan are in operation, and power is being carried as far as Cairo along a new transmission line. As electric power is more generally available we may expect industry to become more dispersed than it is at present. The development of industry in general is still at a comparatively early stage, but even so Egypt is the most highly industrialised country in the whole of Africa after the Republic of South Africa, and the present-day expansion of industry is very rapid. The cotton textile industry is easily the most important form of manufacturing activity; large-scale modern mills have been established in Cairo and in Mahalla El Kubra (see Fig. 113), while there are smaller mills in most towns along the valley and in the delta. Enough textile goods are produced to satisfy the home demand and there is a steady export of fabrics and yarn, mainly to other Arab states and the Sudan, though some exports go to Cuba and even Western Germany.

Oil refining is now undertaken at Suez and Alexandria, while a very useful recently developed industry is the manufacture at Suez and El

Khattara (which lies to the north of Aswan) of fertilisers which are urgently needed by Egyptian farmers. Other industries include food processing (as in the sugar factories of Upper Egypt, mainly in the Thebes Basin, at Kom Ombo and at Cairo), the production of tinned foods, soft drinks, cigarettes, leather goods, paper and soap. A small iron and steel industry has been established at Helwan, but Mountjoy reminds us that locational problems involved in the establishment of such an industry in Egypt are considerable. No coking coal exists in the country, though iron ore is obtained from Aswan. Transport costs are therefore bound to be high, as there is such a lengthy distance between the iron ore and the ports

[*Courtesy of Hulton Press Ltd.*

FIG. 113.—The new Egypt. The Mahalla El Kubra textile factory in the delta.

which must import the coke. Helwan, in fact, lies 500 miles (800 km) from the Aswan ore supply and over 100 miles (160 km) from the Mediterranean ports; costs of production are therefore high, and the plant is a prestige symbol with political rather than genuine economic significance. It is planned to establish an aluminium factory between Aswan and Qena which will use power from the High Dam.

It is noteworthy how the location of industry shows a strong concentration in the Cairo and Alexandria areas, where nearly three-quarters of the total number of factories of Egypt are located and where two-thirds of the total industrial labour force is employed. Such a high degree of concentration can easily be understood on economic grounds, but it is not a desirable state of affairs from the social standpoint which takes into account the regrettable effects of overcrowding and slum development.

The main line of communication in Egypt is, of course, the Nile valley, and most of the important towns lie near the river. Sailing vessels and shallow draught steamers penetrate as far upsteam as Aswan. The main railway links Alexandria, Cairo and the new High Dam near Shellal, just south of Aswan, which is the northern terminus of steamers operating from the Sudan, while an east–west trunk railway links the small coastal towns of Salum, Mattruh and El Alamein with Alexandria, Ismailia and Port Said on the Suez Canal. From Ismailia a rail link runs northwards connecting with Israel, Lebanon and Turkey. We have mentioned the rail link with the Kharga Oasis, while other branch lines serve the delta.

SUMMARY

The greatest single problem facing Egypt today is that of population pressure. Most modern developments in the country are in fact attempts to grapple with this problem—the High Dam scheme, the New Valley Project, agrarian reform and the expansion of industry. An expanding economy is essential if Egyptians are to enjoy higher standards of living than they do at present. Shortage of capital has been a real hindrance to further development, but recent nationalisation of foreign assets will not encourage future capital investment from other countries; neither is it easy to galvanise into activity people who have been accustomed for centuries to a passive acceptance of their lot. Perhaps the most important step forward would be notably to reduce the birth-rate, but this is not something which can easily be accomplished; the experience of Japan in recent years, however, shows that even a revolution of this nature can be achieved.

THE SUEZ CANAL

We should make special mention of the Suez Canal, which runs through Egyptian territory, because of its global, strategic and economic importance. The total length of the Canal is about 100 miles (160 km), though part of that distance lies through the Bitter Lakes (*see* Fig. 114). Even in ancient times the importance of the Suez route was recognised, and as long ago as 1400 B.C. a canal was constructed to link the Nile with the Bitter Lakes, from which point goods were transported overland to the Red Sea. In 285 B.C. a canal built by Ptolemy Philadelphus linked the Mediterranean and Red Seas via the Nile; few traces of these early works now remain.

Various later schemes to make use of the direct isthmus route came to nothing, and even Napoleon's enthusiasm for such a project proved abortive. In the first place his engineers reported that the levels of the Mediterranean and Red Seas differed by 33 ft (10 m), and, secondly, before this report could be proved wrong, the Battle of the Nile dashed his hopes of founding a French empire in the East. It was not until 1854 that Ferdinand de Lesseps, the French engineer, secured from the Khedive a concession to construct a canal along the present route, and this scheme was brought to fruition when the Empress Eugenie opened the new waterway in 1869.

In 1875, Britain, who oddly enough had opposed its original construction, secured a dominant interest in the Canal when Disraeli purchased a large number of shares in the Suez Canal Company from the Khedive of Egypt, and this interest lasted until Egypt assumed responsibility for the Canal in 1956. Fortunately, the Canal does not need to pass through high ground (*see* Fig. 115) as the isthmus of Suez, a flat strip of desert, is low

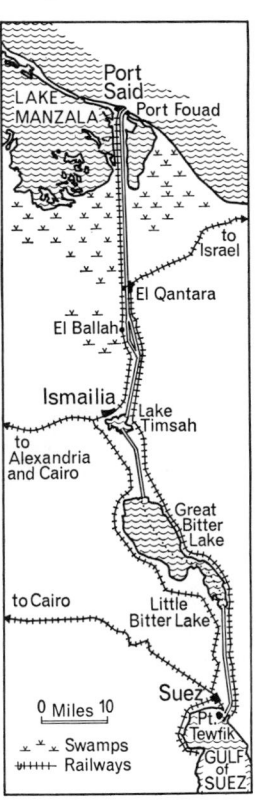

FIG. 114.—The Suez Canal. The railway crosses the canal at El Qantara by means of a swing-bridge. A fresh-water canal which draws its water from Nile via the so-called "Sweet-water Canal" runs roughly parallel with the main Canal a short distance from the western bank. This makes possible cultivation and the keeping of stock, and the comparitively green appearance of the west shore stands in marked contrast to the sandy desolation of the east.

(unlike the isthmus of Panama), while the respective levels of the Mediterranean and the Red Seas are in fact the same. The result of these two features is that no locks are necessary, and this is a great saving of time and money.

Since its original construction the depth of the Canal has been increased to permit ships drawing up to 37 ft (11 m) of water to pass through safely. Except in the Great Bitter Lake, however, ships are not allowed to pass each other when both are in motion; one of them has to tie up while the other is passing. Two measures have been taken to reduce the inconvenience thus caused. The first was the construction of the El Ballah "loop," a new channel about 7 miles (11 km) long, first used in 1951, which permits the simultaneous movement of north- and south-bound vessels. The second was the institution of the convoy system; vessels using the Canal join convoys which leave at fixed times and make the journey in about fifteen hours between Suez and Port Said. Times of departure are so arranged that north- and south-bound convoys pass each other at the El Ballah loop.

[*Courtesy of Hulton Press Ltd.*

Fig. 115.—The Suez Canal. The canal mostly passes through flat monotonous country; the land on the east bank is mainly desert, but there is cultivation on the west bank, thanks to a fresh-water canal.

The great importance of the Canal stems from the fact that it permits considerably shortened sea journeys between north-west Europe on the one hand, and the Middle East, the Indian sub-continent, and Australia on the other. For instance, ships travelling between London and Kuwait save 4000 miles (6400 km) of travel by using the Suez Canal rather than the Cape route; for ships travelling between London and Bombay 4450 miles (7120 km) can thus be saved; and between London and Australia about 1000 miles (1600 km). (For travel between Britain and New

Zealand the Panama route is shorter and is the one generally used.) Great Britain remains the largest user of the Canal.

Traffic through the Suez increased markedly after the Second World War, and the net tonnage of vessels using the Canal went up from 93 million tons in 1953 to 155 million tons in 1958. The chief cause of this is the oustanding increase in mineral oil cargoes from the Persian Gulf area to north-west Europe (including Britain). By weight, oil now accounts for over three-quarters of the total north-bound cargoes, and about three out of every five vessels using the Suez are oil tankers. The constantly increasing size of ocean-going tankers presents a real problem, but it is planned to increase the depth of the waterway. In 1966, 72% of all revenues accruing to the Canal were gained from the passage of oil and its derivatives, so the importance of this proposed measure needs no elaboration. Apart from mineral oil, most of the remainder of the north-bound traffic consists of raw materials (such as ores and oil seeds) and foodstuffs and beverages (such as cereals and Indian tea). Most of the south-bound traffic consists of manufactured goods (including railway equipment and machinery) from Europe destined for the Far East and Australia, together with cement and fertilisers. Note that heavy cargoes to and from Australia which do not need a quick passage still often use the Cape route, as the expense of the longer journey is less than that incurred in paying the heavy Suez Canal tolls. Before the Arab–Israeli war of 1967 the Canal was the U.A.R.'s second biggest earner of foreign currency, cotton being the first.

This section dealing with the Suez Canal was written before the Arab–Israeli war of mid-1967, and it refers in general to conditions as they existed until May, 1967. Since that time the Canal has been closed, and Egyptian and Israeli troops face each other along its banks. Shipping companies have had perforce to arrange their routes to avoid the Canal, and it it not entirely certain that when the Suez is open again they will revert to their pre-war pattern, though some undoubtedly will. The big oil companies, however, are planning to use giant super-tankers which will be too large to use the waterway except in ballast. While such vessels would have been developed in any case, it is clear that the oil companies have pushed ahead rapidly with plans for using them, largely because they are not willing to suffer the risk of repeated dislocations of their shipping arrangements through any future closing of the Suez Canal; more than 100 super-tankers were ordered in 1967 alone after the closure of the Canal.

We must also bear in mind that it is no longer entirely disadvantageous even on economic grounds to use a longer route, for economies of large-scale transport are so great that it will be possible to haul crude oil round the Cape in the giant vessels planned at a lower unit cost than conventional tankers could achieve using the Suez route.* It is estimated that between 1970 and 1975 most crude oil travelling to Europe from the Middle East

*The question of economies of large-scale transport of crude oil is examined at some length in JARRETT, H. R., A Geography of Manufacturing, Macdonald & Evans, 1969.

will be carried in giant tankers which will be using the Cape route, and that as a result very little oil, if any, may be passing through the Suez Canal.

In these circumstances the future of the Suez Canal must be regarded as extremely uncertain, and it is by no means sure that the waterway will ever regain the importance in world affairs that it once had. We may be on the verge of a drastic re-shaping of shipping routes which will take small note of Suez, and it is possible that the cost to Egypt of the 1967 war will be very high indeed before the final reckoning is made.

STUDY QUESTIONS

1. What are the peculiar characteristics of the Nile which make it so valuable a river to Egypt?

2. Why is Egypt "the Gift of the Nile"?

3. Relate the agricultural economy of Egypt to (a) physical, and (b) human factors.

4. What is the place of manufacturing industry in the economy of modern Egypt?

5. Attempt an assessment of the importance of the New High Dam project to Egypt.

6. Critically examine present schemes for the extension of agricultural production in Egypt.

7. Write an essay on the importance of town life in Egypt.

8. What, in your view, are the future prospects for the Suez Canal?

Chapter XXII

TURKEY

TURKEY (296,432 square miles; 567,462 sq. km) is the largest country on the northern side of the Mediterranean. It is in two parts: Turkey-in-Europe (9245 square miles; 23,935 sq. km) and Asiatic Turkey. Turkey-in-Europe occupies eastern Thrace and is separated from the rest of the country by the Bosphorus, the Sea of Marmara and the Dardanelles, which are known collectively as the Straits. Asiatic Turkey is sometimes called Asia Minor, although the eastern boundary of the country lies beyond the peninsula usually recognised by that name. The geographical position of Turkey ensures its international significance, for it controls both the land bridge between Europe and Asia, and the sea route through the Straits between the Mediterranean (Aegean) and Black Seas.

PHYSICAL ASPECTS

STRUCTURAL DIVISIONS

Turkey has the most complex geological structure of all the Mediterranean lands. Earth movements which commenced in the late Cretaceous, were most active in the Tertiary, and continued into the Quaternary, were accompanied by severe folding in the south of the region, by the upthrust of an ancient block in the centre, and by the crushing and further uplift of horsts in the north. The movements were part of the Alpine orogenesis (*see* Chapter I), in which two distinct series of folded mountains, the Alpides and Dinarides, were uplifted and forced towards each other. As they approached more closely, intermediate sections of the floor of the Tethys geosyncline were either forced down to form deep basins such as are found in both the eastern and western Mediterranean, or they were lifted as what are called "median blocks" to form plateaus. The massifs of Mediterranean France, Sardinia, Corsica and the Rhodope were apparently formed in this way, and the central plateau of Turkey seems largely of the same character. The mountains in the south of Asia Minor belong to the Dinarides system and were formed by tectonic thrusts from the south. In the north, pressure from the Alpides—which are represented by the Balkan mountains, the Crimean mountains and the Caucasus—resulted in gigantic faulting and the subsidence of the Black Sea basin; and further faulting along the southern edge of this basin broke up the northern edge of the central plateau into a long series of horsts and rift valleys, the horsts being elevated sufficiently to constitute a mountain range bordering the plateau. At the same time, the central plateau was faulted and dislocated, so that it is made up of a number of blocks squeezed together, irregular in

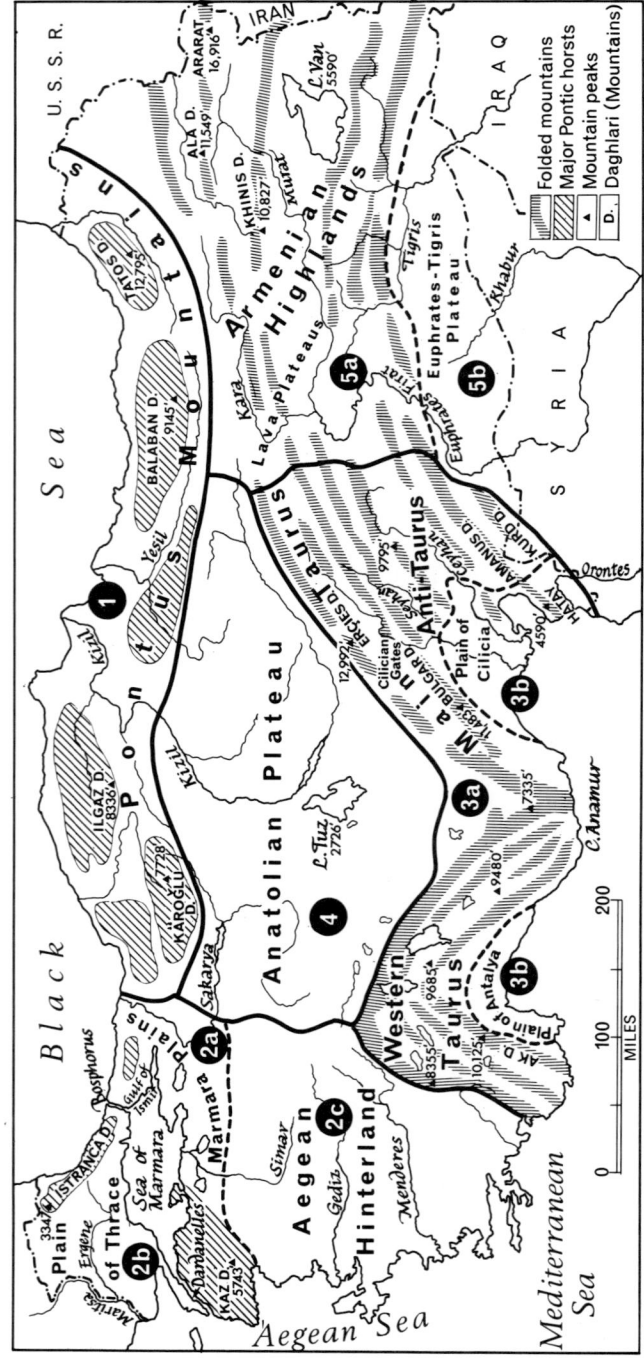

FIG. 116.—Turkey: physical. The numbers refer to sections in the text.

shape and varying in altitude. In the west of the plateau, cross-faulting and the development of horsts and rift valleys, with later subsidence of the land and post-Glacial drowning by the sea, has resulted in the deep basin of the Sea of Marmara and in the greatly indented Aegean coastline. The Bosphorus and the Dardanelles, by the way, are not the result of tectonic movement, but are drowned river valleys of post-Glacial age.

Based on its structure, then, Turkey may be divided into three physical regions: Alpine mountain ranges in the south, and faulted mountain ranges in the north, with a high plateau sandwiched between them. However, since the plateau area changes its character both to the east and west, it may be sub-divided as follows: the main body of the plateau, forming the core of the Asia Minor peninsula, and known as the plateau of Anatolia; the fractured and partially submerged western portion skirting the Aegean; and a more elevated mountain section in the east, which is known variously as the eastern highlands, the Armenian highlands, and the Armenian plateau. Eastwards this section links with the still higher Caucasus and Zagros mountains, but to the south it falls away to the low plateaus drained by the upper Euphrates and Tigris rivers.

A good division of Turkey into geographical region is as follows: (1) the Black Sea coastlands or Pontus mountains which extend from the eastern frontier to the Sakarya river; (2) western Turkey, which is sub-divided into (a) the Marmara lowlands, (b) Turkey-in-Europe and (c) the Aegean hinterland; (3) the Mediterranean coastlands, which include (a) the Taurus and Anti-Taurus ranges and (b) the southern coastal plains; (4) the Anatolian plateau; and (5) the eastern highlands sub-divided into (a) the Armenian highlands and (b) the Tigris–Euphrates plateau. This division of Turkey (see Fig. 116) is not only the basis for an examination of structure and relief, but it also serves admirably for a survey of climatic characteristics and of the Turkish economy dealt with later in this chapter.

1. The Black Sea coastlands

The Pontus mountains run along the north of Turkey for a distance of about 700 miles (1120 km) and shut off the Anatolian plateau from the Black Sea. As we noted above, they are not the result of folding, although folded structures are not entirely absent, but of earth movements which accompanied the foundering of the Black Sea basin in Pliocene times. An extensive series of major faults with a mainly east–west trend, caused by tangential pressure from the north, led to differential radial movements in which blocks of the main plateau of Asia Minor were forced up to great heights. In the west, where the direction of faulting coincided more or less with the present coastline and in fact determined its shape, the Pontus mountains fall steeply to a straight, unbroken coast, except where rivers have built up a few small deltaic plains. East of Sinop, however, the direction of faulting was more north-west/south-east, and was accompanied by much minor cross-faulting. Here the Pontus mountains are a series of ranges in echelon and reach the coast as headlands separated by deep, steep valleys, at the seaward end of which there are deltaic plains; the mountains in this eastern stretch are higher than in the west, and rise imposingly behind the ports which have developed along this indented coast. The Pontus mountains are, therefore, a succession of horsts, some large, some small, some uplifted without tilting, some violently dislocated; and their formation was accompanied by the extrusion of basaltic lavas which form an extensive cover to the eastern Pontus, but which have been mostly eroded in the west.

Prolonged erosion has reduced many of the horsts to peaks. In the west some reach over 7500 ft (2290 m); in the east some of the blocks are topped by volcanic peaks above 11,000 ft (3350 m). Within the Pontus, and running parallel to the coast, are longitudinal fault-valleys occupied by rivers such as the middle courses of the Sakarya, Yenice, Kizil, Yesil, Kelkit and Coruh. (In atlases these may be named Kizilirmak, Yesilirmak, etc.; *irmak* means "river.") The rivers break through to the coast in gorge-like transverse valleys, and do not afford an easy passage through the mountains. In consequence, the Pontus form an extremely difficult barrier to communications, and are penetrated by very few roads and only one railway (from Amasya to Samsun).

2. *Western Turkey*

There is no clear-cut division between this region and those to the east, except that there is more cross-faulting, and that the area as a whole lies at a lower altitude. We find the same ancient and metamorphic rocks (granites, gneisses, marbles and surface lavas), the same horst formation, the same rift valleys; but here cross-faults have produced many small, isolated horsts separated by wide valleys in which rivers have built up flood-plains. Near the sea, subsidence of the land and submergence by the waters of the Aegean have resulted in a coastline broken by a succession of fiord-like or ria-like openings and many island horsts. It is difficult to classify this coastline; its openings show characteristics similar to those associated both with fiords and rias.

(a) *The Marmara lowlands.* The real Pontus ranges may be said to terminate at the river Sakarya, but the displaced horsts continue westwards beyond the Bosphorus to the Istranca Dağlari (Strandja Dagh) in European Turkey. The Asiatic ranges are rarely much more than 1000 ft (300 m) high, but the Istranca Dağlari rise in Mount Mahya to 3347 ft (1020 m). The Asiatic portion subsided in late Tertiary times, giving birth to the deep basin of the Sea of Marmara and drowning the lower end of a rift valley to produce the Gulf of Izmít. The scale of dislocation can be judged by contrasting the depth of Marmara (over 3500 ft, 1070 m) with some of the heights which border it in places (1500 ft, 460 m). To the south and east of the Sea of Marmara are plains of deposition drained by several small rivers; and to this region should be added the flood-plain and delta of the Sakarya.

At the end of the Tertiary, Europe and Asia were joined by the ridge extending from the Pontus mountains. A stream flowing from this ridge to the Sea of Marmara cut back its source in a fault-valley until a channel was opened for the waters of the Black Sea. This is the Bosphorus, a strait which is 20 miles (32 km) long and varies in width from 800 yards to $2\frac{3}{4}$ miles (0·74–4·4 km). A tributary of this stream entered from a synclinal valley in the Cretaceous and Tertiary rocks which today flank the north of Marmara; and subsequent flooding gave rise to the Golden Horn, the magnificent harbour of Istanbul. Another river entering Marmara from the south cut back along a valley carved in faulted limestones and sandstones, to give rise to the Dardanelles, a strait opening to the Mediterranean Sea. Here the rocks are softer, and the Dardanelles, 40 miles (64 km) long and known to the ancients as the Hellespont, may be as much as 4 miles (6·4 km) wide.

(b) *Turkey-in-Europe*. Most of European Turkey consists of the Plain of Thrace, an undulating lowland floored by Cretaceous limestones with a cover of Tertiary clays and sands. The plain is drained by the river Ergene and its tributaries; the Ergene flows to the Maritsa, which forms the whole of the Turko-Greek boundary. Eastwards, the plain rises to the Istranca Dağlari (mentioned above), which form a barrier along the Black Sea coast. To the south, shutting off the plain from the Sea of Marmara, is the slightly folded Tertiary range of the Tekir Dagh, lower than the northern mountains, and rising only to 2382 ft (733 m) at their highest. They are high enough, however, to exclude Mediterranean climatic influences from some parts of the Marmara littoral.

(c) *The Aegean hinterland*. This is defined as the region whose rivers, with the exception of the Simav, drain to the Aegean. As already noted, the drowning of the Aegean coast has produced a very indented coastline, with alternating peninsulas and long, winding inlets, and with many horsts separated by the marine transgression as islands. Although they are so near to the Turkish coast, most of these islands belong to Greece. The peninsulas often rise from the sea in cliffs, and extend eastward as low plateaus; the inlets are drowned rift valleys and are continued inland as narrow plains drained by rivers. Many of the rivers are meandering, due in part to the complicated pattern of cross-faulting which has affected their courses, and in part to silts which have obstructed their flow. A notable example is the river Menderes, which was known to the Greeks as the Meander, and gave its name to all winding streams. The silts are washed down not so much from the ancient rocks of the horsts as from Tertiary and Quaternary limestones, marls and sandstones which have not yet been completely eroded from their flanks. The chief rivers are the Simav, Gediz, Menderes (Buyük Menderes) and Dalaman; the Simav turns sharply to the north, to flow into the Sea of Marmara. All the rivers have deltas which are marshy; some are being reclaimed. The region draining to the Aegean is the most productive in Turkey. River valleys and coastal plains have fertile soils, there is an ample water supply, and climatically it is the most favoured part of the country.

3. *The Mediterranean coastlands*

The south of Turkey is occupied by a great series of folded ranges, the Taurus and Anti-Taurus mountains, arranged in two arcs, a smaller one in the west, and a more extensive one in the east where the folds are continued in the Zagros mountains in Persia. Enclosed by the western arc is the coastal plain of Antalaya (Pamphilia); further east the Cilician Plain is contained by the truncated southern termination of the Anti-Taurus. In the extreme east, the plain of the lower Orontes lies just outside the mountain system.

(a) *The Taurus and Anti-Taurus mountains*. This system differs completely from that of the Pontus. It forms part of the Dinarides and is a series of folded ranges forced up by pressures from the south against the ancient block of Asia Minor. The dominant rock is Cretaceous or Tertiary limestone similar to that found in most Alpine folding, in contrast to the very much older rocks of the Pontic horsts. In both Taurus and Anti-Taurus there are parallel ranges varying in height and continuity, presenting a formidable obstacle between the sea and the plateau of Asia Minor. The Western Taurus, arranged in the shape of an inverted V, rise in the Ak Dağlari to 10,125 ft (3086 m) and in the Anamas Dağlari to 9685 ft (2952 m). Between the northern ranges there are numerous basins of inland drainage with saline or brackish lakes such as Beyshehr (Beysehir) which lies 3773 ft (1150 m) above sea-level. The Western Taurus is an extremely difficult region, almost completely isolated from its neighbours.

East of Cape Anamur the direction of folding changes and swings to the north-east in a great arc towards Armenia and the mountains of Persia. The western arm of the arc comprises the folds of the Main Taurus and, south of these, a series of five parallel ranges known as the Anti-Taurus. Further south again are the Amanus and Kurd Dağlari on the borders of Syria. The Main Taurus are higher but not so difficult as the Western Taurus. The system is narrower and has been split by erosion into several sections separated by river valleys, one series of which forms the Cilician Gates, a relatively easy passage from the interior plateau to the Mediterranean In the south, the highest peak in the Main Taurus (Bulgar Dağlari) is 11,483 ft (3507 m); at the northern end, Quaternary volcanic activity has resulted in many high cones, the most elevated being Erciyas (Erçies) Dagh (12,992 ft, 3960 m).

The ranges known as the Anti-Taurus rise gradually from the Plain of Cilicia and trend north-eastwards, increasing in elevation to about 9000 ft (2740 m), and between the ranges are longitudinal valleys buried at their northern ends under thick sheets of basaltic lava. This northern area is almost impassable; but the lower valleys are wide and floored with fertile alluvium deposited by such rivers as the Seyhan and the Ceyhan. They form extensions of the Plain of Cilicia. The southernmost ranges of the Taurus system are the Amanus and Kurd Dagh. Between the Misis Dagh in the Anti-Taurus and the Amanus the land has foundered, and the deep Gulf of Iskenderun is the result.

Eastwards, the Taurus system is continued into eastern Turkey. It is surveyed below under a separate heading.

(b) *The southern coastal plains.* South of the Taurus a discontinuous coastal plain broadens in the Plain of Antalya, in the Cilician Plain and in the Hatay. The Plain of Antalya is made up of alluvium brought down by the many small rivers flowing from the southern slopes of the Western Taurus. The interior of the plain is fertile, but near the coast there are stretches of malarial marsh. The area is isolated from the rest of Turkey: in the north by the mountain wall, in the south by a shelving, marsh-girt coast. Only two passable roads climb over the northern highlands. The Cilician Plain, known also as the river Seyhan lowlands, is similar to the Plain of Antalya in many ways. It was built up by the silts deposited by rivers, it is flat, and it has marshes; but because the rivers flowing through it—the Seyhan and the Ceyhan—are larger and carry a heavier load, the plain is greater in area. It differs from that of Antalya in that it is more open to the interior via several cols in the Main Taurus and by gaps around the ends of the Anti-Taurus. Roads and railways enter the plain from the north via the Cilician Gates and continue into Syria by passes over the Amanus and Kurd Dagh. South-east of the Cilician Plain is the Hatay, a lowland province of Turkey, occupying the lower basin of the river Orontes. Like the other two plains, it is flat, alluvial and fertile, but it has a smaller proportion of marshland and is much more accessible by land.

4. *The Anatolian plateau*

The Anatolian plateau has a foundation of ancient rocks split in Tertiary times into horsts. These have been cemented together and sometimes completely submerged by outpourings of lava; in the east there are many volcanic cones. The surface of the plateau is broken by ridges of lava or displaced horsts, which enclose basins of inland drainage. In the largest of these is Lake Tuz (Tuz Golu) which is saline. The plateau is ringed on three sides by mountains; to the west it opens to the Aegean coastlands. The general level of the plateau is from 3000 to 4000 ft (910–1220 m); it is somewhat lower in the west, but in the east it rises to 5000 ft (1520 m), with volcanic cones climbing to a further 3000–5000 ft (910–1520 m).

The plateau is tilted towards the north, so that drainage, except in the aretic basins, is to the Black Sea. Most of the rivers, notably the Sakarya, Kizil and Yesil, flow in deeply entrenched valleys through a region eroded to a most irregular topography. Much of the plateau surface has a cover of saline lacustrine deposits which are infertile. The best soils are in the north, wherever river valleys are wide enough to allow the building of flood-plains.

5. *Eastern Turkey*

Most of eastern Turkey is a complex of high mountains, volcanic peaks, lava plateaus and deep valleys lumped together as the Armenian highlands or the Armenian plateau. To the south is a lower plateau through which flow the headwaters of the rivers Euphrates and Tigris, and which may be considered as the northernmost part of Mesopotamia.

(a) *The Armenian highlands.* In eastern Turkey the ranges of the Taurus approach those of the Pontus to form the confused mountain knot known sometimes as the Armenian complex. The Pontus then trend towards the Caucasus, and the Taurus turn south-east to merge with the Zagros. Geologically, the region is one of great instability. Disastrous earthquakes occur frequently (*see* page 16), and much of the landscape is the result of Quaternary vulcanicity, both Pleistocene and recent. In the east, towards the Turkish boundary, earlier extrusions of lava were so vast as to fill the valleys between the mountains and form basaltic plateaus 7000 ft (2130 m) in elevation; more recently, volcanic activity has built such giant cones as Ararat (16,916 ft (5156 m; extinct)) and Nimrud (dormant). A lava flow from Mount Nimrud shut off part of the drainage area of the upper Euphrates, forming a basin of inland drainage occupied by Lake Van. The lavas of the region are too young as yet to have developed into soil, and so their surface is usually barren. For the same reason the waters of Lake Van are brackish rather than saline.

The region was also affected by the glaciers of the Quaternary Ice Age. There are many frost-shattered peaks more than 10,000 ft (3000 m) high, and deep U-shaped valleys are cut in the lavas. It is a well-watered region, and large rivers such as the Euphrates, Tigris and Yesil have carved immense gorges in their upper reaches; lower down, where the valleys are wider, there are more accessible alluvial deposits. Lake Van, too, has alluvial plains on all sides.

On the whole the Armenian highlands are a region of rugged inhospitality, with thin or non-existent soils except in a few places, and, as we shall see, with a most inclement climate and little attraction for human habitation.

(b) *The Tigris–Euphrates plateau.* South of the mountains the land is a plateau which decreases in height southwards, but is never less than 1500 ft (460 m) above sea-level. The surface is undulating rather than hilly, and has been deeply dissected by the rivers Euphrates and Tigris and their tributaries which flow in entrenched channels. The valley floors and river terraces have a cover of alluvium.

CLIMATE

Although Turkey is here included with the Mediterranean lands, only a small proportion of the country has a Mediterranean climate, and this is along the coastal margins. Firstly, there is a contrast between the maritime margins of Turkey and the enclosed "continental" interior; and secondly, the high altitude of Asia Minor, especially in the east, gives most of the country climatic characteristics which bear little or no relation to the relative proximity of the Mediterranean Sea. Moreover, in both the coastlands and the interior many climatic sub-types may be recognised;

and as these correspond more or less with the physical divisions of Turkey given above, the climate of the country will be examined under the same headings.

1. The Black Sea coastlands

The climate of this region may be regarded as sub-Mediterranean. Winters are mild, the average temperature for January, the coldest month, varying little from 44° F (6·7° C). Summers are hot, the mean for July ranging from 70° F (21·1° C) to 75° F (23·9° C). Trabzon, with averages for the coldest and hottest months of 45° F (7·2° C) and 73° F (22·8° C) respectively, may be taken as typical. In the interior valleys of the Pontus mountains, shut off from sea influences, winter temperatures may fall below freezing point, but summer temperatures are much as on the coast. Altitude in the mountains reduces temperature; in the east, for instance, above 7000 ft (2100 m), the peaks are snowclad for the whole of the winter. A feature of this eastern area is the frequency of *föhn* winds in winter, and the consequent rapid rise in temperature. The thermometer at Trabzon has often registered over 70° F (21·1° C) in January, but only for a short time.

It is more in respect of rainfall that the climate of the Black Sea coastlands differs from the typically Mediterranean. The winter half of the year has a greater total mean rainfall annually than in summer, but no month has drought; and in general, precipitation is well distributed throughout the year. Average annual amounts vary from 25 in. in the west to 50 in. in the east near sea-level; Trabzon has 33·4 in., 35% of which falls in September–November. Precipitation in the mountains is much greater, ranging from 40 in. a year in the west to 100 in. or more near the eastern frontier; and much of it may fall as snow in winter (*see* Fig. 117).

2. Western Turkey

In general, the climate of this region has the usual Mediterranean pattern of hot, dry summers and mild, wet winters; but there are some variations from this. In the Marmara lowlands and European Turkey, mean January temperatures are rarely above 40° F (4·4° C), which is lower than along the Black Sea coast. The January average of Istanbul is 41° F (5·0° C). The Plain of Thrace in European Turkey, partially shut off from maritime influences by highlands, has a bleak, almost continental winter with much frost. Summers are hot; Istanbul has a July mean of 73° F (22·8° C). Annual precipitation in these sub-regions averages from 25 to 30 in., but unlike the Black Sea coast, there is a definite winter maximum. Istanbul, for instance, has 28·8 in. annually, of which 68% falls from September to February.

Temperatures in the Aegean coastlands near the sea range from around 45° F (7·2° C) in January to over 80° F (26·7° C) in July (Izmír: 46–81° F (7·8–27·2° C)). Further inland, January temperatures may fall to averages below 40° F (4·4° C). Diurnal ranges in summer may be great throughout

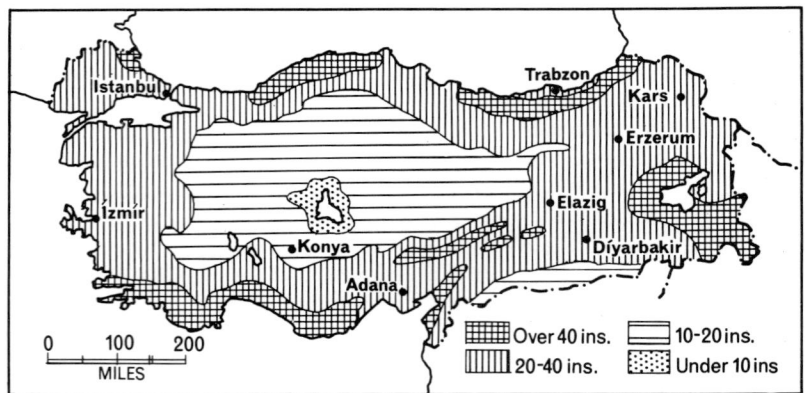

FIG. 117.—Turkey: mean annual rainfall. The stations shown are mentioned in the text.

this sub-region, day temperatures of over 90° F (32·2° C) being common. Annual rainfall averages from 20 to 30 in. along the coastal margins (Ízmír: 26 in.), but inland it may not reach more than 15 in. Summer drought is pronounced everywhere; Ízmír receives only 2% of its total precipitation in June, July and August. Two points of interest should be noted in the climate of the Aegean coastlands: the prevailing northerly Etesian winds in summer temper the midday heat; on the other hand, the sea-facing valleys may suffer very high, enervating humidity for days on end.

3. *The Mediterranean coastlands*

The south-facing slopes of the Taurus system and the plains along the Mediterranean coast show the usual Mediterranean climatic characteristics. The mountains have an annual rainfall of about 30 to 35 in., with a winter maximum; but both in the amount of rainfall and in seasonal distribution of temperature, much depends on altitude and aspect. The coastal plains, sheltered by the mountains and at a lower latitude than the rest of Turkey, have higher temperatures at all times than the Aegean region. Adana is typical; it has a January mean of 48° F (8·9° C) and an August average of 83° F (28·3° C). August is the hottest month in these plains, with maximum temperatures over 90° F (32·2° C). Rainfall averages between 20 and 30 in., nearly half the total falling from December to February. June, July and August are months of drought, but are slightly wetter than on the Aegean coasts; Adana, for instance, has an annual total of 23·8 in., of which 6% (1·43 in.) falls in these months.

4. *The Anatolian plateau*

The altitude and enclosed character of the Anatolian plateau have led to a continental type of climate, with extremes of temperature and a tendency to aridity. Mean temperatures for January average 30° F (−1·1°

C), and for July about 70° F (21·1° C); but diurnal ranges are big, and night minima in winter may be as low as 15° F (−9·4° C), and day maxima in summer as high as 85° F (29·4° C). Annual precipitation is small, varying from around 10 in. at lower levels to 18 in. on hills. Most falls in winter and spring, May often being the wettest month. A feature of the rainfall is its uncertainty. In winter the plateau lies under a high-pressure system which obstructs the passage of depressions, so that totals of rainfall in January and February may be much less than in December. With its collapse in spring, depressions from the eastern Mediterranean can penetrate to the plateau and give rise to the relatively larger rainfall of April and May. June, July and August are the driest months; in fact, there may be absolute drought which extends for weeks. Konya, in the south of the plateau, may be taken as a typical station. Its mean temperature in January is 30° F (−1·1° C) and in August 74° F (23·3° C), and its annual rainfall 11·3 in. In January, maxima average 38° F (3·3° C) and minima 22° F (−5·6° C), and for August the corresponding readings are 56° F (13·3° C) and 92° F (33·3° C). Sixty-eight per cent of its rain falls from December to May.

5. Eastern Turkey

The mountains and plateaus of Armenia have a still more extreme climate. Temperatures at Elâzig, in the west and more favoured part of the region, range from averages of 19° F (−7·2° C) in January to 77° F (25·0° C) in July. Further east, summer temperatures are much the same as this, but the winters are bitterly cold. Kars, near the Russian border, has a January mean of 9° F (−12·8° C), and Erzerum 12° F (−11·1° C), and in both towns readings of −30° F (−34·4° C) have been recorded in that month. Temperatures are still lower on the mountains, and even in summer diurnal ranges may bring night temperatures below freezing point. Rainfall varies with elevation, but on the whole the Armenian highlands have a greater precipitation than the Anatolian plateau, ranging from about 16 in. in the interior to over 30 in. in the north-east. Most of it falls as snow. February and March are the wettest months, and August and September the driest. The climate of the east of Turkey is one of the most inhospitable in the world.

In the south, the plateaus drained by the upper Euphrates–Tigris system have winter temperatures similar to those of Anatolia; Díyarbakir, for example, has a January mean of 31° F (−0·6° C). In summer, the plateaus lie open to hot, dry winds from the deserts to the south, and in the river valleys temperatures during the day may reach 120° F (48·9° C). Precipitation is scanty, rarely more than 10 in. annually and mostly in winter; June, July and August are almost completely rainless.

VEGETATION

The natural vegetation of Turkey varies with the climate, soil and elevation. The Pontus mountains are clothed in the east with luxuriant deciduous forests of Turkey oak, beech, chestnut and alder at lower levels, succeeded upwards by cedars, pines and firs, with Alpine pastures above. In the west where the rainfall is less the forests are less dense. Along the narrow coastal plains there are extensive thickets of hazel, whose nuts are an important export. Forests occur also on the seaward slopes of the Taurus system, but they are smaller and with less varieties of trees. Pines predominate, the chief species being cluster pine, black pine and Pyrenean pine; and there are stands of Turkey oak, cedar, cypress and fir. The Aegean coastlands have Mediterranean evergreen forests on the slopes of the peninsulas and the ridges which extend inland. The chief trees are the kermes oak, valonia oak, wild olive, plane and dwarf pine, with an occasional ilex (holm oak).

The Aegean forests degenerate towards the Anatolian plateau into maquis, and this type of vegetation covers vast areas in the interior of Turkey, nine-tenths of which is treeless. The inner slopes of the limestone Taurus have a discontinuous cover of garrigue, which occurs also in the plains of European Turkey, where it is known as phrygana. In the damper valleys in Anatolia, there are straggling clumps of willows, poplars and chestnut, but in parts of the plateau where the annual rainfall is less than 10 in. or where the soils are saline, the vegetative cover at the best is coarse grass with a short life-cycle, bulbous plants, and xerophilous or halophilous shrubs. In other words, it is dry steppe; and it is continued into eastern Turkey, where it covers most of the less elevated surface, including the southern plateaus. In the Armenian highlands, large areas of the lava plateaus and the volcanic slopes have no vegetation at all. In the northeast, where there is more rain, there are stands of coniferous trees high up the mountain slopes.

HUMAN GEOGRAPHY

HISTORICAL OUTLINE

The first people of whom we have definite knowledge in Turkey were the Hittites who entered Asia Minor about 2000 B.C. and ruled there until the Aryan invasions of the eleventh century B.C. The Hittite power extended to the whole of Asia Minor and occasionally to northern Syria and Mesopotamia; their sculptures and inscriptions have been found at many places from İzmír to the Euphrates. The Aryans founded a kingdom in Phrygia, south-east of Ankara, but in the eight or ninth century B.C. they were displaced by the Cimmerians, a wild Asiatic tribe who entered Turkey via Armenia. In the meantime, Greek colonies appeared on the coast in a chain which stretched from Trabzon (Trebizond) to Rhodes, and a second Aryan kingdom had arisen in Lydia, with its capital at Sardis, about 30 miles (48 km) east of İzmír. By 617 B.C. Lydia was strong enough to drive out the Cimmerians and also to take possession of the Greek colonies, which were too jealous of each other to combine and too weakened by luxurious living to resist individually. The Lydian kingdom ended with the capture of Sardis by the Persians, 546 B.C., and Asia Minor formed part of the Persian Empire until it was invaded and conquered by Alexander the Great in 334 B.C.

After his death Turkey came ultimately into the hands of the Seleucids, but they were never able to establish a rule over the whole country. Rhodes seceded and became a prosperous maritime republic; large parts of the south and west coasts belonged at various times to the Ptolemies of Egypt; and in the north, Gallic tribes crossed the Bosphorus and established the kingdom of Galatia in the middle of the Anatolian plateau. The Greek Seleucids maintained their uneasy rule until the successful invasion by the Romans after 133 B.C., after which there followed over eight centuries of tranquillity during which Asia Minor prospered. The introduction of Christianity and the thorough hellenisation of the region led to the disappearance of native languages and brought about a new unity in tongue and religion.

This period of peace was terminated in the seventh century. First the Muslim Arabs overran Asia Minor and held it for nearly 300 years; and then the Seljuk Turks came from the east in 1067, subjugated both the Arabs and the natives, ravaged the country and ruled without mercy. They accepted the teachings of Islam and imposed them on the indigenous inhabitants. The Seljuk Turks were the first of a long succession of nomad tribes which pressed in from central Asia, looking for better pastures for their animals. The most successful of these incursions was that of the Ottoman (Osmanli) Turks, who appeared in 1227 and within a century were in complete control of Asia Minor. In 1453 they captured Constantinople and began to build an empire which by 1600 extended from Armenia to the middle Danube, and covered the Levant and the coastlands of North Africa as far as Algeria. The Ottoman Turks were ruthless invaders, destroying all in their path; flourishing towns were razed to the ground and agricultural communities exterminated; the Turkish language and Muslim religion were enforced, and all traces of Hellenic culture eradicated.

The Ottoman Empire lasted until the early years of the present century, but at its best it was a ramshackle structure, torn by dissidence and constant rebellions against the cruelly repressive rule of the Turks. Weakened also by a succession of wars with European Powers, decline and decay were inevitable; and the Empire finally broke up in the First World War, 1914–18, after which Turkey was reduced to approximately its present boundaries.

The fact that Turkey became the centre of a vast empire seemed to have had little or no effect on its own inhabitants. In all the turmoil and vicissitudes of the empire, the mother country remained poor, backward and illiterate, with a culture based on oriental ideas and completely severed from that of Western Europe. But after the First World War a regeneration commenced. New boundaries for Turkey were delineated and agreed to by the Western Powers, the sultanate was abolished, and the country became a republic. Under the autocratic leadership of Mustafa Kemal, who became known as Atatürk ("father of the Turks"), the country went through a revolution of political, economic and social change, and the transformation continued after his death in 1938. Educational facilities were extended and the Latin alphabet replaced the Arabic script; Islam ceased to be the national religion and the compulsory wearing of the fez and the yashmak was discontinued; and European clothing and ways of life were encouraged. Politically, Turkey abandoned its oriental outlook and began to fit itself into the European concert of nations (it became a member of NATO), and economically better use was made of its natural resources, agriculture was improved, irrigation extended, and industries and communications developed. Turkey is still relatively backward, but with the help and encouragement of the Western world, it is making rapid progress as a truly democratic state.

PEOPLE

None of the conquering races which invaded Asia Minor, whether from east or west, wholly expelled or exterminated the inhabitants in possession, the vanquished retiring to the mountains or absorbing the victors. In the course of ages there has been the fusion of blood of many peoples and a consequent obliteration of true racial characteristics. Even the name "Turk" is not racially distinctive, for wherever the people accepted Islam they called themselves "Turks," so it is probable that large numbers of the population have no real Turkish blood at all. In the east of the country, for instance, there are about $1\frac{1}{2}$ million Kurds, a semi-nomadic people who came in very early times from the Turan and still live their own lives with their own language and customs. Other minority groups in the eastern highlands include the Circassians and Georgians, and there are many thousands of Arabs mainly from Syria, along the Mediterranean coastlands. Until 1923, there was a large Greek population in European Turkey and the Aegean coastlands, but by the Treaty of Lausanne in that year $1\frac{1}{2}$ million Greeks were exchanged from these regions for 700,000 Turks who lived in Greece. More recently still, the struggle between Greek and Turkish Cypriots has had its repercussions in Greece and Turkey in a renewed exchange of peoples in the Straits region. The result is that the population of Turkey is today more homogeneous than for centuries past.

The population of Turkey is estimated about 32 million (1961 census: 27,809,831). The country is primarily agricultural and four-fifths of the people live in rural areas and only one-fifth in towns. The largest concentrations are around Istanbul, Ankara and Ízmír, which together account for $2\frac{1}{2}$ millions. Other centres of dense population are Bursa and Eskişehir in western Turkey, Konya and Kayserí in the Anatolian plateau, and Adana and Gazíantep in the eastern Mediterranean coastlands. The average density of population is 108 persons per square mile, but it must be remembered that most people live in the west of Turkey and that vast areas of the plateau and mountains are virtually uninhabited.

THE ECONOMY

GENERAL CONSIDERATIONS

Nearly half the surface of Turkey is classed as pasture land (*see* Fig. 118). This includes areas as widely different as the water meadows in the river valleys of the Pontus and the arid steppe in the east of the plateau. Land under the plough or occupied by market gardens and fruit trees takes up about one-fifth of the country, but since peasant farmers usually adopt a two-year rotation of crop and fallow, a large proportion of the cultivable land is productive only in alternate years. The remainder of Turkey is divided nearly equally between forest and unproductive land. About four-fifths of the population is dependent directly on agriculture or pastoralism, and their products provide the bulk of the country's exports, notably in wheat, cotton, tobacco, dried fruits, nuts, wool and mohair.

AGRICULTURE

Prior to 1923, agriculture in Turkey was regarded as secondary to pastoralism, but under the régime inaugurated by Kemal Atatürk, serious efforts were made to improve its status. Rural schools were established to instruct the peasants in new and modern methods; new seeds and equipment were provided; communications were improved; land previously used for pasture was ploughed; irrigation systems were developed; and nomadic shepherds were persuaded to become sedentary farmers. Since the Second World War the increase in agriculture has continued, and in the first two Five-year Development Plans (1963–72) top priority is being given to agricultural development.

A system of extensive agriculture is currently used in Turkey. So to feed the rapidly growing population and leave a surplus for export, it is necessary to increase the area under cultivation at the expense of grassland and pasture; in other words, an increase in agricultural production is possible not through an increase in productivity, but through an expansion of the cultivated area. The plans also aim at the development of intensive farming, the eradication of wasteful farm labour, and the introduction of new export products. So far the plans have been moderately successful. Since 1963 there has been an increase of over 20% in the total of agricultural commodities; but progress is slowed down by peasant conservatism and ignorance, by the perpetuation of wasteful and primitive farm practices, by lack of capital and by the difficulty of transforming nomads into agriculturists.

Turkey's agricultural products cover a very wide range, thanks to varied soil and climatic conditions. The products include tobacco, cotton, hazel nuts, dried raisins and figs, cereals, sugar beet, pulses, oilseeds, citrus and other fruits, vegetables, tanning materials, pistachio nuts, walnuts,

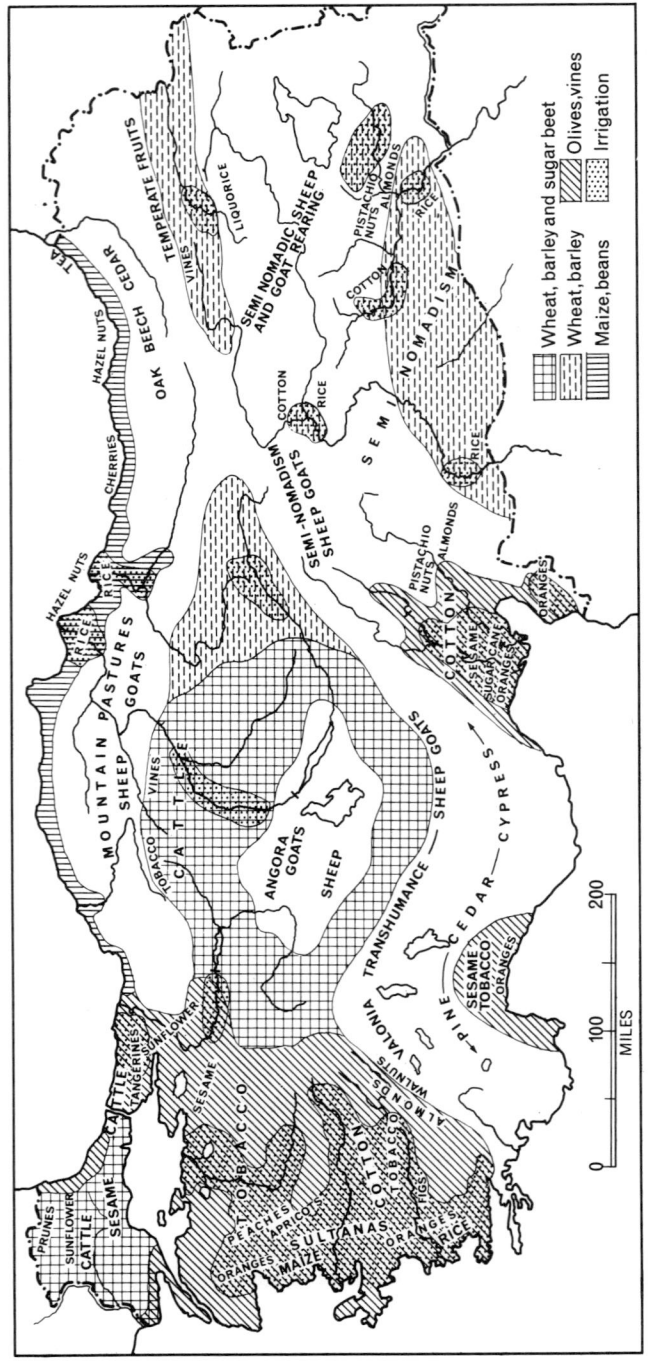

FIG. 118.—Turkey: agriculture and pasture.

liquorice, attar of roses and many others. Of these, cereals are of out-standing importance as a food crop, and tobacco, cotton and sugar beet as commercial crops.

About four-fifths of the crop acreage is given over to cereals, which in-clude wheat, barley, maize, rye, oats, rice and millet, in that order. The chief wheat areas are along the northern and southern margins of the Anatolian plateau, the Plain of Thrace, and the Tigris–Euphrates plateau. Cultivation here is favoured by the undulating surface and by a rainfall of 15 to 20 in. a year. In Anatolia and south-east Turkey, more and more of the neighbouring steppe is being ploughed for wheat. Barley is grown in the same regions as wheat, but to a far less extent; it can withstand drier conditions, and so it is confined more to the steppe margins. In the west of Turkey wheat and barley are grown as winter crops, but in the east where the winters are too cold, spring-sown wheat is more usual. Maize needs more moisture, and is cultivated along the Black Sea coasts, and by irri-gation on the alluvial plains near the Aegean.

The remaining cereals are of less importance. Rye is the most tolerant of poor soils and drought, and is found mainly in the interior of Anatolia away from the salt lake areas, and among the highlands of eastern Turkey. Oats, which with barley is grown as fodder, is restricted to the cooler wheat regions of the north and north-west. Millet needs more heat, and is grown as a summer crop along the Mediterranean coastlands. In this area, too, rice is important in the plains and reclaimed marshlands, and it is cultivated in the deltaic lands along the Black Sea and Aegean coasts, and by irrigation in the Tigris and Euphrates valleys.

Sugar beet was introduced into Turkey after 1923, and its cultivation was so successful in the north and west of Anatolia, where it is grown in rotation with wheat, that it can now supply all the country's needs and leave a large surplus for export. Sugar cane grows in the Mediterranean plains, especially around Adana, but the total output is small and is de-clining. Vegetables are grown everywhere for local consumption, and potatoes in the cooler north and east.

Easily the most important region in Turkey for cotton is the Seyhan basin in the Plain of Adana, which is responsible for over 80% of the total crop. Small quantities are produced also around İzmír and in the Men-deres valley in the west, and in the river valleys near Díyarbekir and Elâzig in the east. Most of the cotton cultivation needs irrigation; and as more water is made available artificially, the acreage under cotton is in-creasing. Raw cotton and cotton-seeds are among Turkey's most valuable exports. Tobacco has been grown in Turkey for centuries and is exported in large quantities. For local use it is cultivated widely in all the coastlands and the marginal areas of the Anatolian plateau. As a commercial crop it is grown in two main districts: the Aegean and Marmara plains and the eastern half of the Black Sea coastlands. The best tobacco occurs with a coincidence of deep, rich soils, rainfall of over 20 in. annually, and a period of drought during which the leaves may be dried in the open air.

The chief oilseeds, after cottonseeds, are sesame, grown in the plains of Antalya and Cilicia, and sunflower, in European Turkey and the Marmara plains.

Most of the rest of Turkey's agricultural products are tree crops, and these may be classified as (a) cultivated, and (b) natural, that is, gathered from forest trees and shrubs. Among the former are olives, vines, figs, citrus fruits, peaches, apricots, plums and cherries; and the latter include hazel nuts, acorns, almonds, pistachio nuts and liquorice.

Olive groves are found extensively on the hillsides of the Aegean peninsulas, the Mediterranean coast and the western end of the Black Sea coast, with the greatest concentrations around Ízmír, in the Cilician Plain and Hatay. Most of the crop is consumed locally, but olive oil is pressed and exported from the regions mentioned. Vines have a wider distribution than olives; not only are they found in all the "Mediterranean" areas, but they occur also on the foothills of the Pontus and Taurus bordering the Anatolian plateau, and in some of the valleys in Armenia. Unlike olives, however, the crop is mostly exported, chiefly dried as sultanas. The best sultanas come from the southern Aegean lands. This is the most important fig region, too. Turkish figs have a high reputation for their flavour, which is said to be the result of fertilisation by an insect peculiar to the Aegean region. The figs are dried in late summer by the hot Etesian winds, and are packed and exported from Ízmír.

All kinds of Mediterranean fruits such as apricots, peaches and pomegranates are grown for local consumption in the coastlands and the western half of the plateau; further east in Anatolia and increasingly in Armenia, temperate fruits, especially apples, are the chief orchard crops. Citrus fruits are comparative newcomers to Turkey, which is strange when one remembers that the Levant just to the south has been growing oranges for centuries. Jaffa oranges, introduced from the Levant, are grown and exported from the Aegean coastlands, and tangerines from the Black Sea/Marmara plains. Cherries and plums are also grown widely in these plains. The cherry takes its name from Gíresun, a small town about 60 miles (96 km) west of Trabzon, which was its original home. Much of the plum crop is dried as prunes at Edirne in Thrace, which is the centre of production. A tree crop of a different character is tea, which has been introduced into the extreme east of the Black Sea coastlands from the Transcaucasian states of the U.S.S.R. The relief, climate and soils resemble those of neighbouring Georgia, which has extensive tea plantations. Turkey is now almost self-sufficient in tea.

More than half the world's hazel nuts which enter into commerce come from Turkey, from the forests which clothe the Black Sea slopes of the Pontus mountains from Sinop eastwards. Smaller amounts are gathered from cultivated plantations along the Aegean peninsulas, where they are sometimes side by side with walnut groves. Almonds and pistachio nuts are gathered wild in the Ceyhan and Tigris basins, but larger amounts now come from organised orchards in the same areas. Acorns of the valonia oak, prized for an extract used in tanning, are collected in the forests on the inner slopes of the Western Taurus, and processed and exported from İzmír. Liquorice is a pea-like shrub which grows wild in the arid steppe of Anatolia and south-east Turkey. The liquorice of commerce is extracted from its long sweet root, thousands of tons of which are gathered annually; it is used in medicine and confectionery.

An increase in the area growing cereals has been made possible by using dry-farming methods and mechanisation, but an extension of the acreage of some crops such as cotton and citrus fruits means either the further development of existing irrigation systems or the building of new ones. Here Turkey has to face certain problems. The rivers which are suitable for irrigation in the north of the Anatolian plateau, such as the Sakarya, Kizil and Yesil, flow in deeply entrenched valleys, so that powerful pumps are required to raise the water to the fields which need it. Nevertheless, there are major systems around all these rivers, and new ones are being constructed along deeper valleys in the Elâzig–Díyarbakir region. Along the coasts there are scores of rivers carrying down silt in such quantities in the wet season as to obstruct their lower courses and form marshes. Irrigation in these cases has to be developed in conjunction with reclamation and river control; and this has been done throughout the Aegean coastlands, near the deltas of the Kizil and Yesil on the Black Sea, and very extensively in the plain of Cilicia. South-east of Ankara, the Kizil has been dammed to provide domestic water to the city, and the impounded lake serves also to generate hydro-electricity and to irrigate market gardens and sugar beet fields.

PASTORALISM

The semi-arid character of vast areas of steppe and mountain slopes have led to the rearing of sheep and goats on a large scale. In the west transhumance is practised widely; eastwards the seasonal movements amount to semi-nomadism or even, as with the Avshars of the Anti-Taurus, to true nomadism. Sheep (32 million) are the most numerous throughout the country, but the largest numbers are in European Turkey, in the east and west of the Anatolian plateau, and in the region south of Lake Van. There is a large export of wool, but its coarseness makes it more suitable for carpets and cheap blankets than for clothing. Efforts are being made to improve its quality by the introduction of merino stock. Goats (21 million) are reared alongside sheep, but they are found also in the more arid districts and in mountain areas where sheep could not find sustenance. About a quarter are Angora goats, which yield mohair, a long, fine, lustrous fibre used in the manufacture of cloth; they are reared mainly to the south of Ankara (formerly Angora). Both sheep and goats are also an important source of milk, cheese and yoghourt (a Turkish word for fermented milk).

Cattle (13 million) are reared in greatest numbers in the wetter districts along the western Black Sea coasts, the Marmara plains and the hinterland of Istanbul. They occur also on a broad zone in northern Anatolia centring an Ankara, where they are fed on barley, oats and vegetable fodder, so that this region is gradually becoming one of mixed farming. In the eastern Black Sea coastlands there are over 1 million water buffaloes, which are employed as farm animals a well as giving milk. Horses, mules and asses are the usual transport animals; and in the southeast there are still about 46,000 camels, but their numbers are diminishing rapidly in face of motor transport.

MINERALS AND POWER

Turkey has a large variety of minerals, but usually the deposits are small and scattered or they occur in places difficult of access, so their exploitation is limited (see Fig. 119). Coal occurs in a long, narrow basin from Ereğli to Amasra on the Black Sea coast, but the output is small, amounting to not more than 5 million tons a year. The coal is of good quality, but is apt to crumble in the handling and washing processes, so that at least a quarter is wasted. The advantages of a coastal position are reduced by the lack of good harbours and poor communications inland. Lignite is found in many scattered deposits on the Anatolian plateau, and is not fully exploited; the largest production is near Kütahya, in the west, where it is used to generate electricity. No significant deposits of petroleum have as yet been discovered in Turkey; there are two small fields at Raman and Garzan, about 60 miles (96 km) east of Díyarbakir, and other deposits occur on the eastern edges of the Cilician Plain. Oil refineries have been built at Batman and Mersín (see Fig. 120).

Iron ore is worked from large deposits at Dívrígí (Divrig) in the eastern highlands, and near the head of the Gulf of Izmít, at Çamdag; it occurs also a few miles south-east of Ízmír at Torbali, on the south coast behind Anamur, and at several places in the Main Taurus, but there is little output from these. Blast furnaces have been built at Karabük, south of the coalfield (see Fig. 121); this necessitates a 600-mile (960 km) rail haul of the ore from Dívríği, and as the Çamdag deposits are nearer and of higher quality, more attention is paid to them. A second integrated steel plant, including blast furnaces, was opened at Ereğli in 1965, but this also lies a long way from the nearest ore field. Turkey is the world's second largest producer of chrome ore, most of which is exported. It is either mined in shallow adits or gathered from open-cast workings, and is associated with ancient, metamorphic outcrops. By far the largest deposits are in the isolated region of Güleman, west of Lake Van, which produces about three-fifths of the total output. Motor transport carries the ore to Erganí, whence it is taken by rail to the port of Mersín, 400 miles (640 km) distant. Surface deposits of chrome occur also in the Aegean coastlands at Fethíye, Bursa and Eskísehír, but are being rapidly exhausted by open-cast workings.

High-grade copper is mined in appreciable quantities at Erganí and in the Black Sea littoral at Trabzon and Hopa, but little is exported; it is used mainly in the developing electrical industry and for armaments.

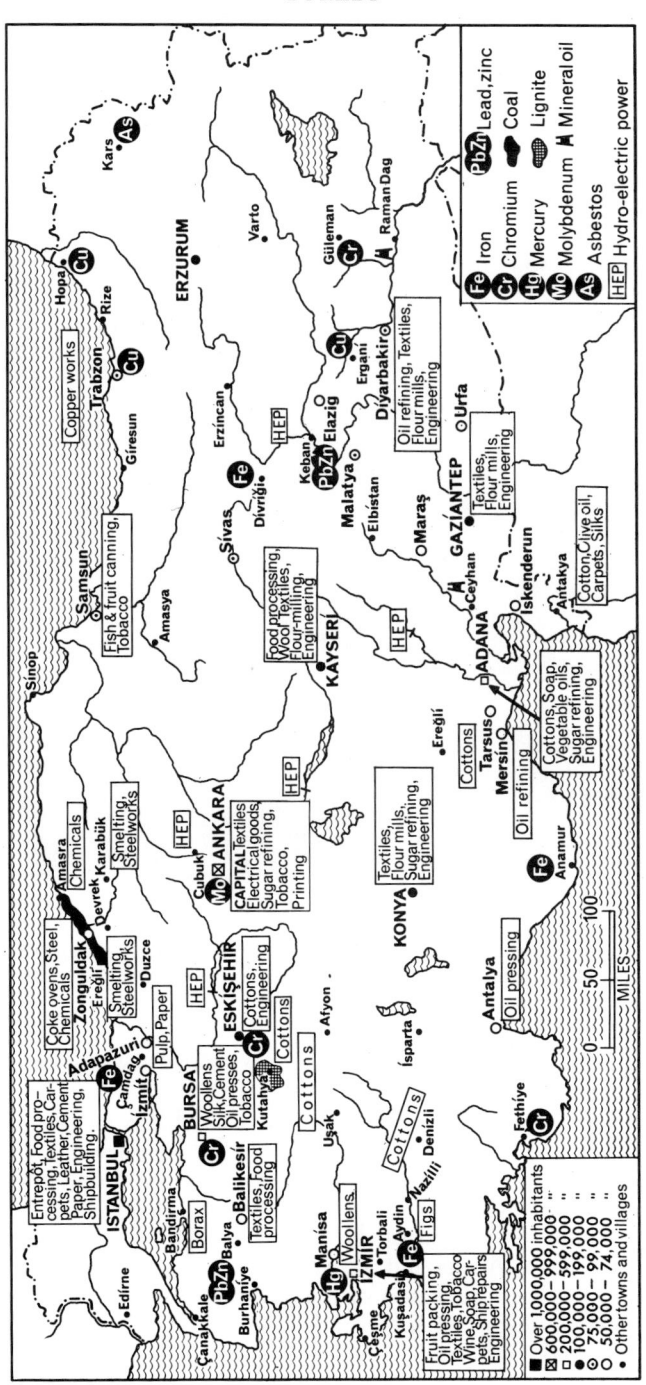

Fig. 119.—Turkey: cities and towns; minerals and industries.

Lead–zinc ores are worked at Balya and Keban, but the output is small. Manganese occurs at many places in the eastern highlands and the total output (20,000 tons a year) puts Turkey among the world's leading producers, but individual deposits are too small to be located on the map. Among other minerals which are exploited in a small way are boracite (borax, at Bandirma), asbestos (Kars), mercury (İzmír), molybdenum (Ankara) and sulphur (volcanic regions). Meerschaum, a whitish clay

[*Courtesy of the Turkish Embassy.*

FIG. 120.—Turkey: oil refinery at Batman. Situated in eastern Turkey, 50 miles east of Díyarbakir, and on the pipeline from the Raman-Garzan oilfields, this small town (pop. 12,600) is growing rapidly. The Tigris plateau in the background is undulating in character.

used in the manufacture of pipes, occurs in western Anatolia, but is little quarried today.

Water power used in the generation of electricity is included in this section. The hydro-power potential of Turkey has been estimated at over 2000 million kWh, but up to the present little more than one-hundredth of this has been developed. The chief resources lie inconveniently in the east of the country; the greatest developments have been in the regions centring on Ankara, Adana and Malatya. At Çubuk, 12 miles (19 km) north of Ankara, the headwaters of the Sakarya have been dammed (*see* Fig. 122), and south-east of the city the Hirfanli barrage impounds the middle Kizil, and both send hydro-electricity to the capital and west

Turkey. The river Seyhan has been dammed to supply power to Adana, and there are prospects of further developments in this region. There are great possibilities in the eastern highlands; already a power station has started to operate at Keban, at the confluence of the east and west branches of the upper Euphrates, called in Turkey the Murat and the Firat.

INDUSTRIAL DEVELOPMENT

Initial efforts towards industrialisation were launched in the middle of the nineteenth century, but they were designed primarily to meet the requirements of the armed forces. Industries in the true sense of the word did not come into being until after the proclamation of the Republic in 1923, and it was then decided to develop them as far as possible on the Anatolian plateau, so as not to upset too much the rich agricultural economy of the Aegean coastlands. Progress for some years was slow, but under the First Industrial Plan (commencing 1933) considerable headway was made in the establishment of such basic industries as iron and steel, textiles, cellulose and paper, ceramics and chemicals, and by the beginning of the Second World War the share of industry in the national economy

[*Courtesy of the Turkish Embassy.*

FIG. 121.—Turkey: iron and steel works at Karabük. The first modern blast furnaces in Turkey, on the edge of the Zonguldak coalfield, have been augmented by others at Erĕgli, but both are handicapped by their distances from sources of iron ore.

had risen from 10% in 1930 to 16% . In the years 1950–62 there were further important developments, especially in power, textiles, cement and sugar, so that by the end of that period the industrial share in the economy had reached 23%. As a result of the first Five-year Development Plan started in 1963, it was expected that by its termination in 1967 the figure would have reached 32%. This was a little too optimistic in a country which is primarily agricultural and pastoral; there have certainly been great strides in industrial development in the past 20 years, but much more rapid expansion of power resources will be necessary if Turkey is to maintain its industrial growth and reach the target aimed at in its current Plan.

In the early years of the Republic, the heavy industry needed by the country was established by the State, and it still retains control of such branches as iron and steel production, weapons and ammunition, ship-building, road and rail communications, mining and power installations. It shares with private enterprise in food processing, woollen and cotton textiles, timber products including paper-making, rubber, plastics, chemi-cals, sugar and oil refining (see Fig. 123), glass and ceramics. The State is responsible for harbour works, and has a monopoly in the manufacture of tobacco, cigarettes and alcoholic drinks. In all its developments, Turkey has had to rely heavily on foreign capital. The chief investors are the U.S.A., West Germany, Holland, Switzerland and France, in that order.

Some detail of the location of Turkey's industries is given in the next section (see also Fig. 119).

REGIONAL ECONOMY

1. *The Black Sea coastlands.*

The narrow coastal plain widens in the deltas of several rivers, notably the Kizil, Yesil and Coruh; but although the extent of cultivable land is limited, it is very productive. Rainfall is abundant and there is no dry season in the east of the region; in the west it is drier and with a tendency to summer drought. Maize and beans are the basic food crops throughout the plains; wheat is also important in the west, and rice is grown in the Coruh valley in the east, and in the interior irrigated valleys around Düsce (18,200) and Devrek (4200). Sugar beet and cotton are cultivated in the irrigated lands in the east, and sunflower seeds (for oil) in the west. In the intermontane valleys rye and potatoes are important crops. The chief commercial crop of the region is tobacco, especially east of Sínop (9900), a small port. The tobacco is processed and exported from Samsun (87,300), the largest town on the coast, and from Trabzon (Trebizond, 52,700), which has the best harbour and was originally a Greek colony. Vines are grown everywhere on the lower hill slopes, but olives are limited more or less to the drier west. Gíresun (20,000) cans cherries from the neighbouring orchards.

The Pontus mountains provide timber and hazel nuts, the latter being sent out from Samsun and Trabzon. Rize (22,300) is the collecting centre and port for tea. Cattle are reared on Alpine pastures, and at higher levels there are summer pastures for sheep and goats. Samsun is the outlet for hides, wool and mohair, and has also fruit and fish canning (anchovies from the Black Sea), and light engineering. It is the only port in the east with railway communications inland. Trabzon has copper works producing blister copper from deposits in the neighbourhood and from Hopa (5000).

One of the few industrial regions in Turkey is in the west, around the

[*Courtesy of the Turkish Embassy.*

FIG. 122.—Turkey: the Sariyar dam on the Sakarya river, about 85 miles (136 km) west of Ankara. This is the most recent hydro-power plant in Turkey and supplies current to a large area, including Ankara and Eskíşehír. The impounded lake is 25 miles (40 km) long. The piece of the Anatolian plateau shown has a surface cover of basaltic lava gullied by winter torrents.

Ereğli–Zonguldak–Amasra coalfield. The development is being undertaken by the State, which controls all the industries there. Zonguldak (54,100) is the centre of mining and has coke ovens, steel works and chemical manufacture, including fertilisers. Ereğli (8850) has new blast furnaces and steelworks and is growing rapidly. Amasra is still only a small village with chemical works. Karabük (31,500), south of the coalfield, had the first blast furnaces and modern steel works in Turkey, and is developing a heavy engineering industry. Zonguldak is the chief port and has railway communication with Ankara. It has a poor harbour; in fact, the absence of good harbours and the difficulty of communications inland have restricted the growth of large towns all along the north coast of Turkey.

2. Western Turkey

(a) *The Marmara lowlands*, including the Sakarya valley, are chiefly agricultural, for they have fertile soils and a climate which approaches the true Mediterranean. Wheat and potatoes are basic crops, and there is a large production of tobacco, sunflowers and rice, the last in irrigated land around several lakes south of the Sea of Marmara. Vines and olives are important, and there are plums, mulberries and almonds. On the higher lands, especially the ridges running to the Bosphorus and Dardanelles, sheep are reared in great numbers, and cattle are herded in the plains. Chrome is quarried in small quantities near Bursa; and at Çamdag, east of Izmít, a large iron ore deposit supplies the blast furnaces of Karabük and Ereğli.

Western Turkey as a whole was well developed by the Greeks, who formed a majority of the population until their expulsion in 1923. The towns of the region show more signs of industrialisation than most others in Turkey, although manufactures are based primarily on local agricultural raw materials. Light engineering, now found in all the larger towns, is an exception; it had its origin in the iron and steel produced since 1923 in Karabük (*see* Fig. 121). The largest town is Bursa (153,600), one of the country's chief centres of the wool textile industry. It also has olive-oil pressing, tobacco processing, and manufactures of cement, carpets, cottons and silk, the last based on the growth of mulberries. Adapazari (80,100) and Izmít (73,700) have paper and cellulose industries; and Canakkale (19,500), which commands the passage of the Dardanelles, is a wool collecting town. Bandirma (28,900), south of the Sea of Marmara, produces borax from local boracite deposits.

(b) *Turkey-in-Europe* is an expanse of steppe on which sheep are reared in the drier parts, cattle in the wetter, and where wheat is grown extensively, with poor yields. The plain is drained by tributaries of the Maritsa, and in their valleys conditions for agriculture are better; here there are large areas under maize, sugar beet, tobacco and sunflowers, and plum trees (for prunes) on the slopes. The marshes of the lower Maritsa have been reclaimed for rice cultivation. The chief town and market of the region is Edírne (Adrianople, 31,900). Helped by irrigation from artesian wells, the Plain of Thrace is gradually becoming a very well-cultivated region, but it is more important as part of the boundary zone protecting the European side of the Straits than as the food-producing hinterland of Istanbul, which is situated at its eastern end.

For over 1500 years the Straits have been guarded by Istanbul (Byzantium; Constantinople), a key point where land routes are crossed by sea

routes (*see* Figs. 119 and 123). The ancient Greek colony of Byzantium
was chosen in 330 by Constantine as the site of the capital of the Roman
Empire of the East (*see* Fig. 124). His new city, Constantinople, on the
harbour of the Golden Horn, protected to the south by cliffs and to the
west by strong walls, was an almost impregnable fortress. The Byzantine
Empire remained the eastern bastion of Christendom for over a thousand
years until at last, after two long sieges and the failure of the West to come
to its aid, the city fell to the Turks in 1453—one of the most critical vic-
tories in European history, for it led to the domination of south-eastern
Europe by the Ottoman Turks. Constantinople was made the capital of
the Ottoman Empire and held that position until 1924, when Kemal
Atatürk moved his capital to Ankara.

When Constantinople was the Turkish capital, the overland trade route
from central Europe to Asia Minor was important, but the Turkish withdrawal from the Balkans and the removal of the capital reduced its value.

FIG. 123.—Turkey: communications.

Renamed Istanbul, the city lost much of its economic pre-eminence.
Fifty years ago it had a population of over a million but when it lost metropolitan status this fell to 700,000. Since 1924 the city has been modernised
and is today the greatest industrial area in Turkey. Besides acting as an
entrepôt for the whole of northern Turkey, it has cotton and woollen
textile and carpet manufactures, light engineering, leather, pottery, paper,
cement, food-processing and shipbuilding industries. The population of
Istanbul—including the suburbs of Galata and Beyoğlu on the northern
side of the Golden Horn, and Üsküdar on the Asiatic side of the Bosphorus—has grown since 1960 to 1,500,000, and is still increasing. It is
more than twice the size of Ankara, the next largest city.

Istanbul and Thrace remain a part of Turkey chiefly as a result of an
"accident of history." As a reward for entering the First World War on
the side of Great Britain and France, Russia in 1914 was promised a strip
of Turkish territory which was to include the Turkish Black Sea coast-

lands and the Bosphorus, including Constantinople. But Russia took no part in the negotiations which followed the Allied victory in 1918, for it was torn by a revolution which commenced the previous year. By the negotiations, the Aegean coastlands of Turkey were to be given to Greece, the southern coastlands to Italy, and the Straits were to become a "special zone," for the time being not allocated to any country. Turkey was to have been reduced to a tiny state on the plateau of Anatolia, but this never happened.

The proposed arrangements were upset by Kemal Atatürk, the "father of the Turks," who in 1923 led his people against the Greeks and drove them from the Aegean lands; and he also forced the occupying forces of Britain, France and Italy to withdraw from the whole of Anatolia. By the Treaty of Lausanne, Turkey's sovereignty over Asia Minor was recognised and the country was given control of the Straits, as well as of the

[*Courtesy of the Turkish Embassy.*

FIG. 124.—Turkey: Istanbul, the Suleymaniye mosque. This was built in the sixteenth century, the best period of Turkish architecture, and shows marked Byzantine characteristics. It is now used as a museum.

small hinterland now known as Turkey-in-Europe. By the same treaty it was agreed that an exchange of populations should take place between Greece and Turkey, so as to make the two countries more homogenous in race. Exceptions were made for many Turkish tobacco farmers in the Greek part of Thrace and for Greek merchants in Istanbul. About 1½ million Greeks were moved into Macedonia and replaced by 700,000 Turks, an exchange, be it noted, more favourable to Turkey; but in both countries the influx of homeless people caused great misery and distress. During the Cyprus crisis there were further expulsions of Greeks from Istanbul.

(c) *The Aegean hinterland* is agriculturally the most valuable and productive part of Turkey. The region shows a succession of broad river valleys between horsts. The floors of the valleys are formed of fertile alluvium mixed with Tertiaries, and the lower slopes of the horsts have enough soil for tree crops. Cultivation is zoned and there is much terracing. At lowest levels are crops of wheat, maize, tobacco, cotton, sesame, flax and hemp; and on reclaimed marshland near the mouths of rivers rice is important. The crops are continued in terraced fields up the slopes, which they share with vines and olives in the north, and with vines and figs in the south. The Menderes, Gediz and Simav rivers have been dammed for irrigation, and citrus fruits are being produced in increasing amounts. Higher up the slopes forests of valonia oak yield acorns, and nuts are gathered from hazel plantations; and still higher, on the horst plateaus, sheep and goats are reared. In some valleys the opium poppy is cultivated for morphine, its derivative, and the production is under strict governmental control; in the valleys of the İzmír district there are mulberry groves, and at Çeşme (3700) a start has been made with tea plantations. Bananas are grown in the extreme south of the region.

Mineral deposits in the Aegean lands are of little importance except for the lignite field around Kütahya (40,000), on the edge of the plateau of Anatolia. This is the largest lignite deposit in Turkey. It is made into briquettes for domestic fuel; fed raw into furnaces for the generation of electricity; and is being used in a new chemical industry in Kütahya to produce tar and lubricating or fuel oils. Kütahya is also a centre for the manufacture of ceramics. Mercury is mined near İzmír; lead–zinc at Balya (1700), a hamlet north of Balikesír; and surface deposits of chrome at Fethíye (7700) and Eskíşehír (153,200), the second largest town in the region.

The chief occupations and industries are concerned with the agricultural products. Small, seedless grapes are dried as sultanas in most valleys, and exported from İzmír; figs are dried and packed at Aydin (35,700) in the Menderes valley; tobacco is processed in most towns; and oil is pressed from olives, sunflower, sesame and linseed. The textile manufacture was started by the Greeks and is important for cottons in İzmír, Eskíşehír and Kazilli (36,600), and for woollens in the same towns and in Manísa (59,200). As a whole, western Turkey is the chief textile region in Turkey.

İzmír (370,900), the third city of Turkey, is the regional capital and chief port. In fact there is no other port on the Aegean coast with more than local importance; Burhaníye (10,300), Fethíye (7600) and Kuşadasi (7000) are the next largest. Although from a map the Aegean coast appears to have many good harbours, this is not so; most of the inlets have steep sides, and the rivers which flow in at their heads are obstructed by marshy deltas. İzmír is an exception; situated on a deep harbour carved out in a horst just south of the Gediz delta, it has good rail and road communications inland. Its position between the Gediz and Menderes valleys has made it the market for their products. It manufactures cottons, woollens, silk, carpets, soap and tobacco; has food processing and fruit canning, and packing sheds for sultanas and figs; and is the centre of a small but important wine trade. It also has light engineering, boat building and ship repairing, and is the headquarters of a sponge-fishing industry. Balikesír (61,000) is the collecting centre for the Simav valley, Manísa for the Gediz, and Aydin for the Menderes.

The inner end of the Aegean lands is marked by a line of towns at the heads of the valleys, serving also the western portion of the Anatolian plateau. Besides being collecting centres for local produce, they are also minor cotton manufacturing towns. They are Eskíşehír, Kütahya, Usak (30,000), Afyon (39,000) and Denízli (49,000).

3. The Mediterranean coastlands

The modern development of Turkey's southern coastlands is really just commencing. In the forests of the Taurus there is lumbering for cedar and pine; but ruthless deforestation in the past has reduced the stands, and new plantations of young trees are carefully conserved. The vanished forests were replaced by garrigue on which sheep and goats are reared by transhumant shepherds, but many areas are bare karst. The coastal plains are too narrow for much development except where they widen in the Antalya, Cilician and Orontes deltaic plains. Much of these lowlands is marshy and is being reclaimed by drainage schemes which are also irrigation systems. The river Seyhan, which flows through the Cilician Plain, has been dammed for irrigation and the generation of hydro-electricity. Maize and autumn-sown wheat are the chief cereals, and increasing quantities of rice are grown in the drained swamps. Sesame (for oil) and vines (for sultanas and larger raisins) are grown throughout the plains, and olives occur everywhere on the slopes. Cotton growing is especially important in the Seyhan part of the Cilician Plain; this area is well irrigated and grows most of Turkey's cotton crop. Cotton is produced also in Hatay, that is, around the Orontes, again by irrigation. Sugar cane grows behind Adana.

The largest city in the region and the fourth in Turkey is Adana (230,000), the market for the Cilician Plain. It has easy communication to the interior via the Cilician Gates, and is connected by railway to eastern Turkey and the Levant (see Fig. 123). Adana has cotton manufacture, cottonseed and olive-oil presses, soap-making, sugar refining, and light engineering, including the assembly of electrical goods. Its port is Mersín (68,500), which deals also with the export of chrome from Güleman and copper from Erganí. It is connected by pipeline to the Raman oilfield and has a refinery. In the east of the Cilician Plain are Maras (54,600) and Ceyhan (32,000) on the river Ceyhan. They are in an irrigated district producing cotton, and are growing rapidly. Tarsus (53,500), between Adana and Mersín, is another expanding town also helped by irrigation. It has newly-established cotton mills.

The chief town in the Antalyan (Pamphylian) Plain is Antalya (51,000). There are no large rivers in the plain, and opportunities for irrigation are limited. Its main products are wheat, sultanas, olive oil and sesame. In the fertile and well-watered Plain of Orontes there is cultivation of maize, cotton and tobacco; and on the surrounding slopes there are olive groves and large herds of sheep. The largest town is Iskenderun (Alexandretta, 64,000), at one time the major port in that corner of the Mediterranean, but now outstripped by Mersín. The administrative centre is Antakya (Antioch, 46,000), which has manufactures of cottons, carpets and silks.

4. The Anatolian plateau

Although the Anatolian plateau forms the heart of Turkey and contains the capital city, it is a region of meagre resources, of pastoralism and extensive cultivation of cereals. In the middle of the plateau is the arid, saline basin containing Lake Tuz (Tuz Gölü), a region of semi-nomadism, sheep and goats. Surrounding this is arid steppe, whose inhabitants eke out a livelihood by the sale of wool, mohair and skins from their flocks. This is the region of the Angora goat and the fat-tailed sheep. The best areas lie in a belt around the edges of the plateau, especially along the foot of the Taurus and towards the Aegean lands, and in the Kizil and Yesil river valleys. Here wheat is grown by extensive methods of cultivation and mechanisation, side by side with primitive, low-yield, peasant farming. Irrigation is not easy, for the rivers flow in deep, entrenched valleys, but systems, mostly small, but more ambitious along the Kizil and Yesil, have been constructed and are being extended; and these have resulted in large crops of sugar beet, fodder crops and the development of mixed farming. One of the chief aims in the current Five-year Development Plan is to increase the agricultural output of the plateau at the expense of pastoralism, and some progress has been made. But complete transformation is a long-term process, and is not possible at all over a big proportion of the region. The best results so far have been around Ankara in the north, Konya in the south and in the better-watered east where irrigation is more feasible. In the Development Plan, too, the towns of the plateau have been singled out for industrialisation, and cotton and woollen manufactures, light engineering and chemical industries have been established.

The towns for the most part lie along the borders of the plateau, in the agricultural sector. The western region is within the zones of influence of the border towns of the Aegean lands, already mentioned. The largest elsewhere are Ankara, Konya (122,700), Kayseri (103,000), Sívas (94,000), Ísparta (36,200) and Ereğli (32,000). Ankara (646,200), the second city of Turkey, was chosen as capital after the Revolution of 1919–22. It was only a small town, less in size at the time than Konya, but was selected partly because it was on the site of an ancient Hittite settlement, and partly because of its central position in the western and more developed part of the plateau. It has grown rapidly as the administrative and commercial centre of the country, and has textile, tobacco, printing, light engineering and electrical industries. Its development, however, like that of Madrid, is somewhat artificial.

5. Eastern Turkey

The mountainous character and the harsh climate of most of the region are not conducive to great economic development; nevertheless, the fertile soils and the presence of available water supplies in the many river valleys, together with a more favourable climate at lower altitudes, have led to the growth of prosperous farming communities and some large towns, especially in the south of the region. On the whole, however, eastern Turkey is more pastoral than agricultural, and its plateaus and mountains are the home of transhumant and even nomadic shepherds of sheep and goats, and occasionally, in the extreme south, of camels. Some of the towns, such as Erzerum in the north and Gaziantep and Díyarbakir in the south, serve as exchange markets for the wool, hair, skins and yoghourt brought in by the nomads.

Most of the agriculture is of a subsistence type, but along the Euphrates and Tigris valleys there is cultivation of wheat, rye, potatoes, fruit, and, in the south, cotton and rice, the last two by irrigation. Eastern Turkey has many mineral resources, most of which are only beginning to be exploited. Chrome is mined in large quantities in the Güleman district, copper ore near Erganí (8400), iron ore at Elbistan (10,300) and Dívrígi (8900), asbestos in the vicinity of Kars (32,000), and lead–zinc at Keban; and petroleum comes from the Raman field (see Fig. 123). All of these except asbestos are exported from Mersín on the Mediterranean.

The largest town and market in the highlands proper is Erzerum (91,200) on the river Aras (Araxes). It is in a region which suffers from earthquakes. In 1939, Erzíncan (36,500), in the upper Euphrates valley to the west, suffered severe damage and loss of life, and in 1966, Varto, a small town about 50 miles (80 km) south, was completely demolished. The two branches of the Euphrates and their tributaries provide irrigation water at several places, and this has helped the growth of Elâzig (60,500), Malatya (84,100) and Gazíantep (125,500), the last the largest city in eastern Turkey. Dams on the river at Elâzig and Malatya impound water for irrigation and for a hydro-electric station which supplies power to Gazíantep and Díyarbakir, for their textile and food-processing industries. Díyarbakir (80,700) is on the Tigris, which is also used for irrigation and may in the future be harnessed for hydro-electricity. In this southern part of eastern Turkey, the Euphrates and Tigris valleys are elongated oases in a region of dry steppe, where nomadic pastoralism is still a normal way of life.

STUDY QUESTIONS

1. Analyse the factors which have influenced the site and importance of Istanbul.
2. Explain how relief and climate influence man's use of the land in Turkey.

3. Attempt a division of Turkey into natural regions and justify the division you make. A sketch map is essential.

4. Make a comparative study of Istanbul and Ankara.

5. With the aid of a sketch map, describe and explain the distribution and density of population in Turkey.

6. Write a concise geographical account of *either* (a) that part of Turkey which is drained to the Aegean Sea, *or* (b) the Anatolian plateau.

7. From a geographical standpoint, compare and contrast the northern and southern coastlands of Turkey in as many ways as possible.

8. Make a critical survey of the development of industry in Turkey in recent times.

Chapter XXIII
CYPRUS

THE Republic of Cyprus (3584 sq. miles; 9280 sq. km) is the third largest island in the Mediterranean, coming after Sicily and Sardinia. It is situated in the Eastern basin, at roughly equal distances from the coasts of Turkey to the north and Syria to the east; the headland of Cape Kormakiti in Cyprus is 44 miles (70 km) from Cape Anamur in Asia Minor, and that of Cape St Andreas 69 miles (110 km) from Latakia in Syria. The island has an irregular shape; its greatest length is 141 miles (226 km) and its maximum width 60 miles (96 km), but while it has an average width of just over 40 miles (64 km) for the greater part of its extent, about 34 degrees E. it suddenly narrows to less than 10 miles (16 km), and from there it sends out a long, narrow tongue of land 46 miles (74 km) in length terminating in Cape St Andreas.

PHYSICAL ASPECTS

PHYSICAL FEATURES AND STRUCTURE

The greater part of the island is occupied by two mountain ranges with a general east–west trend, separated in the west by a broad plain (*see* Fig. 125). Almost the whole of the southern portion of Cyprus is filled by the Troödos range, the highest summit of which is Mount Olympus (6406 ft, 1953 m). Other lofty peaks are Adelphi (5305 ft, 1617 m), Papoutsa (5124 ft 1562 m) and Machaira (4674 ft 1425 m). In the west subordinate ranges extend on all sides from the central mountain mass, terminating along the south-west and west coasts in steep cliffs and headlands. Eastwards the Troödos decrease in altitude, and end in the isolated peak of Santa Croce (Stavrovouni) (2260 ft, 672 m). Extending for more than 100 miles (160 km) in an unbroken ridge along the north of Cyprus is a range known in the west as the Kyrenia mountains and in the east as the Carpas (Karpas) mountains. These are less elevated than the Troödos; the highest peak in the Kyrenia is Buffavento (3135 ft, 956 m), and the Karpas rarely exceed 2000 ft (600 m). The notable feature of these northern ranges is their continuous and unbroken character; they consist throughout of a narrow, rugged, rocky ridge, and descend abruptly on the north to a very narrow coastal plain and on the south to a broad lowland.

This plain, known as the Mesaoria or Messaria, extends across the island between the two mountain masses from the bay of Famagusta in the east to that of Morphou in the west, a distance of nearly 60 miles (96 km), with a breadth varying from 10 to 20 miles (16–32 km). The plain is undulating, and is watered by a number of intermittent streams from the mountains north and south. The chief streams are the Pedias and the Yalias, which follow roughly parallel courses eastwards.

Structurally, Cyprus lies in the continuation belt of the folded mountain-arc of the Anti-Taurus system of Asia Minor. The Kyrenia–Karpas Range is formed by the oldest rocks in the island, consisting chiefly of massive limestones and marble of Cretaceous age, with occasional masses of igneous rock. The Troödos is a great igneous dome of diorite, basalt and serpentine forced up in Tertiary times. The northern range is flanked by Eocene sandstones and shales, and similar rocks occur around the Troödos. Overlying these in patches, and reaching their greatest development on the south side of the Troödos are Oligocene marls. Pliocene and later beds cover the central plain and occur at intervals around the coast.

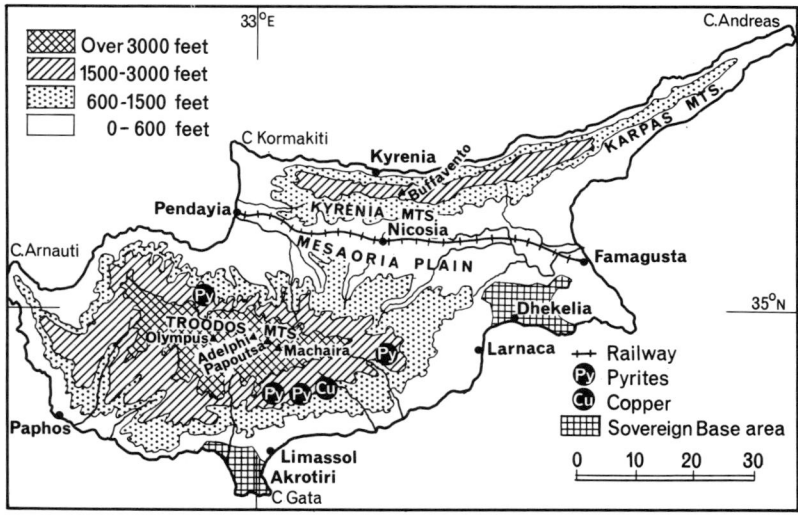

FIG. 125.—Cyprus.

The Pliocene is of marine origin and rests unconformably on all the older beds, including some of the igneous rocks, thus proving that the final folding of the northern range and the volcanic outbursts which led to the basalts of the Troödos were probably of Miocene, that is, mid-Tertiary, times. Fossils of mammals of the early Quaternary have been found in caves in the Kyrenia mountains. Earthquakes of slight intensity are common.

CLIMATE AND VEGETATION

Although Cyprus with its hot, dry summers and mild, wet winters may be said to have a typically Mediterranean climate, there are in its small area some striking variations from what might be considered averages of temperature and rainfall. The mean annual temperature of Cyprus as a whole is about 69° F (20·6° C), the mean maximum being 78° F (25·6° C), the mean minimum 57° F (13·9° C). How misleading these figures are may be seen from the following. Mean temperatures in Nicosia range from 50° F (10·0° C) in January to 90° F (32·2° C) in July; and summer temperatures in the middle of the Mesaoria often reach over 100° F (37·8° C). So much of the island consists of land considerably more than 1000 ft (300 m) in elevation, however, that temperatures in the mountains both in summer and winter are lower in accordance with altitude and may vary considerably from the averages given above.

The mean annual rainfall of Cyprus is about 19 in., but again there are wide differences between highland and lowland; all, however, show the same characteristic of complete summer drought. Precipitation during the months June, July and August is negligible and is usually recorded as "nil." The highest parts of the Troödos may have more than 40 in. annually, but in parts of the Mesaoria the total barely reaches 15 in. a year. Most of the highlands and coastal plains have an annual precipitation of from 20 to 25 in.; Nicosia has 20 in., over 80% falling in the winter half of the year. In winter a centre of low pressure sometimes develops to the south of Cyprus, causing stormy weather; at such times the *levanter*, a strong, blustery wind, may blow from the east.

It is remarkable that in antiquity Cyprus was celebrated for its forests which long supplied the Greek monarchs of Egypt with timber for their fleets, for today the island has a continuous covering of trees only on the higher slopes of the Troödos mountains. At one time both mountain ranges were clothed with oak, cypress and pine, and there were considerable stretches of forest in the Mesaoria. Ruthless cutting for timber and fuel, and the constant ravages by goats, have reduced the forest-clad areas so much that the central plain is now bare and treeless, most of the Kyrenia–Karpas Range is karst with a patchy cover of garrigue, and natural forest is confined to the Troödos. Forests cover 670 square miles (1740 sq. km), 19% of the island. The disappearance of the forests naturally affected the rivers, which are mostly mere torrents, drying up in summer. Even the Pedias, which is the largest, may not reach the sea in summer, and its stagnant waters form unhealthy marshes. Re-afforestation of the lower slopes of both mountain masses in recent years has been moderately successful, but is hindered in the northern range by the porosity of the surface rocks. The chief trees are the cypress, cedar, carob, olive, Aleppo pine, Corsican pine, eucalyptus and stone pine, the last two being recent additions.

The soils of the lowlands are extremely fertile, and they are thus very productive where water is available. The northern and southern margins of the Mesaoria are enriched by silts washed down from the mountains, and these are the areas also where there is most surface water from springs and mountain torrents. They are the chief arable regions. Much of the Mesaoria, however, remains uncultivated because of the porosity of the soil, the summer drought and the absence of irrigation facilities; it is garrigue-covered and used for pasture. One of the problems of Cyprus is soil erosion. Along the south coast the sediments washed down by winter torrents block the lower courses of streams, causing marshes and breeding

FIG. 126.—Cyprus: land conservation works in the Tylliria area. Bench terracing is the main work, covering 2500 donums (1 donum = 100 sq. m; so 40 donum = *c.* 1 acre). The reclaimed land will be irrigated from the Pomos dam, completed in 1967.

places for malarial mosquitoes. Much reclamation has taken place (*see* Fig. 126), notably near Larnaca and Limassol; and throughout the island the threat of malaria has been reduced to a minimum.

HISTORY AND PEOPLE

Cyprus was celebrated in the ancient world for its copper mines. The name of the metal is derived from *aes Cyprium* or *aes Cuprium*, by which it was known to the Romans. As one of the chief sources of copper, Cyprus was of peculiar importance during the Bronze Age, that is, roughly 3000–1000 B.C., but although the island was influenced in turn by the civilisations of Egypt, Crete, Assyria and Phoenicia, it never became itself a centre of Bronze Age culture. Near the end of this period the Greeks established colonies at Salamis, Curium, Paphos, Soli and Kyrenia, and the Phoenicians at Citium, Amathus and Tamassus; and in spite of invasions, first by the Assyrians and later by the Persians, the island remained Graeco–Phoenician until in 333 B.C. it was incorporated into the empire of Alexander the Great. On his death it passed to the Ptolemies of Egypt and remained in their possession until 58 B.C., when it was annexed

by Rome. In early Christian times Cyprus was a refuge from the perse-
cutions which followed the martyrdom of Stephen in Palestine (Acts vii.
56–59), and in A.D. 46 it was visited by Paul (Acts xiii. 4).

After the division of the Roman Empire in the fourth century, Cyprus
became part of the Byzantine Empire, and remained so for more than
seven hundred years. In the last part of this period, however, the Byzantine princes in charge of the island became virtually independent of
Constantinople and tyrannised its people. In 1191, one of these princes
ill-treated the Crusaders of Richard I of England, who drove him from
the island and sold it to the Knights Templars. From them it passed
first to the King of Jerusalem, then until 1489 to a succession of Frankish
kings, and finally through marriage to the Venetian republic. For 82
years the Cypriots were sorely oppressed by Venetian governors and their
lot was made worse by an invasion of the Ottoman Turks. The Venetians
capitulated in 1571, and from then until 1878 Cyprus was ruled by the
Turks. For these three centuries the history of Cyprus is one of cruelty and
repression, of persecution and massacre of its Christian people by their
Muslim overlords. In 1878, however, the Turkish sultan, in return for
help against the Russians, assigned the island of Cyprus to Britain.

The island was a welcome addition to the British Empire, for it is stra-
tegically situated near the entrance of the Suez Canal; and, as in Malta, the
entry of the British marked the beginning of a period of new economic
and social advance for Cyprus. Reservoirs and irrigation systems were
constructed, soil conservation, land reclamation and re-afforestation
schemes introduced, and improved techniques in agriculture developed.
The building of military bases gave employment to the Cypriots, and the
money spent on their upkeep added to the new prosperity of the island.
Many tithes and taxes were abolished; Greek Cypriots, who outnumbered
their Turkish compatriots by four to one, were for the first time admitted
to positions in local government; and separate Christian and Muslim education boards were established. By 1925, when Cyprus became a Crown
Colony, the island had a standard of living higher than at any previous
time in its history.

After the Second World War changed political conditions reduced the
authority of the British in the Mediterranean, but Cyprus was still of
sufficient strategic value to warrant the continuance there of military
bases, even after the loss of control of the Suez Canal and the British withdrawal from Malta. Now, however, a political movement was born in
the island, in which Greek Cypriots called for *Enosis*, that is, political
union with Greece, with a complete evacuation of the British from
Cyprus. The Turkish Cypriots, who formed 18% of the population,
opposed the scheme so violently that civil war broke out in 1954.
Hostilities continued for five years, with the British forces and later the
United Nations trying to act as peacemakers. In 1961 Cyprus became an
independent republic under the joint sponsorship of Greece and Turkey,
but it remained a member of the British Commonwealth, and Britain

was allowed to retain two military enclaves totalling 100 square miles (260 sq. km) and known as the Sovereign Base Areas of Akrotiri and Dhekelia; these two areas, situated on the south coast, are not included in the republic.

The population of Cyprus numbers approximately 588,000, with an average density of 164 persons per square mile. Over 80% are Greek-speaking Christians; most of the remainder are Turkish-speaking Sunni Muslims. Almost everywhere the two peoples live in mixed communities; only in the west of the Mesaoria is there a definite Turkish majority. This mixture of the two elements is an obstacle to segregation, which was suggested during the Enosis struggle. The Greek-speaking people have been affected by the long succession of invaders; Phoenicians, Greeks and Egyptians endowed the original Cypriots with their racial characteristics, but these have been very much modified by incursions, some for long periods, of Assyrians, Persians, Romans, Byzantines, Franks and Venetians. Throughout history the Cypriot has shown lack of originality; he is conservative, accepting innovations such as the modern techniques of agriculture and industry only reluctantly. The Cypriot Turks retain the language, customs and traditions of their forefathers in Asia Minor, and remain distinct in culture from the Greek element, a distinction which is emphasised by the contrasting philosophies of Islam and Christianity.

Most of the people of Cyprus are grouped in nucleated villages and small towns. Their houses are usually of stone, two-storeyed and with flat roofs, and arranged irregularly along narrow, winding streets. With the exception of modern warehouses and factories in the larger towns, there is little impressive architecture anywhere. The Turks destroyed many of the fine churches built by the Franks or turned them into mosques or grain-stores.

THE ECONOMY

In spite of water difficulties (see Fig. 127) Cyprus is the most thoroughly cultivated land in the eastern Mediterranean. Approximately 1 million acres, about 43% of the island, is classed as farmland, and upwards of 40% of the active population is engaged in some kind of farm work. Many of the methods and appliances used are still primitive, but imported techniques and machinery are fast displacing them. It has been very difficult, however, to win the average peasant from his inveterate prejudice against new implements and fresh seeds, and to convert him to rotation of crops, artificial manures and clean land. There are two well-organised irrigation systems, both constructed by the British. One, near Famagusta, provides perennial irrigation; the other, a larger installation in the Mesaoria, uses the stored flood waters of the Pedias and Yalias rivers for summer irrigation.

Most of the arable land, especially in the Mesaoria, is given over to barley and wheat; Cyprus is the only Mediterranean land in which barley is the principal grain crop. In the regions of summer irrigation vegetables

[*Courtesy of the Public Information Office, Nicosia.*

FIG. 127.—Cyprus: Argaka Magounda dam, near Paphos. Built in 1963–64, its
impounded waters are used for irrigation by both Greek and Turkish communities, and also for replenishing the Limni aquifer. The picture shows the effects
of water erosion and dissection in the south-west Troödos mountains.

and cash crops such as cotton, flax and hemp are grown, and where perennial irrigation is possible there are groves of citrus fruits (oranges, lemons,
grape-fruit) and tobacco plantations. Early potatoes, mainly from the
southern coastal plain, are another good cash crop. Vines and olives cover
many of the lower hillsides, and carob beans are produced for fodder, for
use as food by the poorer peasants and for export to the confectionery
trade. There has been a notable increase in recent years in the export of
wine; the native Cyprus wines are strong and pure, but faulty methods of
storage until recently made them unpalatable. Today Cyprus is becoming
noted for its wine of a sherry type.

Animal husbandry is important in Cyprus. In the agricultural regions, where fodder and vegetable waste are available, cattle (35,000) and pigs (44,000) are the chief animals. On those parts of the Mesaoria which are too dry or too saline for cultivation, and on hill slopes above 1000 ft (300 m), sheep (420,000) and goats (190,000) are reared in large numbers. Hillslope grazing, especially by goats, is carefully controlled as part of forest conservation. There are considerable numbers of asses and horses, and mules are reared as draught animals on farms or for pack transport in the hills; there is also a small export of Cyprus mules to the Levant, where they have a high reputation.

After agriculture, mining is the most important occupation in Cyprus and provides between 30 and 35% of the island's exports. The chief minerals are iron pyrites, copper pyrites and copper ore, in the Troödos igneous dome. The mining areas lie to the south-east and north-west of the mountain mass; from the former the ores are exported via Limassol and Larnaca, and from the latter via Pendayia on the bay of Morphou. Because of lack of fuel the pyrites are exported raw, mainly to the United Kingdom and the U.S.A. Some of the copper ore is treated and exported as a concentrate. Deposits of asbestos are exploited in the Troödos in the immediate hinterland of Limassol, and there is a small output of chromite (chromium and iron) from the same region. In some parts of the southern flanks of the Troödos the overlying grey marls have been metamorphosed by igneous dykes; the resultant coloured earths, chiefly ochre and umber, are obtained by open-cast mining and exported for the manufacture of pigments. Marble is quarried in the Kyrenia range and is used for building in the island; little is exported. Gypsum occurs extensively in the Tertiaries of the Mesaoria and the Karpas Range; it is easy to extract, and large quantities are exported, either as unburnt gypsum from the Karpas or as plaster of Paris from Limassol and Larnaca, mainly to the Levant lands. Salt is obtained by solar evaporation from practically inexhaustible salt-water lagoons at Larnaca and Limassol.

Manufacturing industries are on a small scale and are mostly related to the agricultural products. They include olive-oil pressing, cigarette-making, fruit drying (chiefly raisins), soap boiling and the bottling of wines and spirits. There is a growing textile industry, local raw materials being used in the manufacture of woollens, cottons and linen. Craft or domestic industries are important throughout the island. The chief of these is the button manufacture which is carried on extensively in the people's homes. Craft industries usually depend entirely on raw materials obtained locally; the button industry of Cyprus is peculiar in that it is based on the dom nut or vegetable ivory, which is a native of the Sudan and has to be imported. The women of Cyprus have long been noted for their lace-making and embroidery, and their products find a ready market in the growing number of tourists who visit the island from the Levant and Egypt, and even by air from Western Europe. Off the east coast there is fishing for sponges.

Nicosia (103,700), centrally situated in the Mesaoria, is the capital and easily the largest town. It is a collecting centre and market for the products of the plain, and has most of the industries mentioned above, together with light engineering, printing and book publishing. It is connected by railway to Pendayia on the west coast and Famagusta on the east. Pendayia is little more than a rail terminal, but Famagusta (38,500), facing the Levant, handles most of the general imports and exports of Cyprus. Limassol (47,300) is the second town of the island and the chief exporter of its minerals. Larnaca (20,400), the third port, shares the mineral export, especially of gypsum and salt. Limassol and Larnaca are the chief outlets for the wines produced on the south-eastern slopes of the Troödos. The only other towns of any size in Cyprus are the ports of Paphos (10,400) in the south-west, and Kyrenia (3700) in the north.

STUDY QUESTIONS

1. Write a concise geographical account of either Cyprus or the Maltese Islands.
2. "The political problems of Cyprus are a constant menace to the island's economic stability." Which, in your opinion, are its most serious political problems, and how far is this statement justified?

Chapter XXIV

THE LEVANT LANDS. SYRIA

INTRODUCTION: THE LEVANT LANDS

THE name "Levant" (Fr. rising) has a general reference to the east or the Orient, where the sun is seen to rise. In the sixteenth century the Far East was the "High Levant" to distinguish it from the "Near Levant," which was the eastern Mediterranean and its coastlands. Today the Levant connotes the countries between Turkey and Egypt, that is, Syria, Lebanon, Jordan and Israel. They were formerly referred to as the "Near East," but nowadays they are included in the "Middle East" which comprises all the lands between the Mediterranean and Arabian Seas. The countries of the Levant, as they are at present constituted, are creations of the twentieth century, for none of them existed as independent political units prior to 1946. They began to be recognised as potential sovereign states after the Turkish domination of the Levant was broken in the First World War, for in 1919 a mandate was given to Britain to rule Palestine (Israel) and Transjordan (Jordan), and similarly to France to guide Syria and Lebanon, with a view to their ultimate self-government. The mandates were relinquished and sovereignty recognised in Syria, Lebanon and Transjordan in 1946, and in Palestine in 1948. Before 1919, the histories of individual countries in the Levant are largely indistinguishable from that of the region as a whole. For that reason, the historical summaries in succeeding chapters relate only to recent events, and the earlier history of the region is summarised below.

STRUCTURE AND RELIEF

Geologically, the Levant forms part of the region which was trapped and squeezed up by gigantic tectonic pressures exerted by proto-Asia in the north and the advancing foreland of Afro-Arabian Gondwanaland in the south (see page 13). In the north and north-west the pressures resulted in the folded mountain systems of Asia Minor and western Persia, but in the Levant the surface layers of sedimentary rocks suffered only slight wrinkling. These sedimentaries were accumulated on the foreland or basement of Archaean rocks during repeated transgressions of the dwindling Tethys Sea, and the ancient rocks resisted compression except in a very minor way. Although there was little folding, however, there was extensive faulting and dislocation near the edges of the foreland, seen best in the great rifts of the Red Sea and Dead Sea basins and in the numerous faults and rifts in Lebanon and Syria. The earth movements date from the Tertiary period, commencing in the Oligocene and continuing into the

Miocene, and in Syria there are lava outpourings which are probably of Quaternary age.

The folding was near the coast and resulted in a series of north–south mountain ranges such as the Jebel Ansariya in Syria, the Lebanon and Anti-Lebanon mountains and the Judaean platform; and there are minor folds across the Syrian plateau in the Jebel Sharqi, Jebel Buweida, Jebel Bishri and Jebel Abdul Aziz. They are all simple anticlines from which the Tertiary layers have been eroded, to disclose the underlying Cretaceous and Jurassic series. Away from the folded ranges, the Cretaceous and Tertiary strata have been little disturbed except in the Negev, where erosion has exposed a "window" of Archaean rocks. The folding was followed by faulting, mainly along two lines running roughly north–south through the upfolds and parallel to the Mediterranean coast (see Fig. 128). To the west the chief ranges are flanked by a narrow, low-lying and discontinuous coastal plain floored by recent deposits, and to the east they are backed by the relatively undisturbed Syrian plateau (see Fig. 129).

The rift valley of the Dead Sea and river Jordan is a continuation into the Levant of the fault-zone of the Red Sea. There are further dislocations northwards through Lebanon and Syria to the Amanus–Kurd Dagh rift valley in Turkey, but these are not simple continuations of the Dead Sea Rift, from which they may differ in age. The valley between the Lebanon and Anti-Lebanon mountains has a fault only on the western side, and this fault is continued northwards through the Jebel Ansariya until a parallel fault along the edge of the Syrian plateau completes another rift valley, El Ghab, through which flows the lower river Orontes. Transverse faults have produced gaps through the limestone ridges, for example, between the Jebel Ansariya and the Lebanon mountains, and in the Plain of Esdraelon between the Lebanon mountains and the hills of Galilee. The dislocation caused by faulting is greatest in the Dead Sea rift; the floor of the sea is 2598 ft (800 m) *below* sea-level, and the sides of the valley rise steeply on both sides to about 3000 ft (925 m) *above* sea-level. In the Jebel Ansariya and Lebanon mountains, faulting has resulted in steep scarp slopes on the downthrow side (see Fig. 130).

In many places the faulting was accompanied by outpourings of basaltic lavas. These occurred frequently from Pliocene to Quaternary times, and built up plateaus, the largest of which is the great dome of Jebel Druze, over 5600 ft (1723 m) high. Smaller lava sheets occur in the Akkar plateau between the Jebel Ansariya and the Lebanon mountains, between Hama and Aleppo, and in north-east Syria. The main area of vulcanicity stretches from southern Syria across Jordan into Arabia. The older lavas, such as those of the Pliocene in the Hauran, have weathered into a thin, boulder-strewn soil, but those of more recent eruptions in the Jebel Druze and the Leja and Safa regions have not had sufficient time to break down into soil, and remain barren and desolate except in a few moister districts. Lava streams from the Hauran eruptions penetrated the Jordan valley, and impounded Lakes Huleh and Tiberias. The lava barrier at the exit of

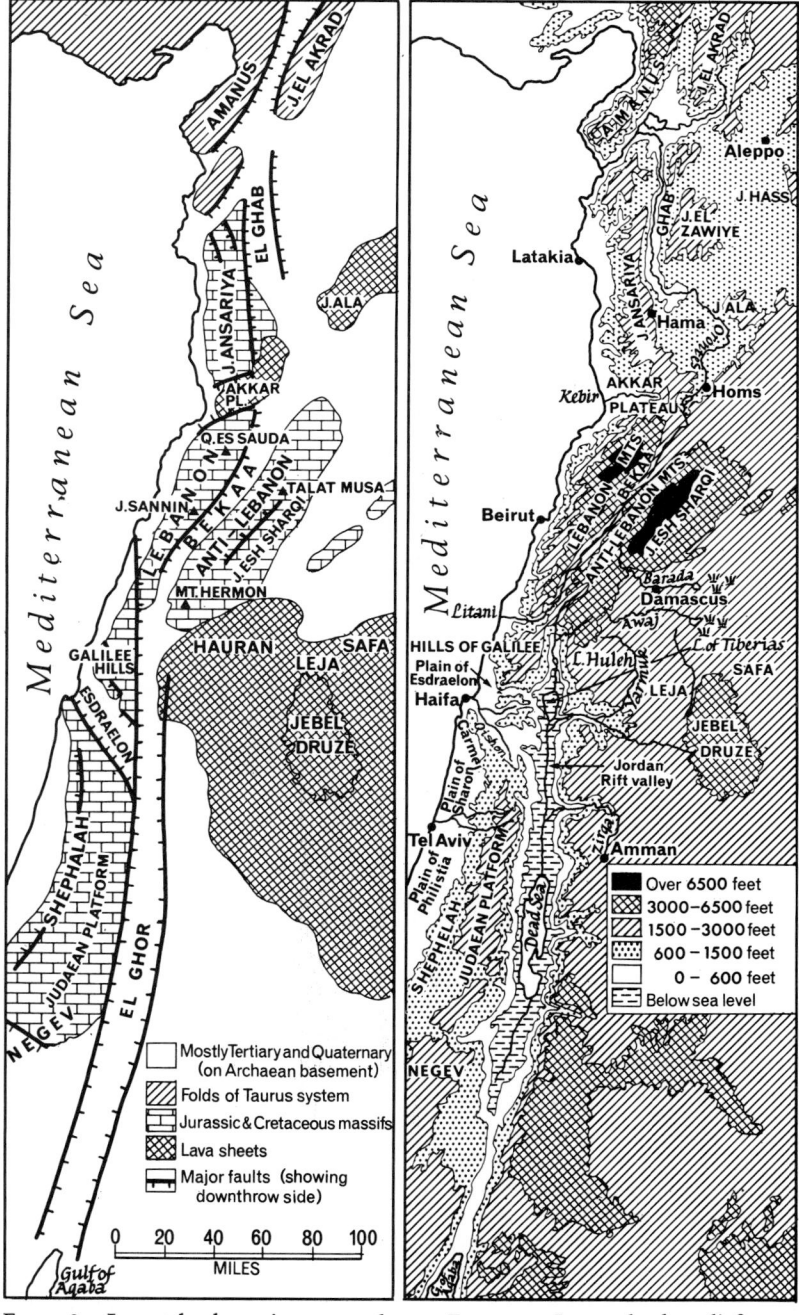

FIG. 128.—Levant lands: main structural features.

FIG. 129.—Levant lands: relief.

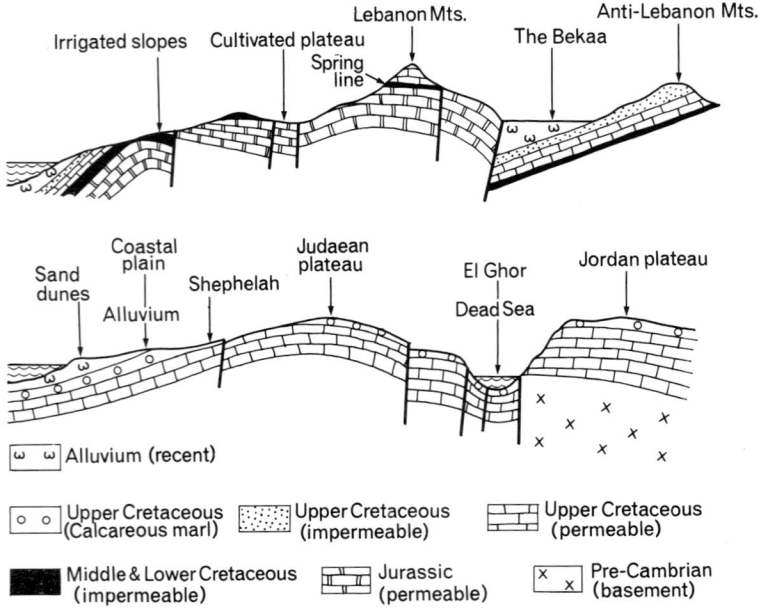

FIG. 130.—Sections across: (a) Lebanon; (b) Israel and Jordan (*based on Fisher*).

Lake Huleh has been lowered by blasting and the lake drained for cultivation. Earth movements along the lines of eruption have not yet ceased;
from time to time there are slight earthquakes such as the one mentioned
at the Crucifixion (Matt. xxvii. 51).

CLIMATE

Details of the climates of the separate countries of the Levant are given
later. Here a general picture is attempted of the outstanding climatic
features of the region as a whole.

The coastlands of the Levant have a Mediterranean climate, modified in
respect of the amount of winter rainfall (*see* Fig. 131). The prevailing
winds in that season are from the south-west quarter and cause variations
in rainfall from north to south. In the north the winds have traversed a
longer stretch of the Mediterranean and carry more moisture than in the
south; in addition, the highlands which encompass the coastal plains are
higher in the north and occasion more relief rain than those in the south.
Winters along the coast are mild and frost is almost unknown; when the
khamsin blows from Egypt, January temperatures of over 70° F (21·1° C)
may be registered. Summers are hot and oppressive, for although little or
no rain falls, the air has very high humidity, causing a heavy precipitation
of dew during the night, and exceedingly unpleasant and enervating moist
heat during the day. The high humidity also leads to a greater incidence of

cloud formation in summer along the coast, a condition rarely found else-where in the Mediterranean at that season.

The highlands form a climatic boundary between the Mediterranean climate of the coastlands and the continental climate of the plateaus in the east of the Levant, and so they are transitional between the two types. The windward slopes have a Mediterranean climate modified by altitude, that is, lower temperatures both in summer and winter and a higher winter rainfall than on the coastlands; summer is a season of absolute drought. Humidity is lower than in the lowlands, so that the hot season is more pleasant and attracts holiday-makers from the coastal region. The winter rainfall decreases from north to south, from more than 50 in. in the Lebanon mountains to less than 20 in. at Jerusalem in the Judaean hills; and it may be in the form of snow which on the highest peaks may remain for months.

The lee side of the mountains, the intermontane valleys, and the interior plateaus have a continental or steppe type of climate, with extremes of temperature, big diurnal ranges and low rainfall. In the interior the steppe conditions change gradually to hot desert; Eilat, for instance, near the Gulf of Aqaba, has an annual average rainfall of only 1 in. Tempera-tures in many places may be less than freezing point in winter nights and may rise to over 100° F (37·8° C) during the day in August, the hottest month. The annual rainfall ranges from 18 in. in the west to less than 10 in. in the east. It should be noted, however, that throughout the Levant the yearly precipitation is uncertain; in 1960, for instance, the whole region received little more than half its annual average. It is periods of drought like this which cause unrest and friction between agriculturist and pastoralist, for the latter's animals in their search for food encroach on cultivated fields and venture even into the towns.

The Jordan rift valley has a climate of its own, governed by its depth below sea-level and the shelter afforded by its steep sides. The mean tem-perature in January (60° F; 15·6° C) is the highest in the Levant, and in July, the hottest month, may reach 90° F (32·2° C). The annual rainfall is about 5 in., and its effectiveness is reduced by very high evaporation, which, with the fall in temperature during the summer nights, also causes heavy morning mists throughout the trough.

HISTORICAL SUMMARY

The Levant forms a large part of the western limb of the Fertile Cres-cent, a zone of fertile river valleys, oases and steppe which stretches from the Nile to the Euphrates–Tigris (see Fig. 132). It lies on a line of easy communication between the seats of the earliest civilisations in Egypt and Mesopotamia and within convenient reach of the cultures which developed later in Greece and Rome. The eastern Levant is steppe merging into desert, and this arid region is unable to support more than a sparse popu-lation; so throughout history it has sent a constant stream of migrants to

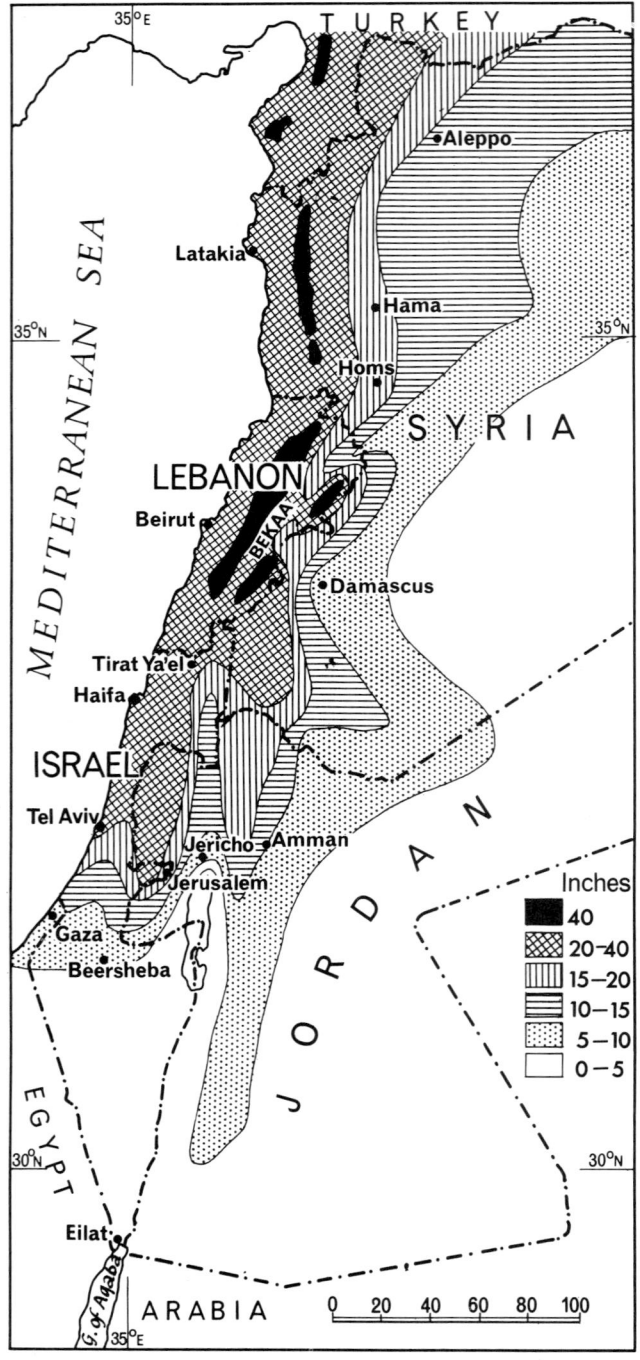

FIG. 131.—Levant lands: mean average rainfall.

the more fertile and productive coastlands. In consequence, the lands of the Levant have been characterised from very early times by racial fusions; their history relates in the first place to the struggle for their possession by Egypt, Babylonia, Assyria, Persia, Greece and Rome, and is complicated by the incursions of less powerful tribes such as the Aramaeans who occupied Syria (Aram was the ancient name of Syria), the Canaanites, Hebrews and Philistines who took possession of Palestine, and the Phoenicians who inhabited the coast from Mount Carmel northwards. Most of these lesser peoples were descended from various branches of the Semitic race

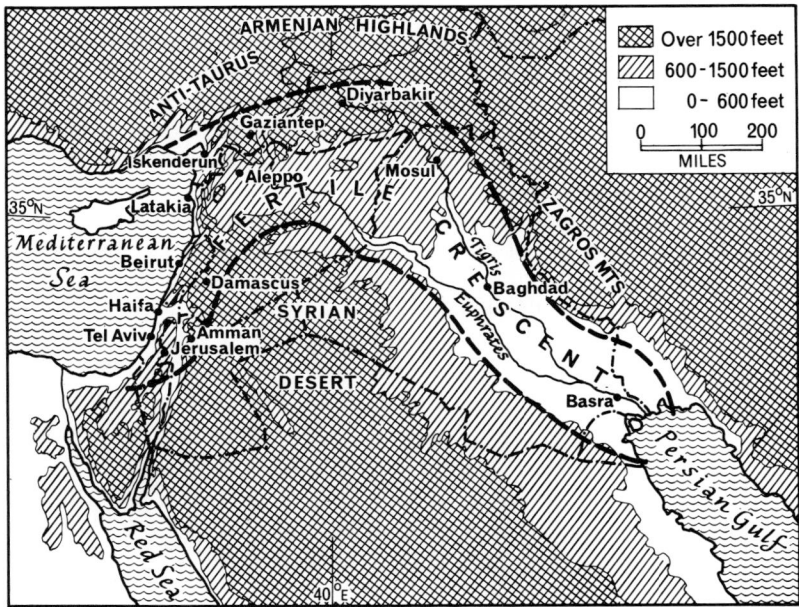

FIG. 132.—The Fertile Crescent.

which moved before 1800 B.C. from Mesopotamia towards the coast. The Phoenicians, against all Semitic nomadic traditions, became a sea-going people.

Until about 1860 B.C. the Levant seems to have been at peace, but from then onwards its boundaries were constantly threatened by invaders. The Egyptians launched a successful campaign and conquered Syria, and at the same time tribes from Asia Minor and Caucasia began to infiltrate via the Syrian steppe. After about 100 years the Egyptians withdrew, for their own country was vanquished by the Hyksos, a branch of the Hittite people of Asia Minor, who held Egypt for more than four centuries. During their rule the ancestors of the Hebrews moved from northern Mesopotamia through Canaan to the delta of the Nile, where they prospered under the Hyksos. In 1580 B.C., however, the Egyptians regained power, drove out the Hyksos, enslaved the Hebrews, and again conquered the Levant, where they remained in control for about 500 years. Their rule was not strict, and they allowed the many petty kindoms of the Levant to become almost autonomous; and when, in the twelfth century B.C., the Hebrews (Israelites), who had been freed from slavery and allowed to leave Egypt, invaded Canaan, the Egyptians did not interfere. Neither did they prevent the occupation of the southern coast of Canaan by the Philistines, a "sea people" from whom Palestine takes its name. The Hebrews ruled Canaan, the "land of Israel" or "the Promised Land," for four hundred years until 734 B.C., and it is mainly on this period of sovereignty that the Hebrews (Jews) base their present-day claims to Israel. In 734, however, the Assyrians conquered Syria and the northern half of Canaan, then known as Israel. The Assyrian ascendancy in the Levant was short-lived, and was succeeded in the next century by that of the Babylonians, who by 597 B.C. had destroyed the kingdom of Judah in the south of Canaan and enslaved its people, thus bringing the sovereignty of the Hebrews to an end.

Meanwhile, the Persians were beginning to build their empire. They overthrew the Babylonians in 538 B.C., and by 525 B.C. had subjugated the Levant and entered Egypt. One of their first acts was to restore the Hebrews to Canaan (Palestine) and make their country a self-governing province of the empire, 537 B.C., but the Hebrews were never to regain full independence until this present century. The Persians remained in power in the Levant until their empire was destroyed by Alexander the Great in the years 334–331 B.C. He inaugurated a period of Greek (Hellenic) overlordship which lasted until the advent of the Romans in the first century B.C. Syria, including present-day Lebanon, was conquered in 64–63 B.C., and Palestine a few years later, and the Levant formed part of the Roman Empire until A.D. 330, when it was transferred to the Eastern (Byzantine) Empire and remained so until early in the seventh century.

During all these invasions and conquests the Levant continued to be composed of many petty states, often semi-independent and frequently at war with each other. The strongest Syrian tribes, centred on Damascus, had constant quarrels with the Hebrews about possession of the land east of the Jordan, mainly of Hauran and Gilead, because of its cultivable value; and there was strife throughout the Levant between the cultivator and the pastoralist. The most stable country seems to have been Phoenicia, which comprised a series of city states stretching from Acco (Acre, in Israel) to Arwad (in Syria), and including Byblus (Jubeil), Berytus (Beirut), Sidon (Saida) and Tyre (Sur). To these ports came silks, perfumes, jewels and luxury goods from the Orient to be transferred from Syrian caravans to Phoenician ships and carried to Egypt, Greece and Rome, together with saffron, umber and Tyrian purple dye (from murex shells) which were produced in Phoenicia itself. There are records, too, of exports of cedar and cypress from the Lebanon slopes, for example, to Jerusalem for the building of Solomon's Temple. The foundation of Alexandria in the fourth century B.C. struck a mortal blow to the mercantile economy of Phoenicia, for the new port changed the trade routes of the eastern Mediterranean. The Romans incorporated the city states into their province of Syria, a name which was applied loosely to the whole Levant; Palestine, for instance, was known as Syria Palaestina.

The way of life was greatly influenced by each of the invaders. New products and methods of cultivation were introduced from Mesopotamia, and new cultural ideas (hellenisation) from Greece and Rome, and all brought with them their own gods and religions. At the commencement of the Christian era, Syria and Phoenicia had a syncretism, that is, a fusion of religions and gods, which would be hard to match. Palestine, however, remained on the whole faithful to the Judaic doctrines inherited from Moses. The Romans, as the latest of the ancient invaders, had the greatest effect on the culture of the Levant. As the centuries passed, they imposed their Hellenistic culture everywhere, obliterating native customs, languages and institutions; the ordinary tongue became *Koine*, a dialect composed of a mixture of Attic Greek and Aramaic. They introduced their gods to the region, as we are reminded at Baalbek in Lebanon, where there are ruins of enormous temples to Jupiter (Baal) and Bacchus. In the later years of their reign, hellenisation was continued and increased, but under Christian auspices; for it must be remembered that Christianity, as well as Judaism, was born in Palestine, and from there spread to the northern Levant, Greece and Rome.

Roman power dominated the Levant and gave the region prosperity until the seventh century, when it was displaced by that of the Muslim Arabs. The movement of Arab peoples was started by Mohammed, the founder of Islam, ostensibly to convert his brethren from paganism; but after his death in 632, his missionary followers added invasion and conquest to their work of conversion. It has been suggested that the Arab invasions were not merely proselytising missions, but were rather a repetition of the migrations of ancient times, when shortage of food at home necessitated a search for new pastures and means of sustenance. In fact, both objectives were achieved; the conquered lands were converted to Islam, often by forceful methods, and the Arabs gained new grazing grounds. By 637 the Levant was in their hands and remained so until the arrival of the Ottoman Turks in 1326. The Turks had already accepted Islam in Asia Minor, and after subjugating the Arabs in the Levant, found their co-religionists ready allies against the Christian Byzantine power in Constantinople. In 1453 that city was captured by the Turks and the Roman opposition broken, and by 1516 the last vestiges of Christian resistance in pockets along the coastlands of Palestine had disappeared, and the Turks were in control of the Levant.

Under the Arabs, and much more so under Ottoman rule, the economy of the Levant fell to pieces, crushed by the dead hand of Islam, and repair did not commence in the region until the final break-up of the Ottoman

Empire early in the present century. It is true that much of the importance of the Levant as an intermediary of trade between Europe and the East had been maintained under the Arabs, even during the Crusades; but with the advent of the Turks the overland route was completely blocked and transit trade came to an end. Merchants began to use a route to the East via Egypt and the Red Sea, leaving the Levant on one side in a kind of commercial backwater; and the opening of the Suez Canal in 1869 seemed to take from the region any hope of economic recovery. The last years of the nineteenth century saw the Levant in a state of complete backwardness, illiteracy and poverty, important to the outside world mainly for the sentimental reasons that it holds the most sacred places of Christianity and Judaism.

The final collapse of the Ottoman Empire came in 1917, and the Turks were driven from the Levant. The victorious Allies, who had promised to set up a number of Arab states in the Levant in return for help against the Turks, established French mandates in Syria and Lebanon, and British mandates in Transjordan and Palestine. A mandate was the power given by the League of Nations (the forerunner of the United Nations Organisation) to govern a region until it was able to administer its own affairs, with a view to ultimate independence. It should be noted that Lebanon, which had never had a separate existence since the days of Phoenicia, was once more to be divided from Syria. This division was a legacy of Turkish rule, for about 1860 the Turks had organised the predominantly Christian Lebanon as a self-governing unit of their empire. In spite of oppression and massacre, the Lebanese had maintained a Christian tradition from Roman times, and the Lebanon mountains had provided refuge and sanctuary for religious fugitives. The mandate over Lebanon was given to the French in 1918 because of their claim to be traditionally the protectors of the Christians of the Levant, and in spite of determined opposition by the Syrians, who for centuries had looked upon Lebanon as a piece of Syria. The French mandate was relinquished in 1946, and Lebanon became a sovereign state for the first time in history.

In Syria the French mandatory government was hotly disputed by Arab nationalists, who demanded immediate independence for their country. They proclaimed the inclusion of Lebanon and Palestine within the boundaries of Syria, installed a native king in Damascus, and took up arms against the French. After a short and bitter campaign the Syrian resistance was broken and the king expelled, but nationalist feeling continued to foment disturbance in Syria and Lebanon, until in 1946 the country, by the termination of the mandate, achieved sovereignty within the boundaries delineated by the League of Nations.

The status of Palestine presented a most intractable problem to Britain, the mandatory power. The mandate was given to prepare Palestine as a "national home for the Jews," but unfortunately in 1917 a promise had also been given to the Palestinian Arabs that they would have a permanent home in Palestine, where they had lived for more than 1000 years. There were in consequence two opposing nationalist parties: the Hebrews (Jews, Zionists) who appealed to Jews throughout the world to return and settle in Palestine, and the Palestinian Arabs who viewed this call for mass immigration with apprehension and were determined to preserve the *status quo*. Under the banner of Zionism Jews in great numbers entered Palestine to cultivate the land, build villages and towns and establish industries. From 1914 to 1939, the Hebrew population increased from 85,000 to nearly 650,000, and it was obvious that such large numbers of new settlers could be accommodated only at the expense of Arab landowners and pastoralists. The Palestinian Arabs began to intrigue with Syria and Egypt to reduce Jewish immigration even if it meant by force of arms. They resorted to acts of terror and murder against the Jews, who set up a self-defence organisation, the *Hagana* (Heb. defence), which after 1945 evolved into the Israel Defence Forces. The Hagana answered violence with violence, and for ten years prior to 1947 Palestine suffered intense xenophobic nationalism, with Jew against Arab and both in opposition to the British administration.

Before 1917, when promises were made to both Arabs and Jews that an independent Palestine would be established, there were substantial minorities of Jews in all the countries of the Levant and in Egypt, living in harmony with their neighbours and respected for their mercantile ability. As the years passed and the Arabs in Palestine saw themselves displaced from their lands by Zionist zealots, feelings of animosity were engendered not only there but also throughout the Arab world, where an attempt was being made to resurrect the Pan-Arabism of the past. In 1945 the Arab League was founded, a confederation of Syria, Lebanon, Transjordan, Iraq, Saudi Arabia, Yemen and Egypt, with the declared aims of political, social and economic co-operation between its members; and it soon became evident that high on the list of its priorities was the extinction of the nascent Hebrew state of Palestine. Nationalist activity was stepped up in the country, amounting to actual civil war, with British troops trying vainly to stem the uprising. Finally, in 1947, the "Palestine question," as it was termed, was brought to the United Nations, who recommended the partition of the country into independent Jewish and Arab states, linked in an economic union, and in the following year, 1948, the British mandate was terminated and Palestine was declared independent.

This was the signal for renewed action by the nationalist adversaries, for neither Jews nor Arabs would accept the boundaries set up by the United Nations Special Committee on Palestine. The Jews proclaimed the new state of Israel and included within its frontiers some of the territory allocated to the Arabs. To prevent this, Arab armies from Egypt, Jordan, Syria, Lebanon, Iraq and Saudi Arabia invaded Israel in May, 1948, with a view to its extermination. After seven months of intermittent and inconclusive fighting, and after United Nations intervention, an armistice was declared and the lines marking the territories occupied at the end of hostilities were agreed upon as the frontiers between the new Arab and Jewish states, albeit reluctantly by both sides. Most of the hill country of central Palestine and Old Jerusalem became part of Jordan, which changed its name from Transjordan; the coastal area around Gaza (the "Gaza strip") was given to Egypt; and a small part of the Mount Hermon range was allocated to Syria. Israel was left as a long, straggling country of irregular shape, with land boundaries 590 miles (945 km) in length, open everywhere to Arab threats of new terrorist raids; and the Palestine question remained without a permanent solution.

In 1919, Britain was given a mandate over a number of small Arab sheikhdoms east of the river Jordan. They were united under the name Transjordan and placed under the rule of an emir, Abdullah. Aided by British financial and technical assistance, the powerful emir guided Transjordan reasonably well along the path of economic progress, and in 1946 the mandate was relinquished and the country became independent. In 1948, during the Arab–Israeli conflict, Transjordanian troops occupied portions of Jerusalem, the highlands of Samaria and Judaea, and part of the Jordan valley, and these were added to Transjordan after the armistice. The country was renamed the Hashemite Kingdom of Jordan, with Abdullah as its first king.

One result of what is known in Israel as the War of Independence, 1948, was the exodus from that country of about three-quarters of a million Arab refugees into neighbouring states. Some went to the Gaza strip or southern Syria, but the vast majority crossed into Jordan, where they remain as destitute refugees in miserable camps on the desert edges and constitute a serious social and economic problem. They are too numerous to be integrated into an economy which is still struggling, and their camps are in areas which are unlikely to become productive, for there is always a shortage of water for agricultural purposes. The relief camps were set up and supported by the United Nations Relief and Works Agency for Palestinian Refugees (U.N.R.W.A.) as a temporary measure, but experience over the past 20 years suggests they are now permanent institutions; in fact, the Six Days War, 1967 (see later), resulted in a further flood of refugees to Jordan, possibly up to a quarter of a million, thus accentuating the problem. Life in the camps is socially and economically of a very low standard, and politically the settlements are hotbeds of unrest and often the headquarters of terrorist bands.

SYRIA

The Republic of Syria (72,234 square miles; 187,014 sq. km) includes within its boundaries climatic types which have led to distinctive Mediterranean, steppe and desert environments, Physically, the country may be divided into (1) the coastlands, (2) the Ghab and (3) the Syrian plateau, and these are also very approximately climatic divisions (see Figs. 133 and 134).

PHYSICAL ASPECTS

REGIONAL DIVISIONS

1. The coastlands

A narrow coastal plain, which is sometimes not more than 4 miles (6·4 km) wide, opens out behind Latakia and near the southern boundary in the lava-covered plain or low plateau of Akkar. The plain is well watered by many streams from the Jebel Ansariya, which also shelter it from cold winds from the north and east. The plain has good soils and a Mediterranean climate, and supports a dense population. Behind it rises the Jebel Ansariya, a dissected limestone anticline which averages about 3750 ft (1133 m) in height and rises to 4500 ft (1370 m) in its highest peak, Nebi Yuness. The eastern slopes of the highlands are steep, but on the west they descend to the plain by broad, wave-cut terraces formed by oscillations in the level of the Mediterranean. The terraces are covered by marine sediments, but most of the range is Jurassic limestone with karst features and little surface water.

2. The Ghab

At the foot of the faulted eastern slopes of the Jebel Ansariya is the rift valley of the Ghab, physically but not structurally a continuation of the Bekaa valley of Lebanon. Its eastern side is bounded by the Jebel Zawiyeh, which is really the faulted and tilted edge of the Syrian plateau. In the south the eastern boundary of the Ghab is much lower, so that the rift almost loses its valley character. The Ghab is drained by the middle course of the river Orontes (Asi); in the south the river has a deeply entrenched valley, but north of Hama, where the character of the faulted trough is more pronounced, it is exceedingly meandering and subject to flooding in the winter. In summer the flood-plain is a stretch of malarial marsh, which is slowly being drained and reclaimed. The southern region has better soils and potential productivity and has a more prosperous appearance.

3. The Syrian plateau

The east of Syria is a vast plateau, the northern portion of the Arabian platform. Over most of its area it averages more than 2500 ft (760 m) above sea-level, but in the north and east it slopes downwards to less than 1500 ft (450 m). The western edges of the plateau have been tilted or folded to form the Jebel Zawiye, and the limestone massifs of the Anti-Lebanon mountains and Mount Hermon (J. esh Sheikh), and in the south are the volcanic outflows associated with the Jebel Druze region. Eastwards the plateau is broken by a discontinuous line of hills which includes the Jebel Sharqui, J. er Rauwaq, J. Buweida and J. Bishri, and runs towards the deeply entrenched river Euphrates. The Anti-Lebanon and their prolongation, Mount Hermon (9145 ft, 2787 m), are an almost unfaulted anticline of Cretaceous and Jurassic limestones. Their crest-line forms part of the frontier with Lebanon. Most of their eastern slopes are waterless, the infrequent rains being quickly absorbed by the porous limestones. At their feet, however, many springs in winter feed small streams which flow to the Syrian Desert in that season, to dry up finally in saline basins. The only perennial rivers are the Barada, on which Damascus is situated, and

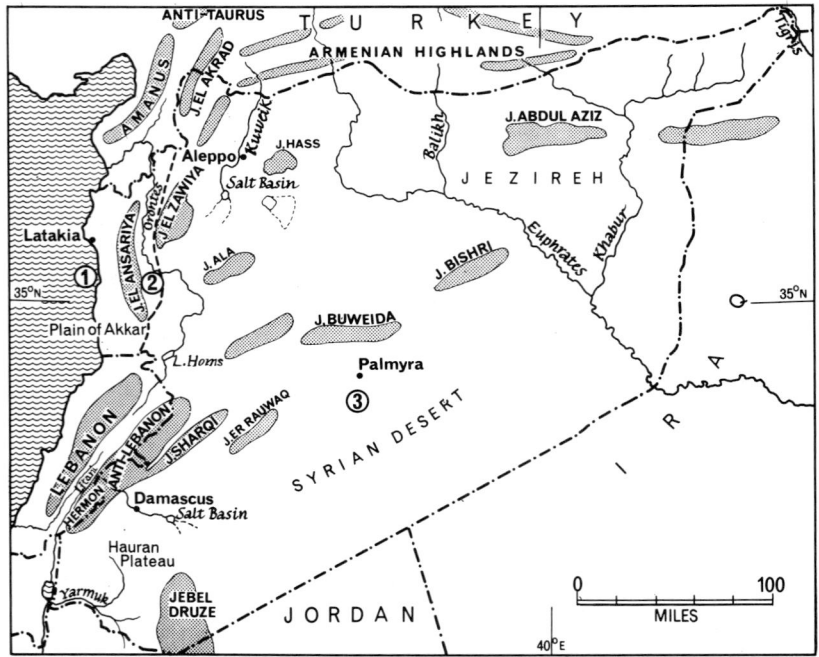

FIG. 133.—Syria: physical features and divisions. The numbers refer to sections in the text.

the Awaj, which feeds the oases of Kiswe and El Hijane. In the north-west of the plateau a similar river, the Qoweiq (Kuweik), flows from the Anti-Taurus mountains in Turkey to water the oasis of Aleppo (Haleb). East of the river Euphrates is the Jezireh (Al Jazira), where the land surface falls in places to less than 1000 ft (300 m), and in the north of the Jezireh the Jebel Abdul Aziz, about 1650 ft (500 m) high, are a continuation of the line of limestone folds mentioned above.

CLIMATE

The general characteristics of the climate of the Levant outlined earlier in the chapter can be applied to Syria. The coastal plain and windward slopes of the Jebel Ansariya have a Mediterranean climate. Mean temperatures in the lowlands range from above 50° F (10° C) in January to over 80° F (26·7° C) in August, the hottest month. The big diurnal range in summer results in a heavy dewfall, but the season is virtually rainless except in the extreme north, where a couple of inches may fall. Temperatures are lower at all seasons in the mountains, but the Jebel Ansariya are not high enough to reduce them more than about an average of 10° F (5·5° C). On the highest peaks, however, they may fall below freezing point, so that here the precipitation in winter may take the form of snow. The annual rainfall amounts to about 38 in. on the plain to 45 in. on the mountains, and is confined mostly to the months of December, January and February. The average annual number of rainy days is about 75.

The eastern slopes of the Jebel Ansariya, Anti-Lebanon and Mount Hermon, the Ghab trough and the western and northern margins of the Syrian plateau have what might be termed a steppe type of climate. Ranges of temperature from winter to summer and from day to night are extreme, and annual rainfall, confined to the winter months, is low. Aleppo has a January mean of 42° F (5·6° C) and the nights may be well below freezing point; its August average is 89° F (31·7° C) and maximum temperatures may be over 100° F (37·8° C). Annual rainfall in the steppe region varies; in parts of the Ghab it may reach 25 in., but in general it ranges from 15 to 18 in.

Most of the Syrian plateau is screened from Mediterranean influences by the coastal highlands, and the mean annual rainfall decreases rapidly eastwards to less than 10 in. and in the south-east to true desert conditions and not more than 5 in., all in the winter half of the year. During the summer the region experiences dry, northerly or north-westerly winds which are drawn to the monsoonal low-pressure centre in the Persian Gulf. Temperatures in that season are consistently high during the day, often reaching 120° F (49° C), and a complete absence of cloud leads to large diurnal ranges. Winters are cold and damp, a small amount of rain being carried inland by depressions from the Mediterranean.

HUMAN GEOGRAPHY

HISTORICAL OUTLINE

The Republic of Syria came into existence in 1946, and since that time its history is of constant unrest both internally and externally. In spite of the armistice which concluded the war with Israel in 1948, Syria, in common with the rest of the Arab League, maintained that a state of war still persisted between the two countries. Diplomatic and commercial relations remained broken off, and the pipeline conveying oil from Iraq via the Syrian plateau to the Israeli port of Haifa was closed; and today, more than 20 years later, these conditions still obtain. Syria was not immediately concerned in the "Suez Crisis" of 1956, but some of its troops fought on the side of Egypt against Israel. In the years which followed, however, the long-standing tension and mutual hatred of Syria and Israel brought about a series of border incidents and terrorist raids, especially after January 1965. At first, these were mainly along the Syrian border with Israel, but before long there were raids across the Jordanian border into Israel. Most of the raids, including those from Jordan, were instigated by Arab terrorist organisations known as *Al Fatah* ("Conquest") and *El Asefa* ("Storm"), which were openly encouraged by the Syrian Government, despite warnings of counter-action by Israel. After the withdrawal of the United Nations Emergency Force from the Gaza strip in May 1967, Egypt also entered the field with renewed raids across the Israeli border, with retaliation by Israel. Egypt has defence pacts with Syria and Jordan, and with them now began to mobilise its armed forces and preach a *jihad* (holy war) to regain Israel for the Arabs; and when Egypt blockaded the Strait of Tiran at the entrance to the Gulf of Aqaba and so prevented Israeli access from Eilat to the Red Sea, it was obvious that war was imminent.

Hostilities commenced in the early hours of 5th June 1967, between Israel and an alliance of Egypt, Syria and Jordan (Lebanon took no active part). Israel took the initiative and engaged all the opposing forces simultaneously; and in one of the most rapid and dramatic campaigns in modern history it gained a complete military victory over its Arab opponents. When the war ended on 10 June (the "Six Days War"), Israeli armed forces were in occupation of an area four times greater than that of Israel before the war started. Its armies captured the high ground on the Syrian border, advanced 12 miles (19 km) into Syria and occupied the garrison town of Kuneitra, 40 miles (64 km) from Damascus. Syria actually suffered far less territorial loss than either Egypt or Jordan, but the blow to its pride was enormous. It still considers itself to be at war with Israel, but the hills from which it used to launch terrorist attacks are now in Israeli hands. Its activities are therefore directed to the fomentation of unrest in the Jordanian refugee camps and to the organisation of frontier incidents along the river Jordan; and as each raid is answered in kind by Israel, there seems at present to be little hope of a peaceful settlement.

Internally, the political situation has been dominated since the beginning of 1965 by a struggle for power between two rival factions in the ruling *Baath* party, who are referred to as "moderates" and "extremists." Syria has no democratic government, and the shift of power from one faction to the other is usually the result of a military *coup* accompanied by violence and bloodshed. In 17 years (1949–66) there have been 10 successful *coups*; and as the two factions have divergent policies relating to both internal and foreign affairs, there has been a lack of continuity in the country's social and economic development.

The moderates, broadly speaking, are in favour of a pragmatic, matter-of-fact, flexible approach to the chief problems, namely, the application of socialism, relations with Egypt and the Palestine question. They advocate a conciliatory policy towards the middle classes—the merchants, shopkeepers, craftsmen, small manufacturers and petty landowners—who in total own most of the wealth of Syria but are little interested in politics. When in power the moderates announced their encouragement of private enterprise, notably in contracting, tourism and craft industries. They oppose military intervention in politics, and are in favour of improved relations with other Arab countries, especially Egypt, with whom in 1958 they formed a political union known as the United Arab Republic.

The extremists, who are supported by high-ranking officers and by religious minorities such as the Shi'ite Muslims and the Druzes, want a stern government and a tough economic programme. They are hostile to Egypt, which in their opinion was a weak partner in 1948 and again in 1956 in the Arab effort against the state of Israel, and as soon as they were in power in 1961 they withdrew Syria from the political union with Egypt. They advocate a sweeping policy of nationalisation, and in 1964, in spite of demonstrations and strikes by merchants, shopkeepers and industrialists in Damascus and Aleppo, they nationalised 95% of the country's industries. In the following year they took control of 25% of Syria's cultivable land and proclaimed a State monopoly in the export of wheat, barley, cotton and cotton-seed, and in addition nationalised 57 cotton ginning mills.

Only about Israel are the two parties in agreement, but not wholly so. The moderates desire the extinction of the Hebrew state by economic and political pressure rather than by violence, whereas the extremists adopt a constant militant attitude towards Israel and have been largely responsible for the terrorist raids mentioned above. The two factions were united in the Six Days War, but since its conclusion they are again at variance, the moderates advocating peace by negotiation, the extremists panting with a desire to avenge the Syrian defeat. Both parties have a basic socialist policy, which bears some resemblance to Communism, but whereas the moderates favour the Soviet Union, the extremists have a leaning towards Communist China.

PEOPLE

Syria has a population of 4,566,000 and an average density of 64 persons per square mile; but since 60% of its surface is desert or dry steppe with very few people, in contrast to the crowded cities of Damascus, Aleppo, Latakia, Homs and Hama, it is obvious that this average is misleading.

The people of Syria are descended mainly from Aramaean stock, as already noted, but they have been almost completely "arabised"; and there are many minority groups such as the Druzes, Kurds, Bedouin and Armenians who preserve their own religious and social customs. The Druzes are more a religious than a racial type, who took refuge in the Jebel Druze to escape persecution and gave their name to the region. They profess a debased form of Islam mixed with animism, and are mostly pastoralists. When recruited into the army they are ruthless, loyal fighters. The Kurds came originally from the mountains of Armenia and the Zagros; in Syria they number about 100,000, and live a semi-independent, pastoral life in the northern steppe. The Bedouin are nomad Arabs (see page 103) who range from the Euphrates to Damascus; their numbers are known only approximately and are estimated at about 200,000, but they are declining. The Armenians are Christians who fled from their home-land in 1915–16 to escape massacre by the Turks. There are about 120,000 Armenians in Syria, chiefly in the cities near the coast, where they are engaged in commerce and in skilled professions such as the law, medicine and teaching.

The mixture of peoples and the great variety of cultures, languages and religions have been a barrier in the past to national unity. In recent years,

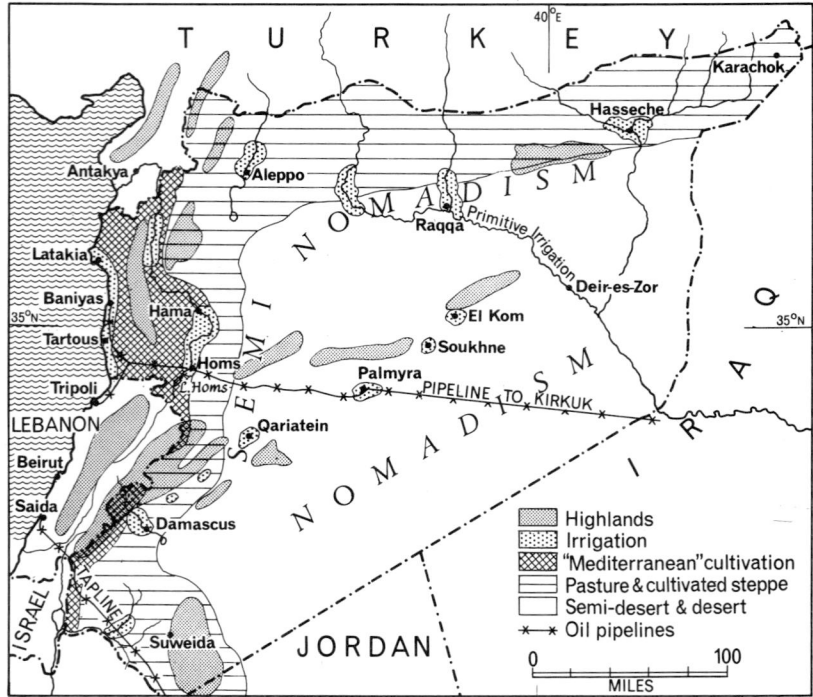

FIG. 134.—Syria: agriculture and pasture.

however, Arabic has become the official language of politics and com-merce, and more widely spoken by most of the people; religious differ-ences have shown a tendency to be ignored; so that today Syria is more integrated as a state than when it achieved independence. Nevertheless, it will take a very long time to weld together such a heterogeneous popu-lation.

THE ECONOMY

REGIONAL ECONOMY

1. *The coastlands.* Tobacco, cotton and olives are grown along the coastal plain, and vines, mulberries (for sericulture) and temperate fruits

on the lower Ansariya slopes, which are terraced for more than 200 ft (610 m). The Plain of Latakia is especially noted for tobacco and cotton, and the Plain of Akkar for citrus fruits, chiefly oranges. The slopes of the Jebel Ansariya have been largely deforested (less than 3% of Syria is counted as forest) and are covered with garrigue; and here and on the scrub-vegetation of the dissected plateau above, sheep and goats are reared by transhumant shepherds.

Latakia (67,604) is Syria's chief port, with a much-improved deep-water harbour. It suffers by having no railway connections with the interior, but better road communications are helping it to compete with Beirut and Tripoli in Lebanon, through which much Syrian traffic passes. Latakia has cotton manufacture, and olive-oil and tanning industries. Baniyas, south of Latakia, is the terminal of the oil pipeline from Kirkuk in northern Iraq, and has large tanker facilities.

2. *The Ghab.* This trough valley, about 10 miles (16 km) wide, provides transhumant flocks of sheep and goats with pasture during the summer, but the unhealthy conditions preclude permanent settlement, especially near the river Orontes. In the north, however, where the valley narrows, the hill slopes are terraced and wheat, barley and olives are cultivated. Farming is difficult because water is scarce on the limestone slopes, and population is sparse. The marshy character of so much of the Ghab is the result of a basalt sill which crosses the valley north of Hama and impedes drainage. A large-scale engineering project is lowering the surface of the sill so as to give a more complete run-off from the waterlogged soils, and already a large acreage has been reclaimed and planted with wheat. Ultimately, the scheme will result in about 200,000 acres (80,000 ha) of arable land, which will be irrigated by waters impounded further up the Orontes.

The middle Orontes valley, that is, from Hama to Homs, presents a contrast to the Ghab proper. Here the river flows in a deeply entrenched valley, but its waters are lifted into irrigation channels by huge, wooden water-wheels known as *norias*. This primitive method, which is traditional along this part of the Orontes, is limited in scope to the immediate vicinity of the river, but it is sufficient to transform the natural steppe into a well-cultivated area producing wheat, barley, vegetables and fruit of all kinds. A recent project, however, is extending the irrigated region considerably; the damming of the Orontes by the construction of an artificial barrier on the basalt sill which holds back Lake Homs has raised the level of the lake, enabling water to flow by gravity into irrigation canals farther from the river than those fed by norias. This has resulted in a great expansion not only in the area under wheat, but in the commercial cultivation of cotton and sugar beet, as well as of subsistence crops such as barley, sesame, vines and apricots. The Homs–Hama region is one of the richest parts of Syria and is beginning to suffer from rural over-population. Conditions of life, however, are improving, largely because of the Syrian land reform of 1958 whereby many estates owned by absentee landlords and worked by indigent share-croppers were confiscated by the State and rented to peasants. But the process of confiscation and redistribution is slow, the more so because it is often in the hands of corrupt officials.

The chief towns of the region are Homs (148,386) and Hama (103,419). Both are ancient markets and craft centres which developed in fertile areas on the edge of the steppe, and, with the increase in cotton cultivation, both have cotton manufactures. Homs controls road and rail communications through the only gap from the coast to the interior, a fault-valley between the Ansariya and Lebanon ranges which gives access to the port

FIG. 135.—Homs: water wheels on the river Orontes. The Orontes valley in the lee of the Jebel Ansariya has little rain, but is one of the most fruitful parts of Syria because of irrigation. Primitive methods of lifting water such as that shown are being replaced gradually by modern systems. A dam is being built near Lake Homs.

of Tripoli (in Lebanon). Homs, therefore, is a rail and road junction and has oil refining, textile, flour-milling, tobacco and sugar industries. Much of its trade passes through Tripoli, since there is no convenient Syrian port. An oil pipeline from Kirkuk branches at Homs to its terminals at Tripoli and Baniyas, and has given birth to an oil refinery in the town. Hama, which is a centre of noria irrigation, has agricultural industries similar to those at Homs but on a smaller scale.

3. *The Syrian plateau.* This region may be divided into, firstly, a belt of settled cultivation along the western and northern edges, and secondly, a wide expanse given over to semi-nomadic pastoralism. The cultivation is centred on the ancient oasis cities of Aleppo and Damascus, the more recent foundation of Suweida, the Druze capital, and the new irrigation works along the Euphrates and its tributary, the Khabur. The so-called "plain" of Aleppo (Haleb) has been occupied since ancient times by seden-

tary peasant farmers whose traditional crops were wheat, barley, vegetables and a small amount of cotton (*see* Fig. 134). The plain is watered by the river Qoweiq (Kuweik), which flows from the Kurdistan highlands and loses itself ultimately in a salt basin. The river is used for irrigation, especially around the city of Aleppo, where, in addition to the crops mentioned, there are vineyards, olive groves and fruit orchards. Aleppo (425,467), the chief settlement, has been known since Babylonian times (*see* Fig. 137). It originated as a defensive site on eight hillocks in the fertile oasis plain and became the economic centre of north Syria and the greatest road focus for eastern caravans. It still retains major importance

[*Courtesy of the Syrian Embassy.*

FIG. 136.—Syria: a village near Aleppo. This is marginal country, where the desert is advancing and agriculture becomes increasingly difficult. Poor crops of wheat, barley and vegetables are grown, but life is a constant struggle for the inhabitants. The existence of the village shows that water is present, but the general aspect is unpromising. The huts of dried mud have no window openings.

as a collecting and distributing market, but in recent years its supremacy has been challenged by Damascus, and in common with other oasis cities which depended on caravan trade, it has suffered because of improved sea communications with the Orient, especially via the Suez Canal. Aleppo was at one time the western outlet for the silks of Bambyce, called *bombazines*, and for the fine cotton textiles of Mosul (*mosulines* or *muslins*), and it was the market for timber and copper from the mountains of Asia Minor, and of wool, hair, skins and livestock from the steppe. The craft industries which originated from these products—connected mainly with leather and metals—still exist side by side with light engineering and cotton manufacture in modern factories. Aleppo is a mixture of ancient and modern. Its gardens which extend for miles along the river banks; its bazaars and *khans* (inns and caravanserais) which are unusually large; its winding, narrow streets crowded with pack animals; and its mosques, citadel and Saracenic wall tell us we are in a truly oasis city. But Aleppo is also a railway centre of more than local importance, and has modern shops, warehouses, factories and hotels.

Damascus (529,963), the capital of Syria, is situated near the northern edge of a small plain called the Ghutah, at the foot of the Anti-Lebanon, 2250 ft (687 m) above the sea (*see* Fig. 137). Through the plain flows the river Barada, which rises in the Anti-Lebanon, runs for about 10 miles (16 km) in a narrow channel and then spreads itself fan-wise over the plain. Damascus is built on both banks of the river about 2 miles (3·2 km) from its exit from the gorge. The Barada loses itself about 18 miles (29 km) east of the city in the marshlands known as Lake Ataiba or the Meadow Lakes. A second river, the Awaj, pursues a similar course south of the Barada, and finishes in the same marshes. The plain is thus exceptionally well irrigated, and its consequent fertility is proverbial throughout the Middle East. The waters of the river are conducted by channels and conduits to all the houses in the ancient city, which is surrounded by ornamental gardens, vineyards, apricot orchards, nut trees and market gardens. Beyond these are fields of wheat, barley, cotton and sesame, with olive groves on the hill slopes to the west. The origin of Damascus is not known, and the popular belief that it is the oldest city in the world has much to commend it. Be that as it may, very early in history it was already a premier "desert port," but of less importance under Turkish rule than Aleppo.

With the emergence of Syria as an independent state, however, the position of Damascus in the centre of a more extensive oasis than Aleppo, plus the fact that it has better communications, has led to its development as the administrative capital of the country, and to a rapid increase in its manufacturing and tourist industries. Damascus has craft industries, especially of copperware and silk brocades, and of cheap carpets and rugs which are sold to tourists, and there are thriving modern cotton factories, flour mills and beet sugar refineries. The city is connected by rail to Beirut and has a first-class airfield which has helped its tourism and its pilgrim trade. The latter has been of some importance in the development of Damascus, for the city is the starting-place for the Hajj pilgrimage from Syria to Mecca, which leaves annually on the same date and brings much trade. It is interesting to note, too, that our word "damask" comes from Damascus. It was applied as early as the twelfth century to beautifully figured silk fabrics which were made in the city and exported to Europe. Later the name was fastened by traders on all fashioned silk fabrics, but today it is given usually to figured cottons and linen, such as tablecloths. The figured silks which are still produced in Damascus as a craft industry are now known as brocades. The term *Damascene* or Damascus steel used in connection with sword blades refers to weapons which had a peculiar streaky or watered appearance; they were made in Persia from a remote period, and marketed in Damascus.

South of Damascus the landscape is characterised by lava flows which form an irregular plateau crossed by basaltic ridges and dotted by extinct volcanic cones, and rising in its highest part to the dome of the Jebel Druze. In the west the lavas are breaking down to form a fertile soil, the result of the slightly greater rainfall caused by the Jebel Druze; elsewhere, the cooling of the lavas has been too rapid and the precipitation too small, so that soil formation has hardly commenced and the surface layers are cindery, dry and desolate. In the west, however, the Hauran plateau is watered by the river Yarmuk and its tributaries, and has great productive potentialities. Unfortunately, most of the streams dry up during the summer, so that irrigation is limited to a narrow band along the Yarmuk; nevertheless, rainfall is sufficient over most of the Hauran and on the lower western slopes of the Jebel Druze for dry-farming of wheat and barley and for the rearing of sheep, goats, asses and even cattle. Dates, citrus fruits

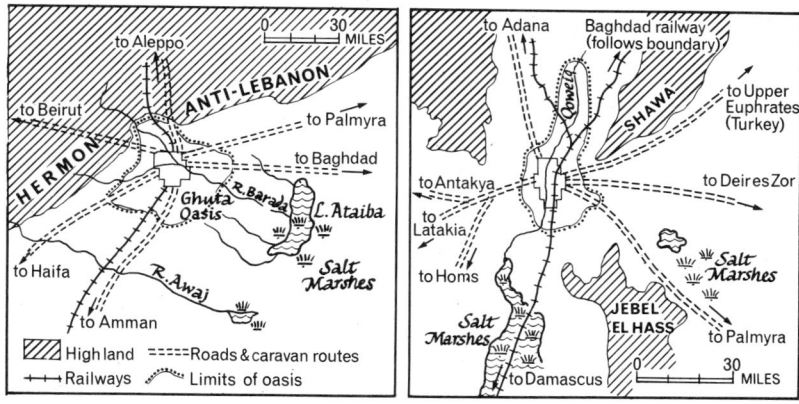

FIG. 137.—Damascus and Aleppo.

and vines are cultivated along the irrigated Yarmuk valley, and there are market gardens around Suweida, the Druze capital, and the many villages.

The Hauran and Jebel Druze are inhabited mainly by the Druzes, who gave their name to the central lava dome. They live to some degree isolated from the rest of Syria, governed by hereditary sheikhs, and semi-independent. In recent years, however, the Druze sheikhs are beginning to acquire commercial ambitions and have shown themselves willing to co-operate with the government in Damascus more than at any time under Turkish suzerainty. There is intense enmity between the Druzes and the Bedouin of the eastern plateau.

The dry farming of wheat and barley in the Aleppo Plain is continued across the Euphrates into the Jezireh which, although it has a low rainfall, is one of the best-watered and fertile parts' of Syria. Along its northern edges there has been a great advance in mechanised farming by Kurds and settled Bedouin, and the extensive cultivation of wheat and barley is somewhat reminiscent of the early development of the Canadian prairie. This region promises to be of outstanding importance as a producer of cereals, for already there is a surplus for export. Its greatest drawback at present is the lack of good communications with the west of the country and the Mediterranean. Along the Euphrates and its tributaries, especially the Khabur, there are primitive irrigation works and an increasing area producing maize and cotton; and there are ambitious schemes to harness the Euphrates for both hydro-electric power and irrigation at Al Tabqa. The largest town is Deir-es-Zor (42,036), the regional capital of eastern Syria, on the Euphrates. Other centres of settlement in the Jezireh are Raqqa, at the confluence of the Balikh and Euphrates, and Hasseche on the Khabir. Of great significance to Syria was the discovery in 1963 of petroleum near Karachok, in the north-east of the Jezireh. Resources are estimated at 1000 million tons, of which 200 million tons are extractable at a rate sufficient for the home market for upwards of 30 years. So far, however, satisfactory exploitation has been prevented by the uncertain political situation in the country.

In the heart of the Syrian plateau a line of small oases lies along the southern edges of the Jebel Sharqi, J. Buweida and J. Bishri. They include Qariatein, Palmyra, Soukhne and El Kom, and, in the ruined Roman temples, tombs and memorial arches of Palmyra at least, show indications that this zone of the plateau was possibly one of great productivity in comparatively recent historical times. It is very doubtful, however, if the past importance of Palmyra was based on its agriculture, for prior to the Roman penetration of the Middle East it was a small Arab oasis. Under the Romans it was transformed from a mere halting-place for caravans to a city of the first rank, the chief market between the Roman and Parthian states. At Palmyra two great trade routes converged, one crossing from the Phoenician ports to the Persian Gulf, the other coming up from Petra and south Arabia. To its market came the chief luxuries of the ancient world, silks, jewels, pearls, perfumes, incense and the like, drawn from India, China and southern Arabia, and destined primarily for Rome. To-day it is merely a collection of Arab hovels whose inhabitants eke out a precarious existence by their sale of water, wheat, straw and salt to nomadic herdsmen, from whom they collect wool, hair and skins in exchange, bartering these in Homs or Damascus for further necessities.

Away from the areas of cultivation the Syrian plateau is covered by dry steppe occupied by semi-nomadic pastoralists and, in the south-east, by hammada (rocky desert). A sparse winter rainfall encourages the growth of tough, patchy grasses in that season, even in the hammada, but in the hot, dry summer the vegetation is scorched and the land becomes bare, so that the herdsmen must move from the south and east to damper grazing grounds nearer the cultivated north and west. The Syrian pastoralists may be divided into the sheep and goat rearers and the camel rearers. The movements of the shepherds and goatherds are much more restricted than those of the camel-herds, whose animals are swifter and adapted to going without food or water for long periods. The grazing grounds for sheep and goats are consequently rarely more than a few days' journey from the cultivated lands, and a large proportion of the herdsmen have a fixed camping place on the edges of oases which they regard as their home and to which they return during the summer. The camel-herds, on the other hand, penetrate far into the desert during the winter, and in summer look for pasture along the irrigated borders of the Jezireh. Summer pasture is becoming increasingly difficult to find in face of the extension of irrigated and cultivated land, and the numbers of nomads and semi-nomads, which were never really large, are gradually declining. This is notably the case with the shepherds and goatherds, who are being attracted to a settled life of cultivation or to work in the oilfields and cities; but even the camel-herds, who look upon themselves as the aristocrats of the steppe and despise the cultivators, are having to give way to the competition of motor-borne traffic and are forced, however reluctantly, to adopt a sedentary life.

ECONOMIC SUMMARY

Since Syria became an independent state it has made substantial advances in agriculture and industry. Nevertheless it is still seriously underdeveloped, for it has no wealth of productive land or mineral resources. Sixty per cent of its surface is covered by desert and dry steppe, inhabited by wandering herdsmen or small communities who depend on subsistence agriculture. This large area of the country supports only about 3% of Syria's population (see Fig. 134). In the remainder of the country—the coastal region and the damper steppe—settled agriculture is typical, but even in the most productive districts around Latakia, Damascus, Homs, Hama and Aleppo, crops such as wheat, barley, beans and olives are grown on a subsistence basis. In the frontier zone east of Aleppo and in the Jezireh, cash crops—cotton, sugar beet and tobacco—are being produced by new irrigation and modern mechanised farming methods, and there are exportable surpluses of wheat and barley. It is true to say, however, that subsistence agriculture remains the basis of Syria's economy, and most of its population is dependent on the soil for a livelihood.

Agricultural development in recent years has been helped by an increase in irrigation and by agrarian reforms. The reclamation of the Ghab and the increase in the area of cultivable land in the valley of the Orontes have already been noted; of more importance are the motor pumps which are now being used to raise water from the rivers flowing in the north of Syria from the highlands of Turkey. The river Kuweik is being utilised in this way north of Aleppo, and the Jezireh is being made more productive by similar pumps along the Euphrates, Balikh and Khabur. An agreement was also signed between Syria and the Soviet Union in April 1966, providing for Russian assistance in constructing a dam and hydro-electric station at Al Tabqa on the Euphrates. The impounded reservoir will provide water for several thousand acres of new, irrigated land.

Land tenure in Syria has undergone much reform since 1958. Prior to this date much of the cultivable area in the west, that is, from Aleppo southwards to the Jebel Druze, was in large estates owned by absentee landlords and worked by poverty-stricken share-croppers, whereas the cultivable steppe along the Turkish border was farmed by what Warriner calls "merchant-tractorists," mostly Armenians, who used the most modern mechanised methods of wheat and barley cultivation, such as are found in Canada and the U.S.A. This type of farming, which is being introduced also in the Jezireh, requires ownership or renting of large units, but in contrast to the west, the workers are well trained in modern techniques, and have guaranteed wages and good living conditions. A Government decree in 1958 ordered the confiscation of large estates and fixed the maximum size of farms at 200 acres (80 ha) for irrigated land and 500 acres (200 ha) for non-irrigated land. As a result the surplus area which became State property was available to peasant farmers, but the rents and taxes are high, so that the new tenants, although they feel more independent and secure, are not much better off materially.

The redistribution of land met with opposition, especially in the north and north-east, where large-scale methods are best used on extensive units; and on the non-irrigated lands, where dry-farming techniques operate, there are still large estates. Elsewhere, the confiscation and re-allocation of land is proceeding, but only very slowly.

Industry in Syria is making fair progress, especially in textiles, but further development is necessarily limited, partly because of the poverty of the country's natural resources, and partly because of the unstable nature of its government, which makes foreign companies reluctant to invest capital in new enterprises. Its industries are largely concerned with the processing of agricultural products, as noted previously, and there has been a notable growth of cement manufacture, which nowadays is regarded as basic in the economy of all emergent countries. Syria's industries and most of its wealth, however, are for the greater part in the hands of middle-class merchants and shop-keepers in the cities of Damascus and Aleppo, and they have not shown very much regard for the interests of the country as a whole but rather for their own enrichment.

Under the heading of industry must be included Syria's share in the oil output of the Middle East. Oil was struck in 1963 at Suwayidia, near Karachok, in the north-east of the country, and is being exploited with financial aid from the Soviet Union. A 400-mile pipeline is under construction from the oilfield to the port of Tartous, to be routed through an existing refinery at Homs. With the exception of this oil and of salt obtained by solar evaporation from saline basins in the desert, Syria seems to be lacking in mineral deposits, but it draws royalties for a pipeline which crosses the country from the Kirkuk oilfield to Baniyas and many of its workers are employed in the maintenance of the line and at installations in the port.

Syria's chief exports are wheat, barley, tobacco, cotton and cotton-seed, wool, skins and live animals; and its imports are manufactured goods, machinery, raw materials, foodstuffs and mineral oil. There is a large adverse trade balance which is partly offset by tourism, foreign aid and remittances from emigrants.

STUDY QUESTIONS

1. Outline and give reasons for the variations in climate in the Levant lands (a) from north to south, (b) from west to east.

2. Describe, and explain as far as you can, rift valley formation in the eastern coastlands of the Mediterranean.

3. Explain how the rural way of life in Syria has been influenced by physical features and climate.

3. Under the headings (a) site, (b) situation, (c) economic activities, examine the rise to importance of Damascus and Aleppo. Sketch maps are essential.

4. Divide Syria into natural regions and justify your division. Give a detailed account of *one* of your divisions. A sketch map is essential.

5. Discuss the geographical factors which led to the early growth of civilisation in the Levant lands.

Chapter XXV

LEBANON

THE Republic of Lebanon (3400 square miles) is the smallest of the Levant countries, yet socially and economically it is perhaps the most advanced state in the whole of the Middle East. It is a mountainous land, the name Lebanon being derived from Aramaic *laban*, "to be white" or "whiteness," referring to the bare white walls of chalk or limestone which characterise large sections of the Lebanon mountains, or possibly to the vista of snow-clad peaks in winter. The country, which extends approximately 125 miles (200 km) along the Mediterranean littoral and at its widest is not more than 40 miles (64 km), may be divided longitudinally into (1) the coastal plain, (2) the Lebanon range, (3) the Bekaa, and (4) the Anti-Lebanon ranges (*see* Fig. 138 (*a*)).

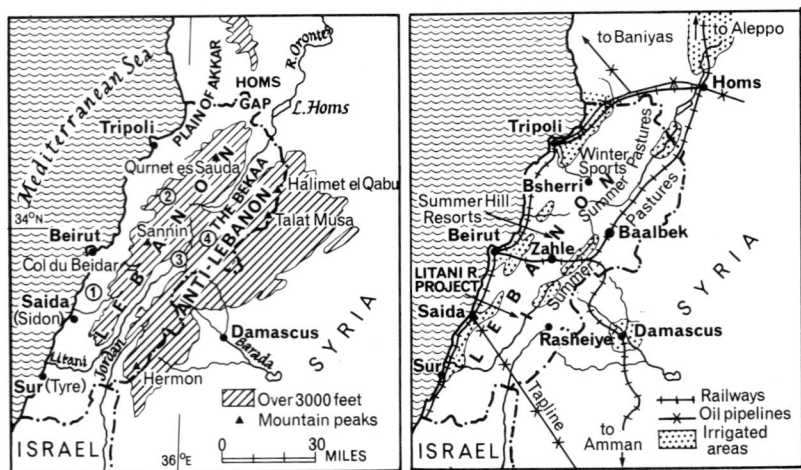

FIG. 138.—Lebanon: (*a*) physical features; (*b*) irrigation, railways, chief towns. The numbers refer to sections in the text.

PHYSICAL ASPECTS

STRUCTURAL DIVISIONS

1. *The coastal plain.* The region between the Lebanon mountains and the sea slopes in an intricate series of plateaus and terraces to the coast, which for the most part is abrupt and rocky, often leaving room for only a narrow path along the shore. The view from the Mediterranean does not suggest the existence of a coastal plain, yet between the mountain spurs which run from east to west and terminate in cliff-girt headlands,

there are sandy beaches backed by discontinuous lowland. This widens in the north to the plain or low plateau of Akkar, in the south at the mouth of the river Litani, and around Beirut, where it reaches its maximum width, a mere 4 miles (6·4 km). The coastal region is crossed by a number of streams, mostly perennial and known as *nahrs*, such as Nahr Akkar, Nahr Kadisha and Nahr Ibrahim, which have excavated deep gorges in the Cretaceous strata which form most of the surface, except in the north, where the Akkar region has a cover of basaltic lava. Brown and chestnut soils are characteristic of the plain, and in the gorges there are small alluvial terraces.

2. *The Lebanon range.* This is a most imposing massif, rising in Qurnet es Sauda to slightly over 10,000 ft (3000 m) and in Mount Sannin to 8140 ft (2481 m). The range, which is roughly 100 miles (160 km) long, consists of a simple anticline which decreases in altitude from north to south, where it falls to the valley of the lower Litani by several elevated and faulted terraces. The anticline is cut by many small, transverse faults, in some of which there are intrusions of lava. The western slopes of the Lebanon mountains rise gradually to the crest of the anticline, but eastwards the massif is terminated by a major north–south fault and falls precipitously to the Bekaa valley beyond.

The Lebanon range is composed predominantly of massive Jurassic limestone which is permeable and easily eroded. This is overlain in the higher parts of the anticline by impermeable clays, sandstones, marls and lignite of the Middle and Lower Cretaceous, above which is a capping of very porous Upper Cretaceous limestone which forms the highest peaks. This structural feature, the alternation of permeable and impermeable strata at high altitudes, is not found elsewhere in the massifs of the Levant, and is of great importance in both physical and human geography. The rainwater and snow-melt which penetrate the Upper Cretaceous emerge as a line of springs along the outcrop of the impervious strata below, and give birth at a height of from 3000 to 5000 ft (900–1500 m) to the many streams which flow down the western slopes to the Mediterranean. The western side of the Lebanon range, which also receives more rainfall than any other part of the country, is well watered; and because its soils, developed and washed down from the varied Cretaceous series above, are fertile and productive, cultivation can be carried on up to the spring-line, that is, possibly up to 5000 ft (1520 m). The best soils lie on the more resistant Middle and Lower Cretaceous rocks which have weathered into easy gradients on which farming is not too difficult; and here religious and political refugees in the past were able to settle and find a livelihood in comparative peace.

On their way to the sea the rivers have carved deep valleys in the Jurassic limestone, notably so in their lower courses, where they have dissected the massif into a number of spurs which reach the coast, as mentioned above. The deeply excavated valleys in the main ridge are enclosed by apparently inaccessible heights, yet these are often crowned by villages, castles and monasteries, built by the mountain dwellers. The only practicable route across the Lebanon mountains is via the Col du Beidar (5000 ft, 1520 m) behind Beirut. This pass to the interior of the country and to the Damascus region of Syria is traversed by a road and a railway, and is a factor in the importance and development of Beirut. A second pass, unsuitable for vehicular traffic in the winter, leads from Tripoli to Baalbek, and crosses the mountains at a height of 8351 ft (2545 m).

The eastern side of the Lebanon range, bleak, precipitous and karst-like, presents a contrast to the west. Major north-east/south-west faulting, with a downthrow to the east, has resulted in a most forbidding topography, with giant cliffs and fearsome ravines. There is little surface drainage over most of the area, but, as is common in karst regions, subterranean streams come out near the foot of the mountains and flow across the Bekaa. None of these is of any size and most are intermittent, drying up in summer. The Nahr Berdani, the largest stream descending into the Bekaa, rises in Mount Sannin, and enters the plain by a deep and picturesque cleft at Zahle. Near by is Lake Yammoune, which lies in a *polje* or basin in the limestone and is fed by intermittent springs; its waters are being harnessed to assist in the irrigation scheme being developed along the river Litani, especially in the Baalbek area.

3. *The Bekaa*. This is a broad valley, from 4 to 12 miles (6–19 km) wide, between the Lebanon and Anti-Lebanon ranges. Superficially it appears to be a continuation of the Jordan rift valley, but structurally it is quite distinct. The fault which bounds it on the west has a different trend to and is not connected with the Jordan system, and the eastern side of the valley, although it rises steeply, is not faulted. The Bekaa is a trough valley not a rift. It is floored by Quaternary deposits, chiefly of alluvium, and has an undulating surface. A slight flexion of the underlying rocks has produced a watershed near Baalbek, the highest point of which is about 3600 ft (1100 m). This separates the valleys of the rivers Orontes (Asi) and Litani, which drain the Bekaa. Their sources are only a mile apart. In its lower course the Litani was captured by a fast-flowing stream which cut back its source through the Lebanon massif. Below the "elbow of capture" the Litani flows to the Mediterranean through a deep, narrow gorge, too difficult for easy access to the Bekaa. The soils of the Bekaa, except in the north where they are thin and stony, are potentially productive; large areas near Baalbek are being brought into cultivation by an ambitious irrigation scheme involving the waters of the Litani and the karst Lake Yammoune. The Orontes valley will benefit by the Syrian Lake Homs development project.

4. *The Anti-Lebanon ranges*. East of the Bekaa rise the Anti-Lebanon mountains and their southward continuation, the Mount Hermon (Jebel esh Sheikh) massif, their watershed forming the boundary with Syria. The Anti-Lebanon range is a simple, almost undisturbed anticline of limestone 67 miles (107 km) long. Its crest has been eroded into ragged peaks, the highest of which are Talat Musa (8642 ft, 2633 m) and Halimet el Qabu

(8005 ft, 2440 m). The slopes are much steeper than those on the west of the Lebanon mountains, and large areas are completely devoid of vegetation. The lower slopes, flanking the Bekaa, have weathered into a rough, reddish region lined with juniper trees, broken by a series of more resistant limestone crests and ridges, bristling with bare rock and crags, and separated by a succession of grassy ravines. The Anti-Lebanon is a karst region with very little surface drainage; consequently, the range has few permanent settlements and is thinly peopled.

The Mount Hermon massif is separated from the Anti-Lebanon by an enlarged fault-valley through which flows the Barada on its way to the Damascan oasis. Like the Anti-Lebanon, is a limestone anticline, but it is more narrowly folded and has several transverse faults in which there are intrusions of basalt. At its highest it is 9145 ft (2787 m) above sea-level. Mount Hermon is more open to maritime influences than the rest of the Anti-Lebanon, so that its western slopes are well watered; nevertheless, it is mostly karst and uninhabited, except at lower levels. At its foot is the uppermost part of the Jordan valley, a fertile alluvial plain.

CLIMATE AND VEGETATION

The coastal region and the lower western slopes of the Lebanon mountains have a typical Mediterranean climatic régime. Beirut, for example, has an average temperature range from 56° F (13·3° C) in January to 84° F (28·9° C) in August, which is the hottest month in Lebanon, and a mean annual rainfall of 37·7 in., 62% of which falls in December, January and February. The surprisingly high rainfall is occasioned by the mountain wall of the Lebanon, which at higher levels may have an annual precipitation of 40 to 50 in. Beirut, unlike most Mediterranean stations, is cloudy at all seasons and suffers in summer, with the rest of the western Levant, from high humidity which makes the heat oppressive and enervating. Many of the coastal inhabitants of Lebanon migrate in summer to mountain resorts which have grown along the line of the Beirut–Zahle roads and railway. The diurnal temperature range in western Lebanon is small at all seasons, rarely exceeding 12° F (6·6° C).

Temperatures, especially in winter, fall rapidly as one leaves the coast and climbs the Lebanon mountains. Snow in winter is common throughout the range, and may rest at high levels for months. The highest peaks may be snowcapped for half the year. The snowfields in the northern part of the range have given rise to winter sports; the Cedars, near Bsherri, is a famous ski-ing resort.

The Lebanon range acts as a rain barrier. The eastern slopes of the mountains have an annual precipitation which is usually less than 25 in., and the valley of the Bekaa, which is in a definite rain shadow, may have less still. The Anti-Lebanon have about 30 in. as a maximum, but the Mount Hermon group, higher and more exposed, may have 40 in. or more. Mount Hermon itself is snowclad for nearly six months. East of the Lebanon range, rainfall becomes uncertain; in some years not more than 50% of the above averages is experienced. Temperatures in the Bekaa and its enclosing mountains are more extreme than nearer the coast, ranging in the valley from an average of 41° F (5° C) in January to 85° F (29·4° C) in August, with an average diurnal range of about 18° F (10° C). Maxima of 100° F (37·8° C) are not uncommon in the summer.

The vegetation of the coast and the western side of the Lebanon has the usual Mediterranean characteristics, but the Bekaa and Anti-Lebanon belong to the poorer region of the steppe, and Mediterranean species occur only sporadically along the watercourses. East of the Lebanon range forest and grassland do not properly exist. The place of the first is taken for the most part by a low brushwood; grass is not plentiful; and the higher ridges support alpine flora only as long as there is snow-melt.

On the western side, to a height of 1600 ft (490 m), the locust tree and stone pine are widespread, but the great mass of the vegetation is of the low-growing type (maquis or garrigue), with small, stiff leaves, and frequently aromatic (ilex, smilax, rock-rose). From 1600 to 6500 ft (490–1980 m) may be called the mountain forest zone, but there are few continuously tree-covered areas. There are sparse woods and isolated trees wherever shelter, moisture and the inhabitants have permitted their growth. For ages the mountain dwellers have exploited the forests for fuel and commercial timber, and their goats have been just as destructive here as in other parts of the Mediterranean. From 1600 to 3200 ft (490–980 m) is a zone of dwarf evergreen oaks; above, up to 4200 ft (1280 m) a tall pine (*P. Brutia*) is characteristic; and higher, between 4200 ft and 6200 ft (1280–1890 m), are the cedar and cypress for which Lebanon is famous. The cedars are shown in Fig. 139. From Biblical and classical times until recently, both species have been ruthlessly cut down and were in danger of disappearing; today they are carefully conserved. Mixed with the cedars and cypresses are a deciduous oak (*Quercus subalpina*) and the rare Cilician silver fir (*Abies cilicica*), and at higher levels junipers (*Juniper excelsa*) and the beautiful *Rhododendron ponticum*, with its brilliant purple flower clusters. Above 6500 ft (1980 m), and reaching to within 300 ft (90 m) of the highest summits, is an alpine flora which consists in the main of low, dense, pillow-like, horizontal-growing dwarf bushes, thorny and grey, completely unrelated to the alpine flora of the Alps and northern Asia and directly connected with many species found in Oriental lands at lower altitudes.

HUMAN GEOGRAPHY

HISTORY AND PEOPLE

In ancient geography the name given to the seaboard of Lebanon was Phoenicia, some account of which has been given in previous pages. Modern Lebanon became an independent republic in 1946, when the French mandate was relinquished. The country had already joined the Arab League in 1945 and took part in the invasion of Israel in 1948. In 1956 and 1967, however, it refrained from any active share in the Arab struggle against the Hebrews, largely because the Lebanese Christians, who form the majority of the population, prefer to deal with the Palestine question politically rather than by force of arms.

In economic affairs the Lebanese go far beyond the purely Pan-Arab aims of the Arab League, and have effected commercial and social ties with the Western world. To this end the economic union which was signed with Syria in 1946 was dissolved in 1950, and Lebanon is now striving to become once more the commercial intermediary between

[*Courtesy of National Council of Tourism in Lebanon.*

FIG. 139.—Lebanon: the cedars. Very little is left of the cedar forests of Biblical times. Most of such trees grow near Bsherri, a ski resort at over 5000 ft (1520 m). The trees average 100 ft (30 m) in height and up to 50 ft (15 m) in circumference, and they have become the symbols of Lebanon.

East and West, as it was in the days of the Phoenicians. In this it is achieving a considerable amount of success, for it is the most advanced of the Arab countries. It is renowned in the Middle East for the quality of its educational facilities, and it has an enlightened and democratic political system in which power is nicely balanced between Christians and Muslims; the President is always elected from the Maronite party, the strongest Christian sect, and the Premier from the influential Sunni Muslims.

Lebanon is usually regarded as an Arab country and Arabic is its official language, yet the majority of its people are non-Arab and non-Muslim.

The total population numbers about 1,750,000, of whom over 50% are Maronite and other Christians, more than 40% Muslims, and the remainder mostly Druzes. It is a very mixed population which on the whole displays the usual characteristics of mountain people, fine physique and vigorous independent spirit, for it must be remembered that most Lebanese are descended from political and religious refugees who isolated themselves in fastnesses in the Lebanon mountains.

The chief Christian sects are the Maronites, Greek Catholics and Greek Orthodox. The Maronites trace their Christian traditions from the days when Lebanon formed part of Roman Syria. Their beliefs were clarified and organised in the seventh century by St John Maron, a patriarch of the sect, after whom they are named; and in the twelfth century they became a Uniate, that is a Greek-speaking, Church in communion with Rome. They were most numerous in the central and northern Lebanon mountains, whence in recent times they have descended to Beirut and the Bekaa. They form about three-fifths of the Christian community. Greek Catholics, who make up another one-fifth, are also a Uniate Church; they live mostly in and around Zahle in the central Lebanon range. The Greek Orthodox, with whom should be included adherents of the Armenian Orthodox, are Syrian by race and Arab-speaking; they are descendants of the Melkists, a Christian offshoot of the Byzantine Church, on whose side their ancestors fought against the Muslims and, eventually, against the Maronites. They are strongest in southern Lebanon, and are among the most progressive of the Christian elements.

The main Islamic sects in Lebanon are the Sunni and the Shi'a. The Sunni, who are orthodox Muslims, are easily the most numerous and influential, especially in the towns and villages of the north. The Shi'a Muslims, whose culture is more backward than that of the Sunni, live chiefly in southern Lebanon, the Bekaa and the Tripoli district. They form a most belligerent religious minority, with great animosity against Israel. The Druzes, who have a peculiar religion derived from Shi'a Islamism and the Bible and flavoured with animism, are a small and unpopular minority in the southern Lebanon range and the Mount Hermon massif. Violent and warlike in temperament, they make good soldiers, and they are often recruited to the Shi'a terrorist bands.

Lebanon, with an average of 548 persons per square mile, has the greatest density of population of any country in the Middle East, despite its mountain environment and its lack of minerals. Nevertheless there is less tendency to over-population than in much larger countries such as Egypt and Syria. The chief reasons for this are, firstly, the remarkable predominance of trading activities in the economic life of the country. Lebanon acts as an entrepôt and distributing centre for a large part of the Middle East, and this gives employment and purchasing power to a big proportion of its inhabitants. Its hinterland extends to Syria, Iraq and Jordan, with which it has reasonably good communications; and its transit trade supports, directly and indirectly, about a third of the total population.

Urbanisation in the Lebanon is untypical of the Middle East, in that there is far less abject poverty in its cities than in those of other Arab states, and there are more opportunities for educational advance and social improvement.

Secondly, although Lebanon's entrepôt services still leave a trade deficit, this is offset by a substantial income from foreign aid, principally from France and the U.S.A., and from tourism, pipeline royalties and remittances from overseas Lebanese. The Lebanon mountains, which are sometimes called the "Switzerland of the Middle East," are renowned for their scenic beauty, and attract annually about 500,000 visitors to their summer and winter resorts; and others are drawn to the country's archaeological treasures of the past (see Fig. 140). Two trunk pipelines cross Lebanon from the oilfields to the east, one from Kirkuk (Iraq) to Tripoli, the other from Abqaiq (Saudia Arabia) to Sidon, and known as Tapline (Trans-Arabian Pipeline). For these, and for the terminals at the ports, Lebanon receives payments from the oil companies, and in addition it benefits by the stimulus given to its economy by local spending on foodstuffs and other commodities by pipeline officials and by employment of local native labour. Money sent by Lebanese abroad to their relatives in Lebanon enables them to live in more comfort at home and slows down the stream of emigration, so increasing the density of population. It is notable, however, that the economy of Lebanon, although it is prosperous, cannot cope entirely with a further increase in its ever-expanding population. There is in consequence a constant trickle of emigrants, possibly 2500 a year, principally to the U.S.A., Brazil, Argentina and Australia.

THE ECONOMY

Lebanon, although its economy depends very largely on its commercial activities, is essentially an agricultural country. At present, 26% of its area is cultivated and a further 16% is cultivable by extended irrigation or improved dry-farming techniques, about 25% is pasture, and 8% forest. The remainder is unproductive mountain, marsh and semi-desert, or is occupied by cities and towns. Of the cultivated land, about 130,000 acres are irrigated, mostly on the terraced slopes of the Lebanon mountains and in the Bekaa; in the latter there are plans for big extensions, as noted earlier. Most farms are small (10–12 acres; 4–5 ha) and are intensively cultivated by their Christian and Druze owners, but in south Lebanon, the Akkar Plain and the Bekaa there are large estates owned by Muslims who practise extensive cultivation. The rural standard of living is higher than in neighbouring Arab countries.

Pastoralism is secondary in Lebanon. Goats (500,000) are the most numerous animals; they are reared mostly on the upper slopes of the Lebanon, in the Bekaa and the Anti-Lebanon, including Mount Hermon. On the Lebanon, where they are allowed to wander almost unrestricted, they have wrought incalculable damage in the forests. Sheep (75,000) are found mainly in the Bekaa and the Anti-Lebanon; sheep-rearing is usually accompanied by transhumance, and journeys of 20 miles (32 km) between winter and summer pastures are common. The largest numbers of cattle (70,000) are in the coastal plains and the irrigated Litani valley, but pigs (7000) are few, and kept almost entirely by non-Muslims. Asses (20,000) and mules (6000) are the chief transport animals; the slopes of the mountains are covered by a network of carefully constructed tracks for their use. There are also 2000 camels in Lebanon, owned by Bedouin in the Bekaa and Anti-Lebanon, nomads who wander in winter far into the Syrian Desert.

Cereals are not important in Lebanese agriculture. The chief is wheat, which is grown mostly on the large Muslim estates; but the total (59,000 tons a year) is small and the standard of production low, and Lebanon has to import further supplies of grain and flour. Maize cultivation has commenced in the Bekaa by means of irrigation, but the total output so far is small. On the other hand the fruit crop of Lebanon, in variety, quality and amount, is of great value, and forms a large part of the country's exports. Many of its fruits, such as the olive, vine, pomegranate, fig, carob, peach, apricot and cherry, are indigenous, and to these have been added at various times the orange, sugar cane, mulberry, strawberry, apple and even the banana. Tobacco is an important crop; cotton in recent years has occupied an increasingly large area, especially on the larger farms; and potatoes are being cultivated with great success in the more elevated and damper parts of the Bekaa.

Industrial developments in Lebanon, judged by Western standards, are small, yet in the past 15 years industrial output has more than doubled. Expansion is by private enterprise, helped by high tariffs against foreign competitors, and has been largely in the field of food-processing, textiles, chemicals and oil-refining. Craft industries, such as lace-making in Beirut and embroidery throughout the coastal region and the Lebanon slopes, find ready customers among the tourists. The tourist industry, which is a large source of revenue, has been mentioned above. Lebanon's industrial development is being viewed with sympathy by the Western world, and in 1965 a trade agreement was signed with the European Economic Community ("Common Market") to give Lebanon "most-favoured-nation" terms. This agreement is noteworthy because it was the first of its kind to be issued to a non-member of GATT, that is, the General Agreement on Tariffs and Trade, an organisation set up to reduce tariffs and increase international trade, to which as yet none of the Levant Arab countries belongs.

Lebanon has one of the best communications systems in the Levant. There are good road networks along the coast, especially around Beirut and the oil ports, Tripoli and Sidon, and main roads across the mountains join Beirut to the Bekaa and Damascus (*see* Fig. 138 (*b*)). A coastal railway gives communication from Homs (Syria) via all the main ports to the southern frontier; originally constructed by the British to run to Cairo, through passage from Syria to Egypt was stopped in 1948, when the Israeli portion was disconnected by the Arabs. Beirut is also connected by a transmontane line to Damascus and Amman, and a branch serves the northern Bekaa. Beirut has a major airport which is a scheduled stop on most air routes from Europe to south-east Asia.

REGIONAL ECONOMY

1. *The coastal plain.* Away from the towns the coastal plains and lower slopes of the Lebanon spurs have intensive cultivation of olives, citrus fruits, cotton, bananas, and market garden produce for export and to supply the urban population. Bananas are cultivated along the floors of deep river gorges where alluvial soils are abundant, water is plentiful and the air is hot, steamy and still. The vine is a notable absentee in the coastal region, for in the humid atmosphere it is liable to contract disease.

The chief feature of the region is its ports, of which Beirut, Tripoli and Sidon are the most important. Beirut (500,000) lies on a promontory south of St George's Bay. It has a good deep-water harbour which has been improved artificially, and is the largest port in the Levant. It houses more than one-third of the country's population and is its capital. It has good communications with the interior and with Damascus and Amman, so that it has become an international entrepôt, dealing with most of the transit trade of Lebanon and with international finance and insurance; and it is also a centre for tourism. Its own industries are food processing, sugar refining and the manufacture of cotton textiles. The modern development of Beirut has been helped by the Arab boycott of Haifa and Tel Aviv since 1948, but is now being challenged by the Syrian port of Latakia.

Tripoli (100,000), the second port and city of Lebanon, lies in the north of the coast and commands the Homs gap to Syria and the northern Bekaa. It has a share in the transit trade of northern Lebanon, but its main importance derives from the pipeline which connects it to Kirkuk, and from its oil refinery and tanker installations. Like Beirut, it has a thriving cotton textile manufacture. South of Beirut are the small ports of Saida (Sidon) and Tyre, mere shadows of the great mercantile centres of Phoenician times. They were built originally on islands, for defensive purposes, but silting joined them to the mainland and spoiled their harbours. Saida (22,000) is the terminal port of the oil Tapline and has a refinery, but Tyre (12,000) has only local importance. Near Jubeil (ancient Byblus) at "one of the most beautiful sites in the world" is the source of the river Adonis, shown in Fig. 140.

2. *The Lebanon range.* The lower western slopes and valleys of the Lebanon mountains are carefully terraced up to about 3000 ft (900 m) and irrigated by the large number of streams flowing from the spring-line above. It is a region of small farms, owned for the most part by Maronites, who practise intensive cultivation of tree crops. Products vary with altitude. The lowest slopes, up to 1000 ft (300 m), are given over to citrus fruits (oranges, lemons), figs, olives and mulberries (for silk), and enough

[*Courtesy of National Council of Tourism in Lebanon.*

FIG. 140.—Lebanon: the cave of Adonis, 27 miles (43 km) east of
Jubeil (Byblus) in the mountains. The cave is in a precipice
650 ft (200 m) high and is the source of the river Adonis (Nahr
Ibrahim). The Adonis of legend was so beautiful that Venus
left heaven to be with him. He was mortally wounded by a wild
boar and from his blood, the legends say, sprang the anemone:
"In stony Lebanon where blooms his red anemone"

(*J. E. Flecker*).

wheat and maize for the farmers' own requirements. From 1000 to 3000
ft (300–910 m) there are more olive groves and this is the zone of vineyards. The grape harvest is used mostly for sultanas and dessert; only a
small proportion is made into wine. This is also the zone for tobacco,
apricots, peaches and plums. The highest cultivated zone, which continues to the spring-line at anything up to 5000 ft (1520 m), has orchards
of apples and pears, and other cool temperate fruits; and there are fields of
potatoes and sugar beet. To the north of the Lebanon, on the lava slopes
which fall to the Plain of Akkar, the chief crops are wheat and barley.

Most of the population of the Lebanon range is in small, nucleated villages, perched very often in easily defended positions on picturesque and apparently inaccessible bluffs, and within easy distance of the farmlands. Many of the villages in the south of the range have developed into summer holiday resorts, to which come the people of the coastal cities to escape the enervating humidity of the lowlands and to enjoy the scenic beauty of the mountains. In the northern Lebanon the winter snows have encouraged the development of winter sports, especially around Bsherri. The tourist industry has led to the building of large hotels on the mountain slopes, and services to the visitors provide added revenue to the mountain dwellers.

3. *The Bekaa.* The trough of the Bekaa is in a rain shadow, and much of its surface is dry, empty and unused. Where water is available, however, as along spring-lines at the foot of the Lebanon and Anti-Lebanon mountains and near the rivers Orontes and Litani, the soils are fertile and productive. The population of the Bekaa is Muslim, and is thinly spread in villages along the spring-lines, where it is engaged in subsistence cultivation of wheat and barley on a dry-farming basis. Near the villages there may be orchards of apricots and peaches, olive groves and vineyards, but their output is negligible. Agriculture is combined with sheep- and goat-rearing, and transhumance is common. A recent irrigation project based on the waters of the Litani and the karst Lake Yammoune (Yammouneh) has transformed a large area in the southern half of the Bekaa, and in the north waters from the Orontes have been made available as part of the Homs development scheme. The irrigated area is gradually being increased, and crops of maize, cotton and potatoes are produced on land which a few years ago was given over to transhumant sheep and camels. A hydro-electricity plant forms part of the Litani Project and provides power to Zahle. Zahle (33,000), at the eastern end of the only good route across the Lebanon range, is a railway junction on the line from Beirut to Damascus. It is situated in the foothills of the Lebanon, away from the floor of the Bekaa, and has a pleasant climate. The hillsides around it are terraced and intensively cultivated by Druze farmers, producing much the same crops as the western Lebanon. Zahle is the largest of the summer resorts and acts as the regional capital of the Bekaa. Baalbek, on the Anti-Lebanon side of the Bekaa, contains famous Roman ruins and is another summer hill station. The Bekaa contains most of Lebanon's undeveloped cultivable land, and the changes made by irrigation schemes in the past few years suggest that the part it plays in the economy of the country will be greatly enhanced in the not too distant future.

4. *The Anti-Lebanon ranges.* The steep slopes of the Anti-Lebanon are of karst limestone with a scanty cover of garrigue. With the exception of a few Muslim villages in ravines which penetrate the foot of the mountains, the range is virtually uninhabited. Herds of goats and sheep are tended on the slopes by transhumant herdsmen whose homes are in the villages below. The western and southern slopes of the Mount Hermon massif to

the south are moister; and Druze farmers carry on terraced cultivation of olives, vines, fruit and tobacco. The chief settlement is Rasheiye, which is little more than a village at the foot of the mountains, near the upper river Jordan.

STUDY QUESTIONS

1. Write a concise geographical account of Lebanon. Illustrate your answer with a sketch map.

2. Give a comparative account of the economic development of Syria and Lebanon.

3. Divide Lebanon into physical regions and give a summary of the economy of each of your divisions.

Chapter XXVI

JORDAN

THE Hashemite Kingdom of Jordan is made up of Transjordan, an Arab state east of the river Jordan, and large parts of Samaria and Judaea, which were added as a result of the Arab–Israeli war of 1948. Since mid-1967, Samaria and Judaea have been in the hands of Israel, but here they will be regarded as still a part of Jordan. The total area of Jordan is about 37,000 sq. miles (96,200 sq. km); the figure is not exact, because the frontiers with Iraq and Saudi Arabia in the eastern desert have never been officially demarcated. Jordan may be divided physically into (1) Samaria and Judaea, (2) the Jordan rift valley known as El Ghor, (3) the highlands of Transjordan, and (4) the eastern desert (*see* Fig. 141).

PHYSICAL ASPECTS

STRUCTURAL DIVISIONS

1. *Samaria and Judaea.* This region, west of the Jordan trough, was formerly a part of Palestine. It is divided into the Samarian uplands in the north and the Judaean plateau or platform in the south. It is a gentle anticline, mainly of Jurassic limestone, which is faulted abruptly to the east, where the land falls precipitously to the Jordan valley. In Samaria the limestones have been eroded more than in Judaea, and the surface deeply dissected into blocks and isolated hills separated by broad, fertile valleys such as those of the rivers Hadera and Yarkon, or by narrow, gorge-like clefts. The average elevation of the Samarian uplands is less than 1500 ft (460 m), and no peak inside Jordanian territory reaches 3000 ft (900 m).

The hill country is succeeded southwards by the continuous, unbroken plateau of Judaea, much of which lies between 1500 and 3000 ft (460–910 m). This is karst country, characterised by wide stretches of bare, dry limestone, with here and there a thin, dusty soil supporting a scanty, thorny scrub vegetation. Many of the hills which rise above the rolling surface of the plateau have shallow valleys carved into their slopes, but there is no surface drainage. The rains are quickly swallowed by the jointed limestone and emerge at the foot of the plateau as intermittent streams which flow across the coastal plain of Israel to the Mediterranean; the chief of these streams is the Rubin. In a few places, subterranean water has dissolved caves and passages which have collapsed, producing basin-like hollows on the plateau surface. The floors of these basins may have a layer of reddish soils, the insoluble residue of the dissolved limestone, mixed with chalky marls. Occasionally there are small springs emerging from the boulder-strewn sides of the basins, sufficient to make the soil cultivable and to allow settlement. Ramallah, Bethlehem and Hebron are the largest of such settlements. Jerusalem, part of which is in Jordan,

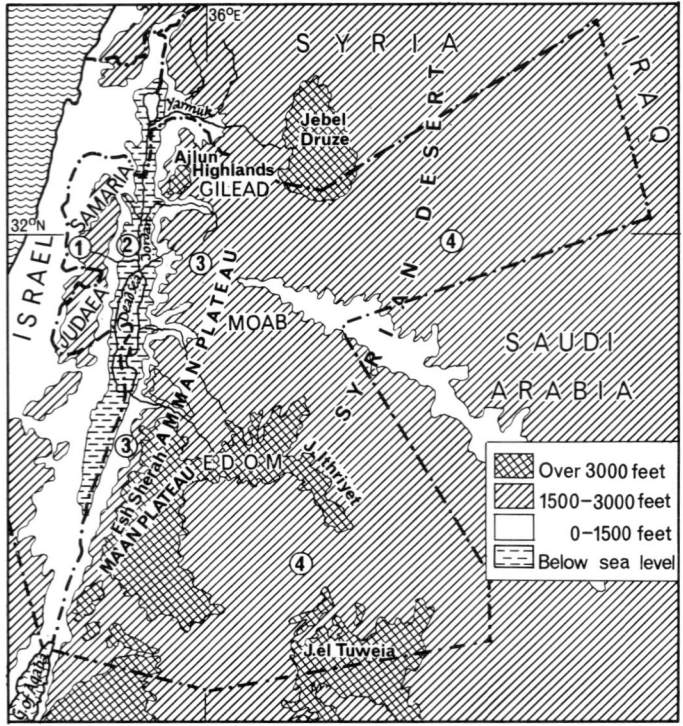

FIG. 141.—Jordan: physical. The numbers refer to sections in the text.

stands on a rocky eminence 2560 ft (780 m) above sea-level, and looks down on valleys which fall to more than 600 ft (180 m) below the general surface of the plateau. All these valleys are now irrigated and productive, but only a small proportion lies inside the Jordanian frontier; the remainder is in Israel.

The south-east of the Judaean plateau is "The Wilderness" of Biblical renown. Here the annual rainfall is not more than 8 in., erosion is slow, and the limestones and marl have weathered into dry, bare, rounded hills intersected by deep gorges, in which there is an occasional stream. It is a wild, inhospitable region, which from time immemorial has been the home of robbers and outlaws or the refuge of the oppressed. David and his followers took to it in order to escape from Saul, and in later days it was a favourite retreat for monks and hermits. There are still one or two Greek Orthodox monasteries whose communities eke out a precarious existence by laboriously cultivating a few patches on the valley floors, but in general the region is incapable of cultivation or reclamation.

2. *El Ghor.* East of the highlands of Galilee, Samaria and Judaea, the land has been let down between two series of parallel north–south faults to form a trough roughly 250 miles (400 km) long, from the north of

Lake Tiberias to the Gulf of Aqaba in the south. The rift, which varies from 2 to 15 miles (3–24 km) in width, has a flat floor which slopes downwards in both directions to a maximum depth of 2598 ft (792 m) *below* sea-level on the floor of the Dead Sea. For most of its length it is bounded on both sides by precipitous cliffs which have been eroded by the torrents of winter to give the narrow gorges, blind canyons, and other forbidding characteristics of typical "badlands." A few perennial streams, such as the Yarmuk and Nahr es Zerqa (Jabbok) from the east, and the Faria from the west, have cut longer, wider valleys, along which steep roads climb from the rift. The name El Ghor is often given to the whole of the rift valley, but it is better reserved for the deeper stretch between Lake Tiberias and the Dead Sea.

The rift is drained by the river Jordan. This river rises about 1000 ft (300 m) above sea-level on the slopes of Mount Hermon. At Lake Huleh, where its flow is impeded by a barrier of basaltic lava across the valley, it is 223 ft (68 m) above sea-level; but from there the gradient increases and at Lake Tiberias (Sea of Galilee), which is the result of another lava barrier, the river surface is 695 ft (213 m) *below* sea-level. Lake Tiberias, a picturesque freshwater lake, 150 ft (45 m) deep, is known to the Hebrews as *Kinnereth*, from its harp-like shape. Below Lake Tiberias, the Jordan winds a sinuous but rapid course to the Dead Sea, whose surface is given variously as 1286 and 1291 ft (c. 393 m) below sea-level, and its depth about 1300 ft (400 m). The distance from Lake Tiberias to the Dead Sea is less than 60 miles (96 km), but so numerous are the meanderings of the Jordan that its actual course measures some 200 miles (320 km). The river bed is in a trench many feet deep, which it has dug for itself in the soft, calcareous soils of the Ghor. Here and there the walls of its incised meanders rise as perpendicular cliffs from 20 to 100 ft (6–30 m) or more; elsewhere it winds itself round the bases of lofty knolls eroded by rain and storm, thrown together in wild confusion and recalling a lunar landscape.

In the north both banks of the Jordan are lined with willows, poplars, tamarisks, eucalyptuses and a wild tangle of aquatic plants, but south of the Zerqa confluence the river becomes increasingly saline and the vegetation disappears completely, giving way to salt marsh. In the spring, when the snows of Hermon melt and its tributaries are in spate, the Jordan overflows its banks and the flood water may spread widely. The Jordan, unlike other famous rivers, has never been a link between cities and peoples on opposite banks; on the contrary, it is and always has been a line of cleavage. Its many rapids make navigation impossible, and there are no towns or villages along its banks in the Ghor.

The Dead Sea, at the lowest level of the Ghor, is a lake of inland drainage nearly 47 miles (73 km) long and up to 9½ miles (15 km) wide. In spite of enormous quantities of water which pour into it from the Jordan and, in winter, from torrents which stream down its mountainous surround, the level of the Dead Sea varies only slightly. This is due to the very high rate of evaporation from its waters, and this accounts also for their unusual salinity; they have a mineral content of 23·4%, as compared with approximately 4% in the open ocean. In the past 40 years this mineral wealth has been exploited for potash, common salt and bromine (from magnesium salts). South of the Dead Sea and the saline encrustations which surround it, the floor of the rift valley rises, and reaches sea-level again about 20 miles (32 km) from the Gulf of Aqaba.

Not all the rift valley is in Jordan. The Jordanian frontier reaches the river Jordan in the north at the Yarmuk confluence, and for over 20 miles (32 km) southwards from this point Jordan shares the Ghor with Israel. The southern half of the Dead Sea, too, is divided between the two countries; and from the southern extremity of the Dead Sea to the Gulf of Aqaba the Jordan–Israeli frontier follows the centre of the rift. The original western frontier of Transjordan was the river Jordan and a line through the middle of the Dead Sea. The boundaries of Jordan in Palestine mark the area of occupation by Jordanian forces at the end of the 1948 conflict.

3. *The highlands of Transjordan.* East of the Ghor is the edge of the Arabian tableland, faulted, tilted and uplifted in places to about 5000 ft (1530 m). The Cretaceous limestones, Eocene sandstones and intrusive lavas which form most of the surface series of rocks have been fractured and dissected into three great plateaus sloping gently to the east. In the north is the Ajlun (Gilead) highland, with Um ed Daraj (4050 ft, 1234 m) its highest point. With an annual rainfall of about 30 in. this is the best-watered part of Jordan. South of Ajlun is the rolling tableland of Amman (Moab), averaging less than 3000 ft (910 m) for the most part, but rising in the south to 4407 ft (1343 m) in Qasr ed Deir and 4960 ft (1512 m) in Jebel el Bukka. Southwards again is the high plateau of Ma'an (Edom), which rarely falls below 3500 ft (1070 m) and has several ridges over 5000 ft (1520 m). Jebel Ram (5700 ft, 1737 m) and Jebel Mubrak (5615 ft, 1711 m) are its highest points.

4. *The eastern desert.* East of the Transjordan highlands and marked off artificially from them by the line of the Hejaz (Hedjaz) railway from Damascus to beyond Ma'an, is the Jordanian portion of the Syrian Desert. It is a plateau which falls gently eastwards to an average height of about 2000 feet (600 m) near the frontiers with Iraq and Saudi Arabia, and becomes increasingly arid. The foundation of Archaean rocks has a thick cover of calcareous and sandstone series, which appear to have been undisturbed by tectonic movements and have weathered into a generally undulating surface, with here and there deeper depressions which are moister and contain oases, as at Azrak and Jafr. In the north, lava flows and extinct volcanoes, an extension of the Jebel Druze and Hauran of Syria, create a black, basalt area which is particularly barren.

CLIMATE AND VEGETATION

Jordan lies climatically in a transition zone, where a Mediterranean régime in the west merges rapidly into one of a hot desert type in the east of the country; and the Ghor, below sea-level, may be said to have a climate peculiar to itself. Temperatures in the Samarian and Judaean hill country are reduced by elevation and range from averages of 41° F (5·0° C) in January in higher regions to nearly 80° F (26·5° C) in August, the hottest month. Jerusalem, for instance, has means for January and August of 47° F (8·3° C) and 75° F (23·9° C), and Nablus 49° F (9·4° C) and 76° F (24·4° C) for the same months. In winter, temperatures may fall below freezing point, and precipitation is in the form of snow, which rarely lasts more than a few days. For most of the year the hill country is swept by strong, westerly sea breezes which usually begin to blow about midday.

The Transjordanian highlands are more extreme, mean temperatures ranging from 40° F (4·4° C) in January to 88° F (31·1° C) in August, and there is a greater diurnal range; maximum temperatures in summer often reach 100° F (37·8° C). Further east, in the desert, winter temperatures are much the same as in the highlands, but the summers are hotter, and averages of 90° F (32·2° C) are common and readings of 110° F (43·3° C) not unusual. Temperatures in the Ghor are high all the year. Jericho, which may be taken as representative, ranges from a mean in January of 57° F (13·9° C) to 88° F (31·1° C) in August, a truly sub-tropical range due to its low-lying, sheltered position.

Precipitation in Jordan decreases in amount from north to south and from west to east, and everywhere, including the eastern desert, there is a maximum in winter. The wettest regions are in northern Samaria and the Ajlun highlands, where there is an annual fall of from 25 to 30 in. West of the Jordan, the annual total decreases southwards, to an average of 19·2 in. in Jerusalem and less than 8 in. in "The Wilderness." The averages, however, do not indicate the uncertainty of the actual rainfall, and this is true throughout the Levant. Jerusalem, for instance, had only 16·4 in. in 1959, as against 28·2 in. in 1961. East of the Jordan, there are small areas in the northern and central highlands with up to 30 in. annually, but in general the total yearly amount is less than 20 in. and more usually about 15 in. In the southern highlands and in the eastern desert there is a gradual diminution to 5 in. or less. The Ghor, too, has these very arid conditions; the annual rainfall at Jericho is 5 in. In the Ghor there is intense evaporation, and this results in great humidity and, especially near the Jordan, very heavy mists in the early morning.

Natural vegetation on the Samarian hills and Judaean plateau is mainly patchy garrigue, with occasional thickets of dwarf oaks and wild olives, and with tufty grasses in the deeper and wider valleys. Southwards, as the rainfall becomes less, trees become more stunted and the garrigue degenerates into thorny scrub until, in the driest area, there are just bare limestones and dusty marls. There are the same types and distribution of vegetation in the Transjordanian highlands, but at lower elevations there are acacias, tamarisks, bulbous plants and tough grasses characteristic of arid steppe. Eastwards, the steppe vegetation gradually thins out, and in the desert there are large areas with no vegetation at all. The moister oases may have date palms, but they do not fruit very well on the Arabian plateau. In the Jordan valley, the dense vegetation south of Lake Tiberias is more tropical than temperate, but, as already noted, the banks of the river nearer the Dead Sea are bare and desolate. Nearer the edges of the rift, however, even in patches along the shores of the Dead Sea itself, there may be sufficient halophilous vegetation to attract nomadic herdsmen in winter.

The hills of Samaria, northern Judaea and Ajlun were at one time forested, but ruthless cutting down of the trees in the past resulted in soil erosion, so that the flanks of the hills are now often bare and gaunt, except where terraces have been laboriously built to contain the soil. From 1920 to 1948, the Jews pursued a vigorous policy of afforestation in Samaria and Judaea, and since that date the Jordanians have taken over the supervision of the large copses of pines and cypresses which are transforming a one-time desolate landscape, and are extending their efforts to Ajlun and even to the lava slopes of the Hauran.

HUMAN GEOGRAPHY

HISTORY

In 1946 the new state of Transjordan was given sovereignty. Prior to 1919 it consisted of a number of Arab sheikhdoms under Turkish rule, but it was then mandated to Britain, given the name Transjordan and placed under the Emir Abdullah. Under British administration Transjordan made slow but steady economic advance in a stable political atmosphere, and in 1946 the mandate was relinquished. In 1948, during the Arab–Israeli war, Jordanian troops marched into Palestine; and when an armistice was declared, by which established battle-positions became stabilised frontiers, they held portions of Jerusalem, and the Samarian and Judaean highlands. These were added to Transjordan and the enlarged state was renamed Jordan. In the following year it became known as the Hashemite Kingdom of Jordan, with Abdullah its first proclaimed king.

Since 1948 Jordan, in common with other members of the Arab League, has had no diplomatic nor commercial relations with Israel, but its attitude towards the Hebrews is neither as bitter nor as uncompromising as that of Syria and Egypt. This may be because in its acquisition of valuable territory it fared better than other Arab countries, or it may be that it is more fearful of the vulnerability of its long land frontier with Israel, amounting to 329 miles. In this regard it is significant that until recently there were relatively fewer border incidents between Jordan and Israel than elsewhere, and that Jordan took no active part in the Suez crisis of 1956. In the Six Days War, 1967, however, Jordan was one of the Arab allies who suffered humiliating defeat. All the Cis-Jordanian territory which was gained in 1948 was recovered by Israel and remains at present in Hebrew hands.

The political future of Judaea, Samaria and Old Jerusalem is uncertain, and in this book they are still considered as a part of Jordan. Their permanent loss to that country would give a crippling blow to its struggling economy, which has been weakened also by the strain placed upon its meagre resources by the flood of Arab refugees, who poured across its frontiers from Israel in 1948 and again in 1967 (*see* page 526). Since 1967 there has been a recrudescence of terrorist raids across the Israeli border with Jordan, both countries being blamed for the incidents. It seems fairly certain, however, that many of them are organised by Syrian and Palestinian malcontents in the refugee camps, for the Jordanian Government, along with Lebanon, seems more ready than the rest of the Arab world to reach a permanent settlement of the Palestine question by peaceful negotiations.

PEOPLE

The population of Jordan is estimated to be 1,752,000, with an average density of 47 persons per square mile. Due regard must be paid to the fact, however, that one-eighth of the total lives in Amman, the capital, and that there are many urban concentrations in Samaria and the refugee camps, leaving vast areas of the eastern desert and southern highlands virtually uninhabited.

Most of the people are Arabs, Sunni Muslims, and are of three types. Firstly, many of the inhabitants of the Transjordanian highlands are descended from the Moabites, Ammonites and Edomites of Old Testament times, and are probably of Aramaean stock, much diluted from the seventh century B.C. onwards by continuous infiltrations of Arabs from the east and south; they are therefore of mixed Semitic blood. From very early times they have been sedentary, cultivating the land, and living in towns, and in this they present a contrast to the second type, the Arabs of the desert. These are the Bedouin, nomads, who probably represent the primitive Semitic race. There has been hostility from time immemorial between the sedentary Arab and the Bedouin, and this undoubtedly is a main factor in the lack of unity or concerted action inherent in the Arab world. The third type of Arab is the refugee from Palestine. Many of these had been influenced by generations of Western and Hebrew contacts and may have been successful farmers, merchants, professional men and skilled technicians with a more advanced culture than most of the native Jordanians. The great majority are still in refugee camps where their skills cannot be used to the full, but many have been absorbed into the general community, to the great advantage of the country's economy.

THE ECONOMY

GENERAL

The economy of Jordan is based on subsistence agriculture and nomadic pastoralism (*see* Fig. 142). West of the Hejaz railway there are many areas potentially of high agricultural value; east of the line is mostly desert and fit for nothing except winter pasture for camels. Climate is the governing factor; and since rainfall is restricted to the winter months and is usually deficient in amount and uncertain in its areal distribution, cultivation by modern techniques is confined to the better-watered regions of Cis-Jordan and the central and northern Transjordanian highlands. East and south of these is the "pioneer fringe," where as far as the 15 in. isohyet cultivation by dry-farming methods is possible but not always successful. Even in the best parts of Jordan the soils are thin and agriculture depends on irrigation.

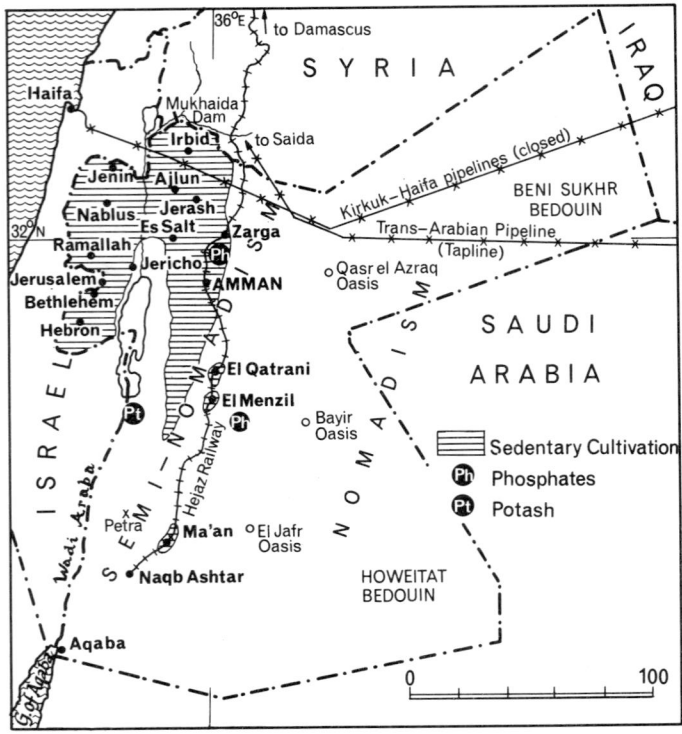

FIG. 142.—Jordan: land use.

The development of irrigation is one of the main items in Jordan's economic programme. The present systems are small and are located for terraced cultivation chiefly in Samaria, Judaea, Ajlun and Amman. Full use of the water of the river Jordan for irrigation purposes awaits a settlement between Israel, which controls part of its flow, and Jordan.

In parts of western Jordan cultivation is intensive and there is some mechanisation, but eastwards farming methods become primitive and little removed from those of antiquity. Land-holdings are usually small, and the peasant farmer combines agriculture with transhumant rearing of sheep and goats. Wheat and barley are the chief cereals in the west, and are now being grown extensively in the dry-farming regions of the east;

but large quantities of grain have to be imported. Sorghum, a grass akin to sugar cane, is grown as fodder and for the extraction of sugar. On the terraced lands vegetables are a main crop, and there are olive groves, vineyards and plantations of figs, almonds and peaches. In total, however, the cultivated area of Jordan amounts to only 5% of the country; the rest is pasture land or waste.

Jordan is lacking in mineral resources. There are deposits of phosphates north and south of Amman, from which over $\frac{1}{2}$ million tons are extracted annually, almost entirely for export. Works have been established on the shores of the Dead Sea for the exploitation of potash and other salts from its waters; and manganese ore has been discovered in a valley east of the Ghor. Trial borings for mineral oil have given negative results except in the south, where a well yields about 7500 tons of oil per annum. Jordan, however, draws royalties for the oil Tapline which crosses its desert *en route* to Sidon. A second pipeline, from Kirkuk to Haifa, has been out of use since 1948.

Organised industry is still in its infancy and is related mainly to the products of agriculture and pasture—food processing, flour milling, fruit and meat canning, olive oil extraction and soap-making. In some cases these are financed by U.N.R.W.A. for the benefit of refugees. Textile, leather and tobacco manufactures are still domestic industries, carried on in small native workshops and bazaars. Jordan has few good roads. The best converge on Amman and Jerusalem, or run along the foot of the Transjordanian highlands to give a north–south route for pilgrims to Mecca. There is only one railway, the Hejaz, also intended for pilgrims; it follows the road from the northern frontier to Naqb Ashtar, about 40 miles (64 m) from Aqaba, which is Jordan's only port. Aqaba has been extended to deal with the export of phosphates.

REGIONAL ECONOMY

1. *Samaria and Judaea.* Much of the surface of these plateaus is dry and barren, but usually has sufficient vegetation for the pasture of sheep and goats, which are found there in large numbers, and are transhumant. In depressions and on terraced hillsides wheat, barley, pulses, tomatoes and vegetables are cultivated; there are extensive olive groves, vineyards and fruit orchards; and in the wetter and broader valleys of the north cattle are reared. Samaria is the best cultivated part of Jordan, but Judaea becomes drier and more barren towards the south, where it is very thinly peopled by transhumant herdsmen.

The only towns of any size are Nablus (202,433) and Jenin (93,780) in Samaria, and Jerusalem (124,643; Jordanian section only), Ramallah, Bethlehem and Hebron (143,149) in Judaea. None may be said to be industrial centres, although Nablus has canning and flour milling, and Hebron tanning and glass manufacture. The region, however, constitutes most of the "Holy Land" and draws large numbers of pilgrims and sightseers, and there is a thriving tourist industry. The walled city of Old

Jerusalem, site of the holy places, lies in Jordan: it is sacred alike to Christians, Hebrews and Muslims. For Christians it is the chief city of pilgrimage, with the Church of the Holy Sepulchre, the Garden of Gethsemane and the Mount of Olives; to the Hebrews the Western Wall of the Temple (the "Wailing Wall") and the Tombs of the Patriarchs are sacred; and the Dome of the Rock, after Mecca and Medina, is the third most holy place of Islam. It should be noted that Jerusalem was partitioned in 1948, and the modern (western) portion of the city left in Israeli hands. Since June 1967, however, the Old City has been in Hebrew occupation, and access by the Jews to the Wailing Wall, which had been prohibited by Jordan since 1948, is once more uncontrolled. At the moment, Jews, Christians and Muslims move freely in the city, and endemic skirmishing has been transferred far to the east, to the banks of the river Jordan, but the future of the Old City remains uncertain. Bethlehem, a few miles south of Jerusalem, contains the Church of the Nativity, and is the second holy place of Christendom.

2. *El Ghor*. It has already been noted that physical and climatic conditions in the Jordan trough are inimical to economic development. Nevertheless, Jordan has ambitious schemes for the transformation of the northern portion of the rift valley, and in the south the waters of the Dead Sea are proving to have commercial value. Limited areas south of Lake Tiberias are irrigated, and wheat, barley and tropical fruits such as dates and bananas cultivated, and in 1965 a start was made on the Mukhaida Dam, which will enable the waters of the Jordan to be utilised more extensively. The dam, which is being constructed by an Egyptian firm, is on the Yarmuk river, about 125 miles (200 km) north of Amman. It will divert the flow of the Yarmuk into the East Ghor Canal, so as to irrigate large areas of land, ultimately it is hoped extending to the Dead Sea. The scheme is noteworthy in that it is entirely a Pan-Arab project, 80% of the cost being borne by Egypt, Saudi Arabia, Iraq and Kuwait, and the remainder by Jordan, Syria, Lebanon and Libya. South of Jericho, potash is extracted from saline deposits near the Jordan, and there are plans to establish works along the Dead Sea shores to exploit the mineral content of the water. The potash is exported from Aqaba, a port at the south of the rift valley.

Away from the irrigated lands in the north, the Ghor is poorly peopled. There are a few villages, chiefly where tributaries of the Jordan debouch into the trough, and their inhabitants exist by transhumant pasture of sheep and goats and precarious subsistence agriculture. Parts of the Ghor are also visited in winter by Bedouin nomads. Jericho (65,000) is the only large settlement in the Ghor. It is situated on a tributary whose valley allows a passage from the rift to Jerusalem and is followed by a good road from that city to Amman. The road crosses the Jordan by the Allenby Bridge, the best bridge point south of the Yarmuk confluence. The Jericho district, terraced and irrigated from the stream and from wells, and with a sub-tropical climate, produces figs, bananas, tobacco, vegetables and the

[*Courtesy of Jordan Ministry of Information.*]

FIG. 143.—Petra: the treasury of Pharaoh seen through a dark and narrow gorge, the only easy way into the basin. This is the most elaborate of the ruins of a city which was mostly carved in the solid, rose-coloured rock.

ubiquitous olive. Jericho is one of the oldest cities in the world, its history going back continuously for at least 8000 years. It was regarded in ancient times as the eastern key to Palestine, and it was taken and destroyed many times. Today, its ancient remains attract many tourists and archaeologists.

3. *The highlands of Transjordan.* These form the core of Jordan, and around them the new state of Transjordan was constituted in 1919. On the whole, it is a poor agricultural and pastoral region, becoming poorer still to the east and south. North of Amman, where the highlands receive up to 30 in. of winter rainfall and there are wide river valleys, wheat and barley are the chief crops on almost all farms; and the terraced hillsides are cultivated for vegetables, tobacco, olives, vines and apricots. Most of the people of the northern region live in large settlements such as Irbid (158,859), Zarqa (130,878), Ajlun, Es Salt and Jerash, from which they go out to tend their farms or to lead their sheep and goats to fallow fields or mountain pastures. The region is being greatly developed; more hillsides are being terraced, large areas are being afforested with pines and cypresses, and extensions of irrigation are planned.

In the south of the region is Amman (341,681), the capital of Jordan. Centrally situated on the eastern edge of the highlands, it is a road focus and an important station on the Hejaz railway. But although it is the centre of administration and has growing industries, it has too many inhabitants for the present state of Jordan's economy, and the imbalance is being increased by the influx of refugees. In consequence, there is much poverty in the city. Amman's industries are connected mainly with food processing and consumer goods, and with craft workmanship.

South of Amman cultivation by irrigation begins to disappear, and in the southern highlands is replaced by dry-farming of cereals. In fact, a belt from north to south along the eastern margin of the whole of the highlands, previously referred to as the "pioneer fringe," is given over to this farming technique, which is carried on by tent-dwelling semi-nomads who are also pastoralists. Cultivation in this zone is not universal, but tends to be concentrated in districts more favoured by soil or rainfall, such as are found around the villages of El Qatrani, El Menzil and Ma'an.

In a basin in the southern highlands, about 25 miles (40 km) north-west of Ma'an, is the ruined city of Petra, which, although not easily accessible, is of great interest to tourists and archaeologists (*see* Fig. 143). Almost enclosed on three sides by rose-coloured mountain walls and watered by the perennial Wadi Musa, it was a strong Arab fortress and one of the most important centres of their caravan trade in ancient times. Many of its ruins are on the banks of the little river, but the most elaborate are hewn in the cliff face; and the rocky walls everywhere are honeycombed with caves excavated to provide homes, storerooms and graves for its inhabitants. The importance of Petra as a caravan centre came to an end in the second century A.D., largely it is said because the Arabs transferred their trade to the growing city of Palmyra (*see* page 538).

Jordan's only mineral deposits of note are in the highlands. Phosphates are mined at Roseifa near Amman, and another deposit south of the city is being exploited. Traces of mineral oil have been discovered in the southern highlands, and there is a small annual output of petroleum. The outlet for the phosphates is Aqaba, which has been specially designed to deal with bulk cargoes. In August 1965, a treaty with Saudi Arabia provided for the exchange of 6000–7000 square kilometres of the coastland to facilitate

[*Courtesy of Jordan Ministry of Information.*

FIG. 144.—Aqaba: Jordan's only seaport is also a winter resort. Once Solomon's harbour, later a Crusader outpost, it became a small fishing village. Today it is an important port with modern hotels. The picture shows: (*a*) the barren plateau in the background, (*b*) the tanker station and oil storage depot, (*c*) the holiday beach, (*d*) the date palm in the foreground.

the development of the port. It should be mentioned that Aqaba is situated in a most inconvenient position for dealing with the West, but Jordan has little alternative (*see* Fig. 144). Haifa is the natural outlet to the Mediterranean, but it is in Israel and is denied to Jordan; and Beirut, also used by Jordan, calls for long and expensive transport.

4. *The eastern desert.* This region is of little economic value to Jordan, except in providing routes to Iraq. It is sparsely peopled by Bedouin tribes such as the Beni Sukhr and the Howeitat, who herd camels and occasionally goats; or by more sedentary Arabs who live in oasis villages

where caravan or nomad routes converge. The chief of these are El Jafr and Qasr el Azraq, which are situated near permanent water supplies in depressions in the desert, and Bayir, which is watered by wadis from desert highlands. Oil pipelines from Iraq and Saudi Arabia cross the desert, and for these Jordan draws royalties.

STUDY QUESTIONS

1. Illustrating your answer by a sketch map, divide Jordan into physical regions and explain your division.

2. Write a comparative account of the economic development of eastern and western Jordan.

3. "Politically and economically, Jordan is the most unstable of the Levant lands." Write a short essay on this statement, showing how far you consider it to be true.

Chapter XXVII

ISRAEL

In 1919 the League of Nations gave Great Britain a mandate to create in Palestine a "National Home for the Jews," but without prejudicing the rights of the Arabs, who at that time constituted the great majority of the population. It proved a task almost impossible to accomplish, and within a year of the relinquishment of the British mandate in 1948, war with the surrounding Arab states broke out and Palestine was invaded (*see* page 525). Under pressure from the United Nations, who had replaced the League of Nations, an armistice was signed by which new frontiers came into being, based on military lines at the cessation of fighting. Palestine was partitioned as a result, and large areas of the original mandated territory became parts of Jordan, Egypt and Syria. What was left is the present Republic of Israel, an irregular, narrow strip some 265 miles (424 km) long, stretching from the borders of Lebanon and Syria in the north to the Gulf of Aqaba in the south, and varying very much in width. North of Tel Aviv, it is only 12 miles (19 km) wide, south of Beersheba it is 70 miles (112 km) across, and from there the triangular Negev tapers to a tip of 6 miles (9·5 km) at Eilat, on the Gulf of Aqaba.

Israel (7993 sq. miles, 20,782 sq. km) is a very small country when compared with Jordan, Syria and Egypt, but because of the irregular shape it was given by the 1949 armistice, it has an excessively long and wholly unsatisfactory land frontier, especially with Jordan. Its boundary with the Jordanian kingdom measures 329 miles (526 km), whereas the corresponding distance along the Mediterranean boundary is 117 miles (187 km). As a result of its victory over the Arab states in June 1967, Israel again took possession of its lost territories and in addition occupied the Sinai Peninsula and a small portion of Syria.

PHYSICAL ASPECTS

STRUCTURAL DIVISIONS

Israel may be divided physically into four distinct regions: (1) the coast-lands, (2) the hill country, (3) the Jordan valley, and (4) the Negev (*see* Fig. 145).

1. *The coastlands.* The coastline of Israel is broken in the north by the limestone ridge of Mount Carmel (1789 ft, 545 m), an outlier of the Samarian highlands, which terminates in a cliff-bound promontory immediately south of the Bay of Acre. North of the headland is the small and very fertile Plain of Acre, which is watered by the lower river Kishon (Qishon) and its tributaries. The soils of the plain are a mixture of terra rossa and decomposed basaltic lava. South of Mount Carmel, the coast

has an almost continuous fringe of sand dunes, behind which there is a rolling plain which widens from only a couple of miles (3 km) in the north to about 20 miles (32 km) in the south. The plain is formed of alluvium brought down by wadis from the Judaean and Samarian high-

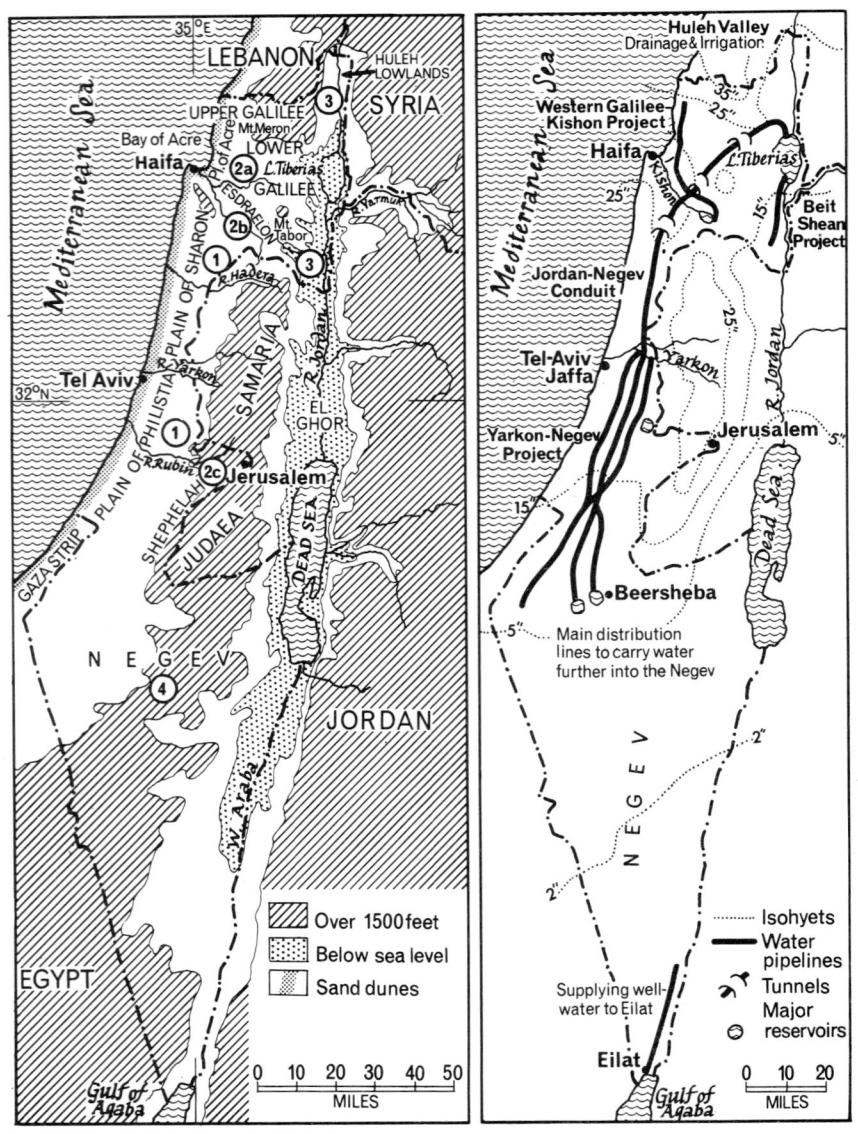

FIG. 145.—Israel: physical. The numbers refer to sections in the text.

FIG. 146.—Israel: national water plan (with mean annual rainfall).

lands, and is interrupted by occasional low ridges of sandstone. North of Tel Aviv the coastlands are called the Plain of Sharon, south of it the Plain of Philistia (or Plain of Judaea).

With the possible exception of the river Rubin, the wadis which cut across the Plain of Philistia dry up during the summer, but since much of their winter flow is absorbed by the limestones of the Judaean plateau and percolates slowly underground towards the Mediterranean, they help to maintain the water-table in the alluvial lowlands. Near the coast, however, the water-table approaches the surface so that behind the fringe of dunes there is a zone of swamps. In addition, the dunes in the south are higher, wider and shift with the wind, blocking the courses of the wadis and causing some of their winter flow to be diverted to the marshlands. Much of the swampy areas has been reclaimed, and the work of reclamation continues; dunes are being fixed by marram and other binding grasses; the lower courses of the wadis are regulated by building controlling walls along their banks; and wells are dug and diesel pumps used to direct surplus surface waters and underground supplies into reservoirs.

2. *The hill country*. East of the coastal plain the land rises to a limestone plateau, which is greatly dissected in the north. Most of this highland is Jordanian territory. The region within Israel may be sub-divided into (a) Galilee, (b) the Plain of Esdraelon (Jezreel) and (c) the Shephelah.

(a) *Galilee*. Upper Galilee is a continuation of the Lebanon mountains and is a limestone plateau averaging nearly 2000 ft (600 m) in altitude. Several peaks rise above the general surface, including Mount Meron (Jarmaq, Atzmon) (3692 ft, 1125 m), which is the highest mountain in Israel. Southwards, the mountain block of Upper Galilee is terminated by transverse faults, and the land descends by a series of giant steps to Lower Galilee, and ultimately to the Plain of Esdraelon. In Lower Galilee, the limestones have been greatly faulted and displaced, and are eroded into low, rounded hills which rarely rise to much more than 1200 ft (360 m) and are separated by wide, sweeping valleys. Above the hills protrude the isolated and more resistant mountain masses of Tabor (1929 ft, 588 m) and Moreh (1689 ft, 515 m).

(b) *The Plain of Esdraelon* is a fault trough which projects inland from and continues the Plain of Acre. It is 30 miles long (48 km) and, at its widest, 12 miles (19 km) across, and links the coast to the Jordan rift. The floor of the plain is flat and has a deep cover of rich, black, basaltic soil on which the little river Kishon has deposited a thin veneer of alluvium. In the south-east of the plain, the rounded, stone-ribbed mass of Mount Gilboa (1631 ft, 497 m) towers above the generally flat lowland. The Plain of Esdraelon used to be marshy and malarial, but as a result of the Western Galilee–Kishon Project it has been reclaimed and provided with a comprehensive irrigation and drainage system. Esdraelon today is the agricultural centre of Israel.

(c) *The Shephelah* is a zone of foothills between the Judaean plateau and the coastal plain. A series of longitudinal faults with downthrow to the west has broken the limestones into terraces which have developed into gentle slopes interrupted by shallow valleys cut by wadis. The soils of the Shephelah are terra rossa and limy clays, and although the rainfall is small, it is sufficient for cultivation, so that the region is of considerable economic value to Israel. Towards the north of the Shephelah, a portion of the Judaean plateau belongs to Israel and provides a corridor to modern Jerusalem, the capital of the country. The plateau, which has karst features in common with the rest of the Judaean highlands, is broken into several peaks, the highest being Mount Herzl (2741 ft, 835 m) in Jerusalem itself.

3. *The Jordan valley.* The physical characteristics of El Ghor, the rift valley of the river Jordan, were described in the previous chapter. Only part of the valley lies within Israel. In the north, and as far south as the confluence of the Jordan and Yarmuk, that is, where Syria abuts on Israel, the whole of the rift is Israeli, and includes the Huleh valley, Lake Tiberias and the valley for some miles south of the lake. East of the Samaria–Judaean highlands, the rift is in the kingdom of Jordan. Elsewhere, the river Jordan, or, from the middle of the Dead Sea southwards, the lowest level of the rift, is the boundary between the two countries Israel and Jordan.

East of the Upper Galilean plateau is the upper valley of the Jordan, enclosed on both sides by faults and a northern continuation of the Ghor or rift valley. Here, however, it is above sea-level. A lava flow across the valley impeded the river Jordan and caused the formation of Lake Huleh and of extensive marshes. The barrier has been lowered by blasting, the lake drained and the swamps reclaimed; the area is now a fertile, productive plain.

Lake Tiberias (*see* page 557) is 13 miles (21 km) long, from 5 to 8 miles (8–13 km) wide, and totals 64 square miles (166 sq. km) in area. It was formed as a result of a lava flow across the rift valley holding back the waters of the Jordan. The river leaves the lake by a gorge cut in the lava barrier, near the southern margin of which it is used for the generation of hydro-electricity. The first power station, at Naharayim on the Jordan, was destroyed by the Arabs in 1948, but has been rebuilt. Its great value is to enable the use of electrically driven pumps which can lift the water from Lake Tiberias, low-lying though it is (695 ft, 212 m, below sea-level), and drive it long distances to irrigation systems. In Israel's most ambitious scheme, water will be carried up to 155 miles (248 km) from the Jordan to the Negev. In the meantime, a conduit from the southern end of Lake Tiberias carries water to an irrigation network in the Jordan valley around Beit Shean, where the lavas have developed into a rich, black soil.

About 27% of the total area of 394 square miles (1024 sq. km) of the Dead Sea is under Israeli jurisdiction. The narrow, marshy, salt-encrusted, western shores of the sea are dominated by precipitous, limestone slopes which climb 3300 ft (1000 m) from the floor of the valley to the Judaean plateau. The cliffs are furrowed with watercourses, some of them perennial like the Wadis Muhawat and Seyal, the majority winter torrents only. South of the Dead Sea, the land rises gradually to a watershed above sea-level, which separates its northward drainage from that flowing to the Red Sea. This southern region is known as the Araba (Arava, Haarava) Desert. The Dead Sea is all that is left of a lake 200 miles (320 km) long which filled the rift valley in Pleistocene times, and whose waters were about the same level as those of the Mediterranean. With the diminished rainfall and increased temperatures which followed that period, the effects of evaporation gradually surpassed the precipitation, lowering the water of the Dead Sea to its present level, which remains remarkably stable. As the water conservation and irrigation projects of Israel, Jordan and Syria are developed more fully, however, there will be a reduced flow to the Dead Sea, and its level will fall until a new and lower state of equilibrium is established.

The saline content of the water of the Dead Sea amounts to about 25% of the total volume. The salinity increases with depth, and at 360 ft (110 m) from the surface the water is chemically saturated. Nearer the surface, the percentages of the mineral content are: magnesium chloride 48·4, sodium chloride 33·4, potassium chloride 7·1, calcium chloride 3·9, magnesium bromide 2·3, magnesium nitrate 1·1, calcium sulphate 1·1, calcium carbonate 0·5, and iron and aluminium oxides 0·1; the remaining 2·1% consists mainly of decaying organic matter washed into the sea. Occasionally, lumps of bitumen float from below to the surface of the sea and are collected, but their occurrence is haphazard and economically they are of little significance. The origin of the bitumen is disputed. By some it is supposed to be loosened by slight earth tremors from strata of bituminous marl on the floor of the sea. The more general opinion, however, is that it occurs here and there in the breccia of some of the valleys on the Israeli side of the sea, and is washed down and submerged, till the small stones by which it is sunk are loosened and fall apart, allowing the lighter bitumen to rise to the surface. Exploitation of bitumen-bearing rocks near Sedom has already begun. The Dead Sea is Israel's greatest single source of mineral wealth.

4. *The Negev.* South of the Hebron hills, an east–west fault separates the Judaean platform from a lower tableland known as the Negev (Negeb). Roughly triangular in shape, with its apex in the south, the Negev has an area of some 4716 square miles (12,214 sq. km), more than half of all Israel. Structurally it is part of the Afro-Arabian Archaean block, and ancient rocks are rarely far from the surface. On this basement rests a thin cover of limestone which has been wrinkled in the east and south of the region to form ridges and high peaks such as Mount Ramon (3395 ft, 1045 m). Eastwards the plateau finishes at the north–south fault which forms the western boundary of the Jordan rift valley, and the land descends to the

Arava valley by slopes which are precipitous in the north and more gentle towards the Gulf of Aqaba. In the north-west the land is a continuation of the coastal Plain of Philistia and is low-lying; and here and on large areas of the north of the Negev plateau there is a thick mantle of loess.

Generally speaking, the Negev has most of the characteristics of a hot desert. Absence of rain, saline soils, extreme heat, isolation, and grotesque, barren landscapes carved out by wind and sand are typical. Yet it is known that in Old Testament times and for centuries later, there were hundreds of inhabited settlements in the Negev, of which Beersheba is the largest survivor. The remains of ingenious systems of water preservation and irrigation have been discovered, and ancient caravan trade routes traced and mapped. Until the Arab invasion of the seventh century A.D., the northern Negev was eminently habitable, but from that date it fell into neglect, the water systems decayed and disappeared, and the desert took over. For over a thousand years the Negev was a desolate wilderness.

In 1943, however, a new era began. Israeli agricultural experts, realising the potential fertility of the loess areas if water could be made available, drilled wells and found ample supplies; and although it was too saline for drinking, it was suitable for agriculture. For drinking purposes, they carefully husbanded the torrential showers of winter, as their ancestors probably did in ancient times. Moreover in 1948 they constructed a pipeline, 105 miles (168 km) long, to bring water from the river Yarkon to the north-eastern Negev, and built new settlements and roads for the Hebrew colonists who began to pour in. The experiment was a complete success; and as new pipelines are being constructed and the irrigated areas extended, the northern half of the Negev is showing a remarkable transformation from the desert of only 25 years ago.

The Negev also has considerable mineral wealth. Huge deposits of phosphates occur near Oron, and further beds, not yet exploited, have been found at Arad. Copper and manganese are mined at Timna, north of Eilat, where proven copper ore reserves have been estimated at 17 million tons. Natural gas has been struck at Rosh Zohar, near the Dead Sea, and near Beeri in the northern Negev. Mineral oil was discovered at Heletz, near Ashkelon, in 1955, and the search for more oil and gas goes on. High-quality glass sands exist near Eilat, and flint clays (for ceramics and furnace linings) in several areas. Other minerals known to occur in the Negev are iron ore (of poor quality), magnesium, mica, chrome and gypsum.

CLIMATE

Despite the smallness of its size, Israel has a most varied climate. In the north it has the typical hot, dry, sunny summers and mild, rainy winters of the Mediterranean climate, but southwards there is a transition to the hot desert type. Over the country as a whole, there is no rainfall at all from the beginning of May to the end of September each year; but along the Mediterranean coast there are high summer humidity and extremely heavy deposits of dew which may amount to one-quarter of the annual precipitation. The highest rainfall is in Upper Galilee, where Tirat Yael has an annual total of 37 in. Southwards, precipitation decreases rapidly: Jerusalem, in the Judaean hills, has a yearly total of 19·2 in., and on the coastal plain Haifa has 24·4 in., Tel Aviv 22·2 in., and Ashkelon 15 in. In the Negev it is lower still; at Beersheba it amounts to 8 in., and then tapers to a mere 1·2 in. annually at Eilat. At Tiberias, in the rift valley, the yearly total is 16 in. The average annual number of rainy days in the northern half of Israel is from 40 to 75, in the Negev from 10 to 30.

Average temperatures range from 45° F (7·2° C) in January in the north to 92° F (33·3° C) in August (the hottest month) in the south. Frost and snow are almost unknown at lower altitudes, except in Upper Galilee; Haifa, for example, has a snow shower about once in 15 years. The following averages for January and August may be taken as representative of Israel's physical regions: Mount Canaan (Upper Galilee) 45° F (7·2° C) –75° F (23·9° C), Jerusalem 47° F (8·3° C)–75° F (23·9° C), Tel Aviv 56° F (13·3° C)–80° F (26·7° C), Tiberias 57° F (13·9° C)–88° F (31·1° C), Beersheba 53° F (11·7° C)–79° F (26·1° C), and Eilat 60° F (15·6° C)–92° F (33·3° C). Very high daytime temperatures may sometimes be registered along the coast during the winter and spring, as a result of the khamsin, a hot wind which blows from Egypt; Tel Aviv, for instance, has recorded 82° F (27·7° C) in January.

HUMAN GEOGRAPHY

PEOPLE

The history of the emergence and development of Israel as a Hebrew state has been summarised in previous pages (*see* Chapters XXIV and XXVI), but it may not have been made very obvious that prior to the outbreak of the First World War in 1914, there were upwards of 600,000 Arabs in Palestine, as it then was, and rather less than 50,000 Jews, that is, just over 8% of the population. By 1922, following the declaration that Palestine would become a national home for the Jews, immigration brought their numbers to 85,000, while the Arab population remained static. Hitlerite persecution of the Jews accelerated the flow of immigrants to Israel, and by the beginning of the Second World War, 1939, there were over 400,000 Hebrews in the country, and by the end of the war, 1946, the number had increased to over 600,000. Following the Arab–Israeli war of 1948 and the partition of Palestine, the new state of Israel came into existence, and thousands of Jews in Samaria, Judaea and the Gaza strip crowded back into it; but in opposite directions went over half a million Arabs to Syria, Jordan and Egypt, where large numbers of them still live in refugee relief camps. By 1950, as a result of further immigration from eastern and central Europe, Yemen, Iraq and North Africa, and of natural increase, the Hebrew population of Israel was $1\frac{1}{4}$ millions, but Arab numbers had shrunk to less than 200,000, most of whom lived in

Upper and Lower Galilee. From these figures, the antipathy of the Arabs against the Jews is readily understandable.

In 1965, the population of Israel was 2,525,600, made up of 2,239,200 Jews, 202,300 Muslims, 55,500 Christians, and 28,600 Druzes, and the average density was 316 persons per square mile. Since then, however, the population has been in a state of flux. Following the war of June 1967, large numbers of Hebrews returned to the Jordanian territories of Samaria, Judaea and Old Jerusalem, or to the Egyptian Gaza strip, to re-occupy lands they had lost in 1948; and many Muslim Arabs and Druzes, fearful of Israeli Zionists, fled across the frontier to the relief camps in Jordan.

SETTLEMENT TYPES

Israel is predominantly an agricultural country, yet 85% of its Jewish population is classed as urban and only 15% as rural. The apparent imbalance is accounted for by the large numbers who go out from the smaller towns to work in the fields, and by the fact that about 37% of all Jews live in the three cities of Jerusalem, Tel Aviv/Jaffa and Haifa, and that the majority of these are concerned with the processing, packing and export of agricultural produce. The Muslim Arabs live mainly near the Israeli borders, but everywhere except in the southern Negev they form minority groups. They are most numerous in the towns and villages of Galilee, such as Nazareth and Shepharam, in the Jerusalem corridor and along the borders of Samaria and Judaea, and in the southern Negev. In the last-named they are semi-nomadic Bedouin, 18,000 in number. Christians, who are also mostly Arabs professing Greek Catholic and Orthodox creeds, are found in all the large towns, but live mainly around the Christian holy places of Jerusalem, Nazareth, Mount Carmel and the shores of Lake Tiberias. The Druzes are in villages in Upper Galilee and on the Mount Carmel ridge.

The immigration of Jews into Israel, which began as a small stream near the beginning of the century but developed into a torrent after 1950, presented the authorities with major problems of settlement and integration. It is the constitutional right of every Jew, no matter from what country, to emigrate to and live in Israel; but when he arrived there he had to be fitted into the community according to his resources and ability. Those who had financial resources and were willing to establish new industries, or those who possessed specialist industrial skills or professional qualifications, might be accommodated in the expanding cities on the coast, but the vast majority of the immigrants were destined to work on the land. For these, new towns and villages had to be sited and built and land made available, and care taken that there should be an even dispersal of the growing population. Towns and villages already in existence were allowed to grow bigger, but small villages and new settlements were carefully controlled, and experiments made to try to secure the most suitable organisation for each in the country's agricultural economy. The cardinal question was: how best to increase farming production and develop a rural population—by creating a large number of small village communities based on individual small-holdings, or to farm the land in large estates owned by public or private companies, using the new immigrants as hired labour working under expert direction.

The second system is economically attractive, for it eliminates waste of man-power and equipment, but it runs contrary to Israel's social aspirations—to root its inhabitants in the soil and give them responsibility, and so develop self-maintaining cohesive communities. On the large estates, the hired labourers would be inclined to move from job to job whenever they saw a more favourable opportunity elsewhere. Both viewpoints had a big influence on Israel's agricultural settlement policy, and both systems are in operation, but more and more it is the community-building approach which is in the forefront, and it is this system which will determine Israel's agricultural future.

There are four major cities in Israel: Jerusalem (Israeli part only, 188,000), Tel Aviv/Jaffa (394,000), Haifa (201,000) and Ramat Gan (100,000). Tel Aviv was founded in 1909 as a suburb of Jaffa, one of the world's oldest ports, but within 20 years it had become the dominant partner. Ramat Gan was a suburb of Tel Aviv, and along with smaller suburbs such as Holon (65,000), Benei Berak (57,000) and Givatayim (36,000) has been given municipal status. In a small region centring on Tel Aviv there is more than one-quarter of Israel's total population. Many of the remainder of Israel's towns are of ancient foundation, and have grown considerably since 1948. These include Beersheba (62,000), Acre (26,500), Ashkelon (25,500), Nazareth (25,300), Ramla (23,200), Tiberias (21,100), Lod (Lydda) (19,400), Safad (Safed, 10,950) and Eilat (5850). Eilat had decayed completely, and was re-established after a lapse of centuries. Some towns, such as Herzliya (28,400), Hadera (26,000), Petach Tikva (55,000), Rehovot (29,900) and Rishon Le-Zion (28,500), have blossomed from villages (generally *moshavot*, *see* below) founded by early Jewish colonists. Others, still small in size, like Qiryat Shemona in the Huleh valley, Qiryat Gat in the Shephelah, and Arad in the Negev, were built in recent years to centralise the industries of neighbouring irrigated districts or to exploit mineral wealth.

It is in the villages, of which there are more than 700 with populations ranging from 60 to 2000, that we find distinctive settlement types, some of them peculiar to Israel. There are five main categories:

(a) *Moshava* (plural *moshavot*). This is an ordinary village based on private land ownership and private enterprise, just as you might find in England. The majority are in the coastal plain and the Shephelah; and some, as mentioned above, have expanded into towns.

(b) *Kibbutz* or *kvutza* (plural *kibbutzim* or *kvutzot*). The kibbutzim are communal or collective settlements, governed by the inhabitants. All property is collectively owned and work is organised on a collective basis. Members give their labour and in return receive housing, food, clothing and social services. There are central dining rooms, kitchens and stores, and communal quarters for children and cultural activities. Individual living quarters provide personal privacy. There are at present about 220 of these collective settlements, ranging up to 2000 in population. They are all mainly agricultural, but in the larger kibbutzim there are industrial enterprises. The kibbutz is excellent in opening up new agricultural land or where environmental conditions are difficult, but as it is based on collectivism, which is not Israel's ultimate agricultural policy, it is intended gradually to reduce their number in the future.

(c) *Moshav shitufi* (plural *moshavim shitifiim*). The moshav shitufi developed later than and is a short step removed from the complete collectivism of the kibbutz. Its organisation is based on collective economy and ownership, as in the kibbutz, but each family has its own house and deals with its own domestic requirements, and work and pay are adjusted to individual requirements and not to the moshav shitufi as a whole. This type of settlement is few in number; there are 20 moshavim shitufiim, none with more than 300 inhabitants. In some, as in the kibbutzim, there is a development of industries.

(d) *Moshav ovdim* (plural *moshvei ovdim*). This is a settlement of co-operative small-holders, and is the commonest type, approaching most nearly to Israel's ideal. There are nearly 350 moshvei ovdim, based on mutual aid and equality of opportunity. Each member has a farm worked by himself and his family, and he can call on the rest of the community for help if needed. Produce is sold and supplies and equipment are bought through central co-operatives, but more expensive farm machinery is owned collectively. The moshav ovdim is governed by a council elected by its members, and the council approves all transfers of small-holdings and acceptances of new members. The moshvei ovdim are purely agricultural; industrial establishments are not permitted. Population ranges from 100 to 600.

(e) *Moshav* (plural *moshavim*). There are over 100 moshavim or small-holders' settlements whose economy is based neither on the collectivism of the kibbutzim and moshavim shitifiim nor on the co-operation of the moshav ovdim. There is no standard type, but the majority consist of members who are more or less independent of their neighbours; and in this the moshavim are very like the moshavot, except that the land is State-owned. The moshavim make use of the Agricultural Union, which is a national purchasing and marketing co-operative set up for the purpose.

The above settlement types are purely Hebrew in origin, but there are also about 30 Arab and Druze villages in Galilee with no definite community plan except possibly that of defence. The Israeli Government is subsidising road-building and the installation of water, electricity and sanitation; and by irrigation, land reclamation, and education in mechanised farming, is helping the Arab and Druze farmers to adopt a better way of life, approximating in some small way to that of the moshavim.

THE ECONOMY

WATER DEVELOPMENT

Irrigation is of primary importance for Israel's agriculture, so before considering the economic development of its soils, it is advisable to examine the extent of its water resources and the use made of them. The annual rainfall, as we have seen, varies from 38 in. in the north to as little as 1·2 in. at Eilat, and it is higher on the plateaus than on the plains and valleys. Moreover, the rain comes in the winter months, and the long, hot, dry spell from April to November is seldom watered by more than the morning dew. Of the rainfall that reaches the ground, about 60% is evaporated and 35% soaks into the underlying rocks; only 5% flows on the surface in a few perennial streams and torrential winter wadis which discharge into the Mediterranean or join the river Jordan, and in time the Dead Sea, to be evaporated. The rain which soaks into the ground flows through cracks and crevices in the predominant limestones, and makes its way to the sea via the pores and interstices of the sandy and alluvial formations in the lowlands.

The purpose of Israel's water development is to make use of the surface run-off as fully as possible, and also—and this is vital to its economy—to utilise the vast supplies of underground water wisely, both as to the amount extracted and the kind of agriculture it is intended to serve. Underground water used to be obtained by digging wells and allowing them to fill by percolation. Nowadays, deep borings are made and the water pumped up by diesel or electric power. There is the danger, therefore, that more water may be taken out than can be replenished by the annual rainfall, so that the water-table is lowered and future supplies imperilled; and there is the further risk, as has happened in the Tel Aviv area, that over-pumping may so reduce the level of the water-table as to allow the salt water of the Mediterranean to invade the wells near the coast, rendering them useless for agriculture until such time as their excessive salt can be removed economically. In the meantime, their waters can be used for cooling in industrial plants or for artificial fishponds. To avoid over-pumping and preserve the store of ground-water, many winter-flowing wadis are diverted and their storm-waters directed underground instead of escaping to the sea; or wells are rested during the winter when surface water is available; or surplus water is injected in winter *into* the wells.

In 1914, the only irrigation system using water delivered by pipeline was a small one around Petah Tiqva, on the Yarkon river, in the middle of the Jaffa orange groves. Elsewhere, water was pumped from shallow wells by small oil-engines, and carried along surface channels. For domestic use, water was borne on donkey-back or in mule-drawn carts from communal wells. Towns like Jerusalem had to depend on rainwater collected from the roofs and stored in underground cisterns. In the 'twenties, under the British mandate, water development centred on supplying old and new settlements in the coastal plain with piped domestic supplies from improved wells, using diesel pumps; the Huleh lake was drained and irrigation pipes were laid from the upper Jordan to the surrounding valley; and a start was made on the Lake Tiberias–Beit Shean Project (*see* Fig. 146). Originally, this was to have formed part of a comprehensive Jordan Valley development plan in conjunction with Lebanon, Syria and Jordan, and work commenced accordingly; but although the Arab riparian states had previously agreed to the project, the Arab League in 1955 vetoed their co-operation and substituted a Pan-Arab scheme for the separate development of the river Yarmuk, a tributary of the Jordan (*see* page 564), which had been included in the comprehensive plan. The Beit Shean project carried water from Lake Tiberias to fertile areas in the Jordan valley; and as the scheme included a hydro-electricity plant, power was available to pump water from the many wells situated there and even to serve part of the Esdraelon Plain.

In the late 'thirties attention was directed to the development of large-scale regional schemes. The largest of these is the Yarkon–Negev Project, aimed at directing the water of the Yarkon and of numerous borehole wells in its vicinity to the northern Negev. The Negev has the largest area of fertile soil in Israel; it is flat and eminently suitable for mechanised agriculture, pipe-laying and road building. But it is almost rainless and can be developed only by supplies of water from the north, and so it is that almost all the major projects in Israel take the shape of pipelines and canals strung out in a generally southerly direction.

The second great scheme is the Western Galilee–Kishon Project, which collects the water of the rich wells and springs of western Galilee and conveys it to the fertile but under-watered Plain of Esdraelon, and to the domestic supplies of all the urban centres. The most ambitious scheme of all, the Jordan–Negev Project, not yet completed, will carry enormous quantities of water from the river Jordan to the Negev, a distance of up to 155 miles (248 km), and at the same time interconnect and supplement other irrigation and supply systems met on its way from north to south. The project is being developed in two stages. The first, to convey water from the river Jordan to the central works of the Yarkon–Negev Project and so augment the flow to the Negev, has been completed; the second, which will take several more years to construct, will extend the main conduit into the heart of the Negev. For this project, great lengths of pipe are required, and pipeworks began production at Ashkelon in 1959.

There is a limit, however, to the amount of water available in Israel for development, and even when the above irrigation systems are completed, only about one-half of the country's total irrigable acreage can be furnished with enough water. It is obvious, therefore, that any further extension must be into the most productive land; and it has been decided that this is the Negev. But further development will necessitate better use of the available supplies by capturing storm-water and storing it in reservoirs, by the recovery of usable water from sewage, and by the de-

[Courtesy of Israel Government Tourist Office.

FIG. 147.—Israel: Eilat, the Sarchin desalination plant. The supply of natural water for the growing port of Eilat is inadequate, so this plant has been installed to desalinate the salt water of the Gulf of Aqaba. Such plants are worked by a vacuum-freeze process. The cost is high, so fresh water is not used in the town for industry.

salination of salt water (*see* Fig. 147). The construction of large reservoirs, however, is not easy where so much of the surface is composed of porous limestones and alluvium; there is a popular objection to the use of water obtained by the treatment of sewage; and desalination, although some progress has been made, is still too costly except for domestic purposes where, as in Eilat, alternative supplies are inadequate.

Finally, it must be noted that the Jews in Israel, by the application of science and technology to the water shortage problem, have set an example to all other countries in the Mediterranean which have poor rainfall. In the space of less than 50 years they have changed their economy from struggling subsistence agriculture and semi-nomadic pastoralism to an ever-increasing productivity and industrial prosperity. Yet their water development is unlikely to lead to industrialisation in the Western sense, at least in the near future, for heavy industry demands the use of very large amounts of water which cannot be spared from agriculture. For instance, it takes over 26,000 gallons of water to produce one ton of paper, and nearly 80,000 gallons for one ton of iron; and the case is similar for many existing and proposed industries. Industrial growth in Israel will depend to an increasing extent on the amount of water that can be spared from its agricultural needs (*see* Fig. 148).

AGRICULTURE

It has already been said that agriculture is the basis of Israel's economy. Its farmers produce three-quarters by value of the country's food and make a large contribution to its exports (*see* Fig. 148). Except for cereals, fodder crops and vegetable oils, for which land and water are insufficient at present, they grow all domestic requirements. This is remarkable when one considers that in the past 30 years the population of Israel has increased more than fourfold; and is all the more striking because the bulk of the immigrants, who man most of the farms, had never held a hoe before their arrival. The rapid development of agriculture brought many problems. The new settlers had to be put on the land immediately and given instruction by a resident agricultural teacher or by settled farmers. They had to be shown how to adapt themselves to a life completely foreign to most of them, to learn to wait for a long time to see the fruit of their labours (it takes 5–7 years for an orange tree to produce fruit), to take part in land reclamation, afforestation, house building and road-making, and above all to live in harmony with the other inhabitants of the type of settlement in which they found themselves. In the past few years, as the consequence of unpleasant experiences in some settlements, it has become the policy to establish small villages, each drawing its inhabitants from one country and from the same social background. In the Lachish area, for instance, Otsam, a village of Moroccan Jews, is next door to Shahar, a village of Jews from Tunis and Tangier, while their next neighbours at the village of Nir Hen are Israeli youths who have left the moshavim where they were born to establish a new one of their own.

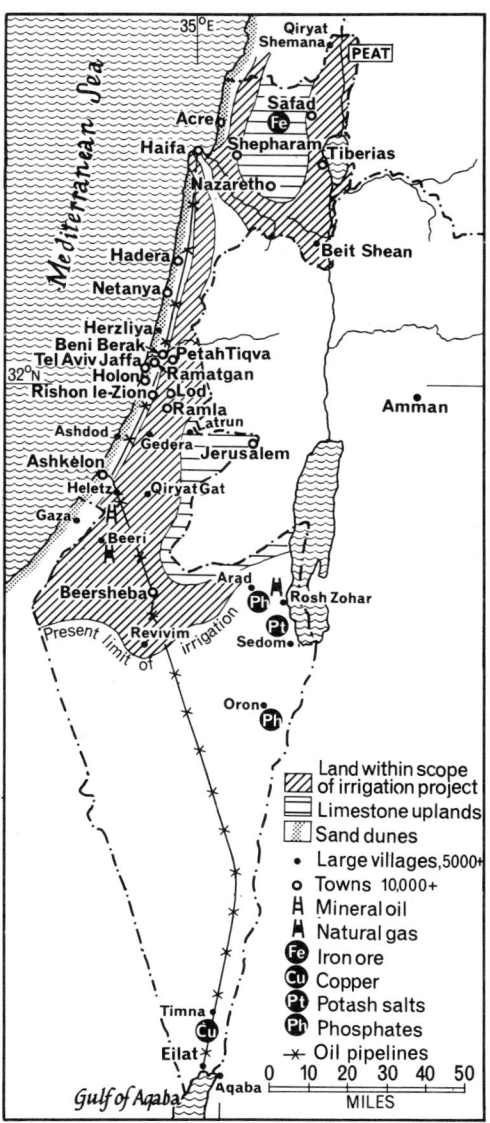

FIG. 148.—Israel: economic. The cities and towns shown are mentioned in the text. There are in addition 40 urban settlements and over 800 villages (100 Arab), of which about 450 have been founded by immigrants, many of them in the Negev.

Methods of farming and crop production depend on the type of settlement (*see* p. 576), and on the amount of rainfall and irrigation and the kind of soil in the vicinity. Soils vary from the heavy black soil of the Jordan valley and the Plain of Esdraelon to the loamy terra rossa in the hills of Galilee and the Shephelah, and from the reddish mixture of sands, alluvium and terra rossa on the coastal plain to the rich loess of the northern Negev. This variety is being exploited for the development of a wide range of vegetables and fruits. Israel can produce the typical fruits of temperate climates, such as apples, pears and strawberries, side by side with sub-tropical bananas and avocados. There has been a striking growth in the area under citrus (75,000 acres) and in the export of oranges (*see* Fig. 149), grapefruit, lemons and tangerines (20 million cases). The groves are found in all areas, even in the newly-irrigated Negev, but the chief regions of production are the coastal plain, especially around Jaffa, western Galilee and the Plain of Esdraelon. There has been an equally marked increase in the area of fruit and vine plantations. This is mainly on the hill slopes of the Shephelah and the Galilean hills. The chief fruits are peaches, apricots, figs and pomegranates. The greatest vine-growing area is in the Lydda district, with centres at Rishon Le-Zion and Latrun.

Olive plantations, for which Israel has always been noted, have unfortunately not kept pace with other agricultural developments, but new methods of cultivation and picking are being introduced to try to increase production. The annual output of olives fluctuates considerably; in 1960, for instance, it was 20,800 tons, whereas in the following year it had fallen to 5000 tons. In vegetable and potato production, on the other hand, there has been a great advance. Vegetables are grown everywhere for local consumption, and for export mainly in the regions of Qiryat Gat, Esdraelon and the Huleh valley. The export of out-of-season vegetables is important.

Israel produces annually over 100,000 tons of grain, chiefly wheat, barley, and oats. It is grown without irrigation on an area of about 300,000 acres, and with summer irrigation on another 15,000 acres. Yet Israel produces only a small proportion of the cereals needed for its growing population. It will always be a grain importer, for it is more economic to use its soil and water resources for other branches of agricultural production.

In recent years Israel has turned to the cultivation of commercial field crops with great success. Cotton, first sown in 1953, now covers more than 60,000 acres in Esdraelon, the southern coastal plain and the northeast Negev, and supplies all domestic demands, besides providing some raw cotton and seed for export. Sugar beet production on an area of 14,000 acres supplies about 40% of the country's domestic requirements. It is grown mostly on the northern edge of the Negev and processed in Tel Aviv and Qiryat Gat. Groundnuts, on over 12,000 acres, are now the most important agricultural export after citrus, eggs and cotton. Roughly the same acreage is devoted to tobacco, particularly in the hill country; most of it is consumed locally.

Animal husbandry is an essential and growing part of Israel's economy. There are 340,000 sheep and goats in the country, of which 200,000 are owned by Arabs. They are reared on the garrigue of the hillsides and on the scanty herbage of the semi-desert Negev and Araba valley, and are kept more for their milk than for meat or wool. In the Jewish sector

[*Courtesy of Israel Government Tourist Office.*

FIG. 149.—Israel: citrus packing station at Tel Aviv. The State-organised Citrus
Control Board supervises the picking, packing and marketing of the whole of
the citrus crop of Israel. Tel Aviv is the chief packing centre. Orange boxes
like these may be seen in any part of the U.K.

efforts are being directed to the evolution of breeds more suitable for
mutton and wool. Arabs also own most of the cattle, but they are usually
of poor quality. About 100,000 are reared by Jews on the margins of the
irrigated lands and in the better-watered regions of the north, about three-
fifths for beef and the remainder for milk. Experiments are being made to
improve the native stock by crossbreeding with Hereford, Brahma and
other stock. Cattle-rearing has stimulated fodder production, and large
areas are now given over to the cultivation of lucerne and clover. Most of
Israel's own meat needs are supplied by poultry, whose numbers may be
realised from the 1000 million eggs produced annually. Eggs come second
in the list by value of Israel's agricultural exports.

Great importance attaches in Israel to forestry development. There is
very little natural forest in the country; most of the extensive tree cover
of the hills was cut down in ancient times and its place taken by dry

scrub and garrigue. Today, the hillsides of Galilee, where they are unsuitable for other purposes, are being re-afforested so as to build up a
valuable natural resource and at the same time prevent soil erosion; and
more trees are planted in the Shephelah and along some 550 miles (880 km)
of roadside. The most recent plantation, of 300,000 trees, was started in
1967 on the slopes of Mount Kesalot, overlooking the Esdraelon valley
near Nazareth, and is called the Churchill Forest.

Fishing is included here as part of Israel's agricultural economy because
half the total fish yield of the country (about 15,000 tons annually) is from
artificial fishponds and reservoirs. In view of the great amount of water
required for fishponds, it is intended to reduce these to a minimum and
expand sea fishing in the Red and Mediterranean Seas.

INDUSTRY

Israel has few industrial raw materials or fuel resources (see Fig. 148).
There is no coal, and the mineral oil and gas deposits will cover only 12%
of the country's fuel needs, even when they are fully exploited. Hydro-
electric power potential is also relatively small and is confined chiefly to
the Beit Shean region of the Jordan. In these circumstances, it is highly
unlikely that Israel will ever develop heavy industries, but will concern
itself more in the establishment of a wide variety of lighter types of manufacture, engineering, processing and finishing.

Most of Israel's mineral resources are in the Negev. The Dead Sea salts
yield thousands of tons annually of potash, common salt, bromine and
magnesia, which are processed on the spot at Sedom and exported via
Eilat. The phosphates of the Negev have led to fertiliser plants in Haifa
and Oron; copper ore is concentrated at Timna; and oil is piped from
Heletz to a refinery in Haifa. In total, Israel's mineral exploitation gives
occupation to a very small proportion of its workers.

The output of electric power amounts annually to about 3000 million
kWh, generated almost entirely in thermal stations strung along the
coastal plain. Of the total, about one-third is used in industry in Tel Aviv,
Haifa and many of the towns enumerated on page 577. There is a wide
range of products such as chemicals, textiles, paper, plastics, leather goods,
glass and ceramics, based mostly on imported raw materials; and there are
works for the manufacture or assembly of electrical goods including
refrigerators and radios, precision instruments, motor cars and tyres, pharmaceutical goods and false teeth. There is also a thriving industry for the
cutting and polishing of diamonds. The bulk of the industrial economy is
concerned with the processing, packing and export of agricultural produce.
Fruit and vegetable canning, juices from citrus fruits, tobacco, tomato
juice and the extraction of vegetable oils are the most important of these.

Israel's economy is helped by a good system of communications. There
are 2325 miles (3720 km) of main roads north of Beersheba, and the Negev
is pierced by a first-class road to Eilat which has been called "Israel's dry-
land Suez Canal." The stretch of coastal railway from Lebanon to Egypt,

now isolated from those countries, has been supplemented by a coastal network amounting to about 450 miles (720 km); and a line is under construction from the southern terminus at Beersheba to Dimona, near the phosphate beds of Oron.

REGIONAL ECONOMY

1. *The coastlands.* The greatest concentration of people, both urban and rural, is found in the coastal plains. As early as 1881, immigrants from Russia established Rishon Le-Zion, south of Jaffa; and by 1900 there were 22 Jewish villages in Palestine, half of them in the coastlands. As more immigrants continued to arrive, they naturally tended to settle where long journeys from the ports could be avoided, and so the coastlands became more and more populated. The soils were comparatively rich and water could be obtained from the rivers Hadera, Yarkon and Rubin, or from shallowly dug wells, so that as the years rolled by the Plains of Sharon and Philistia became dotted with agricultural settlements, and existing ports and inland towns became larger and larger. When large-scale irrigation systems such as the Yarkon–Negev Project were introduced and productivity was increased, the concentration of population was intensified, especially near the ports of Tel Aviv and Haifa. Within a radius of 10 miles (16 km) of Tel Aviv, for instance, lives more than 25% of Israel's total population. To avoid the dangers of over-population, new settlers are now encouraged to live in the less developed Shephelah and the Negev.

Outside the towns the chief occupation is intensive cultivation of citrus fruits and vegetables, largely for the export market; and mixed farming, poultry raising and vine growing occur widely. Based on these, food processing and preparation are the most important industries in all the towns, particularly in Tel Aviv/Jaffa. Marketing of citrus fruit and other foodstuffs is very carefully supervised from their harvesting to their packing and export by the Citrus Control and Marketing Boards and the Agricultural Union, who also supply fertilisers, pest controls and scientific advice.

The largest city in the coastlands is Tel Aviv/Jaffa. (For the population of Israel's cities and towns *see* page 577.) It is the chief commercial and industrial centre in the country, and one of its main ports. Israel's coast, however, is very straight and unbroken, and there is only one good harbour, at Haifa. The harbour at Tel Aviv/Jaffa is totally unsuited to modern shipping, and in 1965 it was declared obsolete and its function transferred to a deep-water inlet at Ashdod, some distance to the south (*see* Fig. 150). The new harbour at Ashdod is not yet completed, but already it deals with large quantities of citrus and Negev minerals which previously were despatched from the larger port. Tel Aviv/Jaffa still remains the centre of coastwise traffic. Together with its satellite towns—Ramat Gan, Bat Yam and Holon—Tel Aviv/Jaffa, in addition to having fruit juice and canning factories, manufactures cotton textiles, leather, chemicals and

[*Courtesy of Israel Government Tourist Office.*

FIG. 150.—Israel: the port of Ashdod. This unique picture shows the beginning of the port which is to become the largest in Israel, outstripping Tel Aviv and Haifa.

motor tyres, assembles motor cars and electrical apparatus, makes dental equipment, and cuts and polishes diamonds.

Haifa, the chief port and deep-water harbour on Acre Bay, is connected by pipeline to Eilat via Heletz. In its refineries it deals with oil from Persia as well as domestic supplies. Up to 1948, it was also connected to the Kirkuk (Iraq) oilfield, but this pipeline is now discontinued by Arab veto. Haifa is the centre of the chemical industry, using Dead Sea salts and phosphates; and petro-chemicals are a by-product of its oil refineries. It shares in the cotton textile industry, and also has light engineering, car assembly, railway workshops and ship-repairing. There are glass works and foundries, and it is hoped to develop the latter into steelworks.

2. *The hill country.* This is mostly agricultural and pastoral, with no towns of any size except Jerusalem and Nazareth. In the north, helped by the Western Galilee–Kishon irrigation project, the valleys of Galilee and Esdraelon produce large crops of wheat, barley, maize and tobacco, and there are considerable areas of mixed farming and citrus cultivation. Cattle- and sheep-rearing are carried on widely, and this is the centre of Israel's olive groves. It also contains most of the natural forest and the new plantations, in which there are many carob trees whose nuts can be used as fodder. This northern region has most of Israel's Arab population. Their farms present a sad contrast to those of the Jews, and play a poor part in the country's economy; and their villages, composed of badly built mud or stone houses huddled as closely as possible, bear no resemblance to the planned settlements of the kibbutzim or moshavim. Nazareth, the chief town, has a large Arab population. It is a road centre and, as the third holy city of Christendom, is a place of pilgrimage.

The Shephelah, the limestone foothills along Israel's eastern border, have fairly fertile terra rossa soil, and water is available from wells. It is a region of barley, wheat, sugar beet, vines, olives and sheep-rearing, and is well peopled. The hills of Ephraim, at the western end of the Jerusalem corridor, are noted for their vineyards. Jerusalem, the capital of Israel, is divided by the Israeli–Jordanian border, only the western sector being Jewish. It is in a good defensive position, but it is too high and too remote to function as the capital of modern Israel. It is the spiritual and cultural centre of the Jewish people the world over, and so of great pilgrimage and tourist interest. Jerusalem's water supply, which used to be obtained from rainwater collected from the flat rooftops, is now pumped through a long pipeline from Petah Tiqva, the heart of the Yarkon–Negev irrigation system. The only other large towns are Ramla, Gedera and Qiryat Gat, which lie where the Shephaleh meets the coastal plain and act as collecting and marketing centres.

3. *The Jordan valley.* The Huleh valley, north of Lake Tiberias, is reclaimed land which is now devoted to cereals, sugar beet and potatoes. Peat, which occurs near the upper Jordan, is being cut for fuel. Safad, on the edge of the region, is a small settlement at the meeting-place of roads from Galilee, Lebanon, the Jordan valley and Syria, but it has only local importance. The Huleh valley has several fishponds. Lake Tiberias is now regarded as the main reservoir for the Jordan–Negev irrigation system, but it is also one of Israel's chief fishing grounds, as it was in Biblical times. Tiberias is a fishing port and tourist centre, for the lake shores have many sacred associations for Christians.

South of Lake Tiberias is the hydro-electric power station and irrigated district of Beit Shean. This is a region of sub-tropical climate, of calm sultry air and rich black soil, where banana cultivation is very successful. Fishponds and fish-breeding stations are numerous. Some of the ponds are of salt water, for there are many saline springs in the west of the valley. The water is too salty for irrigation by itself, but it has been found possible to dilute it with fresh water from other springs in a blend suitable for cultivation. This is done in special mixing plants worked by electric power, with the result that thousands of acres have been added to the area under irrigation. The experience gained here in the use of brackish water has been of great value in the coastal plain and the Negev. The hills flanking the Beit Shan valley have vineyards and new olive groves, and in the lowlands there is intensive citrus and vegetable cultivation, and more extensive growth of cereals and fodder.

4. *The Negev*. The modern economic development of the vast triangle of land in the south of Israel, occupying more than half the area of the country, began only in 1943, when three Jewish experimental stations were set up to explore the possibilities of agriculture in a region which was barren and almost rainless. Within 2 years it was pronounced that the fertile soils in the north of the Negev had underlying supplies of saline water, the torrential showers of winter could be conserved for drinking or to dilute the water from the wells, and that if further supplies of fresh water could be obtained the agricultural development of the Negev was eminently possible. By 1946 there were eleven more Jewish settlements in the north-east, and a pipeline carried water to them from the river Yarkon. At the partition of Palestine in 1948, there were 27 villages, and a second pipeline was begun. In addition, many wells were bored to supplement the piped water. Beersheba, which was made the regional capital, was only a small village of 3000 people, a battered, dusty, broken-down caravan halt in a damp hollow in the semi-desert. Soon it became a transit camp for thousands of colonists who followed the first pioneers; piped water transformed its surroundings into rich, productive land and gave them food; factories were built and shops opened; and a thermal-electricity plant constructed. Today Beersheba, constantly bursting at the seams, has a population of over 62,000.

The area between Beersheba and the Egyptian border has now about 100 villages, in which all the Jewish settlement types are represented. Water is supplied by the Yarkon–Negev Project, augmented by the first stage of the Jordan–Negev Project; and an auxiliary pipeline is under construction to carry purified waste waters from the Tel Aviv district for irrigation, not domestic purposes, to the northern Negev. The loess soils of the region are extremely fertile, and extensive cultivation and mechanisation are facilitated by its flatness. The northern Negev grows greener every year.

Over 125,000 acres (50,000 ha) are at present cultivated, three-fifths under wheat and barley. Of the remainder, half the area produces vegetables, three and four crops a year being possible. Multiple crops offer the advantage of export of out-of-season vegetables such as tomatoes and new potatoes to the markets of Western Europe. Other crops include cotton, sugar beet, groundnuts, sorghum (for fodder) and sunflower seed (for oil), and a start has been made in viticulture and olive cultivation. There are over 5000 milch cows and 7000 beef cattle in the irrigated lands, and thousands of head of poultry, fed on fodder and vegetable waste. Not everything will grow in the Negev, but there are crops (cereals, sugar beet, early vegetables) that grow better there than elsewhere in Israel; the policy is to concentrate on these and find others equally adaptable.

In the south of the Negev there are about 15,000 Bedouin tribesmen, semi-nomadic and engaged mostly in sheep- and camel-rearing. They are being encouraged to develop their poor cultivation by forming Bedouin co-operatives. The Government provides tractors, fertilisers, combines and seeds, and leases suitable land, so that the trend to sedentary farming is accelerated. To date, two such co-operatives have been formed, with members drawn from six tribes.

The southern half of the Negev is as yet undeveloped for agriculture, but exploration shows it to have sources of mineral wealth, details of which have been given earlier. Unfortunately, the Dead Sea salts and phosphate fields lie at long distances from the more developed parts of Israel, and communications are poor and transport costly. Nevertheless they gave birth to industries in Sedom, on the Dead Sea, for the extraction of potash and bromine; at Oron, for the mining of phosphates; at Beersheba, for the making of ceramics and sanitary ware from flint clays; and at Timna, for the concentration of copper ores. Perhaps the most spectacular achievement in the southern Negev was the resuscitation of the port of Eilat, on the Gulf of Aqaba, as Israel's window to the Red Sea and her outlet to the Indian Ocean. A harbour (still unfinished) was planned to deal with bulk cargoes; a road to Beersheba, 155 miles (248 km) away, was asphalted throughout to accommodate heavy lorries; an oil terminal was built and a pipeline laid to Haifa, to carry crude oil from Persia and link up *en route* with the Heletz field; air communication was established with Tel Aviv; and a town was built with amenities intended to attract settlers to its difficult environment. Eilat is a flourishing holiday resort as well as a port for the Negev's minerals. In conclusion, it might be noted that Eilat is one of the few places in the world that depends for some of its water supply on the desalination of sea water (the remainder is piped from wells), and that experiments to harness solar energy on an economic scale are far advanced in the Negev.

STUDY QUESTIONS

1. Using headings of your own choice, write a summary of the geography of *one* of the following: Israel, Lebanon, Cyprus.

2. Write a comparative account of the site, situation and rise to importance of Tel Aviv/Jaffa and Beirut. Sketch maps are essential.

A SHORT GUIDE TO FURTHER READING AND STUDY

The following guide to the study of the geography of the Mediterranean lands does not pretend to be comprehensive, but it contains most of the texts which have been found of value in Sixth Form work. With a few valuable exceptions it is confined to books in English or books translated from the original language. For some of the books listed, editions may have been published at dates later than those given; on the other hand, some of the older books are now out of print, but may be consulted at public libraries. Articles in geographical magazines and journals are kept to a minimum, as they are not always readily available and are often ephemeral in nature. Much up-to-date information about population, production statistics, sources of raw materials, new developments in agriculture, engineering and communications, etc., is to be found in *Geographical Digest*, published annually by Philip (London), and in the *Statesman's Yearbook* (Macmillan). A good atlas is essential. Among the best English atlases are Bartholomew, J. *Advanced Atlas of Modern Geography* (Meiklejohn), Lewis, C. and Campbell, J. D. *The Oxford Atlas* (O.U.P.), *Oxford Economic Atlas of the World* (O.U.P.) and Goodall, G. and Darby, H. C. *The University Atlas* (Philip); and there are many excellent Continental atlases, notably Chardonnet, J. *Atlas International Larousse* (Harrap).

THE MEDITERRANEAN LANDS IN GENERAL, ESPECIALLY PHYSICAL BACKGROUND

Birot, P. and Dresch, J. *La Méditerranée et Le Moyen Orient*. Vol. I. *La Méditerranée Occidentale*. Paris, 1953. Vol. II. *La Méditerranée Orientale et Le Moyen Orient*. Paris, 1956.

Branigan, J. J. *Europe*. Macdonald & Evans, 1966. (Much of the present work is based on this text, along with that of H. R. Jarrett, *see* below.)

Charlesworth, J. K. *The Quaternary Era*. London, 1957. (The standard work on the subject. Somewhat advanced for Sixth Forms.)

Collett, L. W. *The Structure of the Alps*. Arnold.

de Martonne, E. *A Shorter Physical Geography*. Christopher, 1927.

Dury, G. H. *The Face of the Earth*. Pelican, 1959.

Finch, V. C. and Trewartha, G. T. *Elements of Geography*. London and New York, 1957.

Firth, J. V. *The Middle East: A Geographical Notebook*. Harrap, 1963. (A useful and informative summary.)

Fisher, W. B. *The Middle East: A Physical, Social and Regional Geography*. London, 1961.

Géographie Universelle, Vol. VII. *La Méditerranée et les Péninsules Méditerranéennes*. Paris, 1934.

Hance, W. A. *The Geography of Modern Africa*. New York, 1964.

Hardy, M. E. *The Geography of Plants*. Oxford, 1925.

Hare, F. K. *The Restless Atmosphere*. London, 1960. (An excellent summary.)

Holmes, A. *Principles of Physical Geology*. Nelson, 1957.

Jarrett, H. R. *Africa*. Macdonald & Evans, 1966. (By the co-author of the present work.)

Joly, J. *The Surface of the Earth.* O.U.P., 1930.
Kendrew, W. G. *The Climates of the Continents.* O.U.P., 1961.
Lyde, L. W. *Peninsular Europe.* London, 1931.
Miller, A. A. *Climatology.* Methuen, 1953.
Newbigin, M. *The Mediterranean Lands.* Christopher, 1924. (Out of print.)
Newbigin, M. *Plant and Animal Geography.* Methuen, 1950.
Newbigin, M. *Southern Europe.* London, 1952.
Ogilvie, A. G. *Europe and its Borderlands.* London, 1957.
Pounds, N. J. *Europe and the Mediterranean.* New York, 1953.
Robinson, G. W. *Soils.* Allen & Unwin, 1950. (The final chapter, "The Geography of Soils," is a very good introduction to modern soil science.)
Siegfried, A. (tr. D. Hemming). *The Mediterranean.* London, 1948.
Tyrell, G. W. *Volcanoes.* Butterworth, 1931.
Walker, D. S. *The Mediterranean Lands.* Methuen, 1960.
Wooldridge, S. W. and Morgan, R. S. *The Physical Basis of Geography.* Longmans Green, 1956.
Wright, W. B. *The Quaternary Ice Age.* Macmillan, 1936.

THE HUMAN RESPONSE

N.B. Many of the books in the previous section deal also with various aspects of human geography.

Beaujeu–Garnier, J. (tr. S. H. Beaver). *Geography of Population.* Longmans, 1966. (Excellent for its treatment of population movements, but somewhat advanced for Sixth Forms.)
Brunhes, J. *Human Geography.* London, 1952.
Carrier, E. H. *Water and Grass.* London, 1932.
Carrier, E. H. *The Thirsty Earth.* London, 1928. (Out of print.)
Cary, M. *The Geographic Background of Greek and Roman History.* Oxford, 1949. (An outline of regional environment in relation to classical times.)
Daryll Forde, C. *Habitat, Economy and Society: A Geographical Introduction to Ethnology.* London, 1942.
Dumont, R. *Types of Rural Economy.* Methuen, 1957.
East, W. G. *Historical Geography of Europe.* Methuen.
Eastall, R. C. and Buchanan, R. O. *Industrial Activity and Economic Geography.* London, 1961.
Fleure, W. B. *The Peoples of Europe.* Oxford, 1935.
Groves Haines, C. and Walsh, W. B. *The Development of Western Civilisation.* New York, 1941.
Houston, J. M. *A Social Geography of Europe.* Duckworth, 1953.
Houston, J. M. *The Western Mediterranean World: An Introduction to its Regional Landscapes.* Longmans, 1964. (An excellent, detailed survey, but mostly too advanced for Sixth Forms.)
Jacks, G. V. and Whyte, R. O. *The Rape of the Earth.* Faber & Faber, 1949. (A classic study of soil erosion.)
Lewis, B. *The Arabs in History.* Hutchinson, 1950.
Manners, G. "The Pipeline Revolution." *Geography*, XLVII, 1962.
Money, D. C. *Introduction to Human Geography.* University Tutorial Press, 1962.
Morgan, F. W. *Ports and Harbours.* London, 1952.
Semple, E. C. *The Geography of the Mediterranean Region: Its Relation to Ancient History.* London, 1932.

Smailes, A. E. *The Geography of Towns.* London, 1958.
Stamp, L. D. and Gilmour, S. C. *Chisholm's Handbook of Commercial Geography.* 17th edition, London, 1962.
Taylor, Griffith. *Urban Geography.* Methuen, 1961.
Vidal de la Blache, P. *Principles of Human Geography.* London, 1926.

REGIONAL: SOUTHERN EUROPE

Agnew, S. "The Cultural Heritage of the Bas Languedoc." *Geography*, XXXVI.
Buckley, P. *The Spanish Plateau.* Chatto & Windus, 1962. (Excellent photographs.)
Carlyle, M. *Modern Italy.* London, 1957.
Carrington, D. "Corsica." *Geographical Magazine*, XXIII.
Chantal, S. (tr. F. R. Holiday). *Portugal: The Land and its People.* Shell Portuguesa in conjunction with the Portuguese Secretariat of Information, 1950. (Obtainable from the Portuguese Embassy.)
de Martonne, E. (tr. H. C. Brentnall). *Geographical Regions of France.* London, 1952.
"Factual Information on Greece." *National Economy, Series C.* Prime Minister's Office, Foreign Press Division, Athens, 1960.
Fisher, W. B. and Bowen-Jones, H. *Spain.* Christopher, 1958.
"Gibraltar—The Rock." *Commonwealth Today*, 114. Central Office of Information, London, 1965.
Hamilton, F. E. I. "Yugoslavia's Hydro-Electric Power Industry." *Geography*, XLVIII, 1963.
Houston, J. M. "Irrigation as a Solution to Agrarian Problems in Modern Spain." *Geographical Journal*, 1950.
Houston, J. M. "Urban Geography of Valencia: The Regional Development of a Huerta City." *Transactions of Institute of British Geographers*, 15. 1950.
Itinerari del Sud. A series of seven booklets issued by the Cassa per il Mezzogiorno, 1962, through the Italian State Tourist Department, Rome. (An outline account, with English translation, of the proposed development and the completed projects in southern and insular Italy. Obtainable from the Italian Embassy.)
Jurgens, O. *Spanischen Städte.* Hamburg, 1926. (In German.)
Kerner, R. J. (ed.) *Yugoslavia.* United Nations Series. San Francisco, 1949.
Longobardi, C. *Land Reclamation in Italy.* London, 1936.
Lopandíc D. *Yugoslavia: Economic and Tourist Guide.* Privedni Pregled, Belgrade.
McVittie, W. W. *Portugal.* Overseas Economic Surveys. H.M.S.O., 1954.
Malta. Central Office of Information. H.M.S.O., 1965.
Marjanovik P. (ed.) *1,000 Facts about Yugoslavia.* Yugoslavian Publishing House, Belgrade, 1963. (Obtainable from the Yugoslavian Embassy.)
Monkhouse, F. J. *A Regional Geography of Western Europe.* Longmans. (For Mediterranean France.)
Naylor, J. "Irrigation and Internal Colonisation in Spain." *Geographical Journal*, June, 1967.
Ormsby, H. *France: A Regional and Economic Geography.* Methuen, 1950.
Pinchemel, P. *Géographie de la France.* Armand Colin, 1964. (In French.)
Some Useful Facts About Greece. Prime Minister's Office, Foreign Press Division, Athens, 1963. (Obtainable from the office of the Commercial Counsellor, London.)

Statistical Pocket Book of Yugoslavia. Federal Institute for Statistics, Belgrade, 1966.
Terrero, J. *Geografía de España.* Barcelona, 1958. (In Spanish.)
Thompson, I. B. "Land Reclamation in Eastern Corsica." *Geography*, XLVII, 1962.
Walker, D. S. *A Geography of Italy.* Methuen, 1967.
Ward-Perkins, J. "Etruscan Towns, Roman Roads and Medieval Villages." *Geographical Journal*, December, 1962.
Way, R. *A Geography of Spain and Portugal.* Methuen, 1960.
Woodcock, A. G. "The Methane Industry in Italy." *Geography*, XLI, 1956.
Wycherley, R. E. *How the Greeks Built Cities.* London, 1949.

REGIONAL: NORTH AFRICA

Ackermann, E. A. "An Algerian Oasis Community." *Economic Geography*, July, 1936.
Barbour, N. *A Survey of North-West Africa.* London, 1959.
Birtwistle, A. "The Khamsin." *Geography*, June, 1946.
Boak, A. E. R. "The Fayum." *Geographical Review*, July, 1926.
Célérier, J. *Le Maroc.* Paris, 1946. (In French.)
Clarke, J. I. "Economic and Political Changes in the Sahara." *Geography*, April, 1961.
Clarke, J. I. "Emigration from Southern Tunisia." *Geography*, April, 1957.
Clarke, J. I. "Oil in Libya: Some Implications." *Economic Geography*, January, 1963.
Fisher, W. B. "Problems of Modern Libya." *Geographical Journal*, June, 1953.
Fitzgerald, W. *Africa.* 8th edition. Methuen, 1955.
Fogg, W. "The Suq." *Geography*, December, 1932.
Forbes, R. H. "The Trans-Sahara Conquest." *Geographical Review*, April, 1943.
Gottman, J. "Economic Probems of French North Africa." *Geographical Review*, April, 1943.
Hance, W. A. "The Gezira. An Example of Development." *Geographical Review*, April, 1954.
Houston, J. M. "The Significance of Irrigation in Morocco's Economic Development." *Geographical Journal*, September, 1954.
Isnard, H. *Algeria.* Nicholas Kaye, 1954.
Kirwan, L. P. "Land of Abu Simnel." *Geographical Journal*, September, 1963.
Lebon, J. H. G. "Dar Fur." *Geographical Journal*, March, 1961.
Lebon, J. H. G. "The Human Geography of the Nile Basin." *Geography*, 1960.
Mountjoy, A. B. *Industrialisation and Under-developed Countries.* London, 1963.
Mountjoy, A. B. "The Suez Canal at Mid-Century." *Economic Geography*, April, 1958.
Murray, G. W. "The Land of Sinai." *Geographical Journal*, June, 1953.
Nasr el-Sayed Nasr. "Land Use in the Nile Delta." *Geography*, June, 1955.
Peel R. F. "Libya." *Scottish Geographical Magazine*, February, 1941.
Peel, R. F. "Some Aspects of Desert Geomorphology." *Geography*, November, 1960.
"Tunisia." *Geographical Review*, July, 1945.

REGIONAL: TURKEY AND THE LEVANT

Bullard, R. *The Middle East: A Political and Economic Survey.* O.U.P., 1958.
Coon, C. S. *Caravan: The Story of the Middle East.* Cape, 1952.

Dafni, R. *The Negev*. Israel Today No. 6. "The Israel Digest," Jerusalem, 1960.

Dresch, J. *La Méditerranée et Le Moyen Orient*. Paris, 1956. (*See* Birot and Dresch, *above*.)

Erinc, S. and Tuncdilek, N. "The Geographical Regions of Turkey." *Geographical Review*, 1952.

Facts About Israel. Ministry for Foreign Affairs, Information Division, Jerusalem, 1963.

Fedden, R. *Syria*. London, 1955.

Fisher, W. B. *The Middle East*. London, 1961.

Grant, C. P. *The Syrian Desert*. Black, 1937. (A scholarly account of travel across the Syrian desert from ancient to modern times.)

Grollenberg, L. H. *Shorter Atlas of the Bible*. (Has excellent photographs of the scenery and archaeological discoveries of Palestine.)

Harman, A. *Agricultural Settlement*. Israel Today No. 2. "The Israel Digest," Jerusalem, 1960.

Hindle, P. "Aqaba: An Old Port Revived." *Geographical Journal*. March, 1966.

Hourani, A. H. *Syria and Lebanon*. London, 1946.

Lingeman, E. R. *Turkey*. Overseas Economic Surveys. H.M.S.O., 1950.

Prushansky, Y. *Water Development*. Israel Today No. 11. "The Israel Digest," Jerusalem, 1961.

Smith, G. A. *The Historical Geography of the Holy Land*. Hodder & Stoughton, 1935. (Out of print.) A classic geographical and historical treatment of Palestine.

CONVERSION TABLES

Temperature

°F	°C	°F	°C	°F	°C	°F	°C
100	37·8	55	12·8	10	−12·2	−35	−37·2
95	35·0	50	10·0	5	−15·0	−40	−40·0
90	32·2	45	7·2	0	−17·8	−45	−42·8
85	29·4	40	4·4	−5	−20·6	−50	−45·6
80	26·7	35	1·7	−10	−23·3	−55	−48·3
75	23·9	30	−1·1	−15	−26·1	−60	−51·1
70	21·1	25	−3·9	−20	−28·9	−65	−53·9
65	18·3	20	−6·7	−25	−31·7	−70	−56·7
60	15·6	15	−9·4	−30	−34·4	−75	−59·4

Precipitation

in.	mm	in.	mm	in.	mm	in.	mm
60	1524·0	20	508·0	4	101·6	0·5	12·7
55	1397·0	15	381·0	3	76·2	0·4	10·2
50	1270·0	10	254·0	2	50·8	0·3	7·6
45	1143·0	9	228·6	1	25·4	0·2	5·1
40	1016·0	8	203·2	0·9	22·9	0·1	2·5
35	889·0	7	177·8	0·8	20·3	0·05	1·3
30	762·0	6	152·4	0·7	17·8		
25	635·0	5	127·0	0·6	15·2		

Rough approximation 4 in. = 100 mm

Distances / Heights

mile	km	km	mile	ft	m	ft	m
1	1·609	1	0·62	500	152	5500	1676
10	16·1	10	6·2	1000	305	6000	1829
15	24·1	15	9·3	1500	457	6500	1981
20	32·2	20	12·4	2000	610	7000	2134
25	40·2	25	15·5	2500	762	7500	2286
30	48·3	30	18·6	3000	914	8000	2438
35	56·3	35	21·7	3500	1067	8500	2591
40	64·4	40	24·9	4000	1219	9000	2743
45	72·4	45	28·0	4500	1372	9500	2896
50	80·5	50	31·1	5000	1524	10,000	3098

Rough approximation 10 miles = 16 km   *Rough approximation 1000 ft = 300 m*

1 sq. yard = 0·836 sq. metres (m²), *Roughly* 100 sq. yd. = 84 m².
1 sq. metre = 10·764 sq. yd., *Roughly* 10 m² = 12 sq. yd.
1 acre = 0·404 hectares (ha), *Roughly* 10 acres = 4 ha.
1 hectare = 2·471 acres, *Roughly* 1 ha = 2·5 acres = 1800 sq. yd.
1 sq. mile = 2·589 sq. km (km²), *Roughly* 10 sq. miles = 26 km².
1 sq. km = 0·386 sq. mile, *Roughly* 100 km² = 40 sq. miles.

EXAMINATION QUESTIONS

1. Compare the positions and functions of any *two* major ports which are situated on the coast of the Mediterranean Sea.

2. Which of the Mediterranean lands do you consider to be under-developed? Explain the basis for your assessment and indicate the problems involved in the development of these countries. (*Based on* J.M.B.)

3. Discuss the distribution of the major coal resources of the Mediterranean lands.

4. Explain and illustrate with specific examples in the Mediterranean lands, (*a*) entrepôt trade, (*b*) transhumance, (*c*) terrace cultivation, (*d*) the growth of new cities. (*Based on* J.M.B.)

5. With reference to specific areas in the Mediterranean lands, examine the importance to human activities of water conservation and control. (*Based on* J.M.B.)

6. Give a reasoned account of the distribution in the Mediterranean lands of developed hydro-electric power. (*Based on* J.M.B.)

7. What qualities do you look for in a capital city? Illustrate your answer by reference to *two* capital cities of countries which border the Mediterranean. (*Based on* O. & C.)

8. Explain why extensive industrial development in the Mediterranean lands is concentrated in a few localities.

9. Comment on the significance in the development of the states bordering the Mediterranean of any *two* of the following: the Moors, the Pyrenees, the Ottoman Turks, the lower Nile, the Hebrews. (*Based on* O. & C.)

10. "The political unity of a country can be greatly assisted by its physical geography but there are instances of political unity being achieved despite unfavourable physical conditions." Examine this statement with reference to the Mediterranean lands. (*Based on* O. & C.)

11. Write a geographical appreciation of the difficulties at this time of any *one* country which borders the Mediterranean. (*Based on* O. & C.)

12. In what ways is the increasing use of hydro-electric power bringing about a new distribution of manufacturing industries? Give illustrations from the Mediterranean lands. (*Based on* O. & C.)

13. Choose *three* of the following towns and with the aid of sketch maps describe the site, position and importance of each: Nicosia, İzmír, Salonica, Naples, Tunis, Alexandria.

14. Show by means of a sketch map the regions of exploitation of mineral oil in the Mediterranean lands. Comment on the changes in the lives of the native peoples resulting from the development of these oilfields.

15. Explain how far geographical factors have influenced the following: (*a*) the importance of the olive to Mediterranean peoples, (*b*) the large-scale production of citrus fruits in Israel, (*c*) nomadism as a way of life in many Mediterranean countries, (*d*) the large-scale use of hydro-electric power in the North Italian plain.

16. Write a comprehensive geographical account of any *one* large island in the Mediterranean Sea.

17. Write a short essay on *one* of the following: (*a*) transhumance in the Mediterranean lands, (*b*) the chief physical conditions which control the distribution of population in the Mediterranean lands, (*c*) tree crops in the Mediterranean lands.

18. Show how the density of population is affected by the physical structure, climate and natural resources in any *one* Mediterranean country.

19. Discuss, with examples taken from the Mediterranean lands, the connection between the development of new sources of fuel and power and the wider dispersal of manufacturing and other industries.

20. Comment on the relationship between geographical features and distribution of population on the northern coastlands of the Mediterranean.

INDEX

Main references are indicated by figures in **bold type**